Sport, Leisure and Ph
Trends and Dev
Volume

"Sport Sciences in Europe 1993"
Current and Future Perspectives

Sport, Leisure and Physical Education
Trends and Development
Volume 1

European Network of Sport Sciences in Higher Education

2nd European Forum
"Sport Sciences in Europe 1993"
- Current and Future Perspectives -

German Sport University
Cologne, September 8 - 12, 1993

Joachim Mester (Ed.)

Conference Proceedings

Meyer & Meyer Verlag

Die Deutsche Bibliothek – CIP-Einheitsaufnahme

European Forum Sport Sciences in Europe <2, 1993, Köln>:
Conference proceedings / 2nd European Forum Sport Sciences in Europe 1993: current and future perspectives; September 8 - 12, 1993, Deutsche Sporthochschule Köln. – Aachen: Meyer und Meyer, 1994
(Sport, leisure and physical education; Vol. 1)
ISBN 3-89124-222-0
NE: Deutsche Sporthochschule <Köln>; GT

All rights reserved. Except for use in a review, the reproduction or utilization of this work in any electronic, mechanical, or other means, now known or hereafter invented, including xerography, photocopying and recording, and in any information retrieval system, is forbidden without the written permission of the publisher.

© 1994 by Meyer & Meyer Verlag, Aachen
Cover design: Walter Neumann, N & N Design, Aachen
Printed by Druckerei Queck, Jüchen
Printed in Germany
ISBN 3-89124-222-0

CONTENT

Page

GENERAL KEYNOTES

- **BAMBUCK, R.:**
  Ethics, Sport and Sport Sciences 10

- **KÖNIG, W.:**
  Sport in Europe: Political Ideas and Concepts 18

ACTION FIELD 1 • LEISURE AND RECREATIONAL SPORT

- **DE KNOP, P.:**
  New Professions in Sport and Tourism 32

- **GOVAERTS, F.:**
  Sports and Aging 55

- **HACKFORTH, J.:**
  Blue Chip Sports Communication: Presentation and Effect 69

- **LORET, A.:**
  The Needs and Motivations of Sporting Demand 86

- **POCIELLO, C.:**
  The New Conceptions for Sports and Leisure Equipment;
  Prospects and Innovation 95

- **ROBERTS, K.:**
  The Role of Leisure and Recreational Sport in Europe 113

- **RUBINGH, B.:**
  Training Sport Managers 126

- **SOBOTKA, W.:**
  Education, Training and Further Education in Leisure and Recreational Sport ... 133

- **STANDEVEN. J.:**
  Sport and Tourism in the South of England 137

- **WAGNER, P.E.:**
  Current Professional Activities 153

ACTION FIELD 2 • ELITE SPORT

- **ÅSTRAND, P.:**
  Fundamental and Applied Research in Individual Endurance Sports 162
- **BOUCHOUT, J.-P.:**
  Political and Social Conditions of Elite Sport in Europe 174
- **CLAUDE, R.:**
  Legal and Social Status of the Coach 180
- **ENGEL, L.:**
  Training in Visualisation and Bodyawareness as a Way of Changing the Energy Level and the State of Consciousness During Rhythmic, Slow Motion Stretching 193
- **KIRCHGÄSSNER, H.:**
  On the Research in the Combat Sports 205
- **KOZEL, J.:**
  The Coach as a Manager 215
- **MADELLA, A.:**
  The Coach as a Methodologist for Conditioning and Technique Training 232
- **MESTER, J.:**
  Elite Sport: The Present Level of Scientific Research - Legitimation, Designs and Methods. 245
- **REILLY, TH.:**
  Fundamental and Applied Research in Team Sports 260
- **REISCHLE, K.:**
  Fundamental and Applied Research in Aquatic Sports 271

ACTION FIELD 3 • ADAPTED PHYSICAL ACTIVITY

- **BILARD, J.:**
  Adapted Physical Activities and their Professionalization in the Health Sector .. 288

- **DOLL-TEPPER, G.:**
  The Training of Professionals in Adapted Physical Activity 298

- **ELVIN, I.T.:**
  New Professional Orientations in Adapted Physical Activity 309

- **HOLLMANN, W.:**
  The Impact of Physical Activity in Preventive and Rehabilitative Cardiology . . . 317

- **MARTÍNEZ I FERRER, J.O.:**
  New Perspectives of Medical Investigation within the Area of
  Sport for the Disabled 336

- **PEDERSEN, B.K.:**
  Muscular Exercise: The Immune System, Infections and Cancer 347

- **PEITERSEN, B.:**
  Physical Education Teachers and Coaches in the Context of
  Adapted Physical Activity 360

- **RENSTRÖM, PER A.F.H.:**
  Musculosceletal Disorders in Sports and Physical Education 370

- **RODRIGUEZ, F.A.:**
  Educational Aspects in Health Promotion and Adapted Physical Activity:
  Physicans and other Health Professionals 395

- **ROST, R.:**
  The Impact of Physical Activity in Prevention and Rehabilitation of
  Cardiovascular and Metabolic Diseases 409

- **VAN COPPENOLLE, H.:**
  European Master's Degree in APA: A Way of Combining Competencies 431

- **VERMEER, A.:**
  Adapted Physical Activity and Physical Education & Sport Sciences 434

- **WILLIAMS, T.:**
  Sociological Aspects of Sport and Disability: Current and Future Perspectives . . 443

ACTION FIELD 4 • PHYSICAL EDUCATION

- **ALMOND, L.:**
  The Art and Science of Teaching Physical Education 462

- **BRETTSCHNEIDER, W.-D.:**
  Youth and Sport in Europe: Implications for Physical Education 472

- **CARREIRO DA COSTA, F.:**
  Teaching the Teachers: Aims, Methods and Contents 484

- **CILIA, G.:**
  Continuous Formation in Europe 506

- **CRUM, B.:**
  A Critical Review of Competing Physical Education Concepts 516

- **DIETRICH, K.:**
  Unemployment and Occupational Opportunities 534

- **HARDMAN, K.:**
  Physical Education within the School Curriculum: A Beautiful Dream ? 544

- **LAPORTE, W.P.R.:**
  Professional Qualifications in Physical Education 561

- **MEINBERG, E.:**
  Sportpedagogy as a Science 577

- **NAUL, R.:**
  Physical Education Teacher Training - Historical Perspectives. 588

- **PIÉRON, M.:**
  Educational Research in Physical Education 611

- **TELAMA, R.:**
  Physical Activities out of the School System - Educational Aspects 643

TOKARSKI, W.; PETRY, K.:

Summary of the Interview of Conference-Participants by Students
of the Specialism "European Sport Studies" 659

SCIENTIFIC COMMITTEE / ORGANIZING COMMITTEE 661

INDEX 663

General Keynotes

ETHICS, SPORT AND SPORT SCIENCES

Bambuck, R.
Centre National de la Recherche Scientific
Paris, France

In an article extracted from the internal Bulletin of the Paris Freudian School, Jacques DURANDEAUX noted: "If the term 'ethics' is used here, it is only to distinguish between ethics and morals; in this sense, one can have ethics without having morals. I.e., one doesn't do just anything, and one doesn't agree that whatever can be done is to be done. The ethical debate relates to the fundamental principles of discourse and the behaviour which is in harmony with it, while the moral debate relates to the 'necessities' or 'would-be necessities '- rightly or wrongly - induced by these fundamental principles."
These remarks make it possible to throw some real light on the sport-induced problems which have always existed and which we are about to rediscover because sport has permeated our everday lives and influences our individual and collective behaviour even against our will. It has functioned, and still functions, as a carrier of ideologies designed to subdue man. In view of more profitable management, it has been locked behind a set of obligatory rules, regulations, codifications and laws which don't always reflect the needs of the majority.

At the end of the 20th century, it is our responsibility to contribute, via sport, to the recognition of each individual person's dignity:

Dignity through access for all to the whole of sports practice. To arrive at an autonomy allowing us to work out and implement our individual projects of life in a social context; at first close by, then striving for universality, through recognition of the values which guarantee the respect of others and of ourselves.

Dignity through unfettered enjoyment of our physical self, once liberated from all constraints caused by strong ideological pressures. Dignity which organizes the modalities of mutual relationships between people, and which is a warrant of value hierarchies based on the intention to confirm their power. Especially in the world of sports, as it imposes on us the dogmas of a society governed by some sort of ultimate religion. Our intention to advance the limits of knowledge, should also materialize in recognition and respect of human dignity.
The scientist must refrain from seeing man in general and the athlete in particular, as nothing but a "beautiful original creature", a nice object for study, oblivious at the same time of the fact that this "creature" contains a man or

woman who may be disconcerted. This recognition of dignity can neither be reduced to a simple description on which it would depend, nor to a purely legal command on which it would depend by way of convention.

Dignity is also denying to do business in favour of political or cultural purposes, e.g. by assisting in the creation of myths suitable to ornate a hall of fame; myths which impair the universal adoption of the possible achievement of a few champions.

Dignity is also refusing to convert the athlete into a marketable product from which economic profits can be procured in a variety of forms specific to our time, e.g. on the occasion of mass events of doubtful authenticity.

To recognize the dignity of man, says Paul RICOEUR, involves the necessary recognition by each of us of our own human dignity, without which we couldn't call ourselves civilized.

Sport happens to be on the interface of two exemplary problems affecting our world.

Firstly, it is an activity which "by necessity" is strongly codified and in which individual behaviour is strictly subjected to rules. Each instance of non-compliance with these moral regulations is sanctioned by a ban, which may be voluntary. Of course this fact becomes apparent in sport federations and also in non-organized sports practice where singular behaviour by some individuals is equivalent to breach of order, and hence exclusion.

The authority of such a structuring of society comes close to a dogmatic religion in which morals are sturdily observed. To this can be added a tyrannic attitude (in Pascal's sense) of the leaders of the federation, who are the fortunate few permitted to modify or interpret the rules and regulations as they please. My statement is illustrated by the IOC Medical Commission's decision on the occasion of the Albertville Winter Olympics, to have women pass genetic tests in order to be sure they belong to the fair sex, and then make them participate in the women's contests. This occurred without prior discussion with those concerned.

It is interesting to note that the scientists' attitude, too, was stripped of ethical behaviour, inasmuch as they felt they could apply technical orders, and did not have to worry about possible consequences for the individuals to which these tests were administered.

To stay with current affairs, the exclusion of the French football club Olympique Marseille from the European Football Cup contest is the pure type of tyrannic decision. What is beneficial for UEFA is necessarily good for football and, perhaps, also for sport. The emotional effects on the club, the city, the country or the people matter little.

It seems to me that this sanctioning, had it been governed by ethical considerations, ought to have concerned the French officials. They were unable to command respect for the moral and disciplinary rules of their sports organization which had been entrusted upon them.

The religious aspect of sport provides suitable answers to all questions, including those of a moral nature. This leads to a confusion of ethics and morals in sports; hence the superposition of loyalty, fair play, and respect of the referee with the term ethics. All these questions are already settled in the sports code. The justification of such explanations can be found in the "necessities" or "would-be necessities" of sports organization. Sports organization cannot exist without its own moral rules.

In another respect, the question of ethics has reached a point where it doesn't fear that rule breaches, admonitions or calls for moral action might harm their captivation effects. To enter the domain of creativity and innovation cognition requires an autonomy based education, rather than the conditioning of the perfect disciple by a magic word.

Furthermore, as a consequence of the first term, science and sport join forces in a highly ambiguous marriage. First of all, in order to know the real nature of sport one should desecrate it. But we find it very difficult to have it leave its sphere, and place it in the world.

It is no exaggeration to say that the behaviour of certain officials with respect to knowledge of their sport comes close to that of the mighty inquisitors in the peak times of obscurity which this world has known.

On the opposite side, the claims sport has towards science are sometimes a form of pandemonium. Science must know everything in a minimum of time, find remedies for enhanced performance of the human machine, even if it uses prescriptions without prior verification - elsewhere a must in scientific method. In addition, the world of sport is aware of the need to have modern tools at its disposal, and it doesn't hesitate at times to take the scientists as ransom, to have them do a subtler job; e.g. when using them for selection purposes in the selection of individuals, without previously having informed the researcher of the fact that his/her work might be used for this purpose.

Such behaviour is far more widespread than one would think, and - if it occurs in the context of a ban (a selection, too, is excluding somebody from a group) - then the question arises concerning the scientist's ethical behaviour with respect to authority.

Of course, at the end of the 20th century, science has lost its innocence. The high cost of scientific work, the need of recognition by other scientists, the splendid isolation of the world of sports and the defective diffusion of information are further powerful obstacles confronting the scientists. They can provoke in some people an attitude of retreat, concealed behind the excuse to be devoted to pure science, unbiased passion, honour of the human intellect which is always good as such; and leave the applications to the subordinate level, seat of all the perversities.

This is exactly where the ethical question must be asked. How to reconcile the necessities of learning with the respect of human dignity, and in sports, with the farewell to beliefs and the sacred?

Should the scientist conspire with all the authorities, should he/she exclusively direct his/her research work at higher profits and standardization of each discovery? Or should he/she become aware of his/her role as a mediator of knowledge in order to take part in the education of all, lavishly spreading information collected in laboratories to the crowd, particularly to the athletes in their capacity of actors themselves, to allow them build their own projects of life, which then might become a human project embracing the whole life of the individual, not just over a short period, a moment in time of their lives.

The dissemination of learning must be done qualitatively, by respecting all principles of scientific work, i.e. to enrol ourselves in time beyond short-term effects. Do we know for sure today if intensive training in junior athletes is really not harmful to their lives as adults? A certain number of studies, especially some published by parents, appears to prove the contrary.

We can add to these two paths of the crossroads another, even a more delicate one in my home country France, viz. the lack of recognition by the so-called intellectuals of sport as a progressive element. We are today faced with a permanent battle involving all actors in sport, trying to remove sport from the cultural ghetto into which it was forced in centuries of intellectual domination. This implies two consequences, a lack of interest in a large number of scientists who probably think they get too little reward from the subject, and an attitude of reservation, if not even submission or isolation in those who devote themselves to advancing the limits of knowledge and for this very reason have opted in favour of the original milieu which constitutes sport.

In order to meet these difficulties it appears necessary to me to let all those who wish to know sport to get together and exchange views, as happens in other branches of science faced with a moral problem and an ethical question such as the "life sciences" ["science de la vie"] in order to have the role of sport reconfirmed as an element of the evolution of humanity and to consider ethics in peoples' actions, their behaviour and their responsibility.

This firstly requires a permanent emphasis on the principles of ethics in science. In France a centre exists, the purpose of which is to answer questions on ethics asked by scientists, primarily for the "sciences de la vie", but its opening to other branches of science is under way.

However well these principles are conceived or made available, they will never be able to answer all questions, and the risk will always remain that they will serve as a crutch to those who think they can do without ethical considerations. Therefore, in addition to institutions of this kind, one should, in my view, ask all scientists, sports and political leaders, sport participants, teachers, parents, and champions to attend regular meetings, the objective of which would be to expose and oppose confronting points of view, both on ethics in general, and on the specific point of ethics in sport.

This action would expose those who are required to make a choice, important or less important, and of which one doesn't always see the consequences, at a given moment in which they have to assume responsibility.

In my opinion it would have the advantage of illuminating economic problems, both in sports development and in financing research. Ethics and money are facts of our world, too often concealed in our discussions and yet permanently present in our minds. Prof. Jean BERNARD, the former president of the Comité consultatif national de l'éthique, writes in his book "De la biologie à l'éthique" [From Biology to Ethics]: "It is not our duty to make a judgement instead of profits in contemporary societies. But it is important to stress the dangers associated with the evolution of the relationship between profits and the human body. One may at this point wish ethical conscience would revive."

Although it does not reveal such a dramatic picture, the sports community is faced with the same type of question, viz. whether our responsibilities override the development of research for financial profits at all cost, given the expansion of commercial sport.

Let us not seek farther away the use of doping substances in top-level sport training and competition.

The opinion of the Comité consultatif national de l'éthique, upon a request by Professor Jean Paul ESCANDE, President of the National Anti-Doping Commission, and the authors of a report entitled "Pour une éthique de l'intervention médicale dans le sport" [For an Ethics of Medical Intervention in Sports], is rather straightforward on this point: "In general, the role of the physician is to protect health, and that of the practitioner of occupational medicine or sports medicine more particularly, should in the first place be to protect the athletes from possible harmful consequences of their exercise, no matter whether they are professionals or amateurs. Carefulness is all the more required, as the athletes often live in a milieu with multiple pressures (e.g. the quest for top achievement and economic pressures), which may lead them to train too hard, or too frequently take part in competitions. It is the obligation of the sports milieu and its surroundings to get organized in such a way that the quest for performance does not mean sacrificing the athletes' health. As a result, the Comité consultatif national d'éthique considers that endocrine deficits, associated with intensive sports practice, are a result of overtraining. They constitute alarming symptoms. One should, therefore, try to remedy the causes of the deficits rather than compensate for them, while at the same time maintaining the conditions which have provoked them. Such an attitude could be harmful to the athletes' health, who would be the ones to run the risk, themselves often under pressure due to media schedules and economic interests."

Yet, in spite of such principles, we still continue to witness the use of doping in sport.

The doping issue allows us to clearly expose the difference between ethics and morals.

The organization of international sport has the right to ban any help from "illicit" substances figuring on the list drawn up by the IOC and the international sports federations. I would like to make a first remark here: The psychological part of training and competition is concealed. Furthermore, the only sanction proposed is an idiotic punishment: suspension or exclusion. But the fight against doping should give us the opportunity to develop the educational dimension of sport, in order to unmistakably explain and integrate the need not to have recourse to doping if one wants to live the successful life of an athlete and become aware of the real risks encountered. This more than justifies science. First of all, because scientists have as their primary mission an understanding of all phenomena of life, and the relationships between individuals and groups. Thanks to the scientist's work, he/she alone can give us the information we need to form a judgement and an attitude which take into account common interests, and to assume the full responsibility for our acts; to be free to choose in full knowledge of the matter.

One must therefore say that we do not have enough information to discuss the reality of medium-term and long-term doping effects on the athletes' health.

And yet this is what the debate should be about all the time. We ought to communicate on all levels of practice and of understanding of scientific findings, in order to assume responsibility in full awareness of the situation.

It is in this respect that sport has a real impact in its educational role. It touches on universality because its function is not to defend particular interests, but to place humanity in a dynamic process which has as its centre, man in his relationship with the environment.

If it was for morals only, things would be much more simple, the role of the scientist would be limited to finding objectively measurable elements, to explaining the reality and complexity of sport.

I wish all researchers would keep this responsibility permanently in their minds, so they could speak to us on ethical problems which they encounter. This dual existence of the researcher is stressed by Mr François KOURILSKI, Director of the Centre National de la Recherche Scientifique (CNRS), when he tells us that ethics isn't the scientists' subject, but that the scientists are requested to point out ethical problems wherever they come across them in order to reaffirm their place in society.

I don't want to enter here into the debate about the existence or non-existence of a science of sport; this issue has, and will always nurture polemics which unfortunately are conducted to the disadvantage of knowledge about sports. However, every scientist has an obligation to fully assume his/her role in a world in which the progress of science affects that of society at large. The ethical behaviour which we have a right to demand of him/her requests that he/she should be unafraid of running into conflicts with any entity which bases its authority on a reduction of the world. They may go as far as concealing certain realities, as long as the foundations of their authority are not shaking, no matter which destiny will be reserved for man and society.

The violence surging in our stadia is an example. Is it just imported violence, having nothing to do with sports? Or is sport itself not a carrier of violence, via a certain number of educational shortcomings? Still worse, isn't sport itself a means of educational regression, with the trainer-trained relationship still too often resting upon theoretical knowledge?

Scientists should raise all these questions without fear. A good deal of the progress of humanity will depend upon their responses.

Parallel to this train of thought, science should be carried out with man instead of being conducted on man, which implies that people consent to it on a voluntary basis, and that they are given information and follow-up care, especially in the Human Sciences and in Sociology, in order to make them partners associated in a work of exploration from which they can personally benefit.

This question of essential ethics, for the future of humanity, is at the centre of the CNRS reflexion. The year 1991 saw the establishment of the Comité opérationnel pour l'éthique dans les sciences de la vie (COPE). Its duty was primarily to supply scientists, upon their request, with the necessary assistance in view of harmonizing their work with the law or protecting persons who avail themselves to biomedical research. Other needs became manifest following a questionnaire designed for laboratories, particularly in the area of genetic engineering, psychology, and sport. To meet these demands, several colloquies have been organized, or will be organized in the near future.

In January 1994, we shall organize a seminar in Paris entitled "Ethique, recherche et sports. Du particulier au général" [Ethics, Research and Sports. From specific to general]. The objective of the seminar is to identify scientists and sport participants who are interested in sports ethics in order to make sure sports ethics are translated into research ethics.

The seminar will be open to scientists of all branches, representatives of scientific associations in the field of sport, representatives of the sports movement etc. The discussion will touch on four major subjects:

- Healthy Man - Ethical Uncertainties
- Sports Performance and Ethics
- Choice and Responsibility
- Sport and Society.

I would like to find someone who could launch the debate on ethics on the European level. In the course of the discussion, I hope to find not some sort of dogmatic solution to a question, but rather a starting point for permanent reflexion.

SPORT IN EUROPE: POLITICAL IDEAS AND CONCEPTS

König, W.
Ministry of Cultural Affairs, State of North Rhine-Westfalia
Düsseldorf, Germany

Ladies and Gentlemen,

Since the changes introduced in 1989 sport and science have enjoyed an extensive autonomy in the majority of European countries. This is illustrated by such examples as the right of self administration. However, sport and science are also so closely bound to other domains of politics and life, that it would be an illusion to believe they could travel along side paths independent of the great roads of historical development.

As a result of this dependence, the organising committee of this congress has decided to begin the work at hand with a lecture in which four chapters bind together a reminder of our European identity, the description of the present framework of politics and the present state of methods and contents of European sport politics, with the prospects of several future possibilities.

"We must re-open the European building site without leaving it to the demolishers who are already rubbing their hands." This statement of the French Foreign Minister, Alain Juppe, barely four weeks ago, appeals to everyone who has not forgotten the fact that it is the ideal of peace which forms the basis of European unification. The message of the first Haager Congress for Europeans on the 10th May 1948, categorically stated that "the fate of European and World peace is dependent upon this unification." This remains unchanged today; the alternative bears the names of many, far too many, destructed towns and devastated countries such as Sarajevo, Bosnia.

In 1989 when the Dutch cultural philosopher Ton Lemair looked back upon European history at the Catholic University Nijmegen, he described the extreme divergence between the intellectual, musical and technical values and ideals on one side and the violent practices of murdering people and races on the other side and he added: "I have often been ashamed to be European." This tension Lemair described as existing between the diverse possibilities of togetherness of different peoples has determined one thousand years of our history. Its destructive centre is indescribable for anyone who believes the words of Ortega y Gasset: "If we were today to ascertain our intellectual capacities (...), we would come to the conclusion that the majority arises not from our specific motherlands but rather from a European pool. The European in all of us by far dominates the German, Spanish, French,... If we try to imagine a life in which we attempt to live only as defined by our 'nationality', if all the customs, thoughts and feelings adopted from other countries of the World were to be removed from the average German, we would be astounded at how impossible such an existence was; four fifths of us is European common property."

In the framework of this report it is not possible to mention the philosophers and authors, the composers and painters, the scientists and architects, the pioneers of Swedish and German gymnastics, the British sport games and the nordic or alpine winter sports, which, despite belonging to individual nations have left us with a common, binding inheritance. However, right at the very beginning of this congress we should be fleetingly reminded that from Cyprus to Iceland, from Lapland to Andalusia and from the Atlantic to the Urals our history brings us together. And if you are aware of your origins, you will be more successful in determining the goals you wish to achieve.

Our continent has not grown since Edouard Herriot concluded in the French National Assembly in 1925 that: "On a global scale Europe is no more important than a province. (...) My greatest wish is to one day see the United States of Europe." This goal was the same as that described at the same location by Victor Hugo as early as 1851. In order to finally achieve this goal, Winston Churchill, on the 19 September 1946 in Zürich provided the explanation that: "This is the only solution for hundreds of millions of hard working people to regain the simple joys and hopes that make life worth living. The method is simple. What we need is hundreds of millions of men and women to decide ..."

As we know now the path has not been quite this simple. This was realistically predicted by Robert Schuman on the occasion of the foundation of the European Coal and Steel Community: "Europe can not be created in a single hit." However, the goal remained, even through the decades of renewed divisions in Europe, the results of which we have been attempting to overcome over recent years.

In this respect I am optimistic for a quite simple reason: If you have a path strewn with catastrophies and obstacles behind you, you will not retreat along this path, but will rather aim at the already visible goal even if some problems are still to be solved. A clear orientation, good intentions, perseverance and patience are all qualities utilised and developed in both sports and science that continue to be necessary today.

Alain Juppe's "European building site" cannot be completely managed by anyone or from any one location. The building contract is of huge dimensions and without comparison throughout history. It is impossible to develop a building plan right into the finest detail, but instead we have the general idea of a place where we can live in peace and harmony, in which freedom and human dignity are assured. Whoever is of the opinion that this place is called "Utopia" should remember the words of Oscar Wilde: "Progress is only the realisation of Utopia." Therefore building and future planning must occur simultaneously in order to construct the next buildings. At the same time everything present must be tested for future usefulness and be utilised as efficiently as possible or adapted to the new environment.

This process which has been going for decades, has and is today still completely rebuilding European economic and social systems. The dictatorships in Greece, Spain, Portugal and finally in eastern Europe have not been able to withstand this development which is slowly seizing more and more of Europe whilst simultaneously influencing the life of the citizens to a greater extent.

Although one of the fathers of the European unification; Jean Monnet, said that if he was given the chance to start again he would begin with culture, this can not distract from the fact that economic cooperation was a stronger or at least faster catalyst in the unification process. It was the economic measures which permitted the systematic rather than isolated or random development of closer contacts and harmonising measures in education, science, research, culture and sport. This appears surprising when compared to the background of European intellectual and cultural history. However, this can be the only explanation why this congress of sport science establishments is only the second and not the twentieth of its sort.

It is imperative to see this connection in order to realise that, and also why, science and sport will not be capable of escaping from this current of European unification. De facto dreams of complete independence cannot exist forever. Therefore anyone talking about the further development of sport in Europe must at least mention the overall political perspective. If this permits the consideration of only those institutions which have survived and are also of importance to our topic, then we cannot consider the ex-eastern block countries or even the KSZE, the west European Union, the EFTA and other organisations. Only the council of Europe and the European Community which is now developing into the European Union remain.

These two supra-national political levels will be responsible for the further development of Europe including those countries of the former Soviet Union and those resulting from the civil war in Yugoslavia. This is the obvious trend apparent in the important and publically inappropriately received conclusion A 3 - 0189/92 of the European parliament on the 20.1.1993 in the so-called Hänsch Report: "(...) concerning the formation and strategy of the European Union in terms of its expansion and the attainment of complete order in Europe." The report and the conclusion create a clear, realistic picture of the future political order in Europe. In this the parliament requires "(...) the expansion of the European Union to European nations (...) in which fully developed democratic institutions based upon national law and economic structuring exist and in which human rights are guaranteed (...)." This last requirement clearly indicates that the "system of confederal cooperation" demanded by the parliament is geographically and institutionally largely identical to that of the European Assembly in which the member nations must recognise the convention for human rights.

The aims, the tasks, the operational possibilities and the self conceptions of these two political levels differ and will continue to differ which will have considerable consequences for sport and science. The most important difference is the extent to which the regulations made by the respective legislative and executive agencies are bound to the law. Cooperation within the European Assembly will eventually unify over 40 countries the Committee for the Development of Sport (CDDS) already being represented by 37 countries after a rapid influx from east and south east Europe. Cooperation will continue to operate on a voluntary basis and retain a high degree of independence with the exception of national conventions to be ratified separately.

As a result of the very likely inclusion of Austria, Finland, Sweden and Norway into the European Union this will form a new political and legislative domain of which the legislative norms will influence almost all areas of community cohabitance with an intensity that has previously been a characteristic found only in the regulations of national states. The required constitution is currently being developed in the European Parliament, surely a bit late which can easily be explained historically, but still early enough for the formation of a foundation for further developments. In the framework of our topic the question remains whether the combined summation of the rights which are transferred from the national to the supra-national level will eventually justify the definition of a National Federation or "only" a Federation of Nations.

It is therefore very important to us that the discussion concerning the Treaty of Maastricht has lead to an unexpected elevation of the principle of subsidiarity. This contains both a regional and a contents component. Article 3 of the EC contract states that the Community will only become involved when "(...) the aims of the measures concerned cannot be realised on the level of the member states (...)". This can be interpreted in many ways, however the norm should indisputably be to take responsibility wherever it can be filled with life in the most qualified manner. In the areas of educational and cultural politics, in which the Community is only credited with a fringe competence anyway, this fundamental formula provides a greater chance for autonomous, non-state organisations as well as the provinces and regions in Europe than for the national states.

Although sport was given credit for a "Europe of Citizens" in the Adonnino Report (1985), contract processes have failed to mention it. Its position should probably be observed parallel to the regulations of cultural politics. Subsidiarity does not, however mean purely the relinquishment of the above in favour of the lower level or of the state in favour of free organisations. What is often overlooked is that it also means the fundamental right of cooperation, and even the commitment to intervene when the institutions closer to the citizens do not fulfill their obligations. This can lead to considerable consequences in sport if the state takes its responsibility to all citizens seriously, a task which requires more than the responsibility of sport organisations to their members.

After this insight into various strains of development in "big politics", let us observe the institutions which are already involved European oriented sport politics, as these will also play an important role in future.

Although I am quite aware that the non-state organisations have priority, I will begin with the supra-national institutions for two reasons: firstly this will allow a better continuation from the above mentioned and also because it is the Council of Europe which has had a relative long tradition with extensive activities. Since 1966 it has been involved with the complete spectrum of themes in sport, initially in terms of its cultural political programme which explains why those countries who had previously ratified the Cultural Convention of the Council of Europe in 1954 are permitted to participate in the sport political programme.

The cooperation is realised primarily through the following instruments:

1. As a result of the first conference of the sport ministers in 1975, a formal meeting has been organised every third year with informal meetings occurring in between.
2. The Committee for the Development of Sport (CDDS) steers the running work through annual programmes and prepares the ministerial conferences. The national delegations also provide non-state sport organisations as members of the CDDS.
3. Both committees are aided by two sub-committees whose experts are members of the Development of Sport-Sports Research (DS-SR) or the Development of Sport-Sports Information (DS-SI), where the latter sub-committee also helps conduct the work of the Clearing House in Brussels which is a centre for sport informatics.

The contents of the work has followed the charter "Sport for all", which was replaced in the 1992 conference of sport ministers by the far more detailed "Charter for European Sport". The aims are diverse and broadly formulated; all the important areas of sport development are covered by 13 articles. The central demand is that every citizen must be provided with the opportunity to participate in actively sport regardless of other general or individual living conditions. Any government or sport organisation that conscientiously accepts this task has undertaken an endless challenge. The Council of Europe itself is attempting to fulfill this requirement. It is therefore conducting expert seminars and educational courses which have been predominantly directed at the east European countries in recent years through the SPRINT programme with the intent of supporting the development of new sport structures. By the end of this year 17 seminars will have been conducted in Hungary, Poland, Rumania, Bulgaria, the Czech Republic and the Baltic states.

Whereas an independent sport policy is therefore obviously present in the Council of Europe, this is not the case in the European Community. The reason is quite simple: it is not immediately competent in sport, which has at this stage not been mentioned in any contracts. Nothing has changed the present legal situation despite various wishes and complaints, for example the statement has been made since the seventies, primarily by representatives of the European Parliament that sport could be an efficient unification catalyst, also as recently as the 23 February 1993, Freddy Black, Member of Parliament, complained bitterly that the Community made no more money available for Sport Development than for the entertainment of the PR office for olive oil in Copenhagen, which could not be disputed by the commission. At this stage only narrow contact areas therefore exist between the community and sport and of these I would like to mention the most important:

1. The commission supports sport events of which publicity for the ideals of European unification are in turn expected. For example the EC ladies cycle race from Vlissingen (Netherlands) through five EC countries to Cambrai (France) is taking place right now from the 1 - 11 September. This category also includes a sailing tour around the coasts of Europe, team competitions of swimming and weightlifting clubs, and also the dearly paid for opportunity to represent the European Community at the Olympic Games.

2. The many EC promotional programmes, the topical content of which is generally poorly defined also offer many opportunities for sport involvement. I will point out the promotion of handicapped sport through the Helios programme, of youth sport through the programme "Sport for Europe" and of the sport science institutions, including our "network..." through Erasmus. The regional funds can be used for the development of sport facilities if these also serve to improve the tourism infrastructure of a

region and new jobs, in sport as well can be produced through social funding. I could make this list considerably longer.

3. Paradoxically the public and especially the sport organisations have not primarily found out about the effects of the Community policies on sport through these sport promoting activities. This has occurred to a far greater extent through well known conflicts, eg. the argument with the UEFA concerning the number of professional football players from EC countries permitted in each team and the heated debate concerning the settlement of previously regional or national lottery operations in other countries. This broad field is therefore concerned with the effect of the position of European rights on sport and here the regulations for the creation of free movement?? of people, goods, work and capital which came into force on the 1.1.1993, have particularly far reaching consequences. Everything concerned with sport appears to be affected: the free trade of sport goods, the building of sport facilities, logos and emblems, tickets and television rights, taxes and insurance, educational courses and the mutual recognition of diplomas, athlete nutrition and - of course - doping etc.

An explanation of these effects would take hours, however, they have been thoroughly investigated by the British agency, Coopers and Lybrand. I will therefore at this point only draw attention to the interim report of November 1992 which has already been published and which will shortly be followed by a far more extensive representation.

I do not have time to describe the efforts of the European Parliament made towards sport, the decisions of the European Court of Justice, the activities of individual ministerial meetings, the European school sport games, the EC youth games, the sport related work of the European Committee for Standardization CEN/CENELEC or many more although the direct effects on sport are only just becoming apparent. The only reason I cannot mention a conference of the EC sport ministers is because it does not exist.

The mention of all these institutions should have clarified why the political and legal development of the community have made it necessary to pay close attention to the resulting sport related consequences, to recognise the possible uses and to avert dangers. The advice section for general direction X which is most closely involved in the concerns of sport formed the "Sport Forum of the EC" in December 1991 for this reason. The third meeting of this forum takes place on the 23 November, 1993. Here all member states of the EC work together with delegations comprised of four representatives of the state and the non-state sport organisations. This year is to be the first in which this forum is to discuss a work programme related to sport. It must also make decisions on its mode of operation especially concerning a stronger presence in Brussels.

Maybe the fact that the German Sports Federation opened its lobby office in Brussels a few days ago will help.

With this I would like to move over to the non-state organisations:

Once again I must neglect a considerable amount. It is impossible to describe here what importance the many international contacts between sport clubs, especially in border areas has for the European idea. I must also restrict myself to a number of succinct comments in my observations on the work of international trade associations: Despite their exceptional and effective steering of international competitions and harmonisation of rules, despite their friendly and peace promoting work, well above all ideological borders, despite all this their cooperative, mutually agreed upon contributions to the general development of sport have remained inconsequential and humble. Here I can think of nothing to say about more than 90% of all international associations.

The football and athletic associations belong to the few exceptions. Hopefully their solidarity actions, especially towards the development of new sport structures in eastern Europe has an infectious effect.

Similarly, in terms of a general development in sport, few memories of the union of national olympic committees are immediately awakened for me to mention here. Of course this is understandable in a movement in which the Olympic Games play a far greater role than the original Olympic Idea. However, justice requires an indication that this union possesses European spirit in its "Olympic Solidarity" actions and today especially in its aid to athletes and organisations in Bosnia.

The dominant Europe - orientated sport organisation institute is the European Sport Conference. Its greatest success lies in the fact that since 1973 east and west has frequently been brought together and even during the times of bitter opposition between the political blocks the mutual acquainting and exchange of ideas were possible despite all the adversity. The subsequent atmospheric conditions eased several bilateral agreements. Obviously the central themes of the meetings had to remain very general which I would like to illustrate through some examples from the last decade. "Sport as an Educational Factor in Mutual Understanding" (1981), "Europe and the World" (1983), "Youth and Sport" (1985), "Sport and Culture" (1987) preceded the Discussion of Sort Science Questions (1989). Of course a number of concrete themes were also considered such as doping, race discrimination or in 1989 the development of a charter. However, not until 1991 following the political upheaval in eastern Europe could the conference in Oslo decide to modify its work towards a goal of intensification. Work groups were initiated there with the themes "Women in Sport", "Youth in European Sport", "Support for the Development of Sport in

Europe" and "Europe in a changing World" and these are to present reports at this year's conference in Bratislava in a few weeks. The political development of Europe and its effect on sport is clearly indicated by the fact that this conference has 48 member nations, seven guest nations and 9 observing organisations concerning themselves with topics of cooperation.

In this discussion it will surely again become obvious that despite all advances the sport organisations in many European countries can still not be described as completely independent of the governments. This explains the formation of the loosely bound European Non-Governmental Sport Organisations (ENGSO) a few years ago. Naturally ENGSO also has a charter in which cooperation, exchange of information, the search for and representation of combined positions concerning sport political problems are included.

A summary of the existing institutions reveals no quantitative shortages thereof. This could lead many an observer to ironic remarks, but not me. We must realise that this was caused by the course of European history after the war and is an expression of the good will of countless people to finally let that which belongs together grow together again, as was so often stated during the German unification. We can however, not afford to remain uncritical. Some problematic points must therefore be addressed:

1. The report submitted for the conference in Bratislava by the work group "Youth in European Sport", states that: "A cause for uneasiness is provided by the lack of contact and coordination between the various organisations and insufficient utilisation of already existing mechanisms of information exchange." This sentence clearly shows that despite the many conferences, the European partners' knowledge of their work and their specific conditions is still poorly developed.

2. This deficit leads to gaps in the work processes on one side and a doubling or even trebling on the other side.

3. The fundamental papers such as the charters contain very general statements and are open to a wide variety of interpretations. The level of abstraction which has helped avoid conflicts in the past could now be decreased. A more precise description of goals would aid the cooperation of concrete projects.

4. The indisputable determination of all institutions are still lacking in the strategies for the combatting of abortive developments and crisis symptoms in international sport, as are coherent agreement on measures and the required systematic. This deficit could have many causes, but of especial importance is the fact that in recent decades we have all become used a too uncritical attitude towards elite sport which was used as a weapon in the

battle of political systems. If after this dispute, elite sport has lost its leading function for the overall development of sport, then new justifications are required for elite sport and also for "Sport for all" which are relevant to the cultural, social and economic context of the European nations.

5. The working methods are not particularly efficient in all committees. They can not achieve much if they only meet once a year.

6. To me it appears that the complete process is not oriented at "foundations" enough. Here I refer to the schools and sport clubs, the universities and regional or provincial sport organisations and of course especially to the individual citizens of our countries who are well justified in expecting some recognisable benefit for themselves from these summit meetings.

This critic has already provided a basis for changes. What is required?

1. The existing institutions must coordinate their work better and at least partially solve it mutually. If everybody tries to do everything on every level then paradoxically less is achieved than if everyone concentrates upon precisely defined task areas. For example I would regard it as a beneficial step if the working group which in the European Sport Conference has been primarily involved with aid measures for east European countries now leaves this to the more economically powerful European Congress.

2. If one intends to work together with a partner then one should be well acquainted with the conditions. This requirement reveals many deficits. Even those countries which have for many years belonged to the European Congress and can therefore benefit from the work provided by the Clearing House, the DS-SR and the DS-SI, possess far too few people with a proper knowledge of the social conditions and sport structures of the neighbouring countries. How much more extreme is this ignorance with respect to the east European countries where completely new structures must be built for government independent sport! Visits by delegations and conferences are not sufficient to solve these deficits. Detailed analyses are required of the present situation in sport in the individual countries and also the most precise deception possible of the conditions influencing its further development. Science should accept this challenge. An information system should then be built upon this preliminary work which extends far beyond the present capabilities of the Clearing House to the regional and local level.

3. A dominant role will be played by the area of education and continuing education. The two guidelines which regulate the mutual acceptance of educational courses and qualifications within the European Community must be amended by agreement with the other European nations even if this refers only to the employment areas in sport. For example it would be

a considerable step forwards if: the results of the working group 3 of the European Network of Sport Science Institutes concerning the teaching and examination of trainers were recognised by the governments and sport organisations of as many European countries as possible. The more educational systems and curriculums are harmonised, the easier exchange and assistance will become.

4. Partnerships must be developed. There can never be too many. There should be no international conference which does not aim to mediate such direct contacts. These should be developed between sport clubs and sport associations of individual countries, between schools and universities, between cities and regions, basically between all groupings in which sport plays a major role. In order to facilitate such partnerships we need an office which can be contacted by any person or institution interested in taking part.

5. Positive experiences in sport should be systematically analysed and multiplied. This applies particularly to the more novel and specific individual characteristics. This could be a sport possibility for a population with specific handicaps or a new strategy for the expansion of popular sport or a new teaching concept for elite sport trainers or forms of independent economic administration for clubs and associations or maybe a new method of obtaining voluntary staff.

6. This list of ideas could be lengthened indefinitely. On the occasion of the conference of Ministers of Cultural Affairs and Sports in Germany a few years ago a number of suggestions were made towards the intensification of sport contact with France which immediately produced a four sided list of more and more possibilities. However, such fantasies are restricted by economic limitations. Only those who remain realistic in terms of both the goals and the methods can expect increased budgets. Theoretically no sport organisation's or government's budget should still be without a portion designated for European measures. This is especially important for any such organisations which has "European" included in its title.

I appeal to these latter organisations not to restrict themselves to the above mentioned positions concerned with everyday sport but to instead create some European sport political highlights independent of the major tournaments of the sport associations and independent of the political conferences in order to deepen our sense of togetherness. For example I could imagine a European youth sport network which would be easily financed if sport organisations ruled that 1% of the taking at all international sport events in Europe must be made available for this purpose. Similarly a European sport foundation could be financed which would probably also be supported by public funding and sponsorship. Such a foundation could provide a service for the most urgent areas in sport development.

The similarity between sport and culture means that the experiences there obtained should be profited from and transferred to sport. An extension of such a consideration could be that "Europe's City of Sport", in which sport assumes an especially important role for a year is chosen annually, thus providing the opportunity for the cultivation of intensive European contacts. A "European Day of Sport" could also release new initiatives. In my opinion a logical development of recent years in the European network would be the distinction of outstanding sport science or belletristic sport literature with prizes if it has actually succeeded in overcoming national barriers.

Obviously this catalogue of ideas is incomplete and could be supplemented by creative minds. However, this may not necessarily result in an overall concept for the further development of European sport. The time for this has not come, but the present indications are more promising than ever before in our history. Future, concrete conceptions can be based upon fundamental definitions present in charters we have today and we already have countless individual activities which are weaving an ever denser net.

All assistance contributing to future developments is welcome. It was therefore not necessarily wise of the commission of the European Community to state that they were not responsible when a member of the European Parliament, Lord O'Halagan, nominated Saint Bonifatius, a good European, as patron saint. Walter Hallstein, the first president of the commission would surely have accepted such heavenly assistance true to his motto of which I am particularly fond: "If you don't believe in miracles in European affairs, then you're not a realist." We should also be filled with such a belief during these days in Cologne where we are attempting to construct a building on the "European building site" above the door of which one reads the inscription: "European Sport Science".

Action Field 1

Leisure and Recreational Sport

NEW PROFESSIONS IN SPORT AND TOURISM

De Knop, P., Wylleman, P., De Martelaer, K., Van Puymbroeck, L., Wittock H.[1]
Physical Education Department (H.I.L.O.K.) - Vrije Universiteit Brussel
Belgium

1. New professions in sport and tourism

In order to highlight the professional roles Physical Education-graduates can take in the emerging field of tourism and sport, this paper will first look briefly at the factors influencing the employment in P.E. and sport and at the characteristics of P.E. and sport careers. In view of a description of the job market for P.E. graduates, the relationship between tourism and sport and the evolution of sports tourism as a segment of the tourism industry will also be analysed. In conclusion, specific avenues for the evolution and development of P.E. and sport-related professions in tourism and sport will be described.

2. Employment in P.E. and sport

2.1 Factors affecting employment in sport

Several factors, related to specific social phenomenæ and/or to individual motives and attitudes, can be identified which enhance or inhibit the development of employment in P.E. and sport.

First we find that, as modern society removes the natural requirement of movement for individuals (e.g. cars, living in apartments, television as leisure-time activity), physical activity is now tentatively complemented through the efforts of different organisations: for example many companies try to use the values of sports (e.g. improving health, harmonious development, social environment) to <u>keep up</u> the <u>physical condition</u> of their staff and personnel by introducing fitness programmes, organising sports teams and participating in sports events for companies (e.g. survival weekends, adventure incentive trips). As future generations will, on average, grow older, people will act and behave as if they were younger because of their degree of fitness and vitality. Their urge to <u>prolonge</u> their <u>youthfulness and fitness</u> will necessitate more extensive physical training, upkeep and maintenance. Nevertheless, due to today's society witnessing an increasing level of <u>individualisation,</u> leisure activities have become more informal, i.e. less organised: sports are practised more and more within the private sphere (at home). This "cocooning" leads to the fact that less and less people ask for guidance from coaches, trainers, sports leaders, and focus more and more on using (individually or in a group) specific sports equipment (e.g. workout equipment). However, although the actual practising of sport becomes individualised, sports practitioners are also actively in search of opportunities for more social contacts: people spend more time in 'after sports'-activities than in the actual sports activities themselves. These "après"-activities are mostly enjoyed in an establishment where food and drinks can be consumed in a leisurely environment.

Second we find that several social phenomenæ have an (in)direct influence on the evolution of employment in sport and P. E.. Important is the fact that the leisure- or non-working-time has changed drastically: from 70 working hours/-week without holiday at the beginning of the twentieth century, it has evolved towards a 36-hours working week which is currently being negotiated, with extra holidays provided instead of raising wages. From a judicial point of view, we find that the launching of the 'Sport for All' idea by the Council of Europe in 1966, followed by the approval of the 'European Charter on Sport for All' in 1975, and the embodiment of the fundamental rights for physical education and sport in the UNESCO International Charter in 1978, has led to Sport for All becoming a world-wide phenomenon. Although sport was originally a privilege for the upper-class, it became accessible for all, and led to an increased sports participation. Sports has become a major economic force: the gross regional sport product for Flanders is 1.3 % of the total gross regional product of Flanders (or approximately 825 million US dollars) (4). As a result of the 'Sport for All' policy and the resulting large number of sports participants, we find that sport has not only been introduced in the educational system, but also in other institutions, i.e. industrial companies, socio-cultural organisations, youth-welfare organisations, organisations for ethnic minorities, criminality prevention, ... have all recognised the values of sport. As the value of sport evolves from sport as a goal in itself towards sport as a means, the is necessity augmented for wellstructured organisations on a governmental as well as on a private level. Originally manned with voluntary workers, these organisations have professionalised. In the wake of this surge in active sports participation, we find that there has also been an increase in passive sports interest: not only the number of P.E.- and sports-related journals has grown, but also the average amount of hours of sport on television steadily increases (from 2 hours/week in 1970 to 11 hours/week in 1990) (21). We may find however that the positive consequences of these factors may be counterbalanced by two specific developments, the most important of which may be the demographic evolution, i.e. a decrease of the total population in general and of the youngsters in particular. In Flanders for example, an 18% drop of the total population is expected by the year 2040, with a decrease of 500.000 youngsters (18 years old or less) within the same period. As this evolution will result in an increasing proportion of older people in society (25), we may find that in the future elderly people will participate in the same leisure activities as the other segments of the population, although differently: other sports and recreational activities, other levels of intensity and performance. A second important inhibiting factor is of an economic nature: (a) the 1980's economic decline and resulting <u>budget cuttings</u> and the decrease in the numbers of pupils and students which is leading to an oversupply and consequently unemployment, of teachers; (b) members of sports clubs who, due to the <u>economic recess</u> are not willing to pay a substantial, higher membership fee, resulting in sports clubs, especially the smaller ones, not being able to engage their coaches on a professional basis; (c) due to the growing market of sports journalism in magazines and on television, industrial companies have replaced their direct sponsorship of sports clubs and sports federations by advertising through the <u>sports media</u>.

In conclusion we can state that although many individual- and social-related factors can be identified which may enhance the development of employment in P.E. and sport, it is clear that due to the strong inhibiting influence of factors such as the economical recession, the demographic trends, and the changing behavioural patterns (i.e. individualisation, cocooning), the chances for an increased employment in P.E. and sport have strongly been diminished.

2.2 The Characteristics of Professions and Careers in P.E. and Sport

Before contemplating the development of new careers, it is useful to have more insight in three related aspects of professions in P.E. and sport, i.e. (a) the meaning of 'profession(al)', (b) the characteristics of P.E. and sport-related careers, and (c) the current job situation in P.E. and sport.

Physical educators have argued for years as to whether or not physical education is a profession, and as to who is (not) a professional in P.E. and sport. When we look at the <u>P.E. profession</u> from the point of view of its characteristics (e.g. its intellectual activity or body of knowledge, its practical use, its research resulting in new knowledge and ideas, its self-organisation, its communication capacity, its altruism) (17), then we must still accept Charles Bucher's (5) suggestion that the P.E. profession is still emerging, is still in full development. This does not mean however that there are no professionals in P.E. and sport, on the contrary! It is, however, important for these professionals to distinguish themselves more clearly from other so-called 'professionals', such as the person who performs for money, the 'roll out the ball' teacher, the experienced athlete without qualifications, ... Professionals in P.E. and sport have a body of knowledge which is broader and deeper, they translate their knowledge into practical use (e.g. the development and improvement of people's health, skills, and fitness), they perform research resulting in new knowledge and ideas which steadily increases their effectiveness, they are formally self-organised in professional bodies, they have professional publications and meetings, and they help protect or improve people's lives.

But professions in P.E. and sport, and their consequential careers, are more than the sum of their (academic) characteristics. Careers in P.E. and sport are:

1. known as young careers: these professions are fairly young, with new careers coming into existence, e.g. for coaches due to (a) new sports stemming from a new technical evolution (mountain-bike, surfboard, wind surfing ...), (b) new trends (calanetics, step, martial arts ...), and (c) the diversity of the sports activities pursued by a large part of the population (indoor climbing, golf, tennis ...).
2. exercised by young people, because (a) one should be fit to exercise a P.E. and sport profession, (b) the link with health and sport requires a sporty dynamic outlook, (c) very often sport is practised outdoors, (d) the sports activities take place during leisure-time and on holidays, and (e) teaching and training require dynamic people.

These careers have an element of glamour, necessitate great knowledge and skill, are achievement-oriented, offer enormous self-gratification and satisfaction and can provide significant personal and financial rewards at their upper limits.

Nevertheless, when we look at the job situation of these professions (directly or indirectly associated with P.E. studies), we find that although they have an extremely high profile, they also have great difficulties in establishing themselves as secure, consistent professional work opportunities. It is very difficult to acquire and maintain a (permanent and life-time) position in many of these careers, although their appeal to young undergraduates of both sexes is most significant and understandable. In Belgium, for example, there are not many highly technical, specialised and science-oriented P.E. and sport careers requiring graduate studies. Only the P.E. teacher (secondary educational level), university professor, teacher educator, sport scientist, and (in some cases) staff member of sports governmental bodies, require such a qualification. In other professions (among others the coach or trainer, the recreation or sport manager in communities) a graduate study can enhance the job-opportunities. Studies conducted in Flanders, the Flemish-speaking part of Belgium, regarding the employment of P.E. and sports graduates (15, 36, 37) show equal trends, namely (a) most P.E. graduates are employed outside schools, (b) the paramedical sector is becoming an attractive field of employment for P.E.

graduates, (c) schools, although decreasing in importance for employment, are still an important sector of employment, and (d) tourism, although still relatively small, is a new field for employment of P.E. graduates (but less than five percent).
It is with this dual image of P.E. and sport professions in mind, i.e. its youthful, and yet professional characteristics, in contrast to the unclear and unsteady job market, that the professional opportunities in the field of sports and tourism will be studied in more detail.

3. Sports tourism, a new profession?

Although tourism offers employment to only a small number of P.E. graduates at this moment, one can wonder if this amount could not increase in the future. One possible avenue for development of employment for P.E. graduates can be found in the field of sports tourism - an area which has become popular during the past decades. In fact, nowadays, we cannot ignore the importance of sport as a contributing factor to tourism.
As sport may be regarded as the world's largest social phenomenon (24), and as tourism is predicted to become the world's biggest industry in the next century, it would be surprising if such a relationship should not exist. This relationship is twofold : on the one hand sports tourism is becoming a high profile segment of the tourism industry and on the other hand tourism is influencing sports participation and the sports infrastructure.

3.1 The origin of sports tourism

Sport and tourism both have enduring pedigrees and first merged long ago. For example the numerous multi-sport festivals of the ancient Greek and Roman civilisations of which the Olympic Games are probably the best-known, attracted their share of tourists over many centuries (20). Since then, many factors have contributed to the dimensions of tourism in modern society. The same sociological, psychological, economical and cultural factors are standing at the source of tourist and sports activities, i.e. the influence of urbanisation on human behaviour, the change of the community into a society, the changed vision on "the hereafter", and the sociological elements determining human behaviour (e.g. population, education, available free time, profession, income, status) (40). Holidays and tourism have become a real part of life due to these four elements and sport has gained a natural attractiveness. "A world-wide recreation-and-leisure industry has emerged, replete with specialised paraphernalia, catering for a well-advertised and expanding market. New facilities, allied with government-sponsored programmes, have assisted in the promotion of fitness and "Sport for All" movements for a largely materialistic and narcissistic international society" (29). This evolution, together with the development of mass tourism has also changed the face of tourism: the tourist has become more critical, better educated, gaining a greater consciousness of health, demanding more and better infrastructure (e.g. transport, accommodation, sport facilities) and last but not least, demanding more active participation (9, 10). The tourist organisations had to adapt their products to these changing demands, and using modern technology, have created an international sporting playground for the reasonably affluent athletic tourist.

3.2 Sports tourism as a segment of the tourism industry

People have become more and more conscious of the numerous possibilities of "active holidays". In former days, "going on holiday" was mostly associated with the idea of "carpe diem" and "dolce far niente" ; today this attitude is no longer "in", and as far as recreation is concerned, it is considered to be far too insufficient. What is more, owing to changing living conditions, such an attitude could result in greater social isolation, anonymity, routine, all of which are negative aspects of our modern society and working methods. Today, active participation replaces passive consumption. The success of several types of sports and the increasing sports participation proves that today's recreation is more and more focused on a new type of sports person, i.e., an active sports participant. So we may speak of an overlap of the programmes of everyday activity and holiday recreation where more and more sports possibilities are offered. It means that, due to a more active leisure time pursuit, holidays are also becoming more activity-oriented. Sport has indeed become the second most popular holiday activity of the Belgian holiday makers (27.1%) and has experienced a considerable increase in participation during holidays since 1967 (35, 39). This percentage of sports participation has even increased to 30.4% for the holidays spent abroad (38, 39). Furthermore, about 26% of the sports population seems to be active in sport only during their holidays (6). This has resulted in an increased market for holidays with a certain sports content. Using Hahn's and Finger's categorisation on people's motivation to participate in holidays (19), we can see that two types of holidays have augmented during the last decade, i.e. the W-type (i.e. the wood, walking, competition-type) with tracking, tour cycling, tour kayaking, and the A-type (i.e. adventure, suspense, danger, surprise-type) with rafting, hang gliding, tubing, and mountaineering.

Sports holidays seem indeed to be an ideal opportunity to fulfil some of the basic needs of many holiday-makers, i.e. self-respect and self-importance (e.g. tennis, golf, wind surfing), compensation through sports performance (e.g. track, cycling, mountaineering), return to nature (e.g. water sports, mountaineering, orienteering), increasing family-activities, enhancing social contact, body-care and well-being (e.g. yoga, aerobics), and safety and security. This development of trying to fulfil some of the basic needs of tourists by means of sports is becoming very clear :

1. The choice of a camping area is dependent in 35 % of the cases on the presence of possibilities for sport and recreation,
2. The increase of the number of organisations offering club holidays (Club Mediterranée, Club Aldiana, Club Robinson, Holiday Club, Club Escolette ...), 3. The choice of the holiday destination is more and more frequently based on the possibilities for sports practice (e.g., wind surfing, walking paths, tennis, skiing),
4. The tourist organisations use sports pictures and photographs as promotional tools,
5. The authorities (e.g. community, country) are organising sports promotion campaigns during the holiday periods,
6. Sports federations are organising sports promotional campaigns (e.g. on the beach),
7. "Sport for All" mass events attract participants from abroad,
8. Sport and recreation are used to promote tourism for a country,
9. Sports training is a market exploited recently by tour operators mainly in response to demands for (team) training abroad where better facilities and/or climatic conditions are available (e.g., British golf players to Tunisia or Spain, Belgian athletes to Lanzarote),
10. Individual or group travel to sports events of national or international significance are a good opportunity for travel organisations to book flights and hotel accommodations (e.g., French, Spanish and Dutch interest in Wimbledon; Swedish interest in soccer at Wembley; the Olympic Games, ...),
11. The active, sports tourist is considered in the tourist world as a substantial target group (14). In other words, sports and recreation are an essential part of the package offered by tourist organisations.

3.3 Tourism as an influencing factor of sport

Tourism also influences sports: not only are holidays often the start of a leisure time pursuit which is continued during the year (e.g. tennis), but holiday makers on returning home, also compare the sports facilities available during their holiday with those at home, and find the latter more and more unattractive and insufficient (11). According to Opaschowski (27) the distinct reduction of visitors to local facilities at home in the past is indirectly due to an increase in travel intensity because these facilities are no longer adapted to their needs (e.g. the swimming pool which must today offer more recreational opportunities).

3.4 The specific factors affecting sports tourism

Sport and tourism are both following the same trend in participation : while in 1969 only 53 % of the male population in Flanders had ever participated in sport, this had increased to 72 % in 1989. For females the statistics show an increase from 25 % to 56 % (33). A comparison of the holiday intensity during the same era indicates an identical trend: we find that the total holiday intensity has evolved from 34.3% in 1967 to 56.0% in 1988 (3, 39). However table 5 shows us that not all age categories participate in sport on holiday with the same intensity. Primarily younger people (below 35) seem to be active in sports on holiday (39) (see table 1).

Table 1   The activities during holidays of the Belgian population according to age (39) (in percentage).

Age in years	Passive recreation on holiday	Sportsparticipation on holiday
< 5	43.2	30.1
6 - 17	31.7	40.3
18 - 24	38.9	30.7
25 - 34	45.8	30.2
35 - 44	47.4	22.7
45 - 54	35.9	23.4
55 - 64	31.0	14.2
> 65	38.9	6.2
Total	38.1	27.1

These data indicate that the same factors influencing leisure and tourism also have an impact on the development of sports tourism, i.e. education, occupation, income, ... The return to nature and the preference for open air sports activities during holidays can be explained accordingly (12). Furthermore, the quantity and quality of means of transportation make sports trips and vacations possible at more distant locations (31).

3.5 The various appearances of sports tourism

The combination of sport and tourism can be identified within two specific sectors: (a) the holiday with a certain sports content, and (b) the non-holiday with a certain sports content (e.g. business-travel with golf as entertainment, a week of training with relaxation elements, travel of a sports team to participate in a sports event).

3.5.1 Holidays with a certain sports content

Holidays with a certain sports content consist of four different types : (a) the sports holiday, (b) the (organised) holiday where sport is not the main object, but forms an important part of the holiday time, i.e. the club formula, (c) the sporadic participation in sport, provided during holidays, (d) private sports activity on holiday (individual or in group).

<u>The sports holiday</u>
The primary aim and content of such holiday is sport. The best-known form of this sports holiday is undoubtedly the <u>skiing holiday</u>. It has various different appearances: for beginner or experienced participant, for young and old, at a ski school, a ski course, a ski club or privately. The model of this organised skiing holiday however has recently been adopted by various other forms of sport. Holiday concerns, holiday organisations, societies and private sports schools now provide holiday courses, especially in sailing, gliding, riding, golf, diving, mountaineering and surfing : for instance bicycling tours are organised by well known cyclists. Bicycles, all-terrain bicycles, ski equipment, boats, recreation vehicles ... all have grown considerably in popularity in recent years for holiday purposes (7). New active holidays have also been invented. Guerrilla, or combat games which originally stormed the U.S. are now also very popular in Britain (1).

Another form that should not be forgotten is the <u>sport cure</u>. This can be useful for people who are ill or convalescing (e.g. Bad Salzuflen - Germany) (16). Recently a third form has been envisaged : <u>the fitness clinic</u> for healthy people who want to increase and tone up their vitality. There is daily physical training according to a special plan drawn up for each person individually on the basis of a medical examination (22). This form of sport cure will probably prove to be very expensive and it will therefore remain a sport merely for the wealthy.

Finally, we must mention <u>adventure travel</u>. Experienced leisure travellers constantly seek new levels of vacations. Organised travel adventures provide extraordinary experiences under safe auspices, like European hunting holidays, trekking with Sherpas in Nepal, river rafting ... .

The (organised) holiday where sport is not the main object, but forms an important part of the holiday time, i.e. the club formula

One of the most obvious and popular manifestations of this is Club Med., a 40-year old concept which has grown into a US $ 1.3. billion empire, with 110 villages in 33 countries on five continents, whose boast is : "Whatever you fancy, we've got the sport". Its formula of beautiful locations plus numerous activities organised by congenial hosts (Gentil Organisateurs = GO), allied with interesting and varied cuisine, has proved to be one of the most successful offerings in international tourism. This club formula has experienced a recent revival and creates interest by organising short distance club holidays with sports opportunities. Several kinds of tourist organisations have already adopted the principal idea of this club formula and adapted it to their own objectives (Club Aldiana, Club Escolette, Holiday Club, Club Robinson). A quite new form however is the year-around weather-independent club in Western Europe like Center Parcs, Gran Dorado, Sun Clubs, ...Already 7.1 % of the Belgian population today chooses a club holiday during short holidays (39). The origin of this club holiday can be found in social tourism, packed into a commercial product. Center Parcs for instance opened its first club in 1967. Today 12 clubs are being managed in 4 different countries with a level of occupation of more than 95 %. Research explains this success in terms of:

1. Changes in holiday habits : (a) because of the economic crisis the holidaymaker is choosing destinations that are not so far from home ; he/she still wants to go on holiday but during less days ; he/she is more conscious of prices and values, (b) there is a trend to go on holiday more often (but shorter), (c) an increase in demand for more active holidays and animation, (d) a greater need for freedom, (e) special arrangements for specific target groups.

2. The emphasis on the family life : (a) different types of accommodations (from 1 to 12 persons), (b) child-friendliness (baby-sitting, special animation for children, all the infrastructure is adapted to children ...), (c) special arrangements for families.

3. The recreational infrastructure : (a) weather independent subtropical swimming pools, (b) beautiful infrastructure situated in quiet surroundings, (c) many sports and recreational facilities.

4. A professional management.

5. Specific sports courses.

6. The integration of business (e.g. meetings, seminars) and holidays (13).

The sporadic participation in the organised sport provided during holidays-
Sport on holiday as opposed to a pure sports holiday - this is the primary goal of all attempts at integrating sports and games in all walks of life, in this case on holiday. Since 1963 the way has been paved by Marcel Meier from the Magglingen Physical Training College in the Swiss tourist resort of Engelberg. Sport activities were provided under the guidance of sports teachers, e.g. gymnastics, swimming, games, fitness exercises, folk dancing, gymnastics using apparatus and walks in the forest. Other models are the German Spa at Inzell since 1968 (awarding of 11.200 fitness badges to holiday-makers in the course of three years), the "Team Holiday" (exercise teams with potential for individual decision and organisation) held in Ruhpolding (Germany) since 1965, the venture entitled "Dolce-far-Sport" operated in Lezerheide-Valbella (Switzerland) since 1969 with a sport badge as an incentive, and since 1970 the venture "job join in, keep fit" in Switzerland and Wildhaus (Switzerland) and the "Pro-fit-Sport-Holiday" in Arosa (Switzerland) (32).

Today in Belgium the tourist communities (e.g. at the sea-shore) are competing to provide the most elaborate Sport for All programme to their holiday visitors. Some people take part in a promotional action only once (e.g. beach recreation); others are following a training course (e.g. Catamaran-sailing). Where a few years ago commercial companies were organising beach games as a part of their marketing strategy, now almost every tourist resort and even a lot of countries have taken over and elaborated such recreational programmes to attract tourists. Examples are provided in table 2.

Table 2 An overview of sport tourism programmes set up by different European countries.

PROMOTION-ACTION	COUNTRY
"Wanderschuh" (the hiking boot)	Austria
Cooperation between national and regional sportpromotion and local tourist organizations	Austria
Promotion of typical holiday sports (skiing - walking)	Austria
Game-festivals (Spielfest) during holidays	Austria
Cycling tours	Austria, GDR
Specific holiday sport promotion actions (courses for people staying at home, in communities...)	GDR
Lay out of touristic recreation areas with sport opportunities	United Kingdom
Public rights of way	United Kingdom
Sportfederations with a special offer for tourists (sailing and rowing)	Netherlands, France
Outdoors- and sportclasses	France
Promotion-action "Participate in Sport during your Holiday"	France
Outdoor recreation	France, United Kingdom, Austria, Scandinavian Countries
Foundation of research centres for the improvement of the cooperation between the authorities responsible for sport, recreation and tourism (STARPS)	Scotland
Train + bicycle	Belgium
Construction of folk games routes	Belgium
Walking/Cross-country Skiing/Tennis	Belgium
With Bloso in the breakers	Belgium
Sport, health and tourism in the mountains	Italy

Private sports activity on holiday

Sports practice during holidays is of old standing and yet it is a novelty. Ever since people go on holiday to the seaside or to the mountains, they swim or go for a walk. Holiday-makers at camping sites are playing "jeu de boules". At the beach the sporty holiday-makers play volleyball on a field marked in the sand with the big toe. However the offer and the planning of sport on holiday is new. Handbooks and leaflets containing practical instructions are distributed to holiday-makers. In some countries a series of television programmes has been dedicated to promote participation in sport during holidays. Games and sport facilities have been established (cycling paths, swimming pools, ...). Specific infrastructure for storing surfboards, mountain bikes, ... must also be provided. Now special police-units must even be trained for controlling surfers.

3.5.2 Non-holiday with a certain sports content

The best known example of this category is probably the exercise facilities offered by hotels for their clientele : "... as long as the general interest in fitness remains at its current high level, and as long as at least one hotel can claim some advantages by providing this very expensive amenity, fitness facilities in hotels will be an important consideration for any hotel with an eye to capturing the business." (34).

Comprehensive health and sports facilities are becoming mandatory for any resort worthy of the title, and urban hotels which have space restrictions preventing them from providing the extensive sports facilities necessary for qualification as a fully-fledged resort, are nevertheless now providing exercise facilities far beyond what would have been expected a few years ago. Leisure in general and health and fitness in particular form very important aspects of the total package offered to customers (23). Hotels are trying to attract seminars and business-meetings by offering golf and tennis courts besides business facilities. Incentive weekends are also introduced.

Besides, sport is not only an important element of the tourist product but mega-sports events can also generate a considerable tourism-flow, primarily (tourism-flow by attending sports events) as well as secondarily (tourism-flow arising from the attention given by the mass-media to the city, the area or the country where the event takes place). This secondary tourism-flow is giving the city or the area a sportive and international image (city-marketing), e.g. the importance of the Olympics for a city such as Barcelona or for an area such as La Savoie in France. From a geographical perspective there are three basic types of spatial organisations associated with mega-sports events : (a) events which occur periodically at different places over both regular (e.g. the

Olympics, World Cup Soccer) and irregular time spans (e.g. the British and US Golf Opens), (b) events with a long term attachment to a specific place (e.g. Wimbledon Tennis), (c) sports franchises with a general spatial stability. Teams (e.g. la Barça-Barcelona) become a part of a city's tradition, its social fabric, its culture and as such are major attractions for sports enthusiasts (26).

Large-scale athletic competitions conducted on an irregular basis (i.e. one per year or less frequently) have broad-based spectator appeal to a market whose dimensions are not, as yet totally understood by travel researchers. No systematic data base and no valid means of judging the variable effects of different types of mega-events are currently available. Mega-sports events are a powerful travel lure. The biggest draw large international audiences to the host site. Television provides free advertising and promotion to places which regularly stage mega-sports events. Such exposure attracts tourists on a year-round basis.

Unfortunately, there can be no guarantee that benefits will entirely outweigh the costs accompanying mega-events. The citizens of Montreal can attest inflated pre-event expenditures. The Montreal experience was an economic disaster by most standards. Los Angeles (1984), however, was a major triumph for the city and its visitors. Calgary followed in the pattern established by Los Angeles, using the 1988 Winter Olympics to generate both profit and prestige (30). These Olympic Games are but the tip of an iceberg, for they have spawned many similar festivals which also attract regularly thousands of visitors. Several kinds of imitations exist, based on : (a) geographical regions (e.g. Asian Games, African Games, Pan-American Games), (b) physical disabilities (e.g. Special Olympics), (c) religious affiliation (e.g. Maccabiah Games), (d) career or profession (e.g. World Student Games, Law Enforcement Olympics), (e) political (e.g. Commonwealth Games), (f) sexual orientation (e.g. Gay Games) (28). Even multi-sport festivals may, however, not represent the biggest sporting and tourist attraction. It is debatable whether the Olympic Games or the World Cup Soccer is the world's largest sports event (29). Accordingly, travel to hundreds of sports events world-wide is eagerly arranged by tour operators. Some countries are even developing a policy to promote tourism by organising sports events or promoting sports tourism with the purpose of attracting more tourists. Some examples: Portugal some years ago, established the commission "Sport and Tourism" with the task of promoting the image of the country by means of sport. Three categories of sports were chosen : (a) car racing, tennis, golf, horse riding, sailing and other aquatic sports, (b) other Olympic sports, (c) other, non-Olympic sports. Priorities have been put on : (a) big sports events, (b) events with impact on mass media, (c) organisation of European or World Competitions. A second example is the Tourism Authority of Thailand (TAT) which, in close cooperation with the Thai Golf Course Association, is promoting the year 1993 as the "Visit Thai Golf Year" aimed at increasing the number of foreign tourists in Thailand. This campaign expects to attract more than one million golfers annually, while the market today is only 20.000 golfers visiting Thailand. Another example is the Island of Curaçao. Recently the Curaçao Tourism Development Board has conducted an intensive research on the United States and European diving market. The reason for this research is based on the fact that Curaçao has a unique diving-product that satisfies the needs of the affluent diving-market. There are an estimated 1.5 million active divers in the US. of which some 600.000 travel abroad. Furthermore, the percentage of skin-divers travelling overseas has doubled in the past ten years. The Caribbean attracts the lion's share of outward dive travel from the U.S.. Curaçao is now trying to compete by disseminating information on the U.S. as well as the European diving-market (8).

3.6 Areas of professional concern

Sports tourism has proven to be popular. In order to see if this sector of tourism has become an area of professional concern for P.E. students, we have to evaluate this sector according to the standards of a "profession" as elaborated in 2.2. Four out of six characteristics (intellectual activity, practical use, communication capacity and altruism) can be recognised in sports tourism-related jobs. However two other important characteristics of a profession are the existence of a professional body and the research resulting in new knowledge and ideas. Table 3 provides an overview of the international congresses, seminars and workshops on sport and tourism.

Table 3 Overview of international congresses, seminars and workshops on sport and tourism (12).

Data	City	Country	Topic	Organisation
1971	Helsinki	Finland	Active Holiday-making	ICSSPE "Sport and Leisure"-Committee
1975	Bombannes	France	.Sport on Holiday	DSB + Nat. Olymp. Committee of France
1981	Mürren	Switzerland	Sport for All during	Trim + Fitness holiday
1981	Ottawa	Canada	Int. Conference on Winter Recreation	Nat. Capital Commission
1983	Piestani	Czechoslovakia	The Economic Basis of Recreation Services in Tourism	CIEPSS "Sport and Leisure" - Committee
1986	Troia	Portugal	Sport and Tourism Sports Animation in the Tourism Field	Council of Europe
1986	Wingate	Israël	Outdoor Education Recreation & Sport Tourism	ICHPER ICSSPE
1987	Hurghada	Egypt	1ste International Conference for Sports & Tourism (canceled)	ICSSPE
1988	Gmunden	Austria	Staff Training	FISpT + Freizeit Pool
1988	Malaga	Spain	Leisure, tourism & sport	Unisport
1989	Rovinj	Yugoslavia	Sport and Tourism	ICSSPE
1989	Waterford	Ireland	Qualified leadership in Sport and Tourism	FIEP

It can be concluded that a professional body, covering sports tourism does not (yet) exist. Five international organisations have however, put tourism and sport on their working scheme, but not as a regular topic i.e. ICSSPE (International Council for Sport Science and Physical Education) (the Working group "Sport and Tourism" and the Committee "Sport and Leisure"), FISpT (Fédération International du Sport pour Tous) (with the Commission Sport and Tourism, the Staff Training Committee and Events), Trim + Fitness, Council of Europe, and FIEP (Fédération International d'Education Physique). This means that, although the topic "Sport and Tourism" has been recognised by those five organisations as an interesting topic for a single conference, sports tourism is for them not a recurrent area of research, staff training, ...

3.7 Conclusions

Sport tourism is a vast and growing enterprise. The same sociological, psychological, economical and cultural factors are at the source of tourist and sports activities. Sport and tourism are characterised by the same trends in participation. Their relationship is twofold:
1. Tourism is influencing sports participation and the sports infrastructure.
2. Sport tourism is becoming a high profile segment of the tourism industry in various ways: the pure sports holiday, the club formula, the sporadic participation in sports activities provided during the holiday, private sports activities on holiday, sport on business weeks, and travel to sports events.

The significance of sport tourism is however not yet matched in the areas of professional concern. A professional body is not existant and the related literature and research are scarce. More research is needed concerning such aspects as the participation level or trends in sport tourism, the economic importance of sport tourism, the evaluation of sport tourism programmes, the motivation of participants, etc. . According to the overview of the sports and tourism promotional campaigns, it can be concluded that the authorities are involved and have a clear responsibility. Glyptis (18) states however that the evidence from five countries examined, points to a linkage between sport and tourism in the minds of participants, commercial providers and local authorities, but also to a lack of conscious integration - or even resistance to it - by policy makers, planners and public providers at national level. We must therefore presume that tourism, although it is predicted to become the world's biggest industry and sports tourism is becoming a high profile segment of this tourism industry, does not yet meet the requirements for new professions for P.E. students. In order to examine this conclusion some interviews were undertaken as described in the next chapter. The interview scheme was based on the five characteristics of a profession (Flexner, 1983 as cited in 17) to examine if these characteristics are also of major importance for someone who wants a profession in sports tourism.

4. The job market for P.E. graduates in sports tourism

As the demand for holidays is still increasing and as sport is becoming an important factor in tourism, the question remains if these developments offer possibilities for P.E. graduates. To be able to answer this question, we will analyse the job market in tourism. This market consists of the staff responsible for the policy, the administration, the recreation and sport (animation), the technique, the transport, the security and the cleaning up.

To look more closely into the job situation for P.E. graduates in the tourist sector, data were gathered regarding the job market itself, the salary and the educational and selection requirements. Three tourist organisations (i.e. Club Med, Sun Parcs and Center Parcs) as market leaders in holidays with sports possibilities, were questioned regarding their sport and recreational programmes. Club Med is focused on foreign countries, while Center Parcs and Sun Parcs mainly focus on short inland holidays. Information was completed using interviews with P.E. graduates who have been working in the tourism industry [2].

The jobs suited for P.E. graduates are the entertainer and/or the sports animator[3]. However, in the three tourist organisations examined, barely 3 % of the entertainers were P.E. graduates. Club Med. had a higher percentage due to the many part time jobs available during the season. It is striking that there are more undergraduates than graduates doing such jobs. The entertainer can become head entertainer, recreation manager and general manager. Sometimes there is a possibility to continue in a tourist agency with a greater responsibility (e.g. booking hotels, prospecting, providing promotion activities,...), or to become tour operator. Most of the P.E. graduates had few possibilities or little interest in the development of such a career.

The entertainer, with a monthly pay of ± 35.000 Belgium francs gross (approximately 1.100 $)[4], is not well paid. When working abroad, board and lodging are free, with a salary of 30.000 Belgium francs gross (approximately 900 $). Many entertainers are unable to work within the criteria of a decent contract and are therefore unable to receive retirement pay, social security,... Tourism organisations are looking for people with sports experience. A certificate of higher education in P.E. is preferred, but not required. During some periods (mostly out of the season) high level athletes, specialised in one sport, are responsible for a specific course (e.g. tennis, fencing,...). The knowledge of languages is a must. Further, one has to be very flexible and sociable. Organisations prefer people between 20 and 35 years old, who are good looking. Those who have a specific job, such as a life-saver or a ski-instructor, need to have a specific diploma. Sometimes clowns are hired for the recreation club or children's animation, through the mediation of a commercial organisation (e.g. artists bureau).

This data lead us to conclude that those responsible for recreation and sport, are an important part of the tourist organisation staff. Nevertheless, employment for P.E. graduates within this job market is scarce as a result of the unfavourable conditions (e.g. the salary, the contract, ...).

5. General conclusions

Today the situation facing university departments and P.E. institutes has changed significantly from that of two decades ago. The situation is such that the departments of P.E. are faced with the task of responding to multiple crises. This has resulted in a so-called "management by crisis" syndrome as a result of three (interrelated) challenges: (a) trying to keep jobs and positions secured, (b) maintaining quality professional preparation programmes under the P.E. umbrella, (c) trying to create alternative career opportunities for P.E. graduates. With the continued decrease in employment opportunities in the traditional area of P.E. (teaching), P.E. departments are looking for other, more perceived or supposed marketable professional fields such as health and fitness, sports management, ... (non-teaching areas) or have expanded the P.E. umbrella to include other teaching areas such as training and coaching, adapted P.E., recreational sports, sport tourism, ... Although they have not yet been able to provide many alternative career possibilities for their graduates, it is sound to widen the P.E. umbrella.

Our profession has indeed an obligation to help meet the needs of today's and tomorrow's societies by enlarging the traditional concept and scope of P.E. professional preparation programmes. Therefore we support the new P.E. professional preparation programmes in Belgium which are characterised by a general main core, directed towards teaching with introductory courses and options opening the umbrella towards other career options of which (sport)-tourism is one. Tourism, until now, has offered employment to only a small number of P.E. graduates. However, tourism is predicted to become the world's biggest industry in the next century and one of its segments, sport tourism, is a vast and growing enterprise. Although the job characteristics in sports tourism are eminently suited for P.E. graduates, the job situation (e.g. low salary) at this moment in tourism does not allow us to create a separate and specialised professional preparation programme for sports tourism alone. However, to treat the field of sport tourism within a broader package of the P.E. teaching area seems at this moment to be the best strategy to create a new profession. A professional body and more research are needed besides a better job situation before it can be said that animation is a new profession in the field of sport tourism.

References

1. **Algar R.:** Adult activities. Residential holiday programmes. Leisure Management 2: 51-53, 1992.

2. **Amman H.:** Paper presented at the Symposium "Animatie" [Animation] of the NWIT,Breda, The Netherlands.

3. **Boerjan, P.:** De ontwikkeling van het vakantiegedrag van de Belgische bevolking 1967-76 [The development of the holiday-behavior of the Belgian population 1967-76]. Brugge, Belgium, 1978.

4. **BLOSO:** Economische impact van de sport [Economic impact of sports]. Brussel, 1988.

5. **Bucher, C.A.:** Foundations of physical education. St. Louis, Mosby, 1972.

6. **Claeys, U.:** Sportbeoefening in Vlaanderen opnieuw bekeken [Sports participation in Flanders re-studied]. Leuven, SOCK, 1982.

7. **Crandall D.A.:** 1988 Outlook for recreation. In: U.S. Travel Data Center: 1988 Outlook for travel and tourism. Proceedings of the thirteenth annual travel outlook forum, U.S.T.D.C., Nevada., 1987.

8. **CTDB (Curaçao Tourism Development Bureau):** Executive Summary Marketing Strategy. Curaçao, CTDB, 1990.

9. **De Knop P.:** De sportvakantie besproken [The sports holiday discussed]. Unpublished dissertation. Brussel, Vrije Universiteit Brussel, 1979.

10. **De Knop P.:** Sports holidays, a new phenomenon in tourism. In Seguire S. (ed.): Proceedings of the International Congress on Trail and River Recreation, pp. 168-171. Columbia, Outdoor Recreation Council of British Columbia, 1986.

11. **De Knop P.:** Some thoughts on the influence of sport on tourism. In Garmise M. (ed.): Proceedings of the International Seminar and Workshop on Outdoor Education, Recreation and Sport Tourism, pp. 38-45. Wingate, Emmanuel Gill Publishing House, 1987.

12. **De Knop P.:** Sport for all and active tourism. World Leisure & Recreation 3: 30-36, 1990.

13. **De Knop P., Clerbout I.:** Clubtoerisme : een pilootstudie naar het profiel van het cliënteel en mogelijke redenen van succes [Club tourism : a pilot study into the profile of the clientele and possible reasons for success]. Unpublished dissertation. Brussel, Vrije Universiteit Brussel, 1990.

14. **De Knop P.:** New trends in sports tourism. Malaga: ICSSPE, 1992.

15. **De Canck F., De Clercq D.:** Waarheen als licentiaat lichamelijke opvoeding? [Where to as graduate P.E.?]. Bewegingsopvoeding en sportagogiek 3: 12, 1990.

16. **Dieckert, J.:** Holiday sport. In ICSSPE (Ed.). Sport and Leisure, Finland, 1971.

17. **Freeman W.H.:** Physical education and sport in a changing society. New York, Macmillan, 1987.

18. **Glyptis, S.:** Sport and tourism in Western Europe. Loughborough, 1981.

19. **Hahn H., Finger K.:** Animation im Urlaub [Animation at holiday]. Starnberg, Studienkreis für Tourismus, 1975.

20. **Harris H.A.:** Sport in Greece and Rome. Ithaca, Cornell University Press, 1972.

21. **Lambrechts M.:** Sport als bron van inspiratie [Sport as a source of inspiration]. Vlaams Tijdschrift voor Sportbeheer 112: 16-17, 1992.

22. **Larner C.:** Luxuriously healthy. Leisure Management 3: 20-21, 1992.

23. Leisure Management, 1988, 3, 9.

24. **Loy J. Jr., Kenyon G.S., Mc Pherson B.D. (eds.):** Sport, Culture and Society. Philadelphia, Lea and Febiger, 1981.

25. **N.I.S.:** Bevolkingsvooruitzichten 1990-2040 [Demographic prognoses 1990-2040]. Brussels, N.I.S., 1991.

26. **Okrant M.J.**: Sporting events : an untapped market share for travel and tourism. In The travel and tourism research assosiation (TTRA): Tourism research : expanding boundaries. Montreal, 1988.

27. **Opaschowski, H.W.**: Das Freizeitprofil öffentlicher Bader: Was kann Animation leisten? Archiv des Badewesens 3: 71-85, 1983.

28. **Preston, J.**: The pursuit of happiness. West nov.: 26-34, 1990.

29. **Redmond G.**: Changing styles of sports tourism : industry/consumer interactions in Canada, the USA and Europe. In Sinclair M.T., Stabler, M.J.: The tourism industry : an international analysis. Wallingford, C.A.B. International, 1991.

30. **Rooney J.F.**: Mega-sports events as tourist attractions - A geographical analysis. In The travel and tourism research association (TTRA): Tourism research : expanding boundaries. Montreal, 1988.

31. **Ruskin H.**: Selected views on socio-economic aspects of outdoor recreation, outdoor education and sport tourism. In Garmise M. (ed.): Proceedings of the International Seminar and Workshop on Outdoor Education, Recreation and Sport Tourism, pp. 18-37. Wingate, Emmanuel Gill Publishing House, 1987.

32. **Sprecher H.**: Kurortsport - Angebot sportlicher Betätigungen für Feriengäste. Unpublished dissertation. Magglingen, ETS, 1971.

33. **Taks M., Renson R., Vanreusel, B.**: Hoe sportief is de Vlaming? Een terugblik op 20 jaar sportbeoefening 1969-1989 [How sports active are the Flemish? Looking back at 20 years of sports participation 1969-1989]. Leuven, SOCK, 1991.

34. Travelling on Business, March 3: 5-6, 1987.

35. **Vanhove N.**: Het vakantiepatroon en de toeristische bestedingen van de Belgische bevolking [The holiday-pattern and the tourists' expenditures of the Belgium population]. Bruggc, WES, 1969.

36. **Vannieuwenhuyse A.**: Arbeidssituatie van Licentiaten Lichamelijke Opleiding [The professional situation of graduates P.E.]. Leuven, SOCK, 1988.

37. Waumans J.: De tewerkstellingsmogelijkheden van de licentiaat LO in de sport, zowel binnen als buiten de lichamelijke opvoeding [The professional opportunities for the graduate P.E., in as well as outside physical education]. Unpublished dissertation. Brussel, VUB, 1984.

38. WES: Reisgedrag en- opinies van de Belgen [Traveling behaviour and opinions of Belgians].Brugge, WES, 1989.

39. WES: Reisgedrag van de Belgen -1988- [Traveling behaviour of Belgians -1988-]. Brugge, WES, 1991.

40. Zeedzen L.: Vakantiegedrag: een speculatieve benadering vanuit de psychologie [Holiday behaviour: a speculative approach from psychology]. Breda, NWIT, 1973.

Footnotes

[1] Third to fifth authors are in alphabetical order.

[2] The P.E. graduates have been working in the tourism industry, i.e. Sunair, Center Parcs, Solmar-travelling, BVBA Management Recreation Services and St. Paulus youth camps.

[3] The term "sports animator" will be used as a general name for those who are responsible for the sports instruction / guidance as well as the entertainers who provide animation to the guests in a broader context (f.i. a spectacle, conjuring tricks, a fashion parade,...). According to Amman (2), animation is: to help people, through a social intervention process (guidance), to improve themselves (self reliance) and their quality of life. Animation is not only restricted to activities guided by a leader. Indeed it can be divided into four categories: social-ecological (e.g. attractive surroundings), material (e.g. special accommodations, play areas), medium (e.g. video, brochures) and personal (e.g. guided by animators). It is clear that in this case the personal animation has a central place. During the last decade sports activities have become some of the most essential elements of animation progammes, even in tourism.

[4] The salary of a graduate starting out in the educational sector is approximately 1.400$.

Sports and Aging

Govaerts, F.
Université Libre de Bruxelles
Belgium

1. Sport and physical or motor activities

All the sciences of sport possess, doubtless, representation of sport at once common and specific to these sciences. For sociology, the concept of sport calls into play physical activities involving social interactions of a competitive nature aimed at maximal performance in conformity to rules and conventions within groups or communities. These are organized socially, culturally, economically and even politically. Such organization governs the practice of sport while guaranteeing it a permanent institutional character. Like any social institution, sport polarizes the expression of perceptions, representations, actions, values and beliefs as well as constructs of knowledge and techniques. Self-fulfilment as success, self-discipline and competition to achieve it, oriented more towards performance and optimizing physical and psychological effort than towards pleasure, favour mastery of self and human interactions. Everything depends on the social goal attached to respect for the dominant values: courage, perseverance, tenacity and above all the worth of the competition that requires them as well as adherence to rules and discipline. Such a practice can inscribe itself as a profession and become remunerated labour. Or else, it may be a free-time activity engaged in as an amateur, for fun and without pay, or again such a practice may become so highly valued a spectacle that in numerous countries a television channel is reserved for it. And we should add here a supplemental form: sports education, taught in high schools, colleges and universities.

From this enumeration it is immediately obvious that we are dealing with a total social phenomenon, and the list given is by no means exhaustive. Thus, the reality of sport is not well-defined. Everyday language conflates sport with other activities - simple play or outdoor activities.

The same is true of physical activities that are also motor activities but that do not necessarily involve any striving for optimal performance or competition or respect for rules of play or interaction of roles subjected to strict rules of an ethical, technical and institutional nature.

Physical activities do not yet constitute a priority social phenomenon. Whatever prestige is possible for them is often picked up from the aura surrounding sport.

It is with sport that the ideal of performance and of excellence crowned by reward is associated rather than with simple physical activity.

In all cases, though in varying degrees, motor activity is the object of regular and unflagging training, carefully tailored, to be sure, to the abilities and progress of the participants. Its primordial importance to health is not yet known to all or in all quarters, yet it is recognized by all sports sciences [20] as well as by numerous governments [5] [25]. Such training is a source of physical benefits at every age of life. It promotes growth in children and adolescents; enhances health in maturity; and, starting from that period, slows down the process of aging, making it easier to live through late maturity and even old age.

Health through training in sports in respect for one's body and the bodies of others is the great collective value that more and more in the course of the century is associated with the values of striving and endurance. It was sports medicine, of which Albert Govaerts was one of the pioneers, that gave rise to this development, delineating one of the fundamental characteristics not only of elite sports, professional sports or amateur sports, but of all physical activities in the broad sense of the term. These activities are known for providing well-being by getting one into shape and keeping one in condition.

Is this a matter of faith or a scientific conclusion? For years, gerontologists have been telling us this, as have all the sciences of sports, including physical activities [9]. No doubt, in order to obtain quantifiable, experimentally reproducible and relatively reliable observations, one must scrutinize regular motor effort. One must be guided by the parameters of volume, intensity and frequency of exercise on the part of comparable groups in comparable circumstances. These conditions immediately suggest genuine sports training. It is not always easy to distinguish with reliable precision whether one is dealing with sports activities in the narrow sense or, more generally, physical activities.

For this reason, inasmuch as we are accustomed to seeking that precision, our task here, we feel, is simply to pose the problem. The framework in which it is placed is the gerontological sociology of sports in the broad sense.

Here a distinction seems essential. Sports, in the narrow sense, require specific qualities developed with a view to achieving prowess through self-disciplined living focused on intensive training engaged in on an almost full-time basis or at least several hours a day. While physical activities or even sports activities, in the everyday sense, may not be aimed at competition and contests, they, too, require sustained training if results are to be achieved. Here the training is only part of a way of life, not its essence. Needless to say, it is mainly this second type of activity that is taken into account in gerontology or in gerontological sports sociology.

Usually, it is the youthful model that predominates in the societal representations of sports, which are reinforced by the media as they turn sporting events into commercially profitable celebrations of the youth culture [13]. For those no longer young, it is easier to conclude "I'm too old for that" than to try to benefit from such activities.

Obviously, participation in sports and informal physical activities declines with advancing age. This is sometimes more true of women than of men, especially among less educated persons with lower incomes [9] [23]. The initial results for the city of Brussels and Anderlecht in the international epidemiological survey conducted by WHO on the health of elderly persons and their use of services seem to show which important function health plays in the practice of physical activities, at least for subjects aged between 70 and 79 years in 1980. In 1990, the same relationship existed between health and physical exercise. It should be noted that the number of women participating is greater than in 1980. Furthermore, people satisfied with their lives are also those more physically active [2].

2. Slowing down aging and identity-building

Everyone, naturally, wants to slow down the aging process. Not everyone knows that it is a question of quality of life. Judicious use of time becomes instrumental in the achievement of the long-term gratification provided by recreational sports activities. With advancing age, the meaningful use of time can no longer be evaluated in relation to economic production through work. Rather, as one grows older, essential production comes to be a matter of meaningful leisure activities that help keep one in condition physically, intellectually, and even emotionally.

Therefore, society must respond to the need for integration of the aging and the old who require these activities to "keep them in shape." A new commitment by all generations requires abandoning stereotypes of agist fatality [19]. The notions of full development and quality of life that govern the use of time in youth and maturity should guide physical and sports training along the lines of meaningful, expressive recreational activities [12].

Let us examine the relevant criteria: creativity, autonomy, sociability, development of talent, rest and relaxation, personal integration by belonging to the groups of one's choice. All these have the advantage of being able to offset the decline inherent in the marginalization that characterizes agism. They promote the capacity for personal expression in interactions with the environment, from which one is entitled to expect, moreover, artistic, intellectual and playful leisure activities. Agism, as opposed to the above, is a sociological process that affects those advancing in age by a marginalization tending to undermine the self-esteem of those who exhibit signs of age in a context of social interactions which stifle the quality of life.

Forms of personal expression, on the other hand, develop quality of life from the emotional, physical and cognitive standpoints. They are found in most free-time activities. These forms require sensory stimulation, the concentration of attention and the expenditure of energy through effort, all brought into focus through appropriate, regular training.

2.1 The physical and sports activities instructor: a significant partner

This is particularly true of sports. Sociologically, in order for the goal that has been set to be attained, a role must be given both to those practicing the sport and to the trainer. Why? Because the network of norms, behavioural models and values that constitute the role serve as references for existential activities. In so far as one is a member of groups within a social system, one needs the experience of roles, which are a powerful source of stimulation that guides identity structuring or restructuring at different ages in life. In sports,
in the strict sense of the term, the roles are clearly established, constituting a framework for motor activity. As for physical activities, they will be more beneficial to the extent that they are provided with a set of interacting, and not overly constraining, roles.

Apart from the specific needs of the persons concerned, one must also strive to discover the values that might be shaken up in various situations of aging. Connected with this is the need to rebuild the personal identity along three lines: independence of action, a feeling of competence, and self-determination.

Thus, the instructor or teacher of sports or physical activities must ensure the fulfilment a basic function: that of being a significant partner in dialogue. A critical approach on the part of the participants is desirable in order to facilitate a democratic relationship.

In addition to the creation of a climate of sensory stimulation involving the will to expend energy and keep one's attention focused, a genuine conviction of the possibility of imparting a new value to the personal and social identity of participants is essential, in order to encourage the elderly to empower themselves.

The problem, in the last analysis, is to bring about significant integration of aging or elderly persons so as to prevent them from being relegated to the fringes of society. By "significant integration" we mean sharing and dynamically interacting with various members of the group into which one has entered. Concretely, a sports policy requires men and women instructors having precise knowledge of gerontology, geriatrics, medicine, sociology and psychology [22].

The significant-partner role is fundamental. In addition to physical training, it means actively seeking discussions and dialogues in order to draw out from the vicious cycle of low social esteem/low self-esteem that characterizes agism those affected. The significant partner will help rebuild the personal and social identity, ascertaining to what extent certain stereotypes and prejudices tend to undermine one's self-image as a function of one's immediate relationships. The partner will encourage each individual to become an active agent of the improvement of his or her own human condition. The point is to reject the oversimplified role of "old man" or "old woman", which readily leads to the role of the sick or disabled. Otherwise, one is in danger of following the road of social senescence starting with middle age, allowing oneself to be stigmatized owing to outward signs that are purely chronological or biological or to the fact of reaching retirement age.

2.2 Creating kinesthetic awareness

The object, in fact, is to create by these means a kinesthetic awareness, so that every individual may maintain the ability to be physically mobile throughout one's existence, with sureness of movement and alertness of mind.

In addition to the enormous job done by senior citizens' clubs and sports or recreational associations, it is essential to establish motivating information programmes and advisory services to promote kinesthetic awareness. The latter should be included in development plans for persons aged 50 to 100 years, along with knowledge of socio-cultural problems, and with the goal of an active life and intergenerational conviviality.

Despite its heterogeneity, this enormous age group can provide opinion makers and militant family members in support of learning kinesthetic autonomy. The more intense and regular this learning is, starting from an early age, and the more it is practiced at maturity, the better the chances that it will be continued during aging and even into extreme old age. This is the best safeguard against being bedridden and placed into a facility for the elderly, arising from the self-confidence that goes with precise awareness of one's body's capacities.

The growing awareness of the requirements of good health through life style goes hand in hand with training in kinesthetic awareness.

This is not just the awareness of the sensation of movement, as the term "kinesthetic awareness" is more commonly defined. It is also the feeling of "the value of the achievement provided by sport" [6] at the level of awareness of movement as an "expression of neuromuscular coordination" [11].

The notion of healthy aging is spreading. Planners and interested persons are focusing more and more on maintaining or restoring locomotor and cognitive functions. "Regression" coefficients are used to measure them. When they are cited, it would be highly desirable to mention at the same time coefficients of kinesthetic recovery. Thus one would avoid discouraging aging persons, especially sedentary ones, who have not experienced the prevention or the recovery provided by exercise and training. What is more, important research results from sports and physical-education laboratories should be made known to the public, for they would tend to encourage participation in sports.

Such a measure means organizing researchers on a large scale in order to collect and summarize data for computing coefficients and elaborating useful indicators for development policies.

If it is true, as reported by Heikkinen [14], Raczek [21] and many others, that differences in fitness between those who are physically active and those who are not increase with age, one should quickly turn to elaborating coefficients for evaluating those differences, with a view not only to establishing programmes covering the entire life span, but also to promoting supportive learning for fitness.

2.3 Informing the public

At the same time that the public, and especially its elderly segment, is informed regarding these differences, however, it is also important to report that physical training, even when started at age 60, tends to increase reserve capacities as well as the capacity of aerobic energy-producing sources. This is certainly a high-priority information topic [16].

In connection with the popularization of scientific results, in order to instil in persons aged 50-60 years a greater desire to participate regularly in sports or physical activities, an effort should be made to eliminate the fear of accidents or health mishaps due to exercise - a significant barrier in the way of turning intentions into practice [24]. Shephard rightly recommends stressing "self-efficacy" and greater encouragement on the part of physicians.

Emphasis must also be placed on achievement motivation, which depends primarily on education. Of course one cannot hide the fact that in order to have a measurable impact on health and fitness status, regular exercise is a must. In short, kinesthetic awareness combined with health awareness implies an acceptance of a life style for each of stage of the life cycle.

While it cannot be denied that decline during the process of aging depends to a considerable extent on previous life style as well as socio-economic, occupational and environmental (urban or rural) factors [10] [14] [15], one cannot repeat often enough that it is never too late to benefit from adopting a programme of sports or physical activities. Here we have another priority public-information theme.

3. Gerontological and sports sociology vs. agism and homogenization of aging

If we are to help prevent the percentage of depressed individuals from doubling after retirement, we should do well not to consider aging an unavoidable process of deterioration. Let us interpret it as a way of opposing death, a process of resistance and differential growth. One can hope to make it slow down, or at least take place in a state of well-being.

As Yves Camus [4] put it, each organ seems to have its own timetable for growth and decline. While it is genetically programmed, it can still be modulated by the way one lives.

Thus, the rate of aging differs in many respects: physical and intellectual performance vary within a given age cohort, from one society to another, according to socio-economic conditions, educational level or sex, due to differences in life style.

Chronological age is distinct from biological and psychological age. While it is true that greater knowledge and experience can offset the slowing-down of nerve-impulse transmission times and increased disease due to stress, this does not take place to the same extent in everyone.

The socio-occupational or male/female categories subjected to the least favourable working conditions during the economically productive years and having the least access to leisure activities that afford development and relaxation, and also the lowest participation in decision-making, show the greatest signs of premature physical decline.

Nor must we forget that approximately half the persons below the poverty level are over 65. Their dynamic and creative capacities and their ability to adapt and relate have been worn down by the difficulties of survival. They are far less capable of taking rational steps to fight aging, owing to both economic and cultural impoverishment. They certainly do not make up the clientele of sports participation. It is not only the context of destitution that keeps them away from physical activities, but also the psychological aspect of deprivation of an identity providing a sense of one's own value.

Social time stigmatizes chronological aging by attaching to it deficiencies that do indeed result in a loss of status, roles and identity. Agism, which involves stigmatization based on outward signs that reduces the diversity of individuals and situations to the homogeneity of a single social category, is as rampant as racism or sexism. It appeals to widespread notions and images reflecting prejudices.

3.1 Managing advancing age and promoting training

If we recall that identity-building is related to the individual's social insertion, we can but note that opportunities decrease as chronological time advances. It is for this reason that educational gerontologists have spoken out against dividing existence on the basis of socio-economic imperatives [4]. The words of A.M. Guillemard are often quoted: "Retirement is the real cause of aging". While this is exaggerated, it is a factor that should be taken into account as well as the socio-psychological personality destruction.

It is a matter of urgency to change language that associates the later years of life with inactivity and imposed rest, or in other words, a non-role. It is time that we resist the institutionalization of aging and the amassing of inequalities when the ax of retirement falls. By means of expressions such as "retirement age" and "old people", which represent mutually exclusive categories with respect to "youth" and the "prime of life", social time hardens the lines between generations.

Within a context of ongoing education and interdependence with sports education, pedagogic strategies must be transformed. The development activity programmes and the installation of infrastructures require the participation of elderly practitioners just as much as the participation of experts in sports and physical activities. In order to obtain programmes and infrastructures, the elderly must stress their concerns, needs and aspirations and demand the formation of a political will. The exercise of decision-making and responsibility by the elderly will work synergistically with regular physical training.

This is part of the continuing education of the entire population, coming under health policy. Far from giving rise to excessive medical treatment or welfare assistance, training and its holistic context should be conceived of as agents of development and self-transcendence. Their models and their standards of action might be served by gerontological and sports sociology within the framework of a recognized partnership.

3.2 The benefits of regular training

Increased efficiency of certain metabolic processes, optimum maintenance of cardiovascular and musculoskeletal function - such are the obvious benefits of sports and physical activities [1].

Performance at the highest level cannot be an objective for elderly individuals, but rather optimal health and well-being.

The potential advantages are conditioned by constitution, socio-cultural and economic level and physical capacity in relation to chronic diseases. Cognitive functions play a favourable role with respect to them.

Effort and endurance are not necessarily prized by the elderly and are in fact often a matter of discouragement for them. Yet these two values of the sports commitment are fundamental to everyone. In view of the physiological limits that characterize aging, it is precisely those values that maintain the muscular tissue mass, which diminishes the more one remains sedentary. The same appears to hold true of bone density, which is of greater importance for the more active parts of the body [3].

Aging and elderly persons should be systematically warned against the loss of bone minerals that goes with prolonged immobilization. They should be apprised of the impact of exercise on bone mineralization. They should also be informed of an essential fact: "The diminution of muscular performance linked to age is not absolute nor inevitable". Strength, flexibility and muscle performance depend on aerobic metabolism. This is impaired with age. But it can be restored, commensurately with each individual's possibilities.

The following, fairly recent, conclusion should be widely publicized: Suitable programmes can reverse the loss of muscular tissue. This is true to a certain degree and requires regular participation in training to develop aerobic capacity [1].

Very simple stretching, relaxing and strengthening movements will be used to combat stiffness and weakness and in the case of impaired physical capacity. Once these have improved, they no longer limit performance, though it will still depend on cardiovascular function and metabolism. In view of these limiting factors, the degree of fatigue and the extent of recovery, the physical condition must be worked on for flexibility, strength and endurance before one moves on to sports training [24].

If physical condition has not been maintained, one must start from scratch, even if the motor abilities of youth have been maintained. The correlation between volume, intensity and frequency of training sessions must be taken into consideration in finding the proper level.

As noted by Carl Schneiter [24], "a time of less than one hour for running 10 km, achieved by the best octogenarians, is out of range for even 20-year-old sedentary subjects".

Raymond Malesset [18] reports the changes in this correlation with increasing age. For high-energy sports, regular training three hours a week very significantly improves physical fitness in persons aged 60 to 69 years as compared with sedentary individuals of the same age; but in men aged over 70 and women aged 60 to 69, it takes six hours for an equivalent result.

4. Growing, yet insufficient, practice of sports

As pointed out by Walter Tokarski [26], the methodologies used render the comparisons difficult. First of all, the definitions of sports and physical activities used vary, some including and others excluding "soft sports", to use Tokarski's expression, such as walking, individual rather than club-organized hikes, and play activities. Thus, for sports practiced in Germany, the differences in percentage may range from 5% to 25% of the population aged 50 to 64 years. The delineation of age groups, too, usually varies from one study to another. The preponderance of 50-to-64-year-olds and the near-constant absence from the population samples of persons aged over 75 years or combining into a single group all aged over 70 reflect an exclusion process and prejudices that have not yet disappeared and do not adequately account for the increase in life expectancy. Finally, many surveys are limited to sports associations and clubs.

One must therefore exercise caution in interpreting most of the results. They do, nevertheless, reveal some general trends with respect to practices and the nature of the sports and physical activities engaged in.

According to a French survey [4], barely 1% of all persons over 65 years of age regularly practice a sport throughout the year, while 21% previously practiced a sport but no longer do so. Finally, 75% of those aged over 75 have never practiced a sport. A survey conducted in the early 1980s among sports federations and cities and the French community of Belgium showed that the percentage of members over 60 years of age was small, and those few were usually former members who continued their favorite sport. The sex distribution showed at that time that there were three women to one man [17].

The Senior Sports Federation of the French Community of Belgium furnished us with the data for the city of Liège, at our request, by 5-year age groups, from age 50 to 80, and by sex. The data as of 30 June 1993 showed 1133 persons aged from 50 to over 80 years belonging to 54 sports clubs in Liège, including 698 women and 435 men. In each 5-year age group from age 50 to 75, the women outnumbered the men, though the difference gradually diminished starting with age 75. One Liège sports club has some 178 women from 65 to 70 years of age, as against 132 men. This number drops to 103 women and 78 men for the 70-to-75-year age group, 35 women and 33 men for ages 75 to 80, and 16 women and 15 men for those over 80. Gymnastics, walking, swimming and the game of bowls (pétanque) are the sports most commonly practiced by both sexes in Liège.

The survey done in Switzerland in 1989 [7] seems to indicate that Switzerland is one of the countries of Europe with the highest sports participation rates for the age group 55 to 74 years, inasmuch as only about 50% do not engage in any sport or physical activity. Approximately 14% practice a sport less than once a week, 21% twice a week, and 15% more than twice weekly. In other words, in 1989, out of a Swiss population of 1,209,600 persons aged from 55 to 74 years, more than 600,000 had sports activities, the most frequently cited ones being ranked as follows: walking, 45.9%; swimming, 21%; gymnastics,15.9%; bicycling, 15%; running, forest hiking and jogging, 9.8%; and skiing, 8.5%. The dynamic and catalytic action of Pro Senectute, a culture focused on public health since the 19th century, and reduced insurance rates for persons engaging in sports might explain this participation of a far higher percentage of senior citizens in sports and physical activities than is ordinarily observed in Europe (usually not over 25%).

The survey carried out in 1988-1989 on a sample of 10,000 persons in five regions of Germany [15] also deals with the factors that play a role in the practice of sports, from the standpoint of both demand and supply. This is also a survey that has the advantage of dividing the sample into 5-year segments, from age 50 to 79. There was an appreciable increase in participation in sports activities between 1973-1984 and 1988-1989. More senior persons had already engaged in a sport and were more inclined to continue to do so; there was an increase in motivation as well as in the differentiated supply of sports associations, though the latter was still just beginning. In all age groups starting from age 50 and for both sexes, sports participation increased with educational and income level. Between the ages of 55 and 69 years, men who engaged in sports devoted more time to them (4 hours a week) than women, but women consecrated more time to them between the ages of 65 and 70.

The survey further shows - and this is an important fact - that one person out of four in the age range 65 to 75 years engaged in a sport or physical activity on a doctor's recommendation.

5. For a significant, lasting impact

Participation in sports and physical activities seems to have progressed since 1980 in most European countries. This growth is insufficient, however, in the light of the demographic and economic changes taking place in post-modern societies. The working population is diminishing while the non-working population is on the rise, with an ever longer life expectancy.

In Belgium, for example, even back in 1981 the over-60-year-old segment of the population, which then represented only 18%, weighed heavily on health and disability insurance: more than 60 to 70% of the patients were elderly persons [17].

The recession and unemployment of the 1990s have reduced the working population still further through massive lay-offs based on economic considerations. For reasons not only of equity, quality of life and public health, but also from a purely economic standpoint, maintaining the physical and mental autonomy of the senior population as long as possible is becoming a top priority. A political will, concerted action and investments, both national and local, by communities, associations and individuals, to promote sports and physical activities for seniors and supportive publicity campaigns will be less costly than geriatric health care and the institutionalization of the elderly.

There is a growing awareness of this. An example is the pilot project of Aargau canton in Switzerland [27] entitled "Health and Sports for Seniors". The stated objective of this project is "to delay to the greatest possible extent the need for permanent care for senior citizens, bearing in mind that it is not activity but inactivity that engenders the phenomena of wear".

We all know, in each of our countries and in our cities, of successful model experiments whose benefits for the elderly have been undisputed and scientifically controlled.

The problem confronting us in the 1990s is that we must proceed from these pilot experiments or public or private initiatives to a larger, nation-wide and European scale in order to exert a genuine and lasting impact on the quality of life of what will be more than one-fifth of the population and thus reduce the human as well as economic cost of health.

References:

1. Arroyo, J.F., Bengoa, J.M.: Activité physique et besoins nutritionnels chez les sujets âgés. Rev Gériatrie 17, no. 7: 357-364, 1992.

2. Asiel, M.: Enquête épidémiologique internationale sur la santé des personnes âgées et leur utilisation des services, OMS, communication personnelle de résultats pour Bruxelles-Ville et Anderlecht pour 1980 et 1990.

3. Blumenthal, J.A., Emery, C.F., Madden, D.J., Riddle, M.W., Schnielbok, S.: Effects of exercise training on bone density in older men and women. J Am Geriatr Soc 39, no. 11: 1065-1070, 1991/11.

4. Camus, Y.: De la notion du vieillissement différentiel à la conception d'une gérontologie éducative et sportive. Gérontologie 50: 28-32, 1984.

5. Council of Europe, Recommendation (88) 8, April 18, 1988.

6. Diem, C.: Wesen und Lehre des Sport und Leiberserzieung, Berlin, 1960.

7. Eidg. Sportschule Magglingen, Seniorensport, Schriftenreihe der ESSM 50: 1992.

8. Elward, K., Larson, E.: Benefits of exercise for older adults. A review of existing evidence and current recommendations for the general population. Clin Geriatr Med 8, no.1: 35-50, 1992.

9. Foldesi, G.S.: Public opinion of physical activity in the later years of life cycle. Int Rev Sociol Sport 24, no.2: 107-120, 1989.

10. Frändin, K., Meelström, D., Grimby, G.: Functional performance and patterns for physical activity at the age of 76: a lifespan perspective. 3rd International Conference on Physical Activity, Aging and Sports: Physical Activity and Sports for Healthy Aging, University of Jyväskylä, May 31-June 4, 1992. In: Harris, S. (ed.): Physical Activity, Aging and Sports Series v 3,4. Albany, Center for the Study of Aging, forthcoming 1994.

11. Govaerts, A.: La biomécanique, nouvelle méthode d'analyse du mouvement. Bruxelles, Presses Universitaires de Bruxelles, 1961.

12. Govaerts, F.: Les centres de culture populaire: lieux d'expression des personnes âgées et moyens de prévention du vieillissement. Loisir et Société 4, no.1: 109-121, 1981.

13. Govaerts, F.: Belgium: Old trends, new contradictions. In: Olszewska, A., Roberts, K. (eds.): Leisure and Life-Style, a Comparative Analysis of Free Time, pp. 62-83. London, Sage Studies in International Sociology, 1989.

14. Heikkinen, E.: Role of physical fitness exercise in healthy aging. 3rd International Conference on Physical Activity, Aging and Sports: Physical activity and sports for healthy aging, University of Jyväskylä, May 31-June 4, 1992. In: Harris, S. (ed.): Physical Activity, Aging and Sports Series v 3,4. Albany, Center for the Study of Aging, forthcoming 1994.

15. Heuwinkel, D.: Sport für Ältere in einer sportaktiven alternden Gesellschaft. Z Geront 23, no. 1: 23-33, 1990.

16. Korkushko, O.V.: Motor activity in the prevention of premature aging. 3rd International Conference on Physical Activity, Aging and Sports: Physical activity and sports for healthy aging, University of Jyväskylä, May 31-June 4,

1992. In: Harris, S. (ed.): Physical Activity, Aging and Sports Series v 3,4. Albany, Center for the Study of Aging, forthcoming 1994.

17. Levarlet-Joye, H.: Activités du troisième âge. Enquête auprès de la Communauté française de Belgique. Sport 104, no.4: 56-63, 1983.

18. Malesset, R.: Retraite active - Retraite sportive. Paris, Charon, 1987.

19. Neuhaus, Robert, Neuhaus, Ruby (eds.): Successful Aging. New York, Wiley and Sons, 1982.

20. 3rd International Conference on Physical Activity, Aging and Sports: Physical Activity and Sports for Healthy Aging, University of Jyväskylä, May 31-June 4, 1992. In: Harris, S. (ed.): Physical Activity, Aging and Sports Series v 3,4. Albany, Center for the Study of Aging, forthcoming 1994.

21. Raczek, J.: The effects of physical activity and motor fitness in the elderly. 3rd International Conference on Physical Activity, Aging and Sports: Physical activity and sports for healthy aging, University of Jyväskylä, May 31-June 4, 1992. In: Harris, S. (ed.): Physical Activity, Aging and Sports Series v 3,4. Albany, Center for the Study of Aging, forthcoming 1994.

22. Röthlisberger, E.: Quel est l'avenir de la vieillesse dans le sport ?, Macolin 47, no. 1: 2-3, 1990.

23. Rubenstein, J.: Outdoor recreation in two European countries. Int J Aging Hum Dev 25, no. 2: 129-146, 1987.

24. Schneiter, C.: Le sport des aînés, une question de dosage. Macolin 47, no. 1: 4-6, 1990.

25. Shephard, R.J.: Sport, physical fitness and the costs of public health. Sports Sci Rev 13, no. 1: 9-13, 1990.

26. Tokarski, W.: Neue Alte, alte Alte - alter oder neuer Sport ? Seniorensport in Zeichen des Umbruchs. Brennpunkte der Sportwissenschaft 5, no. 1: 22-35, 1991.

27. Weber, U.: Sport des aînés: modèle cantonal pour une tâche nationale. Macolin 47, no.1: 11, 1990.

BLUE CHIP SPORTS COMMUNICATION
PRESENTATION & EFFECT

Hackforth, J.
Institut für Sportpublizistik, Deutsche Sporthochschule Köln
Germany

1. Introduction

The following brief report contains information and results which were taken from a research project conducted over several years, entitled "PRESENTATION AND EFFECT OF SPONSORING AND ADVERTISING IN SPORTS", which will be completely analyzed and brought to its conclusion during these days. The scientific debate over the problematic issue to be discussed here started already on the occasion of the 1984 European Soccer Championship in France (1) and was continued in depth at the subsequent event in 1988 (2). At the end of the 80s these "snap shots" at major sports events by a "single initiative method" were abandoned and instead longitudinal section studies for the period of one year (3) based upon a "multiple initiative method" (4) conceptualized and realized during the years 1990 -1991.

Due to the complex method design, based upon a solid knowledge of literature (5), monocausal types of observation, which had been more often speculative rather than plausible, were discontinued in favour of multicausal patterns of interpretation.

The submitted research initiative and the data gained thereby, as well as the different methodological approach are, to my knowledge, new, and until now, unique to the Federal Republic of Germany; nevertheless, based solely upon this research a number of factors concerning the success or failure of sponsoring activities in sports become clearly apparent!

2. The "Magic Web of Connections"

Three societal subsystems build the basis of the complex structure of connections, which all together go through expansive and innovative developments.

The catch-word "leisure society" (6) documents not only the changed living conditions of the Federal Republic's citizens in regard to the free time at their disposal, but also the relevance of sports and play, from numerous "out-of-the-house" activities with the family, in the circle of friends, in the club, or in commercial leisure establishments. The organized (club, association, DSB) as well as the unorganized (studios, centers, field) sports profited considerably from this changed leisure-time behavior in recent years.

LEISURE SOCIETY SPORTS

Sport, characterized then and now, by extremely positive attributes like success, performance, victory, dynamics, fitness, contest, but also "fair play" has a predominantly positive image and reflects the socio-economic order of the Federal Republic very well (7).

Secondly, expanding activities of the advertising industry are substantiated, in which advertising and sponsoring in and with sports, individual sports figures, or teams, as well as special sports events are in the forefront. The 80's provided for a barely predicted augmentation of the total sponsoring budget, which at the beginning of the 90's was estimated at around DM 1.5 billion.

ECONOMY

Often without a true concept, without recognizable strategy, and only with punctilious realisation; barely with valid success control! That's how enterprises make use of financial resources which are more or less intuitively and emotionally invested or disseminated.

And thirdly, - finally the monopolistic and restrictive media landscape, particularly in radio, had demanded advertising alternatives before the pluralistic opening up of broadcasting (radio and television) since 1984 permits new possibilities and forms.

The state treaty which became effective January 1, 1992 opens up additional sponsoring and advertising opportunities for statefunded establishments, which first became visible on broadcasts of the Winter Olympic Games in Albertville (8). Technical innovations and widening publicity will put its omprint on future developments which also include advertisement activities in all media.

The catch-word "information society" (9) characterized this trend appropriately. All the subsystems named and outlined here show ganins in the "economic" and competition-oriented dimension. So far, a fundamentally congruent development can be ascertained which is being described by catch-words like internationalization, commercialization, and segmentation (10).

3. The Phenomenon "Sports Sponsoring"

In contrast to the traditional patronage of past decades in German sports, sponsoring rests on the premise of an "economically relevant return". The reciprocal give and take between sports and commercial interests will possibly become a mutually beneficial deal through the spread by the mass media. Sports provide events, performers, and media attractiveness (particularly TV); the sponsor provides money, goods, know-how, and organizational skills. In the most effective case an affinity and coherence exists between the type of sport (sports figure) and the sponsor (product) which can enhance the credibility, attention, and effect of the measure taken.

SPORTS-SPONSORING

Provision of money, goods, know-how and organizational skills for sports figures, sport teams, sport events with the goal to receive a relevant return.

The goals strived for by the sponsor can be attempted singularly, in combination, or inclusively. The consumer and potential customer should have an "improved or at least stabilized degree of name recognition, the knowledge of individual products should be actuated, the image transfer via the type of sport, the sports figures or the sports event should occur, and - ultimately - the baying and social habits should be influenced. For co-worker and partner the motivational aspects of sponsoring are at the center as are socially desirable "good-will" activities. The total of the possible goals here too is more than the sum of its parts. A strategy; planned, coordinated, and answerable to different goal categories is to be preferred over a punctilious conception. It remains important that individual goal categories can only be reached over a long-term period and immediate effects seem to be improbable.

SPONSORING SERVES -"SHOULD SERVE"

Name Recognition
Image(s)
Contact Nurturing
Goodwill
Product Actualization
Buying and Social Habits
Co-Worker Motivation

The weakest link in the sponsoring activities in sports and the "black box" for many businesses and agencies is effect and success control. To the question of what the effect of advertising is; there are many, and yet only few answers and initiatives. The same goes for the central question, what the modern mass media can achieve (11).

Until now a homogenous effectiveness theory is still missing; however, there are promising and empirically secured initiatives and conclusions to be drawn into the calculation.

Media influences our knowledge (cognitive effects), partially our opinions and attitudes towards persons, products, and circumstances. Media alone hardly has any influence over our buying and social habits. For that; additional contacts and a number of variables are needed by the citizen and consumer, which are not initiated by the message. If, however, knowledge, opinions/attitudes and behavior are to be influenced, exact knowledge is needed, which is mostly missing in the communications practice.

EFFECT & PROCESS CONTROL

Process Control
Result Control
Media Analysis
Audience Analysis
- Ex-ante /Ex-post -

Therefore process controls during the course of an action or campaign are necessary (concomitant research; evaluation) as much as result controls after a campaign, in which debit and credit conditions must be compared to each other.

In addition, it is imperative to analyze the campaign presentation in the media (particularly TV and newspapers/magazines) as well as conducting audience research, accomplished by multiple interrogations and observations. The combination of media analysis on the one hand and audience analysis on the other is rare or non-existent. If at all, monitoring and clipping (12) should evaluate the media presence or, on the other side, questioning should reveal the knowledge of the audience. Each one separately sometimes, but in combination these effect initiatives are rarely found in reality, at least they are not applied with continuity. One could improve this effect research, if, before the start of a campaign a so-called EX-ANTE poll (O-measure) would be conducted, and after an extended time period past the campaign, an EX-POST study would give further information. Not intuition and personal preferences, but analytical and systematic research methods must govern sponsoring in particular. The postulate for economic deal making mentioned earlier must be scrutinized and evaluated; the irrationality of decisions must yield to provable procedures. Only approximately 30 % of enterprises engaged in sports sponsoring scrutinize themselves or their decisions made (13) - effect and success control, by contrast, offer the instrumentation needed for systematic research.

4. The Research Design

The research plan of the long-term study also directly conditions its results. Therefore the methodological credo and the discovered context of understanding shall be formulated here:

A) A comprehensive and long-term media analysis was compared to a multilayered, representative population poll.

B) In addition, two stadium polls (Cologne and Frankfurt) were conducted with spectators on site.

C) A supplementary laboratory experiment was conducted with two groups.

AD A) From February 1, 1990 to January 31, 1991 sports reporting plus advertising in the general area (TV commercials and print ads) on four national TV stations - ARD, ZDF, RTL-Plus, SAT 1 - 20 daily newspapers - from BILD to WAZ to FAZ, five magazines and weekly papers from BamS to SPIEGEL and STERN - and the sports magazines KICKER, SPORTS and SPORT BILD -was researched systematically and without any exceptions.

This data is to be compared to a three-layered representative population poll, which was conducted together with the market and opinion research institute EMNID (Bielefeld), and was done there within the framework of a multiple issues poll.

At the core of these two interrelated partial studies was our interest to determine media presence, audience knowledge and evaluation. The oral interviews were conducted by way of a standardized questionnaire; but for reasons of fair representation, only in the original Federal states.

AD B) At the center of the oral polling on the occasion of two Bundesliga soccer games in Cologne (170 interviews) and Frankfurt (164 interviews) stood the knowledge and evaluation of the spectators on site or during the sports event. Here it was of interest to see the differences compared to the TV viewers and assessments of the "sports fans" in contrast to the average consumer.

Figure 1: Media-Analysis

Television	Newspaper	Magazines	Sports-Journal
4	20	5	3

Figure 2: Audience-Analysis

1. three wave representative population poll (N= 3,019)
2. two stadium polls (N= 334)
3. one laboratory experiment (N= 38)

AD C) Additionally, experiments were conducted with two groups (38 tests persons) using a manipulated test arrangement in which knowledge, motivations, and emotional reactions were the main focus.

This complex research design was meant to guard against false conclusions and to uncover provable connections. The data input and data evaluation were achieved with the assistance of the statistical evaluation program SAS which was geared to the body of the text and the data structure.

5. Data Analysis and Casework Figures

Over 3,400 single broadcasts with a duration of 1,400 hours total were recorded, analyzed, and interpreted. Approximately 59 days at 24 hours or almost two complete months were monitored and researched! The announcements accompanying the sports broadcasts, their beginning and end, which were evaluated came from two sources: from the program magazine HÖR ZU and.- because of possible changes - from the program schedule of the daily press. The perspective of the co-workers engaged in the study (20 students) has been in all cases the "sportsminded TV viewer". All advertisement and sponsoring forms had to be perfectly perceivable for longer than one second before they could be recorded and analyzed by us.

ANALYSIS - EXTENT TV

Broadcaster	Contributions	Minutes
ARD	1,098	24,039
ZDF	984	21,808
RTLplus	717	15,468
SAT 1	652	23,229
Total	3,451	84,544

While the individual programs and broadcasts ran, all commercials were monitored before, during, and after a sports broadcast, whereby the sports reference, the testimonial, and the type of sport presented were also noted.

The three-layered representative public opinion poll amongst the citizens of the original FRG over the age of 14, included altogether 3,019 persons which were interviewed between March 1990 an February 1991. The questionnaires dealt with knowledge in reference to sponsoring and to the sponsors, particular events and types of sport, as well as prominent sports figures; it also dealt with memorable past performances, ratings and evaluations of the media. The data can be segmented by the usual variables of demography like age, formal education, income, political interests, etc.

6. Results - TV Analysis

Within the researched 12 months, covering four TV broadcasters, a total of 3,191 different product names or business enterprises (organizations) could be traced. To formulate it differently: the average TV sports consumer received a concomitant delivery of 3,000 different "messages" and written texts due to sports broadcasting; from A for "Adidas" to Z as in "Zamek".

TV-ANALYSIS/CONTRIBUTION: FRAMEWORK DATA

Product Names / Sponsors / Business Enterprises   3,191
Advertising Form Contacts   45,976

Furthermore, 13 different types of advertising (sponsoring measures) were noted in the study, from on-site banner advertising to patronage broadcast, from product placement to naming of the sponsor by the journalists. The number of this form of advertising contact - not the frequency of the contacts at or within individual forms of advertising -comes to almost 46,000! The frequencies of contacts within individual types of advertising add up to a surprisingly different figure. Almost two-thirds of all contacts go to on-site banner advertising, according to already published studies, the most effective advertising device (13). While apparel advertising with 10 % of the hominations takes the second position; by comparison product placement (3.2 %), inserts (3.1 %) and the naming of sponsors by journalists (1.7 %) fall off considerably. Traditional, but more likely ineffective possibilities, are on top of the rank order; newer, but presumably more effective presentations, at the bottom of the scale.

PRESENTATION CONTACT OF INDIVIDUAL ADVERTISING FORMS
TV-Analysis Broadcast / Contribution

Rank	Form of Advertising	n=	Percent
1.	On-Site Banner	28,326	61.6
2.	Apparel	5,277	11.5
3.	Outdoor Facilities	2,891	6.3
4.	Tricot	1,908	4.2
5.	Indoor Facilities	1,608	3.5
6.	Product Placement	1,473	3.2
7.	Inserts	1,423	3.1
8.	Sports Equipment	1,268	2.8
9.	Journalist/Moderator	801	1.7
10.	Start Numbers	316	0.7

Which enterprise or which product name had the most TV contacts within the individual forms of advertising is shown on the following exhibit. Coca-Cola, as the top performer, can claim over 1,000 contacts; an enterprise which operates since the 1920's according to the maxim: "Where there is sports, there is Coca-Cola!" Since this business philosophy is adhered to, it is not surprising that they hold the first position in frequency; however, the relative data shows that even Coca-Cola with a 2.5 % share has numerous and intensive competitors. Only ten well-known enterprises are able to reach a share of 1.0 % or more; the greatest number, by far, remains below that figure.

ADVERTISING FORMS-CONTACTS
(TV Analysis Broadcast / Contribution)

Rank	Sponsor	n=	Percent
1.	Coca-Cola	1,196	2.5
2.	OPEL	754	1.6
3.	Ford	688	1.5
4.	Fuji	654	1.4
5.	Adidas	600	1.3
6.	IBM	595	1.3
7.	Agfa	542	1.2
8.	Erdgas	534	1.2
9.	Mita	474	1.0
10.	Atari	473	1.0

BUSINESS BRANCHES - EVALUATION

The business branches evaluation shows - according to a system developed by ZAW -that the five leading branches already claim more than 50 % of all contacts. It is not surprising that the electronic industry leads this tabulation with over 20 %, which is aided by the immense Financial investment of the Japanese industry. The automobile and motor industry is in second position (10%) before non-alcoholic beverages (9 %) and the sporting goods industry (8.6 %).

This evaluation shows indeed a multitude of industries engaged in sports sponsoring, but only half a dozen with permanent and respectable ratings. The product names and enterprises which place far ahead in the individual evaluations always emerge from these branches of industry.

ADVERTISING CONTACT BY BRANCH OF BUSINESS
(TV-Analysis Broadcast / Contribution)

Rank	Branch	n=	Percent
1.	Electronics	8,719	21.9
2.	Automobile / Motors	4,124	10.4
3.	Beverages	3,586	9.0
4.	Sports Equipment	3,412	8.6
5.	Beer	2,415	6.1
6.	Energy	1,800	4.5
7.	Insurance	1,578	4.0
8.	Apparel	1,523	3.6
9.	Watches/Timekeeping	1,407	3.5
10.	Food	1,386	3.4

EVENT SPONSORING

Event sponsoring has in recent years gained importance and has opened up new dimensions, particularly by the quality of possible effects. The traditional "Aral-Pokal" in the equestrian sport was joined a few years ago by new event sponsors like Ford Australian Open" or "Nokia Damen Masters" or "Davis Cup by NEC". Besides the private industry TV broadcasters like RTLplus and SAT 1, the state-funded establishments ARD and ZDF also no longer shy away from naming main and auxiliary sponsors of an event, particularly not when a title sponsoring takes place at the same time. Altogether, until now, this opportunity is used by few enterprises; however, when it happens, the big concerns and international companies are engaged in force.

EVENT - SPONSORING
(TV-Analysis Broadcast / Contributions)

Rank	Sponsor	n=	Percent
1.	Ford	150	28.5
2.	Compaq	60	11.4
3.	NEC	42	8.0
4.	IBM	34	6.5
5.	BMW	25	4.8
6.	Lufthansa	17	3.2
7.	Newsweek	17	3.2
8.	Peugeot	14	2.7
9.	Volvo	14	2.7
10.	Mercedes-Benz	12	2.3

During the research time frame, Ford showed with a 150 contacts and a 28.5 % share the best rating, followed by Compaq, NEC, and IBM; enterprises which are all engaged in tennis, the preferred sport. Surprising in this evaluation is that Mercedes-Benz, official sponsor of the national soccer team, is in 10th place of the rank order with 2.3 % and only 12 nominations. Also not anticipated - enterprises like Coca-Cola and Opel, leading in other evaluations, are not represented among the leaders of event sponsoring. Only Ford appears on the important rank lists twice among the first three positions.

7. Analysis of TV-Commercials

After viewing 8,293 TV commercials, during and after sports broadcasts of the four researched TV channels, 968 different product names or business enterprises could be analyzed. Whether or not ist has been a special advertising from will be determined by further evaluations of the commercials. Every single commercial has been evaluated according to diverse categories and, of course, according to the criterion of repetition (cumulative effect) as well as of the testimonials, the relationship to sports, and to the sport just broadcasted on TV. The analysis of the commercials according to enterprises and product names shows clearly, that only the first four make it to over one hundred frequencies and that already the number 6 of the rank order has only a 1 % share.

TV-ANALYSIS ADVERTISING-COMMERCIALS: FRAMEWORK DATA

Product Names / Sponsors / Business Enterprises   968
TV-Spots   8,293

Mercedes-Benz, so far only noticed in 10th place at event sponsoring, leads in the numbers of the measured commercials. The goal set by the automobile manufacturer becomes clear: to give the products a sporty image and to speak to the sportminded men.

One can report similar facts for Opel (Nr. 3) and Toyota (Nr. 4), whereby three automobile concerns at once are to be found amongst the first four. For the sporting goods manufacturer Nike (Nr. 8) commercials within the framework of sports broadcasts are only logical. The evaluations for Sensodyne, Gillette, as well as Kellogg's and Dr. Oetker are at first surprising, unless the target group men is pre-eminently addressed and pointed to healthy, athletically-oriented nutrition.

8. Audience Analysis

The estimation of the audience, when asked which media advertisement in sports attracts the most attention, is instructive in that it shows which effect quality the citizens attest to the individual medium and to the personal communication.

The unequivocal, stand-out performer is the medium television with over three-quarters of all nominations. The different print media follow with relatively similar evaluations between 14 and 18 %, before radio with only 10 %, and personal conversations at the end with only 3 % of the nominations.

The conspicuity of advertising at visits of sports events is evaluated with 14 % by the audience polled, similar to the print media.

Audience Analysis: "WHERE IS ADVERTISING MOST NOTICEABLE?"
March 1990 / N= 1,027

Rank	Medium	Percent
1.	Television	78
2.	Newspaper Ads	18
3.	Daily Newspaper	16
4.	Sports Magazine	14
5.	Sports Event	14
6.	Radio	10
7.	Conversations	3

Like many sponsors and those in the advertising industry, the audience looks upon the TV broadcasts of sports as the most noticeable source to gain our attention in the most effective way.

NAME RECOGNITION

To the question to name familiar enterprises advertising in sports, an interesting rank order appears. Opel (27 %) is in first position by a wide margin, followed - understandably - by Adidas (19 %), right behind is Coca-Cola (17 %) and then the second sporting goods manufacturer Puma (14 %).

If one disregards the special position of Adidas and Puma, it shows that the two enterprises which are engaged first very massively in recent years (Opel) and second, already traditionally (Coca-Cola), find themselves in the consciousness of the population by this unsupported inquiry. The documented evaluations surprise perhaps by their small percentages, but are valid for a representative cross section of the population.

The then following enterprises are already under 10 % of the replies, whereby the accumulation of Japanese electronic enterprises is as noticeable as the evaluation of Commodore, which is to be viewed as the long-term effect of an already finalized campaign.

Accordingly, three enterprises have asserted themselves - although not in mirror image - in the consciousness of the population which reached in the established contact evaluations of sports broadcasts on television the positions one, two, and five. It can therefore be interpreted that there is a positive relationship between presentation frequency on the one side and the perception and recollection by the audience on the other.

BUSINESS BRANCH KNOWLEDGE

When asking the citizens which branches of business represented in sports advertising are familiar to them, again a finding was established which concurs very plausibly with that of the media analysis. When counting the computer industry to the electronic branch, as was done for the TV analysis, this branch too is with 48 % on top of the population's consciousness.

Audience Analysis: "WHICH BRANCHES OF BUSINESS ARE KNOWN IN SPORTS ADVERTISING?"
March 1990 / N= 1,027

Rank	Branch	Percent
1.	Electronics/Computers	48
2.	Sporting Goods	45
3.	Automobiles	44
4.	Beverages	41
5.	Insurance	28
6.	Food	17

Right behind is the sporting goods industry and automobile branch: a reliable and valid succession! The evaluations for the beverage branch and insurance industry too find corresponding evaluations in the TV analysis. Therefore one can speak of a very homogenous diagnosis, when both analyses are put into relation to each other.

With this the subject effect and subject-structuring effect of the mass media and particularly of television are proved impressively, but also the fact that only few big names or individual branches of business assert themselves in the consciousness of the population.

PRODUCTS AND ADVERTISING PARTNERS

When given a list of well-known enterprises and asked the question who the topical advertising partners are, only three enterprises showed respectable evaluations: Opel with Steffi Graf and Bayern München; Puma with Boris Becker (overlap effect), and Schueco with Franz Beckenbauer reached the best evaluations in 1990, distancing themselves from all others. Here too one finds the plausible explanation that only the intensive advertisers and sponsors, as well as only the best-known sports figures are a guarantor for the proper association and recollection.

Audience Analysis: "WHICH (SPORTS)TESTIMONIAL BELONG TO THE PRESENTED SPONSORS?"
October 1990 / N= 992

Rank	Sponsor	Testimonial	Percent
1.	OPEL	Steffi Graf	37
2.	Puma	Boris Becker	32
3.	OPEL	Bayern München	21
4.	Schueco	Franz Beckenbauer	20

Similar - even if short term - findings can be acknowledged for the German National Soccer Team whereby first effects can be proved for Mercedes-Benz and Müller Milch.

The greater the prominence and the name recognition - the greater the effect; the more intensive the advertising initiative - the more attention it gets.

COMPARISON: MEDIA PRESENCE AND AUDIENCE KNOWLEDGE

Rank	Contact	Commercials	Event	A.A.
1.	Coca-Cola	Mercedes	Ford	OPEL
2.	OPEL	Sensodyne	Compaq	Adidas
3.	Ford	OPEL	NEC	Coca-Cola
4.	Fuji	Toyota	IBM	Puma
5.	Adidas	Kellogg's	BMW	NEC

When the rank order of the three separate evaluations are put into relation to the results of the representative poll, it becomes clear that besides the rather atypical representatives of the sporting goods industry, Adidas and Puma, the two most conspicuous and effective enterprises are Opel and Coca-Cola. But it also shows that merely punctilious investments and merely one-dimensionally executed activities hardly lead to the intended effects with the viewer, citizen, and consumer. The multi-functional strategy is provably an advantage; the most diverse media presence with different impressions more effective!

PRESENTATIONS-INDEX

The following table will attempt to give a summary of all evaluations - which have so far been presented and discussed - and to build an index of the rank order. Point of departure is the sequence of the representative poll (rank of the audience analysis) to which the positions of the contact frequency, the commercials, and of the event sponsoring will be added. Please note: this concerns the comparison of positions, not of frequencics or qualities!

Presentations-Index

Rank-A.A.	Contact	Spot	Event	Index
1. OPEL	2	3	62	3/22.3
2. Adidas	5	50	-	2/27.5
3. Coca-Cola	1	38	-	2/19.5
4. Puma	15	39	-	2/27.0
5. NEC	61	-	3	2/32.0
6. Sony	286	56	-	2/171
7. Commodore	124	-	-	1/124

The undisputed "winner" of this index is Adam Opel AG who is to be found measurably in all researched fields and therefore - as the only enterprise - reaches an evaluation of 22.3 besides the factor 3. If Opel did not hold the 62nd position in the event sponsoring category, the dominance of the enterprise would be even more pronounced.

The second position is taken by Coca-Cola, which could only be tracked in two categories of the media analysis, but takes the best evaluation average with 19.5. The goal of every marketing or sponsoring campaign of every enterprise should be to reach the most pre-eminent positions in all categories. Only then could one speak - cum grano salis (with a grain of salt) - of a good concept and effective strategy.

9. Laboratory Experiment: TV Commercials

The laboratory experiment with two test groups and 38 test persons had among other things the goal to test the frequency, form and the sports relationship of commercials.

LABORATORY EXPERIMENT: TV COMMERCIALS

- Testimonial
- Cumulation
- Thematic Affinity

Under these test conditions manipulated by us - three indicators resulted, which without doubt were responsible for the effectiveness of commercials: The cumulative effect (multiple repetition of an identical commercial) is clearly provable, also the thematic affinity to sports, the type of sport or the sports event, as well as finally the effective entry of testimonials of the sport, according to prominent (ex) sports figures, for which, as other evaluations show, only a few qualify. The two German tennis stars Steffi Graf and Boris Becker were 1990/91 the same positive example as the former team captain of the German National Soccer Team, Franz Beckenbauer. It is also noteworthy, that only national prominence of sports figures (i.e. Carl Uwe Steeb) cannot provide the intended effect, according to our evaluations.

10. Conclusion

Out of the findings of the TV analysis, the analysis of commercials audience poll, and the laboratory experiment, one can formulate five demands for successful advertising with and within sports

DEMANDS

1. **Concordance**
2. **Continuity**
3. **Uniformity**
4. **Universality**
5. **Professionalism**

Marketing, sponsoring, and advertising initiatives in sports must be tuned to each other in an complementary manner, must come together like a mosaic to form a total picture for the viewer or consumer. The character of "concordance" not only relates to the single initiative but also to the multi-event and multimedia. Directly connected to this the fourth factor "universality" which should make clear that all initiatives should have no local or regional boundaries, but instead be global and open to the world.

Many sports campaigns are marked by the punctiliousness of the initiative; concerning the time, the event, as well as the media initiative. This - futile - endeavor is to be countered by the "Continuity" factor, which means long-term, recognizable, and in itself homogenous activities. The continued presence and the continued initiative in sports bring the results and effects which are of the first priority to the sponsor.

Otherwise, everything is "for the birds" and the modern sports sponsoring remains as traditional patronage in the end.

Not only does the key-word corporate identity or corporate communication make it clear how important an inside and outside, homogenous, and uniform image is, but also that campaigns, slogans, logos, and all advertising means must comply with this demand. Also, and particularly, the concurrent philosophy of the enterprise with the sponsored sports figure, event, or association is therefore unrelinquishably important.

Several case studies have discussed the to be expected findings, although ca. DM 1.5 billion are expended, this sum is only made available in exceptional cases on the basis of secured data, analyses, and concepts. The only seemingly rational system of economic deal making is much too often marked by intuitive, subjective, and unsystematic decisions!

Therefore, the only conclusion drawn by engaged enterprises and organizations must be:

1. **Concordance of media, advertising forms, and advertising goals.**
2. **Continued long-term strategies.**
3. **Uniform image and uniform contents.**
4. **Universal, global strategy, and**
5. **Professionalism of concept, realization, and control of sponsoring.**

Only then initiative and success will be in an economic interrelationship.

References

1. **Schumann, Frank:** Und am Rand steigt der Bekanntheitsgrad?, in: Hackforth, Josef (Ed.): Sportmedien & Mediensport, Berlin: 1988, S.57-79.

2. **Hackforth, Josef:** Zwischen Bandenwerbung und Bandenwirkung, in: Herrmanns, Arnold (Ed.): Sport- und Kultursponsoring, München: 1989, S.100-111.

3. **Scholz, Rolf:** Sportmedien & Sportwerbung, Münster: 1988.

4. **Scholz, Rolf / Jens Wernecken:** Untersuchungsdesign, in: Hackforth, Josef (Ed.): Sportsponsoring: Bilanz eines Booms, Berlin: 1994, S. 1-18.

5. **Hackforth, Josef (Ed.):** Sportsponsoring: Bilanz eines Booms, Berlin: 1994.

6. **Hackforth, Josef:** Neue Medien und gesellschaftliche Konsequenzen, in: Das Parlament, Heft B3/1986, S. 3-10.

7. **dito**

8. **Staatsvertrag der Länder**

9. **Donohew, L. / Tipton, L.:** A Conceptual Model of Information Seeking, Avoiding, and Processing, in: Clarke, Peter (Ed.): New Models for Mass Communication Research, Beverly Hills: 1973, S. 243-268.

10. **Arbeitsgemeinschaft für Kommunikationsforschung e.V. (Ed.):** Medienforschung / Medienpolitik, Berlin: 1981.

11. **Hackforth, Josef:** Massenmedien und ihre Wirkungen, Göttingen: 1976.

12. **Mostly used by commercial agencies**

13. **Herrmanns, Arnold (Ed.):** Sport- und Kultursponsoring, München: 1989.

THE NEEDS AND MOTIVATIONS OF SPORTING DEMAND

Loret, A.
Caen University
France

Sporting supply and demand has been subject to serious upheaval over the last fifteen years: new sports have appeared and the definition of the average sportsperson has changed (older, more females...). Things are changing so quickly that it is likely we do not even know today some of the sports we will be taking part in, in five years time. Even if we cannot predict the future, it is possible to hint at developments to come. That is what we do here, setting out the changing trend and an analysis table of the needs and motivations of sporting demand.

Does a type of marketing exist specifically for sport? Or in other words, do sporting products (technical equipment and services) all come under a particular marketing approach? In view of the current sporting ethic and traditions, the answer would certainly appear to be yes. Nevertheless, things will change in time.

Analysing sport simply as a consumable product will probably be perceived as a downright challenge because sport is normally considered as an activity "useful" to the smooth running of society.

1. The new sporting creativity

For many people the ideology of sport seems to be engraved on the very history of western society. Along those lines of thought, sport would be intangible. More so, it would be "natural". A little as if physical exercise through sport was part of modern man's instinctive behaviour. Under these conditions, applying a marketing argument to it would hardly be of any use.

This would however be forgetting two things.

- The first is obvious: modern sport was created totally at the heart of western society during a period stretching from the second half of the nineteenth century to the middle of the twentieth. It is therefore very clear that the sport which our contemporaries take part in were conceived by inventors who thought up and devised the rules and regulations by which we practise the different sports today. It certainly seems, then, that they are the "products" or the "creations" of an industrial society searching for games corresponding to its ideology, if not to its needs. It remains particularly interesting to observe that sporting creativity was exhausted by the middle of the twentieth century. Sporting disciplines invented during the period from 1950 to the beginning of the seventies were extremely rare. Only embellishments of the rules, technical innovations or the development of new equipment, allowed a certain evolution in the sporting world. From that moment, this lack of creativity, which was to last for almost a quarter of century, contrast sharply with the many sporting innovations which have appeared over the last fifteen years. A quick head-count reveals some forty new sports were created since 1975 and every season sees new arrivals.

If it doesn't fail to surprise, this statement must certainly force us to ask a few questions about sport's immediate future. Indeed, nothing seems to show that the current torrent of sporting creativity is likely to dry up suddenly. In this condition, it is likely that we don't know now what sports we will be doing in five years time. Neither do we know what type of equipment and materials we will be seeing in sport in 1995. This situation is totally new, because the stability of the preceding period in sport, unlike what is happening today, would let us know with a fair measure of certainty, the form sport would be taking five years hence. That era is past. Today those in charge of the management of leisure sports must therefore anticipate our future sporting desires and behaviour through marketing and prospective techniques.

- The second parameter to be considered which also comes from a new phenomenon is the change in structure of the sporting population. At the same time as it was producing its regulatory standards by building up arbitration codes, modern sport was generating physical standards (physiological, biomechanical, psychological) adapted to the constraints of producing records. The development in physical standards under the contraint of achieving performances, quickly determined the profile of a typical sportsperson. The sportsperson was a male individual, under thirty years old, and capable of beating records. Today, things have certainly changed. Anyone can be considered (or consider themselves) as sportsperson...even if they are female, over fifty, and, "last but not least", totally uninterested in competition. It is therefore obvious that there is a major change in the know-how and services offered by the leisure-sports organisations. We bet that precise knowledge about these new sports peoples' demands, together with the propositions of appropriate services, will rapidly become the subject of a highly detailed marketing analysis by the institutions (federations, associations, clubs) concerned with their future.

2. Taking the future into account

What will be appearing on the horizon of the year 2000 is thus a real and abrupt change in the European sporting scene. The essence of this huge transformation affecting sport can be phrased as follows: the future of sport will have nothing to do with its past. One must understand that this sybilline phrase would have had hardly any significance only fifteen years ago. Throughout the seventies, sport lived really on its history and traditions. In 1993 it must consider its future. It should be repeated that only those leisure sports organisations which show themselves to be sufficiently creative will have any chance of getting over the hurdle of the century. In 1993, their objective can be defined in this way: they must not ask the market what it wants but what it will want in five years time. This goal will not be attained without placing importance of indepth analysis, because sports marketing presents such a surprising peculiarity: even though they today seek to market a product which is decades old, sports marketing has never been the subject of convincing studies.

As regards the developments of sports practices, the marketing attitude consists of being aware that society's evolution cannot be ignored, as it has previously been. In other words, sport must no longer be considered as a huge, intangible area, set apart from social and cultural change. Today it is essential to be aware that for the most part, sport depends on rules that were thought up years ago. And more seriously, those rules have hardly changed, unlike the social, economic, technological and cultural environments around the sport organisations, which have elaborated them. On a global scale, we can assume that the lifestyles which were current when all the sports rules were made in the first half of the twentieth century are no longer the same as the present ones.

3. A new type of marketing

In view of current mentalities, and especially the weight of tradition, sport marketing presents itself as an approach "of the third type". The first type of approach to marketing is centred on a product designed to correspond to a consumer need, and to satisfy that need.

The second approach to marketing is centred on a service. That is to say something neither material nor stockable. Today, if one considers the weight of history, sport marketing should be based neither on a product, nor a service (although you could be persuaded to think so). It should be centred on its function. In other words, it should imply the educational function towards public health and social integration, inherent to the public service which fell to the French sports organisations at the end of the forties.

Sport marketing must therefore be of a "third", or "other" type of approach, because the commercial data used in the running of sporting organisations are quite different from those which are found at the heart of other companies. Indeed, when a product fails to achieve the expected success, there are two options open to a company:

- to modify the product in line with demand;
- to attempt to modify demand to suit the product.

In France, an associative national sport federation would have difficulty carrying out such an alternative, because it is generally accepted as a "public service". In other words, the very nature of its function sets it on an institutional level. This organisation does partially come from a demand from society. Its social recognition therefore, arises from the conviction that what it promotes is essential to the very society. So, it cannot:

- modify the product, since it is a product of society, which is therefore, by definition beyond its reach. It has only the power to promote the sporting product, not to change it;
- modify the demand, since it is the social demand for sport which causes the organisation to become an institution. For a sport federation, modifying the sporting demand would therefore come back to modifying itself.

Sport marketing relying on history is thus a type of marketing which is radically different from the traditional marketing approach. Traditional marketing centres the company's activity around a number of basic rules: if the tastes of the clientèle change, the company consequently modifies the products or services that it offers.

As opposed to that, a federation seeks to promote the social and cultural function of its own sporting discipline (for example, pleasure in effort and a sense of gratuity, respect for the rules, for the arbiter and for the adversary, thirst for victory, the will to go beyond one's possibilities, etc). If this function no longer fits the demand (or, in other words, is no longer fashionable) there is nothing that can be done to change it. It is not for the federation to say that it no longer answers a need... In France, that is a job for the state, which has delegated its organisational and promotional power for that particular discipline.

Such marketing is therefore quite different from the usual commercial strategies, since it must "make do" to serve the cause of sport as best it can, identified as it is by its social function and its "public service". The essential task for the decision-makers of sport will therefore be to recognise exactly what "public" is concerned by this service. "To recognise" and not "to know", since by definition, the public is known. This recognition (in sense of renewing acquaintance with) will allow a better evaluation of the potential market, and therefore, to carefully discern the true possibilities of the organisation. It goes without saying that such an approach is particularly limited, even if it does seem to be adapted to the conditions presented by sporting organisations in France and, maybe, in Europe.

4. Starting from the needs

A different approach to the problem consists in combining the two different marketing styles, no longer considering sport as a social function, but from the viewpoint of three types of needs and categories of hopes and desires which it then tries to satisfy. Such an approach is a total turnaround of the facts of the problem and of the mentality of the sporting world.

In fact, talking of sport in terms of marketing, implies that the sport product (the activity or the technique) no longer exists only as a regulatory process (arbitration code and know-how), but as an answer to a system of needs which it will satisfy, knowing the player's demand. From then on, marketing applied to sport will essentially be based on a selection of analyses methods designed to produce strategic decision.

An exhaustive study of sporting needs and aspirations remains to be carried out, even if some analyses have sketched the first details of this particular marketing sector. We can isolate five tendencies in the evolution of the sporting demand.

1. The search for autonomy, leading to the rejection of large organisations dealing with widespread sport, which are restrictive and regimented.
2. The search of pleasure, fun and personal achievement, to the detriment of traditional sporting asceticism.
3. The search for vitality and shape in order to feel good physically.
4. The search for a richer communication between individuals, by belonging to small transient and informal groups and no longer to institutional type organisations.
5. The search for harmony between one's physical and mental faculties and the natural and urban environment[1].

It is significant that this analysis does not take into account the real needs of the true sportsmen. That is the fully registered members of sporting organisations "traditionally" followers of institutionalised competitions. Nevertheless, apart from considering that several million individuals (in France) do not constitute a market, it is impossible not to take their needs into account. Even if some analyses currently tend towards their being gradually squeezed out of the French sport scene, I think that it is largely too early to write off as a loss century of institutional and disinterested sporting competition (or amateur, if you will).

5. Formalising the supply of sports "products"

In the light of the study carried out by INSEP's sociological department in 1987[2], it is today possible to envisage a certain number of lines of thought based on the many motivations of the French towards sport. Even if the approach can seem a little old-fashioned I would organize the presentation of those thoughts around the idea of "needs". As a first step towards a more detailed analysis, at the moment being carried out, this presentation has the advantage of being simple. The objective is to give a rough outline for formalising the service supply which will come from leisure organisations currently working in the sport market.

Needs	Motivations	Types of Practices	Search for	Structures Types	Physical Potential	Example of Activities	Criteria of Service
self fulfilment	personal satisfaction	competition	achievement	federations	exploited	athletics	sports meetings
esteem	aesthetics	body building	beauty	body building clubs	sublimated	to develop the muscles	"mirror"
self assurance	fear of ageing	physical maintenance	youth	/	maintained	maintenance gymnastics	support
to belong	social acceptance	distinctive	being valued	club (in the English sense)	shown	yachting	modes
to occupy oneself	to fill free time	play activities	pastimes	holiday centers	used	wind-surfing	liveliness
physical shape	good health	keeping fit	well-being	gymnastics clubs	regenerated	aerobics	personalisation
escape	get out of routines	adventure	change	tour operators	experienced	trekking	logistic
sensation	vertigo	"unlimited"	emotions	paragliding schools	risked	bungy jumping	security

play	amusement	play activities	hedonism	aqualand	amused	"wild" activities	pleasure
learning	progress	pedagogical	progress in learning	sports schools	developed	all activities	training
educating	social integration	educational	formation	school	taught	all activities	didactic
meeting	exchange	group	social interaction	club (in the French sense)	used	mountain biking	minitel phone

The suggested analysis table is organised in eight columns which gradually reveal the new concept around which the service should be structured (last column on the right).

As an example, if one takes the "need to fulfill oneself", one notes that the inferred motivation is an attempt to "find one's way" through competition, leading to the search for results. The structures offering this type of service are the sporting federations (for example the French Athletics Federation). The "physical potential" column seeks to present how the body is used in the particular activity satisfying the need. It is clear, in this case, that the competitor will exploit his physical potential. It is really about an exploitation which can go so far as exhaustion (in the true sense of the term) of the body's resources. An analysis of the chain formed by these different data will lead to those responsible in the organisation to discover the pertinent criteria around which they will organise the production of the service supplied to satisfy the need. The choice of these criteria will allow the organisation to correctly discern its real job. The elements given in the last column, I insist, are purely for information. They are only examples. Thus, we can come to think that the main service rendered by the sports federation to satisfy their members in their search for personal fulfilment is founded around the idea of "meeting" (in the sporting sense: a football match). It is because there are matches that the teams are confronted with one another and therefore classified. The ability to provide a calendar of meeting or matches guaranteeing the reliability of results on the field, on one hand, and in time, on the other, appears to be the principle "job" of the sporting federations.

6. Sport: a polysemic reality

Like all general models, this table simplified the particularly complex reality of sporting needs and services. In fact, it is simply trying to show basic data: that is, the existence not of one market for sport, but several very distinct markets for which demand it would be advisable to supply (or to serve), according to specific forms. The market of sports services and products will therefore have to consider the idea of a "supplied" or "served" market to define and give priority to such segment or segments of the market on which efforts should be focused.

Thus, for example, one can wonder about the market truly "served" by the French Tennis Federation. Is it the sports meetings market, as the media promotion of the Roland Garros Tournament and the considerable number of officially graded players would have us believe ? Or isn't it rather "teaching" if one considers the type of publicity which the French Tennis Federation put on at the time of the French Internationals. The study of the service proposed by that federation leads one to thing that it is serving purely the teaching market. Contrary to appearances in fact, it only serves a very small part of the fixtures market... despite the 1.5 million fixtures that it organises every year. Paradox? Not at all, because those 1.5 million matches are in theory offered to the 1.4 millions members of the federation (these figures are rounded off to give a better illustration. They correspond globally to reality). Which - still theoretically - hardly represents one match per member per year. Obviously, that doesn't correspond to the real service which allows the French Tennis Federation to count nearly 1.4 millions members. From that point, it is clear that the French Tennis Federation marketing service is absolutely right to put the emphasis on teaching, because it is definitely the market which the federal organisation must serve in view of current tennis demand.

7. Appreciating the needs to develop new sports products

Through the nineties, sports innovations will take on two major aspects:

- on the one hand, the appearance of previously unseen technical sporting articles (shapes and materials) and of equally unseen sports grounds with heavy equipment and much more exotic sites;
- on the other hand, the emergence of a new type of needs resulting from the appearance of a deeply original sporting population (more female and decidedly older).

Confronted to this change, we can figure out that the market for sport will be organised around three types of new products.

1. Redefined sports products will concern the older sporting disciplines, trying to bring them up to current fashion, by modifying their perception by a potential public. A good example of redefinition today is "beach volley" which totally revamps the game of volleyball.

Walking in the desert is equally a redefinition of trekking, which was itself an exotic move away from hiking. You hike in the Alps, you trek in Nepal and you walk in the Saharan Tassali n'Ajjer. One could also mention aerobics, which was a redefinition of maintenance gymnastics.

2. **Revised sporting products** will be those where the rules be essentially changed to make them more televisable. Tennis, with the introduction of the tie-break, baskets scoring three points in basketball and the plans to increase the size of the goals in football are goods examples of revision.

We can equally conceive certain rewrites of the rules with the aim of integrating spectacular new mass sports. The case of road-running, which deeply bothers the French Athletics Federation, is significant of the new motivations which are transforming the traditional organisation of marathon. Moreover, the triathlon is only another revision by combination of certain swimming, cycling and running competitions.

3. **Innovative sports products** will be those which will produce an abrupt change at the same time in the diverse areas of technology (shapes, materials, electronic components), techniques (sporting know-how), and public image (especially the symbolic ones).

Windsurfing is the archetypal innovative sporting product. It has allowed the appearance of new heros (for example, Robby Naish) who have conceived hitherto unknown know-how (funboard) and also introduce a particularly surprising counter-culture into sport.

8. Conclusion

The emergence of what I have above called the "new sporting creativity" and of the markets that it encourages (and will encourage), appears very much like a genuine change, whose consequences it would be difficult to calculate. We must bear in mind that the urgent duty to determine precise objectives corresponding to these different sporting markets, is now a priority for all those economically involved. Only a strategic step, taking into account the multiple facets of contemporary sporting reality, will allow the production and development of services qualitatively adapted to the multiple needs and motivations of today's sportsmen.

References

1. In: La lettre de l'économie du sport, N^0 60, January 24th 1990.

2. **Irlinger P., Louveau C., Métoudi M.:** Les pratiques sportives des francais, Paris, INSEP, 1987.

THE NEW CONCEPTIONS FOR SPORTS AND LEISURE EQUIPMENT; PROSPECTS AND INNOVATION

Pociello, C.; Baslé, G.
University of Paris sud-Orsay, Research Center for Sports Cultures
Orsay, France

Ladies and gentlemen. I would like to state that I do not speak here on my own name, but on behalf of the laboratory to which also belong both Jacques Defrance, who is here with us today, and Gérard Baslé. Mr Defrance is in charge of the sociological strictness of our research. Mr Baslé plans and applies a fine methodology to adapt projects and equipment programs that have some kind of social or technological innovation to their various urban settlements.

Within this scholar background, our joint work aims at :

- **understanding the evolution of taste and sports behaviour** in France and other equivalent European countries.

- finding the concrete technical applications to our theoretical research.

Our presence in front of such a big audience aims at establishing contact and finding cooperation on the **prospect and planning for sports and sports oriented leisure equipment**, in their relation to modern urban equipment....

In other terms, our research leads us mainly to the analysis of the **sports components of space urban systems**; which we examine both in the context of the evolution of the sports demand and the transformations of the actual manufacturing process of the Town ....

1. Introduction: Planning or Prospective?

Each one of us here should question himself on the possibilities of expanding and extrapolating his own observations and thoughts to other member countries of the European Community... it's a rule in this kind of gatherings. This means a **knowledge**, as thorough and objective as possible, of facts and conditions (economical, political, technological...) that may define a common environment to the Old Continent... But there has to be also an effort -rather difficult to do- of **decentring** that will inform us on our tendencies, penchants at representation categories (that could be felt as failures by our neighbours)... This teaches us about our own way of seeing and reasoning, which depends so much on our own histories and cultures. The healthy effect of this confrontation in exchanges can be seen instructively through our difference in speech. Whilst it can be seen that it is often spoken of "planning of infrastructures or equipment",... in most European countries, (mainly in the Anglo-Saxon and Germanic cultures) french scholars like (and indulge in) vast and ambitious "prospective thinking" on the same objects. Probably their inventiveness and creativeness is recognized - and they like it unbridled although it is not always in touch with the limits imposed by the **gathering of means** (technical, financial, commercial...) that are necessary for the swift outcome of projects or "genial" concepts... Maybe their taste for conflictive situations and for the dramatization of their controversies pushes them to discard the past and come up with "revolutionary" projects and to conceive forms contradictory to traditional ones, that are therefore difficult to have accepted and done... But, on one hand we willingly admit our penchant for speculation, and our pragmatic neighbours tease us because of that, (is it really a shortcoming to want to totalize and make one's own principles universal?...) on the other hand we have not been seen as "amateurish", although we have such a marked cultural tendency.

In planning; once the desired future conceived, the objectives and it's corresponding products clearly defined, it is expected -and required- that all the means be rounded up and all resources put to work in order to successfully achieve the planned goal.

The **exploratory prospective**, in the french sense, extends to the construction of "possible futures" of any system; considering the weight of the past determinants and the confrontation of the projects and stakes of the different parts involved.

In our point of view the prospective analysis has a double dimension; both **poetical and political:**

The **"poetical"** dimension, which is considered essential, belongs to the realm of creators. It conceives future forms that will become new forms, recognized as innovations and obtained through the disassembling and recomposing of what exists, composed of both imagination and imaginative thinking.

It is up to the **"political"** dimension to carry out the previously created forms trying to influence a policy (or the administrative guidelines); taking into account the different compulsions (especially economical) to which decision makers are compelled.

This, of course, could be the result of a particular culture, an excessive tendency for unrestrained speculation, but it also rests on our conviction of the **imposing power of the Law** on administrative decisions, consequence of the french tradition of centralization. This self-criticism will be the more beneficial if rewarded.

But let's not mock so fast these "french" attitudes, especially at a time in which there seems to be a certain convergence amongst European countries (strange chiasmus effect) in which federal or less centralized countries tend to centralize certain decisions, and an opposite decentralization in hyper centralized countries... (Education, health, sports.)."Prescriptions", "recommendations", "enforcement" "normalizing", etc. appear more and more often in areas such as sports, recreation and leisure infrastructures throughout the member countries. The C.D.D.S. of the European Council regularly registers in all EC countries, these acts of influence that always emanate from the Center in the direction of the Borders [1].

Rationalization choices, cost optimization, the taking into account of the evolution of sports demand of the population as a whole, the evolution of sports equipment industry, etc...; a whole that seems to engage in a complete and simultaneous reorganization of sports national systems is situated in the context of an economic crisis.

2. Innovations and Prospective ...

This transformation movement (sometimes fast, often slow), the disorder and uncertainties that it produces in the whole of the sports systems lead us into **a full span, European wide prospective research**.

Within this context we have to talk of innovations when we refer to projects that aim to answer, in advance, to sports behaviour and taste. and where we refer to "demand evolution", it should become "offer evolution" **because of the appearance of new stakes in the sports and political fields** (urbanistic, social, tourist, economic, commercial...)

In this turbulent era, the future of Europe itself is at stake. We believe that a well tempered -and well led- innovation in the most varied fields of the production of goods and services is essential.

In spite of a growing mistrust of progress amongst consumers it is widely recognized that innovations are necessary in the post industrial world, in fast movements and when new technical systems are spread out into the whole of the production process (T.Gaudin). It is a common phenomena to these highly developed and competitive countries for whom high-tech is a commercial and economic weapon, (and even a "value" in itself), enhanced with the globalization of trade and the toughening of economic warfare... Isn't it considered by specialists, that the amount invested in R&D by companies is an index of the economic vitality and a sign of the modernization of nations...?

We should all take an interest and feel concerned by the prospective of leisure, recreational and sports activities, and the equipment (or infrastructure) planning that makes it possible. It is also possible to **try to act in order to master the future** and anticipate on possible evolutions in our own modest field of intervention.

We believe that intervention and prospective should be closely linked in order to avoid **utopian**, ridiculous and unrealistic "inventor's" creativity, and that it will stay invalid it is not part of a **wide prospective movement** that rationalizes its methods, seeks to separate "heavy tendencies", grasps "new needs" and as long as it isn't accompanied by a **planning strategy** that rounds up men, concentrates resources, mobilizes means and produces (or stimulates) in some way this "demand"...

3. Contradictory Force Dynamics; Field Effect...

But although there are, in our own societies, whole groups that are innovative and propelled by fast movements, there are also others that are stuck in immobility and reactive attitudes... Innovative essays or projects destabilize existing structures and disturb it's agents. They don't act in a void neither they have only followers. Misoneist reactions, (full of hatred onto all that is "new") appear even amongst traditional "proposers" because new products bring competition in a saturated market. It is therefore necessary to place oneself and reason in a context of **contradictory social forces dynamics.**

This means we have to evaluate what is at stake for those in what we call in our jargon, the **"field of sports"**. This is a relatively autonomous social field with it's own history; in which all parties compete to insure the benefits, whether social, professional, economic or symbolic, produced specifically through it.

These actors are not attached to one of the two functions that A. Loret points out as"educative" or "merchant" but to one of the four main functions of sport, which we have identified as: integrative, statutory or ethical, educational and academic, play, tourism and adventure, economic, communicative and merchant, which are more or less legitimate social uses and functions of sport that compete and interact both at national as well as local levels.

General tendencies of evolution of these complex systems can be understood by observing the adaptation **reactions of these fields to the "heavy" constraints of the environment**, such as economical, social, cultural and technical, by taking into account their adjustment or reorganization efforts, according to defined historical contingencies, by analyzing the internal regulations of this field, the movements of synergic forces and the changes of strategy of those involved.

Attitudes unto these innovations may vary according to the differences of **national political cultures** that define thought patterns and actions and induct privileged organizational structures[2] , according to the economical means of each country, rich or parsimonious, according to authoritarian positions or centralized habits, or, on the contrary, according to liberal attitudes, flexible and inclined to encourage regional initiatives. Sometimes they might be felt necessary and therefore encouraged, or elsewhere feared and rejected.

It can be also said that the perception will not be the same according to the importance that each nation gives to these different functions which produce the political legitimation and the social definition prevailing in Sports within the whole social body. Attitudes may therefore be very contrasted unto those technical and social innovations related to sports.

4. Main Environmental Variables

In spite of the national cultural political differences, and the particularity of the national fields of sports, the weight of the common environmental constraints makes it possible to anticipate on a near future and to design "possible futures". Some of these evolutions are already on their way nowadays within the European field of physical activities and leisure sports.

Which are the main environmental variables that may have the strongest and lasting impact on national sports systems, to produce similar effects and guide the production of new products, such as equipment?

We can rely on the viewpoint of the CDDS text **"Préparer l'avenir" (Preparing the future)** inasmuch as demographic economic, social and cultural changes go.

-1: **Demographic changes:** The diminution and aging of population, the changes in the age pyramid may have paradoxical effects on the rate of activities. The practice rate increases with age in a population ever so conscious of physical hygiene, paying more attention to the body, recreational activities, well being and health. This has a high cost in radical transformation of sports projects.

It should also be expected, at the narrow end of the pyramid, to find a greater autonomy of the teen-age sports culture which produces new sports ways and questions the functioning of traditional organizations, ill prepared to apply their influence on restive, open and changing customers.

-2: **Economic and productive.** The growing importance of robotics and computer technology at work and the reduction of physical effort, the growing importance of the service sector and of intangible investments in all production and distributing levels, which are trademarks of our post industrial societies, should enhance and increase active leisure time in the direction and sense of sports high tech. Female professional activity that acts directly on the investment in sports activities will contribute to broaden the image.

The non working population, unemployed and young school drop-outs, low income population with plenty of free time, should form a second segment of potential users inasmuch as sports may constitute for them a positive means of social reintegration. But their demand quite inspired by classical sports, differ strongly in relation to definitions and century old organizations.

New actors to the sports scene will appear with the concomitant development of leisure industries at a local level, the apparition in towns of new stakes such as local development, urban communication, tourist development, real estate value increase and at nation-wide levels, sports business and the merchandising of services, which bolsters them to increase their influence and so decrease the autonomy of structures and destabilize them. The growing importance of the media and the merchandising of sports puts a lot of pressure on the traditional ethics of the sports and the effort to keep it free, educational and uninterested.

-3: **Social and cultural changes,** linked to the renewal of generations, to the development of a "young" culture, to the evolution of mentalities and ways of life, will bring around deep transformations in the nature, the variety and the directions of the social demand for sports activities. The continuous increase of the level of education will bring a higher level of demand of services and products on behalf of the users, but also a greater volatility and versatility. Thought should be given on the research of quality and the adaptation of products to these new expectations.

5. The "Heavy" Tendencies of the Evolution of Sports in France and in Europe

We have built a socio-historical theoretical model that permits us to define certain tendencies deemed long lasting in regards with the rather big inertia of this system, in order to grasp the complex **interactions** amongst the different institutions and agents within the **field of sports** (internal variables) and the effects of the reorganization that the environment imposes according to the **different contingencies** of recent history (external variables). We have represented in the following diagram (Fig. 1) the four main functions that structure in our country both the cultural field as well as the field of sports, and which are integrative, educational, recreational and commercial (O.Donnat, 1989).

Fig. 1 The French Field of Sports Economic Social and Political Environment (1980 - 2000) Strategic and Functional Analysis

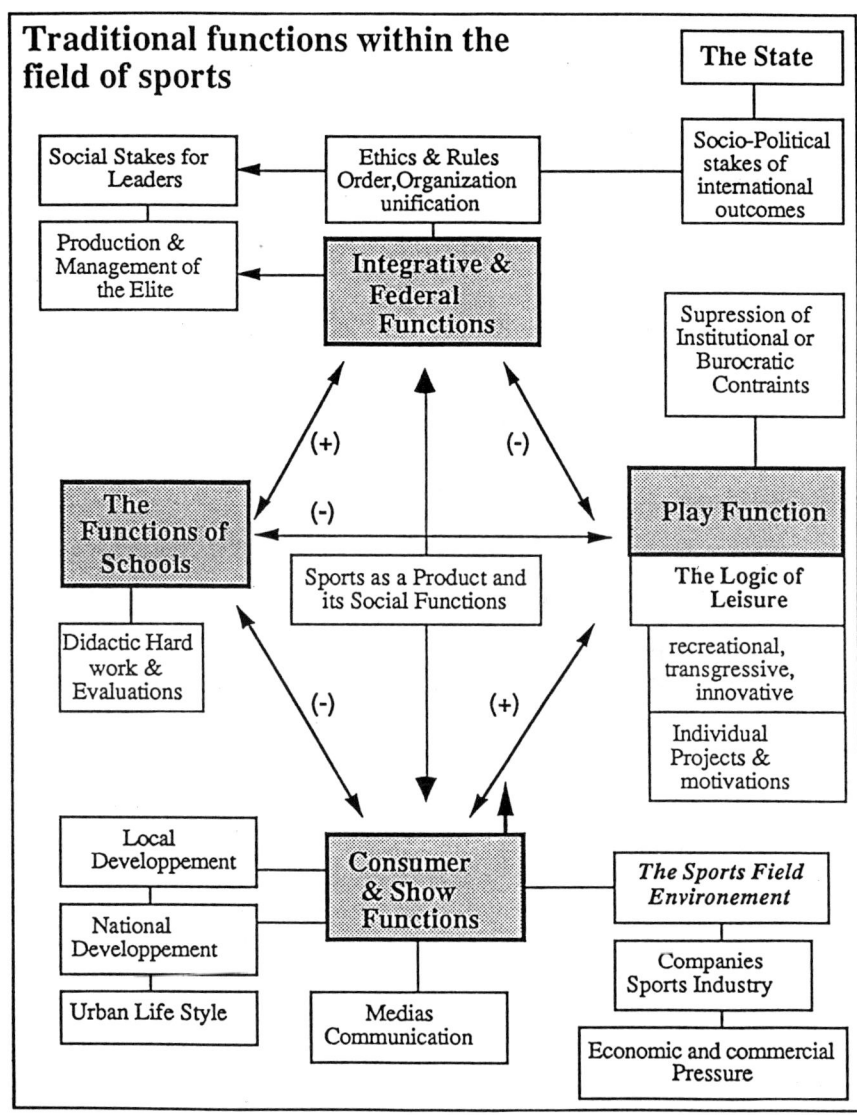

Within the context of the economical growth of the sixties through 1975, there was a growth of the strong synergic bind between the educational and federative poles, under the strong, centralized influence of the state, in the context of a considerable growth of the socio-political stakes related to the results of the international sports stars. These stakes were themselves bound to the growing impact of these huge events, representations of the pacific (or pacified) competition amongst competing Nations and to the fast increase in number of private T.V. sets. Within this context, physical education became sports oriented, (something that was self-evident to some teachers but that was the consequence of this policy) and progressively transformed sports into a school subject.

With the economical crisis and the State's disengagement, this relation is reversed and the system is **re-organized on a different and long-lasting basis, in the context of the years 1980 - 2000**. There is a tendency for a strong synergy to be formed between the economic, industrial and commercial worlds, who try to satisfy individual private and solvent customers and the ever growing group of those who practice in the hyper-valued sphere of recreational leisure, adding themselves to the inventors of "free" games, turbulent and individualistic, transgressive in a sense. This renewal that pleases the young generation, is in opposition to the traditional school and sports framework.

Which are the general effects of this upheaval of the field of sports on the products offered by it, and on the demand of activity?

We make a clear difference between **"heavy tendencies of evolution"** and **"future bearing achievements"**.

The former are the strong, deep, long lasting tendencies upon which experts tend to agree, and that respond in a clear way to the internal regulation of the field imposed by the environment (external) that we have previously mentioned. Whereas in regards with the latter there is no consensus. Those achievements considered as "bearing" are the result of somewhat more personal constructions - and therefore more risky - that design a long term alternative amongst other possible ones. Some of those concerned, sensing an eventual loss of their profits, or even of their own existence, will forge a resolute opposition rhetoric against them. Vigorous interventions at local levels can maim or even annihilate their effects.

But, some "future bearing achievements" -anticipated in 1985- have since proven themselves to become reality (see further on "the topic of adventure") This urged us to look into the intellectual process which permitted us to foresee them.

* We have pinpointed **four main "heavy tendencies"** in the evolution of leisure sports within the whole population

-1: A mass tendency associated to a great diversification of activities:

Each sport broadens its social recruiting base, but at the same time the "customers" become less exclusive or faithful. New activities appear and develop, whereas sports blow up into multiple practice modalities adjusting to the personal tastes of its adepts.

-1: A strong feminization in the whole:

This tendency - noticeable throughout Europe - affects all sports although in different manners. This feminization tends to modify the practice of sports, and of their image, in the sense of a sweetening of confrontation and aesthetic movements.

-3: A lengthening of the sports life cycle:

There is a tendency to push back the age of abandoning the chosen sport and sometimes there is even an increase in activity through age. This of course means important changes in sports and a deep transformation of personal projects.

-4: A quest by city dwellers of an organization without restraint:

City dwellers try to avoid compulsive structures and school like or selective competition-oriented clubs.

* And we postulate the existence of **five "future bearing achievements"**

-1: An individualization, or rather a personalization of activities and their adaptation.

This means the effort to adapt closely to personal projects, possibilities and personal, or family oriented dispositions of users. Singular behaviours mean an important growth of the expressive power of movement. Expectations of a greater motor and decision autonomy is pressing amongst deserters. They indulge in verbal delectation and this exchange permits intense emotions within small groups of cultural pairs.

-2: A certain "transfer" and "ecological awareness" of activities, a quest for space.

We observe a quest for new settings which appears in the relative transfer of traditional equipment and the transformation of their use (baby swimmers, diving equipment, kayaks or leisure in swimming-pools for example), and a development of outdoors activities. This taste for free space, landscape discovery, natural territories to assail and cross, may take the tendency to drift from space to spaces.

-3: A combination, a concatenation, even a hybridizing of diverse activities.

The seasonal binding of activities is a clear example, and activities can be closely combined in pairs or in threesomes at a time. But this profusion of new activities, thus produced, is accompanied with a greater versatility of a public willing to shorten the learning period and to attain the pleasures of mastership faster.

-4: A greater part of technology (instruments, sports devices).

There is a greater sophistication and a simultaneous increase of instruments and sports equipment. Invention and use of vehicles is typical of the so called Californian sports. They permit the exteriorization of energy (A. Leroi-Gourhan) and offer the exultant experience of acrobatic mobility at a minimal cost. Through this multiple piloting, the exploitation of "soft" energies permit the discovery of new space, movements or sensations.

-5: An adventurous set-up of activities:

The taste of youth to transgress established values, the paradigm of "going away" and "travelling", breaking away from home and the paternal figure, affects the field of sports, through cross country expeditions, touring, escape away from the beaten track and "off limits" exploration and wandering by the young generation. As in most adventures, they are distinguished by the discovery of the unknown and the encounter of danger. The absence of laws, rules and of a discipline imposed from outside, express the reject of institutional constraints and the acceptance of on site sanctions. Within the small autonomous group, there is a tendency to boast of one's feats, cleverness, intelligence and resourcefulness. -which is the strength of the weak- and to perform initiation rituals. (Fig. 2)

Fig. 2 The Concept of a Sports-Adventures Site and it's Variations

6. Technical Solutions in Urbanistic and Architectural terms

It is possible to prepare the future in account to these foreseeable (or supposed) evolutions, conceiving sophisticated technical solutions that try to avoid the drawbacks of these tendencies.

In this process, **a fundamental difference between innovative "concepts" and adapted "products"** has to be introduced. As such, a concept can only be presented through illustrations and has no programmed or architectural reality. It can only be illustrated through visual images stimulating for the spirit, but since it is a concept it can not be "grounded", and a "construction cost" can not be estimated.

Only once a thorough adaptation of the project to it's defined urban functions, to specific geographic sites, to qualified urbanistic projects, to quantified needs of a local population is done, then the concept can be varied, worked out, calibrated, adapted to answer to these sometimes naïf or treacherous questions.

The starting point is quite simple: **It is a question of integrating in these new concepts of equipment, the main aspects of identified evolution**, which appear perfectly as specific examples in ecological, individual, high-tech activities of speed and thrill and acrobatic mobility at a lesser cost, of which youth, it's main promoter, is so fond of. It is therefore necessary to conceive all possible urban adaptations and find artificial areas that permit the practice of these activities in urban or suburban areas.

These activities may be classified in four groups according to the way the out-doors instrumentation is appropriated. There is the climbing, sliding, rolling and flying. Technical and technological feasibility of these urban sports adventure areas has been proven with a concern of the quality of the environment, surfaces and materials for the comfort and pleasure of those who practice and the possibilities to transfer the basic skills acquired in these areas onto natural ones. Special attention has been given to the restrictions of space in crowded areas and high real estate values.

The multiplicity of proposed activities is an answer to the versatility of tastes of a public whose loyalty is sought. It might be possible to start with a neighbourhood activity, advance into an other one pass from one to another, to link them, to combine them in twos or threes.

It is self understood that the manager of the grounds will **organize regular outings and expeditions to natural areas**, to validate and improve skills and share in small groups these new experiences and joys.

But the concept will not be reduced exclusively to the self evident **initiation and perfecting of skills, nor to spectacular competitions** (or friendly ones).[3]

It is based on four other functions that can articulate both the equipment and the urban environment.

It is also an axis of economic development and a business distribution center (building and distribution of sports products) a showplace of the best products in the market.

The resort (Fig.3) is **an encounter site of cultural exchanges** related to local activities (crafts, repairs, reduced models, technological improvements, the working principle of various devices, acquaintance with nature...). It is also a specialized **research laboratory** (management, computerization, export..) and eventually a **training center**. A technical or engineering school could be associated.

Fig. 3   A Variation of the Concept Associated to the Hotel Business and Centered on the Enhancement of Tourism

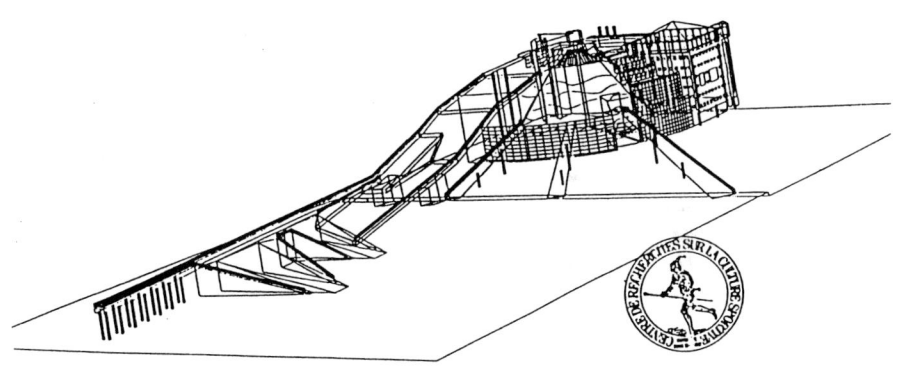

The urban environment in which the concept is to be inscribed, must be systematically explored, testing the potential of the five social and urban functions with which it will combine. This functional adjustment effort of the concept is the first phase of it's adaptation to it's multidimensional implantation context, and considers the objectives of local sports policies in a more general vision of local urban development.

7. Conclusions

We have to plead in favour of a **prospective research on sports like leisure activities of European city dwellers** (which concern the most: women, children, elderly people as well as teen-agers and young adults) with the pretext of the **innovation of sports and leisure facilities**, according to the demands, expectations and needs that can already be identified today.

New projects can be conceived and carried out in the context of a combat to obtain existing sports areas and a rough battle to conquer the urban space. They can only come to life by playing in the most favorable geographic urban and social conditions with **new actors**.

Those innovative sports leisure devices we have briefly referred to are not expected to replace existing traditional sports equipment because they respond to a real and legitimate need of the population (school children, competitors, sports elite, shows ...) but only pretend modestly, to **complement existing urban equipment**.

As from the appearance of the first prototype, a **deep change in the local offer** is to be expected, to the prejudice of the restrictive traditional competitive sport.

But our experience in the analysis of existing equipment and the drainage of users as well as the systematic test of the **reaction of users** (and competitors) **to innovative offer**, (G. Baslé, 1989) supports our belief of massif acceptance of new projects. **Traditional athletes** openly support, at least in France, the opening onto stimulating leisure activities, that they find recreational and complementary to their activities.

On the other hand, the leaders and spokesmen of associations and federations, often organized in lobbies, are not just unwilling but plainly hostile to these innovations. They claim never to have enough space for their own sport! They claim that "efforts should not be dispersed nor athletes distracted."

Those that have not yet benefited of existing private or public facilities -especially inner city youth- massively and enthusiastically adhere to these innovative projects.

We have not tried to list all existing facilities (which is impossible), nor to examine the efforts for improvement of classical equipment here and there in Europe in order to reintegrate it to the urban fabric (and the totality of urban functions) away from which they have progressively abstracted themselves through specific use and reducing their functions in the process (competition, shows).

It can hardly be expected for classical sports facilities to be modified to adapt to new forms, because they are meant to organize intentional events and are adapted to produce big shows. They are ever more worried to avoid violent outbreaks.

We could mention the efforts in modernization and renewal of facilities such as swimming pools in a quest of quality, improved management and to render them more pleasant. Other kinds of equipment, subject to **international normalization** and cost saving **industrial standardization** (through scale economy) were not, we understand, apt for our analysis.

We should not neglect the **difficulties of generalization of our observations** (or speculations) in this essay of **equipment prospective** based on **similar tendencies of evolution in Europe** through **factors deemed common** (mainly economical, social, urbanistic and technological), knowing the differences in policies and organizational structures, the differences in national strategies that determine choices, the financial differences as well as the historical and cultural contexts in which national sports systems are listed. Is it necessary to stress that the actual difficulties in the building of Europe are of similar origin and akin?

Outside of the political will of Nations, powerful forces of homogenization are at work producing similar effects in Europe. It might be our chance to work together...

References

A) European Council

1. Sports information bulletin; European Council; CDDS. "Préparer l'avenir;" Introductory document ; Preparatory meeting: September 28th-29th 1989.

2. Sports information bulletin; European Council; CDDS. Germany; Le Plan d'Or-Est; n° 32, March 1993, p. 2811.

3. Sports information bulletin; European Council; CDDS. Netherlands; Sports facilities manuel ; n° 32, March 1993, p. 2812.

4. Sports information bulletin; European Council; CDDS; Synthesis report: Les Sportives & leisure facilities; New challenges to planning and architec-ture; n° 33 June 1993, p. 2907.

5. Sports information bulletin; European Council; CDDS; Germany; Planification of local sports infrastructures, n° 33 de June 1993, p. 2924.

6. Sports information bulletin; European Council; CDDS; United Kingdom, Prescriptions for the equipment for sports & leisure, n°34, Sept 1993, p.3004.

B) Work done by the Research Centre of Sports Culture

1. **Pociello** (C. **& staff),** Sports et société; Paris, Vigot, 1991.

2. **Pociello C.,** "Structure et évolutions des loisirs sportifs dans la société française" (1975-1995), Research report at the Ministry "de la Jeunesse et des Sports (Mission Technique de l'Equipement)",Tome 1; September 1989.170 p.

3. **Pociello C.,** "Etude de faisabilité du "Site d'Aventures Sportives"; Construction du catalogue, sélection des espaces et premiers agencements architecturaux," Research report at the Ministry "de la Jeunesse et des Sports (Mission Technique de l'Equipement)", Tome 2, December 1989; 70 p. plus appendices and 40 illustrations.

4. **Baslé G., Pociello C.,** "Etude de fréquentation d'un équipement sportif et de loisirs; "L'Archipel" de Petit-Couronne: analyse de l'existant et test de l'offre d'innovation ", DEA theses -STAPS de l'UPS, 1989. 130p.

5. **Baslé G., Pociello C.,** "Méthode d'adaptation du "Site d'Aventures Sportives": Analyse de la demande sociale", SEJS, UPS Orsay / CRCS, Jan. 1990, 140 p.

6. **Pociello C.,** "Les tendances d'évolutions des pratiques de loisirs sportifs; à la recherche d'un modèle d'analyse prospective," in Revue Mappemonde, special N°: "L'expansion internationale des sports," 1990.

7. **Pociello C.,** "Prospective et innovations dans les loisirs sportifs," in; ""Le sport Moderne en question", Innovations et changements sociaux": AFRAPS Lyon, Jacques Cartier, Oct. 1990.

8. Hillairet D., "Prospective et Innovation des Sports à Technologie Elevée ("Système P.I.S.T.E".)" Doctorate theses for STAPS, University of Paris Sud-Orsay, 1991; 3 tomes plus appendices; 1400 p.

9. Baslé G., Pociello C., "Espaces et équipements sportifs et de loisirs; Etude de définition des besoins pour la Région de Paris-La Défense. Rapports de 1ère et de 2ème phase à l'Etablissement Public d'Aménagement de la Défense"; CRCS/ ISC, 1992.

10. Baslé G., Pociello C., "Espaces et équipements sportifs et de loisirs; Phase de créativité; Scénario possibles: Proposition d'un équipement innovant de grand rayon d'action; Le "Site d'Aventures sportives" Rapport de 3ème phase à l' Etablissement Public d'Aménagement de la Défense"; CRCS/ ISC, 1992.

11. Baslé G., Pociello C., "Espaces et équipements sportifs; innovations, prospective et management; in Sports & management; directed by A. Loret Paris, Dunod, 1993, (in print)

12. Defrance J., Pociello C., "Structure et évolutions du champ sportif français; Essai d'analyse "fonctionnelle", historique et prospective;" in "Revue internationale de Sociologie du sport," 1993

13. Pociello C., "Courants et contre-courants sportifs; Essai de compréhension des évolutions du champ sportif français". in "Communication au Congrès "Sports et citoyenneté" "Town of Brest, November. 1992 will be published in "Actes du Congrès" 1993.

14. Pociello C. (1987-89), "Réalisation d'illustrations, d'axionométries et de maquettes pour la présentation du "Site d'Aventures Sportives"", Congres, Meetings & Expositions (for the University of Paris Sud Orsay), and presentation brochure for territorial Community.

Footnotes

[1] Eg the European Council's "Sports information report"; CDDS, particularly The golden Plan-East- The Netherlands; Sports facilities manual- Germany; Planning and local sports infrastructure.- UK, Prescriptions for sports and leisure equipment; for the sole year of 1993. These documents are listed in the bibliography.

² Just by one example the interest and complexity of these cultural and national differences can be seen. Southern European Latin countries, (Italy, Spain, Catalonia, Portugal...) the way participants are computed is strongly conditioned by a quite restrictive "masculine" social definition of sport. In effect, the competitive, pugnacious, energetic, ascetic dimensions of sports activities are mainly identified, and therefore legitimized. The "virile" dimension is valued when counting participants. It can be seen to what extent the culture and history have an influence in the social definition of what is to be called "Sport" and therefore contribute to favor certain functions. On the other hand, the french controversy amongst experts following the distortions of french sports practices according to several polls (INSEP, INSEE) are mainly due to the considerable broadening of the social definition due to the increase of female participation. Practices, projects, functions, and the image of sport is therefore upturned. Will policy follow?

³ Special care will be given to the arrangement of the areas to increase the attractive potential of the equipment and seeking to enhance the most expressive and aesthetic movements. It is based on four other functions that can articulate the equipment with the urban environment.

THE ROLE OF LEISURE AND RECREATIONAL SPORT IN EUROPE

Roberts, K.
Department of Sociology, Social Policy and Social Work Studies
University of Liverpool
UK

1. What is recreational sport?

All sport has a recreational aspect. Sports are games, and nowadays all types of games are usually leisure time activities for the players or spectators. Both players and spectators may treat their games extremely seriously. Enjoyment of sport is conditional on a desire to win or improve, and knowledge that competitors are doing their best. Even so, sports remain 'just games'. The outcomes are rarely serious issues for the wider societies. In this respect sport differs from business, politics, military affairs and even the state of family life.

Rather than distinguishing recreational from non-recreational sport, it makes more sense to separate elite sport, amateur club sport and do-it-yourself sport. The latter variety is not new but it accounts for much of the growth in sport participation in most European countries since the 1950s, and this growth is indicative of broader trends in popular leisure.

2. Structural differentiation

The physical basics of present-day sports - the motions of running, throwing, swimming and so on - have been foundations for play throughout the ages. However, most present-day sports, the games played in industrial societies, were invented quite recently. Their rules were mostly codified, and the sports were initially organised and promoted by modern voluntary associations, and the most fertile period for these developments was the late nineteenth and early twentieth centuries. It is beyond the scope of the current discussion to explore the connections between the genesis of modern sports on the one hand, and industrialisation, urbanisation and modernisation on the other. Suffice it to say that at the start of the modern sporting era most sports were 'owned' by voluntary associations and amateur clubs. Ideals of sportsmanship nurtured during this period were closely entwined with ideas about amateurism. Sports were to be played for the sake of the games themselves, for the intrinsic enjoyment. Some believed, and still believe, that such a sporting ethic could unite humanity. The founders of the modern Olympic movement had such a vision and imagined (wrongly) that the ancient Greeks had shared this aspiration.

Elite, professional or topsport evolved out of amateur club sport when the most successful teams and individual performers found that they could attract large spectator audiences who were willing to pay for the entertainment. From the beginning there was tension between the professionals and the original amateur sports governing bodies. In most sports this tension was eventually resolved by structural differentiation. Professionals now usually play in separate teams and clubs, and participate in professional competitions. Elite sport has thus been able to become part of the modern entertainment industry. Its leading players are now professionally trained, highly paid entertainers. Professional sport has become sufficiently different to require separate streams of research, papers and sessions at major sports symposia (see 11).

Amateur club sport and professional sport have always been surrounded by a great deal of self-organised play in streets, parks, the sea and public swimming pools. Amateur club players have always practised informally, outside their clubs, while some spectators have been inspired in private play to emulate their heroes' skills. Do-it-yourself sport is not new, but since the 1950s there has been an explosion in this type of recreation in most of the world's more prosperous countries. More and more people have begun jogging, swimming, surfing, sailing, skiing, playing golf, tennis, squash, badminton and so on without becoming members of any clubs. Hence the paradox that has arisen in some European countries of rising levels of sport participation alongside static or even declining club membership.

Actually there has been no general decline in club sport. The 1960s and 70s were years of growth for all types of sport in most European countries.

Table 1 gives the number of participants in selected sports in Italy in 1974, 1981 and 1983. Participation in every listed sport rose during this period. Across Europe at that time the equivalent figures usually revealed the same upward trend.

Table 2 describes trends in the number of federation players in Portugal who were active in selected sports in 1970, 1978-79 and 1984-85. There was growth in a well-established team sport such as football, and in the younger sport of handball, and, indeed, in almost every sport for which information was collected.

Table 1

ITALY
Number of participants (in 000s)

	1974	1981	1983
Handball	884	855	811
Football	853	1094	1243
Fishing	511	568	617
Winter sports	124	144	177
Basketball	107	185	224
Athletics	91	138	118
Volleyball	85	153	226
Motorbike riding	65	97	116

Source: (1).

Table 2

PORTUGAL
Association or Federation members who were active in selected sports

	1970	1978-79	1984-85
Handball	3635	8631	10692
Athletics	2409	6832	8978
Badminton	169	124	1112
Football	28723	56459	65724
Swimming	684	729	1721

Source: (9)

All sports may be organised by clubs. Also, all sports can be practised privately. However, sports differ in the likelihood of their players becoming club members. The figures in Table 3 are from The Netherlands in 1987 but they would tell basically the same story had they been collected in any European country in any year since the Second World War. Most Netherlands soccer players (65 percent) in 1987 were club members. It is

Table 3

THE NETHERLANDS 1987
Percentages of participants who were club members

Sport	%
Soccer	65
Badminton	35
Sailing	12
Swimming	11
Running	10

Source: (4)

difficult to play soccer properly without joining a team. Just over a third of badminton players were club members, only a half of soccer's proportion, while in sailing, swimming and running no more than 12 percent of the players belonged to clubs. The latter games can be played to high standards by solitary individuals or small groups of friends who may see little benefit in club membership.

Team sports are the most likely to involve club membership and these games are not in decline, but throughout Europe there has been stronger growth in other kinds of sport. This is illustrated in Table 4, from France, which shows that the proportion of adults participating in team sports rose from 12.0 to 15.8 percent between 1973 and 1981. However, over the same period there was more growth, in percentage terms, in individual sports and forms of exercise that did not require club facilities. Again, the trend would have been much the same in the 1970s and 80s no matter which European society was examined.

Table 4

FRANCE
Percentages of adults taking part in different types of sport

	1973	1981
Gymnastics, physical exercise, walking, jogging.	18.6	34.8
Individual sports such as athletics, swimming, riding, judo, tennis, skiing, sailing.	25.5	31.9
Team sports	12.0	15.8

Source: (7)

The growth of do-it-yourself sport has changed the role of many clubs that have their own buildings, equipment or playing fields. Many clubs have experienced an influx of players who neither wish to compete nor, in many cases, develop their play to the highest possible standard. In addition to organising their members' sporting lives, therefore, many such clubs now operate on quasi-commercial lines by providing facilities that are available to customers - individuals, family groups and friends - who pay to use the resources for private play. The growth of do-it-yourself recreation has also encouraged a switch in public policy away from embracing leisure as a collective responsibility towards treating it as a private matter, but best left to individuals' choices and, increasingly, to their personal budgets (5).

3. The spread of sport participation

The post-war years up to 1980s were a growth era as regards sport participation in Europe. This was the case throughout the continent, East and West, and north and south. Part of the explanation was simply that sport was among the many forms of recreation that benefited from a general growth of leisure. Hours of work were trimmed; leisure time is vital for recreational sport because regular play is time demanding. However, leisure time alone is insufficient to generate sport activity. Most adult participants are full-time employees or full-time students who also, in many cases, have part-time or temporary jobs. Equally to the point, sport players have above-average participation rates in most other leisure activities (3). They tend to lead the busy leisure lives associated with the 'harried leisure class' (6). 'Finding the time' rather than 'filling time' is their main leisure problem. Groups outside the paid workforce - housewives, the retired and the unemployed - have below-average sport participation rates. Sport is not a time filler but a form of recreation which requires the time management skills associated with time pressure in education and employment.

The spread of prosperity in the post-war era will have been as important as the increased availability of leisure time in the rise of sport activity, especially in do-it-yourself sport. Participation will have been aided by, even if it was not wholly dependent on, more people being able to pay user charges, transport costs to recreation places, and the costs of private sports equipment and clothing. Increased vacation entitlement, a form in which work-free time for Europe's paid workforces has expanded rapidly since the Second World War, and people's ability to afford to fill their vacations with out-of-home, and often away from home, leisure ventures, will have been another factor in the rise of sport activity since do-it-yourself sport is frequently a holiday pursuit. The growth in the popularity of these activities, however, has depended not only on people having holiday time, but also the cash to 'go away' then pay for active recreation.

Changes in women's roles will have contributed to the spread of sport activity. Women have gained greater independence. In East European countries full-time labour force participation by women was standard throughout the communist era, while in western market economies the proportions of married women in employment rose during the 1950s, 60s and 70s. This led to more adult women having their 'own' money, and feeling that they, like men, were entitled to independent leisure. The chances are that female sport participation would have risen, and the gender gap narrowed, without any special campaigns by sport providers.

Trends in education will also have contributed to the rise in adult sport participation during the post-war decades. Schools have broadened their sports curricula and augmented traditional team games with sports that are more likely to be retained into later life stages. Simultaneously, schools have promoted sport for all rather than just the most talented. Increased educational participation in late-adolescence will also have been favourable to sport. Young adults who remain in full-time education retain access to the heavily subsidised facilities that are available in most schools and colleges, and, equally important, are in daily contact with same-aged friends with whom to play. Youth and young adulthood are critical life stages in sport careers (13). If individuals acquire broad stocks of sporting skills and interests when young, and continue to play into their 20s, the chances are that they will then continue to participate for many more years. The best way of boosting adult sport participation is to reduce drop-out among young people, and the best known strategy for reducing this drop-out is to retain young adults in education for as long as possible.

Increased provision for sport by the public, voluntary and commercial sectors from the 1950s onwards has been partly a response to growing demand, but will also have been a causal factor in the spread of sport participation. Recreational preferences respond to opportunities. Governments in most countries have realised this, and have regarded sport as a desirable leisure time activity worthy of subsidy, and have therefore created or subsidised facilities for people to play.

4. Individualisation

All the above trends could have led to higher levels of sport activity inside or outside clubs. The crucial development favouring do-it-yourself sport has been individualisation. This is not a wholly new phenomenon. Industrial employment has always been of individuals, modern democracy has always enfranchised individual citizens, and individuals have long been held responsible for their own actions in courts of law. Nevertheless, individualisation has accelerated in recent years.

Individualisation should not be confused with privatism. The latter term refers to home and family centredness which lead to disengagement from the wider society. The significance of such a trend, especially amongst the working classes, was widely debated in the 1960s and 70s. However, privatised lifestyles are not necessarily individualised. People can share common experiences in their jobs, homes and leisure irrespective of whether they interact and become aware of these similarities, while people can lead outgoing but still individualised ways of life.

A crude measure of individualisation is how many other people in a person's social network share the same biography having grown up in the same neighbourhood, gone to the same local schools, entered similar types of local employment, then continued to live as neighbours. The trend over time throughout Europe has been towards individuals who know each other sharing less in common with one another. Experiences of life increasingly underline each person's unique individuality rather than express membership of a common social category.

Greater individualisation in recent years has been a product of higher rates of geographical mobility, the break-up of former concentrations of employment in traditional industries, and the increasing complexity of education and training systems and careers therein. Individualisation has both objective and subjective dimensions. People with distinctive life experiences are likely to be conscious of their individuality and the features that distinguish them from other people that they know. Individualised persons may or may not feel in control of their own life trajectories, but the dominant tendency today seems to be for people to regard their life courses as personal creations, and, among young people at any rate, to feel that they themselves will be responsible for constructing their own futures (2).

As a result of these broader trends, leisure activities have increasingly become individual decisions, or projects involving just current friends or family members if not solitary individuals, rather than long-term group commitments. Leisure skills, including sporting skills, have become portable individual assets which people augment and carry from place to place and group to group. Commitments to teams and clubs have become temporary in most instances, like the club commitments of professional elite players. Provisions for participant sport have partly encouraged, but they have also adapted to this trend. Public sport facilities have normally been created for, and been made accessible to all members of the public. Subsidies to voluntary associations have often been conditional on the facilities being made available to the general public rather than exclusive to club members. Commercial providers in particular have responded to the growing demand from individuals for opportunities to play do-it-yourself sport. Golf courses, fitness centres and leisure complexes offering various mixtures of experiences have created opportunities to play sport for all with the financial means, and no other commitment has been expected. Membership systems in the commercial sector are typically more a method of advance payment than a means of restricting access to a particular social group or involving players in the management of the facilities (14).

In East Europe individualisation has spread rapidly since the collapse of communism (12, 16). Until the reforms young people from given neighbourhoods normally attended local schools where most of them were prepared for local employment in state owned or state managed firms, farms or government departments. Once obtained public sector jobs could normally be relied on to last for life. Housing was also provided through public allocation systems in which entitlements depended on membership of a social category. Recreation outside the home was catered for mainly through firms, trade unions, party organisations and other branches of the state. Individualisation could develop only around the fringes of socialist systems whereas it became a central trend once these systems disappeared. Many large state enterprises soon collapsed. Others became leaner and more competitive. They were joined by much larger numbers of private businesses, mostly small businesses, few of which can offer anything resembling the life-long security of the former socialist systems. In post-communist Europe housing is now being marketised, and leisure likewise. Opportunities are increasingly individual choices and are governed primarily by individuals' ability to pay.

Individualisation does not mean that opportunities in leisure, or in employment for that matter, have ceased to be influenced by the familiar predictors of age, gender, socio-economic origins and current status. The new situation is rather that these 'determinants' now form a multitude of individualised configurations. So any single 'predictor' has ceased to be a useful guide to an individual's most likely leisure practices, and individuals have less reason than formerly to be conscious of the constraints and opportunities that they share in common with all other members of particular social categories.

5. Saturation?

Since the 1970s there have been signs of the previous steady growth in sport activity faltering. Individualisation is continuing but this trend merely shaped rather than caused the earlier growth in sport activity. The clearest and most dramatic reversals have been in Eastern Europe during the dislocations prior to and following the collapse of communism. Consumer spending declined in many of these countries while the sporting infrastructures, the state sports organisations, collapsed, and spending on the maintenance of sports facilities declined. Between 1976 and 1984 the sport participation rate among Poland's adults almost halved (see Table 5). There was a similar downward trend in Czechoslovakia during the same period (see Table 6). There have been no equally steep cases of decline in Western Europe, but in particular countries, within specific socio-demographic groups, there have been reversals, as among The Netherlands' 18-24 year olds between 1983 and 1987 (see Table 7). Such reversals may have been due to the economic difficulties which followed the end of the '30 glorious years' and the deeper recessions that have returned to the Western economy since the 1960s. Such economic difficulties may prove temporary, but additional longer-term trends are now operating against a continuing rise in sport participation.

Table 5

POLAND
Percentage of adults playing sport on a typical weekday

1976	1984
1.1%	0.6%

Source: (8)

Table 6

CZECHOSLOVAKIA
Adult sport participation (in percentages)

	1978	1984
At least once a week	10.3	8.4
Less than once a week but at least once a month	5.1	3.1
Less often	84.6	88.5

Source: (10)

Table 7

THE NETHERLANDS
Percentages of different age groups who were sport participants

	1979	1983	1987
18 - 24	74	81	77
25 - 34	69	76	75
35 - 54	51	61	62
55 - 64	30	41	43

Source: (4)

Virtually all governments are now seeking to contain if not reduce their social spending. Sport can longer rely upon forever increasing public subsidies. 'User pays' has become a widespread policy. Furthermore, the ageing populations of all the developed countries, with population growth in the retired age groups certain to continue well into the twenty-first century, will operate against further overall increases in adult sport participation rates.

More fundamentally perhaps, sport participation in the economically advanced countries could be pressing its limits of natural growth. Leisure trends usually peak at some point. This has proved the case with television viewing. Also, the former long-term decline in hours worked by full-time employees is no longer running. By the end of the 1980s the majority of adults in most West European countries were sport participants on a broad definition, meaning that they engaged in some physically energetic recreation at least once a year. Diminishing returns apply as surely in sport as in other spheres; the higher the level of participation, the more difficult it becomes to win additional participants. Further rises are likely to depend upon changing what, up to now, have been the basic social contours of sport participation.

For example, it will be necessary to close the differences traditionally associated with age, sex and socio-economic status by involving larger numbers from the very groups that have always been the hardest to recruit into sport. Alternatively, or in addition, further rises in participation could depend upon persuading existing participants to play more sports, or to take part in their current sports more frequently. Up to now most sport participants have been 'casuals' (15). 'Serious' athletes who play the several times a week considered necessary to derive physical health benefits have been a relatively small minority among all sport players. Increasing the number for whom sport is a form of serious or committed leisure is likely to be difficult because sport is a time demanding form of recreation and leisure time is no longer increasing among the socio-demographic groups that are most likely to play, and there is increasingly intense competition for all groups' leisure time and money.

6. Emergent trends and issues

Rather than any strong expansion or decline, a clearer future trend is likely to be towards even greater structural differentiation; among recreational sport players themselves as well as between this group and other participants. Such differentiation normally occurs as leisure taste publics mature. There are likely to be clearer divisions between casual and serious players, and among the latter according to their particular sports and factions thereof. Structural differences are now well established in publishing, and increasingly pervade tourism. Experienced tourists seek something more demanding or specialised than standardised mass packages. Likewise, generations that have been in sport since their childhoods, particularly those who treat their own play seriously, are likely to distinguish themselves from casual participants. Providers, the owners and managers of sport facilities, are therefore likely to be rewarded for identifying market niches rather than offering something for everyone. If overall participation levels stabilise, as is likely, market success will depend more upon capturing existing participants than attracting newcomers to sport. So providers are likely to seek distinctive identities, offering something manifestly novel in their sport repertoires, fitness or training regimes. Likewise, clothing and equipment providers will fashion distinctive products, or at least distinctive packaging.

Debates about the role of the public sector are likely to focus more upon which participants to service rather than how to promote sport for all. In an era when government support lags behind demand for recreational sport there is likely to be greater competition between the claims of casual and dedicated players. The latter will argue that their exceptional commitment, and the scale and variety of the benefits that flow from their participation, should be accorded greater priority than the whims of casuals. If commercial operators, and voluntary clubs that operate on commercial lines, become increasingly keen to attract existing participants, which is where the main scope for short-term market success will probably lie, public policy might concentrate on influencing longer-term trends in participation which could mean ensuring that sound foundations are laid in childhood, and that young adults have every opportunity to continue in sport.

Amid these trends, the 'politics' of recreational sport will be less of a concerted campaign for more resources and participants than a series of internal struggles for shares of the cake. As argued above, the rise of recreational sport in post-war Europe accompanied broader processes of individualisation. These trends have left sport less equipped than ever before in modern history to act as unified lobby representing common goals and interests.

References

1. **Belloni M C:** 'Italy'. In: Kamphorst T. J., Roberts. (eds): *Trends in Sports*, Culemborg, Giordano Bruno, 1989.

2. **Evans K., Heinz W.J., (eds):** *Becoming Adults in England and Germany*, London, Anglo-German Foundation, 1993.

3. **Gratton C., Tice A:** 'Sport participation and health'. *Leisure Studies*, 8, 77-92, 1989.

4. **Kamphorst T.J., Giljam M:** 'The Netherlands'. In: Kamphorst T.J., Roberts K.(eds): *op cit* 1989.

5. **Lengkeek J.,** 'Collective and private interest in recreation - the Dutch case': *Leisure Studies*, 12, 7-32 1993.

6. **Linder S.**, *The Harried Leisure Class*, New York, Columbia University Press, 1970.

7. **Malenfant C.**, 'France': In: Kamphorst, T.J., Roberts K, (eds): *op cit* 1989.

8. **Olszewska A.**, 'Poland: the impact of crisis on leisure patterns': In Olszewska A. Roberts K, (eds): *Leisure and Life-Style*, London, Sage 1989.

9. **Pais J.M.**, 'Portugal': In Kamphorst T.J., Roberts K., (eds): *op cit* 1989.

10. **Rak V.**, 'Czechoslovakia': In Kamphorst T.J., Roberts K., (eds): *op cit* 1989.

11. **Roberts K.**, 'The disintegration of sport': In Williams T., Almond L., Sparkes A., (eds): *Sport and Physical Activity*, London, Spon 1992.

12. **Roberts K.**, 'Young adults in Europe': In Vereniging voor de Vrijetijdssector, *Internationalisation and Leisure Research*, Proceedings of a Conference: Tilburg 1992.

13. **Roberts K., Brodie D.A.**, *Inner-City Sport: Who Plays and What are the Benefits?* Culemborg, Giordano Bruno, 1992.

14. **Roberts, K., York C.S., Brodie D.A.**, 'Participant sport in the commercial sector', *Leisure Studies*, 7, 145-157, 1988.

15. **Stebbins R.A.**, *Amateurs, Professionals and Serious Leisure*, Montreal, McGill-Queens University Press, 1992.

16. **Wallace C.**, 'Youth, citizenship and social change in East and West Europe', paper presented at International Youth Conference on *Youth and Social Changes in Europe: Integration or Polarisation?*: Moscow, 1992.

Training Sport Managers

Rubingh, B.
Sport Management Instituut, Rijksuniversiteit Groningen
The Netherlands

1. Introduction

Managers in sport are just like other managers in society, they run an organisation. During the last decades however, sport has changed, and these changes have influenced the management of sports organisations. An increasing need for special training programmes occurred, which meant the start of a new sport management training programme based on the needs of sport managers in the field.

In the Netherlands in the three years beginning in 1988, three courses have been developed; a middle management, a higher management and a Masters course. The courses have been developed by the Sport Management Institute (SMI), a joint venture among universities, sport federations and the Dutch government.

At this moment over 100 managers have completed the sport management training programme. Amongst them are leading figures (directors) within Dutch sports organisations.

During the development of these courses a lot of new concepts and theories were born. It seems appropriate to share some of our experiences with others.

2. A training concept

The following three different perceptions form the basis of the training concept which is used by the Sport Management Institute:

1. looking at the training of the sport manager from an educational point of view,
2. looking at the training of the sport manager from a sport point of view,
3. looking at the training of the sport manager from a management point of view.

2.1 The educational point of view

It is often said that adults learn differently, with more difficulty than children. Since children are born to learn, the ability to learn decreases when one gets older. Recent studies however, point in a different direction, that adults do not learn differently and therefore should learn as easily as children. Reality proves that this is not the case. If adults learn in the same way as children, then what is the cause for not learning as fast and easy as children? The theory of experience concentration answers this question.

In the initial phase of the sport management programme, SMI was confronted with numerous applications not for studying sport management, but for teaching it. So at the start there were more teachers than students. Of course most of the teachers did not fit into our programme, but more important it gave us our first hint, people in sports, probably believe that they have a lot of expertise which fits into a sport management programme. The second hint was dropped by some of the students who, at the beginning of the course, said when answering the question what they wanted to learn, that they already knew a lot but that this programme should give them the tools to structure their knowledge. The study progress gave us a third hint. The students showed a lot of resistance to new theories and concepts during the first months of the programme. However, after some weeks it was as if we were breaking a window, and a fresh wind could blow in.

Adults have, depending on their age and the different environmental settings a lot of experience. Mostly the experience has been obtained in a limited area. For example, a child that grew up in a garage and later becomes a mechanic in the same garage will translate all new experiences to his garage experience. Driving through a new city, he will notice other garages because he is focused on this topic. This is called experience concentration. Because everybody has certain experiences, we are looking to the world through a filter made up of our experience concentration. In most cases this filter helps us to filter all the unnecessary information and build up our (concentrated) experience. New experiences and new knowledge are translated to old experiences. This helps to understand and to filter what is important. So it is for example easy to understand the theory of formal organisational structures if one works in an organisation, because the new theory can be applied to own experiences. Students tell you that it makes learning easier. Some theory however is neglected simply because it cannot be translated to earlier experiences. The advantage of experience concentration is therefore that people can learn easier by recognizing and translating new theory to their earlier experiences. The disadvantage is that people are less open to new theories and experiences unless they are directly connected to their own (concentrated) experience. You could say that they filter new information.

Sport managers working in a sports organisation find themselves more and more in a changing environment which is becoming increasingly complex and diverse. Managing a sports organisation based on old limited perceptions is not enough, they have to look beyond sport and sports organisations. The consequence is that they have to be open to new ideas, new theories and concepts, able to work on new directions for sport management.

2.2 The sport point of view

Sport is a very important entity in our western society. Now-a-days you can participate in sport through your entire life. A high participation percentage and the attention paid to sports by the media prove a high and close involvement. But sport is not as clear as it seems to be.

Most of us were confronted with sports when we were young. Through the years we have created a solid image in our minds. When we talk about sport, we must be aware of the fact that everyone has a different image associated with the word 'sport'. Because of its entanglement in society and its variety of appearances, sport creates a many-sided image in people's heads.

If you raise a discussion, you may notice that if the subject is sport, everybody has an answer and everybody knows something about it. Is it one of the few subjects one can talk about, without fear, since the subject is not as serious as real life?

Besides the fact that a sport manager is confronted with his image of sport, created over the years (the experience concentration handicap), he is also confronted with colleagues, employees, members and spectators who all have their own image of 'sport'.

Yet images play an important role in the efficiency and effectiveness of organisations. The image is closely linked to the activity to be realised (see Fig. 1).

Fig. 1

(common?)		
IMAGE ↓	=	what image do we have of the situation?
VISION ↓	=	where do we think it will lead to?
MISSION ↓	=	why are we doing it?
OBJECTIVES ↓	=	what are we doing?
ACTIVITIES	=	we are doing it.

Related to Morgan, Images of Organisation (1987), for example it makes quite a difference when one employee sees the organisation as a battle field while another sees it as a network.

Based on Morgan's statement (Imaginization, 1993) that an organisation has no presence beyond that of the people who bring it to life, sports organisations are composed of a variety of people who all have their own image of sport and therefore bring sports organisations to life in different ways.

One of a (sport) manager's major concerns is, whether all images of participants in the organisation lead to the same direction. Do we all have the same idea of what this organisation is all about and what we want to accomplish? However, because of this high and lifetime involvement all participant have their own varying images and it is a very firm image built over a lifetime, and difficult to alter.

Let me give you an example of this predefined image. A student is in his last year of studying physics. His marks so far were extremely high and his work-placements good. A larger European car company invites him over for an interview at the company and offers him a contract right after his study. He is very surprised, because he had told them that he so far he had no experience with cars. Over the phone he expresses his surprise on which the personnel manager gives the next reply: "I see, but you have to understand that we see it as a great advantage that we have the opportunity of giving you your first experience in a car company".

From the car company's point of view, the moment the graduate enters the company it starts working on the image of cars of the new employee. It is quite easy to form a desired image with a person who is not pre-occupied with other images. The car company hopes that the image arising is not too different from the images of fellow employees.

Comparing this situation with a sports organisation, we may conclude that all who want to work in a sports organisation are pre-occupied with an image. Often people are very eager to work for a sports organisation because they love the sport, etc. People entering a sport organisation already have made up their minds, they bring along their own image. A manager of such an organisation has great difficulty in creating a mutual image and shared understandings in the organisation. A mutual image and shared understandings are necessary to tackle the challenges facing modern sport organisations as we move from a mechanistic to an information based world (Morgan, 1988, Peters, 1987), where there is a need for more creative, intuitive, empowered approaches to management.

The manager of a sports organisation is confronted with a variety of images of sport and of the sports organisation by colleagues, employees, members and other stakeholders. It is an important challenge to build a mutual image which underlines the mission statement. It is probably difficult to accomplish but a lot easier to work with, if participants in an organisation all work in the same direction and with the same image of sport and of sports organisation.

One of the major inspirations of leadership for the coming years will be the ability of the organisation to create an image of the future which is shared by all its members. "We must learn to find common images for the future that create real engagement and not just followers." (Senge, 1990)

In summary, it appears very important to create a mutual image amongst the members of an organisation. In sport it seems a lot more difficult to create that mutual image because individuals have a pre-occupied image created over a lifetime involvement in sport.

2.3 The management point of view

Recent developments in management theory show great attention for the phenomena 'learning organisation'. Organisations that discover how they can use at all levels, the willingness and ability of their members to learn, will be up front in the future.

The principle of the learning organisation tells us that it is no longer sufficient to have one person at the top who is the organisation's brain. The organisation as a whole has to think. Sports organisations in a way have already been composed of thinking members. Compared with other organisations one can assume that members of sports organisations are much more involved. This could be the reason why sports organisations often accomplish the impossible and can fulfil an enormous amount of work. However, if the opposite occurs big mistakes are made and a lot of energy is lost. The most important aspect of a learning organisation is the mutual goal, and a mutual image of how to get there. By adjusting the images within sports organisations, learning organisations could arise with hardly any energy. Aspects such as involvement, expertise and empowerment are often sufficiently present in sports organisations. The problem however, is how to lead all this energy into one direction. An instrument which could be a key factor in sports organisations therefore, may be inspirational leadership 'to create a mutual image'.

The fact that most people involved in sport and sports organisations have their own image built over a lifetime involvement (experience concentration) in sport, can be a handicap. However when a manager has the capability of reading all those different images and adjust them to a mutual image, a powerful and learning organisation is born. Therefore management should know the variety of meanings sport has to all stakeholders.

The three aspects discussed all influence the curriculum of our sport management programme. The sport manager working in the field is using a subjective concept to tackle the day to day problems. This concept is based on practical experience (experience concentration) and theoretical knowledge. To use the positive aspects of the students subjective concepts, we try to integrate new theory into old concepts. The negative aspects of experience concentration can be tackled by way of reflection on his/her own practice and a variety of other practical situations and subjective concepts (different images). The groups are composed of managers with a wide variety of experiences and backgrounds. SMI has experienced a lot of added value in training sport managers by using these different experiences in its didactical working forms. Fellow sport managers often broaden the narrowed image built by 'experience concentration'. SMI therefore, has made this diversity in a class a selection criterium for entrance. The education is problem-oriented for which theory is constantly translated to practical situations of the student. The theory provided is an integration of several knowledge areas, into an interdisciplinary field of 'sport management'. Key subjects are management and organisational theory and practice, sport marketing management and financial management. Within these subjects aspects of law, decision making, negotiating, public relations, research, etc. are integrated. All this has to lead to a professional working concept (see Fig. 2).

Fig. 2

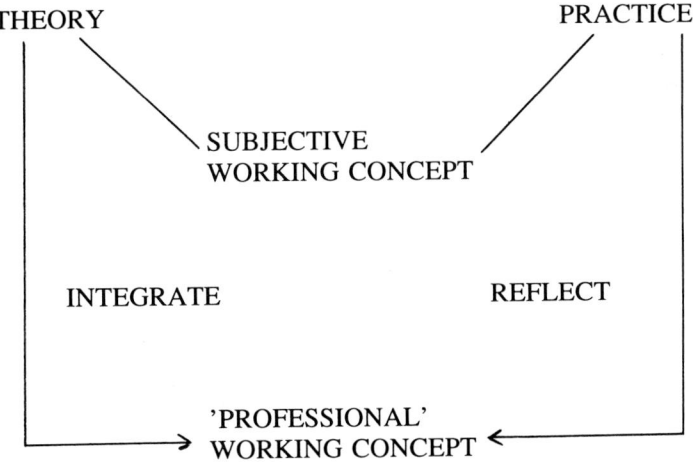

3. Summary

Educational theory on adult education and latest organisational and management theories are translated to sport. This translation was used by SMI for the realisation of its training programmes. Such a translation has consequences for training programmes for sport managers.

Experience concentration, images of organisations and the learning organisations are three aspects which can be translated to sport. Surprisingly they all lead to the same conclusion. The image of the members in a sports organisation, more than in any other organisation, seems crucial for its success. A solid image formed over the years and built by so-called experience concentration seems a handicap which is more obvious in sports organisations than in any other organisation. Principles of a 'learning organisation' seem to be more present in potential than of xx organisation. The importance of creating a mutual image seems obvious.

Hypothesis/assumption
This article underlines the assumption that sports organisations require inspirational leaders, who can create aspiring images with a charismatic approach. In this case the potential energy in these organisations can be directed to the principles of a learning organisation.

Education, Training and Further Education in Leisure and Recreational Sport

Sobotka, W.
Österreichische Turn- und Sportunion
Wien, Österreich

Most of the education for training and further education in sport is more or less competitive sport oriented.
Therefore, it was necessary to establish a broad possibility for recreational and leisure sport.
The situation in Austria took care of 3 different aspects in this matter:

1. Broad education
2. An education system with the possibility to start with a basic education and continue by specialisation
3. To organise the training in our sport federations and therefore support the clubs in this matter.

Education for everyone is organised by the state institutes for physical education on a level where no entrance prerequisites are necessary. Therefore, everyone can join such an education.
The start is a youthleader education and a basic recreational and leisure instructor.

There are two possibilities to go on with a further education: one is a higher education as trainer for recreational and leisure sport. The second is the specialisation towards concrete subjects in leisure and recreational sports:

- sport for older people
- sport for youngsters
- mother and child sport
- sport for handicapped people.

All this education is mainly organised by the state federations and executed by the state institutes for physical education. To get higher participation rates these education programs are held in a compressed form in the holiday season in summer.
The briefly described topics will be further explained in my paper in detail.
The discussion of this important topic begins with an analysis of the present situation in sport education.

The education for training and further education in sport was and at least so far is more or less competitive sport oriented.

The main reason for this statement is that the structure of sport is very strange in the aspect of money.

There is a big deficit in money involved in sport and money spending habits.

If you look at the total money available for sport, most of the money is spent for competitive purposes. On the other hand most of the money earned or spent for the sport of normal people is coming out of leisure and recreational sport.

Therefore, the need to support this type of sport with properly educated trainers and instructors is bigger and bigger.

If we look at the education structure, the beginning of sport education (beside the education for teachers in physical education) was more or less set up to educate trainers for high level sport and a good example are all the trainers for skiing, tennis and soccer.

The main goal was not to reach many people for this type of education; it was only designed to get well educated and selected trainers for competitive sport.

But society has changed very fast in the last decade and the years of the sport visitors are being followed by the years of the active sport participants. SPORT is an integral part of our society life and we are living in a so called "LEISURE TIME SOCIETY".

Active sport means being active in leisure time and if the sociologists are right the main leisure time now is sport.

Whether this will also be true in ten years is the important question and a good and effective education system is therefore necessary.

Therefore the societies have to take care of education, training and further education for "instructors" and "Trainers" to fulfill the need of our leisure time society and supply it with adequately educated people.

In Austria, 3 different aspects had to be taken into account to be successful with this task:

1. The need of a real broad education system to reach as many as possible

2. A special system which is offering the possibility to start with a very broad basic education to reach as many people as possible, as mentioned above but on the other hand to open the door for a great variety of special education for recreational and leisure sport.

3. To organise an operating platform for training in the different sport federations and sport clubs under educated guidance.

Education for recreational and leisure sport is organised by the state institutes for physical education in very close connection with the big sport federations.

In Austria the 3 main sport federations are mainly taking care of leisure sport. Education is free for everyone and it is organised on a level that no entrance exams are necessary and also there are no real prerequisites for this type of education. Therefore, everyone can obtain such an education.

The start is a youthleader education or the basic recreational instructor.

This type of education is designed as a 2-semester course which could be held in the form of semester education with about 28 hours a week or as it is normally done as a 3 full week course which is normally divided in 3 portions and these courses are held mainly in the holiday season.

The normal fluctuation rate is not bad, there are only 20-30% drop out rates. Each course ends with an oral and practical examination and each successful participant gets a "State certificate" which has official character.

90% of participants pass the courses at the first attempt.

Each course has 3 main subjects:

1) So-called necessary topics fulfill the Austrian education laws like religion, German, history, political education.

2) theoretical subjects like: anatomy, psychology, pedagogy, sport psychology, training science, audiovisual aids, methodology group dynamic, sexual pedagogy.

3) practical subjects: practical sport (especially leisure sport), practical methodical sport, special methodic sport education, athletics, swimming, ball games.

The rate of these 3 parts is about
1 - 10%
2 - 40%
3 - 50%.

After having finished this basic education you can go on with a further education towards a trainer for recreational sport which is 4 semesters and specialises in such topics as:
- anatomy and first aid
- special gymnastics for disabled people
- also special spine problems and physiotherapy
- biomechanics, English, massage and a larger variety of topics on practical leisure sport
- functional gymnastics and also health gymnastics.

This education could also be used as a professional education in sport.

The second form is specialisation:

- recreational sport for children
- recreational sport for senior citizens
- recreational sport for mother and child
- sport for handicapped people

basic education - 100%
further education - 2%
specialisation about 20-30%

All together about 500 fitness instructors are educated in Austria.

300 basic fitness instructors or youth leaders
180 special fitness instructors
20 fitness trainer.

The fluctuation problem is severe. If you look after 5 years how many are still working practically in sport clubs or sport federations 60-80% have disappeared. The real practical value of the education system is therefore rather low but because the interest in the last 10 years has been rising it is now satisfying for the sport federations and sport clubs.

Main problems:

Further education on a weekend base organised by state.
More financial help for trained and educated trainers.

SPORT AND TOURISM IN THE SOUTH OF ENGLAND

Standeven, J.
Chelsea School of Physical Education, Sports Science, Dance & Leisure
University of Brighton
UK

1. Introduction

Whilst this paper, a case study of the links between sport and tourism, takes as its focus Southern England in dealing with inbound and outbound visitors as well as domestic tourism, the discussion extends into mainland Europe and further afield to other parts of the world.

The connections between sport and tourism have been established for close to two hundred years with British tourists 'inventing' the modern sport of mountaineering in the European Alps early in the nineteenth century. The first mountaineers climbed in order to research the effects of altitude upon the body, but by 1827 the Britons Frederick Siade and Yeats Brown's unsuccessful attempt to climb the Jungfrau was described as 'for the fun of the thing', and Cieare (1975) reports:

> .. continental critics expressed shock at the complete lack of any scientific justification for their attempt".

Between 1854 and 1865 some 180 of the highest Alpine peaks were first climbed with more than half of these conquests made not by patriots but by British tourist climbers. Thus mountaineering as a sport became associated with the privileged classes of British society who could afford both the time to travel and the equipment and guiding services needed to attempt the ascents. One hundred and fifty years later privileged British sport-tourist participants can be found trekking in the Himalayan foothills of Nepal (Faux,1993).

By the end of the nineteenth century the French aristocrat Baron Pierre de Coubertin 'invented' a new incentive for travel with the rebirth of the Olympic movement, and the first celebration of the Games in Athens rated as much a 'tourist event' as a 'sporting event'. McFee (1990) describes the 1896 Games as an "attraction" and sees them as an event which brought sport-tourist spectators to Athens; part, perhaps, of the European 'Grand Tour', a status symbol of elite society at that time.

Other innovations, such as the mass production of the bicycle, enabled a broader segment of the British population by the 1930s to combine a sporting activity with a tourist or holiday experience, and more than 10 million people are said to have visited the countryside for pleasure (Tornlinson & Walker, 1990). Links between sport and tourism are not, then, in any sense new, though trends and influences in recent years have given their relation renewed meaning.

However, in Britain this relation has remained largely unrecognised at policy level until very recently with government involvement in sport and tourism split between different Departments. Nevertheless, the Sports Council, in its 1988 strategy document, acknowledged the importance of joint initiatives between the Council and the Tourist Boards (Sports Council, 1988). These connections have recently been given a higher profile following the Conservative government's re-election in April 1992 and the establishment of the Department of National Heritage (DNH). The DNH, which groups related areas together, has been created to co-ordinate and direct the development of the various leisure-related sectors; it gives cabinet status to sport, the arts, tourism and broadcasting.

The Sports Council (South West) and the West Country Tourist Board became, in September 1992, the first regional agencies to publicly acknowledge the possibilities for collaboration in the issue of a joint policy statement 'Tourism and Sport'. They state:

> "There is a need for more co-ordinated strategies at both regional and local levels to take greater account of the close functional links between tourism, sport and active recreation in the region".
> (WCTB & SC (SW) 1992)

The document presents tourism and sport as part of a larger leisure industry which it claims "should be considered more comprehensively to ensure a proper 'consistency of fit' with wider social and economic aims", and it makes 25 joint policy statements.

An extract from a leaked 1993 DNH letter shows the importance now being attached by central government to such collaborative planning and the promotion of joint initiatives:

> "Ministers are anxious that we become more active in promoting collaboration between DNH-sponsored bodies, both national and regional".

The letter goes on to advise administrators of the need to consider:

- "the interdependencies, and any conflicts, between their own objectives and activities and those of other sponsored bodies. . . particularly local authorities;

- the extent to which they are currently collaborating with others to achieve their objectives;

- the potential for extending that collaboration and their plans to do so".

There is little doubt amongst these agencies that future funding will depend, in part, upon plans for collaboration between these previously disconnected bodies.

This attempt in Britain to forge connections between formerly separate sectors of the leisure industry will require people to work together in new ways, problematising relations between the different interest groups in the public sector and between industry and government. In analysing these new connections, high level policy shifts have to be taken into account. The potential benefits of a co-ordinated approach to sport and tourism have to be set in the context of the potential disbenefits of the political agenda.

A theoretical model which visualises the changing relations between interest groups as an activity embedded in parameters of power on different levels forms the final section of this paper. Working out the new policies and bringing about change will cause activists to come into contact and potentially conflict with one another as they share the situational space between them; their relation being dependent upon their relative positions of power. David Botterill's (1992) 'visualisation of activist space' is projected as a potentially useful model through which to analyse the changing relationships.

This paper takes as its starting point a clarification of key terms such as region, sport, tourism, activity holidays and holiday activities.

Working definitions are followed by a number of examples of sport and tourism connections from the different regions within the south of England. The economic and sports development justifications for the sport-tourism relation are demonstrated through the links examined.

2. Key terms

Working definitions of key terms are necessary to enable an adequate interpretation of the examples that follow. Region, sport, tourism, activity holidays and holiday activities are terms open to varied understanding.

Region has been variously defined as:

"Any circumscribed territorial unit" (Rodman)
"A geographic area unified culturally..." (Young)
"A complex created by man and which man can destroy" (Gottman)
"Any one part of a national domain sufficiently unified ... to have a true

consciousness of its own customs and ideals, and to possess a sense of distinction from other parts" (Royce) (all cited in Matthews, 1981).

Young's definition goes beyond Rodman's in its emphasis upon a sense of shared meaning. This is developed in Royce's fuller account which focusses on the consciousness of the inhabitants, the customs and ideals they share and the sense they have of their own distinctiveness.

Southern England possesses no easily identifiable unifying concept. In a recent seminar called to address regional identity and cultural policy in the South East, the region was described as an 'elusive entity' (Lawrence & Tomlinson,1993).

Regions are quite often social constructs which use different boundaries for different purposes and these can be altered at will; by definition, then, a region so defined may lack homogeneity since it will have no cultural imperative. The definition of region used in this paper is closest to Rodman's and Gottman's definitions, since the territorial unit to which it refers is differently defined by the agencies concerned. The Sports Council, for example, has three regions that cover Southern England, dividing the country into the South East, the South (or the central area), and the South West. The Tourist Board's, meanwhile, use four regions to cover the same territory - South East England Tourist Board, the Southern Tourist Board, the West Country Tourist Board (whose region differs from that of the Sports Council) and the now defunct Thames and Chilterns Tourist Board. This serves to emphasise the complex relations involved in forming the new collaborative associations which are being required to secure government approval and future funding.

Defining **sport** is no simpler than defining region. However, for the purposes of this paper it is appropriate to use the four characteristics of sport provided by the European Sport for All Charter (Council of Europe, 1980).

In the Charter's terms sport includes:

* all competitive games and sports which are characteristised by the acceptance of rules and response to opposing challenge
* outdoor pursuits/survival sports;
* aesthetic movement of 'body oriented' sports e.g. figure skating;
* so called 'exercise sports' e.g. yoga, keep fit etc. (Council of Europe, 1980).

This characterisation allows for a wide range of different sporting activities.

A major question with the definition of **tourism** is whether or not to include day trips. So far as domestic tourism is concerned within Britain the British Tourist Authority works with a definition that excludes day trips:

> "For domestic tourism a tourist trip is defined as a **stay of one or more nights away** from home for holidays, visits to friends or relatives, business, conference or any other purpose except such things as boarding education or semi permanent employment".
> (British Tourist Authority/English Tourist Board 1990)

The Tourism Society's definition may be more useful in that its time frame includes day trips:

> "Tourism is the temporary short-term movement of people to destinations outside the places where they normally live and work, and their activities during the stay at these destinations; it includes movement for all purposes as well as day visits or excursions".
> (BTA/Tourism Society 1981)

Activity holidays, according to the definition used by Leisure Consultants in their recent research, are distinguished from other trips by three key features:

> "involvement in physical or mental **activity** as a **main purpose** of the holiday and which is carried out on an **organised** basis".
> (Leisure Consultants, 1992)

This reasonably excludes lying on the beach as the basis for a holiday to be called an activity holiday, but it includes a study course or attendance at a sporting event. Its requirement to be on an 'organised basis' also excludes, according to Leisure Consultants definition of 'organisation', a large number of boating, skiing, walking, fishing, golfing, cycling and other sporting trips that are participated in casually by individuals on an independent non-group basis. Their definition therefore excludes packaged ski trips taken by groups of friends unless tuition is bought as part of the package. Participation in a golf tournament qualifies a holiday to be defined as an 'activity holiday' and therefore to be included in Leisure Consultants research, but a holiday purely for golfing with friends is excluded. Whilst it is understood that this is the basis upon which the Leisure Consultants study has to be interpreted, its definition of 'organised' may be thought altogether too narrow, and for the purposes of this paper an 'activity holiday' is defined as one that has an activity as its **main purpose**. Thus organised trips as defined by Leisure Consultants and DIY (do-it-yourself) activity holidays are considered in this discussion. Playing an occasional game of volleyball on the beach or taking a short country walk are excluded unless they are the main purpose of the holiday. These kinds of activities can be classed as **'holiday activities'** since they may be seen as an 'active' rather than a 'passive' use of time, but given that their pursuit is not the main purpose of the holiday they are not classed as activity holidays.

3. The context

It is reliably estimated that almost two thirds of UK residents take some kind of holiday trip in a twelve month period. In 1991 this produced 114m trips totalling around 617m nights, of these 20m trips and 222m nights were spent abroad (English Tourist Board,1992).

In 1991 16.8 million international tourists arrived in Britain ('inbound' visitors); just over half of these arrivals were from Western Europe, the European Community alone producing 40% of the total. In the same year UK residents took more than 20 million trips abroad ('outbound' tourists). The most popular destinations were EC countries and the USA. Most of both the inbound and outbound visits were for holiday purposes.

There is growing evidence in Britain to demonstrate that holidays in which people are active, or in which involvement in activity is the main purpose of the holiday, are now a significant element in the total holiday market. A recent survey (Leisure Consultants, 1992) showed that around 15% of British adults took an activity holiday which represents nearly 7 million people and almost a quarter of all holiday takers. The English Tourist Board estimate that 29 million trips totalling 159 million nights included activities as part of the holiday. Holidays in which participation in activity was the main purpose of the holiday accounted for just under half of those trips. If the definition is narrowed to take account only of those holidays in which the activity is organised, and to exclude DIY activity holidays, then around 10 million trips (7 million within the UK and 3 million abroad) took place. Over half of the activity holiday takers (56%) participate in sport of some kind; and 20% attend sports events as spectators. Two thirds of activity trip holidays are taken within the UK, one third of them abroad.

"Other sports" which include walking and cycling are the most popular category accounting for almost half of all active sports participation holidays; water sports (excluding swimming) account for almost a quarter, skiing and golf take up around 15% each.

Outbound activity holidays emphasise skiing and water sports, other active sports are less important and golf is much less important. Leisure Consultants identified 40 countries in which it was possible to take an activity holiday though Europe is the single most popular continent, and France the most popular country.

Abercrombie and Kent Travel of London claim to have served 'the sophisticated traveller' for nearly three decades, and in 1991 they published for the first time 'The World of Sport and Adventure'. This brochure offers eleven different sports holidays in more than a dozen countries: for example scuba diving in Kenya; polo in Argentina; golf in India and a raft trip through the Arctic. The pursuits featured have been chosen to "appeal to the dedicated and amateur alike" and emphasis is placed on "the acquisition of new skills". In addition to their generic brochure, and as well as a specialist ski brochure, the company also produces 'The World of Fishing' designed to offer a wide variety of international fishing in some of the world's most exciting destinations, 'Cavalry Tours' - a unique collection of well researched rides throughout the world, and 'Walking Safaris' a careful selection of off-the-beaten path walks through Spain, the USA, Nepal and Tanzania.

Children's activity holidays are estimated to cater for between 2.7-3.7 million children in the twelve month period. Just under half the children are unaccompanied by family or other adults. The overseas holidays accounted for around .7 million of the total. Like the adult market, children's activity holidays have increased and are forecast to increase further.

Two thirds of those who took an activity holiday took just one in the twelve month period, but one third took more than one and 18% took more than two. Activity holidaytakers involving sports participation were more likely to be young (under 35), male, from AB or C1 backgrounds, and from London and South East England.

When results from the leisure day visitor survey are taken into account (Baty & Richards, 1991) alongside the growth of activity holidays, the popularity of outdoor activity trips becomes more evident. Of these, walking type activities were the most popular form of recreation closely followed by swimming/sunbathing. In the three regions that form Southern England outdoor activities were the most popular reason for a day trip, though the levels of participation (27% - 32%) did not reach those achieved in parts of northern England (Cumbria 56%; Yorkshire & Lancashire 37%).

Sport-related consumer spending has been estimated to amount to some £9.75bn in 1990 prices; excluding gambling, the total is £6.91bn. The most recent analysis of the economic impact of sport prepared by the Henley Centre (1992) shows that central government income from sport-related economic activity amounted to £3.56bn mainly derived from forms of duty and tax. On the other hand, central government spending on sport totalled £533m in 1990 prices, spending mainly in the form of grants to local authorities and the Sports Council. Local authorities spending on sport-related activity (£1.33bn), however, exceeds income (£906m) and is mainly directed towards defraying the staffing costs and running expenses of sports facilities. Government income from sport hugely exceeds its expenditure and the ratio has been widening; income to expenditure was 6.7 to 1 in 1990 compared to 4.5 to 1 in 1988. The sector provides jobs for around 467,000 people (Henley Centre, 1992).

In terms of sheer economic value, tourism, if domestic trips are included, is worth considerably more to the national economy than sport which raises the question of the strength of their symbiotic relation. Economic benefit is a powerful tool in the hands of developers. As one recent commentator put it:

> "A symbiotic relationship between sport and tourism is possible
> - so long as the figures tally".
> (Dresser,1993)

4. Illustrative examples

Six examples are detailed below. Outbound tourism in the form of the ski holiday; one example from each region of Southern England - the South West, South and South East -; water sports holidays as an example of inbound sport-tourism, and the preliminary report of a new survey which is predominantly domestic tourism.

It is probably the packaging of ski holidays over the last forty years that has led to the increased popularising of sport-activity tourism to the outbound British holiday market. Placing the ski holiday in the perspective of activity holiday-taking, shows that more than one in five of those who took a sportactivity holiday went skiing (Leisure Consultants, 1992). This recent research found that whilst just less than half of those who went skiing (47) made only one trip, 53% made at least two, and one in four made more than two ski trips in the year (Leisure Consultants, 1992).

With around 653,000 people taking skiing holidays worth some £214 m (199-1/92) (Mintel,1992), skiing is now said to account for around 20% of the total European holiday market (Wood, 1993). Given its promotion through travel agents and specialist holiday brochures, some find it surprising that the ski market is actually no larger than the market for motor boat cruising, cycling, golf or horse riding in terms of its popularity as an activity holiday. If the more limited definition of activity holidays as used by Leisure Consultants is taken then skiing again ranks alongside golf with 10% of skiers buying tuition.

At one time skiing was seen as an activity for the 'royal, rich and famous', but the offer of inexpensive, largely self-catering packaged holidays brought the sport to the mass market and enabled thousands of less privileged people to enjoy the beauty of the mountains together with the exhilaration of skiing. However a noticeable change has taken place, levels of participation have declined in the last two years, most significantly in London and South East England which reflects the severity of the recession in this region. Mintel also observed:

> "Skiing holidays have decreased most significantly among the middle income groups. Skiing has moved away from becoming a mass market activity, towards being a sport for the well off".
> (Mintel, 1992)

The sport has once again become an elitist minority activity. Just 50 % of the ski market in 1989 was taken up by skiers in social groups ABC1 (senior management/professional - skilled non-manual employment type). By 1990 63% of skiers were from this sector of the population,and in 1993 one study found they formed 100% of the respondents. Skiing as a highly commercialised tourist activity depends upon a market relation and it is this that has forced countless would-be participants out of the sport. Austria has been the most popular destination for British skiers taking 36% of the market, France was second, but rising, with 31%.

The Manor House Hotel near Okehampton, a market town below the northern edge of Dartmoor in Devon, testifies to the value of the sport-tourism mix as a means of selling hotel beds. For the past five years The Sporting Manor has seen 95% year-round occupancy of its one hundred and twenty-seven bedrooms. This country house hotel boasts two eighteen hole golf courses and covered golf nets, a pitch and putt course and a croquet lawn, three swimming pools, sauna and solarium, squash courts, outdoor and indoor tennis courts, outdoor and indoor bowls, covered shooting range for archery, air rifle and air pistol, a badminton hall, and access to a range of outdoor activities including water sports, rock climbing, pony trekking and country walking. The aim is to provide activity based holidays in a superb setting on the edge of Dartmoor National Park with a country club atmosphere. The ingredients and the recipe for this success story are not new, Center Parcs begun developing the concept in 1968. Some major differences include the size of the development (Sherwood Parc in Nottingham accommodates 3,500 visitors at any one time) and the hotel base compared with the holiday village concept. Small or large, the phenomenal occupancy figures achieved testify to the attractiveness of the sport-tourism mix.

A city in Southern England which is taking both sport and tourism seriously, and claims to be getting its figures right is Portsmouth where the local authority is harnessing sport as a vehicle to bring tourists to the city and to help it to change its industrial dockyard image. Securing a stage of Le Tour 1994 (no longer the Tour de France), the director of leisure services for the city is convinced of the value of spectator sports events in the promotion of tourism on the one hand and sports development programmes on the other. He cites examples of the Portsmouth International Triathlon and the Great South Run as major events within his current portfolio, an investment programme which costs the city some £100,000 but which generates £2 m annually in tourism revenues. Whilst this is a major justification for the investment, the director feels strongly about the "sport development policy":

> "International Athletics and the Great South Run helped to increase the membership of the local Joggers Club from 400 to 800 in two years, and the International Triathlon reslted in the local club increasing 4-fold, with two members in the national squad. "
> (Interview with David Knight, the Director,1993)

Economic benefits are carefully weighed not only against costs but against social benefits and disturbance. The political agenda in Portsmouth takes account of local residents feelings and the city has made its choice of sports concentrating on eco-friendly cycling, athletics and bowls.

Eastbourne, one of the more traditional resorts of Southern England, sees its tourism market boosted annually when it hosts the Ladies International Tennis Tournament the week preceding the Wimbledon Championships demonstrating the way in which spectator sport can generate tourism revenues. Attracting many of the worlds best players to a comparatively small town of 80,000 people generates an estimated £2.2 million revenue from the 31,000 spectators in one week. Only 13% of the visitors to the 1993 tournament were residents of the town, 40% came from beyond the South East region and 2% were inbound from overseas. Almost 50% of the total audience chose to stay in the town for the week. Being aware of the increasingly strong link between water sports and holidays and of the lack of marina facilities on the South East coast, Eastbourne is currently developing a new facility at the Crumbles. According to a recent survey, the South of England had two thirds of all coastal marinas in the UK and around 56% of water sports participants (Leisure Consultants,1989). Of the 22 coastal resorts listed in the British Tourist Authority's The Watersports Island, a brochure designed to attract visiting yachtsmen (and women), no less than 14 are in Southern England. Brighton is Britain's largest facility with berths for 1,800 craft and a growing popularity amongst mainland European boatowners, particularly the French. Portsmouth, with its great maritime heritage has a natural harbour and an extensive new marina.

Britain is a Mecca for boating holidays. There are said to be more live-aboard cabin hire boats in Britain than in the whole of the rest of the Western World put together. Around 440,000 people take boating holidays on the country's 2,000 miles of inland waterways each year; about 87% are UK residents and 13% are inbound tourists principally from Europe (ETB,1990).

A survey in 1986 found that 55% of those who take part in sailing do so only when on holiday, pointing to the potential for sports development 'at home' (Veal,1986). This phenomenon was not limited to sailing but applied even more to swimming (80% of all those who swim outdoors), and to fishing (40% of all who fish), golf (30%), tennis (28%) and walking (24%). Participants, then, are often willing (or able) to try out a sport whilst on holiday but fail to pursue it throughout the rest of the year.

A new recreation activity survey is currently being conducted in South East England (University of Brighton,1993) based on 28 rural sites around the Sussex Downs. At each site, 500 self-completion surveys are being distributed by hand, 100 in each of the months of May through to September. The results available for inclusion in this paper refer only to the month of May when the return rate was 60%; the full results are not expected before November.

From the May database, 75% of the visitors were on a day trip, 25% were staying overnight. Of the staying visitors 61% were based inland, 39% at the coast. Just 5% of the visitors were inbound. Of these 58% were from Europe, 20% from the United States and 22% from the rest of the world. There were slightly more men than women (52% to 48%), 65% were in social groups ABC1, 18% in C2 (skilled manual occupations) and only 3% in groups DE. Since this social categorisation is based on the respondent's own assessment it is subject to people's overstatement of their social grade. Thus the data so far confirms that a large proportion of our population are not participating even when day trips are included.

Unsurprisingly, walking was the most popular activity; just over a third of the respondents claimed they were using footpaths. Cycling, especially mountain biking, has recently attained renewed popularity; it was the single most popular sport attracting 8% of the visitors. Informal games, mainly of the type played with children such as rounders, were participated in by 7%. Kite-flying (3%), which is rarely treated as a sport in Britain, was more than four times as popular as horseriding or angling (7% each).

These early results from the Downlands survey indicate the relative popularity of different recreational activities, and, when the research is complete, will provide a measure of the scale of activity being undertaken in an environmentally sensitive area of Southern England. The increasing number of visitors, the growth of new sports such as mountain biking and hang-gliding, and the need for new built facilities and improved communication systems are placing growing pressures on the countryside of the region. The changes in the European Common Agriculture Policy will have a major impact on the rural economy causing farmers to look for new ways to make their land more profitable. The challenge will be to balance development and use with conservation.

But environmentalism is not just a concern of the state. A forthcoming report states:

> "(environmentalism) has become an issue of consumer priority where a large sector of the market..... are seeking greener products and higher quality, and local and national action groups are more prepared to react, adversely, to proposed new built facilities".
> (Standeven & Tomlinson,1993)

Certainly, Leisure Consultants found activity holidaytakers placed importance on the environment, on the contribution a holiday can make to personal health and well-being, and developing individual capabilities (Leisure Consultants,19-92).

One of the most significant observations in all sport-tourism data relates to 'who' participates. Every piece of evidence indicates that participants are drawn from an elite minority and the anticipated growth can reliably be forecast to extend opportunities to yet more of the same wealthy social groups. It is these more privileged groups who are both the participants in tourism and the participants in sport. Commercial interests, which must inevitably control provision of most of the opportunities, will seek to stimulate demand amongst the more well-off and to attract repeat business from those already in the market; the incentive to attract consumers with less disposable income will be minimal. Market economics secures benefits for very limited sectors of the population.

Experienced forecasters see the holiday business as fundamentally a growth market rising by 16% in total holiday trips by 1996, and within it activity type holidays will expand significantly, organised trips alone comprising 14.5% of all holiday trips compared with 12.5% at present (Leisure Consultants,1992). Given the current level of interest, the potential for expansion, the addition of the larger DIY holiday market and the leisure day trip visitor, a very significant growth factor can be confidently anticipated. Increasing usage, however, will lead inexorably towards increasing environmental impact. What measures need to be taken, not simply to secure a more participatory and just opportunity to engage in sport tourism, but to allow expansion to be sustained within the terms of local, national and global environmental interests?

Given the potential for sports development from the sport-tourism relation what opportunities exist to widen the base of the sport market and to extend it to sectors of the population not currently participating? If there is a social agenda it is difficult to see what this is or could be, other than at the most local level, since participation is heavily skewed towards the better-off. What, then, can, or should be the relation of government to this phenomenon? The research question is 'can the sport tourism relation, even given that it can be made more widely available, transform non-regular/non-participants into people with active leisure lifestyles'?

5. Conclusions

There can be little doubt that the political agenda is being economically driven. In analysing the attempts Britain is making to forge new connections between formerly separate sectors of the leisure industry high level policy shifts have to be taken into account. A changing ratio of government leisure-related income to expenditure is evident, increasing the income and reducing the expenditure. Alongside this it is important to take a political reading of central government's initiative in creating the Department of National Heritage and the promotion of collaboration between its sponsored bodies. It would be naive to suggest that the government's purpose is simply to improve the quality of life of all citizens by offering them more integrated services. Thirdly, the significance of central government's attempts to restructure local government, introducing a new system of unitary local authorities to replace the present two-tier town and county systems and the threat this could pose for local authority leisure departments. As Henry has indicated:

> "Leisure may become a service area of greater financial significance. However, the political significance of leisure is likely to decline..."
> (Henry, 1993)

Local authorities in Britain have not, and are not, simply accepting re-organisation as inevitable. They have a genuine concern to serve their local constituency and are engaged in political negotiation for survival (without doubt motivated by the double-edged need to avert unemployment). These negotiations are going on in the context of new power relations as central government seeks to increase its authority over more locally based bodies.

The benefits of the co-ordinated approach to sport and tourism are thus set in the context of the disbenefits of the political agenda within which they are framed. The "quite different and often complex structures of power that operate around any single issue" and the accommodations that are acted out between them on different levels identify the potential of theorising the sport-tourism relation through David Botterill's (1992) tourism initiated 'visualisation of activist space'. By identifying three basic parameters of power (socio-cultural historicities, economic and industry structures, and political system/discourse) that are acted out on several levels from local/regional activity through to national, international and transnational levels, it provides a framework for the analysis of the changes that are taking place. Botterill states:

"The proposition here is that activists working to change any given situation in tourism will best make sense of any resistance to change as being due to the constraining power of any combination of the parameters in the model". (Botterill, 1992)

Sport and tourism can share increasing points of contact in the formation of cultural policy. The potential for Southern England to benefit from this relation will depend upon its ability to attract tourists (domestic and inbound) and the capacity it has to initiate and sustain collaboration and partnerships between different agencies. Working out new relationships is rarely a smooth process - indeed Botterill's model suggests that it will be characterised by negotiation and conflict within the region and between the region and the rest of the country. But Southern England is closer to regions within mainland Europe, and particularly to parts of Northern France, than it is to some other regions within the UK. Implicitly, sport-tourism collaborators in Southern England should seek their counterparts in the Netherlands, Belgium, North West France and Northern Spain as well as within the UK. Cultural development, in which the sport tourism relation may play a vital role, should not be restricted by language, nor bound by political or geographical division.

References

1. Baty, B. & Richards, S. (1991) 'Results from the Leisure Day Visitor Survey 1988-89' in Employment Gazette, May

2. Botterill, T. David, (1992) 'Working for Change in Tourism: Tourism Concern, the First Three Years' in J. Sugden & C. Knox (1992) Leisure in the 1990s: Rolling Back the Welfare State, Leisure Studies Association Publication No.46, Eastbourne: University of Brighton

3. British Tourist Authority/English Tourist Board Research Services, (1990) Tourism Intelligence Quarterly, Vol. 12 No.1, July

4. BTA/Tourism Society (1981) Tourism in the UK - The Broad Perspective, London : British Tourism Authority/Tourism Society

5. Cleare, J. (1975) Mountains, London: Macmillan

6. Dresser, G. (1993) 'Push on the Waterfront' in Leisure Week, March 5

7. **English Tourist Board** (1990) 'Boating Holidays - Opportunities in Britain' in Insights

8. **English Tourist Board** (1992) 'Tourism by UK Residents in 1991' in Insights, September

9. European Sport for All Charter (Council of Europe, 1980).

10. **Faux,R.** (1993) 'On the trail of breath-taking views' in The Times Saturday Review, February 20

11. **Henley Centre** (1992) The Economic Impact of Sport in the UK in 1990, London: Henley Centre/Sports Council

12. **Henry,I.** (1993) The Politics of Leisure Policy, London:Macmillan

13. **Lawrence,L. & Tomlinson, A.**(1993) LSA Newsletter No.35 - May 1993, Leisure Studies Association, University of Brighton pp26-31.

14. **Leisure Consultants** (1989) Boating and Water Sports, Sudbury,Suffolk: Leisure Consultants

15. **Leisure Consultants** (1992) Activity holidays: the growth market in tourism, Sudbury, Suffolk: Leisure Consultants

16. **Matthews,J.** (1981) Quantitative and Statistical Approaches to Geography, Oxford: Pergamon Press

17. **McFee,G.** (1990) 'The Olympic Games as a Tourist Event: An American in Athens, 1896' in A.Tomlinson (ed), Sport in Society: Policy, Politics and Culture, LSA Publication No. 43, Eastbourne: Leisure Studies Association, pp.146-157

18. **Mintel** (1992) Leisure Intelligence, Vol. 3, London:Mintel

19. **Sports Council** (1988) Sport in the Community: Into the 90's. A Strategy for Sport 1988-1993, London:Sports Council

20. **Standeven,J. & Tomlinson, A.** (1993 forthcoming) Sport and Tourism: A Report to the South East Regional Council for Sport, Crystal Palace: The Sports Council

21. Tomlinson,A. & Walker,H. (1990) 'Holidays for All: popular movements, collective leisure and the pleasure industry', in A.Tomlinson (ed) Consumption, Identity and Style: marketing, meanings and the packaging of pleasure' London: Routledge.

22. Veal,A. (1986) People in Sport and Recreation 1980. Summary of Data from the 1980 General Household Survey for England and Wales, Centre for Leisure and Tourism Studies, London: Polytechnic of North London

23. West Country Tourist Board & The Sports Council (South West) (WCTB & SC (SW)(1992) Tourism and Sport, Exeter and Crewkerne

24. Wood,C. (1993) 'Is the Brit skiing holiday going out of fashion?' in Daily Mail, May 1

CURRENT PROFESSIONAL ACTIVITIES

Wagner, P.E.
Wagner/Schlichter Consultancy Group
Groningen, The Netherlands

Ladies and gentlemen,
I am very pleased to have the opportunity to give a presentation about the current state of professionalism in and around sports organizations. Maybe it is a good idea to start by explaining my own concern with the field of sport and management.
My own background is consultancy in policy and management problems of professional organizations.
As Director of the Wagner/Schlichter Group and professor at the Sport Management Institute in the Netherlands I have been involved in several cases and discussions in and around the Dutch sport infrastructure concerning the following points:

First case: What is the influence of societal movements on the future perspective of sports organizations?
In this case the combined effects of developments such as: the change in the sporting population on aspects of age and culture, the change in responsibility the government is willing to make for the sports infrastructure, and the change to more consumer oriented orientation of those people who participate in sports and sport organizations, are significant.

Second case: What organizational developments will be necessary to ensure the continuity of the Dutch Sports infrastructure?
A stronger market orientation, product innovation and cost effectiveness are self evident conditions to ensure the continuity of the sport infrastructure in the current societal context.

Third case: The challenge for sport managers to manage, participate and survive in this process of societal change and organizational developments and the skills they need to support this process in an appropriate way. At the Sport Management Institute we have of course gathered a lot of experience on improving management skills and applying organizational concepts.
Improving managing skills and applying concepts from organizational theory in a highly dynamic context is not a one way stream. It is an interactive activity from which both theory and practice can benifit.

The aim of my presentation is to approach current activities of sport managers from an organizational theory point of view. I want to illustrate that this approach can help in placing sport management as a profession in the societal perspective predicted for the future.

The subject can be looked at under four main headings:

First of all I would like to mention some characteristics of the way the sports infrastructure is organized in the Netherlands, since this is a major frame of reference for what is to follow.
Then I wolud like to mention some features of organizational theory which in my opinion are very relevant to the theme we are discussing here.
Thirdly I will give my opinion on what kind of organizational interventions and professional developments are needed to prepare the sports infrastructure for the future.
Finally I would like to conclude the presentation by emphasizing some statements of what I think is the preferable profile for sport management and sport managers.

Let's go back to the first point: some characteristics of how the sports infrastructure is organized in the Netherlands.

- Our supply structure is very complex. For this typical Dutch structure we have a typical Dutch word which cannot be explained in proper English because it does not exist in the English language. But when I explain it in a direct way I would scall it the societal mesofield. It refers to private non-profit organizations which are supported by governmental money to fulfil a task with societal relevance. Sports organizations are considered to fulfil such tasks.

  The large number of volunteers who find a mission participating in these organizations is a strong legitimation for governmental spendings (especially from the local government) on sport organizations.

  Another reason for the government to support these organizations is that the government needs these organizations for implementing governmental policy in health care and welfare.

  On the other hand the sports organizations depend on the government for financial support and in this way the entanglement between the public and the private sector becomes very complex. To share responsibility and to participate in each others decision-making is an essential part of Dutch culture and folklore. An illustrative joke about the Dutch is that we have as many churches and political parties as we have inhabitants.

  I believe that now-a-days in Holland we also have as many consultants as we have decision makers.

This attitude of course, has its advantages and disadvantages for the existence of sports infrastructure and the possibility to manage it in a successful way.
An important characteristic of the Dutch system is the way top-class sport is anchored in recreational sport. They are both brought forth by the same associations and clubs.
In the Netherlands highly professionalized commercial leagues for top-class sport have not assumed enormous proportions. I think that it has something to do with our culture of entanglement.

There are some developments which I think are so important, because of the influence they will have on the future sport infrastructure, that I think they should be mentioned here:

First of all the common opinion about the desirable role of the government in public life is changing. The effect is that the government is withdrawing its concern in the sports infrastructure. When the government withdraws its support, the group of organizations that together form this infrastructure is suddenly confronted with a political and financial vacuum.

At this moment there is a political movement to transform the supply side sports economy supported by governmental money into a market oriented economy in which the customer has to pay for the welfare or commercial services he has ordered.

The success of this movement depends on the fulfilment of a few conditions:

At first there has to be a market or something like a market has to be created. From a market perspective we have to see organizations as exchange mechanisms. Organizations are only able to function well as an exchange mechanism, if they have an answer to the following essential questions.

- What is the so-called mission, or societal reason for existence of the organization?
- In what business does the organization operate, what are the services that are provided and who are the potential clients?
- In which way is the organization competitive or even has a competitive advantage? Things such as cost effectiveness of the supplier, a unique sports product or a full service concept can be thought of.
- How is this advantage communicated to the other market parties, especially the (potential) customers?

For most organizations these questions are easy to ask, but not as easy to answer. Maybe, for some of you these business oriented questions appear far

away from sports organizations reality. These organizations have always focused their attention on governmental policy and money.
Now they have to develop a business strategy to survive the market situation of the future.
This requires a lot of analysing and conceptualization.

A second point in this movement towards a market situation is that developing a market is an interactive process among organizations. When a lack of market orientation is a common problem in a whole field of organizations, the market has to be developed. Therefore, an intervention at the meso level is needed. The creation of a power center may help to bring about a leverage in market exchange.

In this market orientation sports organizations are confronted with changing demands.

Sportsorganizations are basically product-oriented. For example, we assume people are interested in hockey, and the club provides a range of hockey products which are more or less intensive and competition oriented.
Top-class sport and recreational sport products are brought forth by the same clubs; obviously we assume they need the same organization and support structure, or at least don't have opposite interests.
But I think the situation today is that top-class sport and recreational sport are influenced by different societal developments which ask for a different future strategy. In top-class sport the globalization of the media forces a top-class sport product to be competitive at an international level to remain attractive to the media and the related sponsors. Wanting to be competitive at an international level, forces a sports organization to conform to the general professional standards for that type of sport.
So the top-class sport organizations must make a clear strategic choice: or develop the sports infrastructure in relation to international standards (this the will usually mean further professionalization and commercialization), or accept the end of the top-class sport status in that form of sport.

In recreational sport the strong product orientation does not fit the orientation of the consumer anymore. The consumer doesn't focus his choice on the main product sport. No, the recreational sportsman or sportswoman wants a broad leisure concept. This concept has to fulfill a set of wishes in terms of health, pleasure, social contact and lifestyle expression. In both top-class sport and recreational sport the function of sports is moving from goal towards medium. The organizational forms we have now are not appropriate for the function society imports to sports. Even if the product definition of the suppliers in this case does not fit to the product definition of the customers anymore, the sports market is not to be defined in a unique way. For the spenders of time and money (governments, companies and individual citizens) spendings for top-class sport can be carried out in a lot of alternative ways and sport in itself is not the issue for the allocation of time and money.

I would like to show you some marketing trends for the nineties which show the orientation of the citizens, as individual consumers. I also want to show you some issues which indicate what individuals consider an important collective responsibility for society.

Firstly, let me present the marketing trends for the nineties:
The American marketing specialist Faith Popcorn (believe me that is her real name) distinguishes ten major trends important for this decade in her book 'The popcorn report'.

Trend	**Interpretation**
1. Cocooning	Homing
2. Adventure	Make casual things more exciting
3. Spurt out	Tolerance for more kicks
4. Ego trip	Strong orientation on individual development
5. Non career orientation	A more balanced attitude towards working life and private life.
6. Staying young	Activities are not linked to specific ages anymore
7. Health fanatism	Focus on healthy food and a fit body
8. Consumentism	A critical attitude to supply quality
9. '99 lives	Identification with a pluriform lifestyle
10. Save our society	protect the environment

The additional issues for collective responsibility are:
1. safety
2. environmental protection
3. social and cultural integration

As you may see, we now have an interesting overview of the individual and societal issues in which sport and recreation has to find its position as a medium for identification.

What challenge does this change in marketing situation mean for sports and recreational organizations?
Traditional sports and recreational organizations must make a change from a sports product oriented organization to leisure concepts that appeal to the trends I have mentioned.

Top-class sports organizations will develop in another direction: as a facility concept for a highly professional media related product.

It must be clear that the movements I have mentioned to this point: the withdrawal of the government from the sports infrastructure, the orientation to the market of the recreational sport and the professionalizing of top-class sport are a challenge to renew organization and management in sports.

Now I would like to mention some features from organizational theory which I think can contribute to this process of renewal:

From a theoretical point of view it is very efficient to describe some images with which the nature of organization can be described.

Which images predominate?

- The organization as a family, in which hundreds of thousands of people participate, especially during the weekend. The core of this type of organization is that the participation of volunteers is not only a resource for the creation of services, but is also value in its self.

  This demands a special attitude of the professionals in the organization. They have to be able to manage participation and motivation.

  In this sort of organization there must always be a critical balance between the family orientation, in which the professionals are supportive, and the service orientation, in which voluntary participation is supportive to the professional forthbringing of services. In these organizations, with a complex culture, human relations and human behaviour are very critical and easy to transfer to another image:

- The organization as a battlefield of complex constellations of interests combined with a frequently poorly elaborated control system in the organization and 'the always being there' attention of the press provides a high risk for battlefields. It is interesting to see that on one hand sport is taken as a proposal for business management on themes such as leadership and team management and on the other hand professional sports organizations are not able to control their own business and management system. This is very important, because sports organizations are today not able to function as an isolated system anymore; sports organizations function as an exchange mechanism between their stakeholders.

  This brings us to the third image:

- The organization as an exchange mechanism. This organization is seen as an open system in continuous exchange with its public, its professionals, its volunteers, its financial supporters, the local and national policy makers and the other suppliers of leisure products.

To function as an open system makes certain demands on the people who participate in it. They must be sensitive, and need to have a sense for the existence of counter veiling power and how to deal with it.

Organizations function as a part of a bigger network with shared and adversative goals. As a part of the network they are interdependent.

The contribution from organizational theory should be to support the whole network of sports organizations with concepts to help them to be capable of redefining their position in the network.

What is needed is an intervention at meso level. Only by interfering at meso level is it possible to innovate the infrastructure in such a way that the competitive edges are linked to the right allocation of resources. In such a highly institutionalized context as the sports infrastructure, market forces are not enough to push innovation.

What kind of context is needed to realise such intervention successfully?

Firstly: The collective awareness of the group of suppliers that they need eachother to get their problems solved.

Secondly: Interests should not be in total conflict with each other, but rather network partners should be willing to make some concessions to contribute to the soundness of the whole network.

Thirdly: Coaching a network on its capability to change is extremely difficult. If you compare the situation of changing the sports infrastructure to processes of complex change at big companies, those companies have the advantage that they at least have a kind of power center to manage the change process.

So a power center must be created, and therefore there must be a minimum consensus about the type of change and intensity that is needed.

In this presentation I have drawn your attention to the need of change in the sports infrastructure. A changing role of the government, changing demands in leisure society and the globalization of our social economy structure demand it.

The world of sports has to prepare!

Finally I would like to conclude my presentation by emphasizing some statements on what I regard as a preferable profile for people who can contribute in the mentioned process.

1. Those people must be capable of transforming the value of sports into other societal issues and movements. A logical consequence is that these people have a broad interest in society and not only read the sports section in Monday's newspaper.

2. They must be capable of managing a sports organization as an exchange mechanism. The management style has to be pluralistic and service oriented.

3. The management of complex situations, conceptual overview and strategic insight is required.
   This is what we try to lecture at the University of Groningen.

Thank you very much for your attention.

Action Field 2

Elite Sport

Fundamental And Applied Research In Individual Endurance Sports

Åstrand, P.-O.
Department of Physiology and Pharmacology, Karolinska Institute
Stockholm, Sweden

1. Introduction

The energy expenditure during endurance sports is almost exclusively covered by the metabolic pathways demanding an oxygen supply, the so called *aerobic* processes. During very intensive exercise, e.g. during the finish of a race, a break down of carbohydrate (glucose and glycogen) can support the aerobic processes. In this *anaerobic* energy yield the end product is lactate and its accumulation is one candidate for fatigue. Therefore the efficiency of the oxygen transport systems securing an adequate oxygen transport from ambient air to the "power plants", the mitochondria in the skeletal muscles is very decisive for good performance in such sports. In addition the availability of optimal substrates, particularly carbohydrates, is of importance.

European research has been devoted to efforts to solve the question: what is/are the limiting factor(s) for the oxygen transport system, effects of training and de-training on this system, on enzyme activity, capillary density, substrate utilization, how diet and water balance can affect endurance. Elite athletes in endurance events are characterized by (i) very high values for maximal oxygen uptake. For good performance two additional factors are of importance: (ii) ability to exercise at a high percentage of this maximum for long periods of time and (iii) an efficient technique, a low energy cost of movement. Various aspects of endurance in sports are discussed in a recent IOC Medical Commission publication (15).

2. Limiting factor(s) for maximal aerobic power (oxygen uptake)

At present there is a general agreement that the central circulation is decisive for the maximal oxygen uptake during exercise in which large muscle groups are involved (see 14). The individual's maximal cardiac output, the haemoglobin concentration of the blood and the ability of the lung to oxygenate adequately the blood returning from the tissue are of paramount importance as determinants of maximal aerobic power. (For discussion see references 3, 8.) There are reports that subjects with very high maximal oxygen uptakes when related to body mass are unable to fully oxygenate the returning venous blood and the resulting desaturation will limit this maximum (6). One explanation for this relative "handicap" can be that a high cardiac output in relation to the pulmonary vascular bed implies a high speed in the transit of red cells through the pulmonary capillaries. Therefore, the time for equilibration of alveolar and arterial oxygen tensions becomes too short.

3.1 Effects of training

A typical effect when training at intensities demanding a high oxygen uptake, say exceeding 70% of the maximum, will increase the heart's stroke volume and therefore the maximal cardiac output and oxygen uptake. The maximal heart rate remains unaffected. If anything, endurance athletes may have a peak heart rate which is slightly lower than the average for persons at the same age. Factors behind the increase in stroke volume at rest as well as during exercise is an increase in heart volume (13) and blood volume favouring the filling of the heart during diastole. Regulatory factors may also be of importance for the enhanced stroke volume. There is a definite limit in the individual's response to a given training program. Trainability appears to be largely genetically determined (for discussion and references see chapter 14 in ref. 15). Endurance athletes who train daily for many years stay more or less stable in maximal aerobic power, they just maintain it until age will set a limit. Master athletes in endurance events are characterized by a high maximal oxygen uptake but in most cases there is a decline with age beyond the 3rd decade (16).

3.2 Effects on skeletal muscle

Numerous studies have demonstrated a significant increase in mitochondrial density as a consequence of endurance training with a proportionate increase in mitochondrial enzymes in the muscles engaged in the training (for references see 1). If one expresses the skeletal muscle's oxidative capacity for a sedentary individual in one "unit", the endurance trained elite athletes have a three-"unit" capacity. From such data we can conclude that with aerobic training there is a shift in the trained muscle to greater reliance on oxidative metabolism. Another effect of this training is an increase in capillary density in the muscles. This higher density will reduce the distance between blood and cell interior, which enhances the exchange rate of gases, substrates, and metabolites. The surface area available for this exchange also increases. With more capillaries in a given tissue volume, more blood can flow through the vascular bed per unit of time. The so called mean transit time (MTT) is increased, which allows a more complete exchange of material. The primary advantage of high capillary density in highly endurance trained muscles is probably that it allows for an adequate MTT at high flow rates, thereby promoting a more complete exchange of materials as compared with the situation in an untrained muscle. It was stated that a high blood flow rate in the pulmonary capillary bed may prevent an optimal oxygenation of the passing red cells. In contrast to the response in skeletal muscles, endurance training will not increase the capillary density in the lung tissue. For optimal performance in endurance sports, carbohydrate is an important substrate in the energy providing metabolism in the engaged muscles. The stores of carbohydrate, mainly as glycogen, are however, limited. Therefore the enhancement of fat metabolism in endurance trained muscles has a glycogen saving effect - it takes longer time to empty a given glycogen store because the relative contribution of fat metabolism is increased. Danish studies published already in 1939 described the effects of training on the metabolism in active muscles and how diet could improve performance in endurance events. The mentioned changes in capillary density and enzyme patterns as consequences of endurance training can explain the modifications in choice of substrate induced by this training. (For detailed discussions see chapters 12, 23, and 30 in ref. 15.)

The combined results of these effects on performance can be illustrated by the following example: An untrained person with maximal oxygen uptake of liters per minute may be able to exercise at 90% of this maximum for some 20 min before exhausted. If after a period of training the maximal aerobic power has increased to 3.0 liters per minute, the submaximal rate of oxygen uptake of 2.25 liters per minute will demand only 75% of this new maximum. The trained person can tolerate this metabolic rate for some min, i.e., there is a 4.5-fold improvement of endurance that apparently is not limited only by the potential of the oxygen transport system. Peripheral factors have key roles for endurance.

3.3 Economy of movement

There is a wide variation in energy cost at a given speed in running, cross country skiing, swimming, less so in bicycling, even in elite athletes. Svedenhag (17) reports that there was a surprisingly wide (about 20%) variation in the oxygen cost of running at a given speed between runners of similar performance capacities. He claims that prolonged training may significantly improve running economy even in elite runners.

3.4 Training principles

For details, consult Shephard and Åstrand (15). It was pointed out above that individuals respond differently to a given training program. Training adaptations in the skeletal muscle, whether for strength or endurance, are limited to the muscles actually involved in the activity trained. As an example, an athlete concentrating on running may have a maximal oxygen uptake of 6 liters per minute. During maximal efforts in swimming the peak maximum may be about 5.5 liters per minute. After intensive swim training it may reach the 6-liter level. The problem for the athlete and the coach is to develop an optimal program. Scientific support is at this stage limited. It is still some sort of a trial and error business. An extreme example is the training program for a soccer team. Is soccer an endurance event? Well, with exception of the goal keeper the players will cover an average distance of some 12 km during the 2 x 45 min game. It is quite evident that the training program must be adapted to the individual and her/his tasks. Today many top athletes are professional and it is logical that they devote more time for training than was the case when amateurship dominated. There is a risk of "overtraining" and injuries. There are data indicating that mitochondrial adaptations in skeletal muscles are maximized with 1.5 to 2 hours of daily training (8). To reach the individual's innate potential for maximal oxygen uptake less time is required (see below).

3.5 Lactate threshold

The physiological basis for the threshold concept is the observation that up to a certain exercise intensity the blood lactate concentration does not increase or is only slightly elevated but remains low during continuous exercise. With further increase in work rate lactate is accumulated in muscle and blood and at some stage exercise must stop or intensity reduced. An inadequate oxygen supply to the muscle is probably not the only explanation for the lactate formation. The role of lactate accumulation per se as a cause for fatigue is under debate. However, it is beyond the scope of this article to give a detailed discussion of the threshold concept. (For discussion and references see chapter 22 in ref. 15.) Untrained persons may pass this threshold at a work rate as low as 50% of maximal oxygen uptake. Endurance trained athletes can exercise at an intensity demanding 85% or even higher percentage of maximal aerobic power without an undue accumulation of lactate in muscles and blood. High correlations are noted between the lactate threshold and long-distance running speed because this threshold is dependent on several variables which are all related to performance including maximal aerobic power and oxygen cost of running. The average percentage of maximal oxygen uptake at the race pace in marathon has been found to range from 60% in slow up to about 85% in elite marathon runners (17). He reports that the estimated percentage of maximal oxygen uptake during a race was the same, in average 80%, in both elite runners (mean time 2:21) and good runners (2:37) but it was significantly lower in the slow runners (3:24).

It is quite popular to establish speed and/or heart rate at a fixed lactate threshold (it may a concentration of 2 or 4 mmol per liter of blood) and a training guide for the athletes is than based on these data. However, it is different to run at a certain speed on a treadmill compared with running on a track or in the terrain. The heart rate can be affected by environmental temperature, dehydration, to mention only two factors. My personal believ is that application of the lactate threshold concept in a training regime has its limitations.

4.1 Why are records in endurance sports improving?

Fig. 1 illustrates how the time to run 5000 m has gradually decreased during this century. When compared with 1910 the world record keeper runs about 16% faster today. There is a similar improvement in the 10000 m distance. In the marathon world records are not registered for obvious reasons. However, on average they are run about 20% faster today than at the beginning of the century. It is interesting to note that the record in the 100 m sprint is 10% faster now. However, time taken manually cannot be directly compared with an electronic registration. In technique events like the long jump the improvement is 22%, in the high jump 26% and in the shot put event 49%.

Several factors, which vary in importance depending on the characteristics of the sport, must be considered:

- selection from a larger and healthier population
- better training methods and preparation
- improved techniques
- psychological aspects
- scientific support
- doping
- physiological aspects

A more detailed discussion of these factors will be published elsewhere (2) and therefore only a few aspects will be considered here.

4.2 Selection from a larger and healthier population

More and more individuals, particularly women, are attracted by sports activities. An increasing number of nations are represented in the sport arenas. Now it is more socially acceptable for young girls to participate in sports in developing countries. As preventive and curative health measures become more successful throughout the Third World, millions of teenagers will have the chance to enjoy sports. These factors make it more likely that individuals with talent for a particular sport will have the opportunity, motivation, and means to train and be noticed by the experts.

4.3 Better training methods and preparation

Training volume has increased and training methods have improved dramatically. Today, top athletes are not "true amateurs" as in the days when the Olympic oath included the statement that athletes did not compete for their economic status. Certainly, top athletes have always managed to make money from their sports, but today this is permissible and can involve large sums. In other words, athletes can now devote more time to training and they can train year round in an optimal climate.

4.4 Improved materials

Technical innovations have played an important role in the performance explosion in many events, the introduction of artificial surfaces on tracks improved conditions and, most importantly maintained consistent lane quality throughout a competition. Previously, the inner lane of the track often deteriorated as it became worn by many feet. The Pan American Games in 1967 were the first major event to be held on an artificial surface. However, better shoes and tracks cannot explain the superiority of modern athletes. Ronald Clark's time of 27 min 39.4 s for 10000 m on a cinder track in 1965 is not far from Henry Rono's time of 27 min 22.5 s on an artificial surface in 1978.

4.5 Scientific support

It is difficult to prove to what extent medical science has helped athletes in their pursuit of new records. Often the athletes have been one step ahead, applying trial and error methods, followed by the physiologists (for example) whose studies may reveal mechanisms that can explain why a particular regimen can enhance performance. With regard to diet and water balance science has definitely been very helpful for the athletes. Scientific data supported the belief in the beneficial effects of a warmup before high-intensity exercise.

Unfortunately, many athletes are injured during training and competition. Physicians and physical therapists try, often successfully, to enable the athlete to return to the arena as quick as possible. Methods for treatment and rehabilitation are examined critically. If successful, they are then available to anyone.

No doubt, athletic performances have stimulated the research!

4.6 Doping

It is a tragedy that so many athletes, coaches, and physicians break the rules in their ambitions to win and break world records. It is only in a few disciplines that pills can improve performance beyond what the athlete can achieve through will power and stimulation from a cheering crowd. Actually, she/he usually performs better without such doping. However, many coaches and athletes appear to be willing to uncritically adopt new concepts claimed to improve athletic performance. "Blood doping" will definitely significantly increase maximal oxygen uptake which is of importance in many endurance sports. It is now believed that the hormone erythropoetin, which stimulates the production of red cells in the bone marrow, is being misused. A recent favourite has been an intake of creatine which may improve explosive, repetitive strength efforts (Balsom et al., 1993). In low concentrations it is a normal item in the food, particularly in meat and it is therefore questionable whether it can be classified as doping when consumed.

4.7 Physiological aspects

Are the athletes today superior in their physiological potential compared with their predecessors? As pointed out, a high maximal oxygen uptake is essential for success in sports engaging large muscle groups in all-out efforts for several minutes or longer. In activities in which the body weight is carried, this aerobic power should be related to body weight (oxygen uptake in $ml \cdot kg^{-1} \cdot min^{-1}$ or $ml \cdot kg^{-0.75} \cdot min^{-1}$). However, in exercises such as rowing and swimming, oxygen uptake is given in $liters \cdot min^{-1}$. In 1937, Robinson et al. (11) reported that Don Lash, who held the world record for the 2-mile race, attained when running on a treadmill a peak oxygen uptake of 81.5 $ml \cdot kg^{-1} \cdot min^{-1}$. Today, elite runners reach similar values but they run much faster. In 1936 the world record for 5000 m was 14 min 34.3 s. In the 1960s Kipchoge Keino dominated in middle and long distance running. His maximal oxygen uptake was 83.5 $ml \cdot kg^{-1} \cdot min^{-1}$ and at that time his best time for 5000 m (13min 24.2 s) was 8.8 % faster than the 1936 record. Today, the record is 12 min 58.4 s, adding 3.2 % to Keino's speed. Evidently new training methods have not created endurance athletes with significantly higher maximal aereobic power than observed more than 50 years ago. But they run much faster. This fact is intriguing. As mentioned, better shoes and tracks can only partially explain the improvements. Apparently modern training principles allow the athletes to exercise at or closer to maximal aerobic power for longer periods of time. Another reason for improved performance may be a higher power and capacity of the anaerobic pathways. However, no data are available to confirm this hypothesis.

As mentioned there is a personal limit for maximal oxygen uptake. For example, a Swedish cross-country skier who in 1955 had just qualified for the national team had a maximum of 5.48 $liters \cdot min^{-1}$ at that time. In 1963 it was about the same (5.60 liters), but he had trained almost daily during the intervening 8 years and had successfully participated in two Olympic games and two world championships, winning several gold medals. Another skier reached 5.88 liters·min^{-1} in 1955 (82.5 ml·kg^{-1}·min^{-1}). In repeated tests he never exceeded that value. His last gold medal in Olympic games was won in 1964 (in the 50 km race). There are few longitudinal studies of top athletes in running disciplines. As stated above, there are indications that running times improve despite a stagnation in the maximal aerobic power. Training can induce a slight improvement in running economy and the ability to run faster before a continuous accumulation of lactate sets in.

Apparently it is rare that an athlete has top values for all three components essential for spectacular performance in aerobic events: high maximal aerobic power, high lactate threshold and good economy in movements. Joyner (8) speculated that a marathon runner with this fortunate combination of qualities could finish after 1 hour 57 min!

5. Altitude training

Is training at high altitude beneficial to the oxygen transport system? Acclimatization is essential in the preparation for optimal performance in events demanding high aerobic power if the competition takes place at high altitude. The 1968 Olympic games in Mexico City were not the first challenge forcing athletes to face new environmental conditions. In the 1960 Winter Olympic games in Squaw Valley the athletes had to gasp at an altitude of approximately 2000 m.

It is a common belief that training at high altitude will also enhance performance at lower altitudes. The history of world records does not support this hypothesis. In 1968 the cream of the world's athletes spent long periods of time in Mexico City or at similar altitudes. New records would be expected at sea level if a sojourn at high altitude elicited an additional improvement in maximal aerobic power. However, in 1968, when all Olympic candidates were extremely well prepared, there were no new world records in middle- and long-distance running. Ten cross-country skiers who stayed at 2100 m altitude for two weeks and trained at 2700 m attained just the prealtitude values for maximal oxygen uptake when tested again at sea level (10). It has been suggested that an optimal preparation could be to stay for some time at quite high altitude but to do the training at altitudes below 1500 m. Such programs would be quite sophisticated - and costly. More research is needed to settle this question.

6. How to find young talents for competitive sports?

Rowland (12) has recently summarized the literature related to effects of training with emphasis on aerobic responses in children. He concludes that the pre-pubertal children appear to be capable of responding to endurance training with improvements in maximal aerobic power. Such adaptations are qualitatively similar but apparently quantitatively less as compared with those in adults. For details see also Grana et al. (7).

In this context it should be mentioned that the five best Swedish tennis players (1985), who were also ranked among the top 15 players in the world, actually tried many sports up to the age 14. Only at that age did they start to specialize in tennis. They were compared with a control group of players who were as good or better when 12 to 14 years old. Those players specialized much earlier in tennis, they trained more and had matured earlier. Therefore they performed well but apparently they were not gifted enough to reach world class (5). It is positive if one can generalize and conclude that children and young teenagers should be stimulated to try many sports but wait with concentrating on one event until after they have reached puberty maturity. In my opinion competition in marathon and triathlon should not be allowed before the age of, say, 18 years.

One conclusion from the above-mentioned study of tennis players is that performance at the age of 12-14 years was not a good predictor of future elite achievements. Malina (9) points out that with few exceptions, interage correlations for indicators of growth, fitness, and cardiovascular status are generally moderate too low and thus have limited predictive utility. A boy who starts specializing in high jump or basketball and stops growing when 170 cm tall has picked the wrong event if his ambition was to be champion in that event.

7. Gender

In swimming world records the highest speeds attained by women is, on average, 91.4 % of those reached by men. In track events women are relatively slower with top speeds at the 90.9 level. In speed skating, women reach 93.2 % of men's world record speeds. In cycling the percentage is 87.1 %. The largest difference between women and men in world records in track and field events is noticed in the high jump with the women's cross bar reaching 85.7 % of the men's record and in the long jump, in which event the best woman has jumped 84.0 % of Mike Powell's 895 cm. We have no explanation as to why women are particularly "inferior" in jumping. It may be explained by gender differences in strength. In sports testing strength (bench press, squat, deadlift) the weight handled by women is on average 60.7 % of the men's world record (range 55.9-68.1 % in weight classes 52-82.5 kg).

It is interesting to follow the developments of results for women and men over the years. In 1950 the highest speed during the 100 m run for women was 88.7 % of the best male performance but the figure is 94.6 % today. In

1950 in the 800 m race the highest speed for women was 80.2 % of that of men. However, few women competed over long distances, even if the 800 m race appeared in the Olympic games as early as 1928. In the high jump the women's record was 81% of the men's best result in 1950, 83% in 1960, 84% in 1970, and, as mentioned, close to 86% in 1990. In the long jump the figures are 77%, 78%, 77%, and 84% respectively. The women's records have gradually crept closer to the men's levels. There are speculations, which have gained worldwide interest in the mass media, that women will eventually catch up with men's world records, in the marathon before any other events. Whipp and Ward (18) extrapolated from world record progressions, expressed as mean running velocity versus historical time for men and women respectively and concluded that women will overtake men in the marathon by the year 2000 and in the 200 m sprint by the year 2050. If this were to happen it would be tempting for a female marathon runner to masquerade as a man and race in the men's event in the next century. Whipp and Ward ignore the fact that there are basic genetically fixed differences that are decisive for physical performance demanding muscular strength and high aerobic power even when related to body mass. For example women cannot compensate for their lower haemoglobin concentration during maximal aerobic efforts through "natural methods". There are no physiological data indicating that women have a particular high potential for long-distance events such as the marathon.

References

1. **Åstrand P.-O.:** Why exercise? Med Sci Sports Exerc 24(2):153-162, 1992.

2. **Åstrand P.-O.:** Introduction - man as an athlete. In: Harries M., Micheli L.Y., Stanish W.D., Williams C. (eds.): Oxford Textbook of Sports Medicine. Oxford, Oxford University Press. In press.

3. **Åstrand P.-O., Rodahl K.:** Textbook of Work Physiology. New York, McGraw Hill, 1986.

4. **Balsom P.D., Ekblom B., Söderlund K., Sjödin B., Hultman E.:** Creatine supplementation and dynamic high-intensity intermittant exercise. Scand J Med Sci Sports 3:143-149, 1993

5. **Carlson R.:** The socialization of elite tennis players in Sweden: an analysis of the players' background and development. Sociology Sport J 5:241-256, 1988.

6. **Dempsey J.A.:** Is the lung built for exercise? Med Sci Sports Exerc 28:143-155, 1986.

7. **Grana W.A., Lombardo J.A., Sharkey B.J., Stone J.A. (eds.):** Advances in Sports Medicine and Fitness, vol 3. Chicago, Year Book Publishers, Inc., 1990.

8. **Joyner M.J.:** Physiological limiting factors and distance running: influence of gender and age on record performances. In: Holloszy J.O. (ed.): Exercise and Sport Sciences Reviews, pp. 103-113. Baltimore, Williams & Wilkens, 1993.

9. **Malina R.M.:** Growth, exercise, fitness, and later outcomes. In: Bouchard C., Shephard R.J., Stephens T., Sutton J.R., McPherson B.D. (eds.): Exercise, Fitness, and Health, pp. 637-653, Champaigne, Ill., Human Kinetics Books, 1990.

10. **Mizyno M., Juel C., Bro-Rasmussen T., Mygind E., Schibye B., Rasmussen B., Saltin B.:** Limb skeletal muscle adaptation in athletes after training at altitude. J Appl Physiol 68(2):496-502, 1990.

11. **Robinson S., Edwards H.T., Dill D.B.:** New records in human power, Science 85:409-410, 1937.

12. **Rowland T.W.:** Aerobic responses to physical training in children. In: Shephard R.J., Åstrand P.-O. (eds.): Endurance in Sports, pp. 381-389. Oxford, Blackwell Scientific Publications, 1992.

13. **Rost R., Hollmann W.:** Cardiac problems in endurance sports. In: Shephard R.J., Åstrand P.-O. (eds): Endurance in Sports, pp. 438-451. Oxford, Blackwell Scientific Publications, 1992.

14. **Saltin B., Strange S.:** Maximal oxygen uptake: "old" and "new" arguments for a cardiovascular limitation. Med Sci Sports and Exerc 24:30-37, 1992.

15. **Shephard R.J., Åstrand P.-O. (eds.):** Endurance in Sports. Oxford, Blackwell Publications, 1992, Also in German: Ausdauer im Sport. Köln, Deutscher Ärzte-Verlag, 1993.

16. **Sutton J.R., Brock R.M. (eds.):** Sport Medicine for the Mature Athlete. Indianapolis, Benchmark Press, Inc., 1986.

17. **Svedenhag J.:** Endurance conditioning. In: Shephard R.J., Åstrand P.-O. (eds.): Endurance in Sports, pp. 290-296. Oxford, Blackwell Publications, 1992.

18. **Whipp B.J., Ward S.A.:** Will women soon outrun men? Nature 355 (6355): 25, 1992.

Fig. 1

The world records for the 5000 m track event follow a relatively straight line from 1920 onwards. The introduction of an artificial track surface did not noticeably improve the records. Extrapolation to the world record of the year 2000 is tempting. The photograph shows Lasse Wirén (Finland) winning the 5000 m race at the Olympic games in Munich. (By permission Pressens Bild AB.)

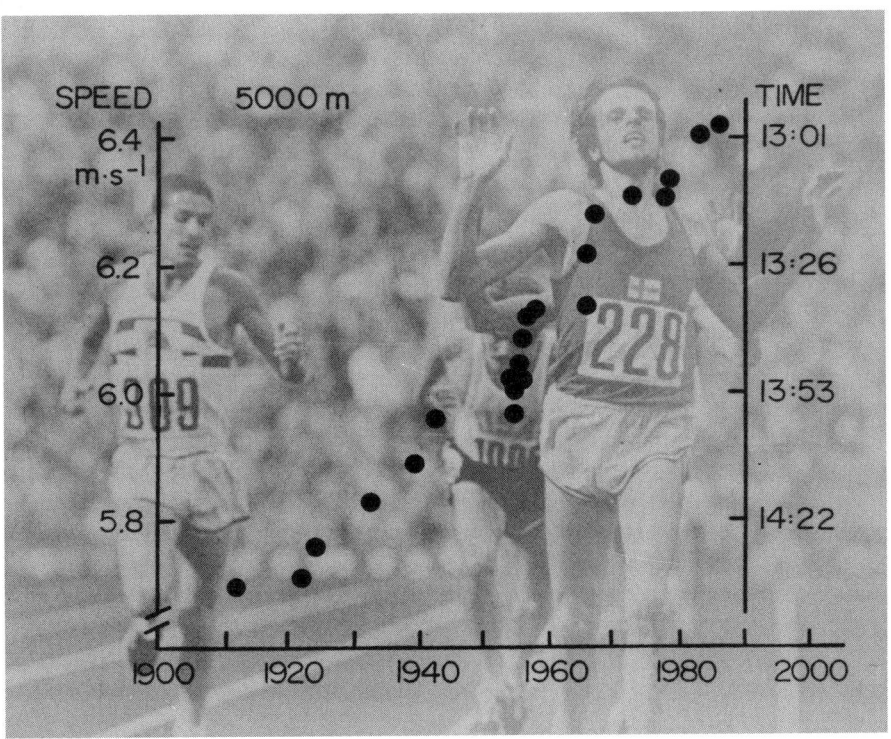

Political and Social Conditions of Elite Sport in Europe

Bouchout, J.-P.
Bureau de la Vie de l'Athlète au Ministère de la Jeunesse et des Sports
Paris, France

1. Introduction: Justification of the topic and terminological definitions

It is difficult to imagine talking about the current situation and development perspectives of elite sport without talking about the political and social conditions in which it takes place. My own approach will be to focus on the elite athlete in my paper, and to view him/her in the centre of a reality which can be considered as a "system". Elite sport today mobilizes numerous structures, governmental and non-governmental, economic and social, professional and voluntary. We have to identify correctly each of these factors and to establish their relationship in such a constant and complex pattern that only a systematic approach will enable us to analyse them.

One must admit that the political conditions of elite sport in a European context full of contrasts have led to a variety of social realities in elite sport practice. We shall see, however, that the building of Europe on the one hand, and the opening of the countries of Eastern Europe to the market on the other, join forces to increase common elements in the social and political conditions of elite sport.

Let us first clarify some terminological definitions of elite sport and Europe. As far as the latter term is concerned, there exists, of course, a great choice of definitions. Geographical Europe, political Europe, sports Europe. I suggest to relate to the last mentioned definition. Neither the European Community with its 12 member states nor the 19 prospective members of the Single Market cover European sports reality. The Council of Europe already comes much closer to this reality, since it comprises 31 European countries. The Association of European NOCs counts 47 members today. In 1990, its membership was only 33, a good illustration of the institutional changes shaking Europe and, as a consequence, European elite sport. As far as elite sport is concerned, I would propose to restrict this term to those athletes who by pertinent national authorities are recognized as participants, or having the potential to participate, in major sports events such as Olympic Games, World Championships and European Championships.

2. The current situation: The diversity of national realities

An outcome of the above definitions is that elite sport in Europe is particularly striking in its diversity. Incidentally, the Olympic Movement has come to revive its own philosophy and specific action for what was conveniently called "the smaller European countries" - small not in terms of quality, of course, but in size and consequently by the number of athletes. The increase in ACNOE (Association des Comités Nationaux Olympiques d'Europe) members might suggest that this distinction could last and this aspect of reality will be enforced. The diversity of the political and social conditions of elite sport primarily results from the differences in the way responsibility is shared between governmental and non-governmental organizations in each European country. Although the "All State" model which numerous countries of the European East used to have now seems to disappear in Europe, it does persist in other parts of the world. Thus, two major patterns are identifiable: A very decentralized one in which honorary action is dominant and the roles of the family, club, and local political authorities are decisive, and where the sports movement has a great deal of autonomy since it receives subsidies. The decision on how these subsidies are used remains with the sports movement itself. Examples are the Scandinavian countries, as described by Mr. Stefan LINDEBERG in February 1993 on the occasion of an ACNOE seminar on elite sport: Sport seems to have become an integral part of national culture. On the opposite side, we have a pattern which rests on a much more centralized system, whether governed by a single sports movement, as in the Italian reality, or exemplified by the French reality characterized by what Nelson PAILLOU, Honorary President of the French NOC, called a "3rd Way", i.e. a very strong partnership between public authorities and the sports movement. This partnership is particularly obvious in the French elite sport commission (Commission Nationale du Sport de Haut Niveau C.N.S.H.N.), where all major policy guidelines in favour of elite sport are decided upon, or in the joint management of the "Fonds National pour le Développement du Sport" which financially assists the sport federations, especially with elite sport programs.

This model rests on relatively strong professionalization of the measures taken in favour of elite athletes.

These different political and social conditions in elite sport thus lead to very different situations for elite athletes, who are more or less cared for, more or less supported in the management of their sporting and professional careers.

However, beyond these differences, a certain number of constants recur in the national realities which I shall now point out.

3. Analysis: A growing number of constants

It is more or less acknowledged throughout Europe that success in sport rests on different concepts which by now are well known. It is therefore not surprising to see that the political and social conditions of elite sport show more and more constant elements.

One can advance four such concepts: the pluridisciplinary approach, individualization, responsibilization, globalism.

- Globalism. Sporting excellence presupposes that the elite athlete is assisted in every respect: In training, of course, but also in his/her social life, particularly as far as professional training and integration are concerned. This is why it is universally agreed that education, professional training, and work must be brought into line through special complementary training modalities, which are adapted to sporting needs.

- Responsibilization. The more successfully the athlete looks after him/herself 24 hours a day throughout the year, for 10 to 15 consecutive years, the better the sporting career. Far from replacing the athlete's responsibility through excessive care, this concept on the contrary encourages the individual involved in elite sport to assume responsibility; cf. the Norwegian example.

- Individualization. In training and competition as well as in social life, all measures have to be adapted to the specific needs of every individual who is considered a unique and independent person.

- The pluridisciplinary approach. The plurisdisciplinary approach must obviously in the first place be understood as a pluridisciplinary approach to sports. This concept has led to the creation of training bases or institutions/schools which facilitate the cross-sectional tackling of problems in sport. Success in sports is the result of a growing amount of joint expertise. The dual coach-athlete relationship is now largely obsolete everywhere in Europe. The idea of a coaching team is dominant. It allows technical and tactical competence to be added to media, engineering, dietetic competence etc. Success comes about through the very important contribution of a large number of specialists, whether in the field of physical conditioning, mental conditioning, regeneration or social care.

I would like to insist on this latter aspect, which seems to me to have been put into the debate most recently. It was discussed with respect to training, management, and integration of elite athletes at the ACNOE seminar held in Paris on 24-26 February 1993. The seminar relied on the findings of an inquiry to which 26 NOCs had responded. All of them declared to have identification systems for elite athletes, which enabled them to adapt their measures to the needs of the athletes forming the national elite. Incidentally all of them distinguished several categories of elite athletes. For example in France, e.g. the first category of elite athletes is composed of athletes classified as "France-élite" (those who obtained the best results) and "France-seniors" (national team members in the major international events). A second category concerns athletes classified as "France-jeunes" (participants in international events for juniors). Still another category has been defined recently. It regroups elite athletes who are "shuffled" to facilitate transition between the sporting career and professional integration, via different support measures.

In addition, a list of "hopes" and "training partners" has been set up to identify athletes likely to benefit from individual accompanying measures, without being recognized as elite athletes.

Social care in elite sport is at first directed at "training" aspects. 19 out of 26 NOCs indicated in the inquiry that there were scholarships for elite athletes, and 13 NOCs said protocol agreements were being implemented between schools and universities, which offered elite athletes special training facilities. In France a special Baccalaureat session is organized each year for athletes who, due to sports schedules, miss the national examination (100 athletes from 28 federations in 1993). Furthermore, an inquiry made by INSEP in 1991 listed 628 special courses of studies with 6.000 athletes enrolled as students, of whom 1.000 were recorded in the elite sport list of athletes. Otherwise, about 100 elite athletes benefit each year from special admission formulas to PE teachers' diplomas.

Social care is also characterized by a variety of measures in favour of professional integration. They are increasingly regarded as indispensable for success in sports, notably due to the fact that the sporting career in some sports tends to last longer. These measures include jobs made available in different parts of public service and governmental administration (8 NOCs said this possibility existed in their country). They also include assistance by public or private companies, which at their own cost offer elite athletes opportunities to combine their sporting careers with initial experience in professional life. Sometimes they even offer permanent job perspectives. In France 400 elite athletes benefit from professional integration conventions that have been signed between the Ministry of Youth and Sports and the private sector.

Thus, social care provides many measures for elite athletes, among them assistance and orientation (diagnosis, ability and motivation assessments), training and professional integration. More and more countries set up structures or services which make it easier to follow elite athletes during their sporting career and beyond. The British, German, Norwegian and French systems were discussed in detail at the ACNOE seminar. Their objectives and programs show great analogies. They differ only in the action taken. But all of them aim at what the Norwegian Thor Ole RIMEJORDE calls a "flexible system".

4. Outlook: The political and social challenges of elite sport in Europe

In a global elite context European athletes take a perfectly honorable rank (European athletes won 55% of the medals at the Barcelona Olympics). It seems that the situation of elite sport in Europe can surely still be improved; subject to two conditions:

- The first one refers to reducing those menaces which loom large over sports ethics and which should be done away with altogether. These are: violence, doping, money.

To master the problems of violence, various measures are required, inter alia a revalorization of the rule, and of its warrant the judge, the referee, who should be given a genuine statute. The French law on the organization and promotion of physical education and sport mentions judges and elite referees, but practical action to enforce their recognition has not yet been taken.

Doping constitutes a permanent threat to the equality of chances and a danger to the health of the athletes. General action is powerful, as demonstrated at the recent World Conference on the fight against doping held in London. However, a lot has still to be done to make it more efficient, especially in view of harmonizing the efforts by the three principle authorities involved: the IOC, the international sports federations, and the national bodies charged by competent governmental authorities to implement anti-doping programs, since many countries still have adapted legal provisions or rules to fight against doping.

Money can also constitute a danger for sports ethics, if the financial powers (public or private) take the lead over sports logic. Furthermore, solidarity among nations and sports organizations needs to be strengthened in order to make sure all have a fair chance of access to elite sport.

If being an elite athlete implies rights, it must also imply obligations. To define the one and the other, plus the modalities of their control, seems to be a major task for the future of elite sport. Let the athletes speak up and share all big decisions concerning elite sport; this is a must. At the same time, the athletes have to respect a certain number of constraints, without which sport wouldn't function. In France, e.g. a charter of elite sport has recently defined the rights and obligations of each party involved: the athlete, the club, the national teams, the prep units, the organizers of events, etc. A growing number of individual conventions state which objectives are to be pursued during the sports year, which funds may be claimed, which obligations and limits are imposed on the elite athlete and his/her federation. There are good reasons to imagine that contractual relationships will come about, including the inevitable risk of legal action. Let alone other consequences, such as the exposure of a real subordination of the athlete vis-à-vis the national federation, which if it went along with payments, would have the federation assume the employer's role and the elite athlete that of the employed person. This is far from the original amateur status invoked on various occasions ever since modern Olympism has come into being, and involves a lot of problems (fiscal status? social security? unemployment?...)

- The second condition for better elite sport results relates to the follow-up which athletes are given. Follow-up in a strict sense: How to give each elite athlete the chance of self-realization, in sports and in society. The concept of coach, which continues to be a central one in elite sport to this day, has developed a lot. It should be allowed further progress in favour of a more competitive understanding of the follow-up team, which takes care of all elite sport aspects. This care will be increasingly professionalized and diversified. How will those teams operate in the future? One major challenge for elite sport will doubtedly be the active and fruitful participation in this development of the different members of the European Network of Sport Science Institutes, whether university or non-university ones, specifically via suitable training programs and efficient research work.

5. Conclusion: Towards a genuine culture of elite sport

The building of Europe, particularly in sport, should welcome challenges and contrasting points of view. Nobody wants a uniformity which is harmful to the expansion of national cultural identities. This also applies to elite sport. If the political and social conditions of elite sport have a tendency towards harmonization, and we have seen that it is possible to identify some elements of such a harmonization, there will still be enough variance from one country to another for meetings to be held, as our meeting today, which bring together scientists, sports leaders, business partners and government officials.

However, given these constants, are we not witnessing the creation of a genuine European elite sport culture? We have every reason to believe that different impulses from one country to another contribute to it, as does the Forum induced by the European Community, or the getting closer of sports organizations, as illustrated by the ACNOE initiatives.

I would like to wish the athletes in European elite sport evolution a good hand in that a humanistic approach to the problems will keep the individual athlete at the centre of the "system" which I have only roughly sketched here.

The Legal and Social Status of the Coach

Claude, R.
Ecole Nationale de l'Education Physique et des Sports
Luxembourg

1. Introduction

The vocation of coach has been known for a long time in Europe. Since the beginning of modern sport in the 19th century and the progressive specialisation in different sports disciplines, the influence of the coach in modern sport has been increasing. Although this sport-related vocation has a long tradition, regulated and structured coach education is quite recent; it is difficult to define a clear common, legal and social status for the coach within the EEC countries. There are, in fact, important differences between the various European courses of study and the qualifications for this vocation.

Moreover, the time allocated to the work of the coach varies: it may be occasional, seasonal, part- or full-time employment. Finally and especially, it is difficult to separate clearly the voluntary coach from the professional coach.

Thus it is not easy to define a common, European status for the coach, without conducting a comparative analysis of the situation in the different countries of the EEC, and of community law involving all countries.

2. The coach: his tasks and his activity fields

The specialised literature abounds in definitions of the coaching vocation. The simplest states that the coach trains the sportsman and assists him in competitions.

To determine this vocation more clearly, it may be helpful to refer to the "work" of the coach. The term "work" is rather hazy; it may be more appropriate to speak about tasks and activity fields from which to define the characteristic features. It is possible to define the social status of a vocation as "the unique features of the organisation controlling a group of individuals in pursuit of a specific group of tasks". The legal status is determined by the statutory regulations defining the working conditions of this specific group.

The European Network of Sport Sciences has proposed a European structure of 5 levels of coaching education, describing clearly the tasks and the activity fields of a coach. It is not necessary to reiterate the subject in this document, but it is important to note that the coach may hold a plurality of roles as coach, manager, psychologist, teacher, scientist etc.

The division of coaching tasks is not fixed and may include one or more tasks depending on the vocational environment. In a high-level environment, the work will be highly specialised and the variety of tasks restricted; the coach may be assisted by managers, psychologists, training assistants, doctors and physiotherapists...

Thus it is not possible to speak about consistency of tasks, as these vary according to the work environment. As the coach normally has a limited contract, he may be very mobile with a changing hierarchy of tasks. This is not without consequences for education and especially for continuing education; the vocation of coach is not stereotyped and is indeed in permanent evolution; - the coach educators have to be aware of this.

3. Coaching qualifications in the different countries of the EEC

The voluntary sector is by far the most developed, and without this sector it would be impossible to maintain sport in society. The professionalization of coaching employment is a recent phenomenon, still evolving and often difficult to define when compared with the voluntary sector.

In Europe there is a consensus definition of voluntary activity as unpaid activity, which may not exclude payment of expenses. Heinemann and Schubert define voluntary activity as "freely consented and non-remunerated provision of services in the interest of and within a non-profit organization" (1).

France is the only country to have established legal conditions to distinguish clearly between voluntary and vocational activity. It is interesting to quote within this context Article 43 of recent French law (13th July 1992): "Nobody is entitled to teach, to supervise, to promote a physical or sporting activity for payment, as a main or a secondary occupation, in a regular, seasonal or occasional way, nor to style oneself as a teacher, an instructor, an educator, a coach or other similar title, if he does not hold a degree, depending on the education level to which it corresponds, and on the vocations to which it gives access, as registered on the authorized list of degrees in physical and sporting activities".

It may be recalled that in France:

a. A vocation is considered as remunerated activity starting at a level of 20.000 French francs a year; this narrows considerably the voluntary activity fields.

b. the qualification for the vocation is the possession of a degree entitling the holder to practise this profession.

- the title of the coaching certificate is protected;

The coaching vocation is regulated by the state, with the consequent existence of two education systems for coaches, one designed for the voluntary sector under the authority of the federations, the other for the professionals under the authority of the State.

In the other countries of the EEC the situation is slightly different. The qualification for the vocation does not depend upon the State but upon the sports movements and it often varies from federation to federation, from country to country, even within one country.The regulations are very often non-existent and unrelated to the conditions of the free market, and so it is difficult to get a common European approach. The absence of a common standard for the qualifications offered by the sports organisations (or the complete lack of qualifications) is unfortunately the most frequent situation in Europe. It is the market itself which regulates and controls the situation, without any interference by the state, and dependent entirely upon the sports market-place.

The role of the State in the different countries and the philosophical approach concerning the responsibility of the State for the well-being of the citizens, may be seen differently depending upon a centralized or a decentralized state. The centralized state (Welfare State) does not delegate. It takes all decisions considered necessary to guarantee the well-being of the citizens. It tries to give the best possible qualifications to the coaches by legal regulation of the coaching profession, in order to protect the sportsmen against hazards incurred by sports practice supervised by non-qualified people.

By contrast, the decentralized state delegates part of the power to the sports organisations which are considered able to resolve the problems of qualified supervision. So it avoids all direct interference in the regulation of the coaching profession, but on the other hand helps the sports organisations in their efforts.

This diametrically opposed attitude between the centralized state, e.g. France, and the attitude of most of the other European countries, shows clearly the difficulty of establishing a common European status for the coach.

Although there is actually great disparity of regulations within the different countries, it is important to know that the vocation of the coach has already been partially structured by various aspects of Community Law, such as two directives appointing a general system of mutual recognition of vocational education. (2)

4. The two general systems for the recognition of diplomas

The free circulation of citizens is a fundamental right registered under the Treaty of Rome, which means that a professional wanting to exercise a vocational activity within another country of the Community, may practise under the same conditions as the citizens of that country. This is true for the coaching profession. A publication of the Commission (3) states: "Any vocational activity recognises this principle, and this includes sport-related and artistic professions, if remunerated."

It is interesting to consider what the above mentioned guidelines understand by the term "vocation", to analyze how this concerns the vocation of the coach, and to define the influence of these guidelines on the national and eventual European status of the coach.

The guidelines depend on some essential principles and it is necessary to keep in mind two principles of particular interest. First they apply to all regulated vocations, to employers, employees, and the self-employed. Furthermore, they contain definitions concerning the special features of the vocation as well as the regulation of the vocation.

4.1 The vocation

Depending on the guidelines, you normally practise a vocation if remunerated. But, in sports, this situation is not as clear. Between a volunteer and a full-time professional, there may be intermediate situations which are not always clearly defined.

The question is now to ask whether occasional or half-time activity is to be considered as an occupation in the sense of a vocation.

An answer is given by the European Court Of Justice. It offered the definition of a worker, as "a citizen of a member-state, practising a wage-earning activity and subject to a national system of social security, under any appellation whatsoever. It excluded persons exercising an independent activity, depending on freedom of association and free provision of services. This notion does not only cover full-and part-time employees, but all persons who may be considered as equivalent."(4)

It is interesting to keep in mind that all the intermediate, vocational forms of activity, from the moment they come under labour law, are to be considered from a judicial point of view as labour. All the different categories of remunerated occupation of the coach, including the occasional, the part-time and the seasonal, should fall under the guidelines guaranteeing the recognition of diplomas. It is necessary to consider these intermediate forms of labour if we try to define a European status for the coach.

4.2 Regulation of the vocation

The two guidelines stipulate that there is a regulated vocation every time admission to the vocation or the exercise of the vocation are directly or indirectly dependent upon the possession of a diploma. This regulation may consist of legal dispositions, administrative or even vocational regulations (the existence of collective conventions or vocational arrangements is considered as evidence of the regulation of the vocation).

It is interesting to keep in mind that a vocation may be regulated by legal dispositions depending upon public interest (decrees, orders...) or upon private interest. The question is then to know if the sport-related regulations are of private interest. Are they legal or not?

The sports associations, in order to achieve their goals and to be well organised, set themselves standards and rules, because without these, cohesion and organisation of associations would be impossible. This internal structure of association within the rules may vary in complexity, depending upon the development of the association. It represents the so-called statutes or internal regulations. These rules accepted by the majority of the members affiliated to the association, confer to this association the power of arbitration in the affairs of the sport concerned.

According to Jean-Claude Germain, (5) " there are many impartial and strong objections to the implementation of the regulations and orders relating to sport". Besides, the community guidelines put on equal terms the legal and regulated dispositions, without distinguishing between regulated dispositions of public or of private interest. It would be interesting to see the European Court of Justice give a decision on this point, in order to clarify this essential question.

This would mean that every federal statement specifies the possession of a degree for a part-time or full-time remunerated coach as obligatory. This is equivalent to judicial regulation of the vocation.

France is the only member-state where all the sport-related vocations are regulated at all levels of sports practice. Very often, a regulation for coaches only exists above a certain level of sports practice, and does not exist for certain minor sports disciplines. The reason is clear, because the sports organisations simply don't want to abolish the voluntary sector and so mortgage their financial situation by being forced to appoint coaches.

In conclusion:

    a.   the community directives (89/48 EEC and 92/51 EEC) give a definition of the idea of vocation in general, adequate for the coaching vocation in all forms in Europe. The coaching vocation is put on equal terms with the other vocations, which will have favourable consequences for its further development.

b. the coaching vocation is directly affected by Community Law and it would be an illusion to attempt to avoid this, by arguing that sports regulations are placed outside the Community Law.

c. the opportunity is open to European coaches to devise common statutes, based on Community Law, and so compensate for the lack of national regulations. These statutes could, in the manner of the European structure of five levels of coaching education, elaborated by the European Network of Sport Sciences, define minimal standards controlling the qualifications for the vocation, and the conditions of work. In order to achieve such an aim, all professionals in Europe should rally and initiate, together with all interested social partners, the development of a European proposal defining the social and legal status of the coach.

The working conditions of the coach, comprising the qualification, the remuneration, the different forms of work and the impact of community law on the national regulations have now been analysed.

In a strict sense, the expression "working conditions" indicates the clauses retained in the individual contracts of employment (payment, working schedules...).

But in a wider sense, it applies to the social organisation of the vocation, which also concerns the working conditions, because it fixes the frame in which each employee operates.

In order to continue logically, it is now time to consider the individual contract of the coach engaging him to his employer, relating to the education and the social organisation of the vocation.

5. The labour contract of the coach and the contracting parties

The relationship of the coach and his employer is normally fixed by a labour contract.

"The labour contract or the contract of employment is a contract by which a person contracts, for a certain time, fixed or not in advance, to work for another person and under his orders, against a remuneration which this other person contracts to pay to him" (6).

The difference between the independent activity and the paid activity is the criterion of subordination which links the employee to his employer. The wage-earner is submitted to the directives of his employer, who defines the conditions of the exercised activity: time schedule, place of work, payment, etc.

The wage-earner takes profit, in the exercise of his vocation, under the general conditions of labour law and social protection.

The vocation of coach is characterised by a defined period of activity for one employer. The labour contracts are fixed for a defined period. In many of the national regulations concerning the legal status of the private employee, the vocation of coach is not quoted as a paid activity. The question now is to determine if the activity of the coach is to be considered as wage-earned or as independent.

Sports clubs tend to classify the coach in the category of independent vocations which would consequently free them from compulsory dependence upon the labour law. The classification of the coach in one or another category depends on the ties which link him to his employer. Most coaches are to be considered as wage-earners, which seems to be ratified by a judgement of the Luxembourg Court of Appeal in the case of a football coach against his club for incorrect dismissal. The result of this jurisdiction is that:

a. it does not matter if the tie of subordination has been determined and defined by the admittance of the contract, or if it results simply from the effective labour conditions in which the vocation is practised.
b. there is a recent trend to relax the criterion of legal subordination and to recognize the character of a labour contract according to conventions where the employer's influence concerning the execution of the work is not basic.

There are grey areas between wage-earning and independent vocations. Following the above-mentioned jurisdiction, the judges, in case of dispute, generally decide in favour of the employee.

In most cases, the activity of the coach has to be classified under the status of the wage-earner or private employee.

In Europe, there are three categories of status for coaches:

1. Paid coaches, as state or local authority officials, delegated to the federations or the clubs. This situation exists mainly in France and there are very few coaches concerned.
2. Paid coaches, as private employees of sports associations. This is by far the most representative category. The number is quite difficult to estimate, because many practise this activity as a second, occasional or part-time job. It is tacitly accepted that some of them may not declare this income to the tax authorities. This explains why it is so difficult to quantify the employment-market.

3. Independent coaches working especially for leisure and tourist activities, such as tennis, horse riding and others. Their number is limited, but it is growing. The sports services market-place for full-time coaches is relatively small, with the supply probably greater than the demand, especially after the opening of the eastern borders.

If all the forms of coaching-related labour are considered, the sport-related working market is becoming more important and represents a significant economic factor. Unemployment in Europe grows increasingly and forces the member-states to devise solutions: They take particular interest in the less developed economic sectors and the coach-related labour market will probably not escape attention. Sport is a field generating employment for the future and there is some optimism about the quantitative development of the coach-related labour market.

6. The education of the coach

The development of coach education is not identical in the different countries of the Community.

1. There are countries which have a long tradition of coach education structures, and other countries that have only recently established these structures. The common work of the European authorities responsible for coach education under discussion by the European Network of Sports Sciences in Higher Education including the development of a European structure of five levels for coaching education, will have a positive influence on the development of this education.

2. The different education levels are not equally developed. Level 4 and especially level 5 are less developed and indeed non-existent in many countries. Provision at level 1, 2, 3 is by far the most frequent, and is taught within all the countries.

The quality of the education offered is improving from year to year. There is a growing tendency to raise the qualifications, because of the requirements of the labour market, and levels 4 and 5 will develop more and more.

Vocational education is one of the most essential components of employment policy and from this base it is possible to organize vocational structures. From this point of view, the tradition of coach education within the different countries of the EEC and the acceptance of the European scale of five levels for coach education by the participating agencies, could be considered as the starting point for the elaboration of European status for the coach. This could be the beginning of harmonisation of the working conditions of coaches. Vocational education has to be developed up on a large scale and has to fit the variety of tasks of a coach's activity. It is necessary to guarantee good articulation between the initial and the continuing education structures, the latter being very important for a vocation characterised by flexibility and continuous evolution.

It is necessary to think about the validation of professional competencies and about the process of certification for supplementary knowledge acquired during continuing education.

Moreover, it is necessary to involve the participating agencies in the planning of educational policy and the elaboration and evaluation of the training structures. With regard to this education, the European Network of Sports Sciences in Higher Education should be the meeting place for the teachers (trainers) and the participating agencies.

7. The participating agencies

The general aim of a trade union is the defence of the interests of the employees against those of the employers. The defense of the vocational interests is a characteristic of a trade union, but is certainly not the exclusive objective of the union. The aim of trade unions is not only to control or to defend, but also to take part in the organisation of vocational, economic and social life.

Effectively, the vocational coaching organisations in Europe very often organise their corporate actions through general associations rather then traditional unions. They are not always directly involved in the wider organisation of vocational life. There are conventions and agreements between coaching associations of the same disciplines and the relevant federations, but they rarely include the wider organisation of vocational life.

The organisation of vocational coach education at national level is characterized by:

1. a multitude of vocational organisations, related to the range of sports disciplines;

2. the consolidation of these different organisations under an umbrella organisation, representing the national agencies. These organisations, although existing in most of the big countries, have nevertheless been created quite recently.It is a problem for them to constitute a traditional trade-union, which explains why they want to integrate, as for instance in Germany, into the existing, interprofessional trade-unions.

At the instigation of the Common Market and in order to defend their interests, some of the vocational, disciplinary organisations convened a meeting at European level. An organisation representing coaches of different sports disciplines was established at the beginning of this year, when the "European Association of Coaches" was created, representing all coaches from levels I to V. Its main aim is now to establish European criteria for the social organisation of the coaching vocation.

It is desirable that this European statute with reference to the coach should receive the support of the employers' associations, as a consequence of the common consultation between the participating agencies. The initiation of such consultation is difficult because:

1. there are several governmental and non-governmental organisations in Europe, the most representatives being ACNOE (Association of the National Olympic Committees in Europe) and ENGSO (European Non-Governmental Organisations);

2. the European Association of Coaches, recently created, has to gain the necessary representativity in the years to come in order to assume its assigned mission.

3. the nature of the vocation itself; the vocational activity is nearly always for a fixed term, and the remuneration of the coach is mainly based on the results obtained. The discrepancy between levels of remuneration can be significant. A European coaching statute for all sports disciplines and accepted by every employer, is impossible to achieve. In the first instance, one has to work out the reference criteria for this statute, so that these can serve as a discussion basis for all the conventions to be worked out by the different national coaching organisations with their federations.

The idea is not to harmonize or to work out uniform and identical European statutes, but to agree on certain common principles to introduce in the different national conventions. The national specifications and the variety of the sports disciplines should in this manner be respected.

8. Conclusions

1. The vocation of coach is in continuous evolution, and from the economic point of view it will become more and more important in the future. The sport-related market-place will have a tendency to expand during the coming years.

2. Professionalization is progressing, though it has not yet stabilised. Flexibility characterises this vocation and employment is often precarious, seasonal or part-time. There are national initiatives planned to stabilise this vocation, and to transform occasional and intermediate work into full-time work.

3. The relatively well developed coach education currently found in most countries will consolidate at each level (I - V), and the quality of coach education will improve because of the collaboration between universities, sport-related institutes and non-university coach education structures.

4. conventions or negotiated joint agreements are rare and the profession is not organised at a European level. The process of professionalization and the social organisation of the vocation will accelerate up because of the mobility of professional coaches, and will be founded on Community Law.

5. it is important to create a European meeting place to discuss for initiatives to analyse employment and qualifications, and to study and define the organisation of this vocation. This meeting place should provide a forum for the employers, the coaches, the teachers and the public authorities interested in the development of this economic activity.

Currently, there is no European legal and social status for the coach. However, all the conditions now exist from which this can be established.

References

1. **Alaphilippe F., Bournazel E.:** Le Dirigeant Sportif Bénévole. CNOSF. Droit et Economie du Sport.

2. **Bouchout J.P.:** Exposé au "Groupe Delbeccha" sur une enquête relative aux métiers du sport dans les différents pays de la Communauté Européenne.

3. **Bouchout J.P., Camy J.:** Les métiers du sport: repères et axes de réflexion. Assises Nationales des Métiers du Sport.

4. **Bourdeau Ph.:** L'Escalade en France. Pratiques sportives et débouchés professionnels 1989-1990. Les Métiers du Sport.

5. **CEDEFOP:** Répertoire Communautaire des Profils Professionnels. Fiche d'information.

6. **Document:** Les Premières Assises Nationales des Métiers du Sport. Emplois et Formations. 19 et 20 décembre 1991 à Paris.

7. **Document CEDEFOP:** Les organisations d'employeurs, partie prenante au développement d'une politique européenne de formation professionnelle.

8. Echelle européenne de cinq niveaux de la formation des entraîneurs. Documents I et II du Réseau Européen des Instituts en Sciences du Sport. 1992.

9. **France:** Loi no 84610 du 13 juillet 1992 relative à l'organisation et à la promotion des activités physiques et sportives.

10. **Francois G.:** Brevet d'Etat d'Educateur Sportif 1er et 2e degré. : Sciences Juridiques. Vigot, Collection Sport et Enseignement.

11. **Gaudemar J.P.:** Formation et Développement Régional en Europe. La Documentation Française.

12. **Kreiss Fr.:** Die Europäische Gemeinschaft und der Sport. Auswirkungen auf sportbezogene Ausbildungsgänge und Tätigkeiten.

13. Les perspectives de l'emploi dans les domaines de l'enseignement et de l'animation des activités physiques et sportives, et de loisirs en Charente-Maritime. Etude réalisée par le Centre de Droit et d'Economie du Sport de Limoges.

14. Les Instituts non-éligibles dans le programme Erasmus. Rapport de la Commission 4 à l'Assemblée Générale du Réseau Européen des Instituts en Sciences du Sport. Octobre 1991.

15. Le Guide du Dirigeant de Club. CNOSF.

16. L'acte unique européen et le sport. Revue Juridique et Economique du Sport.

17. Le schéma directeur des Formations. Jeunesse et Sports, France.

18. L'encadrement technique des activités physiques et sportives en dehors de l'école: voies de formation, qualification et marché du travail. No 63 Bulletin du Centre d'études et de recherches sur les qualifications.

19. Pour une prospective des métiers et des qualifications. La Documentation Française.

20. Qualifications professionnelles pour l'enseignement et l'animation sportive dans la Communauté Européenne. Jeunesse et Sports, France.

21. Regard sur les métiers du sport. Résultats d'une enquête réalisée en 1989 dans quatre départements français. Jeunesse et Sport.

22. **Weis E.**: Exposé sur les métiers du sport à l'heure du grand marché européen. Luxembourg.

Footnotes

[1] **Heinemann K., Schubert M.**: Ehrenamtlichkeit und Hauptamtlichkeit in Sportvereinen. (page 14). Bundesinstitut für Sportwissenschaft.

[2] Directive 89/48 relative à un système général de reconnaissance des diplômes d'enseignement supérieur qui sanctionne des formations professionnelles d'une durée minimale de trois ans.

Directive 92/51 relative à un deuxième système général de reconnaissance des formations professionnelles, qui complète la directive 89/48/CEE.

Journal officiel des Communautés Européennes.

[3] Guide des Professions dans l'optique du Grand Marché. (page 10). Office des publications officielles des Communautés européennes.

[4] La Cour de Justice des Communautés européennes (page 65). Office des publications officielles des Communautés européennes.

[5] **Germain J.-Cl.**: Les sportifs et le droit (page 23). Collection Scientifique de la Faculté de Droit de Liège.

[6] Statut légal de l'Employé Privé.(page 15). Chambre des Employeurs Privés du Grand-Duché de Luxembourg.

Training in Visualisation and Bodyawareness as a Way of Changing the Energy Level and the State of Consciousness During Rhythmic, Slow Motion Stretching

Engel, L.
The Danish State Institute of Physical Education
Copenhagen, Dänemark

1. Introduction

In the holistic understanding of wholeness, the interplay of mental and physical aspects are a fascinating key to a deeper understanding of the important role that our mind, "our inner attitude" has on our way of moving and acting in our life. From our practical work we have the experience that greater body awareness and sensitivity is a way of directly experiencing the interrelatedness of ourselves with our surroundings and that this direct experience is an important way of altering our understanding and our responsibility for ourselves and our surroundings. We were curious to find out if these simple training modes (colourvisualisation, low stretching and running) could help normal people to get a feeling of better bodyawaremness, deeper relaxation and greater sensitivity and to find out the differences there might be between these different ways of training.
Optimal health is characterised by high energy and psychological and physical harmony and well-being. Many investigations show a relationship between regular aerobic exercise and physical and psychological well-being (King, Taylor, Haskell and DeBusk 1989). Different relaxation techniques, visualisation and/or meditation techniques also show a relationship between these kinds of exercises and both physical and psychological well-being (Walsh 1982, Ikemi et al., 1986).

2. Purpose

The main purpose of this study was to investigate the physiological, the psychological and the subjective response to 3 different training techniques: One mental technique, colour visualisation, one purely physical training, running, and one rhythmic, slow motion stretching.

3. Method

The investigation took place during the spring and autumn 1988. 64 subjects were randomly divided into 5 groups, four training groups and one control group. The training took place three times a week half an hour each time during two month. The control group did not have any kind of training until everything was finished.

Group 1 had a purely mental training in the form of colourvisualisation, group 2 and group 5 learned a psychophysical slow-motion stretching synchronised with stomach breathing and group three did a running program with high intensity with the purpose to improve their conditions. Group four was a special group of persons with secondary braindamage on 8. They were trained with slow motion stretching. Everybody were highly motivated.

4. Physiological tests

We measured Meg on m. frontals in my volt (DeGood and Crisholm 1977) and EEG in alpha % of the total amount of brainwaves (Dilbeck et al. 1981) and condition in ml O_2 per kilo per minute (Andersen L.B. et al. 1987). All parameters were measured before the training started and when the training period finished.

5. Psychological tests

We measured state-anxiety and trait-anxiety (Spielberger, Gorsuch and Lushene 1970). We measured creativity with Remote Associate Test (Mednick S.A., Mednick, M.T. 1967). We measured the mood in relation to the training before and after a session after 2, 4 and 6 weeks. We used Mood Adjective Checklist Nowlis V. 1966. We registered three different kinds of mood

Factor 1: Peace, relaxation
Factor 2: Humour
Factor 3: Tiredness

6. The interview

The slow motion stretching group and the controlgroup were interviewed in the middle of the period and in the end. The controlgroup were asked to lay down and relax as best they could and we measured EMG and alpha % as we did in the test situation and asked them how the relaxation had functioned for them. The slow motion stretching group did their training as usual and then laid down and we measured EMG and alpha % and asked them how the training had functioned this specific day and in general. We were specially interested in their experience of the body, the intensity of the situation, visualisations and metaphors and their general experience of this kind of training. We asked them to tell with their own words what they had experienced and eventually we added the following questions:

1) How was the training/situation for you today?
2) How is the training normally?
3) Has the training had any kind of influence on your everyday life? ex. your feeling of energy, your way of reacting in situations with stress?
4) If you should describe your experience with an image or a metaphor, what would it be?
5) What kind of training do you normally do?
6) Have you been meditating or doing other kinds of selfregulating techniques earlier in your life?

7. Results

Slow brainwaves and muscle tension. All measurements are taken with close eyes after 20 minutes of rest as the baseline and then after the training session. All values are mean S.D. values.
$P< 0.05*$, $P< 0.01**$, $P< 0.001**$.

As you can see in the diagram their is a significant rise in the alpha % for group 1 (the visualisation group) and for 5 (the slow motion stretching) and for group 3 (the running group). Group 6 (control) has not changed. The EMG is significantly lowered for group 1 (colourvisualisation) and for group 3 (running). The controlgroup has not changed.

	Alphaini%		Alphafin%		EMG ini MyV		EMG fin MyV	
Gr 1	29%	±12	48%*	±15	2,2	±0,9	1,4*	±0,3
Gr 2	33%	±13	42%	±20	2,2	±0,8	1,9	±0,7
Gr 5	25%	± 8	35%*	± 6	2,2	±0,6	1,9	±0,4
Gr 3	27%	± 9	32%***	±11	2,5	±0,9	1,7***	±0,1
Gr 6	33%	± 3	31%	±10	2,1	±0,7	2,3	±0,7

8. The condition

All values are mean S.D.values.
P< 0.05*, P< 0.01**, P<0.001**.

As you can see from the diagram both before and after the training all groups have a relatively high condition. Only the running group does have a significantly better condition after training.

	Max. O_2 uptake ini		Max. O_2 uptake fin (ml O_2/kg/min)	
Gr1	51,3	± 6,0	52,6	± 8,1
Gr2	50,0	± 7,8	51,0	± 8,0
Gr5	57,4	± 6,4	57,9	± 8,2
Gr3	53,4	± 8,1	57,9***	± 6,9
Gr6	55,5	± 12,1	57,3	± 9,3

9. State Anxiety and Trait Anxiety

As you can see in the diagram there is no change in state anxiety neither for the training groups nor for the control group. Trait anxiety is significantly lowered for group 1, 2 and 3 (colourvisualisation, slow motion stretching and running). The controlgroup has not changed.

Stai	Stateanxiety		Traitanxiety	
Groups	ini	fin	ini	fin
Colourvisualisation Gr. 1 (n=12)	31,6 ±6,1	31,6 ±7,8	36,1 ±7,5	31,4* ±5,9
Slow stretching Gr. 2 (n=13)	31,4 ±4,6	33,3 ±8,9	37,8 ±8,9	34,5* ±9,2
Slow stretching Gr. 5 (n=12)	29,5 ±5,2	32,1 ±5,0	32,6 ±6,4	31,8 ±5,6
Running Gr. 3 (n=14)	29,1 ±5,1	29,4 ±8,2	30,4 ±5,9	27,4* ±4,6
Control Gr. 6 (n=13)	33,5 ±	34,6 ±4,7	34,1 ±8,0	34,0 ±6,2

10. Results from the interview

Overview of the subjective experience from the group with slow motion stretching.

Overview of subjective experiences. Slow stretching.											
Subject no	85	63	92	88	64	62	74	97	95	73	93
1 Heaviness	yes	yes	yes	yes			yes	yes	yes	yes	
2 Warmth		yes	yes				yes	yes			yes
3 Peace-harmony		yes	yes	yes	yes	yes	yes				
4 Vibrations		yes			yes			yes	yes	yes	yes
5 Bodyfrontiers		yes		yes				yes		yes	yes
6 Visualisations							yes		yes		yes
7 Time-space						yes			yes		
8 Unity						yes					
0 Negative experiences											
Earlier experience	think the body	yoga mental		taik-wondo	creative visualisation	breath	breath		karate	music	
Positive ordinary days changes	more guts	better relaxation		physical balance		less stress	more peace		less stress		breath of view
Metaphors	sea old village	beach sea clouds		water sun frost		emptiness	light joy unity		drip floating colours		open sky

- Heaviness:
  8 persons tell that they experience heaviness or lightness f.ex expressed: "I had a feeling that heaviness and lightness changed. "For the moment I am very stressed, but I experienced heaviness.
- Warmth:
  5 persons had experiences with warmth f.ex: Today I am relatively bad at relaxing compared to normal, but I felt warmth". " I experience an electrical stream of pleasure".

- Peace - harmony:
  6 persons express that it has been pleasant, a good relaxation.
- Inner movements/vibrations/pulsations:
  6 persons have experiences of pricking sensations. I could feel my pulse very clearly. I had a waving feeling from the middle of the body.
- Different sensing of the body and of the frontiers of the body:
  5 persons experience a different sensing of the body. Parts of the body disappear. The body is floating.
- Visualisations:
  3 persons tell that they experience vivid spontaneous visualisations. Floating crystals. Movements of floating and glittering colours.
- Time-space:
  2 persons have experiences that their feeling of time changes.
- Unity:
  1 person expresses the experience as a oneness, an oceanic feeling of gliding away. A positive emptiness.

Nobody in the training group has negative experiences. More that half of the group tell that the training has had a positive influence on their way of reacting in the everyday life.

Metaphors for the experience:

The sea. Looking over the sea. Running along the sea. The sound of waves. The sky. White clouds floating on a blue sky. To disappear in the open sky. The sun shining. Clear and frosty air. A feeling of light and joy. To be dropshaped. Floating, glittering colours. The colour yellow. Emptiness.

11. Interview with the controlgroup

They experience the same qualities but fewer persons have the positive experiences and none have experiences oneness and transcendence of time and space. They also have negative experiences like cold feet, impatience, restlessness, irritation etc.

Concluding it can be said that it basically are the same qualities but that the training group have more positive and deeper experiences than the controlgroup.

Overview of subjective experiences. Controlgrupp.													
Subject no	65	67	70	76	78	79	80	81	82	89	90	96	97
1 Heaviness	yes	yes				yes	yes		yes	yes			yes
2 Warmth	yes			yes					yes				
3 Peace-harmony		yes		yes		yes	yes	yes					yes
4 Vibrations				yes	yes			yes					
5 Bodyfrontiers	yes							yes					
6 Visualisations		yes			yes								
7 Time-space													
8 Unity													
0 Negative			yes								yes	yes	
Earlier experience	yes	yes	yes			yes	yes	yes				yes	
Metaphors	yes	yes		yes	yes	yes		yes	yes			yes	yes

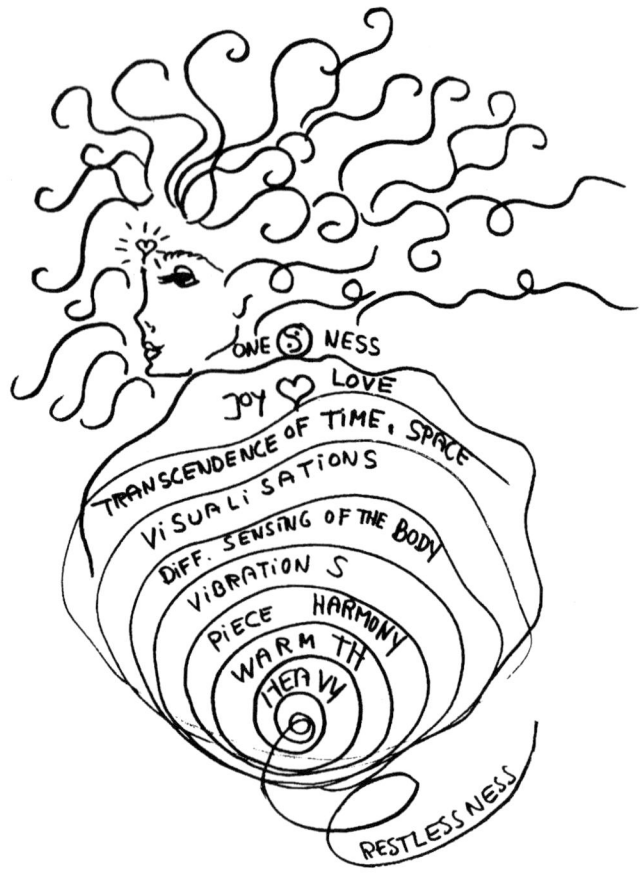

The model should be read as a visualisation of the layers of experience that came out of the interviews of the training group and the controlgroup. There seems to be 4 different layers of experience towards the ultimative experience of total oneness. You have the negative spiral then you enter the beginning relaxation with beginning positive feelings of heaviness, lightness, piece, harmony, then you go into a deeper relaxation with a different sensing of the body and the body frontiers, and then you come into states of altered consciousness where the feeling of time and space change or disappear. There is a positive relation between the intensity of the experience and the alpha %. Beginners normally easily get experiences from the beginning and the middle level while only very few have experiences from level three.

We can conclude that all three techniques have a significant better ability for physical and mental relaxation. The mood before and after training is changed in a positive way, as a feeling of less nervousness and less tiredness. Levels of anxiety go down generally and more than half of the group feel that they react in a more positive way in stress situations. For more that half of the group there are beginning experiences with altered way of sensing the body and the frontiers of the body and a few directly experience altered state of conscious-ness as a transcendence of time and space and an experience of oneness: A flow experience.

Deep Experience	Level	Alpha % fin
Neutral or negative	0)	26 alpha %
Beginning relaxation	1)	37 alpha %
Deep relaxation	2)	34 alpha %
Altered state of consciousness	3)	40 alpha %

12. Discussion

As we can see from the results all these techniques have an effect on physiological and psychological parameters and a positive influence on the subjective feeling of well-being an the ability to cope with everyday stress. In this design we have been training in a holistic way as close to a normal training situation as possible. The results do not indicate any difference on the three techniques in relation to the ability to physical an mental relaxation and a subjective feeling of well-being. In all three training modes there is a significant rise of the alpha%. This is in agreement with many other investigations, particularly different meditation techniques (Delmonte 1984). It is a common view in the literature that a high alpha% correspond to mental calm and piece (Orme-Johnson and Gelderloos 1988). These effects are connected with the relaxation response (Benson et al. 1974) and are not unique for one specific technique. They are registered from so different techniques as relaxation procedures, meditation, hypnosis and here with colourvisualisation and slow stretching and running with high intensity for half an hour. We do not know the exact elements that are of importance for the individual to be able at will to enter a state with high alpha%.

One important element might be the ability to relax in the situation and yet be totally there. It would be interesting to investigate furthermore the role of the eyes in this ability to change the state of consciousness. We think that it is of importance that the eyes are very relaxed. Ex the level of alpha% is somewhat higher in the group with colourvisualisation compared to slow stretching and to running. There is a positive correlation between the subjective feeling of intensity and depth of the training situation and the level of alpha%. One difference on these techniques beside that they are passive and active is that the mental training goes on with the eyes closed while stretching and running is performed with open eyes. Even if we stressed that the persons had to relax the eye and the eye muscles as much as possible ("soft eyes") this did not succeed for all especially because it was a relatively short training period, only 8 weeks. Many investigations that you can not expect a result until after 12 weeks of training (Brown and Engler). Most investigations that are interested in these kind of changes ex meditationtechniques nearly always have subjects who have been training the technique for years.

Many investigations touch on the relation between anxiety levels and the ability to reach a high alpha%. Ex persons with high anxiety or depression cannot go into a high alpha % level (Bick 1989). It is also especially among beginners that there is registered asymmetry in the spreading of the alphawaves, with more experienced subject the alphawaves cover both sides of the brain (Earle 1981). It is necessary that the anxiety level is relatively low to open for the possibility of high alphalevels. In our investigation we could not find a relation between anxiety levels and alphalevels but there was a correlation between subjective experience of intensity and alphalevels. We think it might be because the level in our material is relatively low. It is not uncommon to find levels up to 60-80 % of alpha % in relation to experience of altered states of consciousness. We believe that it is the level more than the rise that is of importance (Echenhofer, F.G. and Coombs, M.M. 1987).

It would be of interest to investigate furthermore how these effects could be applied in active sports and movement training both for elite purpose and for broader purpose of quality in movement and life as a whole. Could we isolate some elements as f.ex the role of the eyes, the over-all muscle economy, the importance of rhythm, the importance of length of the training seance.

References

1. Andersen L.B., Henckel P. and Saltin B.: (1987) Maximal Oxygen Uptake in Danish adolescents 16-19 years of age. Eur. f. Appl. Physiol. 56: 74-82.

2. Benson H., Beary JF. and Carol MP.: (1974) The relaxation Response. Psychiatry, vol. 37, pp. 37-46.

3. **Bick CH.:** (1989) EEG mapping including patients with Normal and Altered States of Hypnotic Consciousness under the Parameter of Posthypnosis. Intern. J. Neuroscience, vol. 47, pp. 15-30

4. **Brown DP.:** (1980) The stages of Mindfulness Meditation: A validation Study. The Journal of Transpersonal Psychology, vol. 12, no. 2, pp.143-192.

5. **DeGood DE., Crisholm RC.:** (1977) Multiple Response Comparison of Parietal EEG and Frontalis EMG Biofeedback, Psychophysiology, vol. 14, no. 3, pp. 258-265.

6. **Delmonte MM.:** (1984) Electrocortical Activity and Related Phenomena Associated with Meditation Practice. A Literature Review. Intern. J. Neuroscience, vol. 24, pp. 217-231.

7. **Dillbeck MC., Bronson EC.:** (1981) Short-term longitudinal effect of the transcendental meditation technique on EEG power and Coherence. Intern. J. Neuroscience, vol. 14, pp. 147-151.

8. **Earle JBB.:** (1981) Cerebral Laterality and Meditation: A Review of The Literature, The Journal of Transpersonal Psychology, vol. 13, no 2, pp. 155-173.

9. **Echenhofer FG., Coombs MM.:** (18987) A brief Review of Research and Controversies in EEG Biofeedback and Meditation: The Journal of Transpersonal Psychology, vol.19, no. 2, pp 161-171.

10. **Ikemi A., Tomita M., Kurofda M., Hayashida Y., Ikemi Y.:** (1986) Self-regulation Method: Psychological, Physiological and Clinical Considerations. Psychother. Psychosom. Vol. 46, pp. 184-195.

11. **King AC., Taylor CB., Haskell WL., Debusk RF.:** (1989) Influence of Regular Aerobic Exercise On Psychological Health: A Randomized, Controlled Trial Of Healthy Middle-Aged Adults, Health Psychology, vol. 8, no 3, pp. 305-324.

12. **Mednick SA., Mednick, MT.:** (1967) Examiners Manual, Remote Associate Test. Boston: Houghton Mifflin. Danish Version by Hans Weltzer.

13. **Nowlis V.:** (1966), Final Report on the Development of A Mood Adjective Check List (MACL) Contract No 668 (12), Office of Naval Research, USA.

14. Spielberger CD., Gorsuch RL., Lushene E.: (1970) Manuel for State Trait Anxiety Inventory. Consulting Psychologists Press. Palo Alto. Ca.

15. Orme-Johnson DW. & Gelderloos P.: (1988) Topographic EEG Brain Mapping during yogic flying. International Journal of Neuroscience vol. 38, pp. 427-434.

16. Walsh R.: (1982) A Model for Viewing Meditation Research, The Journal of Transpersonal psychology, vol. 14, no. 1, pp. 69-84.

ON THE RESEARCH IN THE COMBAT SPORTS
(CONDENSED VERSION)

Kirchgässner, H.
Fakultät Sportwissenschaft, Universität Leipzig
Germany

1. Preliminary remarks

If within the framework of a mainly performance sport-related event of this congress is to speak about the research in one group of sports, it requires first the recognition of relatively exactly determined groups of sports and its implications and secondly the existence of theoretical positions related to the groups of sports.

It is in first line to determine the specific nature of the groups of sports in question, i.e. in this case the exact determination of combat-specific requirements and the resulting necessary performance prerequisites as well as the presentation of scientifically based training methodic solutions.

Starting points for the derivation of the theoretical positions related to the groups of sports are theory-based sport-specific research and development works but also the generalization of positive experiences made in the training of the combat sports.

In my opinion, the theory of sports and groups of sports should be starting-point and aim of sport-specific research.

Such theoretical positions for the combat sports have been elaborated on the basis of long-term and purposeful sport-specific research in boxing, fencing, judo, and wrestling (1, 3, 4, 5, 9).

2. Some selected combat sport-specific theoretical positions

As mentioned above, the following theoretical basic positions have mainly emerged from the generalization of sport-specific research, also from the transformation of scientific results of other events to combat sport-specific questions. A discussion on advantages and disadvantages of inductive and deductive approach for the cognitive gain would be interesting, but could be dealt with at another forum.

In my opinion it is undisputed that safe findings and positions related to groups of sports for theory-based research and development work as well as for training-methodic principle solutions in the different sports are of fundamental

significance. Previous investigations show the general transferability of the training methodic findings to non-olympic combat sports.
An essential prerequisite for the elaboration of the theory of combat sports is the characterization of specific activity requirements.

2.1 Specific activity requirements

A combat sport is defined as "a sport or an event where two sportsmen or sportswomen compete for the victory in direct combat after appropriate preparation and with observation of specific rules" (8).
As to closer characterization of the combat sport there are different trials of explanation, mainly from game-theoretic (10) and activity-oriented or action regulating (2) view. The starting-point is always the characterization of the specific activity requirements. Direct conclusions for the well-aimed and requirement-oriented development of the necessary performance prerequisites can be drawn from them.

Combat sport-specific activity requirements are:
- Active direct combat against opponents on the basis of different strategico-tactical basic behaviour and individual fighting concepts.
- Permanently changing fighting situations that must be recognised, analysed and solved on the basis of lightning quick decisions (key signals!) by individual competition-proof fighting actions.
- Fast sequence and fluent transition of actions of different action groups (attack, counter attack, defence).
- Risk of premature defeat by KO, Ippon and victory by fall or by sport-specific injuries.
- Victory or defeat depend on every advantage no matter how small when the course of the fight and the scoring are directly influenced by referees and judges.
- Adaptation to new competition rules and scoring systems (e.g. box-pointers, passivity rules in wrestling and judo, changed competition time in fencing).

This evaluation shows clearly that combat sport activities put highest requirements to the sportsmen. The performance prerequisites for top-level sportsmen can only be developed with training concepts that link the direct connection between the requirements to training and competition and start from the realistic individual loadability of the sportsman.
From the point of view of combat behaviour we can strongly generalize successful sportsmen's fighting dynamics and characterize it as follows:

1) - Clearly offensive fighting dynamics with enormous prevalence, with distinct self-confidence and great psychologic stability of the so-called "victory sportsmen".

2) - The successful fighting dynamics is characterized by increasing pace of fighting, a higher density of actions and greater toughness in the fighting dynamics.
3) - Highly dynamic fighting by intended change of pace, intermediate and round spurts, fluent transition from offensive to defensive actions and vice versa and more frequent change of distances and transitions from stand to ground..
4) - The bouts are waged with greater tactical variability and technical-tactical versatility. The basis for it are long-term individual fighting concepts that orient specially to the shaping of strong individual qualities and particularities.
5) - Keep the eye on the creation of fighting situations ("special actions") that are necessary for the application of highly perfected individual fighting actions and use persistently all chances of attack.
6) - World best athletes' fighting dynamics is characterized by originality and surprising individual fighting actions that impress judges and spectators as well.

The registration of characteristics of the world best athletes' combat behaviour in the various sports is of principle significance for the derivation of topical and prognostic training requirements. The perfection of the necessary competition analysis and corresponding analysis methods is a basic concern of the applied research in the combat sports.

From this short characterization of combat sport-specific requirements it follows that specially the psychologic requirements to a combat sportsman are high.
This underlines the great value of the combat sports for the shaping of young personalities.

2.2 Combat behaviour

In preparation of the term combat behaviour reference should be drawn from the aspect of following the "central" term of behaviour to the multiple determination of human behaviour which necessitates an integrating approach of different scientific disciplines to the behaviour research.
Personality psychological fundamentals of interpersonal behaviour are mainly significant for the determination of the term of combat sport behaviour.
Depending on the special requirements to the combat sport the following contents, forms and main aspects must be determined:

> "Combat behaviour is the way of acting in the directing sports combat between two combat sportsmen and characterizes the interpersonal correlation in situations.

It is totally directed to gaining the victory and is characterized by the well-directed and unconditioned use of all chances in the various kinds of sports on the basis of the competition rules stability and originality. The regulation mainly takes place consciously, but includes different regulation levels.

The more exact characterization of the four main aspects of combat behaviour underlined in the definition, as awareness in the sense of a situation-related behaviour, single-mindedness, stability and originality turns under the aspect of determination of subjective and objective combat sport-specific requirements into an essential starting point of the derivation of requirement-related training-methodic ways of approach and also into a starting-point for sport-specific research and process-supporting scientific measures.

A concise characterization shall contribute to better understanding:
- Situation appropriateness as the whole of the behaviour that on the basis of specific perception thinking and decision processes realize a great correspondence between objective requirements to the situation and subjective performance capacities.
- Single-mindedness as the whole of the behaviour that allows the sportsman on the basis of a stable competition attitude, of a high level of specific volitional qualities and an outstanding psycho-physical condition to realize his victory-oriented fighting concept with good quality.
- Stability as expression of a positive psycho-emotional digestion of load which allows the sportsman to maintain even in situations of highest psychological load the organization and quality level of combat behaviour necessary for the realization of the aim, the coping with the situation or the gain of victory, and
- Originality as expression of surprising fighting dynamics directed to the individual particularities, to the uniqueness of the personality.

The relevance of this characterization for the perfection of the training systems in the combat sports is underlined by the 1992 Olympic Games analysis which states:

"The victory-decisive combat behaviour constitutes the magnitude and set of aims for the renewal of the training concepts in the combat sports."(11)

The characterization of the present competition behaviour of world best athletes is the starting-point for the derivation of prognostic performances in the combat sports. Therefore, the permanent improvement of the competition analysis is an important task of applied research. The explanation of the term fighting situation is significant in this connection.

2.3 Fighting situations

The determination and characterization of dominating fighting situations are directly connected with the precision of combat sport-specific requirements to actions.

By fighting situations as specific requirements to actions we understand the concrete relations among the sportsmen including the decision for the continuation of the combat in a certain fighting phase. They depend on the competition rules, all useful information for the situation and the individual performance prerequisites of both athletes. The determination and characterization of dominating fighting situations in connection with the assignment of action-relevant situation characteristics are of fundamental significance for the improvement of single-mindedness and quality of specific training, specially the fighting situation training. Finally it is the derivation of concrete, i.e. situation-related behaviour which must be developed according to different interpersonal performance prerequisites with more-year individual concepts of development. The scientist who trains combat sport and the interested coach were faced with the following questions and problems in the past:

- Determination and characterization of significant situations and derivation of certain rules of behaviour.
- Can action-relevant signals (key signals) be filtered and transformed into training methods?
- Which sport-specific classification stands the test and is practice-relevant?
- Determination of useful effective solutions of the situations in the sense of fighting actions in direct connection with the qualification of the specific competition analysis.
- Permanent perfection of the training systems with relation to the requirements (situation training, behaviour training etc.).

The above mentioned questions were basically solved to a large extent and sports-related differentiated. But we cannot start from scientifically founded theoretical positions for the group of combat sports. The present level of solution of the problem is not satisfactory from the point of view of training-methodic application of activity-oriented positions.

A practicable attempt of division is the classification to situation characteristics, such as:
- the position of the fighters within the limited competition site
- the competition rules (standard situations!)
- noticeable body positions of the opponent
- the distance and mensur between two fighters
- particularities of the opponent's fighting dynamics
- certain "nodal points" of the course of the fighting.

The division made due to practicable reasons is differently applied in the sports and is partially reflected in the training means catalogues and the specific approach to the situation training. The fighting actions are understood as solutions of situations and classified mainly from the strategic-tactical point of view as gaining a win of points, saving an advantage, neutralizing a "critical" situation in some sports (6).

3. Selected topical research points in the combat sports

Based upon the high complexity of the performance structure in the combat sports and the dominance and partial compensation ability of single performance factors, a variety of development and research works in the various sports was written in the previous years. In the former Soviet Union, e.g., series of books on specific combat sport problems were published yearly. A survey on these publications is offered in two documentations by the Institute for Applied Training Science.

The majority of sport-related research was and is strongly oriented to practice and based upon theory only in exceptional cases. Its significance for the renewal of the training and competition systems in the single sports is considerable. The following topical examples prove it.

3.1 On the competition analysis

The permanent further development and perfection of the competition analysis is a point of concentration in the performance sport research of the combat sports.

The quickly developing informatics in the previous years offered new ways to formulate differentiated aims and to make the competition analysis the decisive starting-point for the long, medium and short duration training control.

General aims of the competition analysis are:
- the registration of international development trends as an analysis of the international performance level within a sport or an event and the determination of prognosis-oriented requirements.
- the registration of the sport-specific competitive performance and fighting behaviour of the sportsman and derivation of recommendations for training.
- to draw up an analysis of opponent to find individual victory strategies against potential opponents in the competition or "types of opponents" and the permanent perfection of an international opponent card index (data bank).

The methodic approach to the investigation and evaluation of the analysis data is similar in all combat sports. Basic prerequisites are correspondingly coded systems of competition protocolling, practicable observation and analysis protocols and appropriate programmes for the information processing.

Training methodic orientations and individual recommendations can only be given by consulting the results of sport-specific performance tests.

3.2 Motor simulation / Force measuring apparatus in training

In order to register exactly sport-specific performance prerequisites as magnitudes of control specially in the strength oriented sports of wrestling and judo trainager systems were introduced which simulate sport-specific motor requirements. Defined motor parameters are registered and computer-based evaluations made. They constitute a basis for specific training derivations.

The endeavours to register sport-specific complex performance prerequisites was leading progressively to the establishment of measuring apparatus which put complex competition-specific requirements. Within the so-called force measuring apparatus in training a computer-based index-oriented training is realized which guarantees specific stimulus structures and informs directly the sportsman on the achieved results and the quality of execution of his specific exercises.

The sportsman is put into feedback training situations which motivate him extremely and push him to the border of his performance capacity (13).

In principle the endeavours are recognizable in the combat sports that the force measuring apparatus in training should be integrated more and more into the training systems and sport-related measuring and information systems be perfected according to the requirements. Experiences of a concept-based and interdisciplinary approach to the development sport-related measuring and information systems were gathered specially at the Institute for Applied Training Science.

In order to support the process of training in the sports associations the establishment and further perfection of complex sport-related trainer advising systems enhance main endeavours. Strongly simplified it means that exact training recommendations for a certain sportsman are to derive from the different analysis and measuring data. (12)

A special problem in the combat sports consists in the fact that top-level performances with strongly differing individual performance structures can be achieved and medium-duration training recommendations are to direct to "potential main opponents" or "types of opponents".

The individual arrangement of training is the basic principle of preparation of top-level performances in the combat sports. The basis for it are individual development concepts (IDC), individual training plans (ITP), individual norms and finally competition-related individual fighting concepts.

This shows another large and comprehensive range of tasks for the applied research.

Short duration opponent-related fighting recommendations come up at present with the help of the modern data processing and interactive video systems.

3.3 Investigation in the combat sports

It was tried to show the important points of further development of the training and competition systems in the combat sports from the point of view of necessary specific research; finally it is to refer to further important points of combat sport-specific research and development works.
Further important points are:

- determination of the efficiency of combat sport-specific competition-like training means on the basis of modified load requirements
- investigations on the actional speed and the behaviour of decision from the aspect of complex sport-specific requirements
- further development of the measuring and information systems with the aim to derive requirement-related individual training tasks
- bio-mechanic single investigations to determine the effect of the course of strength and speed in selected fighting actions
- medical checks of sport injuries and following consequences, mainly in boxing
- precision of sport-specific behaviour requirements and derivation of training-methodic consequences depending on the changing competition rules and evaluation systems.

4. Outlook

It goes without saying that the permanent perfection and further development of sport-specific competition analyses, of the training diagnosis and control as well as the force measuring apparatus in training will remain an essential point of the applied research in the combat sports in the coming years.
The perfection of the training and competition systems in the combat sport is directly depending on the general development in top-level sport such as commercialization, professionalization and change of value. Thus, ethic-moral, social-psychological and pedagogical problems of the combat sports will have to be elaborated scientifically in the future.

References

1. Barth B.: Abriß einer Theorie und Methodik der Strategie und Taktik des Wettkampfes im Fechten. Diss. B. DHfK Leipzig, 1978.

2. Barth B., Kirchgässner H.: Ansätze zur Nutzung der tätigkeitsorientierten Konzeption der Sportpsychologie zur Verbesserung des Trainings in den Zweikampfsportarten. In: Wiss. Zeitschr. d. DHfK. Leipzig 26/2, 37-48, 1985.

3. Barth B., Kirchgässner H.: Zur weiteren Profilierung trainingsmethodisch orientierter Wissenschaftsdisziplinen - dargestellt am Beispiel der Zweikampfsportarten. In: Wiss. HS-Zeitschr. d. DHfK. Leipzig 28/2, 102-113, 1987.

4. Kirchgässner H.: Persönlichkeitspsychologische Grundlagen und trainingsmethodisches Vorgehen bei der Herausbildung des Zweikampfverhaltens. (Ein Beitrag zur Erarbeitung einer Theorie und Methodik der Zweikampfsportarten Boxen, Fechten, Judo und Ringen). Diss. B. DHfK Leipzig, 1983

5. Kühn J.: Theoretische Grundlagen und trainingsmethodische Empfehlungen zur Neugestaltung der technisch-taktischen Ausbildung im Nachwuchstraining der Sportart Ringen. Diss. B. DHfK Leipzig, 1989.

6. Kühn J.: Trainingsmethodische Ansatzpunkte einer ziel- bzw. aufgabenbezogenen Klassifizierung von Kampfhandlungen und Kampfsituationen im Ringen. In: Wiss. Zeitschr. d. DHfK Leipzig, 29/1, 55-62, 1988.

7. Lehmann G.: Zur Präzisierung von Ziel, Aufgaben und ausgewählten Inhalten des Nachwuchstrainings im langfristigen Leistungsaufbau der Zweikampfsportarten. Diss. B. DHfK Leipzig, 1980.

8. Schnabel G., Thieß G. (Hrsg.): Lexikon Sportwissenschaft Bd. 2, 998. Sportverlag. Berlin, 1993.

9. Müller-Deck H.: Trainingsprinzipien zur Entwicklung technisch-taktischer Kampfhandlungen im Judo: Ein Beitrag zur Theorie und Methodik der technisch-taktischen Ausbildung in den Zweikampfsportarten. Diss. B. DHfK Leipzig, 1983.

10. Tünnemann H.: Zur Weiterentwicklung der Trainingskonzeptionen im Freien und Klassischen Ringkampf. Diss. B. (Entwurf). Forschungsinst. f. Körperkultur und Sport Leipzig, 1979.

11. Tünnemann H.: Analyse des Olympiazyklus 1988/92 und Ableitungen für die Trainingsstrategie in den Zweikampfsportarten. In: Weltstandsanalyse 1992 - Tendenzen der Leistungsentwicklung in den Olympischen Sportarten, Inst. f. Angewandte Trainingswissenschaft. e.V. (ed.). Leipzig 116-140, 1992a.

12. Tünnemann H.: Stand und Perspektiven eines Beratersystems im Kampfsport, dargestellt am Beispiel Ringen. Referat auf dem 3. Workshop Sport und Informatik, Schifferstadt 22.06.-24.06.1992 (1992b).

13. Meßplätze für moderne Traingskonzeptionen des Spitzensports.
Dokumentation zum Seminar des BAL 25./26.11.91 in Leipzig Heft 1. 1992.

THE COACH AS A MANAGER

Kozel, J
German Coaches Academy
Cologne, Germany

"Coach" and "coaching" are terms which today are no longer used in sports only. The coach is generally seen as an expert who prepares other people for special situations. In the sports sector we associate the term "coach" with the voluntary sports instructor, the physical education teacher, the professional coach in competitive and top competitive sports. The diversity of the tasks to be performed by a coach in his capacity as the central reference person of the athlete becomes clear if you consider the great number of influences which the athlete is exposed to. Among those who take an interest in the athlete are the sports manager, the press, his boss at work, the service personnel who are in charge of the sports equipment, medical, psychological and biomechanical experts and others.

The coach therefore is not only responsible for his athlete in technical terms but, due to his pedagogic, psychological and organizational capabilities, must also be capable of influencing the athlete's development.

In many respects the functions of a coach can therefore be compared to those of a manager or - generally speaking - to the functions performed by a manager in industry and trade. In order to make this clear I will use this contribution of mine:

1. to describe the scope of duties to be fulfilled by a manager,

2. to describe the scope of duties to be fulfilled by a coach,

3. to compare the duties to be performed by a manager with those to be performed by a coach and

4. to review the training of coaches as to whether questions of management are sufficiently dealt with.

1. The Manager's Scope of Duties

The following statements are taken essentially from the encyclopaedia of management.1) Management is the translation / the realization of aims with the help of assistants. A manager must therefore have the following basic skills (Fig 1):

Fig. 1

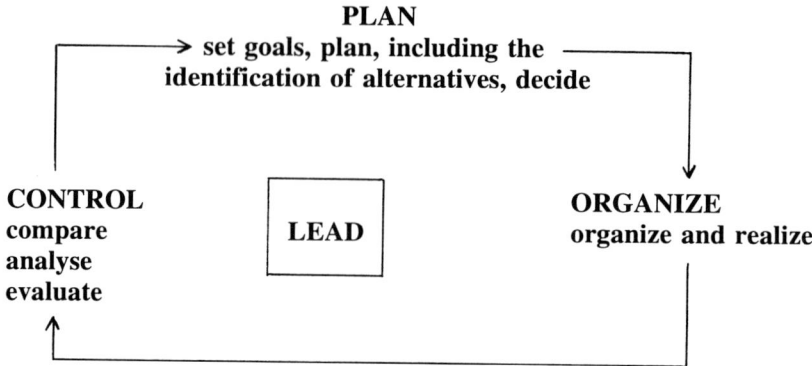

The emphasis which is placed on each of these activities depends on the various hierarchical levels at which a manager is employed (Fig 2):

Fig. 2

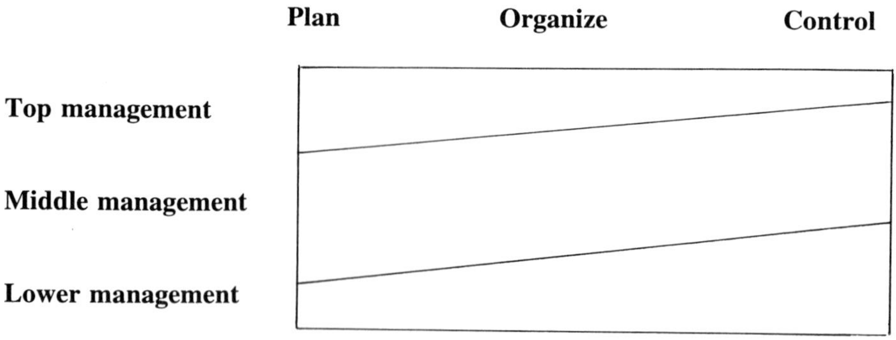

1.1 Planning

"Planning" refers to the designation of management objectives and the short-term, medium-term and long-term business policy pursued by an enterprise to achieve these objectives. Planning thus presupposes a capability for conceptional and imaginative thinking - in other words, creativity. This phase is determined by

- the previous development of the enterprise,
- the financial, material and personnel preconditions necessary to achieve the objectives of the enterprise,
- the identification of internal or even external motives and, last but not least:
- the search for alternative solutions and options. After existing alternatives have been presented and evaluated this phase is concluded with decisions which specify the procedures and description of criteria which give an indication as to whether and to what extent a performance has actually been affected.

1.2 Organization

Organizing is the administrative work which the manager has to do and which takes up the most time. To organize means to build up a structure on the basis of which the objectives advised can be achieved. The organizational structure defines subareas within which staff members are allowed to act independently. The organizational structure is complemented by statements of work and standards of work, which show the staff members what they must do, what capabilities they have but also what responsibility they bear.

In particular, this includes, inter alia:

- delegation of decision-making powers, i.e. transfer of clearly defined competence and responsibility as well as clear-cut accountability for the results achieved;
- introduction of qualification requirements for individual positions, i.e. specification of the occupational, technical and human requirements to be met by individual staff members;
- clarification of personal relations, i.e. specification of the channels of communication, definition of the information policy to be pursued, definition of competences and areas of responsibility with regard to internal and external relations;

1.3 Control

Control means: monitoring and comparing.

In particular, this includes, inter alia:

- the establishment of an information system as well as determination as to which data will be needed in which way, where and when.
- review of the results gained, i.e. comparing the actual value with the rated value;
- correcting measures, e.g. to correct adverse developments and if need be, the introduction of more effective and economic structures and procedures.

These planning, organizing and controlling functions can be represented by the following feedback control system (Fig 3)

Fig. 3

Management Feedback Control System:

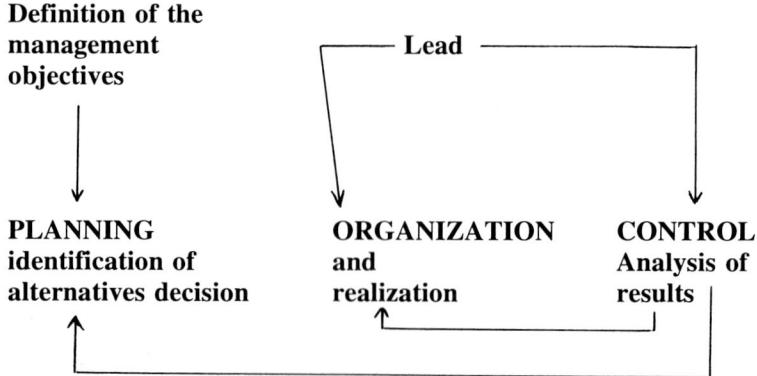

Since, at the beginning of my briefing, "management" has been defined as "the translation/the realization of aims with the help of assistants", then to "MANAGE" can, in most cases, also be equated with to "LEAD". It is the task of the management to direct the enterprise, i.e. to direct the staff to achieve the objective set, and to verify and ensure that the staff identifies with the objectives set.

These management measures include, inter alia:
- the selection of qualified personnel;
- training and schooling of individual staff members;
- promotion through further systematic on and off the job training;
- staff counselling.

To LEAD, however, also means to influence other people. This is possible by the way of sanctions (reward and punishment). The modified way of influencing other people is by recognition and criticism and last but not least by motivation. Unlike the two ways mentioned first, motivation does not require any special balance of power or authority. In this context, it is important for us to know the needs of the staff, since the design of the work itself and of the environment essentially contributes to the satisfaction of the staff and thus has a motivating effect.

2. The Coach's Scope of Duties

In order to accomplish his tasks the coach must have basic knowledge of the science of sports not only with regard to the science of training but also in the fields of kinetics/ biomechanics, sports medicine, sports psychology and sports education. In this respect the coaching of coaches does not differ much from the training of sports teachers (graduate sports teachers, sports philologists). Sports teachers and coaches must be capable of transferring the findings of the science of sports to both the concrete learning and training process.

Unlike the sports teacher the coach must, however, have very good up-to-date knowledge of particular types of sports, knowledge that especially former top athletes can rely on as a result of their own motoric experience. Special knowledge of particular types of sports can be developed only in the tense atmosphere of top competitive sports and in the extreme situation in which coaches and top athletes are.

What is more, the complex requirements of his job demand from the coach a "personal and moral qualification", which gains special importance last but not least in view of the recent discussions on doping. RÖTHIG understands by this the capability to build up a "pedagogic relationship with the athlete".2)

However, the more the trainer is engaged in top competitive sports the more he will also have to deal with the question of how to plan and organize training and competitions. A more comprehensive description of the coach's job could be seeing the coach

- primarily as an educator who stimulates the athlete's self-education (which means that he must be a teacher who has been coached in pedagogy and psychology),

- as a technician comparable to a master or foreman in industry and,
- last but not least, as an organizer and manager.

The German Sports Federation has formulated an image of the coach's job 3) which reaches down into the following areas of activity and associated tasks. In this context, the possibility cannot be excluded that in practice some areas of activity and tasks may overlap:

2.1 Training management, i.e.

planning - execution - evaluation - analysis -management - control of coaching and competition processes

- teaching, improving and stabilizing general and sport-specific techniques of moving,
- teaching general and sport-specific capabilities with regard to physical fitness as well as teaching sport-specific tactical know-how and skills,
- analysis of the current level of performance (coaching and competition checks),
- development of perspective and master training plans (multiyear coaching plans), annual plans (preparation, competition, transitional period) and operational plans (macrocycles and microcycles) for cadres or individual members of a cadre,
- evaluation of coaching plans, competition results, coaching courses, coaching and competition records (coaching documentation).

2.2 Coaching - Counselling - Care

- counselling and coaching during training and competitions,
- conveying appropriate personal, social and factual quality standards according to the athlete's psychological and physical capabilities (success management - failure management),
- coaching of cadre members in their social environment, that is school, work, vocational coaching, family, armed forces, friends etc.,
- providing general health care as well as continuing medical and physiotherapeutical care with regard to prevention, regeneration and rehabilitation,
- direction and execution of compensatory coaching programs (e.g. whole-body gymnastics/remedial gymnastics) for athletes engaged in types of sports/events involving special orthopaedic impact structures,
- execution of rehabilitating coaching programs after acute injuries sustained at sport,
- counselling athletes on sports equipment and sportswear
- counselling athletes on questions of nutrition and leading them to a sportsmanlike way of life

2.3 Coordination - Management

- Coordination of general dates fixed by the specialized sports organization as well as of the special schedules of athletes (competition calendars)
- Participation in the structural planning of the specialized sports association and coordination of the structural plans of the umbrella organization, the state sports federation and the clubs with the appropriate coaches and athletes.

2.4 Organization - Administration

- Organization and supervision of medical care/sanitary control and physiotherapeutical care;
- organizational accomplishment of the tasks listed under "Coordination"
- basic data processing knowledge.

2.5 Public Relations Work

- Interviews, comments and reports on questions and problems of specific types of sport events;
- providing detailed information to the media;
- description and explanation of specific problems of the sports federation (especially in the field of coaching as well as with regard to the provision of health care to cadre members);
- popularization of particular types of sports / events.

2.6 Advanced coaching - Continuation coaching

- Participation in specialized and general advanced coaching education seminars at the national level (if applicable, at the international level);
- continuous exchange of special and general experiences with fellow coaches at different levels of performance.

2.7 Teaching - Scientific Work

- Coaching and advanced coaching of sports instructors and coaches in competitive sports;
- planning and execution of coaching meetings/coaching seminars on behalf of the federation at the national level;
- counselling of full-time, part-time and voluntary fellow coaches;
- proposing scientific studies.

3. Comparison of the Duties/Activities of a Manager and those of a Coach

Despite the differences in the representation of the individual areas and the description of the tasks to be accomplished the duties/activities of a manager have been found to be largely identical with those of a coach when comparing them with each other.

The focal point of the coach's job is the management of coaching, which is understood to be the coordination of all measures relating to the planning of coaching, of the execution of coaching and thus of the organization and implementation of the entire coaching process as well as of the competition and coaching checks. These are definitely the duties/activities of a manager, a fact which is also substantiated in practice when considering the example of the roster of a national coach of the year 1993:

From an example of 31 days of the month, the coach spent

- 10 days on meetings and conferences (at four different places in Germany)
- 3 days on making diagnoses of the performance of the national team members
- 14 days on desk work and direct coaching of athletes.

3.1 Planning/Planning of coaching

The designation of an objective to be achieved in sports, taking into account the previous development of an athlete and his future capabilities, corresponds to the managerial area of PLANNING. The individual planning steps are shown in table 1: 4)

Table 1

	Stage	Designation	Question
Objektives	1	Specifikation of planned objektives	What do I want to achieve in what period of time?
Planning steps: Plan and decide		How do I intend	to achieve it ?
	2	Situation analysis	-What is the situation?
	3	Development of planning alternatives	-Which options do I have?
	4	Assessment of the alternatives	-What advantages and disadvantages do they have?
	5	Selection and elaboration of the best planning alternatives	-Which option shall I choose?
	6	Decision	

The situation analysis and the collection of planning data, e.g. the volume of coaching required, coaching intensity, coaching units, frequency of competitions, the social environment as well as performance/problems at school, provide the basis for the development of alternatives/options. During the planning phase certain principles are to be observed in accordance with BECK, 4) which help to facilitate the subsequent decision-making process and minimize certain risks which can never be excluded:

- the data must be as complete as possible to permit large scale planning.
- the information must be correct.
- planning must be continued for several years which is the only way to ensure a systematic and long-term conceptual preparation of future decisions and actions.
- planning must be adaptable to new sets of data, all the more so since the conditions which were valid during the preparation of a plan may change:
- the planning efforts made must always be in proportion to the reliability and applicability of the plan.

In order to be able to make factual decisions the individual planning data (decisive criteria) as well as the information available on possible alternatives should be summed up/juxtaposed in a matrix of consequences.

BECK 4) presented the following example of a matrix of consequences (table 2)

Table 2

Decisive-criteria		Option C (present option)	Option B alternative 1	Option C alternative 2
1.1 Volume of training	hrs/week	20	20	10
1.2 Intensity of coaching		average	high	very high
1.3 Coaching period	days/week	3	5	4
1.4 Training units	per week	12	10	7
2. Frequency of competitions	per season	20	15	30
3. Social environment		strained	slightly strained	highly strained
4. Performance at school		below average	average	far below average

In order to be able to objectively evaluate the alternatives identified the individual planning data/decisive criteria are now given different ratings and, having been assigned absolute numbers, are allocated to the various alternatives and juxtaposed in an evaluation matrix (table 3). The totals of these ratings then provide a highly objective order of priority and may considerably facilitate the decision-making process.

Table 3

Decisive criteria	Rating	Option A	Option B	Option C
1.1 Volume of coaching	5	5	5	3
1.2 Intensity of coaching	20	10	15	20
1.3 Coaching period	15	5	15	10
1.4 Coaching units	20	15	10	5
2. Frequency of competitions	10	10	5	2
3. Social environment	15	10	15	5
4. Performance at school	15	5	15	0
	100	60	80	45

In the example shown here B would thus be the best solution.

3.2 Organization/Implementation

To organize means to provide the framework required for the proper execution of coaching. This includes the selection and coordination of personnel (coach, scientific assistants, parents, teachers etc.), the selection of suitable material (sports equipment, sportswear) and the determination of the infrastructure (sports facilities, time available at the sports sites). The definition of clear-cut capabilities and responsibilities, when determining the organizational structure and peripheral conditions will reduce the risk of possible problems arising in the implementation phase. The establishment of a well functioning information system is also extremely important in view of the coach's future control function. I suppose I do not have to name any examples of bad planning or failures which occurred only because information was transmitted from the top level downwards (and vice versa) or at one and the same level either not at all, too late, too slowly or too early in order to highlight this problem.

3.3 Checks/Coaching and Competition Checks

How effective planning and organization have been can be seen when comparing the performance aspired in coaching and competitions with that actually achieved. Unless a coach directly coaches the athlete - which is frequently the case especially with national coaches, he is dependent on the transmission of coaching and competition results. A coaching documentation which contains the main characteristics of the coaching actually done permits a systematic and objective coaching control. The conclusions to be drawn from this will enter into further planning and organization.

Like in management, the entire process of coaching control is unthinkable without LEADERSHIP. Here the leading function of the coach does not refer exclusively to the athlete but also includes caring for and counselling the people surrounding him; the staff. Important measures to be taken are, inter alia, the coaching of staff members and the demonstration of how individual staff members (assistant coach, home coach) can accomplish their tasks and discharge their duties.

LEADERSHIP can, however, not prevent the occurrence of disruptive quantitative as well as qualitative factors, 4)

i.e. disruptive <u>quantitative</u> factors, such as:
- unavailability of the coach because he is sick
- insufficient number of coach sessions
- adverse timetable at school
- inadequate coach space etc.

and
disruptive qualitative factors, such as:

- personal problems (wife, girlfriend, family)
- the athlete's mental instability
- communication problems between the athlete and the coach problems at work and or school
- bad coach's etc.

The solution of these problems makes special demands on the coach's personality and the distinctness of his managerial qualities. Here it becomes clear whether the coach has succeeded in building up a pedagogic relationship with the athlete and/or his environment.

4. The coaching of coaches

Coaching and advanced coaching of coaches is an important component of top competitive sports. It is the task of the Federal Committee For Top Competitive Sports and of the Coaches Academy to continuously provide coaching and advanced coaching to national coaches and the scientific-technical personnel of the Olympic bases in accordance with the requirements and outline conditions of competitive sports. It is especially the task of the Coaches Academy to put the coaching of coaches on a solid scientific basis and to impart maximum knowledge of specific types of sport in view of the great importance of sports and the constantly increasing findings regarding the conditional factors influencing an athlete's performance. "An athlete's performance is not accidental but the result of several years of work, using all aids that science offers." (The former president of the German Sports Federation made this assertion in many statements)

Within the framework of a survey/demand analysis the German Sports Federation has developed a thematic catalogue of advanced coaching measures for top coaches. 5)

Regarding the subject "The Coach as a Manager" the results of the analysis are highly interesting:

Three areas of responsibility have been identified, which break down into appropriate duties 90% of which correspond to the functions performed by a national coach:

1st area of responsibility: managing, which breaks down into the following individual tasks:

- set objectives,
- plan,
- decide,
- organize,
- coordinate,
- control.

2nd area of responsibility: acting as a leader, including the following individual tasks:

- rate and judge persons,
- delegate and agree upon objectives,
- promote persons,
- motivate persons and
- solve problems and conflicts.

3rd area of responsibility: future-oriented thinking (innovative functions), including:

- the provision as well as the gathering of information,
- foresighted thinking and
- creativity/innovations.

When asked how much of their working time they spent on the three areas of responsibility mentioned, national coaches were found to spent 50% of their time on the basic tasks of management. Managerial tasks accomplished in cooperation with other persons take up about 30% and the innovative functions about 20% of the coach's time.

When further asking the national coaches which of the tasks mentioned they found very easy - easy - not so easy - not easy to accomplish the following result was obtained (table 4):

Table 4

Basic tasks	
Plan	89%-
Set objectives	88%-
Organize	73%-
Coordinate	66%-
Decide	46%
Control	33%
Leadership	
Motivate Persons	74%-
Promote persons	72%-
Delegate and agree objectives	68%-
Rate and judge persons	65%
Solve problems and conflicts	33%
Future-oriented thinking	
Inform and gather information	76%-
Creativity/innovation	76%
Foresighted thinking	74%

This indicates that especially "deciding", "controlling" and "solving problems and conflicts" are considered to be tasks which are "not so easy" or "not easy" to accomplish. The obvious deficiencies in these areas must be the subject of future advanced and continuation coaching of national coaches.

The Coaches Academy also considers these problems within the scope of its coaching programs. "Sports organization and administration" is being taught at the Coaches Academy and is also included as an examination subject in the study and examination regulations. The three coaching phases provide, inter alia, for the following general lectures:

- basics of sports organization and administration
- introduction to data processing
  in the first coaching phase;
- planning and organization
- sports marketing
- psychological coaching
- leadership and leadership behavior
- statistics and data processing (use in sports organization)
  in the second coaching phase; and

- structural questions in sports (role of the coach and public relations work)
- psychic preparation, counselling and care
- mental disposition and motivation
- control procedures applied especially in coaching and competitions
- psychological training (application)
- statistics
- data processing (use in training and competitions)

in the third coaching phase.

Close cooperation with the Management and Administrative Academy of the German Sports Federation and the sports federation of the State of North Rhine Westphalia gives the Coaches Academy the opportunity to make the graduate coach familiar with the problems of management and qualify him appropriately by offering supplementary continuation coaching courses to him.

I have tried to explain to you why the coaching of coaches and especially the top coach's job is absolutely comparable to the coaching of managers and the job of a leader/manager respectively. In top competitive sports the coach's original function, that is to work on/ with the athlete, is definitely performed at the expense of planning and organizational activities. The proof of a coach's leadership qualities is in the art of finding qualified cocoaches or assistant coaches who are willing and able to achieve the objectives set and to resolutely pursue the common course, that is to "realize aims with the help of assistants". Here parallels between the management of an industrial enterprise and the management of the enterprise of "top competitive sports" are clearly visible.

References

1. **Management Enzyklopädie** Bd. 4, S. 366 ff 1971.

2. **Röthig u.a. (Hrsg.):** Sportwissenschaftliches Lexikon (6. Auflage) S 516.

3. **Deutscher Sportbund:** Berufsbild des Bundestrainers in der Fassung vom 24.07. 1986.

4. **Beck, E.:** "Management im Bundesleistungszentrum Fechten Tauberbishofsheim." Beiheft zu Leistungssport, April 1981.

5. **Deutscher Sportbund:** Fort- und Weiterbildung der Bundestrainer. Analysen, Struktur und Konzeption 1993-1996, April 1993, S. 41-46.

THE COACH AS A METHODOLOGIST FOR CONDITIONING AND TECHNIQUE TRAINING

Madella, A., Manno, R., Beccarini, C., Carbonaro, G., Cei, A.
Scuola dello Sport
Rome, Italy

1. Introduction

The aim of this work is to analyse the relationships between the theoretical knowledge and the practical action of the coach, with reference to the specific requirements of the different sport events. Starting from these considerations we are going to develop some further reflections on the different profiles of the coach and the best educational strategies and procedures to be implemented.

The coach is a skilled professional whose main goal is to allow his athletes or team to perform at the best level at any time with reference to planned goals. This target may seem apparently reductive, if compared to the great quantity of tasks carried out daily by a coach. It is nevertheless a quite complex objective, particularly for the following reasons:

- The achievement of this goal has a curricular basis, as it depends on the cumulation of various developmental stages integrating the effects of maturation and training. It is reasonable to predict that the sport curricula of the elite athletes in the future will last normally between 10 and 20 years. Most of the top level athletes today share a similar background of training and competition. The analysis of the relationships between training and performance development is a central aspect of the activity of the coach.

- A long-term training practice must be based on a very strong and long lasting motivation that should be supported by the coach and modified according to the individual characteristics. The personal history and the social origin of each athlete may require different motivational techniques.

- The complex of the social and biological factors acting on the individual within a specific organizational context, may attract an athlete to a specific sport or event, but it is necessary that the sport participation keeps up and reinforces the athlete's commitment to the discipline. This should occur for all the time needed to achieve the top performance.

- Most of the instructional procedures needed to increase the chances of success of an athlete or a team in a specific sport are not easily codified in normative stages or mandatory skills. This is confirmed by the contradictory results of the analysis of the teachers' and coaches' behaviour. This scientific discipline has not yet demonstrated a clear and unambiguous relationship between coaches' (or teachers') behaviour and achievement of the athletes, at least on the basis of the observational studies of the frequency of specific behaviours (24, 29). This means that the coach should be able to skilfully manage a network of social relations in an open way, with an adaptive attitude that is particularly useful to operate in a very changing environment (3,4).

A further point to be considered concerns the new context of the coach's action. In the most effective and developed situations, the coach works in close collaboration with other professionals, each with his own specific knowledge. The ability to develop and design plans in cooperation with others is therefore a new requirement for the coach but also a new source of stress.

These and other conditions make clear that for such a long period and in such a variable environment, the professional skills of a coach should never be reduced to standardized models, easily communicable and well defined in the competencies required. The professional history of the coaches is, on the contrary, determined mainly by their personal experiences and these, in turn, are influenced by the personality, the professional and cultural context and the individual perception of the situational characteristics. Investigations on expert coaches in many sports have shown that they perceive their experiential knowledge as more effective than formal education (1). That means that each coach should develop and plan specific teaching strategies to guide the athletes and the team in an original way, adapted to the situation and to the specific sport needs. The practical experience of the coach is therefore the key point for the development of effective instructional programs.

2. The coach and sport specificity

It is an impossible task to assess exhaustively all the needs and the competencies needed by coaches working in different sports. It is however clear that the role of the coach takes on distinct aspects in the different sports. For example, in the team sports, the coach is more involved in the social dynamics of the group than in the physical preparation or in injuries rehabilitation programs. Conditioning programs are often administered by other specialists, comparable to a coach from a professional viewpoint, who should operate in close agreement with the decisions and actions of the head coach.

Along with the social problems of the group the major role in determining the coaches' effectiveness in the team sports is played by the knowledge of the technique and the tactics of the event at the individual or collective level. At the top competitive level, there is also a very high frequency of competitions and a marked turnover of coaches in a team (19). That may explain the fact that coaches seldom act on the long term processes (physical preparation, tactical individual preparation or time consuming skill modifications) but prefer to work on the collective tactics and middle-range planning.

Within this context, the most important aspects to be stressed remain the practical experience of the coach, his previous personal competitive experience, his leadership skills and the ability to interact with the media or with other professionals or managers (16). A good proficiency in these abilities improves the consideration of the coach, both by the athletes and the club and influences positively the motivation of the athletes and their perception of physical self-efficacy (30,23,10).

Among the specific skills required is the ability to select the proper tactics and strategies to be applied during the matches and the best composition of the team. It is not common among coaches to pay much attention to the issues of the physical preparation, even when it is aimed at the specific needs of the game. Another aspect which is often neglected by the coach concerns the information about technical and tactical learning. Motor learning research deals with the processes affecting the perception and the decision making process of the players during their competitive activity, but the results often appear too far from the practical needs of the coaches. However, the attention paid to these topics has grown in the last years. The coaches have started to realise that the effectiveness of the tactical models proposed in practice depends on a constant motor and cognitive learning process and effective social relationships and cooperation of the athletes.

A second group of sports that imposes different tasks to the coach is made up by the individual sports. Individual sports may be classified into various subgroups with very different orientation of the preparation. The first group includes the sports based on automatic movements aimed at an aesthetical evaluation by a judge that is decisive for the final ranking. Typical events within this group are gymnastics, ice and roller dancing, diving and others. In these sports, the relationship between the coach and the athlete is individual and the role of the coach is very active and creative because he is involved in a continuous process of observation aimed at providing a continuous and congruent feedback. Good manual skills are required in these sports for spotting, that is to help the athlete to "feel" movements, that are usually acrobatic, complex, and - at least apparently - very dangerous.

The coaches' attention is generally placed on the technical details of the exercise, that is for example the contacts with the ground or the apparatus, the body positions during the flights, etc. In these sports, coaches are usually former athletes with a good knowledge of the specific needs and social environment of these events. The social world of these sports are generally exclusive because the athletes develop their technique in a cumulative and combined way. This requires a long-term process that is very gradual and individualised and starts at a very early age. The diagnosis of the individual needs decides most of the coaches' choices and a proper time management is also required. The body of theoretical knowledge supporting the practical action is often well developed but sometimes superficial because scientific knowledge on these topics is quite limited due to the difficulty of measuring the specific factors of the performance in these sports as is the case for expression and creativity.

A second group of individual sports includes those events in which the performance is mainly based on power or endurance. The events included in the first group are, on the contrary, essentially based on precision and elegance. In this second case, the athletes strive for the maximum power output or mechanical efficiency either on a given distance, in running, swimming, rowing, cycling, cross-country skiing or in jumping or throwing an implement.

In these events, the applied sciences have already produced a great amount of knowledge that heavily affects the role of the coach. The coach usually places a great emphasis not only on the coach-athlete relationship but also on the training program, that is on the contents of the training process. The training schedules and the drills selected must produce an adaptive response and selective modifications in the organism. These modifications have to be controlled as much as possible through tests and a qualitative and quantitative evaluation of training particularly in order to avoid the risks of overtraining.

In such events, another important group of skills must be considered. These skills have a more theoretical base as they allow the coach to single out and preview the individual reactions to training at different times, not only for a short period but also during the long- and middle-term planning. This planning also includes stages in which the performance is reduced intentionally to achieve a better performance in the future (peaking). In such a disciplinary area, the practical experience may be interpreted only through correct theoretical knowledge. This greatly influences the communication between the athlete and the coach, as it happens frequently during practice that the coach estimates the possible outcomes of training in terms of performance. Even the tactical aspects in endurance sports are strictly dependent on the specific level of physical fitness achieved in training so that a "winning surprise effect" is seldom possible.

There are nevertheless also some psychological skills that have special importance. Studies and experience indicate that successful coaches show a greater ability to communicate, to interpret individual sensations, experiences, intuitions, a more effective leadership style, a good ability to take the others' standpoint (12). Creativity and "rational" improvisation my also play a major role. Moreover the coach shall always control the effect of each training program through various evaluation forms and tests supported by a strong theoretical, methodological and statistical knowledge.

Other groups of individual sports can be examined for this discussion:
- combat sports
- shooting sports
- driving sports

In all these cases, the element of specificity are far more relevant in determining the courses of the coach's action. For instance, in the shooting sports, the coach is particularly concerned with training routines based on very specific training loads and aimed at achieving a long lasting and stable concentration. In the combat sports (wrestling, boxing, karate, judo and so on), the pedagogical moves of the coach are aimed at improving the anticipation and the complex reaction times of the athletes through a continuous evaluation of the strategy and effectiveness of the information processing activities carried out by the athletes.

3. The coach and the athlete's performance: theory and practice

We have emphasised the variability and the originality of the specific functions of the coach. There are also many areas of knowledge that might increase the effectiveness of the coaches' action and the reliability of their competencies. This body of knowledge is organized in more or less structured theoretical areas and can also make it easier for the coach to develop a proper methodology based on the findings of scientific research.

Such methodological orientations are organised in a solid body of, as yet developing knowledge, that makes up the so-called theory of training. This discipline puts together scientific data and theories with information extracted by the coaches or, better, by the coaching community from everyday practical experience. This acquisition of new knowledge sometimes proceeds in a non-scientific way, often characterised by improvisation, creativity and authority as it is aimed primarily at solving everyday practical problems.

Training theory is the primary starting point for the action of the coach, as it prevents the training process from being reduced to a simple trial and error approach or the pure reproduction of tradition and authority. Following such an approach, the individual coach could risk being able to evaluate the results only at the end of his professional career. This would obviously cause many mistakes that could be easily avoided simply by having known the results of previous experiences generalized in a specific body of knowledge.

Training theory must consider all that is produced in the sport sciences or, more precisely, in the science applied to coaching. The most relevant and confirmed information is selected and integrated in a flexible way with what is already known. Because of its practical and operational character, training theory aims at producing interpretative models that are very simplified and synthesise, often in a loose form, processes that are much more complex. For a purposive determination of these models, it is very useful to combine the outcomes of the simple observation and description of the action of the coach with a critical evaluation of the effects carried out during the daily practice and the long time periodization.

The success of the coach during his activity increases his motivation to effectively play his role and enables him to continue to work effectively. The coach should always adapt his own methodology to the team or the group he is working with, so to meet the expectations and the preferences of the athletes, thus facilitating a positive perception of his action (3,19). The management of such dynamics is a relevant point for the success of the coach and of the organisation that has hired him.

4. The theory-practice relationship: a basic issue in coaches' educational programs

We have emphasised the operational and practical side of the coaches' work that should be developed in the long period, through a very intensive engagement of the athlete (or the team) in training. Such effects are the consequence of a training practice aimed at modifying the current conditions of the athlete through the increase of his/her fitness and the learning and refining of new skills.

A coach should also guide the team during the preparation by teaching and refining the roles and by guiding the players towards a higher cohesion to achieve the best possible performance. Important changes also occur in the group interaction and organization.

Many disciplinary areas in the science applied to sport, study these phenomena and produce data and information. These sciences can help to establish some models useful for interpreting the transformations and, in a certain way, to predict their effects. It is however, not correct to believe that the mechanical integration of knowledge produced in different disciplinary domains would be the best strategy for coaching education programs. In fact, such an apparently logical consequence does not always correspond to the best operational conditions, because the access to a true interdisciplinary knowledge is a very complex process, probably never to be wholly achieved by a single individual.

The achievement of this interdisciplinary approach for the institution responsible for the coaches' education is expensive both in terms of budget and time and implies a basic knowledge which is not always shared by all the participants.

Rather than looking for a general competence in the applied sciences, that is a too large domain, it is more useful to develop a more sensitive attention to the domain of the sciences applied to training. This is quite a limited context even if it is derived from the previous one and is connected to it both for the method and the contents.

In particular the theory and technique of training, that is a relatively independent discipline within sport sciences, associates simplified models of the development of the performance to a dynamic synthesis of the coaches' experience in very different contexts. The theory and technique of training is aimed at integrating principles common to any sport or, at least, groups of sports, with the specific needs of each event. Such theoretical area may not always be defined as strictly scientific, as it is primarily aimed at an applied knowledge. Moreover, the design of true experiments in this domain would be a hard and time consuming process that would probably never even approximate the true epistemological requirements of an experiment.

On the contrary, it is possible to arrange some limited analytic experiences to uncover the differences between alternative strategies of action put at work in training. Small groups and case studies would be very fruitful for this purpose, while a traditional scientific approach would impose so many limitations resulting in incompatibility with the possibility of testing the whole complexity of the process and the actual nature of the top sport performance. The results, though rigorous and accurate, would never meet the expectations and the needs arising from real practice. Some limited studies have recently been carried out with an experimental attitude that will contribute to the foundation of more developed theoretical models of training. These models might get a practical value if they are connected to experiences made during training processes which have both significant duration and appropriate contents. Moreover, it is questionable that the only resource to develop the coaches' knowledge on the training processes is the traditional empirical (or experimental) approach to knowledge. Hermeneutic and qualitative methodologies may also contribute to the development of testable knowledge thus providing an additional way of acquiring valid information (32,14,21,13).

5. What interdisciplinary education for the coaches?

It is clear that the understanding of the performance, its direction and control, are related to various scientific disciplines with very different contents, methods and standards. The natural sciences permit the understanding of the biomechanical functioning of the body, the cell functions, the changes in the muscle fiber properties and more general organic changes and the role and functioning of the nervous system. On the other hand, the behavioural and social sciences provide useful information on the best strategies and behaviour to improve the performance, and might develop in the coach a better perception of his own behavior and of the group dynamics (22,18,25). The coaches' certification programs have from time to time preferred some approaches rather than others: for example some years ago biochemistry and biomechanics have been the most common educational topics. Later, the teaching and communication skills have become more popular.

A basic interdisciplinary stance cannot be avoided (15) although most of the single sport disciplines my probably be better understood starting from a single disciplinary approach. The claim for a multidimensional disciplinary preparation for the coach, is however difficult to support to its full extent and it is appropriate here to point out its limits and possible dangers. Even if it might apparently convey more information from a quantitative standpoint, it could, on the other hand, engender a great risk of confusion, trapping the coach amid what has been called "a great log jam of diverse....information" (5). To avoid the risk of confusion, the program of preparation should therefore be strongly selective, simple and rigorous and should try to relate the theoretical model of training with that of the discipline and with the practical consequences for the daily practice and long term planning. This is a major issue for the institutions responsible for the coaches' education programs which should usually not be left to the initiative of the individual.

6. Educational programs for professional and amateur coaches

Starting from the analysis of the contents, it is clear that through properly structured educational cycles it is possible to achieve suitable operational ideas and strategies, but it is not possible to achieve an orientation valid for all sports without practical experience. Much of the methodological knowledge of the coach, by definition, is tacit and cannot therefore be taught within a formal program. However, practical experience is only possible for those who were former athletes and/or have been working for a long time in the practice. Moreover, the development of a professional profile must also be based on the cumulation of several experiences, even those made by the "amateur coaches", that, in a certain way, cannot be substituted although they are not able to deal with all the aspects of the modern optimisation of the performance.

We also believe that it is not possible to detect in advance the subjects who may have the greatest chances of success in the coaching career. It is however possible to identify persons with good motivation, practical skills and knowledge of the events and let them enter the educational process to convey the basic theoretical knowledge useful to enhance their performance. These processes of knowledge transmission should be carefully checked in order to avoid a fault common to many coaches' certification program, that is the reduced amount of changes produced by the program in the participants (28). The educational programs should also pay some attention to the need for creativity and innovation, with purposeful teaching methods and situations based on concrete problem solving and a continuous exchange of experiences (5,4). In other words, a compromise is to be reached between a pure experiential knowledge and "low-impact" certification programs. A coach should not receive credentials with only an experience background, although in order to reach the top levels some experience requirements are needed, in particular a successful experience in coaching good athletes and a positive attitude towards change and innovation.

Such a flexible system is now accepted in many countries as it appears to be the most fruitful for the professionalization and the growth of the knowledge. The sport federations in particular benefit from this system that can reduce the costs and reward the most expert or motivated persons even if their chances to get an academic degree are strongly reduced. Organizational conditions should aid the coaches to integrate experience and education. In developing these coaching programs it is very important to select effective organizational forms suitable for the needs of the participants. In most of the cases a continuous education with multiple levels of certification and frequent returns is the best strategy especially when coupled to partial forms of distance learning. A well designed "clinical" experience with systematic supervision by experienced coaches might enable preservice or beginner coaches to stay in the field or enter it with a more thoroughly consolidated knowledge.

7. Which activity levels for the coach?

The background and the status of the coach may be differentiated according to many aspects: the specificity of the sport, the weight of the tradition and the scientific preparation. In the past, for example, many coaches of different sports in Eastern Europe, were involved in an educational itinerary characterised by a full academic background, specific studies and a close partnership with the coaches on the field. In Western Europe, former athletes were dominant, at least in the clubs, particularly in cycling, wrestling, weight-lifting and other events. Due to the lack of a purposeful education, some of them were more interested in the outcomes (competitive results) than in the process. In the last years, this situation has gradually changed and a more detailed professional image of the coach is now emerging. Following the process of modernization of the sport practice, new roles and professional profiles are developing. Among them, we can identify the fitness and strength coach, the instructor of special populations, the expert in talent search, the technical director who is characterised by a managerial attitude, skilled in managing resources according to a true business plan. Many educational institutions active in sport in various countries are currently developing an effort to identify detailed profiles of coaches specialised in youth sport. As youth sport coaches are usually less prepared, it is very important for the sport federations to organize suitable educational programs. The sport clubs are very interested too in the success of these programs because the commitment of young people to sport is strongly dependent on the competencies of their coaches.

In general, with the growth of the athletes' qualification, a higher level of specialisation becomes more important for the coaches, even if some exceptions are possible. This is also confirmed by the limited amount of available studies. Haslam (17) has found that there is a great interest toward the psycho-social components at the basic levels and a balance between social and biological sciences at higher coaching levels. In fact, a coach with a good background in the social sciences may greatly influence with his behaviour and strategies the initial decision to participate, the whole process of socialisation into a sport and later the development of a specific motivation (10). Durand (9) has also indicated the plurality of the motivations directed at various targets by the young athlete, therefore stressing the need for purposive psychological skills by the coach himself.

References

1. **Baria, A, Salmela, J, Coté, J., Russell, S., Moraes, L. Baier, G., Wang, R., Pristarincha, M.** (1993) An international and comparative analysis of coaching process in gymnastics, Sport Proceedings ISSP Congress, Lisbon.

2. **Brunelle, J**. (1987), La formation des intervenants en Activitès physiques. Proceedings of the AIESEP World Convention, Trois Rivières.

3. **Chelladurai, P., Arnott, M.** (1985), Decision styles in coaching: Preferences of basketball players, Research Quarterly, 56,1: 15-24.

4. **Cieslinski, W., Perechuda, K.** (1993) Heuristics methods as the tool of the development of the coach; Sport Proceedings ISSP Congress Lisbon.

5. **Colwin, C.** (1991), Swimming into the 21st Century. Champaign: Human Kinetics Press.

6. **Cotè, J., Trudel, P., Salmela, J.** (1993), A conceptual model of coaching, ISSP Congress, Lisbon.

7. **Cotè, J., Salmela, J., Boria, A., Russel, S.J.** (1993), Assessing the coaching process of experts in gymnastics. Sport Proceedings ISSP Congress, Lisbon.

8. **Crespo, M., Balaguer, I., Atienza F.** (1993), Variables influencing leadership styles in tennis coaches. Proceedings ISSP Congress. Lisbon.

9. **Durand, M.** (1987), Le sport et L'enfant, Paris: PUF.

10. **Escartì, A., Garcia-Ferriol, A. Cervellò, E.** (1993), Relationship between the Perception of the Coach's Competence with Physical Self-Efficacy and Motivation Level, Proceedings ISSP Congress. Lisbon.

11. **Graham, G.** (1987), The developing Physical Education Teacher and Coach: Empirical and Research insight in Proceedings of the AIESEP World Convention, Trois Rivières.

12. **Gravelle, L.H, Deschenne, L.G.** (1987) Enhancing the coach athlete relationships. Proceedings of the AIESEP World Convention, Trois Rivières.

13. **Griffin, P. , Templin, T.J.** (1989), An overview of qualitative research, pp. 399-409 in Darst, P. W. et al. (eds) Analyzing Physical Education and Sport Instruction. Champaign: Human Kinetics.

14. **Groessing, S.** (1978), Consideration of the scientific character of sport pedagogy, pp. 84-92 in Sport Pedagogy: Contents and methodology, Haag H. (ed) University Park Press.

15. **Grupe, O.** (1971), Einleitung in die Sportwissenschaft, Sportwissenschaft 1:7-18.

16. **Hagedorn, G.** (1987), Trainer - die soziale Rolle eines integrierten Aussenseiters, pp. 58-70 in The Physical Education Teacher and Coach Today, Volume I, Aiesep WeltKongress 1986, Heidelberg.

17. **Haslam, J.R.** (1990) Expert assessment of the national coaching certification program, theory component. Canadian Journal of Sport Science, 15(3) 201-212.

18. **Horne, T., Carron, A.V.** (1985), Compatibility in coach-athlete relationships, Journal of Sport Psychology, 7: 137-149.

19. **Isberg, L.** (1993), What does it mean to be an elite coach in team sport, Sport Proceedings ISSP Congress, Lisbon.

20. **Kruger, A., Casselmann, J.** (1985), A comparative analysis of the top level track and field coaches in the USA.

21. **Locke, L.** (1987), Qualitative research as a form of scientific inquiry in sport and physical education, Research Quarterly, 60, 1: 1-20.

22. **Osterhoudt, R.G.** (1978) The body of knowledge, pp. 29-34, Sport studies, in Sport Pedagogy: Contents and methodology, Haag H. (ed) University Park Press.

23. **Patrickson, G., Eriksson, S.** (1990), Young Perception of their coach. International Journal of Physical Education, 27 (4).

24. **Pieron, M.** (1986) Analisi dell'insegnamento. Roma: Società Stampa. Sportiva

25. **Prapavessis, H., Gordon S.** (1991), Coach-player relationship in tennis, Canadian Journal of Sport Sciences (Supplement 3): 229-233.

26. **Roehr, G.** (1990) Sportpaedagogische Erkenntnisse zur Fuehrung trainierender Kinder im frühen Schulalter, Theorie und Praxis der Koerperkultur 165-171.

27. **Salmela, J.H, Draper, S.P, Laplante, D.** (1993), Development of expert coaches of team sport, Proceedings ISSP Congress, Lisbon.

28. **Siedentop, D.** (1987), The practice of sport pedagogy- physical education and coaching - Proceedings of the AIESEP World Convention Trois Rivières.

29. **Silverman, S.** (1991), Research on teaching in physical education, Research Quarterly, 62,4:352-364.

30. **Smith, R.E. Smoll, F.L., Curtis, B.** (1979), Coach effectiveness training: A cognitive- behavioral approach to enhancing relationship skills in youth sport coaches, Journal of Sport Psychology, 1: 59-75.

31. Tinning, R. (1982), Improving instructional model of coaching, Sport Coach 4, 37-41.

32. Widmer, R. (1978), Physical education as theory in sport pedagogy: Contents and methodology, Haag H. (ed.) University Park Press.

33. Wilke, K. (1991), Didactics of high level competitive sport - an academical approach or an artisan education of coach, in Tenebaum, G. and Eiger, D. (eds), Coach education: proceedings of the Maccabiah-Wingate International Congress. Netanya, Wingate Institute, pp 7-24.

ELITE SPORT
THE PRESENT LEVEL OF SCIENTIFIC RESEARCH
- LEGITIMATION, DESIGNS AND METHODS -

Mester, J.
German Sport University
Cologne, Germany

1. Legitimation

After the first main approaches to scientific research in elite sport, e.g. in the context of work physiology (e.g. ÅSTRAND 1970; HOLLMANN 1976) or psychology (e.g. HACKER 1978; WELFORD 1976), in Germany the interest of various scientific branches in human capacity and adaptability has been growing more and more. The field of elite sport nowadays can be regarded as a major field of scientific research of nearly all areas of sport sciences and sport related sciences. Here there may be divided two groups of scientific areas. On the one hand those having relatively strong connections with their scientific "mother branches" using the corresponding methods, e.g. sports medicine, sports psychology etc. On the other hand those approaches that have been developed in sport of its own, e.g. "training science," "movement science," "human movement studies" etc. (see Fig. 1).

Fig. 1: Scientific Branches in Elite Sport

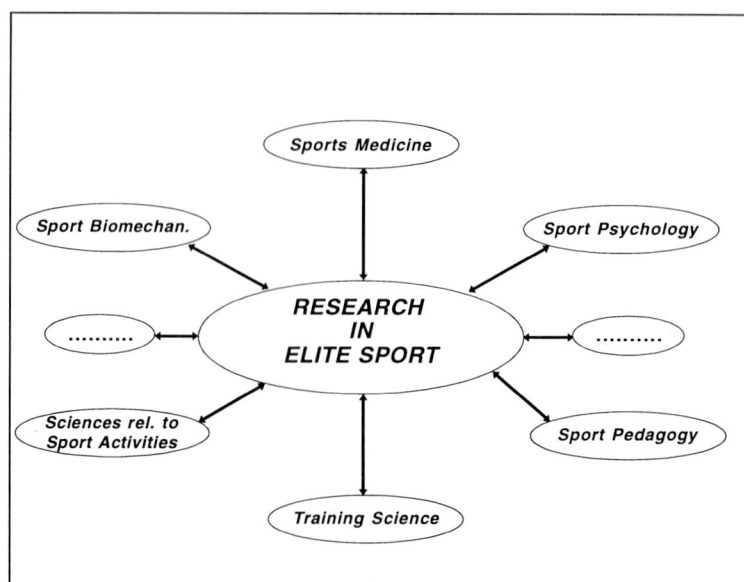

The specific influences of these different scientific approaches in the past often lead to problems of transfer of the results. In elite sport this has to be regarded as a major problem because often the great expectations of the athletes and coaches caused non sufficient fundamental research advancing the period of application. Especially the situation in the countries of the former "Eastern Block" proved the danger of too strong political influences. Actually there are several various threats to research in elite sport that can be summed up as follows:
- Unbalanced influences by governments,
- unbalanced influence by commercialism and
- unbalanced expectations of athletes and coaches.

These aspects may lead to
- an insufficient public control and scientific discussion of scientific results,
- to a disrespect of ethical standards and
- finally to disappointment on all parts.

It is therefore absolutely necessary to define standards for scientific research in elite sport. This research can be regarded as an integrative and interdisciplinary scientific investigation of the theoretical implications of sport to optimize the performance. At the same time the risk of injury and harm for the athletes must be minimized. Research in elite sport stands for research for human beings and research with human beings and this requires the highest standards of scientific conscientiousness and accuracy as well as of control of aims and methods.

The areas of the different activities in research may be described by the "DAAP-Model":
- **D**iagnosis of the state of performance,
- **A**nalysis of the causality of performance,
- **A**nalysis of the development of performance and
- **P**rognosis of the process of performance.

2. Designs

In the past most of the research with fundamental orientation focussed on the model of so-called "General Limiting Factors." These factors stood mainly for certain physiological elements, such as "strength," "endurance," "speed." Early investigations carried out by sports medicine/physiology mostly concentrated on parameters of the cardiovascular system. They led to the models of endurance like the following one (see Fig. 2). As this is very well known, it does not need any explanation.

Fig. 2: Model of Aerobic and Anaerobic Endurance (HOLLMANN 1976, 1990)

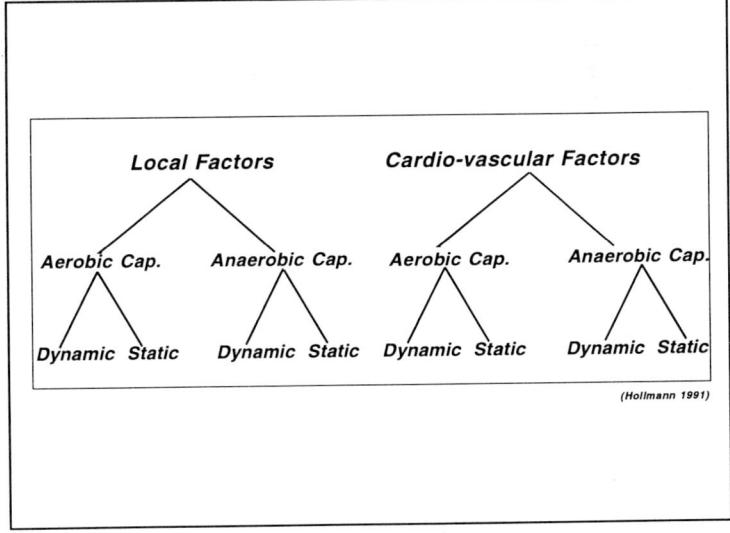

At similar level of differentiation is the model shown first by BÜHRLE et al. (1983) for the phenomenon of muscle strength, in the sense of "speed strength" or "power." As in most sports it is necessary to produce a certain amount or a maximum of strength in a minimum of time, this parameter of "power" is a very important one.

Fig. 3: Model of Muscle Strength ("power") (mod. BÜHRLE et al. 1983)

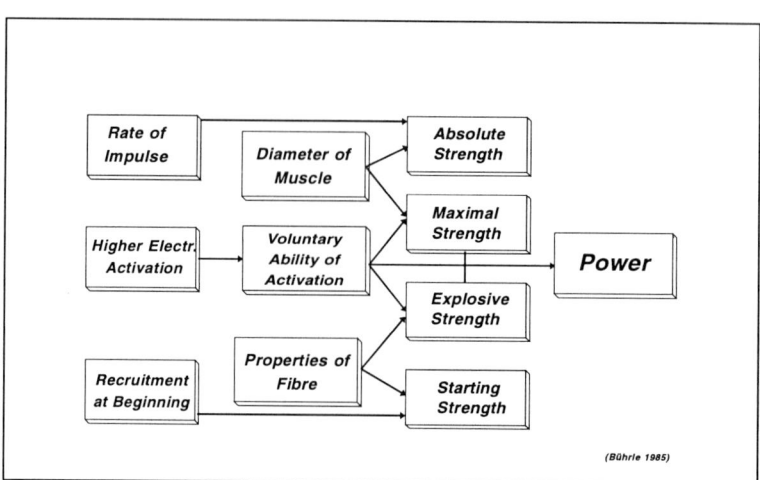

The level of differentiation shown in Fig. 2 and 3, of course, can be characterized to be rather general. Furthermore the investigations leading to these models have normally been carried out in characteristic sports. The parameter of "power" mostly is connected with jumping events, e.g. in track and field, the parameters of endurance connected with running, swimming, cycling, rowing etc.

These models then have often been applied to sports that are very different concerning physiological or psychological strain. Even if there is a certain similarity between some sports, this application in the past often led to misinterpretations and misapplication. The eccentric component of a normal drop-jump, for example, cannot be compared with the eccentric event in alpine skiing, although in both cases a clearly eccentric mode of contraction can be proven. The eccentric phase in a normal jump event has the goal of producing a maximum of "reactive energy", whereas in alpine skiing this phase should render a modulation of ground-reaction forces for an optimum of ski-control.

The models mentioned above allow a systematic localization of specific elements of performance at a rather general level. Models of this kind were supported in the course of the further scientific research especially by investigations concerning energy yield and supply and adaptability of the biological systems of the athletes in elite sport (e.g. HUIJING 1992; SALE 1992). These results were of great importance because of the high training loads that hardly can be increased in most sports. In many cases rising the training load does not lead to an improvement of performance but to the contrary, often named "over-training-syndrom" (e.g. NEWSHOLME 1992).

The protein-metabolism here is a strong indicator of former and actual adaptation events. If the total energy requirements and expenditure cannot be fulfilled by normal food intake, the metabolism shifts towards its own structural protein mass. Furthermore much training efforts are directed to raise muscle mass or to create a certain adaptation mode (e.g. explosive strength). So the status of the protein metabolism seems to contain a lot of information about the actual adaptation and probably also about the adaptability. Obviously these investigations are a very important element of scientific research in elite sport (e.g. MADER 1984; YOUNG 1981) (see Fig. 4).

Fig. 4: Adaptability to Training Load (MADER 1990)

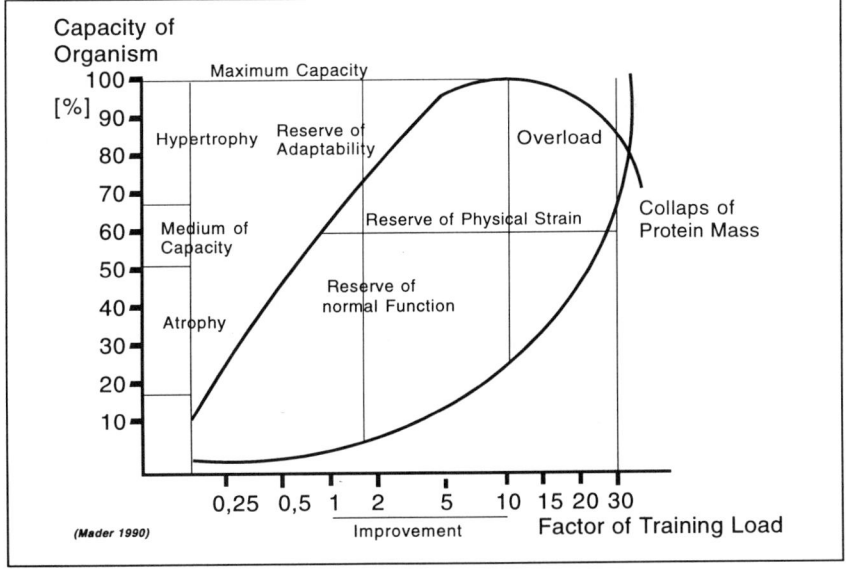

The figure shows the function between training load in a logarithmic scale and the adaptation capacity of the organism. Between about 20 and 50% of the maximum capacity the area of muscle atrophy can be situated. If on the other hand the training load is too high, there is no further hypertrophy but a collapse of protein mass. This is usually accompanied by a loss of performance. Thus the present level of scientific research is generally directed towards the cellular area (e.g. HENRIKSSON 1992).

3. Methods

Still one of the major problems in elite sport is the variability itself and the periodical change and duration of performance. Since the first systematical approaches in analysing training and competition periods (MATWEJEW 1956, 1975), this problem has been focussed. Nowadays at the border of adaptability in elite sport it is one of the objectives of training to reduce the variability of performance. Especially in athletics it is rather easy to quantify this variability and to compare between the various events (see Fig. 5).

Fig. 5: Variability of Performance in Athletics (World Championships 1993)

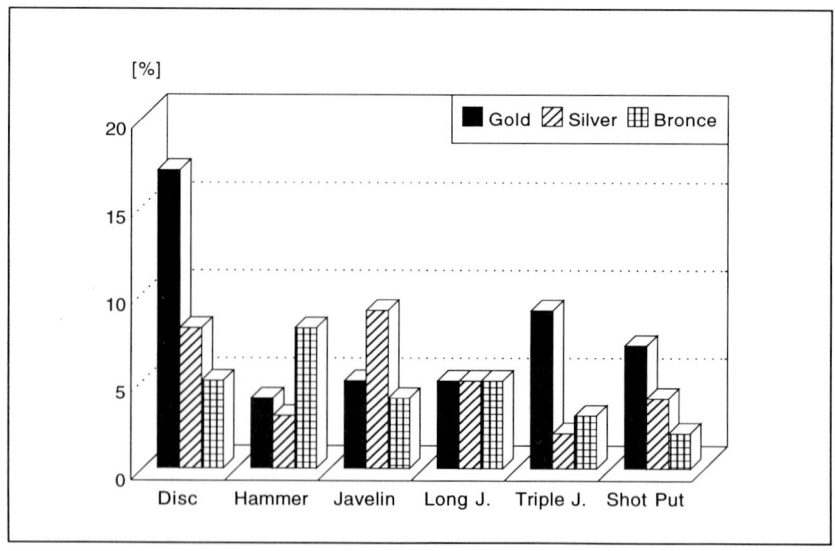

The figure shows for certain events the individual variability between the given number of trials for the first to third place in the competition. Only in Discus Throw a variability of more than 15% in the various trials can be regarded and this only for the gold medalist. In all other events the intraindividual variability between the best and the worst trial is less than 10% with an average of about 5%. The absolute range of this small variability may cause problems for the accuracy of the methods to be used for diagnosis in elite sport, especially for those methods used in field-tests.

On the other hand usually in the training of elite sport scientific investigations in the sense of diagnosis of performance can be carried out only very few times in the course of a year. This causes severe problems in describing the variability and a possible development of performance. The following figure illustrates this by using the data of jumping-tests as a criterion for speed-strength (see Fig. 6).

Fig. 6: Time Series of Jumping-Tests

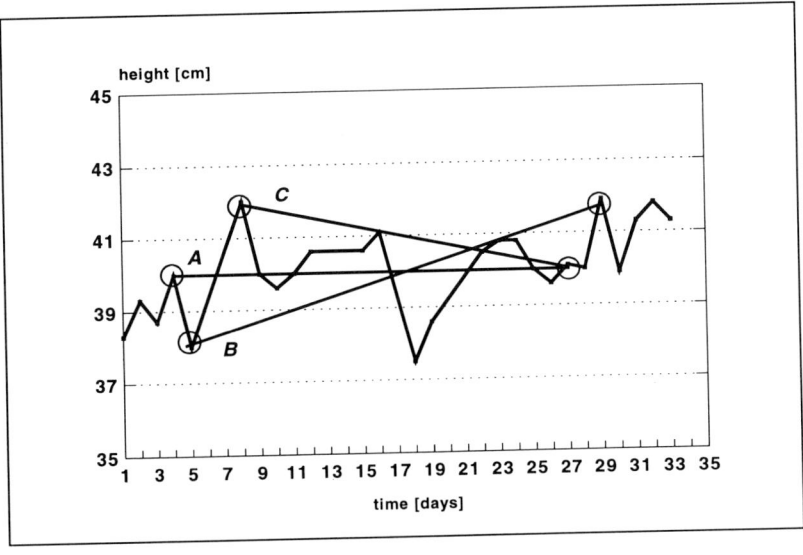

The figure shows the variability of performance in the course of 35 days. If in this time only two measurements would be carried out this could lead to severe misinterpretation of the real variability. Taking the first measurement of the jumping-height e.g. at the fourth day and then the second measurement at the 27th day, this would suggest no change of performance (line "A"). If the first data were collected on the fifth day and the second measurement was taken at the 29th day an improvement of jumping height would be the result (line "B"). Taking the first data at the 7th day and the second one on the 27th day a loss of performance would be suggested (line "C").

Of course, the (true) periodical characteristics of the variability of performance can only be detected if the number of measurements per given period of time is great enough. This requirement, however, is difficult to fulfill in the practical situation of elite sport, at least, if complex and expensive methods are necessary. The only solution is to develop methods which are simpler and easy to handle.

If this requirement then is fulfilled, methods of time series analysis and single case studies are the proper approach for the diagnosis of performance and the analysis of development. The first major question is whether a trend concerning the training can be proven. This analysis of trend should be carried out after investigation of the "Base-Line" as a characteristic of "normal" variability. The following figure shows the results of such an analysis with the given data of the jumping-height.

Fig. 7: Time Series of Power in Strength Training

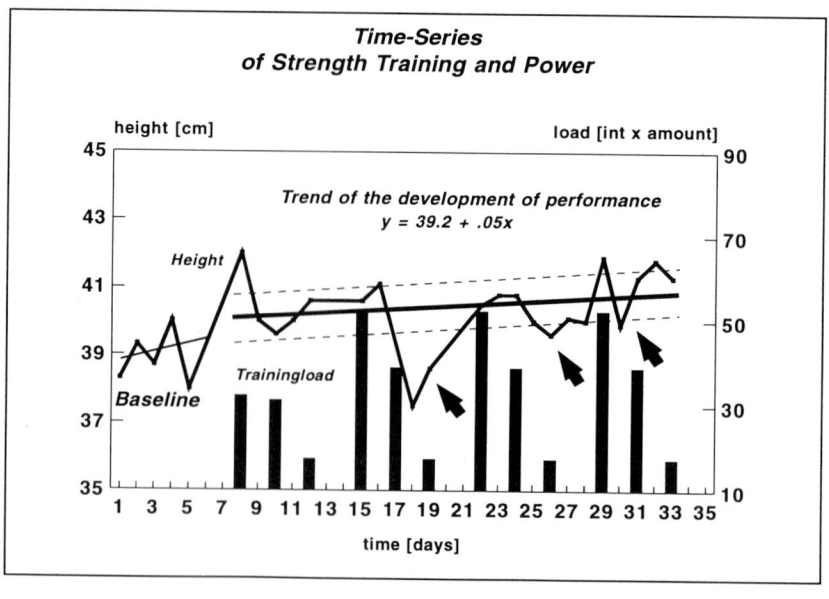

For these data a linear trend can be proved. In the course of the training period the jumping-height improved following the regression equation y = 39.2 + 0.5x. Being the origin of the development, training was quantified by defining the "training load" as product of training amount and intensity. This allows the statement that the improvement of jumping-height is due to the strength training in the given period of time. The question of the periodical changes resp. the variability of performance in the course of training cannot be answered (e.g. MORITANI 1992).

This problem can be analysed by using autocorrelation methods resp. the correlation of a time series with itself (SCHLITTGEN, STREITBERG 1987). The autocorrelation coefficients for the given data show significant values of .45 with a lag of "4" indicating periodical changes of the jumping-height within four days. This result of the jumping-height as indicator of power, of course, can be of high value for planning the performance in the context of competitions.

As common parameters for training-load normally the "amount", i.e. for example the duration of training and the "intensity," for example running-speed, is used. It is of great importance to find out the proper balance between amount on the one hand and intensity on the other. In many sports before competitions a rising of the intensity is used to optimize performance. It is often quite difficult, however, to find out the influence of changes in amount or intensity on performance as both parameters are linked closely together.

One method in the frame of time-series analyses is cross-correlation. The results of such a cross-correlation are shown in Fig. 8.

Fig. 8: Cross-Correlation between Training Load and Power

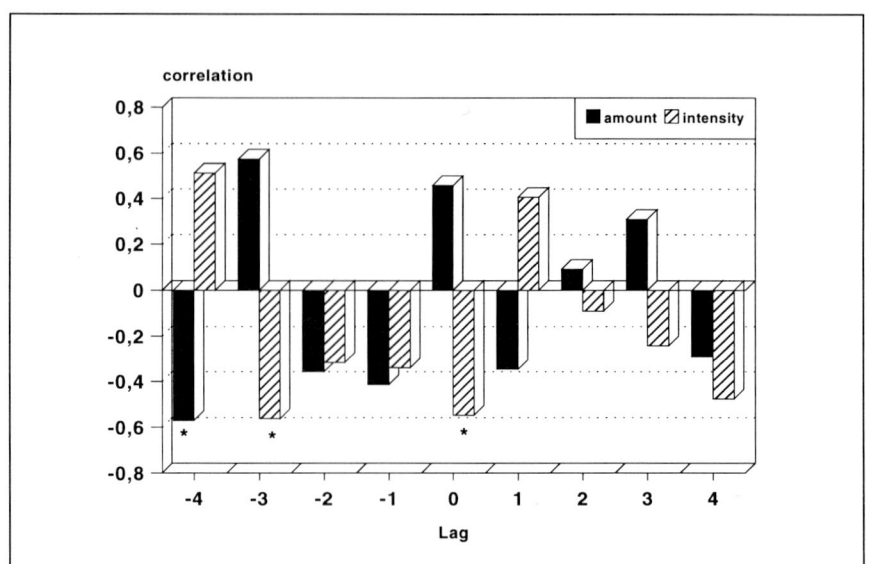

The figure illustrates that significant coefficients of cross-correlation exist between lag -4 and -3, that means, in a similar time context as in autocorrelation concerning the periodical changes of performance. Obviously the amount and the intensity of training play an inverse role in the influence on jumping-height in the course of time. While there is a negative significant cross-correlation between amount and jumping-height the intensity shows positive values at the lag of -4. At the lag of -3 this changes to an inverse result. There is a positive cross-correlation for the amount and a negative value for intensity.

The use of methods of time-series analysis and single-case studies can contribute to prove trends in the development of performance. Then these methods allow to detect periodical changes in the variability of the performance indicator. Finally these methods may reveal interrelationships between parameters of training, such as amount and intensity, and the development of performance indicating variables in the course of time. Thus it would facilitate to analyse the process of adaptation, especially at the limits of adaptability.

Most of the methods nowadays used in scientific investigations in elite sport naturally try to work out the results with a maximum of accuracy and methodological precision. On the other hand even data collected with biomechanical or physiological methods include a methodological error not smaller than 1-2%. In elite sport the absolute range of performance is relatively small. If, for example, there is an improvement of 3 - 5%, a top performance can be reached. As in most cases one single method cannot be sufficient for diagnostics of a complex structure of performance complex approaches and the use of combined methods are necessary. The methodological error, however, produced by these combined methods easily can reach the range of variability of the criterion (see Fig. 9).

Fig. 9: Complex Scientific Approaches

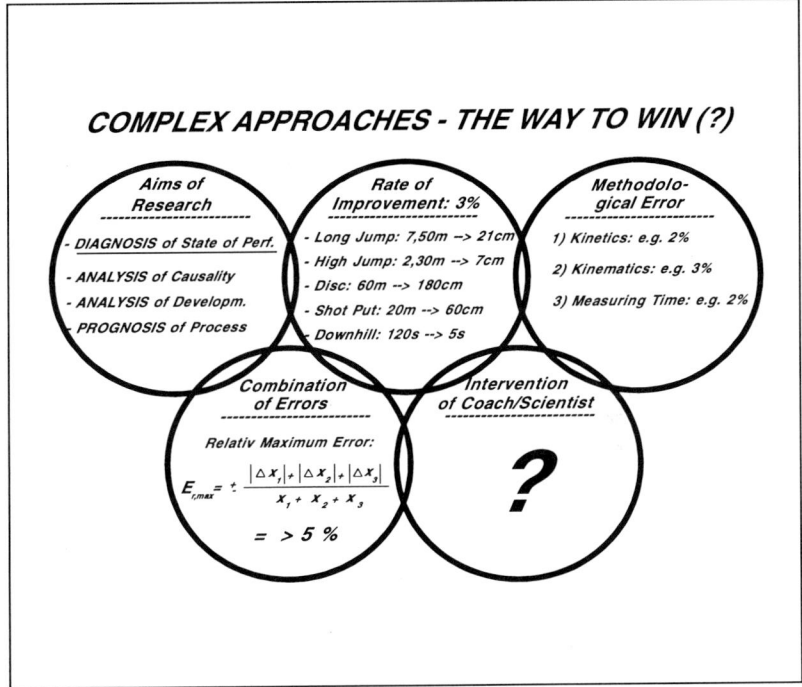

The figure shows some examples to illustrate the problem of carrying out complex diagnosis in elite sport. A rate of improvement of e.g. +3%, would lead to severe changes in quality of performance. This would mean +21 cm in Long Jump on a given value of 7.5 m and -5 s in Alpine Downhill on a given value of 120 s. On the other hand the methodological errors for kinematic or kinetic devices are usually not less than 2%. Following the rules of computing "combined errors" this surely would lead to an error rate of > 5%. Obviously thus it is scientifically not quite easy to detect the reasons for differences in performance. Furthermore after the diagnosis, the intervention of the coach and/or the scientist in the training is to be carried out. Here other errors in this process of treatment surely can occur.

This raises the question for future ideas of diagnosis. In the actual situation of elite sport the major problem is quite often to keep the athletes healthy (COMMANDRÉ et al. 1989). On the ethical basis this, doubtless, is the most important goal. The individual response on a given training load can be very different. This refers to adaptation rate as well as to health-maintenance. At the limits of adaptability it therefore seems to be more important to focus on the rate of change of performance for the individual athlete as to gather so-called "General Factors" that determine the performance.

Time-series analyses of this kind yet require at least 50 measurements per given time that should be regarded and equidistant periods in which the measurements are taken. These requirements are often difficult to fulfill in the situation of training and competition in elite sport. There are, however, any other methods in the statistical sense to test significant changes in performance for the individual athlete.

Following the requirements of time series analyses on the one hand and those of scientific explanation of performance on the other, it is necessary to develop research models with methods on various levels of abstraction and differentiation (see Fig. 10).

Fig. 10: Scientific Research in Elite Sport: Methods at Different Levels

[Figure: RESEARCH IN ELITE SPORT — Methods on Different Levels of Complexity. Chart showing Methods Level 3, Methods Level 2, Methods Level 1, and Perform. [cm] plotted against Days (2–38).]

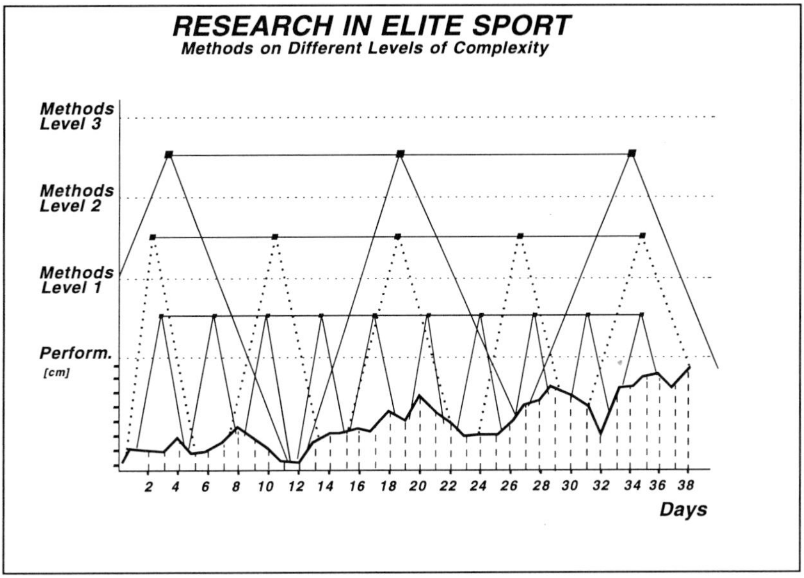

The figure shows symbolically a model of applying methods at different levels of abstraction and complexity. At the lower levels methods should be involved that are easy to use and that thus can be applied frequently, e.g. force measurements as indicators of muscle strength. As these parameters only can describe the development of performance, at higher levels methods with more scientific complexity and evidence must be used. These methods, e.g. parameters of metabolism, then could be applied to explain the actual performance and changes in performance. The higher methodological level thus could "look" at the lower level and contribute informations on variability of performance and even in the sense of prognosis of performance.

4. Summary

1. As scientific research in elite sport is directed towards human beings and as it carried out with human beings it requires as highest ethical standards as possible. This is of special importance because of the growing influences of commercialization in elite sport. Scientific results of research in elite sport must be discussed in public as well as all other scientific work should be carried out under public control.

2. The actual designs of scientific investigation in elite sport are formed by growing differentiation of objectives and methods. There is a growing concern about the transformation of the results into practical application. The key element can be located in an improvement of the education of coaches.

3. In many areas of elite sport the limits of adaptability are reached and the training loads hardly can be increased. So the designs of research should be oriented more to the analysis of individual changes of performance than to detecting "general factors" that may influence the performance.

4. The methods to be used for detecting individual changes can be found in time series analyses and single case studies. Thus, trends and periodical changes of performance can be analysed. As these methods can only render a description of changes in performance, it is necessary to use methods with a higher degree of complexity and explanation. The methods thus can form a model with various levels of abstraction and scientific differentiation.

References

1. **Åstrand, P.-O., Rodahl, K.**: Textbook of Work Physiology. McGraw-Hill 1970.

2. **Balsom, P.D. et al.**: Creatine supplementation and dynamic high-intensity intermittant exercise. Scand J Med Sci Sports 3:143-149, 1993

3. **Bührle, M., Schmidtbleicher, D., Ressel, H.**: Die spezifische Diagnose der einzelnen Kraftkomponenten im Hochleistungssport. Leistungssport 13 (1983) 11.

4. **Commandré, F.A. et al.**: Diagnostische Prinzipien. In: Dirix, A., Knuttgen H.G., Tittel, K. (Hg.): Olympia Buch der Sportmedizin. Deutscher Ärzte Verlag. Köln 1989.

5. **Hacker, W.**: Allgemeine Arbeits- und Ingenieurspsychologie. Deutscher Verlag der Wissenschaften. Berlin 1978.

6. **Hollmann, W., Hettinger, Th.**: Sportmedizin - Arbeits- und Trainingsgrundlagen. Schattauer Verlag. Stuttgart 1976 und 1990.

7. **Komi, P.V. (Ed.)**: Strength and Power in Sport. Blackwell. Oxford 1992.

8. **Henriksson, J.**: Cellular Mechanism and Endurance. In: Shephard, R.J., Åstrand, P.-O. (Eds.): Endurance in Sport. Blackwell. Oxford 1992.

9. **Huijing, P.A.**: Elastic Potential of Muscle. In: Komi, P.V. (Ed.): Strength and Power in Sport. Blackwell. Oxford 1992.

10. **Mader, A.**: Eine Theorie zur Berechnung der Dynamik und des steady state von Phosphorylierungszustand und Stoffwechselaktivität der Muskelzelle als Folge des Energiebedarfs. Habilitationsschrift. Köln 1984.

11. **Mader, A.**: Aktive Belastungsadaptation und Regulation der Proteinsynthese auf zellulärer Ebene. Dt. Ztschrft f. Sportmed. 41:40-58, 1990

12. **Matwejew, L.P.**: Periodisierung des sportlichen Trainings. Moskau 1959 bzw. Bartels und Wernitz. Berlin 1975.

13. **Moritani, T.**: Time Course of Adaptation during Strength and Power Training. In: Komi, P.V. (Ed.): Strength and Power in Sport. Blackwell. Oxford 1992.

14. **Newsholme, E.A. et al.**: Biochemical Causes of Fatigue and Overtraining. In: Shephard, R.J., Åstrand, P.-O. (Eds.): Endurance in Sport. Blackwell. Oxford 1992.

15. **Sale, D.G.**: Neural Adaptation to Strength Training. In: Komi, P.V. (Ed.): Strength and Power in Sport. Blackwell. Oxford 1992

16. **Shephard, R.J., Åstrand, P.-O. (Eds.)**: Endurance in Sport. Blackwell. Oxford 1992.

17. **Schlittgen, R., Streitberg, B.**: Zeitreihenanalyse. Verlag Oldenburg. München 1987.

18. **Welford, A.T.**: Skilled Performance. Foresman and Company. Glenview 1976.

19. **Young, V.R.**: Skeletal muscle and whole body protein metabolism in relation to exercise. In: Poortmans, J., Niset, B.: Exercise and Hormon Regulation. University Park Press. Baltimore 1981.

Fundamental and Applied Research in Team Sports

Reilly, Th.
School of Human Sciences, Liverpool John Moores University
UK

1. Introduction

There are difficulties posed by team sports that are not evident when international sports are investigated by sports scientists. The major one is the identification of performance itself, individual contributions towards the team effort and individual characteristics that influence the performance. In distance running for example there is a definite measure of performance in race time and in physiological variables such as maximal oxygen uptake (V02max) or lactate threshold that can be related to this performance. Team sports are more complex but this should not be a deterrent to those attempting to show links between theories of sports science and performance in team sports.

In the realm of theorists are scientists, statisticians, lecturers, medical and paramedical personnel and engineers. Their work may impinge on sports practice but they are not necessarily dependent upon it. Practitioners include the professionals directly concerned with games or team sports. They include managers, coaches, trainers and players. Perhaps also supporters and administrators should be considered.

2. Characterisation of Team Sports

Team sports may conveniently be distinguished as indoor or court games and outdoor field games. The former group would embrace basketball, handball, ice-hockey, netball and volleyball. The latter would cover games such as baseball, cricket, football, hockey, hurling and lacrosse. These illustrate the variety of sports there are. National sports, such as hurling in Ireland or shinty in Scotland, have enormous local appeal: the All Ireland hurling final is played on the first Sunday in September before a capacity crowd of 65,000. Goals are 160 m apart, teams are 15 a-side and the ball may be hit with the caman (stick) over 100 m. Analysis of the fitness, skills and safety requirements of such games presents a considerable intellectual challenge to the sports scientist.

It appears that more effort has been made in applying science to football than to other team sports. This is evidenced by the work of the World Commission of Sports Biomechanics (under the patronage of the International Council for

Sports Science and Physical Education) in promoting sports science conferences related to sports. Conferences focusing on specific sports are held every 4 years, the longest history being in swimming with its Seventh World Congress scheduled for Colorado Springs in September 1994. Other specialist groups include Science and Golf, whose Second Congress is at St. Andrews (Scotland) in July 1994 and Science and Racket Sports, the inaugural Congress for which was held at Liverpool in July 1993. Team sports are exemplified by the Science and Football Congresses, the third of which is scheduled for Cape Town (South Africa) at the time of the Third Rugby Union World Cup in Summer 1995.

3. Sports Science Support and Football

The complexity of relating science and football is underlined by the inclusion of various football codes within the brief. These include association football (soccer), Rugby Union, Rugby League, Australian Rules, American football and other national codes such as Gaelic football. Nevertheless the body of knowledge is far enough advanced for academic programmes to be validated for specific applications to football. At Liverpool John Moores University, the first Science and Football Diploma was offered in September 1991. This one-year course is concerned with soccer in the main, is run in conjunction with the professional clubs on Merseyside and attracts students from European Community countries as well as from Japan.

Other indicators of the acceptance of scientific applications to soccer are the increased outlet for publication of information. The European Society of Team Physicians in Football has its own periodical, Science and Football, published courtesy of Barcelona F. C. This complements the volumes published as Proceedings of the World Congress of Science and Football (Reilly et al., 1988; Reilly, Clarys and Stibbe, 1993). There are also many research reports referring to football that are published in the sports science journals. On the practical side professional soccer clubs are increasingly willing to take on scientifically trained personnel among their staff. These include specialists in nutrition, physiology, training, fitness and psychology.

Sports Science support in England is formalised by linking sports science institutions with systemisation of coach education. The National Coaching Foundation, established in 1983, sponsored a network of 16 National Coaching Centres where guidance, counselling and fitness testing services are offered to athletes. The "sports science education programme", administered by the National Coaching Foundation, was set up in 1988 to provide a service to the various national governing bodies of sport. Sport science support includes physiological monitoring of top performers and guidance of training programmes, biomechanical analysis and dissemination of educational material and psychological preparation for competition. The system operates under accreditation of scientific laboratories and personnel to ensure quality control of services. Most of the major team sports are included among the 42 projects currently funded (Reilly, 1992).

Amongst the institutions contributing towards the sport science support programme is the Football Associations' National Human Performance Centre at Lillishall. Projects embrace cricket, women's hockey and Rugby League in addition to soccer. This is the one laboratory (or centre) external to academic institutions that is dedicated to a specific sport. Besides, the predominance of research work in team sports has been on soccer, due most likely to its worldwide appeal. Consequently, soccer features mainly in the content of the following sections.

4. Research in Soccer

Research into soccer may be categorised as : - (i) biological aspects, (ii) behavioural aspects. The former would include work-rate (exercise intensity), physiological demands, fitness profiles, training, nutrition, biomechanics and injuries as main thrusts. Behavioural topics would cover match analysis, skills analysis, stresses, team cohesion and special groups. Other issues such as talent identification are explored elsewhere in a more global long-term endeavour.

In one of the first applications of motion analysis to professional soccer, it was presumed that work-rate could be expressed as distance covered in a game, since this determines the energy expenditure. Activities were coded according to intensity of movements, the main categories being walking, jogging, cruising, sprinting whilst other game-related activities such as backing, playing the ball and so on were investigated. The method of monitoring activity was checked for reliability, objectivity and validity (Reilly and Thomas, 1976), and results from the applications have appeared in various outlets (Reilly, 1990; 1993).

On average playing soccer entails a change in activity every 6 s, an appreciable burst of energy output every 30 s and an all-out sprint every 90 s. The overall distance covered is about 10 km for outfield players and between 3 and 4 km for the goalkeeper. Most of the activity is sub-maximal and aerobic, although the critical runs may be anaerobic.

The distance covered in possession of the ball is about 2 % of the total. Hence 98 % of the activity is concerned with movement off the-ball or one-touch plays. Superimposed on the activity profile are the frequent acceleration, deceleration, angled runs and game-related actions such as tacking and jumping that add to the physiological demands of match-play.

Distance covered in a game, although a crude measure of performance was found to be related to aerobic fitness (VO2max). It also differs between positional roles, midfield players covering the greatest distances and possessing the higher aerobic fitness values. The aerobic emphasis is reflected also in analysis of muscle biopsies of soccer players which tend to show biochemical characteristics similar to endurance-trained athletes (Reilly, 1994). It is further underlined when the training responses of soccer players are analysed with traditional radio telemetry, short-range heart rate telemetry (Sports-tester) or blood lactate concentrations (Reilly, 1990).

There is a likelihood in field games that work-rate drops towards the end of the match. This is confirmed in soccer where the fall-off in work-rate appears to be inversely related to aerobic fitness (Reilly, 1994). It has been shown that this form of fatigue is determined by initial glycogen stores in the thigh muscles, those players starting with low glycogen levels being less capable of sprinting towards the end of play (Saltin, 1973). For this reason attention is directed to dietary preparation for team-sport competition (Jacobs, 1988) and this is increasingly accepted by professional clubs.

The style of play interacts with the physiological demands and individual roles. The direct method of soccer players places great reliance on physical fitness of outfield players since they are expected to put pressure on opponents who have possession of the ball. This is a characteristic style of some English clubs and contrasts with a more methodical build-up of offensive plays in European Community countries. It was applied with reasonable success by the Ireland international team which qualified for the finals of the European Nations Championship in 1988 and World Cup in 1990. The relatively greater success in the latter tournament might be explained by the longer recovery between matches that the fixture list permitted and a generally available carbohydrate-based diet in Italy.

The Irish style of play tends to even out differences in work-rate between playing positions. Nevertheless it has evolved to accommodating individual differences. For example, team membership for the 1994 World Cup qualifying matches included Manchester United's Roy Keane k.nown for a high work-rate and 1993 "player of the year" Paul McGrath (from Aston Villa) whose training programme is habitually hampered by a chronic knee injury. It acknowledges the acceptance of team managers to consider building teams around exceptionally gifted players, such as happened with Paul Gascoigne for England and Diego Maradona for Argentina.

Activity profiles during matches can be interpreted in terms of training needs and programmes. They also can form the basis for which the acyclical patterns can be translated into experimental models for laboratory-based studies of physiological responses to exercise. This is a major challenge to contemporary sports scientists.

Matches may also be analysed with a view towards understanding tactical aspects. The computer-based analysis of matches is designed to follow the play and identify patterns. Methods designed for studying football (Hughes, 1992) have been modified for other team sports, including the court as well as the field games. The method utilises video-recordings of whole matches and computerised notation of position of action, the player and the action involved. More accessible methods include computer-controlled dual-video systems for analysis of Bundesliga soccer (Winkler, 1991).

It has been possible to isolate certain soccer skills for laboratory investigations. An example is the study of dribbling a soccer ball under controlled conditions (Reilly and Ball, 1984) and at different speeds of movement. Oxygen uptake and blood lactate were each elevated by dribbling the ball, the increment being similar at each speed. One of the implications is the better training stimulus provided by working with the ball for a given speed of movement. Contributions to the additional energy expenditure are the alterations in stride rate to control the ball and also to deceive opponents.

Extra physiological costs are also apparent when players move backwards or sideways (Reilly and Bowen, 1984). This is represented both in oxygen cost and perception of effort. It suggests that these features need to be incorporated into the training programmes of players.

5. Research in Other Team Sports

Methods of analysis of movements in soccer have been applied to other football codes. This has enabled relative times in various activities to be compared between the football games. The exercise intensity appears to be higher in Australian Rules and soccer when expressed as percent of maximal oxygen uptake as an average. In contrast American Football presents an anaerobic challenge to metabolism and its players tend to have high maximal strength values (Reilly, 1992).

Specific skills such as kicking a ball have been studied in the laboratory, from biomechanical and anatomical perspectives. In addition to the soccer placekick (De Proft et al., 1988), the drop-kick and punt as used in the other football codes (McCrudden and Reilly, 1993) have been examined.

The physiology of field hockey has been comprehensively reviewed, including consideration of characteristics of players, demands of the game, training and other factors (Reilly and Borrie, 1992). The physiological and ergonomic consequences or dribbling in hockey have also been studied (Reilly and Seaton,

1990; Reilly and Temple, 1993). Similar positional trends to those noted in soccer are also evident, the highest aerobic power values being found in midfield players.

Computer-aided analysis of performance in field hockey has been applied in the same manner as to the football codes. Franks and Nagelkerke (1988) demonstrated how feedback on individual contributions to team play can be provided by a systematic approach to match analysis. The link between performance and fitness is evidenced in the increased acceptance of field tests. These include sports specific tests for women's hockey validated by Reilly and Bretherton (1986) and for soccer (Ekblom, 1989; Bangsbo, 1991).

There is a wealth of laboratory investigations with implications for the major court games. Research concerned with drop jumping and the stretchshortening cycle of muscle activity has relevance for basketball and volleyball where jumping is an important skill. Their relevance is adumbrated in reviews that attempt to synthesise scientific studies for practitioners (MacLaren, 1990).

6. Training

The required fitness profiles of players must be invoked by a systematisation of training. Components of training for team sports include warm-up, flexibility, fitness work (weight-training, circuit-training, running and so on), skills practice, team drills and games. The emphasis placed on each varies according to the sport, the imminence of competition (day of work), the stage of the season, the fitness of the team as a whole and the environmental conditions. In some cases specific attention may be given to individual needs, for example specialist training drills for goalkeepers.

Typically games players compete at week-ends, sometimes also in mid-week. The typical weekly programme shows a build-up in daily energy expenditure which peaks in mid-week and a taper in preparation for competition. This cyclical approach towards distributing the training load is supported by physiological principles (Reilly and Thomas, 1979).

There is also a need to consider the phase of the competitive season. Professional soccer players have traditionally placed emphasis on endurance training pre-season to the detriment of strength training. Whilst the training is effective in enhancing aerobic power, it can have adverse effects on muscle strength. There is a recognition now that a smooth transition of training rather than an abrupt change is called for.

Training is ineffective if it promotes injury, and especially in team games where practices are too rough. Intervention studies of soccer players have demonstrated that flexibility work, particularly for hamstrings and adductors groups, can reduce injury incidence (Ekstrand, 1982). Retrospective studies of games players (handball, hockey, rugby union and soccer) have shown that proper attention to warm-up can also reduce injury occurrence (Reilly and Stirling, 1990).

Recurrence of injury may also be prevented by a systematic approach towards rehabilitation. Facilities for accommodating monitoring and regulation of training muscle strength are available in the form of isokinetic dynamometers. Such methods enable training regimes to be set so as to compensate for limb asymmetries or counter flexion-extension imbalances. Individuals cannot afford to carry weaknesses into team games, as they will be more vulnerable to injury in situations of physical contact (Fowler and Reilly, 1992). Generally, pressure to return key players to competition restricts the period of rehabilitation.

Maintaining a consistent team line-up is an important ingredient in producing team success. There is statistical evidence that final position in League football is correlated with the number of players used in the season (Reilly, 1975). The reasons for this are manifold and are probably part of a spiral effect whereby team cohesion and morale is improved the longer the team stays together. Success also breeds a disinclination to report injury so that selection is not compromised. The whole area of group cohesion and its relation to psychological variables within the team is an important area of research for the future.

7. Special Groups

Team sports have traditionally emphasised male events and this has been reflected in the balance of research in team sports between the sexes. Studies of hockey, lacrosse and netball are as numerous for women participants as for men, though these sports are relatively neglected compared to soccer.

Studies on soccer have traditionally been focused on male players. There has only been a handful of studies concerned with women players or the women's soccer game (Davis and Brewer, 1993). A similar state exists with regard to women's rugby (Kirby and Reilly, 1993), though this may be remedied as the game gains in world-wide appeal.

There is also a need to focus on young players. Skills need to be taught during childhood but training at a young age has probably been over-emphasised. The adverse consequence is drop-out or burn-out, or incurrence of injury.

Some attention has also been given to the specific demands and fitness requirements for veteran's team sports. This has been an important part of the 'sport for all' campaign but also gives a focus to the elite player postretirement.

Finally, some consideration should be given to referees who represent one form of elite participant. Studies of professional soccer referees have shown the relatively high exercise intensities sustained throughout a game (Catterall et al., 1993). This is despite being about 15 years older than the average player and being rewarded with considerably less remuneration.

8. Future Directions to Research in Team Sports

At any occasion of reflection, it is prudent to make projections for future endeavours. The Sports Council (London) recently commissioned reviews to provide state-of-the-art information about biomechanics, physiology, psychology and inter-disciplinary sports science. These were in turn synthesised to identify the most pressing areas for research in sports science. Many of the areas identified are directly related to team sports (Reilly, 1992).

The more urgent research needs could be described in terms of progression from the young performer to the adult elite athlete contemplating retirement. Among the many areas identified were:

(i) talent identification and development programmes;
(ii) optimal training for multiple-sprint sports (games);
(iii) optimisation of technique training via biomechanics and motor skills analysis;
(iv) physiological modelling of competitive games;
(v) overtraining and burn-out;
(vi) group dynamics and stress management.

The dynamic nature of team sports means that now research topics will constantly be thrown up to challenge researchers. It should be mentioned that games are aleatory or subject to chance and consequently performance cannot ever be completely pre-determined. There are also elements of art as well as science in the expression of performance and this is underlined by the exceptionally gifted players who grace the competitive environment.

References

1. Bangsbo, J.: Anaerobic energy yield in soccer: performance of young players. Science Football 1 (5): 24-28, 1991.

2. Catterall, C. , Reilly, T. , Atkinson, G. Coldwells A: Analysis of the work-rates and heart rates of association football referees. Brit. I. Sports Med. 27: 193-196, 1993.

3. Davis, J.A., Brewer, J.: Applied physiology of female soccer players. Sports Med. 16: 180-189, 1993.

4. **De Proft, E., Clarys, J.P., Bollens, E., Cabri, J., DuFour, W.:** Muscle activity in the soccer kick. In: Reilly, T., Lees, A., Davids, K. , Murphy, W. (eds.): Science and Football, pp. 434-440. London, E. and F. N. Spon, 1988.

5. **Ekblom, B.:** A field test for soccer players. Science Football 1 (1) : 13-16, 1989.

6. **Ekstrand, J.:** Soccer Injuries and their prevention. Medical dissertation No. 130, Linkoping University.

7. **Fowler, N., Reilly, T.:** The use of anisokinetic muscle function dynamometer in the rehabilitation of soccer injuries. Communication to North Western Injuries Research Group (Manchester), April, 1992.

8. **Franks, I.M., Nagelkerke, P.:** The use of computer interactive video technology in sport analysis. Ergonomics 31: 1593-1603, 1988.

9. **Hughes, M.:** Notational analysis in football. In: Reilly, T., Clarys, J., Stibbe, A. (eds.): Science and Football 11. pp. 151 - 159. London: E. and F. N. Spon, 1993.

10. **Jacobs, I.:** Nutrition for the elite footballer. In: Reilly, T., Lees, A., Davids, K. Murphy, W. (eds.). Science and Football. pp. 23-32. London: E. and F.N. Spon, 1988.

11. **Kirby, W. J., Reilly, T.:** Anthropometric and fitness profiles of elite female Rugby Union players. In: Reilly, T., Clarys, J., Stibbe, A. (eds.): Science and Football II, pp. 27-30. London : E. and F. N. Spon, 1993.

12. **MacLaren, D.:** Court games: volleyball and basketball. In: Reilly, T., Secher, N., Snell, P., Williams, C. (eds.): Physiology of Sports. pp. 427-464. London: E. and F.N. Spon, 1990.

13. **McCrudden, M., Reilly, T.:** A comparison of the punt and the drop kick. In: Reilly, T. , Clarys, J. , Stibbe, A. (eds.): Science and Football II, pp. 3 62-3 66. London : E. and F. N. Spon, 1993.

14. **Reilly, T.:** An ergonomic evaluation of occupational stress in professional association football. Unpublished doctoral thesis, Liverpool Polytechnic.

15. **Reilly, T.:** Football. In: Reilly, T., Secher, N., Snell, P., Williams, C. (eds.): Physiology of Sports pp. 371-425, London: E. and F.N. Spon, 1990.

16. Reilly, T.: Strategic Directions for Sports Science Research in the United Kingdom. London: Sports Council, 1992.

17. Reilly, T.: Science and Football: an introduction. In: Reilly, T., Clarys, J., Stibbe, A. (eds.): Science and Football II, pp. 3-11. London, E. and F. N. Spon, 1993.

18. Reilly, T.: The physiological profile of the soccer player. In: Ekblom, B., Knuttgen, H. (eds.): The Olympic Handbook of Sports Medicine: Football. Oxford: Blackwell, 1994.

19. Reilly, T., Ball, D.: The net physiological cost of dribbling a soccer ball. Res. Quart. Exerc. Sport 55: 267-271, 1984.

20. Reilly, T., Borrie, A.: Applied physiology of field hockey. Sports Med. 14: 10-26, 1992.

21. Reilly, T., Bowen, T.: Exertional costs of changes in directional modes of running. Percept Motor Skills 58: 149-150, 1984.

22. Reilly, T., Bretherton, S.: Multivariate analysis of fitness of female field hockey. In: Day, J.A.P. (ed.): Perspectives in Kinanthropometry, pp. 135-142. Champaign, Ill., Human Kinetics, 1986.

23. Reilly, T., Seaton, A.: Physiological strain unique to field hockey. J. Sports. Med. Phys. Fit. 30: 142-146, 1990.

24. Reilly, T., Stirling, A.: Flexibility, warm-up and injuries in mature games players. J. Sports. Sci. 8 : 185 - 186, 190.

25. Reilly, T., Temple, J.: Some biological consequences of dribbling a hockey ball. In: Lovesey , E. J. (ed.): Contemporary Ergonomics 1993. London: Taylor and Francis, 1993.

26. Reilly, T., Thomas, V.: A motion analysis of work-rate in different positional roles in professional football match-play. J.Human Mov't Stud. 2: 87-97, 1976.

27. Reilly, T., Thomas, V.: Estimated daily energy expenditures of professional association footballers. Ergonomics 22: 541-548, 1979.

28. Reilly, T., Clarys, J., Stibbe, A. (eds.): Science and Football II. London, E. and F.N. Spon, 1993.

29. Reilly, T., Lees, A., Davids, K., Murphy, W. (eds.): Science and Football. London, E. and F.N. Spon, 1988.

30. Saltin, B.: Metabolic fundamentals in exercise. Med. Sci. Sports 5: 137-146, 1973.

31. Winkler, W.: Match analysis and improvement of performance with the aid of computer-controlled dual-video-systems (CCDVS). Science Football 1 (4): 6-10, 1991.

FUNDAMENTAL AND APPLIED RESEARCH IN AQUATIC SPORTS

Reischle, K.
Institut für Sport und Sportwissenschaft, Universität Heidelberg
Germany

1. Prolegomena

Prior to discussing the specified subject "fundamental and applied research in aquatic sports", I would like to acquaint you with the way the contents of this contribution are structured:

- as an introductory step, I will outline the problems and fields of activity of sports research and will present generally recognized scientific criteria;
- secondly, differences between the characterizations "fundamental" and "applied" will be established and intersecting areas outlined;
- subsequently, I will present sports-specific types of enactment, in order to define the position of this contribution.

The first three items of the subdivision referring to science theory will be dealt with briefly, followed, in appropriate consideration of the subject matter, by:

- presentation of the specific preconditional factors for the action field "AQUATIC SPORTS", which in turn call for decisions pertaining to methods in training practice, e.g. in the training of techniques.
- presentation of approaches to find solutions under consideration of fundamental research and applicability in swimming sports and trends in research concerning swimming sports; implications for other aquatic sports can be deducted from the problem complex and subject matter specific to the sport in question. The following topics will be treated in this paper, in representation of overall research in swimming sports:
- (bio) mechanics of propulsion in swimming;
- training of motion techniques in the action field "AQUATIC SPORTS" and didactics of training of techniques;
- diagnostics of characteristics of motion techniques.

1.1 Sports as a Research Object

According to [1], the criteria applicability, reference to the problem and institutional recognition, are, apart from an independent subject matter and its theoretical orientation, decisive for defining a science. The characterization of the research object of sports science and the quality of orientation of its theory serve as a model for the overall constitutional discussion with respect to the theory of science.

The object of sport science is ambiguous and ambivalent, its appearance is differentiated in the sport types enacted by institutions and those practising sports: school sports, instrumental (preventive and rehabilitative) sports, performance-oriented sports and professional sports. Common denominator for the types of enactment listed above is the formal object 'sports activity' - formally, sport is "social, intentional play" [2], which is also instrumentalized.

As a first step, sports science, with regard to its individual disciplines, finds its orientation in the theories of the basic sciences and is "in search" of comprehensive theoretical approaches. This, among others, in order to establish systems organising the abundance of facts and connections and in order to uncover structures of analogies.

The "Stress-Strain-Concept" [3] is an example for a theoretical approach incorporating several disciplines.

Discussions about the object of sports research and scientific and theoretical criteria of delimitation are by no means finalized.
Sports science can currently be identified as an applied science incorporating several disciplines, with predominantly discipline-specific theoretical references.

1.2 Basic and Applied Sports Research

Current questions pertaining to research of aquatic sports, which are investigated with empirical methods and/or theory-oriented examinations of plausibility, are, among others:

- How does propulsion work in swimming?
- Which characteristics of technique and which constructional elements, such as abilities of coordination and physical condition, are relevant for performance and activity?
- How does locomotive learning work?
- By means of which diagnostic methods can progresses in motion techniques be monitored?

For trainers, questions are answered for the time being, whenever they have access to information procedures which after an appropriate period of exercise guarantee that for example;

- cycle distances at a given cycle frequency are increased;
- the combination of the pull-press-phase with the leg strokes of the swimmer is organized more effectively.

In contrast, the scientist with his orientation towards fundamentals, and whose research does not primarily aim to deduct practical consequences directly, but rather to examine hypotheses, will rather study;

- propulsion in swimming, in order to compare e.g. efficiency factors of various cyclic endurance sports (running, cross-country skiing, speed-skating and swimming) with each other;
- progress in learning, in order to compare various theoretical approaches of locomotive learning with each other.

These four examples show, that cognitive interest determines the perspectives from which problems are formulated and treated scientifically. Principally, the alternatives "applied and detached" research do not exist. In most cases, we can immediately discover elements of basic research in applied research and elements of applied research in basic research.

2. The Field of Activity of 'Aquatic Sports' and a Definition of Position

In the field of activity 'AQUATIC SPORTS', the following orientations are important, according to [4]: learning, training, practising, playing, trying, comparing, reflecting and discussing. The sports environment water is thus not only a 'vehicle' for the four styles of swimming, for starting and turning, but first of all a strange element;

- with which participants in swimming courses sometimes have to get acquainted at first;
- which poses a challenge to be mastered to participants in courses and to competitive athletes;
- in which participants in courses test their own possibilities and explore external conditions;
- in which 'skilled' swimmers experiment with 'variations in techniques';
- in which competitive athletes compare themselves with others;
- in which new coordinated movements can be learned and practised;
- in which training can be performed for purposes of competitive sports as well as prevention and rehabilitation;
- in which 'skilled' swimmers propel themselves by means of locomotive patterns, which invite discussion.

In this contribution, we will look at the orientations or rather types of imparting skills: learning, training, practising, experimenting, discussing and reflecting.

3. Analysis of Conditional Factors from the Perspective of Locomotive Technique

In deep-snow skiing, volley ball, jogging and swimming, the preconditions relating to situations, locomotion, structure of movement and apperception (apperception: conscious comprehension of perceptional contents) as well as requirements are only partly comparable. If we want to design concepts for biomechanical techniques and formulate strategies for learning and training of techniques, we need an analysis of conditions specific to the sport concerned as an indispensable aid in the decision making process.

3.1 Theory

The Situation of the Space of Movement

Conditions prevailing in a space, in which movement takes place, provide initial data for the design of the propulsion concept. The following conditions are decisive:
- a swimmer propels himself by means of hitting- and bound vortex (e.g. at the hands) which he provokes himself. Contrary to endurance sports on land with a given "firm support" (reaction of a rigid counter support), the swimmer first has to create "support" and at the same time he has to lift his body forward in swimming direction, over the "support" which he has created. During the cycle of motion, e.g. during the pull-press-phase, the situational conditions of the space of movement water, which are constant at the beginning, are changed by the actions of the swimmer. This is, because values and directions of the reactive flow force elements, pressure drag and dynamic lift, depend on the bound vortex, e.g. at the hands and forearms, on the direction of movement, the speed of movement and the angle of attack, e.g. of the hand. The model variables mentioned above permit construction of a propulsion model with larger or smaller illustrating power.

Locomotion and Structure of Motion

The following preconditions of locomotion and structure of motion provide initial data, which, among others, have to be taken into account in training of techniques: Swimming is a cyclic endurance sport with a markedly high level of demand on coordination, because of the **high density of events per time unit** in the motion cycle. The chronological coupling of the partial movements 'left arm/right arm', "arm pull/leg stroke', 'arm pull/turning or lowering of head during inhaling and exhaling' and 'arm pull/rolling movement around the body axis' occur in approximately one second. On top of that, the angle of the joints as well as angular velocities of the partial movements change several times in the course of the motion cycle.

Apperception

The analysis of apperceptive conditions provides data which form a decisive factor for the selection of relevant reference systems and thus the design of the biomechanical concept of technique and locomotive learning. This is so, because trainers, swimmers and sports scientists are not able to GRASP propulsion in swimming through naive, or direct visual and tactile perception or through the idea of movement, which is adequate for propulsion movements with a firm support. This statement can be confirmed by three perceptional conditions:

- Changes of position can always only be indicated in relation to a given reference system. When watching partial movements, our perception system orientates itself at the reference system which is being moved (rest of the body) and not at the water. Motions of arms and legs in the water are thus perceived by trainers and swimmers in **relation to the body and not in relation to the water**, i.e. the actual chronological and spatial structure of the movements effecting propulsion cannot be perceived with the 'naked eye', as the perception system, so to speak, 'betrays' the observer.

- During fast movements directly opposite to the direction of swimming, i.e. during hydrodynamically wrong propulsion movements, swimmers have the **most intensive tactile 'feedback'**. During self-observation, this execution of motion, which according to the hydrodynamic concept of propulsion is wrong, appears to the swimmer as the most effective one with regard to propulsion.

- Also for top swimmers, **locomotion on land,** i.e. "push-off from a firm support" is taken for granted, and on land all those partial movements are the most efficient ones, which work as directly as possible opposite to the desired direction of movement (e.g. "jump and reach").

3.2 From Theory to Practice

The analysis of conditional elements confirms that swimming, viewed from a situational, technomotoristic and apperceptive perspective, is a technomotoristically demanding sport. This leads, among others, to the following consequences:

- **biomechanical studies and interpretations** of motion are indispensable in order to design, together with further investigative approaches, a data and theory-based propulsion model, which permits, among others, the deduction of technique characteristics with relevance to propulsion and efficiency for learning.
- Trainer and swimmer not only have to know the characteristics of techniques which are taken from the propulsion model, but they also have to have a GRIP on their biomechanical meaning ("KNOWLEDGE and CAPABILITY"), because:

- perception is controlled by expectation, i.e. knowledge of motion techniques guides attention during motion control, and produces, among others, a 'déjà-vu experience' and thus information safety;
- perception is the perception of meaning, because "(...) not verbal contents of communication, but the meaning of the message is stored (..)", i.e. characteristics of techniques which were understood as important can be recalled in the long run;

- In the course of technique training units, a demand on the coordinative abilities specific to swimming has to be made with challenging technique exercises.

4. A Biomechanical Propulsion Concept

4.1 Theory

The first data for the design of the differentiated propulsion concept were supplied by cinematographic analyses. With the aid of chronocyclography and the pulsed light method, it was possible to register **directions of movement, changes of direction and changes of speed** of a given point on the surface. The space lanes projected into the image level represent the absolute space lanes relevant for a propulsion analysis based on theory - the reference system here is the water or a stationary point outside the self-propulsing system. The **morphological analysis** of the 'frozen' movements on the photograph provides the cinematic data for the interpretation of propulsion:

- the direction of movement changes several times during the pull-pressphase and the stroke phase;
- on the sagittal, frontal, and transverse level, movements are preferably aligned diagonally to the swimming direction, in case of the butterfly leg stroke, the orientation of movement is never opposite to the swimming direction;
- regarding the speed of a marked wrist for example, this is characterized by two to three maximums. These maximums are always reached before changes of direction;
- the point of surfacing of the hand lies, in swimming direction, before the point of immersion;
- motion sections directly opposite to the swimming direction are not as pronounced in cases of swimmers with a high level of locomotive technique;
- immersion angles between the horizontal axis and the "movement lane" are of an optimal acute shape in cases of top swimmers.

The theory-based, fluidic explanations of cinematic motion patterns of [5], [6], [7], [8], [9], [10] [11] are followed by the hydrodynamic experiments of [12], [13] and [14].

The theory-based interpretation of empirical data has had the following result: the differentiated propulsion concept corresponds to a very large extent to the theory of propeller propulsion [15], the theory of the "tail fin thrust" [16] and the theory of the flight of birds and insects [17].

The advantages of the diagonal pattern consist in the fact, that
- depending on the swimming style, "support", which swimmers can use for push-off, is created two to three times,
- the speed of hitting vortex, e.g. on hand and forearm, is higher;
- acceleration distances are longer in a "zic-zac-pattern";
- shovelling of water can be performed with optimal speed. In comparison, the underwater pull in the "opposite-to-the-swimming-direction-pattern" is already finished before the "inert mass" of the swimmer has been accelerated sufficiently;
- the areas of hitting vortex remain comparatively small, so that it is possible to considerably increase cycle frequency with a given contraction power.

The differentiated propulsion concept has been confirmed and further developed by, among others, the following three current solution approaches:

1.) In the breast stroke version with the "undulating pattern", the differentiated propulsion concept has been put into effect in extenso. [18] prove with their differentiated analysis of the "undulating pattern" that the arm pull with vertical motions, e.g. preferably with "lift" propulsion, is extremely efficient. In comparison to the "flat pattern", vertical motions in the "undulating pattern", and thus accelerating distances during the upward and downward sections are double in length; and in addition to that, two upward sections can be utilized during the pull phase.

2.) The work group of the Vrije Universiteit in Amsterdam (HUIJNG/HOLLANDER/de GROOT, de GROOT/van JUGEN/SCHENAU, TOUSSAINT) has proved, that "(...) propelling efficiency and distance per stroke are improving when the propulsion is mainly based on lift propulsion." [19].

3.) The **'vortex approach'** is used by [20] to explain lift propulsion in turbulent flow conditions with the MAGNUS effect. The vortex approach does not only represent a further differentiation of the lift concept, which does not yet take turbulent flow conditions into account, but it also has direct effects on motion technique: swimmers have to create a bound vortex by outward and inward rotation of arm and hand, so that the speeds of hitting vortex and bound vortex are added up and low pressure is created (='lift').

4.2 From Theory to Practice

In the differentiated propulsion concept and the vortex concept respectively, three motion actions are decisive for propulsion, e.g. during the pull-press-phase:

- hitting vortexes are provoked by diagonal motions (e.g. during the inward part), which are to be executed with optimal speed and direction and an optimal angle of attack.
- simultaneously, bound vortexes are created through rotation motions.
- simultaneously with the diagonal and rotation motions, the humeral muscles (among others, M. teres major, M. latissimus dorsi) responsible for retroversion (here: backward movement of the arm) have to contract, in order to prevent an anteversion of the arm (here: lifting the arm forward from the deep position) from impairing acceleration of the swimmer.

5. Didactics of Technique Training

5.1 Theory

For technique training, the significant orientations or methods of imparting knowledge: learning, practising, training, trying, reflecting and discussing [4], as explained above, are decisive.

Analysis and evaluation of conditional elements have had the following results: Swimming is a technomotoristically demanding endurance sport, which requires specific capabilities of strength and optimal mobility.

The defined profile of requirements proves the importance of technique training units for swimming training.

Apart from strategies of technique training following 'reference theories', "anecdotal evidences", i.e. discussed and reflected training experiences, also play an important role. Development and differentiation of motion regulation is presently being explained by two diametrically opposed approaches of learning theory:

- the motion programme concept, or the information processing approach ("motor system approach", according to [21]);
- ecological realism or the self-organization approach ("action approach", according to [21]).

5.2 From Theory to Practice

It is possible to allocate more or less clearly definable guidance measures to these diametrically opposed approaches, because either verbal and optical information procedures ('motor system approach') or interactions with a changing "learning environment" have a predominant function in learning and monitoring. For the sport of swimming with its "learning environment", which is constant at the beginning, it is possible to create interaction effects by varying motion technique and/or varying operational conditions [22]. When viewed from outside, technique training, in which technique is acquired ('technique acquisition') and by which technique is adjusted with the aid of complementary strains ('technique adjustment') can be subdivided into sections and it is possible to allocate guidance strategies and information modalities, which are specific to individual phases, to these sections.

1.) **Simplification and feedback strategies** are adequate for the first steps in a technique and for the acquisition of coupling, with the "strategy of aggravating execution conditions" [23] and the "strategy of assigning meaning" gaining more and more importance in the course of the "learning-training-process".

2.) For technique adjustment, the strategy of **'tuning by complementary training'** is adequate. The goals of this strategy are expansion, differentiation and tuning of cognitive, coordinative and conditional capability potentials. Complementary training has, among others, the following contents:

- **technique exercises with additional cognitive tasks**
- **vigilance units,** i.e. training of permanent attention
- **feature sprints,** i.e. the swimmer has to direct his attention to a defined technique feature during sprints.
- **technique-specific muscle-building** in the water with motion patterns specific to swimming, e.g. diving pull (BA) in vertical position with a 150[N]-weight belt.
- **competition-specific units** with additional, straining tasks during swimming.

Starting point for the remarks regarding technique training were two diametrically opposed approaches of learning theory, which can, among others, be related to the phases of acquisition of coupling and adjustment of technique:

- copying pre-set specifications of motion technique is one goal of coupling acquisition;
- experimenting with technique and details of motion, under consideration of the strategy "tuning by complementary training" is one crucial point in technique adjustment.

6. Monitoring Technique Training

6.1 Introduction

EXAMPLE 1

Evaluation of a competition analysis in longitudinal section shows that the cycle distance of a female back-stroker (100m) has, with a comparable cycle frequency ($f=45min^{-1}$), increased by 32cm (1.73m ->2.05m).

EXAMPLE 2

Mechanical performance of a crawl-stroker, measured with the 'power-rack' is comparable to the standard of his cadre.

Thus, diagnosis is a "comparison of ACTUAL to ACTUAL value" or a "comparison of ACTUAL to TARGET value" [24]. This means, that either changes are measured or individual strong points or weaknesses are assessed.

6.2 Theory

The identified causes for deficits in technique play a decisive role for the selection of guidance measures; and the effects of guidance measures have to be monitored. This means that **monitoring and guidance of technique training** complement each other.

The diagnostic instruments used for monitoring technique should ideally fulfil the following requirements:

- diagnostic methods have to be **valid,** i.e. methods of force diagnosis have to guarantee that force potentials which are specific for swimming are also measured;
- selection of **influencing variables relevant to performance and action** is an essential prerequisite for monitoring and guidance of training.

One distinguishes between
a) influencing variables with hypothetical performance relevance
b) influencing variables with logic performance relevance
c) empirical and statistical influencing variables.

Relevance for performance and learning can thus either be proven empirically by "anecdotic evidences" or by considerations of neuromuscular and biomechanical plausibility.

- the **measuring error, or objectivity coefficient** of the method used has to be estimated or rather calculated and the value of 'motor variability' has to be taken into account in measurements of changes. This means, that methods of diagnosis have to be **objective and reliable**. Reliability can

then be used for the calculation of **standard estimation errors and confidence intervals**. An estimation of the confidence interval is indispensable for the evaluation of changes or deviations, because a change or deviation is present when confidence intervals, e.g. in 'comparisons Actual-to-Actual' do not overlap, or when the change is larger than the "critical difference" [25]. In this case "(...) it is possible to confirm a gain in training as significant to the athlete" [24]. Scientific examination of measuring errors is thus not sufficient or only a makeshift solution e.g. in the cinemetric analysis of competitions, because it is not possible to assess motor variability by this method.
- the supplementary quality criteria of **standardization** and **economy** have to be investigated;
- methods used have to be **free from retroactions** as far as possible.

Diagnostics of motion technique as well as diagnostics of conditional capabilities are in a certain dilemma, and lactate diagnostics are no exception to this: on the one hand, evaluation can only be performed after calculation of confidence intervals, and on the other hand it is often impossible, due to the low number of test persons, to deduct confidence intervals.

The following ways out of the dilemma present themselves:
- lowering the conventionally determined significance levels of 99% and 95%, which are "definitely high" [26].
- inclusion of qualitative methods in performance diagnostics of sports motoricity.

Particularly effective are methods which guide attention, e.g. in video analysis, by quantified values and characteristic curves.

6.3 From Theory to Practice

On the following pages, three methods of diagnosis are introduced: the frequency step test, the SVPCC-system, and the cinemetric competition analysis.

EXAMPLE 1: FREQUENCY STEP TEST, A TRAINING EXPERIMENT

When applied as a training experiment, technique practices, for example the "frequency stairs", become test items. Experimenting in this context means: the independent variable of cycle frequency (f) is changed continuously by the test person, and the effects on the dependent variables of cycle distance (Lx) and swimming speed (Vs) are evaluated.

An error estimation, which is also relevant for cinemetric competition analysis, is a requirement for evaluation.

EXAMPLE 2: COORDINATION OF MEASURED VALUES IN PRECISE CORRESPONDENCE TO IMAGES AND INTERACTIVE EVALUATION WITH SENSOR-VIDEO-PC-COUPLING

The characteristic speed curves are registered with the aid of the "cable control method" (ASM-Sensor). In this method, the swimmer is connected to the speed sensor via a longitudinally stable traction cable. The resolution in time amounts to 100 measured values per second, which is sufficient for the analysis of swimming techniques. With a cycle duration of 1.32 seconds - this corresponds to a frequency in minutes of 45.45[min^{-1}] - and a cycle distance of 1.71[m], a speed value is thus registered every 13/100[sec] or 1.7[cm].

The precise coordination of measured values with images represents a solution approach which permits **interactive evaluation of the execution of motions** because biomechanical parameters are assigned to each video image. Interactive evaluation means: on the one hand, it is possible, with the aid of video images, to interpret characteristic biomechanical curves by simultaneous analysis, and on the other hand, qualitative and quantitative peculiarities of the course of a characteristic curve guide attention during analysis of the video image.

The characteristic biomechanical curves registered with the SVPCC-system, or number and shape of maximums and minimums of the characteristic curves, i.e. qualitative and quantitative biomechanical variables, guide, in principle, attention during evaluation of technique. Through adequate guidance strategies and information modes relevant to action, technique training can then be optimized on the basis of the 'SVPCC-diagnosis'.

EXAMPLE 3: CINEMETRIC COMPETITION ANALYSIS

In cinemetric competition analysis, time sections, cycle distances and cycle frequencies of distance sections, as well as starting- and turning times are measured. Swimmers are evaluated through intraindividual **ACTUAL$_1$-ACTUAL$_2$-Comparisons** and interindividual **TARGET-ACTUAL-Comparisons**. A change is reported, when it is larger than the estimated measuring error. It is not possible to calculate a confidence interval, because retesting under identical conditions is not possible.

7. Synopsis

The following aspects of the enactment type "performance-oriented competitive athletics" were treated in this paper:

- **conditional elements** with regard to situation, structure of motion and apperception
- **the hydromechanical basis** of swimming techniques

- **didactics of technique training**
- **technique diagnostics**

This selection does not mean that e.g. the sectors of motivation, periodization, lactate diagnosis, endurance, strength, mobility and coordination, which are interesting for research and relevant for training and competition, are less important.

The subject matters; planning of training and lactate diagnostics were only left out because they have already been treated in differentiation in literature.

Criteria for the selection of the subject matter were:
- the field of research and thus competence of the speaker.
- treatment of a sector with deficits in research, this does particularly apply to the training of techniques.
- outline of research development, this does particularly apply to the sector of biomechanics.
- a further criterion was the lecture time of 40 minutes, which does not permit adequate treatment of all sectors.

References

1. **Barthel, K.M., Adrian, M.J.:** Three Dimensional Hand Patterns of Skilled Butterfly Swimmers. In: LEWILLIE, L., CLARYS, J.P. (eds.): 2nd Intern. Symp. on Biomechanics in Swimming. Baltimore 1975, 154-160.[8]

2. **Brown, R.M., Counsilman, J.E.:** The Role of Lift in Propelling the Swimmer. In: COOPER, J.M. (ed.): Selected topics on Biomechanics. pp. 179-188 Chicago, 1970.[6]

3. **Colwin, C.:** Fluid Dynamics: Vortex Circulation in Swimming Propulsion. In: ASCA (ed.): World Clinic Yearbook. Chicago 1984, 38-46. [20]

4. **Counsilman, J.E.:** The Role of Sculling Movements in the Arm Pull. In: Swimming World 10 (1969) 1, 6-7, 12 u. 43. [5]

5. **Ehni, H.W.:** Handlungsorientierte Sportdidaktik. In: GRÖSSING, St.: Spektrum der Sportdidaktik, pp. 173 - 206. Bad Homburg, Limpert, 1979. [4]

6. **Feld, R., Thierer, K., Wilke, K.**: Der Einfluß der Seitbewegung der Hand beim Kraularmzug auf den Vortrieb - eine Untersuchung der hydrodynamischen Wirkung des Kraularmzuges. In: Leistungssport - Informationen zum Training. Berlin (1978)14, 4-30. [12]

7. **Hertel, H.**: Struktur, Form, Bewegung. Biologie und Technik. Mainz 1963. [16]

8. **Hossner, E.J.**: Beim Fertigkeitslehren im Sport: Keine Angst vor Überforderungen! Sportpsychologie 2: 17-20, 1993. [23]

9. **Kaufmann, F.X.**: Nationalökonomie und Soziologie. Zum Problem der Interdisziplinarität in den Sozialwissenschaften. In: KÜNG, E. (ed.): Wandlung in Wirtschaft und Gesellschaft. Die Wirtschaft und Sozialwissenschaft vor neuen Aufgaben, p. 35. Tübingen, 1980. [1]

10. **Letzelter, M.**: Soll- und Ist-Werte in der Trainingssteuerung, pp. 142-147. In: HAGEDORN, G., KARL, H., BÖS, K. (eds.): Handeln im Sport. dvs, Clausthal-Zellerfeld, 1985. [24]

11. **Lienert, G.A.**: Testaufbau und Testanalyse: Weinheim, Beltz, 1969. [25]

12. **Makarenko, L.P.**: Schwimmtechniken. Berlin 1978. [11]

13. **Nachtigall, W.**: Flugmaschine Fliege. In: V. DITHFURT, H. (red.): Mannheimer Forum - ein Panorama der Naturwissenschaften. Mannheim 1981/82, 83-145. [17]

14. **Nachtigall, W.**: Biophysik des Schwimmens. In: HOPPE, W. et al. (Hrsg.): Biophysik. Berlin, Heidelberg, New York 1978, 525-544. [17]

15. **Persyn/Colman/van Tilborgh** 1992. [18]

16. **Plagenhoeff, St.**: Patterns of Human Motion. New Jersey 1971. [7]

17. **Prandtl, L.**: Führer durch die Strömungslehre. Braunschweig, 1960. [15]

18. **Rackham, G.W.**: An Analysis of Arm Propulsion in Swimming. In: LEWILLIE, L., CLARYS, J.P. (eds.): Swimming II. Proc. 2nd Intern. Symp. on Biomechanics in Swimming. Baltimore, London, Tokyo 1975, 174-179. [9]

19. **Reischle, K.**: Das Antriebsproblem beim Schwimmen - Entwicklung, Stand und Ergebnisse biomechanischer Analysen. In: Leistungssport 6(1976)4, 302-210. [10]

20. **Rockmann-Rüger, U.**: Laufen lernt man nur durch Laufen. Sportpsychologie 1: 17-23, 1991. Sportpsychologie 1: 1991 [22]

21. **Schleiauf, R.E.**: A Hydrodynamic Analysis of Swimming Propulsion. In: TERAUDS, J., BEDINGFIELD, E.W. (Eds.): Swimming III. Baltimore 1979, 70-109. [13]

22. **Schmidt, R.A.**: Motor control and learning: A behavioral emphasis. Champaign, Human Kinetics, 1988. [21]

23. **Toussaint** 1992 [19]

24. **Willimczik, K., Daugs, R., Olivier, N.**: Belastung und Beanspruchung als Einflußgrößen der Sportmotorik. In: OLIVIER, N., DAUGS, R. (eds.): Sportliche Bewegung und Motorik unter Belastung, pp. 6-28. dvs, ClausthalZellerfeld, 1991. [3]

25. **Willimczik, K.**: Theorie der Sportwissenschaft - Die Begründung einer Wissenschaft über ihren Gegenstand. Bielefeld, 1991. [2]

26. **Willimczik, K.**: Statistik im Sport. Ahrensburg, Czwalina. 1992. [26]

27. **Wood, T.C.**: A Fluid Dynamics Analysis of the Propulsive Potential of the Hand and Forearm in Swimming. In: TERAUDS, J., BEDINGFIELD, E.W. (eds.): Swimming III. Baltimore 1979. [14]

Action Field 3

Adapted Physical Activity: Prevention, Rehabilitation, Sport for the Disabled

Adapted Physical Activities and Their Professionalization in the Health Sector

Bilard, J.
Applied Physical Activities Program, University of Montpellier 1
France

1. Introduction

In 1989 the Ministry of National Education announced a sharp decrease in openings for physical education teachers in the public school system. The French universities have responded to this challenge by developing new training programs geared to the private sector. Using the School of Physical Education at the University of Montpellier, France, as an example, we would like to show how over a ten-year period we have developed an important role for physical education specialists within the medical and social service sectors. Our objective is to explain how we currently prepare Adapted Physical Activities (APA) students for future professional work.

We will first present France's current national health policy. Next, after describing the specialized training in APA that our students receive, we will show how the different objectives for APA are determined for the various target populations. We will then show, by reference to the national collective bargaining agreements for employment that exist in the private sector, how students can be prepared to function in a professional setting after two, three, or four years of training. To conclude, we will discuss the future of this professionalization in terms of the current medical and social policies and the costs linked to health spending.

In France there are approximately five million people who are considered to be "disabled" and who are thus covered by existing legislation derived from the Disabled Persons Act of 1975. Public health policy is defined by the Ministry of Health and Social Services and is enacted by both the national public hospital system and nonprofit organizations in the private sector. Since the law of decentralization has passed, the provision of social services has been assigned to the various departments of France.

France has five schools of physical education (Lille, Besancon, Nancy, Strasbourg, and Montpellier) currently offering a specialized curriculum in Adapted Physical Activities at the following degree levels:

- baccalaureat & 2 years (DUEST),
- baccalaureat & 3 years (Licence), and
- baccalaureat & 4 years (Maitrise).

The first professional APA curriculum was created in Montpellier in 1982 and today we offer specialized degrees, including the doctorate (PhD), with two levels of professionalization:

- Licence: 250 hr of specialized training and field work, and
- Maitrise: 500 hr of specialized training and field work.

Our department, of which I am the director, has eight professors who are also researchers at the Sport, Health, and Development Laboratory financed by the Ministry of National Education. More than 200 graduates are now working in the medical and social service sectors and 50 of them in the Languedoc-Roussillon region are field work supervisors. This is a valuable network for ongoing field placements.

The need for physical activities in the health sector is defined in the different official texts derived from the national health policy. For example, the Disabled Persons Act of 1975 emphasizes that (1) access to sports and leisure activities for adults with physical, sensory, or mental disabilities is a national obligation and (2) disabled children in specialized settings must benefit from physical and athletic education opportunities according to their needs. The 1984 Sports Act specifies that disabled adults must have access to physical and athletic opportunities by the organization and development of appropriate programs in specialized settings.

Lastly, a series of recent directives (1980) from the Ministry of Health and Social Services has redefined the role of Adapted Physical Activities for disabled children and adolescents:
"For mentally disabled or maladjusted children and adolescents and for those with physical or multiple handicaps, physical and athletic education is indispensable."

In these texts, APA professionals are considered to be necessary for the fulfilment of these obligations: **"Instruction in physical and athletic activities for these populations must be carried out by qualified personnel and special-care institutions must have on staff at least one full-time physical and athletic education (PAE) instructor if the capacity is greater than 150 children or adolescents."**

Let us now turn our attention to the specific physical activity programs adapted to the needs of the different populations and pathologies, and to the professional grades which have evolved from these adaptations.

2. APA for mentally disabled or maladjusted children and adolescents

These children and adolescents are placed in centers run by private, nonprofit organizations having contracts with, and thus supervised by, the Ministry of Health and Social Services (rehabilitation, medical-educational, or medical-professional institutes). The medical, educational, and social programs of these centers must be approved by the state in order to ensure that the necessary budget is allocated. Once an overall budget has been established between the state and an individual organization, the president of the board of directors hires the staff necessary to fulfil its stated program objectives.

The official instructions published jointly by the Ministries of Health and Social Services and of National Education in December 1989 define the conditions for assuming responsibility for mentally disabled or maladjusted children. These texts (amendment 24 of the 1956 executive order on the disabled or maladjusted child) give a great deal of importance to the role of physical and athletic activities in both educational (academic learning) and social (daily living skills and social integration) programs. Physical and athletic education is considered to be **"an indispensable discipline which contributes to the overall development of the child and adolescent."**

2.1 For young, mentally disabled children, psychomotor education must be a part of the earliest training proposed in rehabilitation centers:
"Psychomotor education, which helps to develop body mastery and the language of gesture, is a basis for all subsequent academic learning. Psychomotor skills can be developed by educational games, rhythmic activities, physical education, etc.
Its specific objectives are the following: an awareness of space and time, the coordination of movements, and the development of dexterity and gestural precision."

2.2 For mentally disabled or maladjusted adolescents, physical and athletic education must be widely mobilized because it **"responds to the needs and general interests of the child and adolescent,** i.e., the need to have all one's capacities stimulated; the need for a positive self-image and the resulting increase in self-confidence; the need to be able to adapt to one's physical environment; and, lastly, the need to establish social and interpersonal relations."
These clearly defined needs have determined the specific goals of APA in the centers responsible for this population:
- maximal development of one's possibilities for action and reaction in the physical and human environment,

- the transmission of cultural education (these activities are different from the other physical practices of the institution because of their social aspect), and
- academic preparation (concretization of abstract notions, learning to avoid over-exertion)."

As an independent element of the center's overall program, the specific APA program must be the responsibility of qualified personnel. As previously stated, a minimum of one full-time instructor is required for physical education aimed at psychomotor development and educational, athletic, and leisure activities in a center with more than 150 mentally disabled or maladjusted children or adolescents.

In 1980, a national collective bargaining agreement formally established the titles of **Instructor and Professor of Physical and Athletic Education (PAE)**. This agreement, signed by both national unions of employers and the unions of child-care workers specialized in working with the disabled, was accepted by the Ministry of Health and Social Services. It defines the conditions for employment, the job functions, and the salaries for the two professional grades (DEUG or Licence/Maitrise).

The title of Professor of PEA is reserved for those possessing either a Licence or Maitrise in the Sciences and Techniques of Sports and Physical Activities (STAPS) with a major in APA. The teaching load is twenty hours per week, and starting salary is approximately 10,000FF gross monthly.

3. APA for children and adolescents with motor disabilities in special education centers

The public and private centers responsible for minors with motor disabilities must provide physical and intellectual education in order to develop the maximum of a child's potentials. This obligation must be fulfilled in such a way that the child is prepared for participation in an ordinary school setting. The objective of the medical-educational team is to "permit access to sports and other leisure activities. Athletic practice requires adaptation of techniques, teaching methods, and materials but many leisure sports are accessible to the physically disabled. These sports must have a social aspect and public use of the athletic installations in these specialized centers must contribute to the social integration of the physically disabled children and adolescents."

Athletics is a specific discipline whose teaching must be ensured by a staff with the proper credentials.

In these centers the staff employed for physical or athletic training are hired according to the guidelines set down in the national collective bargaining

agreement of 1951. A memorandum of 1988 specifies that these staff will be responsible for the overall education of the children and adolescents by means of physical and athletic activities. This agreement recognizes two levels of qualification:
- Grade two PAE instructors for those with a DEUG or DUEST STAPS.
- Grade three PAE instructors for those with a License or Maitrise STAPS.
The teaching load in small groups is 27 hours per week and the starting salary for full-time grade three instructors is approximately 10,000FF gross monthly. A recent circular restated that PAE is normally under the responsibility of the Ministry of National Education.

4. APA for children and adolescents with pulmonary deficiencies in special education centers:

These centers are for children and adolescents medically unable to follow normal schooling. The center staff must therefore ensure a proper education. The physical and athletic activities which are part of that education have a dual function: In addition to their leisure and social aspect, these activities must also be designed to adapt and/or readapt the child to physical effort. The staff therefore have both an educational and therapeutic role.

These medical and educational institutions are often run by insurance companies or state health funds which have their own national collective bargaining agreements defining the different professional grades of employment in APA. For example, in centers run by Securite Sociale (France's national health care system), all positions are classed in three grades according to university degree (DEUG, Licence, or Maitrise).

5. APA for multiple-handicapped children and adolescents in special education centers

Although the treatment teams of these centers recognize that the development of social interactions is particularly important for these children, group-oriented games, swimming activities, APA, etc. give way to the pressing needs for respiratory kinesitherapy.

Treatment predominates and the recruitment of personnel specialized in APA is not a specific goal in the orientations proposed by the Ministry of Health and Social Services. Certain of our students, however, do work in these settings to provide a more complete motor readaptation.

We are today very much aware of the crucial role that physical and athletic activities can play in the personal development of disabled children and adolescents. Indeed, this education is considered necessary to prevent or reverse

social isolation and to prepare the child or adolescent for the fullest possible participation in daily social life.
Let us remember that, according to Article 1 of the Disabled Persons Act of 1975, the provision of opportunities for sports and other leisure activities is a national obligation. Physical and athletic education has thus attained a specific position in the overall educational and social programs of special care institutions by distinguishing itself from those physical practices with a therapeutic goal provided by paramedical professionals trained in psychology or the health sciences. In great part this evolution has been due to the militant action undertaken by athletic organizations for the disabled (Federation Française du Sport Adapté for the mentally disabled and Federation HANDISPORT for those with physical disabilities) and by the APA professionals working in these settings. Simultaneously, the growing use of such terms as "handicapped" or "disabled" in national politics and economics rather than "ill" or "sick" has had the effect of emphasizing the social needs of these persons, rather than the strictly medical.

This emphasis on social needs is enhanced by such concurrent trends as a certain rejection of psychiatry, the disengagement of Securite Sociale from locally-run social service organizations, and the increase in the private, non-profit sector of services capable of responding to the needs of all populations in difficulty in terms of social adaptation.

6. APA for socially disadvantaged children and adolescents

Athletic activities can be a means of maintaining a strong, positive integration between the residents of disadvantaged neighbourhoods and the greater community. On an individual level, these activities can be used to develop and maintain a strong, positive self-identity.

With the support of the state, (the Ministries of Towns and Cities, of the Interior, of Youth and Sports), local organizations have created youth programs in disadvantaged neighbourhoods that combine physical activities, sports, cultural activities, educational activities, etc. Numerous posts have thus been created for graduates of our APA program by municipal and departmental Offices of Sports. These posts have been both summertime-only and year-round. The employment contracts have been defined by public sector national bargaining agreements and take into account the degrees of the personnel (DEUG/DEUST, Licence/-Maitrise).

Although many official texts define the educational, therapeutic, and social obligations towards disabled children and adolescents, few specify the role of APA for adults who are ill, disabled, in difficulty, or without resources.

It should, furthermore, be recalled that since the law of decentralization has passed, the French departments are responsible for social services and the creation of programs for adults.

7. APA for mentally disabled adults

The 1984 Sports Act states that access to sports and leisure activities is the right of all citizens and that those centers working with the disabled must have adapted physical activity programs. Adults with mild disabilities generally attend work-oriented day programs and live in group homes. The APA in these centers are in keeping with the basic work orientation (two hours per week for each adult), but also provide opportunities for physical relaxation and, for certain clients, preparation for participation in a sports club. Those adults with severe disabilities, and who are thus unable to work, live in specialized group homes. Physical activities, especially group play, are highly encouraged in these homes to counteract inactivity and immobility and to contribute to the overall quality of life of the residents.

Many APA professionals work in these centers and their employment is defined by the 1951 collective bargaining agreement (PAE instructor - grade 2 or 3).

8. APA for the adult psychiatric population

Psychiatric patients are hospitalized in either public hospitals or private clinics. Adapted physical activities are a key part of the therapeutic program and are designed to develop better body-image and self-image and better communication with others and the environment; they may also be used primarily to improve depressive states.

Because the public hospitals do not have specific terms in their collective bargaining agreements for the hiring of physical education professionals, recruitment of APA specialists is very difficult. Indeed, APA as a psychotherapeutic technique is usually employed by staff psychiatric nurses or psychologists. Furthermore, because of the current policy of closing down hospital beds and conferring care to smaller, local facilities, the future for APA professional recruitment is not bright in the public hospital sector. Only certain institutions specialized in the long-term treatment of severe psychiatric cases have physical activity programs.

Some of our graduates have taken the initiative and created their own APA programs such as "Centres de gymnastique douce et de thérapie à médiateur corporel." The staff of these centers meet regularly with psychiatric clients and teach various techniques for mind/body work. They work in close collaboration with the traditional service network which normally follows these patients. Such programs, in agreement with third-party payers, also accept more and more of the long-term unemployed and people without resources. Another example of the initiative of APA professionals in Montpellier is the creation of a network to assure the integration of mentally disabled adults into the various local sports clubs. These professionals are paid from the membership dues and the various grants and subsidies from federal and local governments.

9. APA for adults with spinal cord injuries

Since 1945, APA have been principally used as a rehabilitation technique for adults with spinal cord injuries, first with only paraplegics and now also with tetraplegics. The APA programs are carried out in private specialized centers and have overall rehabilitation and leisure goals. Indeed, they differ from kinesitherapeutic programs by their group and game orientation, their emphasis on social interaction, and a close association with the specialized sports club HANDISPORT.

APA professionals work in spine injury services thanks to the collective bargaining agreement of 1951 and are considered as PAE instructors.

10. APA for adults in rehabilitation centers

Post-operation or post-trauma rehabilitation is carried out in private centers. Adapted physical activities are viewed as the logical extension of paramedical techniques and are designed to help the patient to regain and/or maximize his or her physical capacities. In addition, they complement more socially-oriented goals by introducing patients to leisure activities that are an intrinsic part of our culture. The positions open to APA graduates are those presented in the 1951 agreement above.

11. APA for cardiovascular and pulmonary patients

In both public hospitals and private clinics for the chronically ill, APA are an integral part of the retraining programs to increase work capacity. Under medical supervision, the APA professional is part of the therapeutic team and usually intervenes in phase two of the overall rehabilitation scheme. In this way, patient discharge planning can include regular participation in one of the specialized clubs, such as Heart/Health or the Breath Club. In the private clinics, positions are defined either as PAE instructor under the conditions of the 1951 convention or as work therapist-sports instructor in the national bargaining agreement for private hospitals and clinics. The APA professionals employed by the specialized athletic clubs are paid by the hour from the membership dues.

12. APA for the elderly

The creation of retirement homes has not kept up with the increasing number of elderly citizens and it has thus been difficult to keep this population involved in an active life. The role of APA in the geriatric field is important, but the existing homes do not have the budgets for full-time APA professionals. To address this problem, positions have been created and funded by the Direction of Departmental Solidarity of Herault in order to bring APA programs to all retirement home residents. A further goal is to encourage regular leisure outings among the different homes.

These job positions are of limited duration, however, as their primary function is simply to demonstrate their importance in maintaining a high quality of life for the elderly. The expectation is that employment will progress over time as the homes themselves begin to allocate a part of their budgets to this job function. Although APA for adults are closely associated with medical care and therapies, they are unique in that they alone address the issue of social reintegration. For this reason, many cardiovascular and pulmonary rehabilitation centers have hired APA staff. These professionals have not only certain overall medical responsibilities but, what is most important, they are the key personnel who will work with the center residents on their reentry into the community. This "de-medicalization" has helped society to view such people not as ill, but as handicapped or disabled, making it far easier to work at their social and professional reintegration. This shift in thinking, which has reduced national and private health insurance costs, has increased the employment opportunities for APA professionals in the medical and social service sectors. These private institutions, which function in a competitive climate, now view APA as a "must", indicating both the high-quality care offered by the institution (above all if the APA professional is a researcher!) and the commitment of its medical team to prepare clients for a return to a normal social life.

Paradoxically, job openings in the health sector exceed the number of students currently enrolled in the APA curriculum at the School of Physical Education. This fact emphasizes the need for a greater commitment on our part to attracting and training such professionals. However, as we hope to have shown, the awareness of the importance of physical activity for all people has only grown and the concept of sports-health is still alive and well. Health preoccupation is ever present in our society, fed by the narcissism and egocentrism encouraged in our highly competitive world. Our APA professionals, representing a public health perspective, can justify their presence at all levels by the very definition of Adapted Physical Activities, i.e., "physical activities with a therapeutic aim: rehabilitation, education, recreation, or competition for those people with disabilities, dysfunctions or handicaps."

References

1. **Bilard J.**: L'éducation et la rééducation corporelle des enfants et adolescents "inadaptés". In: Brunet F., Bui-Xuan G. (eds): Handicap mental, troubles psychiques et sport, pp 89-112. Clermont Ferrand, FFSAAFRAPS, 1991.

THE TRAINING OF PROFESSIONALS IN ADAPTED PHYSICAL ACTIVITY

Doll-Tepper, G.
Institut für Sportwissenschaft, Freie Universität Berlin
Germany

1. Introduction

To many professionals in the field of physical education and sport science in Europe the term "Adapted Physical Activity" is still quite new 2,10). During the 1970's and 1980's more and more teachers and researchers from European countries were introduced to the developments in North America focusing on physical education and sport for persons with social news where the term APA was already being used.

Especially in the second part of the 1980's initiatives were started to set up networks in Europe and - at the same time - to play a more important role in the already existing worldwide network, the "International Federation of Adapted Physical Activity (IFAPA)". This organization had been established in 1973 in Quebec using for the first time the term "adapted physical activity" instead of "adapted physical education".

The following definition of "adapted physical education" was published in 1952 by the Committee on Adapted Physical Education in the US: "Adapted physical education is a diversified program of developmental activities, games, sports, and rhythms suited to the interests, capacities, and limitations of students with disabilities who may not safely or successfully engage in unrestricted participation in the vigorous activities of the general physical education program." A European branch of IFAPA, the "European Association for Research into Adapted Physical Activity (EARAPA)" was founded in 1987 and in 1988 an EARAPA Seminar was held on "Recent Research and Perspectives on Adapted Physical Activity in European Countries" in Newcastle.

In this seminar the participating experts agreed on the following definition of <u>adapted physical activity:</u>

adapted:	requiring adaptations which may be educational, technical and/or structural
physical activities:	movement experiences (participation may be motivated by therapy, rehabilitation, education, recreation and/or competition),

and their application is directed to the interests, needs and capabilities of individuals with impairments, disabilities and handicaps as defined by the WH0. Based on this definition professional training programmes both on an academic and a nonacademic level were identified in different European countries which included either the whole range or parts of the area.

2. The Professions and Disciplines Involved

When we were preparing the 7th International Symposium "Adapted Physical Activity - An Interdisciplinary Approach" in Berlin 1989 we had chosen the motto for good reasons. It was our objective to unite experts of all disciplines using movement, physical activity, and sports to the benefit of disabled, ill, or aging individuals.

We found the experts to be connected with or coming from different scientific and practical areas:

-physical education;
-adapted physical education;
-sport sciences/human movement sciences;
-medicine/sports medicine;
-psychology;
-special education;
-rehabilitation/rehabilitation sciences;
-physiotherapy;
-occupational therapy;
-therapeutic recreation;
-dance therapy and other movement therapies.

Concerning leadership in these areas an excellent overview is given by SHERRILL (1988)5. Obviously various aspects of "adapted physical activity" are presented to a larger or smaller degree in training programmes of different professions, e.g. there is a clear tendency to offer movement - or sport-related topics in special education and rehabilitation sciences at university level. Physical education courses in many universities and colleges are either modified in such a way that APA aspects are included (this will be explained in more detail later) or additional courses in APA are offered to the students providing them with a specialization, e.g. in wheelchair sports, in recreational activities for individuals with mental retardation.

3. Professional Training Programmes in APA - a European Perspective

On the non-academic level most European countries offer some training for coaches specializing in sport for the disabled/adapted physical activity. However, with regard to high competitive sport there seems to be a great lack of

well-trained coaches. This, however, can be seen as a worldwide existing problem.
SHERRILL (1993)7) - on the occasion of VISTA '93 - and DOLL-TEPPER (1993)1) on the occasion of the World University Games' Conference have pointed out that a masterplan for coach development is urgently needed. In this context the following issues need to be addressed:

Current issues:

- Who is preparing the coaches?
- What kind of cooperation between sport organizations, sport organizations for the disabled and the institutions in higher education can be developed?
- What is the role of the athletes with a disability?
- Can athletes with a disability become coaches and teachers?
- What kind of competencies are needed?
- Do we need specific curricula for the training of coaches and teachers in the area of disabled sports?
- Should the training programmes focus on disability or rather on sport?
- What kind of quality control can be introduced?
- How do we recruit potential coaches? (Do we want them to come from the able-bodied sport movement, from rehabilitation and medical areas?)

In most countries there is also a lack of instructors and coaches in the area of sport for all/recreational activities for persons with a disability. Only recently, some sport organizations and community-based institutions started to offer courses dealing with physical activity and sport in integrated settings. Here some parallel developments can be identified with regard to the integrated and/or segregated school settings.

The preference of a segregated or integrated model depends on various factors:

- philosophical approach
- facilities
- support services
- number and qualification of staff
- skill level of participants.

The following key philosophical approaches have to be taken into consideration in this context:

- Normalization principle
- Social role valorization
- Independent living

In the 1960's philosophical approaches in many countries especially in the United States of America, Scandinavian countries and in The Netherlands stressed the importance of participation of persons with a disability in the mainstream of society. The so-called normalization principle (NIRJE 1992)4 which described the necessity for each individual - despite a disability - to have access to all areas of life including physical education and sport played a key role in this process.

WOLFENSBERGER (1983)11) and VERMEER (1988)9) pointed out that stigmatization can be reduced on two levels: through heightened competence and through an improvement of social image which can especially be achieved in physical activity and sport.

In the overall development of individuals the acquisition of independence (see HAHN 1981)3) and self-determination (see NIRJE 1992)4) are of crucial importance. These experiences are strongly linked to the self-perceived well-being and are important factors contributing to an improved quality of life. Persons with a disability can be characterized as individuals who are experiencing more dependence and less autonomy than most other members of society. In the process of education in general, and in particular in physical education and adapted physical education, it is therefore of great significance to offer a broad spectrum of different opportunities in which individuals with a disability can experience and achieve more independence.

As already defined, adapted physical activities refer to movement, physical activity, and sports in which special emphasis is placed on the interests and capabilities of individuals with limiting conditions. Through these activities improved competence and thus greater independence can be achieved.

Philosophical aspects also play an important role when decisions concerning the placement of a student/child with a disability have to be made. SHERRILL (1993)6) distinguishes four levels with regard to the continuum of placement options for physical education instruction:

Level 1: Regular Physical Education
Level 2: Partially Integrated Physical Education
Level 3: Separate Physical Education
Level 4: One to One (A tutorial system in which the teacher works with one student)

However, such a continuum of placement options will only be found in very few schools in Europe. In general, a comparison between European countries and the USA concerning the schooling of children with disabilities shows many differences. This is also true for professional training programmes. Many universities in the US and Canada offer undergraduate, graduate and postgraduate/doctoral programmes in adapted physical education/activity and/or therapeutic recreation.

As already mentioned, these terms have only recently been introduced into European countries. Therefore, professional training programmes are often using different terms. Programmes in colleges and universities in European countries however might have some similarity as far as aims and contents are concerned.

This statement can be illustrated by the training programme offered by Deutsche Sporthochschule Köln in the area of "rehabilitation and sports for the disabled". It is an example of very sound professional training covering the different areas of sport for persons with a disability which presents an opportunity to the students to achieve a diploma in this area of physical education and sport science.

When trying to identify reasons for the differences in professional training programmes, both with regard to contents and amount of these programmes in Europe, it becomes clear that the legislative situation of each country has to be taken into consideration.

The following comparison between the US and Germany concerning law requirements e.g. with respect to adapted physical education can serve as an example to explain some reasons for differences.

Fig. 1: Comparison between USA and Germany

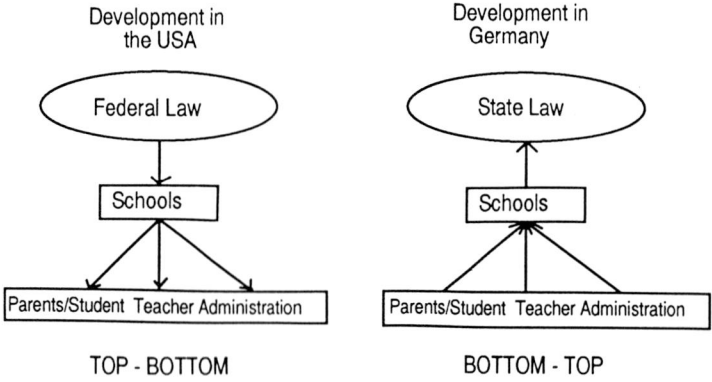

Before looking into current and future developments in APA in the departments of sport science/human movement sciences and physical education it needs to be mentioned that some universities in Europe include into the training opportunities for physicians and other health-related professions also therapeutic and rehabilitation aspects of physical activity and sport.

On the academic level in physical education/sport science there exist different training opportunities for professionals which offer compulsory and/or optional courses in adapted physical activity, using sometimes different terms such as psychomotor therapy, sport for the disabled, rehabilitation etc. in undergraduate, graduate and postgraduate programmes.

Concerning specialists in physiotherapy, occupational therapy, psychomotor therapy there are various forms of professional training existing in Europe, either offered by state or by private institutions or organizations.

With regard to training programmes, e. g. in physiotherapy and in psychomotor therapy, great differences can be found between Germany and Belgium - to give just one example: Physiotherapy in Germany is offered as a professional training on a non-academic level. In Belgium it is possible to achieve an academic degree in physiotherapy. Psychomotor therapy can be studied at the Katholieke Universiteit Leuven (Belgium) on a post-graduate level. This one-year study programme is open both for physical education and physiotherapy graduates. In Germany, psychomotor therapy programmes are mainly offered to students and professionals by organizations such as "Aktionskreis Psychomotorik" without any connection to universities or colleges. Consequently, no academic degree can be obtained. There are only two exceptions: the two-year-postgraduate programme titled "Motologie" at the University of Marburg and the most recent plans to introduce such a degree at the Pädagogische Hochschule Erfurt.

But in general, there are very few of these training opportunities in Europe. An analysis of professional training in adapted physical activity in Europe led to the conclusion that there was a need to develop improved training opportunities.

As a consequence, a "joint venture" of representatives of universities coming from different European countries was created and the postgraduate programme "European Master's Degree in Adapted Physical Activity" was initiated based on the ERASMUS programme. It started in 1991 with 9 universities participating, having selected Leuven as host university.

EUROPEAN MASTER'S DEGREE IN ADAPTED PHYSICAL ACTIVITY PARTICIPATING UNIVERSITIES 1991/92

Fig. 2: EMDAPA - a new degree in Europe

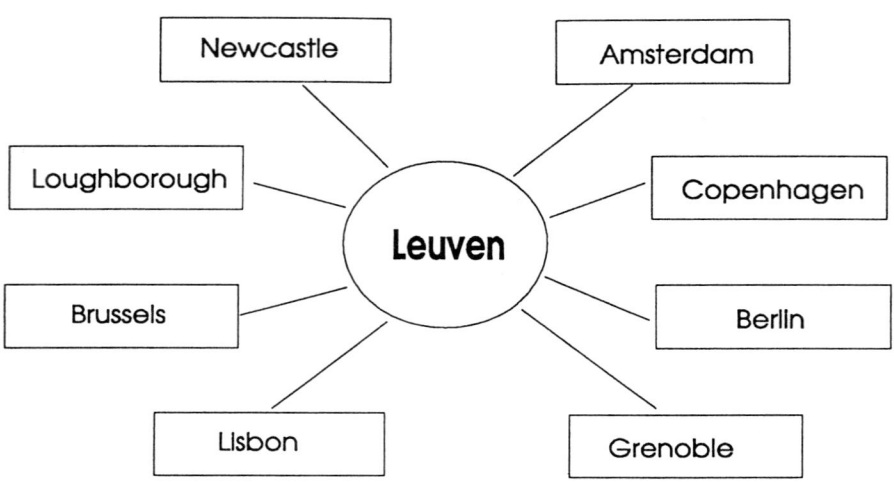

This programme is structured as follows:

- First phase: all students participate in a four months programme in APA, lectures are given by the representatives of the participating universities;
- Second phase: students work in a research project. They are based in one of the participating universities and they finish their studies by handing in their thesis and by doing a final examination.

Currently, 22 universities are participating in this project (see: VAN COPPENOLLE's(9) presentation). In addition, specialization courses (= summer school) in adapted physical activity have started in September 1993 (see: DE POTTER's presentation).

4. Future perspectives

Concerning the current situation and future perspectives in the professional training in physical education and sport science I would like to make a distinction between training programmes being offered (I) by each individual university or college and (2) by those "supra-national", European programmes.

ad (I) :
Based on the current situation which can be described as follows some new directions will be indicated:

Table 1: Current situation: Teacher Training in Physical Education

Preservice (University/ College)	Sport Science - Sport Medicine - Sport History - Sport Sociology - Sport Pedagogy - Sport Psychology - Biomechanics - Exercise Physiology	Sports - Basketball - Volleyball - Handball - Soccer - Gymnastics - Rythm. Gymnastics - Athletics - Swimming etc.	APA optional/ compulsory courses
Postgraduate (University)	e.g. Motologie (Marburg) Psychomotor Therapy (Leuven)		
Inservice	State Educational Agency Local Educational Agency Teacher Associations Private Organizations		

Currently, there are initiatives underway, e.g. at the Free University of Berlin, to integrate specific areas of adapted physical activity/education and sport for persons with a disability into the practical and theoretical courses. The key word for this development is INTEGRATION, or even INFUSION.

Changes especially in the curricula of basketball courses have led to an integration of wheelchair basketball skills. These have been taught as part of the basketball courses since the wintersemester of 1990/91.

In sport science courses a change with regard to adding different aspects of "adapted physical activity/sport for individuals with a disability" area to the curricula is also being discussed. The following topcis could be taken into consideration:

- the historical development of sport for the disabled/the Paralympic movement (in sport history classes);

- therapeutical approaches for individuals with psychic problems; motivational factors in athletes with a disability (in sport psychology classes) ;

- pro's and con's of integrating children with disabilities into regular schools and physical education classes (in sport pedagogy classes) ;

- sociological aspects of elite sport for athletes with a disability (in sport sociology classes);

- analysis of motor behaviour of individuals with impairments and disabilities (in sports medicine/exercise physiology classes).

Similar "inclusion" developments can be observed with regard to inservice training of teachers and only recently also concerning the training of coaches in some European countries.

When looking into future directions there is also a trend towards developing

<u>cooperation models</u>

including e.g. classes/schools; colleges/universities and sport clubs/community based programmes.

Fig. 3: Cooperation Models

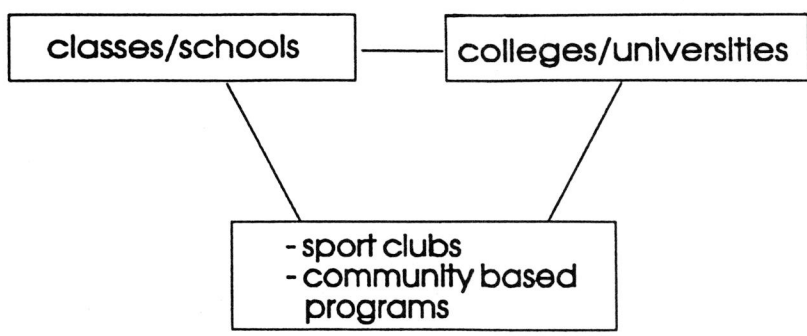

These cooperation models are aiming at offering improved physical activity programmes and at developing new strategies for teaching especially in integrated settings. In this context the evaluation of the training programmes including teacher and student behaviour play an important role.

Finally, when trying to identify future trends in the area of European programmes it becomes clear that closer cooperation between EG and EFTA countries which are already included in programmes based on ERASMUS with central and Eastern European countries will take place and should strongly be supported by the professionals and the relevant institutions and organizations. The excellent examples of European cooperation in the development of the "European Master's Degree in Adapted Physical Activity" - in English language - and the setting up of socialization courses in adapted physical activity - in French language - should serve as an encouragement to intensify cooperation between universities/colleges of different European countries in order to offer greater opportunities for the mobility of students and staff covering both of the area of research and professional training.

References:

1. **Doll-Tepper, G.:** The Preparation of Coaches: Issues for Sport Pedagogy and Higher Education - Paper presented at the CESU/FISU Conference. Buffalo, N.Y., July 1993.

2. **Doll-Tepper, G., Dahms, C., Doll, B., Von Selzam, H. (Eds.)**: Adapted Physical Activity - An Interdisciplinary Approach. Berlin - Heidelberg - New York 1990.

3. **Hahn, B.**: Behinderung als soziale Abhängigkeit. Gammertingen 1981.

4. **Nirje, B.**: The Normalization Principle Papers. Uppsala 1992.

5. **Sherrill, C. (Ed.)**: Leadership Training in Adapted Physical Education. Champaign 1988.

6. **Sherill, C.**: Adapted Physical Activity, Recreation and Sport - Crossdisciplinary and Lifespan. 4th Edition, Dubuque 1993.

7. **Sherrill, C.**: Coaches in the Paralympic Movement: Training, Roles, Responsibilities, and Ethics - Paper presented at VISTA Conference. Jasper, Canada, May 1993.

8. **Van Coppenolle, H./Simons, J./Neerinckx, E./Vanlandedewijk, Y./Verwilt, M. (Eds.)**: Textbook European Master's Degree Adapted Physical Activity. Leuven 1993.

9. **Vermeer, A.**: Der Einfluß von Sport auf persönliche Kompetenz und soziale Stellung von geistig Behinderten. In: Motorik (11) 1988, 17-23.

10. **Williams, T. (Ed.)**: Research and Perspectives on Adapted Physical Activity in Europe. Loughborough 1990.

11. **Wolfensberger, W.**: Social Role Valorization: A New Term for the Principle of Normalization, in: Mental Retardation (21), 1983, 234-239.

NEW PROFESSIONAL ORIENTATIONS IN ADAPTED PHYSICAL ACTIVITY

Elvin, I.T.
University of Northumbria at Newcastle
UK

1. Introduction

In introducing this paper I recognise that our European nations, together with the social and economic fabric of our cultures are undergoing significant change. We need to address economic factors, such as the recession in the world's economy, high levels of unemployment across the community, with many long term unemployed, and a workforce which is not sufficiently qualified in vocational skills and competencies.

Important changes are evident in the demography of Europe, especially the growing population of elderly people. There is the need to increase and promote awareness of citizens' rights and equity issues. Social welfare education and training and health care also represent fundamental problems in a period of tremendous change. The prospect of continued advances in technology, associated with some form of planned economic recovery and ambitions for reducing unemployment, are perhaps offset by the risks of political instability and an education infrastructure that appears to lack the necessary resources to provide for an economic recovery. Certainly we need to readdress the questions posed in the 1980's, and I am not convinced this was only a UK problem, when there appeared to be a focus on the accumulation of personal wealth as the true measure of a successful economy with insufficient consideration given to equity and welfare issues.

2. European Partnerships

Nevertheless Europe does offer tremendous potential for trade and partnership, in areas where markets, needs and skills can be brought together for the common good. In the relatively brief life span of the European Community and the Erasmus Bureau higher education has accumulated valuable experience in organising and promoting joint initiatives. The European Master's degree in Adapted Physical Activity, for example, provided an opportunity for nine Universities from seven member states to address the professional, vocational and academic needs of students in an area where interests and expertise were diverse, both in geography and in discipline, and where no equivalent programme existed. Colleagues contributing to the degree would admit, however, that there is much still to be determined concerning the future development of the programme. Indeed a review of the course is already underway. Our experience over the last three years has taught us a number of things. We have learned that there is much to be gained from partnerships between Universities, particularly where specific academic areas can be developed into new courses, trans European applied research opportunities can be cultivated and an appreciation may be acquired of European professional opportunities. On the one hand what the European Master's degree in APA has done is commendable, but on the other hand it signals the need for more partnerships to be formed and a wider network of courses to be made available to students. The European Master's degree in APA is now complemented by a second programme in APA at first degree level, organised and taught by a combination of French speaking institutions.

A future map of higher education in Europe should show numerous partnership programmes offered by a growing number of institutions across the community. The Erasmus Bureau has supported the development of these partnerships, encouraging each ICP programme to welcome new members. Whilst this philosophy is sound, and the economics a necessity, the principle of cooperation should not discourage the creation of new programmes through a rigid requirement to conform to existing modes of delivery. If there is to be life after Erasmus, and we must all plan for this, we should seek a shared view of the future. What are we working towards and what are the aspirations of students and the needs of the market? Various combinations of institutions in higher education, working in partnership, and with the active support of key non-government agencies, need to recognise that the learning outcomes to European qualifications must be vocationally oriented and competence driven. Academics can no longer determine course objectives and content without close reference to and the support of the professional community.

Course planning committees and review mechanisms should involve key agencies from outside education. Programme delivery also needs to benefit from colleagues who actually work in the professional field. Indeed academics should be continually updating their skills and their appreciation of current practice by spending regular amounts of time working in the area of their teaching expertise. At another level we should consider replacing the traditional research dissertation as the qualitative outcome to higher education by a study programme combined with research that is applied directly to the professional area.

3. Current professional orientations

As a part of the preparation for this paper a letter was sent to over 200 organisations in Europe. The purpose of that letter was to identify current trends in education and training linked to professional orientations and APA.

Replies were received from institutions in higher education, plus national and regional agencies responsible for providing opportunities to participate in sport and recreation. People are becoming more aware, particularly as employment law develops, that equal opportunities legislation continues to highlight the lack of programmes in APA.

4. Higher Education

It is apparent that the higher education sector is moving inexorably towards a modular or unitised approach to course provision. It is also apparent, particularly with the development of many inter-institutional links, that students are benefiting from more choice than ever before. We now have students gaining credits from courses taken at a variety of institutions, and some of the choices have been made across national boundaries. The movement towards a two semester year has certainly helped in this direction, although European Universities have not yet sought to harmonise their semester dates. Universities have also begun to recognise that people with education or training needs that are linked to continuing professional development, may require sympathetic time tabling and the accommodation of both part time and full time modes of teaching. Teaching methods are also beginning to encourage greater interaction between the student and the professional domain, course content is being rewritten to accommodate innovatory practice, and student enterprise and capability is being recognised as pertinent to their professional development.

The UK over the next few years will see a significant impact on course design and teaching delivery from National Vocational Qualifications (NVQs). As consequence of NVQs academics will become obliged to assess students by their competence in a vocational context rather than by traditional academic methods. The course validation process, including course reviews, is at last seeking much greater empathy with the professional sector and its expectations. European governments are bound to recognise that a commitment to resourcing higher education must have an outcome which produces added value. The product of higher education will be measured by the contribution the graduate can make to the professional world, rather than the quality of the course undertaken and the intrinsic value of that programme to the student.

5. Non University Sector

The contribution being made by non University and non governmental sector organisations has become increasingly important. Not only are they closer to the practical issues concerning professional development, they are also able to encourage and co-operate with higher education in promoting applied research and undertaking specific job related training programmes. This sector involves government funded agencies, disability organisations at national and regional levels, national governing bodies of sport, local sports and recreation clubs, organisations who seek integration in a variety of activities and events, colleagues who are essentially concerned with the rehabilitation process, a variety of professional people and volunteers or helpers in a number of settings. Although there are too many to detail here some examples may help to illustrate the potential.

The Paralympics have provided some wonderful examples of successful event management; certainly there has been widespread and justified approval of the excellence demonstrated in Barcelona in 1992. The skills of planning, organising, and controlling such a major event amply testify to the importance of professional skills in an applied setting. However, sports events for most people take place at a local level and it is here that we must concentrate our efforts to develop appropriate competencies.

Trail orienteering, for example, became a joint initiative between the British Orienteering Federation and the University of Strathclyde, and is now part of the orienteering programme in the UK which is proving to be popular. The real significance of this initiative and the resulting value of trail orienteering actually lies with the intention of the British Orienteering Federation, to integrate people with disabilities into mainstream orienteering. The need to train organisers and helpers and to have effective communications between the organiser, Disability Sports Associations and the disabled competitors is clearly essential. Large orienteering events in Sweden have also gained a reputation for successful integration, incorporating classes and courses for disabled competition and holding integrated prize giving ceremonies.

As Havenhand (1993) suggests we must breakdown the stereotypes applied to people and begin to apply more relevant training to those in need. National Governing Bodies of Sport, when seeking to define a strategy for the next five or six years, should address the potential for APA within their sport. If they are prepared to consider a flexible response to need it is possible that sports and their administrators could provide a significant contribution.

6. Public Sector Agencies

Within the UK an ever increasing number of local authorities are appointing Sports Development Officers for People with Disabilities. It may well be that initiatives in sports development are a consequence of central government legislation which saw the introduction of compulsory competitive tendering for the management of sport and recreation facilities. Such requirements have enabled local authorities to retain an element of ongoing control, and some flexibility, with regard to sports development programmes at the levels of participation, performance and excellence. The skills required in development positions include a combination of teacher, coach, manager and administrator. Whilst we have education and training programmes in each of these areas there is still a relative lack of provision which focuses on a combination of skills in an emerging professional area.

In addition to positions which are disability specific, or are governed by organisations with a particular brief, there is an important need to recognise the potential contribution to APA by development officers who focus on one sport or on one group of people. Development officers with responsibility for youth, women, the elderly, performance sport or a combination of outdoor activities also need the awareness, techniques and skills to work with all people in their area; whether they have a disability or not. Development officer positions have increased significantly in response to local authority initiatives, changes in extra curricular school activity and an acceptance by many National Governing Bodies of Sport that they are directly responsible for the long term well being of their sport.

7. Focusing on Professional Skills

Clearly every development officer should have an appreciation of special needs and of the contribution that programmes of adapted physical activity can make. Good coaching practice is afterall the application of a skilled approach to the needs of an individual or team and the most effective method of improving technique, skill and performance in competition. We must be careful, however, to ensure that any person, teacher, coach, leader, motivator or administrator, has a thorough understanding of adapted physical activity and of the potential needs of different populations of people.

There are dangers in confining such responsibilities to those with a specific job brief to develop APA. There is also a compelling argument that personnel working primarily in APA should spend time working with professionals who would not normally or naturally commit themselves to programmes in APA. We need to look for a cascading system of continuing professional development where all personnel are capable of working with all groups or individuals.

8. European Examples

It is apparent that Germany is providing a response to some of the fundamental concerns associated with promoting APA. There are a number of regional authorities and universities, including Rheinland Pfalz, North Rhine and Westphalia, Berlin, the University of Heidelberg and the Deutsche Sporthochschule, Köln where there has been a clear response. Not only are agencies of local government producing discussion papers, handbooks and directories; they are also actively encouraging a cross section of people from sport and recreation to develop required skills.

One of the most important of these areas of development and of added professionalisation will be the training of volunteers. Governments must also appreciate that many people, including those who are themselves disabled and even in receipt of invalidity benefit, can make a positive contribution to their life and to the lives of others if they are encouraged to undertake voluntary roles in promoting APA. Tens of thousands of people volunteer to promote physical activity, including people who work in APA or special needs clubs. The threats that can be imposed to invalidity benefits when making voluntary contributions to community welfare projects should be removed. Indeed there is a further important role here for education in providing the skills where by individuals with a disability can undertake training which encourages a contribution in APA.

Leadership qualifications, targeted grant aid, a system of sports competitions for different needs can then be underpinned by defined aims and objectives which acknowledge and welcome practical support from a variety of agencies and individuals.

The University in Heidelberg has produced a course for sports graduates, offering a different qualification and one which relates to prevention and rehabilitation. The Deutsche Sporthochschule, Köln offers a basic study programme which then encourages students to choose a specific area of study. Rehabilitation sport is one such specialism.

9. Physical Education and Adapted Physical Activity

Various initiatives are being taken in different parts of Europe relating to the teaching of physical education and integration within mainstream situations. This paper does not seek to address the detail of such initiatives, but it is important to recognise that although schemes are being developed within schools, there is no consistent approach to integration across Europe, and that we still lack an effective means of identifying and promoting good practice. Just as there are different needs relating to the physical education curriculum so teachers respond with a variety of attitudes towards integration. Teacher training in Europe would undoubtedly benefit from a requirement to include a special needs component and from an appreciation of the issues surrounding social integration, mainstreaming and adapted physical activity. We cannot appreciate the limits to integration, mainstreaming and APA until there is enough experience and expertise to make meaningful judgements.

Over the last thirty years colleagues in North America appear to have led the way with programmes in APA and with the production of associated literature. This should not confuse us in Europe. The status of physical education still needs to be improved and adapted physical activity must be seen as an integral element of the subject and its teaching. The Physical Education Association of Ireland (1989) endorses the view that there is much to put right and that despite the literature review of Aherne (1989) the status of Adapted P.E. is low. Providing a link between the value of physical education, adapted physical activity with health and fitness may prove to be the real challenge of the 1990's. Certainly little will change in mainstream education without the political will and our political masters must be constantly informed by us that there are needs that must be addressed. Politicians will remain out of touch unless they are properly briefed.

There seems little doubt, however, that health, fitness and positive life styles will become increasingly important through the 1990's. The focus on sport, competition and winning will, for most of us at least, becomes rather secondary to the need for exercise and maintaining good health. In this respect we all have special needs.

The call for social justice and equity then becomes important for the bottom 100 per cent!

10. Conclusion

Article 2 of the European Sports Charter states that, **"sport means all forms of physical activity which, through casual or organised participation, aim at expressing or improving physical fitness and well-being, forming social relationships or obtaining results in competition at all levels."** Article 4 supports the view that all people should have opportunities to take part, including required measures to **"exercise such opportunities effectively."** Disadvantaged persons, including those with physical or mental disability, should also be able to access sports facilities.

It is clear that in order to support any policy of equal opportunity it may be important to call on a variety of professionally trained and competent people.

Whilst it is apparent that teachers, coaches, leaders, motivators and administrators have an important role so it is necessary for politicians, policy makers, planners, lawyers, researchers, consultants, architects, doctors, media specialists, engineers, local authority managers, recruitment officers, people with staff management responsibilities, personnel officers, physiotherapists, health psychologists, nurses, equal opportunity, community care, welfare and occupational health staff, plus volunteers and helpers to have appropriate, well informed education and training support.

There is a compelling argument that states all persons involved in any programme of professional training should be required to study disability within their vocational context. In calling for the development of integration within our mainstream education programmes we can reach beyond any acceptance of minimum standards of service as acceptable. There is scope for programmes of professional education and training to include specific reference to the needs of people with a disability and in particular to endorse the message that adapted physical activity can make a significant contribution to the quality of life for many people. Some opportunities will emerge as nil or low cost options, but it is for those working in APA to persuade colleagues who are not that the extra effort is to the benefit of their students.

A variety of agencies and institutions must take and share the lead. We must avoid prior assumptions, taking a functionalist perspective whenever possible. Normal suggests an alternative is acceptable. There should be only one normal. Everyone has needs. Certainly there is a real need for European legislation, whether it is mandated by individual member states or by the European Parliament itself.

THE IMPACT OF PHYSICAL ACTIVITY IN PREVENTIVE AND REHABILITATIVE CARDIOLOGY(1)

Hollmann, W.
Institute for Cardiology and Sports Medicine
German Sport University, Cologne
Germany

1. Introduction

The significance of physical training in the prevention of the so-called degenerative cardiovascular diseases was studied using 4 different approaches: Experimental investigations, animal attempts, clinical and epidemiological investigations.

4 methods were used in order to determine the effects of physical training: a comparison of athletes and sedentary individuals, athletes in untrained and trained states, sedentary individuals before and after a training program, and prolonged bed rest followed by a training period.

In 1949 we started with investigations about the effects of exercise and physical training on the healthy and diseased human being. For the purpose of a dosed physical exercise the method of spiroergometry was used. Introduced by Knipping and Brauer in 1929, 1949 - 1954 we applied a crank ergometer exercise in a standing position (Fig.1).

Fig. 1   The principle of a spiroergometrical examination in connection with a crank ergometer, used in Cologne from 1949-1955.

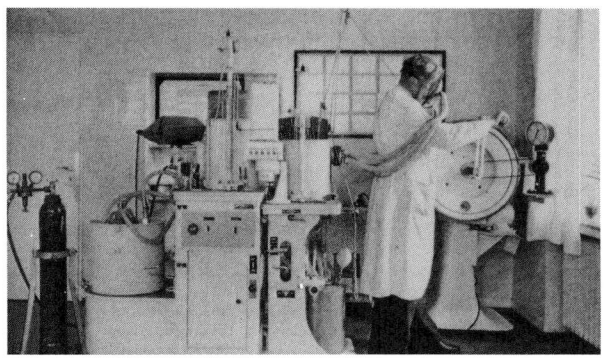

In 1954 we introduced the bicycle ergometer work in connection with the continuous registration of gas metabolism and respiration at the Medical University Clinic of Cologne. At the same time a semi-automatic blood pressure device was constructed for measurement during bicycle ergometer exercise (Fig.2). The principle allowed heart catheterisations and catheterisations of venous and arterial vessels during a dosed exercise with determinations of lactate, pyruvate, blood sugar levels, electrolytes a. o. At the beginning of the 1960's we added the registration of the ECG (10, 11, 13, 14).

Fig. 2 Spiroergometrical examination being based on a bicycle ergometer in conjunction with a half-automatical measuring of the blood-pressure during exercise (1944/45) in Cologne.

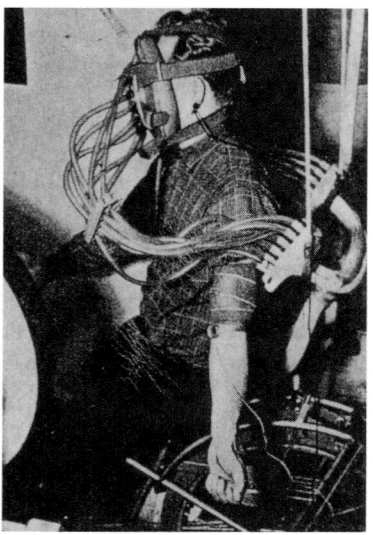

In 1957 we began with determinations of the aerobic-anaerobic transition during an incremental physical exercise in connection with different types of work (crank ergometer in a standing or sitting position, bicycle ergometer in a sitting or supine position). The first publication about the results of the determination of this aerobic-anaerobic threshold was published in 1959 (Pan-American Congress of Sports Medicine in Chicago/USA). A monograph in which the results from 1949 up to 1963 were comprised, was published in 1963 (10).

In 1962 Bergström described the method of needle muscle biopsies. From that time a lot of experimentally based investigations have been done related to the effects of physical exercise and physical training on muscle metabolism and the hormonal regulation in relation to aspects of health and of the prevention of degenerative cardiovascular diseases. The discovery of the existence of HDL-cholesterol and many further details of the lipid metabolism at the end of the 1960's and the beginning of the 1970's supported the interest in those investigations. The actual relevant knowledge to the topic "Health, fitness, and physical activity" was discussed and comprised by the World-Consensus-Congress in Toronto/Canada, 1992.

2. Effects of lack of exercise (longer lasting bed rest)

The technical development influenced strongly our lifestyle particularly after the end of World War II. New technical devices and automatisation reduced the caloric consumption within most professions and in our leisure time. For instance it is supposed that in West Germany the daily caloric consumption for men was reduced between 1950 and 1990 by 600 Kcal, for women by 450 Kcal. Therefore a lack of exercise developed more and more. For an examination of the consequences a prolonged bed rest is suitable. In 1958 we showed that a 9-day period of bed rest provoked approx. 20 % loss of maximal oxygen uptake. The heart volume, determined by X-ray investigations in 2 different plains, was reduced by 10%. The heart frequency, the respiratory minute volume and the lactate level in the blood increased significantly during a submaximal bicycle ergometer test after the bed rest. The heart frequency measured at the same time in body rest was significantly higher after a 14-day period of bed rest. All the symptoms mean that the vital oxygen demand of the heart increased significantly, while the prerequisites for the oxygen supply decreased. Therefore a prolonged bed rest causes an additional loading of the heart but no relief (11, 13).

Saltin et al. (1968) demonstrated the same effects and described at the same time an increased urinary calcium excretion as an indication of bone demineralisation. It appears that gravitational stress on the long bones is essential for normal bone growth and for the conservation of a given condition (11).

In 1965 we published metabolic disorders in orthopedical patients after a prolonged bed rest. There was a pathological course of the blood sugar curve after a double load with 30 g glucose in a distance of 60 min (Fig.3).

Fig. 3   The effects of a prolonged bed rest for the blood glucose tolerance in healthy persons and after remobilization in comparison to a group of healthy persons without bed rest.

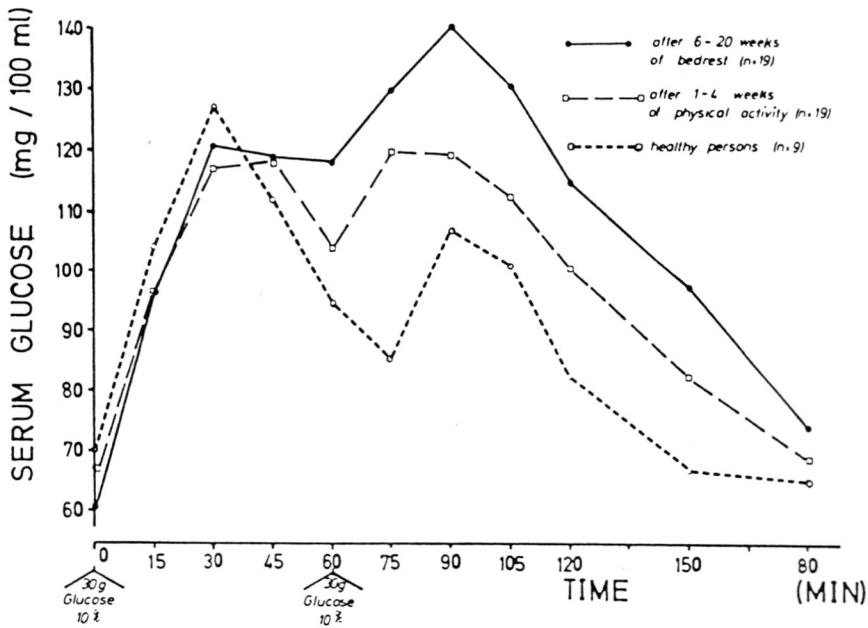

Fig. 4 Intra-arterial blood pressure values during different types of exercise. Only walking and running does not provoke an increase of the diastolic blood pressure (21).

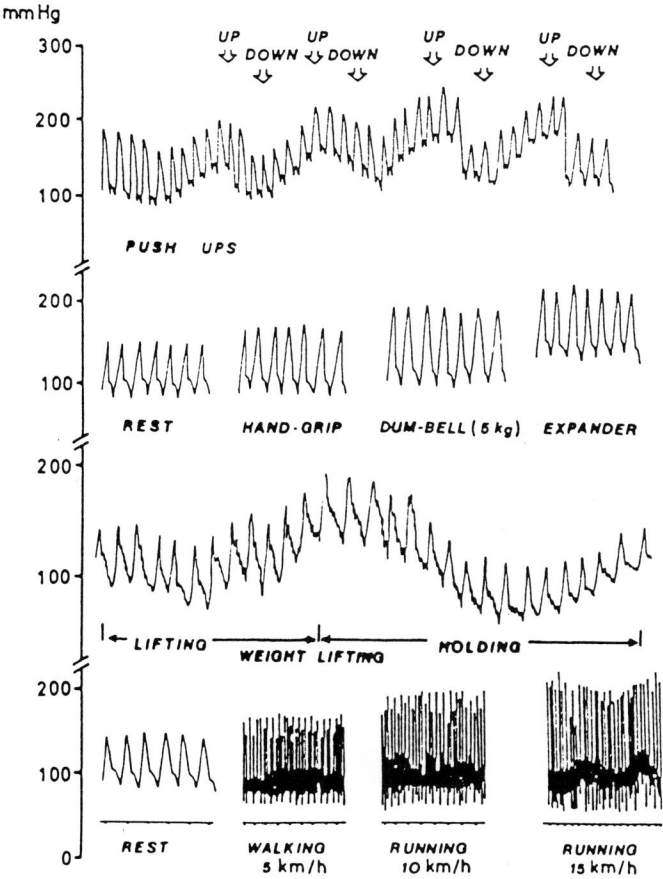

Today it is known that lack of exercise reduces the sensitivity of insulin receptors of the muscle cells. Therefore the blood insulin level increases and provokes the so-called metabolic syndrome with disorders within the lipid metabolism, the carbohydrate tolerance and the blood pressure regulation (13) (Fig.4).

In summary it can be stated that lack of exercise has many detrimental effects for health and physical performance capacity.

3. Recommendations for carrying out endurance training

There are 5 fundamental components of physical fitness: coordination, flexibility, strength, velocity, and endurance. Especially endurance training in connection with an improvement of coordination may be an essential factor in influencing cardiovascular diseases (1-14).

Within endurance training, it is to be differentiated between aerobic and anaerobic exercise intensities and between local and general endurance training. General aerobic endurance involves dynamic exercise of large muscle groups including more than 1/6 of all skeletal muscles. The important question is: What is the most suitable quality and quantity of physical exercise in order to reach health-promoting effects? Optimal types of sports are those which grant a maximum of adaptations desirable for health with a minimum of stress for the exercising person. The effects of different sports events can be examined by simultaneously measuring hemodynamical factors (heart rate and intra-arterial blood pressure) and the size of the anaerobic metabolism (registering the arterial lactate level) (Fig.5).

Fig. 5 The blood lactate level in the arterialised blood during an incremental exercise test in relation to given submaximal oxygen uptakes. 1 = Crank exercise, 2 = bicycle ergometry in a supine positon, 3 = bicycle ergometry in a sitting position, 4 = step test, 5 = running on a treadmill. The lower the lactate level related to a given oxygen uptake the more recommendable the type of exercise for the preventive and rehabilitative cardiology.

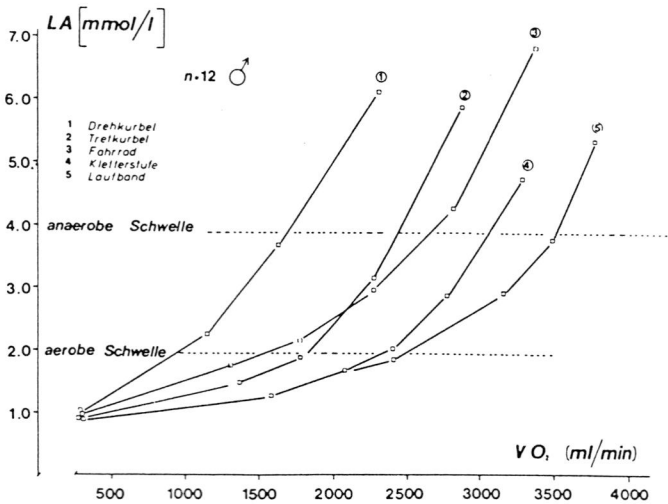

The greater the oxygen intake for a submaximal exercise load and the smaller the simultaneous arterial blood pressure and the arterial lactate level, the more desirable is the event. Examinations on this subject led to the following recommendations:
Frequency: 3 x weekly;
Duration: 30-90 min;
Intensity: 180 - years of age = maximal pulse frequency during continuous effort (rule of thumb) (13, 14).
Recommended events of sports: fast walking (so-called wagging), uphill-walking, slow running (jogging), cycling, swimming, long-distance skiing, rowing. Not so effective for the cardiovascular system but including also other kinds of motoric strain are games like tennis, hockey, basketball, soccer.

4. Some effects of endurance training

There are the following adaptations in the stressed skeletal muscle:
- an increase in number and size of mitochondria (22);
- a rise in the activity of some anaerobic and aerobic enzymes (11);
- an increase in intra-muscular content of glycogen (4, 22);
- an enlargement of the number of capillaries and of the capillary surface (22).

We described very highly significant negative correlations between the mitochondrial volume and the arterial lactate level, the capillaries/muscle fibre and the arterial lactate level, the capillaries mm2 and the arterial lactate level, and the capillaries/mm2 at a given submaximal exercise load (22) (see Fig.6-10).

Fig. 6   Volume of the mitochondria in three muscle fiber types in normal subjects (UNTR), physical education students (ST), and endurance trained athletes (ATH) (22).

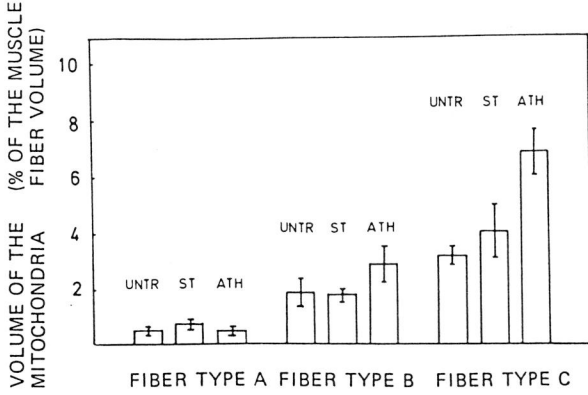

Fig. 7 The relationship between the number of mitochondria per 100 μm² in the central part of C-fibers and the relative VO2max. Untrained persons, physical education students, and endurancetrained persons (22).

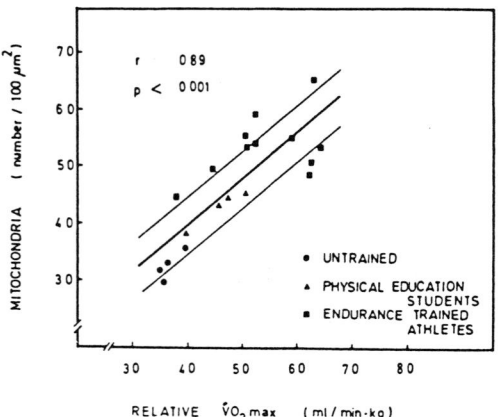

Fig. 8 The relationship between the volume of mitochondria and the lactate level in the arterialised blood in untrained and endurance-trained male persons. The more mitochondria the less lactate production for a given submaximal exercise intensity (22).

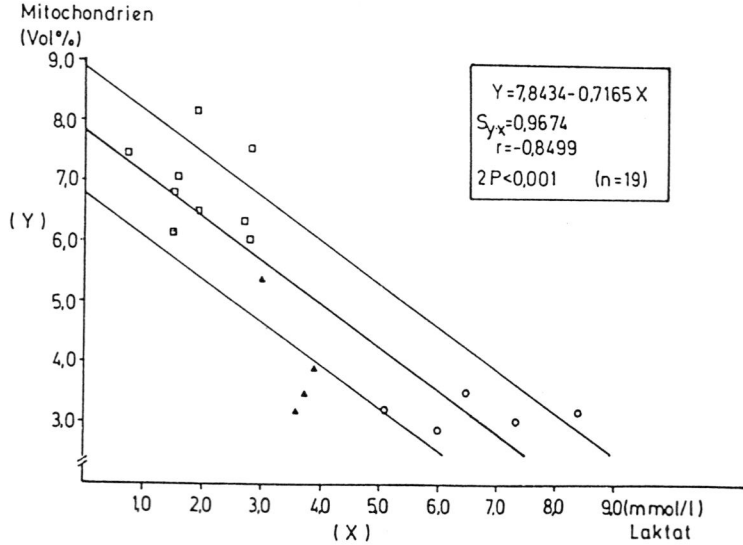

Fig. 9 Number of capillaries per mm2 and number of capillaries per muscle fiber in M. vastus lat. in untrained subjects (UNTR), physical education students (ST), and endurance-trained athletes (ATH) (22).

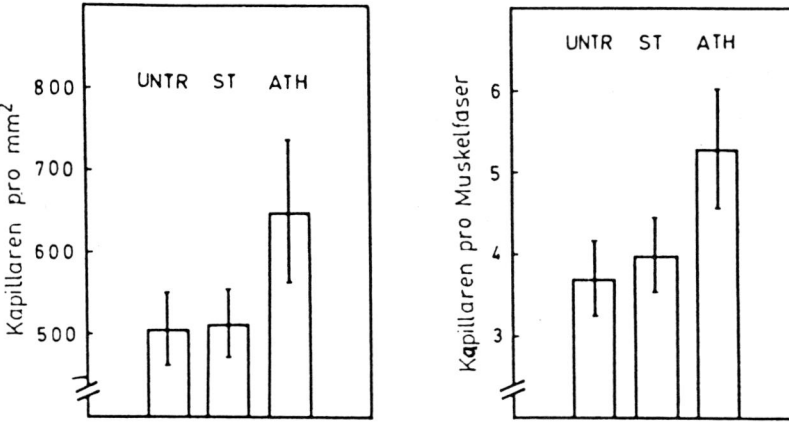

Fig. 10 Relationship between the density of capillaries and the pulse frequency at an exercise intensity of 190 W.

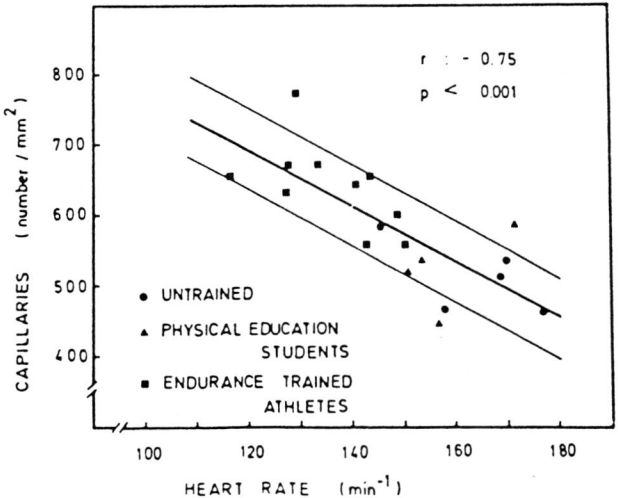

The significance of these peripheral adaptations for the heart can be clearly proved by endurance training conducted with one leg while sitting on a bicycle ergometer. If persons are trained with one leg for 6 weeks 3 times weekly for 30 min in every training session, the heart rate declines significantly when exercise is done with the endurance-trained leg at a given submaximal exercise load, accompanied by a reduced respiratory minute volume. The same person does not show any significant changes of heart rate and respiratory minute volume compared with the values before the training when using the non-trained leg (11) (Fig.11).

Fig. 11 Heart rate before and after an one-legged endurance training on the bicycle ergometer performed by the endurance-trained (upper figure) and with the untrained leg (lower figure). The right side demonstrates the respiratory minute volume during different load intensities in using the endurance-trained or the untrained leg before and after the training period.

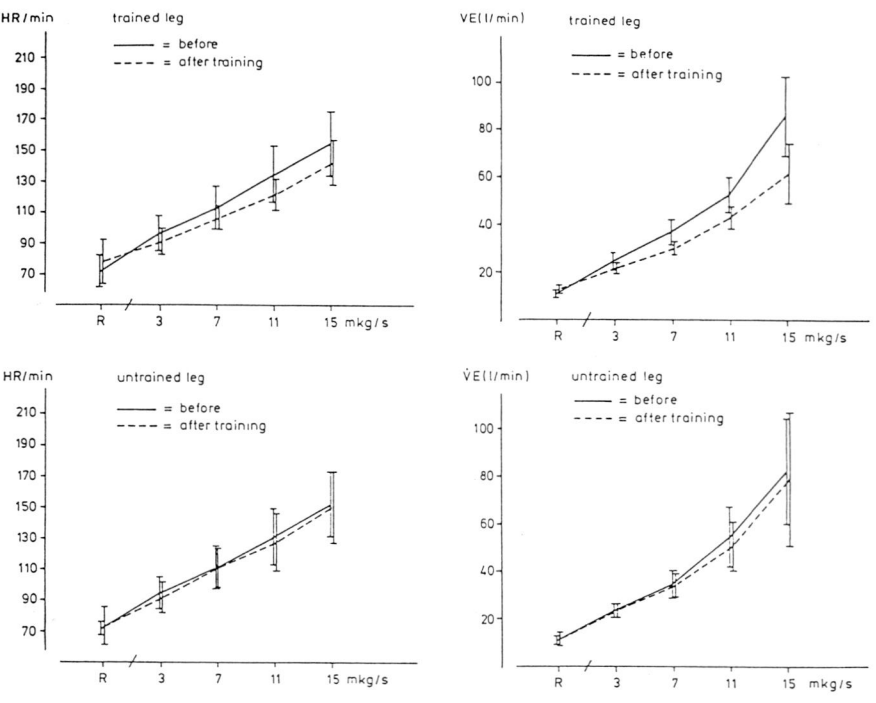

The myocardial oxygen demand can be determined non-invasively by using the product of heart rate and systolic blood pressure. If the heart rate decreases for a submaximal exercise load, the oxygen demand of the heart muscle is lowered, too. This effect cannot be seen when the same person is using his untrained leg.

5. Effects of an endurance training on the heart

The main adaptations are:
- reduction of the heart rate at rest and for submaximal exercise loads;
- lengthening of the diastolic period;
- acceleration of diastolic relaxation;
- enlargement of the stroke volume;
- decrease of catecholamine release;
- diminution of the systolic blood pressure;
- stabilization of the electrical activity (10, 11, 12, 13, 21, 23)

Fig. 12 Significant reduction of the systolic blood pressure after a 6-week endurance training on the bicycle ergometer with two different groups of healthy male persons within the 3. decade of life. One group performed the training program with an exercise intensity according to 3 mmol/l lactate, the other one with 7 mmol/l lactate. (ET = using the one-trained leg, ZT = using the untrained leg). A 3. group (right side) represented healthy female persons of the same age.

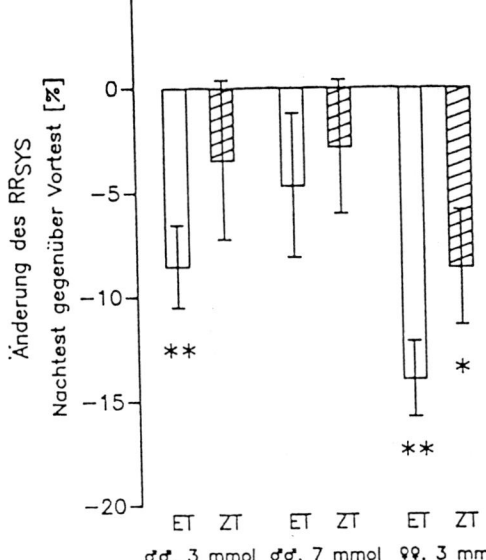

Most of these adaptations are responsible for a reduction of the oxygen demand of the heart muscle. The prolonged diastolic period causes a lengthening of the intramuscular phase of blood supply. The practical consequences can be explained in the following scheme: If an untrained coronary patient can master a load intensity of 75 watts without complaints, then this person may reach, e.g., 125 watts without complaints after training. The difference between 75 and 125 watts practically functions as a safety zone that prevents an incongruity between the myocardial oxygen demand and the oxygen supply.

6. Effects of endurance training on the blood

There are numerous influences of endurance training. The most important one may be that the rigidity of the membrane of the erythrocytes declines. Therefore, the plasticity of erythrocytes increases and the flow properties are improved within the capillaries. At the same time factors such as the adhesiveness and aggregability of the platelets decline, which opposes thrombosis. The content of fibrinogen is reduced (13).

The practical significance of these changes for the prevention of ischemic heart diseases is unknown. Today it is supposed that 98 % of all heart infarctions originate from microthrombosis. Therefore, the effects of endurance training on the blood could be very important.

7. Effects of endurance training on lipid metabolism

We performed cross-sectional and longitudinal investigations of the effects of endurance training in 2 groups of 353 and 24 male subjects between 18 and 82 years of age. In another group of 47 male subjects the changes of the plasmalipoproteins were observed during the first hours and days after a 3-hour run (5-7).

The most important results were:
The concentrations of beta-lipoprotein, total, and LDL-cholesterol were reduced in the blood of endurance-trained athletes. At the same time, the concentrations of alpha-lipoproteins and of HDL-cholesterol were increased. Elite rowers had a direct correlation between total and HDL-cholesterol and an inverse correlation between triglycerides and HDL-cholesterol.
The quotient HDL2/HDL3 was higher in endurance-trained than in untrained persons.
One day after a 3-hour run, the concentration of total and VLDL-triglycerides and of the total VDL-, and LDL-cholesterol were significantly reduced.
The quotient of non-esterised cholesterol/total cholesterol and of non-esterised/-esterised cholesterol increased significantly 3 hours after this run. 1 and 2 days later, these quotients were significantly reduced. The HDL-cholesterol level was

significantly higher one day after a 3-hour run than before it.
One day later, an increase of HDL3-cholesterol (p < 0,001) and 2 days after the running an increase of HDL2-cholesterol (p < 0,05) were to be seen.
The quotient apolipoprotein A-I/A-2 increased significantly 2 days and 4 days after a 3-hour run (p < 0,01) (5-7).
The activity of the lecithin-cholesterol-acyltransferase increased significantly 3 hours after the run (p < 0,01). 2 days later, the activity of this enzyme was decreased in comparison to the resting values (p < 0,05).
The increased HDL-cholesterol, in particular the HDL2-cholesterol, as a result of endurance training might be important for its anti-atherosclerotic effect. It is possible that changes of plasmaproteins after endurance training are the sum of delayed reactions after repeated intense endurance strains (7).

8. Effects of endurance training on some hormones

After a 3-hour run changes of growth hormone (GH), cortisol, and glucagon were not significant (7). Noradrenalin is significantly reduced in endurance-trained persons, related to submaximal exercise loads. As catecholamines are "oxygen-robbers", it is apparent that the oxygen demand of the heart muscle also decreases for an unchanged exercise load as a consequence of the reduced catecholamines in the cell.

Beside of the decreased noradrenalin and adrenalin level in the blood related to a given submaximal exercise load, there is also a reduction of the insulin level. This change is the consequence of an increased sensitivity of the insulin receptors in the muscle cells. As a high insulin level in the blood can favour atherosclerotic developments, this effect of training may be of a specific benefit.

9. Animal attempts

In my opinion the most convincing experiments with animals were performed by Kramsch et al. (16). A representative number of adult male Maccaca-monkeys was divided up in several groups with different nutrition and exercise. One group conducted three times weekly a 1-hour run on a treadmill with a load intensity which was 50% of the maximal performance capacity. The duration of the training was 18 months. Following this time the group continued the program of training but received within the next 24 months a strictly atherogenic diet. Then the animals were killed and the internal organs and the vessels were investigated. The authors compared the results with a sedentary group of monkeys with normal food and another one with an atherogenic diet.

The endurance-trained group had significantly higher HDL-levels and significantly smaller LDL- and VLDL-levels in the blood. A coronary insufficiency was only to be seen in the non-trained groups. The post-mortem-investigation demonstrated an intensive atheriosclerosis of the coronary arteries with several stenosis. The endurance-trained monkeys differed in 4 factors: the pathological changes of the coronary arteries were smaller, the intima was thinner, the arteries had a smaller accumulation of collagen and a far greater diameter of the lumina of the coronaries (16).

10. Epidemiological studies

The role of lack of exercise in causing coronary heart disease has been extensively investigated. Most studies have focused on middle-aged persons. Here should be cited only the investigations of Morris et al., 1980 (18), Paffenbarger et al., 1986 (20), Leon et al., 1987 (17), Kannel et al., 1986 (15). The salient epidemiological features of the association between lack of exercise on the one hand, physical training on the other hand, and coronary heart disease are as follows:

The risk of coronary heart disease is on average two-fold higher in subjects who have low levels of exercise compared with those with higher exercise levels. This doubling of risk is not markedly lower than the relative risks of coronary disease ascribed to hypercholesterolemia, arterial hypertension or cigarette smoking. Lack of exercise was an independent risk factor. Exercise also protects older men. The relative risk of coronary heart disease in unfit men is approximately 2-3-fold greater than in fit men. The relative risk of being an unfit male may approach 8.0 when compared to men with the highest fitness (e.g. the upper 20% of fitness).

11. Physical exercise in cardiac rehabilitation

Oertel started in 1875 the so-called terrain-courses in Munich/Germany. Cardiac patients had to perform daily a fast walking or an uphill-walking. The exercise intensity was dosed individually. The author described good results.

In 1955 Knipping et al. performed in the Medical University Clinic in Cologne the first dosed training program with heart infarction patients. Unfortunately the results were never statistically evaluated. Based on the experiences of Knipping et al., Gottheiner began dosed walks with heart infarction patients in Ramatchen/Israel in 1958. In 1965 the first ambulatory heart infarction groups were founded in Germany. They had to train twice or three times weekly under medical supervision. Today there are more than 3000 groups of out-patients with heart diseases who perform an exercise program in Germany.

The objectives are an improvement of self-confidence, a faster rehabilitation, a better control of risk factors and of the lifestyle in connection with the medical supervision of the training, and perhaps to acquire some of the biochemical and biophysical adaptations cited above.

O'Connor et al. (19) performed a meta-analysis of 22 randomized exercise trials involving a total of 4554 post-infarction patients followed for an average of 3 years after randomization. The relative risks in the pooled exercise group vs. the pooled comparison group were significantly reduced for total mortality (relative risk = 0.80), cardiovascular mortality (0.78) and fatal re-infarction (0.75). Sudden death was significantly reduced in exercisers at one year (relative risk = 0.63).

Thus, existing data suggest that endurance exercise in patients who survive a myocardial infarction results in a 20% reduction in the overall mortality rate.

12. Conclusion

Physical training, especially endurance exercise is clearly important in the primary, secondary and tertiary prevention of coronary heart disease. The cause may be many biochemical and biophysical adaptations which counteract the development of degenerative cardiovascular diseases. At the same time risk factors are reduced as well as hypertension and cerebrovascular stroke. Recommendations about the quality and quantity of exercise training are given, but knowledge about frequency, intensity, duration and type of exercise is incomplete. Exercise training should belong to the habits of our every-day-life like dental hygiene. If sports would be unknown till today, sports would have to be invented by medicine (Table.1).

Table 1 The possible effects of a suitable physical training with benefits for health.

Conclusion

Suitable physical training can combine the following effects for health:

- O2 -demand of heart muscle ▼
- O2 -supply of heart muscle ▲
- antiarrhytmic
- blood pressure ▼
- blood flow properties ▲
- antithrombotic
- LDL Lipoproteins ▼
- HDL Lipoproteins ▲
- triglycerides ▼
- insulin level ▼
- catecholamines (reaction) ▼
- body weight ▼
- mood ▲

13. Summary

Exercise training is used worldwide for purposes of the preventive and the rehabilitative cardiology. After some historical remarks the consequences of prolonged bed rest as a type of lack of exercise are described. It follows the recommendation of a suitable quality, quantity and intensity of exercise training for preventive medicine. Peripheral and central adaptations are described as well as the significance for hemodynamic and metabolic changes. Animal trials with primates also give clear evidence about positive effects of exercise training. First convincing results are also delivered by the cardiac rehabilitation of heart infarction patients in connection with physical training. The main reasons for a protective importance of endurance training may be peripheral and central metabolic and hemodynamic adaptations which reduce the oxygen demand of the heart muscle. The flow properties of the blood are improved, combined with an anti-thrombotic effect. Endurance training induces alterations in the lipoprotein metabolism which could be useful for protection against arteriosclerosis as well as changes in the hormonal regulation. Most of the epidemiological studies confirm the physiologically expected results.

References

1. **Assmann G.:** Lipidstoffwechsel und Artherosklerose. Schattauer, Stuttgart-New York 1982.

2. **Berg A., Johns J., Baumstark N., Kreutz M., Keul J.:** Changes in HDL-subfractions after a single extended episode of physical exercise. Atherosclerosis 47, 231 (1983).

3. **Bergström J.:** Muscle electrolytes in man, determined by neutron activation analysis on needle biopsy specimens. A study on normal subjects, kidney patients, and patients with chronic diarrhoea. Scand. J. Clin. Lab. Invest. 14 (Suppl. 68): 1962.

4. **Björntorp P., Fahlén M., Grimby G., Gustafson A., Holm I., Renström P., Schersten T.:** Carbohydrate and lipid metabolism in middle-aged physically well-trained men. Metabolism 21, 1037 (1972).

5. **Dufaux B., Assmann G., Mader A., Hollmann W.:** Nephelometric determination of apolipoprotein A-I in endurance-trained athletes. Spring meeting, Dresden: The European Atherosclerosis Group, 1979.

6. **Dufaux B., Assmann G., Order U., Hoederath A., Hollmann W.**: Plasmalipoproteins, hormones and energy substrates during the first days after prolonged exercise. Int. J. Sports Med. 2, 256 (1981).

7. **Dufaux B., Liesen H., Rost R., Heck H., Hollmann W.**: Über den Einfluß eines Ausdauertrainings auf die Serum- Lipoproteine unter besonderer Berücksichtigung von HDL bei jungen und älteren Personen. Dt. Z. Sportmed. 30, 123 (1979).

8. **Gordon T., Castelli WP., Hjortland MC., Kannel WD., Dawber TR.**: High density lipoprotein as a protective factor against coronary heart disease: Framingham Study. Am. J. Med. 62, 707 (1977).

9. **Haskell W.L., Montoye HJ., Orenstein D.**: Physical activity and exercise to achieve health-related physical fitness components. Public Health Rep. 100, 202 (1985).

10. **Hollmann W.**: Höchst- und Dauerleistungsfähigkeit des Sportlers. Barth, München 1963.

11. **Hollmann W., Hettinger Th.**: Sportmedizin - Arbeits- und Trainingsgrundlagen. Schattauer, Stuttgart - New York 1990.

12. **Hollmann W., Liesen H., Rost R., Heck H., Satomi J.**: Präventive Kardiologie: Bewegungsmangel und körperliches Training aus epidemiologischer und experimenteller Sicht. Z. Kardiol. 74, 46 (1985).

13. **Hollmann W., Rost R., Dufaux B., Liesen H.**: Prävention und Rehabilitation von Herz-Kreislaufkrankheiten durch körperliches Training. Hippocrates, Stuttgart 1983.

14. **Hollmann W., Rost R., Liesen H., Dufaux B., Heck H., Mader A.**: Assessment of different forms of physical activity with respect to preventive and rehabilitative cardiology. Int. J. Sports Med. 2, 67 (1981).

15. **Kannel W.B., Belanger A., D'Agostino R., Israel I.**: Physical activity and physical demand on the job and risk of cardiovascular disease and death: The Framingham Study. Am. Heart J. 112, 820 (1986).

16. **Kramsch D.M., Aspen AJ., Abramowiz BM., Kreimendah T., Hood WB.**: Reduction of coronary arterosclerosis by moderate conditioning exercise in monkeys on an atherogenic diet. N. Engl. J. Med. 305, 1483 (1981).

17. Leon A.S., Connett J., Jacobs DR., Rauramaa R.: Leisure-time physical activity levels and risk of coronary heart disease and death. The multiple risk factor intervention trial. J. A. M. A. 258, 2388 (1987).

18. Morris J.N., Everitt MG., Pollard R., Chave SP., Semmence AM.: Vigorous exercise in leisure-time: Protection against coronary heart disease. Lancet II, 1207 (1980).

19. O'Connor G.T., Buring JE., Yusuf S. et al.: An overview of randomized trials of rehabilitation with exercise after myocardial infarction. Circulation 80, 234 (1989).

20. Paffenbarger R.S., Hyde RT., Wing AL., Hsieh CC.: Physical activity, all-cause mortality, and longevity of college alumni. N. Engl. J. Med. 314, 605 (1986).

21. Rost R., Webering F. (eds.): Kardiologie im Sport. Deutscher Ärzteverlag, Köln, 1987.

22. Schön F.A., Hollmann W., Liesen H., Waterloh E.: Elektronenmikroskopische Befunde am M. vastus lat. von Untrainierten, Trainierten und Marathonläufern sowie ihre Beziehung zur relativen maximalen Sauerstoffaufnahme und Laktatproduktion: Dt. Z. Sportmed. 31, 343 (1980).

23. Weidemann H., Meyer K.: Lehrbuch der Bewegungstherapie mit Herzkranken. Steinkopf, Darmstadt 1991.

24. Wood P.D., Haskell W., Klein H., Lewis S., Stein MP., Farquhar JW.: The distribution of plasma lipoproteins in middle-aged male runners. Metabolism 25, 1249 (1976).

Footnotes

[1] supported by: 1. Institute for Sports Sciences of the Federal Republic of Germany, 2. Krupp-von-Bohlen-und-Halbach-Grant, 3. Eckloff-Winterstein-Grant

NEW PERSPECTIVES OF MEDICAL INVESTIGATION WITHIN THE AREA OF SPORT FOR THE DISABLED

Martínez i Ferrer, J. O.
Paralympic Division, COOB'92 and Catalana Federation of Sports for the Disabled
Barcelona, Spain

1. Functional classification

The main difference between Olympic and Paralympic sport is the medical--sport classification process made prior to the competition among disabled athletes.

This process must ensure equal opportunity to all participants in order not to put those athletes with serious handicaps at a disadvantage as compared with slighter disabilities, and also in order to allow the both physically and psychologically best prepared participants to compete for the final victory.

No disability is equal to any other, although they may be grouped within a single clinical entity as, for example, D8 paraplegia with an L2 level, or amputation above or below the same joint since their locomotive repercussions are always different. Thus, so that a perfect equality might exist, we would have to hold competitions for a single athlete, which would give rise to a loss of the principal element of competitive sports, that is competitiveness, as it happened in Seoul'88 Paralympics where the paralympic finals were held with only 3 athletes. The greater this sense of competition, the greater the chances of success in sport as in integration and standardization.

Nowadays, the only methods that have been shown to effectively solve this problem are the FUNCTIONAL EVALUATIONS AND CLASSIFICATIONS FOR DISABLED ATHLETES, which consist of evaluating and classifying athletes in groups as similar as possible in terms of disabilities, while attempting to ensure that the number of athletes included assures an acceptable level of competition.

This new system of functional classification has achieved a better balance among the different physical disabilities and the high competition level. In Barcelona'92, the international federations of sport for the disabled as well as the COOB'92, took on this responsibility in order to continue the evolution of sport for the disabled becoming a top-class competition sport and to guarantee conditions of equality.

1.1 The evolution of evaluations and classifications

As may be imagined, this evolution is parallel to the one of competitive sports for disabled athletes.
Mainly after the second World War, sport as a rehabilitation element was introduced in the United States and Great Britain.

What began as recreational sport, became a competitive one. The first classifications among athletes were made by a simple evaluation method, by evaluating pathological sequelae and forming groups of paraplegic persons, amputees, visually impaired persons etc... Eventually subgroups were formed since it was obvious that although the pathology in each group was the same, the degree of affectation was very unequal among them.

Sport for the disabled grew, both in the number of participants and in persons interested in promoting it. This fact favoured the creation of international federations which grouped different athletes with similar disabilities.

· **ISMGF (ISMWSF)**, which grouped those athletes with spinal injuries.
· **ISOD**, which grouped the amputee athletes and those called "Les Autres".
· **CP-ISRA**, including athletes affected by cerebral palsy sequelae.
· **IBSA**, grouping athletes with visual impairment.

Specific evaluation and classification systems were formed for each of these groups, given as a result a total of 31 different classes of physical sequelae and 3 of the sensory kind with 5 different evaluation systems.
However it was obvious that for the development of this sport, this great number of classes and systems of evaluation was neither useful nor valid under many circumstances, especially in the organization of multifederational championships and the organization of Paralympic Games.
Imagine the task of carrying out each event, for instance 100 metres in athletics, 31 times for women and 31 for men, and so for each speciality and modality.

These difficulties were previously detected. Thus, national federations of sports for the disabled did not have enough athletes in each class to ensure a competition. Therefore, many of these federations decided to create their own evaluations systems to meet all their needs. A clear example of this was the Spanish Federation (FEDMF), which in 1971 began to work on a unified evaluation and classification system based mainly on the concept of functionality, which was an attempt to quantify the real disability of the athlete through a medical-sports evaluation record without giving too much importance to the origin of the disability.
This method, called "Método Español", is in 1993 developing a computerized system of classification that facilitates the athlete's classification in relation to the physical needs of each sport, without having to be evaluated for each sport.

Also certain sports sections of the international federations, among them wheelchair basketball and swimming, were to develop alternative integrational methods, based on the concept of functional evaluation, specific for its respective sport, for the development of their competitive structure. So, basketball was to unite its athletes, whatever their disability, since it was impossible to create teams and competitions only for amputees, paraplegics or athletes with sequelae from poliomyelitis. On the other hand, swimming was to evolve toward an integrated system to reduce these 31 classes, both male and female and their different styles and lengths, which transformed swimming competitions into veritable and interminable sport marathons.

These experiences created the new concept of evaluation and functional classification that are nowadays the only possible solution to the evolution of competitive sports for the disabled.

Now, I am going to explain in a general way, the necessary concepts and structures for the development of a method of functional medical-sports evaluation, unique in its type, which can group all the needed information concerning different disabilities and at the same time can compare them correctly.

Secondly, the method should desine a classification system, specific for each sport, which grouped all the necessary potentials for its practice so as to classify the athletes according to their needs.

1.2 Basic elements and structure of functional evaluation and classification

A functional system should have, for its preparation and development, a multidisciplinary team that includes all the elements that can bring together the essential concepts that should be present in such a system:

· **Rehabilitation physicians:** these physicians should bring all their experience on evaluation and the state of the various disabilities that exist, and that can benefit from the practice of competitive sports.

· **Physical therapists:** these professionals are the best prepared to determine precisely the true degree of disability of each athlete, following the evaluation criteria established by the medical teams.

· **Sports physicians:** these physicians should be specialists in sports for physically and sensory disabled and bring all the physiological and biomechanical concepts of adaptation of competitive sports, with the adaptation being dependent on the pathological sequelae presented by the athletes.

· **Coaches:** the coaches will bring, with great scientific precision, all the specific technical criteria for each type of sport, which can be very helpful for the study and integrated classification of each sport.

• **Active athletes:** these athletes, with their practical experience, will serve as means of quality control for modifications, possible improvements and correction of errors for a concrete disability. They will also bring all their experience with the previous methods of evaluation and classification.

After analyzing all necessary elements, we should structure the methodology of the evaluation and the later functional classification. The basic structure should consist of four different levels of action:

Level 1: Evaluation of the degree of disability

In this level, the degree of disability is evaluated, in real terms or as a percentage of the athlete, as a result of the sequelae caused by a causal injury. For this, we shall carry out a medical-sports examination of anatomical areas with biomechanical importance that will mainly consist of:
- Muscular test of anatomical areas. Active.
- Goniometric test of the joints of the aforementioned areas. Active.
- Kinetic test of the aforementioned joints, which will give us their degree of permeability. Passive.

With these tests, we will be able to classify the athletes in absolute values.

Level 2: Medical-sports evaluation

In this second level we will not even attempt to perform a conventional medical-sports evaluation, with morphophysiological tests, strength tests, field tests, etc.. which should be done under other circumstances as, for example, when registering with a national federation. The evaluation consists in measuring general sports functional physical ability and the corresponding physiological adaptations that the disabled athlete uses in general to practise sports, by using a simple sports test where the following aspects are evaluated.
• Psychological factors: such as the principal sports motivation among others.
• Physiological factors: specially "neuromuscular response", the quality of which will be evaluated by parameters such as speed, reaction time, acceleration, skill, flexibility and strength (both dynamic and static), among others. Homeostasis factors shall also be considered, as well as thermoregulation factors, although given less importance.

This will give us a percentage of general sports functional adaptation in specific sport, which is very important in classifying disabled athletes for competition.

Level 3: Specific sports functional ability

In this level we will attempt to measure objectively, sports functional adaptation in a specific sport, using the two aforementioned levels, to extrapolate the most significant factors for each sport and to control the main factors in each sport in particular and to measure more thoroughly the various biomechanical, physiological and technical characteristics of each as well as the adaptation to its practice on the part of the athletes.

Thus, in this third level, we will fill in the blanks remaining from the first two levels of evaluation of generalized characteristics and methods, while reducing the real time of measuring, frequently, thanks to the computer system, this process becomes automatic and completely objective.

Level 4: Criteria for functional classification

The first three levels establish the evaluation of the disabled athlete for the practice of sports, and were predominantly medical-sport-type levels. Now, we should design the optimum classes for competing in specific sports. This level should be based on technical-sport aspects.

Here, different criteria could and must be applied and frequently several of them at the same time, depending on the particular characteristics of the sport and on the disabled athletes who practise it.

· **Statistical criteria:** athletes grouped numerically in intervals of values, obtained by the evaluation in previous levels or by the grades in statistical studies.

· **Medical criteria:** basic concepts or criteria chosen in the general evaluations by which athletes with similar sequelae are grouped together, always under medical criteria.

· **Sports criteria:** criteria of a compensatory type, frequently used in team sports for balancing the competitive potentials of the athletes of the team.

· **Functional criteria:** criteria of positive adaptation of the sequelae to the sport, even though the level of evaluation is similar. Here, it would be very important to introduce a significant difference between congenital sequelae and those resulting from accident.

· **Organizational criteria:** criteria used to guarantee a minimum of competitive participation among the groups. These criteria should be linked to the organizational needs, such as technical, economic, social impact needs...

1.3 Objective of functional evaluations and classifications

Systems of functional evaluations and classifications are nowadays an essential element in the evolution of competitive sports in a logical manner, so that they will not only be understood by us, but also by all those involved in sports; athletes, coaches, directors and, above all, fans and spectators so as to help the process of sports improvement.

However this is not the only objective to be achieved. Even more important is the cultural and social integration that can be obtained by the disabled thanks to the dissemination of their competitive sports. Therefore, we should structure our competitions in a logical manner so that they could be understood by the public, the functional evaluations and classifications are a very useful instrument for this, as well as facilitating fair balance at the sports competition.

2. Biochemical research in adapted sport

A short review of the most representative projects of the biochemical research that were carried out during the organisation and development of the IX Paralympic Games, must be done. Although some of them still continue being in a phase of analysis, it may be interesting to comment them both as a scientific orientation and as a reference to future studies.

These studies can be mainly divided into three groups:

- Biomechanical functional research.
- Research to be applied in medical and social rehabilitation.
- Research related to drug dependence.

2.1 Biomechanical functional research

2.1.1 Study of the morpho-physiological characteristics of the disabled athletes

The final aim of this study is to establish appropriate skills to use both as a pattern and as a guide for studies related to the disabled, so once the morpho-physio-biochemical patterns are clarified, we will be able to carry out the corrections and adaptations of the disabled's training.
Three different types of studies were performed based on the cineanthropometry (by William Ross' method), ergometry (taking notice of the aerobic, anaerobic and mixed capacities, on the cycloergometer or the ergometer of arms according to the disability) and computerised dynamometry (Permanyer's model).
After the first results, new variations have ebbed and flowed, mainly scientific, from the models of training in order to be applied to each group of physical and visual handicaps.

2.1.2. Study of the balance by means of the "Balance Master" in disabled athletes

The main purpose of this study is to prove the existence or non-existence of alterations of the balance in visually impaired athletes and amputees of lower limbs and to obtain values of reference to the different disabilities, comparing this to a control group without disabilities.

The balance is a physiological condition of the individual based on the continuous integration of the information that reaches the brain by:

- Proprioceptive Sensitiveness: thanks to the mechanoreceiver of the esqueletic muscle system that convexs informations of the tension on the system structures.
- Vestibular System: placed in the inner ear that controls the head position with regard to the rest of the body.
- Sight: it informs us of the body situation related to the environment.

This integrated information in the Central Nervous System has Effective Guides, the Cerebellum and the Extrapyramidal System that in each moment, either static or dynamic, modulates the position and/or the movement.

These two disabilities have been chosen because both of them cause alterations in any of the parts that keep the balance.

The "Balance Master" is a system for studying and treating the alterations of balance and position. It objectively measures the representation of the Center of Gravity in a horizontal level, its oscillations and situation.

The system is formed by three main parts:
1) Platform of load divided into two parts, with receivers of load in each one of them.
2) Software to process the received information by the platform.
3) Screen where the data and the position of the person can be seen all the time.

In this study, the estimated data has been:

- Control resting on both feet with open eyes.
- Control resting on both feet with closed eyes.
- Alienation of the center of gravity, in a theoric center indicated by the machine (apart from the visually impaired individuals).
- Control resting on the left foot.
- Control resting on the right foot.

These tests were performed with the athletes on a platform in a relaxed position facing the screen during 20 seconds that lasted each phase of the exercise. The position of the person on the platform was determined according to the rules of the "Balance Master" (alienation of the external peroneal maleolus in the transversal line and of the external part of the foot in the anteroposterior lines marked with S, M and T related to the height of the tested individual).

Visually impaired athletes:

In the light of the results, it has been demonstrated that the studies on the blind population have a worse balance than those on population without visual alterations, although the former develop compensated mechanisms on the level of the proprioceptive and Vestibular System that offer a little improvement upon the results without being comparable to those of the control group, but improving thanks to the learning.

Amputee athletes:

We may conclude that amputee athletes with an A2 level (above the knee) or an A4 level (below the knee) have a worse balance than the model group with no disabilities. However, there are no statistically significant differences between the athletes that rest on just one intact foot and athletes of the control group.

Furthermore, when we eliminated sight in the amputee athletes in the test "Control resting on both feet with closed eyes", the deficit of proprioception that represented a partial or complete absence of an inferior limb, adding the absence of visual impairment, the whole control over the balance is lost.

The study applications:

The results of this study can be mainly applied in the following two different structures:

- Medical-sports classifications: they allow us to quantify the balance and, consequently to include that element, with so much biomechanical importance, as a new factor of objective evaluation.
- To improve the balance by a specific and quantitatively controlled learning, able to improve, in a great way, the sport activities of the disabled athletes.

2.2 Research to be applied in medical and social rehabilitation

2.2.1 Study of gait in athletes whose inferior limb has been amputated

This study has been performed following two different systems of gait control:
- Electronic baropedometry (by a platform, Kistler's model).
- Course of computerised dynamometric gait.

The first system allows us to determine the distribution of pressure in a static phase, using percentages, not only of the forefoot's prints but also retrofoot and, secondly, the study of the plantar phase in the course of the step in a dynamic phase.

Thanks to the second system, we are able to register the forces exerted in the three axes of the space during the different phases of gait, noticing the parameters as: length and velocity of the step, time of unipedal support, double support and complete duration of the step.

The main aim of this study was to take advantage of the opportunity of studying a gait pattern of the different amputee athletes, since they are the point of reference in a rehabilitation stage.

Significant results:

- The weight during gait is equal in both limbs, lying between 60% and 40% in the intact foot in static position.
- The duration of the gait seems to be quite similar once it is compared with control group without disabilities.
- The time of support is longer in the amputees of the femoral limbs than in tibial amputees.
- The gait changes depending on the prosthesis used, noticing that the Flexfoot sports foot does not resemble the pattern of the amputee athletes.

All those results continue being analysed in order to be applied, as soon as possible, to clinical rehabilitation.

2.2.2 Evaluation of the social integration of the Paralympic athletes

By means of interview and an anonymous questionnaire, we have tried to search for the indications of the social integration in the adapted sport, interviewing the disabled athletes who have participated in the Paralympic Games.

Following the main nature of this study, this investigation was divided into two important purposes, taking note of the specific indications in each case:

- Sociological characteristics of the participants.
- Incidence of the competitive sport practice, caring for the social situation of the disabled individual.

All the information obtained by the questionnaires (quantitative methodology) is being statistically analysed. On the second hand, the content of the personal interviews (qualitative method) is also being thoroughly analysed, establishing different areas, which will provide the indications of motivation.

Once the process has reached the end, we intend to publish the results, evaluating the psychological and psychosocial indications in the competitive sport practice for the disabled. That will help the professionals related to the subject not only to recognise the positive psychological benefits in the sport practice in that collective but also to include it in the medical rehabilitation as an integrative factor, both physical and psychological, necessary for the social integration process of the disabled.

2.3 Research related to drug dependence

2.3.1 Evaluation of the pharmacological therapy used for disabled athletes

This study intended to start a line of future work concerned with antidoping control, quite common nowadays, among the top level competitions for the disabled athletes.

The main objective of this study is to know the athletes' toxic and pharmacological habits, since those factors can influence, in a great way, the actual regulations of the antidoping control, equivalent to that of athletes without disabilities as well as the International Olympic Games regulation and lists of forbidden products, not taking notice of the treatment that some athletes must take because of their established sequelae, such as the athletes with medular lesions.

Summary of the results:
- 63% of the inquired athletes took treatment forbidden by the IOC.
- Among this pharmacodependent group, 86,2% belonged to the group, whose lesions were mainly medular.
- The pharmacopedy used by the aforementioned group was basically due to the following causes: - Neurogenic bladder.
    - Reiterative urinary infections.
    - Muscular spasms.
- A significant number of athletes with different sequelae were under treatment to avoid pain.

These results are quite clear, since they demonstrate the serious necessity to develop a specific regulation of the antidoping control, made by the International Federations in the disabled sports, directed at this collective.

2.3.2 Urinary disfunction in Paralympic athletes

A comparative study has been carried out to search for all the adapted solutions for the athletes with urinary disfunctions in order to find a solution of this serious problem and take special measures in the training as well as in the competition.

Not only was this analysis done on a level of prescribed pharmacology and techniques of the diuresis used, but also of the machinery and material of incontinence used.

Such a study will be of great importance to make an ulterior study of the new regulation and lists of forbidden products to apply in the antidoping control of the disabled athletes.

References

1.   **Any authors. (ed.):** ¡ Ánimo ! Inténtalo otra vez: Los minusválidos y el deporte. Ministerio de Asuntos Sociales, Spain, 1989.

2.   **Any authors (ed.):** Blocs 1: Las Paraolimpiadas, algo más que una competición deportiva. Fundación Guttmann, Spain, 1990.

3.   **Any authors (ed.):** Proceedings: I Paralympic Congress Barcelona'92. Fundación ONCE, Spain, 1992.

4.   **COOB'92 (ed.):** General and Functional Classification Guide. COOB'92, Spain 1990.

5.   **COOB'92 (ed.):** Paralympics'92 Official Report. Enciclopèdia Catalana, S.A., Spain, 1993.

6.   **Doll-Tepper G., Dahms C., Doll B., Selzam H.V. (ed.):** Adapted Physical Activity: An interdisciplinary approach. Springer-Verlag, Germany, 1990.

7.   **Goodman S. (ed.):** Spirit of Stoke Mandeville, the story of Sir Ludwig Guttmann. Collins, Great Britain, 1986.

8.   **Hernández R., Martínez J.O., Montesinos M.A., Sánchez-Girón O. (ed.):** Evaluation Handbook, Spanish Method. Excma. Diputació de Barcelona, Spain, 1990.

9.   **Ramsey Musselwhite C. (ed.):** Juegos adaptados para niños especiales. Ministerio de Asuntos Sociales, Spanish version, 1990.

10. **Williams J.G.P., Sperryn P.N. (ed.):** Medicina Deportiva. Salvat S.A., Spanish version, 1982.

Muscular Exercise:
The Immune System, Infections and Cancer

Pedersen, B. K.
Center of Muscle Research, Department of Infectious Diseases
Rigshospitalet, University Hospital
Copenhagen, Denmark

1. Introduction

During the past few years there has been a growing interest in exercise-induced changes in the immune system. This research interest is stimulated by 1) reports of increased frequency of upper respiratory diseases among athletes, 2) the finding that several physical stressors (e.g.surgery, trauma, burn, hypoxia, hyperthermia) induce changes in the cellular immune system and 3) the possibility that the increased levels of some neuroendocrine factors (e.g.catecholamines, betaendorphins, growth hormone, cortisol) during stress may modulate the immune response. This chapter will focus on the effect of acute exercise and fitness level on the immune system. Furthermore the links to infectious diseases and cancer will be discussed.

2. The effect of acute physical exercise on the immune system

2.1 Leucocyte subpopulations

It is well known that severe physical exercise induces changes in the composition of blood mononuclear cells (BMNC). During severe physical exercise lasting 1 hour natural killer (NK) cells, but also B and T cells are recruited to the blood. Simultaneously the composition of T cells are altered, meaning that the CD4/CD8 ratio decreases. Following severe exercise (maximum 2 to 4 h) the lymphocyte concentration decreases and the concentration of monocytes increase (28,32,33,41,43).

2.2 Natural Killer cells

Natural killer cells are thought to play an important role in the first line of defence against viral diseases, furthermore, NK cells are believed to play a role in resistance to cancer (15,29). It has been shown by several people that NK cells are highly influenced by physical exercise (reviewed in 28,30,31). During physical exercise the absolute concentration and the relative fraction of cells expressing characteristic NK cell markers such as CD16 and CD56 (32,33) are increased. Simultaneously the NK cell activity (the function of NK cells) is increased. Young, healthy, relatively untrained male students performed bicycle-exercise for 1 h at 75% of VO2max. At the end of the exercise period the NK cell activity of BMNC, either unincubated or in vitro incubated for 1 hour with interferon-α (IFN-α), interleukin-2 (IL-2) or the prostaglandin-inhibitor indomethacin increased at all times studied. During exercise the IL-2-enhanced NK cell activity increased significantly more than the IFN-α and indomethacin-enhanced NK cell activity (32). When BMNC were incubated with IL-2 for 3 days (lymphokine-activated killer cells (LAK)) the LAK activity of cells from blood sampled at the end of the exercise period were highly significantly increased (42). These data indicate that during exercise NK cells with a high IL-2 response capacity are recruited to the blood.

Two hours after maximal exercise (bicycle ergometer, 1 h, 75% of VO2max) the NK cell activity dropped to a low point. The decreased NK cell activity was probably not due to fluctuations among the NK cells since the proportion of CD16+ cells was normal. Strong evidence suggests that the post-exercise down-regulation of NK cell activity was due prostaglandins released by the elevated number of monocytes. In agreement with this, increased prostaglandin production was found after work and the NK cell activity of monocyte-depleted mononuclear cells did not decrease after exercise. Furthermore, indomethacin in vitro and in vivo fully restored the suppressed NK cell activity (33). Recently it was shown that the post-exercise suppressed LAK-activity was also abolished by indomethacin in vitro (42).

2.3 Proliferation of lymphocytes

It is well known that although the numbers of lymphocytes in the blood are increased during exercise the ability of lymphocytes to proliferate in vitro following stimulation with phytohaemaglutinin (PHA) decreases (reviewed in 28). Niels Tvede et al. showed (43) that the decreased PHA response during bicycle exercise was not due to a changed proliferative response per CD4+ cell, but caused by a decline in the contribution of the CD4+ subgroup to proliferation. The ability of BMNC to proliferate following stimulation with IL-2 is increased during physical exercise. It was shown that the increased IL-2 sensitivity was not caused by an increased expression of IL-2 receptors, but due to increased fraction of CD16+ cells (Tvede et al., unpublished data).

2.4 B cell function

The levels of salivary sIgA were suppressed in cross-country skiers after a race (40) and after a hard 2 h bicycle ergometer session (22). In order to study the mechanism behind the suppression of immunoglobulins a plaque forming cell assay was used, this assay allows us to identify the individual immunglobulin-secreting cells. Stimulation of cells with poke weed mitogen (PWM), interleukin-2 (IL-2) and Epstein-Barr virus (EBV) resulted in significant decreases in numbers of IgG, IgA and IgM-secreting blood cells during as well as 2 h after bicycle exercise, with reversal to preexercise levels 24 h later. The fraction of CD20+ B cells did not change in relation to exercise, suggesting that the suppression of immunoglobulin-secreting cells was not due to changes in numbers of B cells. A decline in the percentage of T cells, mainly CD4+ cells, was measured only during exercise with normalization after exercise. Therefore the B lymphocyte suppression, most pronounced 2 h after exercise, was presumably not due to changes in T lymphocytes also indicated in the experiments using EBV-stimulated cultures, since EBV acts directly on B lymphocytes. Two h after exercise an increased level of CD14+ monocytes was observed. Purified B cells produce plaques only after stimulation with EBV and in these cultures no exercise-induced suppression was found. Addition of indomethacin to IL-2 stimulated cultures of BMNC partly reversed the post-exercise suppressed B cell function. Altogether it was concluded that the exercise-induced suppression of the PFC response was mediated by monocytes (41).

2.5 Cytokines

Cytokines are polypeptide products of activated lymphocytes, monocytes and other cell types that participate in a variety of cellular immunoinflammatory responses. They act as molecular signals between immunocompetent cells (7). Cytokines can be detected in supernatants from stimulated BMNC or in plasma-samples. Supernatants from LPS-stimulated supernatants from BMNC isolated in relation to severe physical exercise showed increased production of IL-1α, IL-1β and IL-6 2 h after severe bicycle exercise lasting 1 h (13). This increase could at least partly be ascribed to an increased fraction of monocytes among the stimulated BMNC suspension. Following a marathon increased IL-6 in plasma was found (27), others have found increased plasma-TNF-α (8). Cannon et al. (3) have found IL-1β in muscle tissue up to 5 days following eccentric muscle work. Recently we have found increased concentration of IL-6 in plasma during severe bicycle exercise (Ullum et al., unpublished data).

2.6 Physical exercise at different intensity

Six persons exercised on a bicycle ergometer for 1 hour at 75%, 50% and 25% of VO2max with intervals of several weeks. Blood samples were collected before, an the end of exercise and 2 hours after. During light, moderate and severe exercise the immune system was generally enhanced, especially the NK and LAK cell activities were markedly increased. Two hours after severe exercise the NK and LAK cell activities and the IL-2 production of PHA-stimulated BMNC were suppressed. Following moderate and light exercise there was no immunosuppresssion. Following severe exercise the monocyte concentration increased two to three fold, but was not enhanced following exercise at less workload. Indomethacin in vitro abolished the decreased NK and LAK cell functions and reversed the suppressed IL-2 production (42). With some generalisation it can be concluded that the immune system is enhanced during light, moderate and severe exercise, however, only severe exercise induces a post-exercise immune suppression, that is mediated by prostaglandins.

3. Possible mechanisms of action

In relation to exercise the concentration in the blood of a number of stress hormones, including adrenaline, noradrenaline, growth hormone, beta-endorphins and cortisol are increased. Severe bicycle exercise also induces a rise in body temperature to 39.5^0 C; this increase in body-temperature is due to hyperthermia and not to a prostaglandin-mediated fever reaction, since pretreatment of test-persons for two days with indomethacin did not inhibit the exercise-induced rise in rectal temperature (Pedersen et al., unpublished data). We have investigated the possibility that stress-hormones or heating of the body are responsible for the exercise-induced immunemodulation.

When healthy, young male students were given intravenous injection of adrenaline to obtain plasma concentrations identical with those observed during bicycle exercise (75% of VO2max, 1 hour) it was shown that the modulation of BMNC subsets, NK activity and lymphocyte function was closely mimicked by administration of adrenaline. However, adrenaline caused minor increase in neutrophil concentration as compared with that induced by exercise (19,43). In vitro adrenaline, even in supraphysiological concentrations, has minor effects on immune functions.

Recently we have obtained results showing that in vivo injection of growth hormone in humans had no effect on BMNC subset, NK activity, cytokine production or lymphocyte function, but induced a highly significant increase in neutrophil concentration (17).

Fiatarone et al. (10) showed that when naloxone was administred in vivo to young women who underwent a maximal bicycle ergometer test, the rise in NK cell activity was no longer significant; however the rise in cells expressing the CD16 marker (NK cells) was not significantly altered as compared with the group receiving placebo. In another study we have obtained conflicting results. When healthy young men were given an epidural analgesia that blocked the afferent impulses and inhibited increase in betaendorphins and ACTH during exercise, this did not inhibit the exercise-induced increase in NK cell function or NK cell concentration. Based on these results we do not think that the betaendorphin response plays an important role in exercise-induced modulation of NK cells (Klokker & Pedersen, unpublished observations).

During bicycle exercise (75% of VO2max, 1h) only a minor increase in cortisol concentration is found (0.63 umol/l before and 0.79 umol/l) (32). It can not easily be predicted from the literature how this minor increase in cortisol concentration can account for the exercise-induced immunomodulation, but cortisol may play a role in exercise training of longer duration.

To examine the selective effect of hyperthermia on the immune system normal healthy young volunteers were immersed into a hot water bath whereby their rectal temperature increased to 39.5 C. In vivo hyperthermia induced alterations that resembled the changes observed in relation to exercise. Hyperthermia induced, however, only minor increases in plasma-adrenaline and -noradrenaline concentrations (18).

In conclusion we find that adrenaline can account for the effect of physical exercise on NK activity, BMNC subsets and proliferative responses, while adrenaline together with growth hormone may be responsible for the increase in neutrophil concentration following exercise. Whether stress hormones are responsible for changes in plasma IL-1 and IL-6 remains to be illucidated. It is furthermore not clear whether the increase in body temperature during exercise can explain part of the immunomodulation in relation to exercise.

4. Training degree

The influence of training degree on the immune system has not been as extensively studied as the effect of acute exercise.

The main problem while examining if the immune system is dependent on training status is to eliminate the effect of acute physical exercise. However, most studies show that the effect on the immune sysstem of physical exercise lasting 1 h is undetectable 20 hours later. In studies on the immune system in trained versus untrained it is important that the testpersons are allowed only to perform minimal physical activity 20 hours before blood sampling. The NK cell activity were found to be elevated in 29 top-trained elite cyclists compared to sex- and age-matched controls. We were unable to find differences in T and B cell subsets or proliferative responses to mitogens and antigens (27,34). The elite cyclists were examined during a period of high (summer) as well as low (winter) training degree after 20 hours at rest. At both examinations the NK cell activity was elevated in the trained group, however, the mechanism behind the elevated NK activity differed between the two seasons. During the winter period the fraction of NK cells was increased, but the study performed during the summer period indicated that the NK cells were activated (27,34).

In a study by Nieman et al. (26) mildly obese premenopausal women performed 15 weeks of walking exercise training (five 45 minutes sessions/ week, brisk walking at 60% HR reserve) and in the study by Crist et al. (4) elderly volunteers performed a 16 weeks exercise program (three 60 minutes/ week consisting of at least 20 minutes of aerobic exercise/session at a HR of 50% of the HR reserve. Both studies showed that resting levels of NK cell activity increased in response to training.

5. Training and disease

5.1 Acute illness

The classic work by Russell (37) showed that exercising during the polio incubation period worsened the disease. This has later been confirmed in experimental animal studies (46). In mice infected with Coxsackie B virus enforced swimming raised mortality and virus replication in the heart markedly increased (48). There are, however, also studies showing that the clinical severity of viral hepatitis is not dependent on the patient having performed physical activity at any time of the disease (24).

5.2 Chronic illness

For many years patients with rheumatoid arthritis (RA) have been excluded from exercise training fearing that it would be harmful to their joints. However, during the last decade a number of studies have shown that exercise training is beneficial to RA patients with low disease activity (for references, see 21). Stimulated by a study which showed that it was possible to induce changes in the immune system of patients with RA who performed a single bout of exercise (21), we examined the effect of eight weeks bicycle training on the immune system in a controlled, randomised study and found no changes in NK cell activity, lymphocyte proliferative response or cytokine level (2). It was concluded that it is possible to train people with RA to increase the fitness level of these without inducing changes in disease activity (2). Training of HIV-positive patients induced significant increase in the concentration of CD4+ cells (20). In a recent publication this finding could, however, not be reproduced (36). It is not known, how acute exercise influences the immune system of patients with severe immune deficiency.

6. Clinical observation

6.1 Training and infections

Several studies have explored the relationship between exercise and upper respiratory diseases (URTI). These studies are based on self-report and do not include a clinical examination or laboratory work-up. Increased frequency of URTI has been reported in a study including 1550 runners who took part in a 56 kilometer race compared to matched controls. Those who ran faster race times reported more symptoms, indicating a dose-response relationship (35). Nieman et al. (25) showed that the marathon runners who actually ran the marathon reported more symptoms of URTI during the week following the race than similarly experienced runners who applied but did not participate in the race for reasons other than sickness.

Heath et al. (14) followed a cohort of 530 runners. Those who ran less than 10 miles had the lowest odds ratio for respiratory diseases, while the odds ratio more than doubled for those running more than 17 miles.

The effect of moderate exercise was studied in a 15 week study including 36 mildly obese women who were randomly assigned to a walking or nonexercising group. The women in the exercise group experienced fewer URTI symptom days and increased natural killer cell numbers than their sedentary controls (26).

6.2 Training and cancer

Acute physical exercise especially influences the NK cells and these cells are thought to play an important role in the defence of malignant cells. It would therefore be of interest to know whether a relationship exists between training and development of cancer. Hoffman-Goetz and McNeil (16) reviewed the evidence linking exercise with natural immunity and cancer. In an American study (11) the prevalence rate of cancers of the reproductive system (uterus, ovary, cervix and vagina) and breast cancer was determined for 5398 living alumnae, 2622 of whom were former college athletes. The relative risk of non-athletes/athletes for cancers of the reproductive system was 2.53 and for breast cancer 1.83. It was concluded that long term athletic training may lower the risk of these cancer forms. The association between physical job activity and colon cancer was examined in a 19-year-follow-up study of 1.1 million Swedish men (12). The relative risk of colon cancer in men employed in sedentary occupations was estimated at 1.3. However, in these epidemiological studies the possibility of exercise-induced changes in the immune system as underlying mechanisms were not discussed.

There are several important experimental studies on exercise and tumors. Voluntary exercise administered during the promotion phase of carcinogesis inhibits the development of mammary tumors (6), whereas forced exercise promotes tumorigenesis (40). In line with this Uhlenbruck (46) showed that moderate exercise training reduced tumor growth in mice, whereas intense exercise enhanced tumor growth and size. With respect to transplanted tumors exercise either inhibits (1) or has little effect (5) on primary tumors. Recently it was shown that exercise that is discontinued and followed by intravenous injection of tumor cells does not reduce the subsequent incidence of pulmonary metastases. In fact, greater tumor multiplicity was observed in the lungs of exercised mice, suggesting a poorer prognosis for this group (23).

7. Conclusion

Exercise-Immunology is a new field. We know much about how exercise influences the immune system. We have begun to understand some of the underlying mechanisms. We know little about the clinical significance of exercise. However, several studies suggest that a relationship may exist between exercise and the development of infectious and malignant diseases. These studies are in accordance with immunological studies suggesting that moderate exercise enhances the immune system while severe exercise is followed by immunedepression.

Future studies will show whether the undesired effects of training on the immune system can be avoided by careful monitoring of the immune system which could warn the athletes when they are more susceptible so they could modify their training and reduce the risk of serious infections. However, it is yet too premature to draw global conclusions and to give guidelines to athletes about exercise and diseases.

References

1. Baracos V.E.: Exercise inhibits progressive growth of the Morris hepatoma 7777 in male and female rats. Can. J. Physiol. Pharmacol. 67: 864-870, 1988.

2. Baslund, B., K. Lyngberg, V. Andersen, J. Halkjær Kristensen, M. Hansen, M. Klokker and B.K. Pedersen. The effect of eight weeks bicycle training on the immune system of patients with rheumatoid arthritis. J Appl Physiol, accepted for publication, 1993.

3. **Cannon JG, Fielding RA, Fiataorne MA, Orencole SF, Dinarello CA, Evans WJ.** Increased interleukin 1 Beta in human skeletal muscle after exercise. Am J Physiol, 26: R451-R455. 1989.

4. **Christ D.M., L.T. Mackinnon, R.F. Thompson, H.A. Atterbom and P.A. Egan.** Physical exercise increases natural cellular-mediated tumor cytotoxicity in elderly women. Gerontol. 35: 66-71, 1989.

5. **Cohen LA, Boylan E, Epstein M, Zang, E.** Voluntary exercise and experimental mammary cancer. In: Exercise, Calories, Fat and Cancer. M.M. Jacob (Ed), New York: Plenum press, pp 41-59, 1992.

6. **Cohen LA., Choi K., Wang C.X.** Influence of dietary fat, caloric restriction and voluntary exercise on N-nitrosomethyiera-induced mammary tumorigensis in rats. Cancer Res. 48: 4276-83, 1988.

7. **Dinarillo CA, Mier JW.** Lymphokines. N Engl J Med 317, 940-945, 1987.

8. **Espersen GT, Elbæk A, Ernst A, Toft E, Kaalund S, Jersild C, Grunnet N.** Effect of physical exercise on cytokines and lymphocyte subpopulations in human peripheral blood. APMIS 1990, 98(5), 395-400.

9. **Evans WJ, Meredith CN, Cannon JG,Dinarello, Frontera WR, Hughes VA, Jones BH, Knuttgen HG.** Metabolic changes following eccentric exercise in trained and untrained men. J Appl Physiol 1986, 61(5): 1864-1868.

10. **Fiatarone MA, Morley JE, Bloom ET, Donna M, Makinodan T, Solomon GF.** Endogenous opioids and the exercise-induced augmentation of natural killer cell activity. J Lab Clin Med 1988, 112: 544-552.

11. **Frisch RE, Wyshak G, Albright NL, Albright TA, Schiff E, Jones KP.** Lower prevalence of breast cancer and cancers of the reproductiove system among former college athletes compared to non-athletes. Br J Cancer 1985, 52: 885-591.

12. **Gerhardsson M, Norell S, Kiviranta H, Pedersen N, Ahlblom A.** Sedentary jobs and colon cancer. Am J Epidemilogy 1986, 123: 775-780.

13. **Haahr PM, Fomsgaard A, Tvede N, Diamant M,Halkjær Kristensen J, Pedersen BK.** Effect of physical exercise on the in vitro production of IL-1, IL-6, TNF- , IL-2 and IFN- Int.J.Sports Med. 12, 223-227, 1991.

14. **Heath GW, Ford ES, Craven TE, Macera CA, Jackson KL, Pate RR.** Exercise and the incidence of upper respiratory tract infections. Medicine and Science in Sports and Exercise 23(2): 152-157, 1991.

15. **Herberman RB.** Natural killer cells: their role in defenses against disease. Science 214: 24-30, 1981.

16. **Hoffman-Goetz L and MacNeil B.** Exercise, natural immunity, and cancer: causation, correlation, or conundrum, in Exercise and Disease, Watson R.R. and Eisinger, M, eds., CRC Press, Boca Raton, FL, 1992, 37.

17. **Kappel M., Hansen M.B., Diamant M., Jørgensen J.O., Gyhrs A., Pedersen B.K.** Effects of an acute bolus growth hormone infusion on the human immune system. Hormone and metabolic research, accepted for publication, 1993.

18. **Kappel M, Stadeager C, Tvede N, Galbo H, Pedersen BK.** Effect of in vivo hyperthermia on natural killer cell activity, in vitro proliferative responses and blood mononuclear cell subpopulations. Clin Exp Immunol 1991, 84: 175-180.

19. **Kappel M, Tvede N, Galbo H, Haahr PM, Kjær M, Linstouw M, Klarlund K, Pedersen BK.** Epinephrine can account for the effect of physical exercise on natural killer cell activity. Journal of Applied Physiology 70(6), 2530-2534, 1991.

20. **LaPerriere A, Fletcher MA, Antoni MH, Klimas NG, Ironson G, Schneiderman N.** Aerobic exercise training in an AIDS risk group. Int J Sports Med 1991, 12: S53-S57.

21. **Lyngberg K, Tvede N, Halkjær Kristesen J, Andersen V, Pedersen BK.** Physical exercise induces modulation of the cellular immune system in patients with rheumatoid arthritis. Scandinavian Journal of Medicine and Science in Sports. 1991, 1, 167-173,1991.

22. **MacKinnon LT, Chick A Van As, Tomasi T.** The effect of exercise on secretory and natural immunity. Adv Exp Med Biol. 1987, 216A: 869-876.

23. **MacNeil B, Hoffman-Goetz L.** Effect of exercise on natural cytotoxicity and pulmonary tumor metastases in mice. Med. Sci. Sports Exerc. 25: 922-928, 1993.

24. Nefzger M, Chalmers T. The treatment of acute infectious hepatitis: ten-year follow-up study of the effects of diet and rest. Am J Med 1963, 35: 299-309.

25. Nieman DC, Johanssen Lee JW, Arabatzis K. Infectious episodes in runners before and after the Los Angeels Marathon. Journal of Sports Medicine and Physical Fitness 30: 316-328, 1990.

26. Nieman D.C., S.L. Nehlsen-Cannarella, P.A. Markoff, A.J. Balk.Lamberton, H. Yang, D.B.W. Chritton, J.W. Lee and K. Arabatzis. The effects of moderate exercise training on natural killer cells and acute upper respiratory tract infections. Int. J. Sports Med. 11, 467-473, 1990.

27. Northoff H, Berg A. Immunologic mediators as parameters of the reaction to strenous exercise. Int J Sports Med 1991, 12: S9-S15.

28. Pedersen BK. The effect of physical exercise on the cellular immune system - mechanisms of action. A review. Int. J. Sports Med. 12, 1, S23-S29, 1991.

29. Pedersen BK. Natural killer cells in relation to disease. A review. Allergy 40: 547-557, 1985.

30. Pedersen BK. Effects of exercise on the immune system - with special reference to natural killer cells. - review. Submitted for publication.

31. Pedersen BK. Exercise and Immunity - Mechanisms of action. Med Sport Sci 1992, 37, 25, 1-6.

32. Pedersen BK, Tvede N, Hansen FR, Andersen V, Bendix T, Bendixen, G et al. Modulation of natural killer cell activity in peripheral blood by physical exercise. Scand J Immunol 1988, 26: 673-678.

33. Pedersen BK, Tvede N, Klarlund K, Christensen LD, Hansen FR, Galbo H et al. Indomethacin in vitro and in vivo abolishes post-exercise suppression of natural killer cell activity in peripheral blood. International Journal of Sports Medicine 1990, 11: 127-131.

34. Pedersen BK, Tvede N, Christensen LD, Klarlund K, Kragbak S, Halkjær-Kristensen J. Natural killer cell activity in peripheral blood of highly trained and untrained. International Journal of Sports Medicine 1989, 10: 129-131.

35. **Peters E, Bateman E.** Ultramarathon running and upper respiratory tract infections. An epidemiological study. S A Med J 1983, 64: 583-584.

36. **Rigsby LW, Dishman RK, Jackson AW, Maclean GS, Raven PB.** Effects of exercise training on men seropositive for the human immunodeficiency virus-1. Med Science Sports Exercise 1992, 24:6-12.

37. **Russell WR.** Poliomyelitis, the paralytic stage and the effect of physical activity on the severity of paralysis. Br Med J 1: 465-471, 1949.

38. **Thomsen BS, Haahr PM, Rødgaard A, Tvede N, Hansen FR, Steensberg J, Halkjær Kristensen J, Pedersen BK.** Complement receptor type one (CR1, CD35) on erythrocytes, circulating immune complexes and complement C3 split products after short-term physical exercise and training. Int J Sports Med, 1992, 13: 172-175.

39. **Thomson HJ, Ronan AM, Ritacco KA, Tagliaferro AR, Meejer LD.** Effect of exercise on the induction of mammary carcinogenesis. Cancer Res. 48: 2720-2723, 1988.

40. **Tomasi F, Trudeau D, Czerqinski D, Erredge S.** Immune parameters in athletes before and after strennous exercise. J Clin Immunol 1982, 2: 173-178.

41. **Tvede N, Heilmann C, Halkjær-Kristensen J, Pedersen BK** Mechanisms of B lymphocyte suppression induced by acute physical exercise. J. Clin. Lab. Immunol. 1989, 30: 169-173.

42. **Tvede N, Kappel M, Halkjær Kristensen J, Galbo H, Pedersen BK.** The effect of light, moderate and severe bicycle exercise on lymphocyte subsets, natural and lymphokine activated killer cells, lymphocyte proliferative response and interleukin 2 production. Int J Sports Medicine, 14(5):275-282, 1993.

43. **Tvede N., M. Kappel, K. Klarlund, J. Halkjær-Kristensen, M.Kjær, H. Galbo and B.K. Pedersen.** Evidence that the effect of bicycle exercise on blood mononuclear cell proliferative responses and subsets is mediated by epinephrine. Submitted to Int J Sports Med, 1993.

44. **Tvede N, Pedersen BK, Hansen FR, Bendix T, Christensen LD, Galbo H et al.** Effect of physical exercise on blood mononuclear cell subpopulations and in vitro proliferative responses. Scand J Immunol 1989, 29: 383-389.

45. Tvede N, Steensberg J, Baslund B, Halkjær-Kristensen J, Pedersen BK. Cellular Immunity in highly-trained elite racing cyclists during periods of training with high and low intensity. Scand J Med Science Sports, 1, 163-166, 1991.

46. Uhlenbruck G, Order U. Can endurance sports stimulate immune mechanisms against cancer and metastasis? Int J Sports Med 1991, 12: S63-S68.

47. Weinstein L. Poliomyelitis - a persistent problem. N Engl J Med 1973, 288: 370-371.

48. Woodruff J. Viral myocarditis. A review. Am J Pathol. 1980, 101: 424-479.

Physical Education Teachers and Coaches in the Context of Adapted Physical Activity

Peitersen, B.
The Danish State Institute of Physical Education
Copenhagen, Denmark

1. Introduction

The purpose of this paper is to identify the educational and social challenges inherent in the creation of new innovative approaches to integrating APA dimensions into the professional training schemata of physical education teachers and coaches.

First, appropriate didactical perspectives directed at the ever expanding subject area knowledge base will be discussed. Second, methodologies appropriate for establishing new initiatives will be identified and briefly described. Third, findings from a few recent studies will be presented as a means of identifying the positive potential and future implications of this focus within the sport pedagogy profession.

Finally, the role of Sports pedagogy as a sports science discipline and as a key element in integrating programmes will be discussed.

2. New educational challenges

As recently as fifteen years ago, there were only two popular job titles for those professionals interested in physical activity: physical education teacher and/or trainer/coach. Currently the list of appropriate job titles looks more like this:

- animateur
- head coach
- consultant
- fitness assistant
- leisure time sports manager
- project manager
- recreation coordinator

This listing clearly documents the radical conceptual changes that have taken place in the field of physical education.

The more popular current conception of physical education has placed an increased emphasis on both the broader concept of movement and the social importance of recreation and physical health.

Recently the term Sports has been used to depict a wide spectrum of physical activities ranging from the extremes of informal activities on one end to institutionalised and internationalised sports at the other end.
Sociologically, new participant groups have emerged and a resultant change in the nature of sports is imminent.
In general, physical activities have maintained a dominant role in European cultures and this has resulted in creative educational challenges emerging in physical education study programmes in a variety of countries.
In addition to the educational challenges and social demands, the study of physical education is currently under intense scrutiny.
The sport sciences are relatively new academic disciplines when compared to other well established disciplines (i.e. Mathematics, Physics), and are characterized as multidimensional and more amorphous. A well integrated study of physical education should be a multi-disciplinary programme that aims both at vocationally-oriented and that attainment of high scientifically standards.
In regards to this suggestion, Telema (1990) has recognized potential problems in the professional preparation of physical education teachers. His suggestion is that the problems in sports sciences are caused by the multidimensional nature of the disciplines, the administrative differentiation of the programs, and the students' assumptions of study and teaching.

Fig. 1: **Problems of academic professional training in physical education and sports**

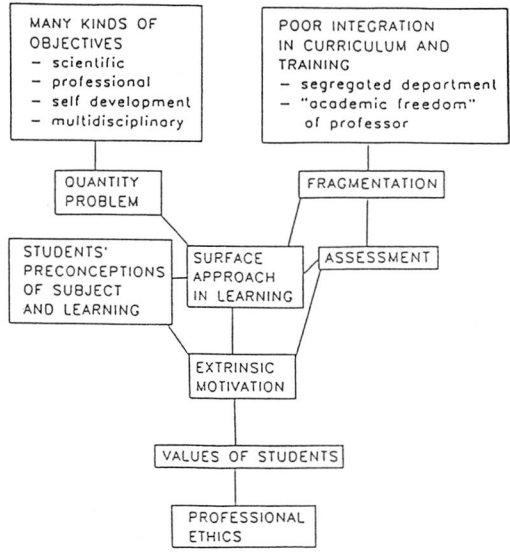

2.1 Adapted Physical Activity

One increasingly important participant group in the newly defined world of sports are those that are classified as "handicapped".
The movement to provide educationally and socially integrated recreational experiences for differently-abled persons continues to gain momentum in all venues.
In 1968, The Council of Europe launched its "Sport for All" charter. Article 1 of this charter states: "Every individual shall have the right to participate in sport".
The Council of Europe extended that right to those at a physical disadvantage, excluded from participation in sport which is often regarded as the prerogative of only healthy young men in their prime. The charter addresses all groups: the elderly, the unemployed, migrants, prisoners and differently-abled. In 1986, the Council adopted a "European Charter for Sport for All: Disabled Persons". This Council envisioned this effort as serving as the impetus for this population to seek or restore contact with the surrounding environment while re-establishing recognition as an equal and respected citizen.

Currently, the term "Adapted Physical Activity" is used world-wide to describe all aspects of this field. The term can be defined as follows:

Adapted Physical Activity:

Specific
>   movement, physical activity, and sports in which special emphasis has been placed on the needs, interests and capabilities of individuals with limiting conditions. (cf. 7th International Symposium "APA" Berlin 1989)

Generic
>   Adapted: requiring adaptations which may be **education, recreation,** or structural in nature.
>   Physical activity: movement experiences (participation which may be motivated by **therapy, rehabilitation, education, recreation,** and/or **competition**)

Application
>   limited to interests, needs, and capabilities of individuals with impairments, disabilities, or handicaps as defined by the World Health Organisation. (cf. European Association for Research into Adapted Physical Activity 1989)

As a result of the increasing attention placed upon the health and well being of individuals, a special focus has been directed at the need for physical activity for individuals with disabilities. Across Europe the trend is towards greater acceptance and inclusion of individuals with disabilities in all societal scenarios, specifically physical education and sport. This trend suggests new directions to be taken by creative and innovative professional teacher preparation programmes.

3. Didactical consequences

Realistically, reflecting on the complexity of teacher preparation at training institutions, it seems almost impossible to tackle and include the multitude of needs and demands of modern society.

This current situation is analogous to the confusion in the mid-seventies when certain academic subjects were inundated with new knowledge.
The heterogenous curricula of the European colleges demonstrate different backgrounds and philosophical intentions; but, a common point to begin discussion could be to identify the form and content most appropriate for teacher education programmes given the nature and demands of society.
What kind of curricular structures and pedagogical strategies need to be implemented within teacher preparation programmes to create the opportunities for teachers to treat teaching as a moral, political, and social act?
Questions and considerations of this sort belong to the didactical area, and can be translated into various conceptions of curricular.

Curriculum orientation, as defined by Crum (1990) is an assumption that general curricular decisions, namely decisions on objectives and contents of education, are dependent on value-bound views concerning (a) children and their potential and desirable development, (b) the expected and the desired changes in the social-cultural context, (c) the role of schooling, and (d) considerations concerning the connections between (a),(b) and (c). He further identified five physical education curriculum orientations;

      a.   the biologistic training-of-the-physical concept,
      b.   the pedagogistic education-through-movement concept,
      c.   the personalistic movement education concept,
      d.   the conformistic sport socialization concept, and
      e.   the critical-constructive movement socialization concept.

There has been an obvious neglect of integration and implementation strategies which would parallel the curricular developments due to an ambiguity of roles and responsibilities of different service agencies and organizations.

3.1 Planning to teach the disabled

A well-balanced P.E. teacher training programme, as a central element, exposes students to the didactical process of decision making in the teaching profession. In most didactical models, the learners' background, etc., is an essential factor in the development of any teaching unit.

When framed in a pedagogical perspective, the terms "disabled", "handicapped", and "impaired" all have a negative connotation. The progressive term of "differently-abled" is more constructive and positive in the pedagogical process.

Of special interest to all educators should be the research findings from adapted physical activity which provide new and essential insights for didactical considerations.

Recent adapted physical education research has focused on (a) effective teaching/learning of individuals with disabilities, (b) effects of integration, (c) assessment techniques, and (d) effective programmes. Physical activity programmes for individuals of varying ability, classification (e.g. elderly people with anorexia, mild to severely retarded) and content (psychomotor, fitness, development etc.) have been internationally explored. Although some international differences do exist, research tends to support (a) the positive effect of instruction/training programmes, (b) an improvement in performance, (c) a positive change in attitude, (d) the positive benefits of integration, and (e) similarity more than difference.

Specific studies targeted programme effectiveness, performance evaluation, mainstreaming effects, behaviour management approaches, and early intervention programs.

In a recent review of research literature, DePauw(1990) characterizes factors which could influence physical activity of disabled participants including attitude, integration, psychological and sociological factors. Examples of factors which influence physical activity are:

(a) The inclusion of disabled individuals with able-bodied individuals enhances motor performance, increases appropriate behaviour, and improves social interaction. (Studies conducted of autistic, mentally retarded, blind, and physically disabled subjects).

b) Attitudes toward disabled individuals are generally positive and can be changed. The acceptance of those who are disabled is directly related to one's attitude. Those who feel more competent had a more positive attitude toward disabled subjects. Practicum experiences were found to be effective in changing attitudes.

(c) Disabled athletes (wheel chair, cerebrally paralysed, blind) were found to exhibit similar perceptions, cognitive behaviours, and psychological profiles as able- bodied athletes. Self-concept was found to be variable and dependent on the individual's level of physical activity.

DePauw suggested that these results be incorporated in the development and implementation of programmatic parameters for physical activity that can benefit all individuals including those with impairments (DePauw,1990).

3.2 The school setting

To date, local and national legislation has been supportive of mainstreaming policies to enable social and academic gains. Physical education settings specifically offer evidence that (1) effective teaching can occur in mainstreamed environments, and (2) the behaviour of mainstreamed students is similar enough to warrant their inclusion in regular classes (Vogler, van der Mars, Cusimano, and Darst, 1992).

Only by incorporating all this relevant information into the didactical subject matter will the students be able to develop, refine and transform the language and categories in which teachers think about their work. The aim is to infuse the teaching profession with a new set of insights and understandings about the schooling process.

4. Prioritizing approaches for curriculum and teaching aims

One of our partner universities, the American Adelphi University, has redesigned their Physical Education Teacher Education (PETE).
The programme's conceptual framework is constructed around four interdependent curricular components which have been used to guide the development of innovative programme features.
One of the four curricular components is the Infusion Component. This component emphasizes transactional processes and experiences between students and faculty, directed at blending subject matter content with pedagogical themes.
In the infusion phase, which runs over a year, four selected major pedagogical themes guide the programme in building a matrix.

The matrix of differently-abled looks like this:

Fig. 2: **Adelphi University Teacher Development Team Matrix**

DIFFERENTLY-ABLED MATRIX	VISUAL	AUDITORY	AMPUTATION LOWER	WHEELCHAIR	ED/LD AT-RISK	MR	TERMINOLOGY	AMPUTATION UPPER	ORTHOPEDICALLY LIMITED MOBILITY
BADMINTON								X	
BASKETBALL				X					
GROUP GAMES	X								
LIFETIME SPORTS		X							
RHYTHMS & DANCE						X	X		
SOCCER									X
TENNIS				X					
TRACK & FIELD								X	
TUMBLING					X				
VOLLEYBALL			X						

This figure identifies the selected pedagogical themes which have been purposefully introduced and explored in the context of physical activity in the subject matter content courses. (Barrette and Fiorentino, 1993).

Student simulation is the chosen method of experiences/learning. The inability of most educators to project themselves into the psychological space of the disabled persons can most probably be overcome by applying the method of simulation.

Inspired by this innovative programme, my own institute will integrate our infusion component of differently-abled perspectives in a matrix like this:

Fig. 3: DHL's koblingsmatrix - 1993/94 (The Danish version)

Forelæsning	Dato	AT	FO	HÅ	BA	VO	SV	KE	RY	RG	OR
Metode i undervisningen	29.10.93			43-44				43-44			X
Motivation	19.11.93								46-47		
Social læring	26.11.93		47-48								X
Progression-Regression	03.12.93						48-49	X			
Undervisningsdifferentering	04.02.94							5-6			
Teknik træning	11.03.94			10-11			10-11				
Præstation	18.03.94					11-12					
Video feedback	25.03.94	12-13									
Projekt arbejdsformen	08.04.94									14-15	
Tillid-tryghed	15.04.94								15-16		
Visualisering	06.05.94				18-19						
* Handicap	1 week	←					→				

This means that our undergraduate students will be exposed to the inter-relatedness of subject matter and pedagogy.

As a result of exposure to The Adelphi Model of infusing differently-abled thematic scenarios into physical education content courses, a student knows:

- The definition of visual impairment, and the specific activity modification guidelines associated with visual impairment.

- The definition of auditory impairment and specific activity modification guidelines associated with auditory impairment.

- The definition of/categorization of amputation classifications and specific activity modifications guidelines associated with amputations.

- The definition of orthopedic impairments (crutches, limited mobility, wheelchair) and specific activity guidelines associated with orthopedic impairments.

- The definition of emotionally-disturbed children and specific activity modification guidelines associated with emotionally-disturbed children.

- The definition of learning disabled children and specific activity modification guidelines associated with learning disabled children.

- The definition of At-Risk children and specific activity modification guidelines associated with At-Risk children.
- The definition of mentally retarded and specific activity modification guidelines associated with mentally retarded children.
- The definition of Down's Syndrome and specific activity modification guidelines associated with Down's Syndrome children.
- The definition of mainstreaming, reverse mainstreaming, adaptive programs and adapted programs.
(Fiorentino, 1993).

Examples of differently-abled thematic infusion scenarios in physical education content courses include:

1. Volleyball methods and amputations: The effects that lower body amputation has on mobility, coordination, balance, timing and accuracy.
2. Group games and visual impairment: The effects that visual impairment has on the increased dependence on auditory and kinesthetic input as well as the distractibility with increased noise.
3. Tennis methods and orthopedic impairment: The effects that orthopedic impairment (wheelchair) has on mobility, eye-hand coordination, balance, and timing.
4. Rhythms and movement methods and amputation: The effects that amputations (upper and lower body) have on mobility, coordination, balance differences and social reactions.

5. The role of Sport Pedagogy

Research indicates that a crucial element of attitudes to integration is perceived competence which in turn is partly a function of the quantity and quality of teacher training prior to any mainstreaming experience (Center and Ward, 1987).

To develop a relevant competency in students depends heavily on the place of sport pedagogy and its content in the teacher training programme.

The quality aspects depend on the issues brought up in the sport pedagogy area and how students are encouraged to adopt a perspective that challenge the students to ask "why?". In the adapted perspective we are looking for a competency that enables the student to narrow the gap between presented theory and experienced practice and combining the notion of technical rationality in the teacher education process with the reflective teaching approach (Hellison and Templin, 1991).

It is not relevant to adhere to a functional-technical education alone. The shape and content of school subjects are in constant process and debates concerning the the contents and the teaching methods of physical education are likewise. So it is not simply a matter of finding the best and most efficient ways of improving teaching and learning. The notion of a science of sport pedagogy involves much more than the development of "better" teaching techniques and in the planning procedures the didactical reflective process, the focus is on the main questions when dealing with didactics: What - How - Why. Understanding <u>what</u> is being taught and <u>why</u> are as important as knowing <u>how</u> to teach it.

For an optimal preparation of future physical education teachers and their skills and attitudes towards the integration of differently abled it is crucial to give sufficient recognition to the role of sport pedagogy in the teacher training programmes.

References

1. Barrette, G & Fiorentino, L, (1993). Teaming + Timing = Transformation. Developmentally appropriate teacher education. Paper presented at AIESEP Conference, Trois-Rivieres, Quebec.

2. Crum, B (1992). Competing orientations for PE curriculum development; The trend towards a consensus in the Netherlands and an international comparison. In T. Williams, L. Almond & A. Sparkes(eds). Sport and Physical Activity: Moving towards excellence. London. E & FN. Spon.

3. DePauw, K. P (1992). Current international trends in research in adapted physical activity. In T. Williams, L. Almond & A. Sparkes(eds). Sport and Physical Activity: Moving towards excellence. London. E & FN. Spon.

4. Hellison, D. & Templin, T. (1991). A reflective approach to teaching physical education. Champaign. Human Kinetics.

5. Telema, R. (1990) Problems of meaningful learning in physical education and particularly in teacher training. In R. Telema, L. Laakso et al.(eds). Physical education and life-long physical activity. Jyväskylä.

6. Vogler, E. W. Van der Mars, Cusimano, Darst (1992). Experience, expertise, and teaching effectiveness with mainstreamed and nondisabled children in physical education. APAQ. vol 9 no 4 1992 p. 298-314.

Musculoskeletal Disorders in Sports and Physical Education

Renström, Per A.F.H.
University of Vermont, Department of Orthopaedics and Rehabilitation
Burlington, Vermont; USA

Physical activity and sports are an integrated part of many peoples' lives. Young individuals have a need for motion and sports offer a natural way of using their energy. Sports and physical education should, therefore, be a natural and integrated part of the school curriculum. The importance of students' participation in sports and physical education is not appreciated everywhere. With increasing age, health aspects are more important and because of this, there is a continuous explosion in participation in different kinds of physical activity after the younger and more competitive years.

Sports and physical activity can present a danger to health in the form of sports injuries. Competitive sports are characterized by increasing demands and intensity and duration of training. There is a decreasing time for recovery of fatigued tissues, and, thereby, an increased risk for injury. With increasing demands, there is also an increasing specialization, even in younger age groups which can be a risk factor for overuse injuries. Overall, there is a potential increasing risk of injury for all levels of athletes. This fact is not only causing problems for the athletes themselves and their teams, but there is also an enormous cost for society involved. In order to break this vicious circle, there must be an increased focus on prevention of injuries and of recurrence of injuries, as well as on education in how to correctly manage these injuries. This means that there is an increasing need for people involved in athletics to be more educated. Athletes, parents, coaches, teachers and especially physical education teachers, need health education including prevention, correct management of injuries and other health aspects.

The aim of this presentation is to discuss some factors of importance in prevention and management of injuries in sports and physical activities, and how adequate measures can be taken by people involved in these activities. It is of great importance that teachers in for example, physical education, are well educated and trained in prevention and management or orthopaedic sports medicine problems, as they deal with athletes and active people on a daily basis.

The approach to this presentation is to initially discuss prevention as this is of general importance. We will use the sequence of prevention presented by Van Mechelen, (21) as the base for this presentation. This sequence includes first a discussion of the extent of the injury problem, which can be described by injury incidence and by severity of sports injury. Secondly, the etiology of injuries must be established, as well as the mechanism of injury. The third part of this sequence is introducing measures that can reduce future risks and severity of injuries.

1. The Extent of Sports Injury Prevention

1.1 Injury incidence

The incidence of sports injuries depends on the method used to register the injuries, i.e. whether it is prospective or retrospective. The methods used to establish the population at risk are important, as well as the representativity of the population. Sports injuries are preferably expressed as the number of sports injuries per exposure time, e.g. per 1,000 hours of sports participation.

Van Galen et al. (12), found in the Netherlands, 3.5 injuries per 1,000 hours spent on sports. 1.4 injuries per 1,000 hours were medically treated.

There is a difference in incidence of injuries of different sports. In an investigation in Holland, indoor soccer was the highest with 8.7 injuries per 1,000 hours. Basketball was #10 with 4.4 injuries per 1,000 hours and swimming was #20 with 1.2 injuries per 1,000 hours. The incidence rate of injuries in physical education classes varied between .75 (27) and 11.7 per 100 sports injuries per year (4).

> **Message:** The Injury Incidence in Sports and Physical Activity is too high.

1.2 Severity of sports injuries

This is evaluated by the nature of sports injury, the duration and age of treatment, sporting time loss, working time loss, permanent damage and costs. The nature and duration of treatment can be evaluated from an epidemiological point of view. Only 25% of all injuries registered called for medical attention of a general practitioner or a medical specialist. Sprains were the most common type of injury, and the ankle was the most injured area according to Austin et al. (3). The actual number of days lost from sports, or until the athlete returns to sports activities, are often reported as a measure of injury severity. Sandelin et al. (33) found that 71% of injuries were minor, which was defined as absent from sports less than one week, 20% as moderate, i.e. absent from sports for one to three weeks, and 9% as severe.

The severity of an injury depends on how an injury is defined. The Council of Europe defines sports injury as the result of participation in sports with one or more of the following consequences: Reduction of the amount or level of sports activity, a need for medical advice or treatment, or an adverse social or economic effect (12).

> **Message:** Most Sports Injuries are Minor, but Severe Injuries Occur.

1.3 Cost

Sports injuries cost society billions of dollars in both direct and indirect costs. Sports trauma made up for 10 to 15% of all accidents in West Germany (34). Forty years ago sports injuries formed 1.4% of all injuries in the emergency rooms. Today, 10% of all traumatic injuries treated in the emergency room hospitals in all countries are sustained in sports (12). Overuse injuries have, however, gradually become more common, but they are not included in the casualty department records.

The direct and indirect costs in the Netherlands associated with medically treated sports injuries have been estimated to run up to 225 million U.S. dollars (35). The annual costs of sports injuries in West Germany in 1983 was over 2,500 million U.S. dollars (34).

2. Sequence of Prevention: The Factors and Mechanisms, which Play a Part in the Occurrence of Sports Injuries.

Sports injuries result from a complex interaction of identifiable risk factors of which only a fraction seems to be possible to identify. To exemplify the etiology of factors and mechanisms for injury, we will use running as an example.

An average recreational runner has an overall yearly incidence rate for running injuries of about 37 to 56%. The distribution of running injuries according to medical diagnosis can be seen in Table 1. Distribution of overuse and acute running injuries are seen in Table 2.

Table 1: Frequency of the 10 commonest medically treated injuries sustained by 987 male and 663 women runners. Clement (9).

	Males %	n	Females %	n	Total %	n
Patellar pain syndrome*	24.3	262	27.9	206	25.8	468
Tibial stress syndrome[t]	10.7	115	16.8	124	13.2	239
Inflammation Achilles tendon	7.9	85	3.2	24	6.0	109
Fasciitis plantaris[tt]	5.3	57	3.9	28	4.7	85
Inflammation patellar tendon	5.6	60	2.8	21	4.5	81
Iliotibial friction syndrome	4.6	50	3.8	28	4.3	78
Metatarsal stress syndrome	3.3	36	3.0	22	3.2	58
Tibial stress fracture	2.4	26	2.8	21	2.6	47
Tendinitis m. tibialis posterior	1.9	21	3.2	14	2.5	45
Tendinitis m. peroneus	2.0	22	1.6	12	1.9	34
Total	68.0	735	69.0	510	68.7	1244

* Patellar pain syndrome (chondromalacia patellae) is a disorder of the kneecap.
[t] Tibial stress syndrome (shin splits) is caused by strain on the points of attachment of the foot flexors.
[tt] Fasciitis plantaris is a disorder of the sole of the foot.
Tractatus iliotibialis syndrome is pain in the outer side of the knee.

Table 2: Distribution of overuse and acute running injuries (%).
Van Mechelen (23).

	Ijzerman & van Galen 1987 (n = 644)	Marti et al. 1988 (n = 877)	Ooijendijk & Van Agt 1990 (n = 64)	Van Mechelen et al. 1991 (n = 44)
Overuse Injuries	54	73	73	75
Acute Injuries	46	27	27	25

Musculoskeletal injuries result from a complex interaction of intrinsic and extrinsic factors.

2.1 Extrinsic factors

Training factors such as running too often, too fast, or for too long may be causes of injuries in both inexperienced and experienced runners. Running experience results in a better adaptation to running from a biomechanical point of view. Lack of running experience or running to compete are risk factors which are probably difficult to deal with in terms of prevention other then through health education. Weekly running distance is a strong determinant of running injuries. The role of running frequency and weekly running time are unclear (22).

Previous injuries are an important independent risk factor for running injuries, although the mechanism still needs clarification. Distribution of recurrent and new running injuries can be seen in Table 3.

Table 3: Distribution of recurrent and new running injuries (%).
Van Mechelen (23).

	Marti et al. 1988 (n = 1994)	Macera et al. 1989 (n = 300)	Walter et al. 1989 (n = 620)	Van Mechelen et al. 1991 (n = 44)
Recurrent Injury	21	70	46	30
New Injury	79	30	54	70

In summary, running injuries are significantly associated with lack of running experience, running to compete and excessive weekly running distance and previous injury.

A dissociation exists, on the other hand, between running injuries and running frequency, warming up and stretching exercises, body height, malalignment, muscle imbalance, restricted range of motion, running frequency, the level of performance, stability of running pattern, shoes and in-shoe orthosis and running on one side of the road (22).

Concerning the shoes, the important shock absorbance of running shoes does not seem to be denied by epidemiological studies. The shock absorbing qualities of wet running shoes are reduced. Running shoes lose between 30 and 50% of shock absorbing characteristics after as much as four times long-term running (10). The role of running shoes in running injury prevention remains, however, unclear.

Different running surfaces as such do not cause running injury risk, although it should be kept in mind that bias probably plays an important role. According to Nigg (24), sports surfaces have been shown to be involved in tripling and quadrupling the frequency of injuries selected towards activities. This is, however, sports dependent. In sports such as tennis, the playing surface can vary considerably. Unforgiving surfaces such as asphalt are often fatiguing for the legs, and can produce overuse problems of the knee. Inconsistent and unforgiving surfaces such as indoor carpets may cause sudden unexpected stops and can cause ligament sprain injuries to the knee and ankle joints. Inconsistent and unforgiving surfaces such as clay are less likely to result in overuse injuries. Sliding into the lines on clay can, however, result in knee pain.

> **Message:** Many running injuries can be prevented by analyzing extrinsic factors and by modifying training routines.

2.2 Intrinsic factors

Intrinsic factors such as age, have not been found to be associated with running injuries. It has been speculated that the association may be biased by factors such as running experience, weekly running distance or running speed. Gender per se does not seem to be an important risk for running injuries. Body mass index is not related to running injuries, but perhaps taller runners are at a greater risk. In summary, age, gender, body mass index, running hills, running hard surfaces, participating in other sports, and the time of the day are not significant associated with running injuries (22).

Biomechanics of the lower extremity play an important role in the development of some overuse syndromes about the knee. In 40% of injured runners' malaligaments, such as foot insufficiency, lower extremity muscle stiffness, genu varum and high-Q angle were factors causing injury (18). Excessive pronation results in compensatory internal rotation. This transverse rotation must be absorbed by the knee and can cause knee problems. It can lead to a more proximal problems, e.g. in the hip region or the back. Cavus feet are associated with injuries on the lateral side of the lower extremity. Bony malalignment can cause increased hip anteversion, leg length discrepancy, abnormalities of the lumbar spine and increased lumbar lordosis which may all predispose to biomechanical overloading of the knee. Specific anatomic malalignments and abnormal biomechanics of the lower extremity are, however, not correlated with specific injuries on a predictable basis.

Iliotibial Band Friction Syndrome: An example of the importance of malalignment is the etiology of the iliotibial band friction syndrome. Training errors, such as running downhill or on tilting roads are associated with the injury in 42% of athletes suffering from iliotibial band friction syndrome. The dynamics of the role of malalignment is such that at 30° the iliotibial band rubs over the lateral femoral epicondyle and a bursa can be irritated and form pain. Foot abnormalities associated with iliotibial band friction syndrome are excessive pronation, heel varus, cavus feet and forefoot pronation. Excessive pronation results in decreased lower leg internal rotation. The iliotibial insertion site at Gerdy's tubercle is drawn anterior and medially and, thereby, the iliotibial band will be tighter and friction will cause bursitis. This means that when treating the iliotibial band, the cause of the injury should be treated, as well as the symptoms.

The importance of malalignment as a cause of running injuries is still not clear. The cause of running injuries are so multifactorial and diverse that any specific single measure proposed will probably be of help to only a small minority of runners. There should be a broad approach to these problems.

Message: The underlying cause of injury must be established for successful treatment.

Message: Runners should be taught to respect the language of their body.

Overuse Achilles tendon injury: An example of how malalignment can be of importance for injuries are Achilles tendon injuries. Achilles tendon injuries have a 5% incidence in soccer players, 5.5% among tennis players and 4.3% among dancers.

Training errors such as a sudden increase in mileage, or change in activity, are the primary etiological factor in more than 75% of all Achilles tendon overuse injuries. Causative training errors also include increased interval training, running on sloping trails, on hard or slippery roads, or on soft beaches.

Achilles tendon problems are linked to increased pronation. Compensatory pronation may occur in tibia vara of 10° of more, forefoot varus, leg length discrepancy, ligamentous laxity and muscle weakness and tightness.

At the University of Vermont, a study was carried out with the hypothesis that foot malalignment will induce Achilles tendon overuse injury. It was found that increased foot pronation of 10° increased the local strain on the medial side of the Achilles tendon with 1.4% (32).

Tendinitis has been the clinical term applied to virtually all painful tendon conditions. Histological examination of tissue taken from a pathological tendon, however, often fails to reveal inflammatory cells. A modified classification of tendon injuries has, therefore, been suggested (Table 4).

Table 4: Injury-producing situations for the anteroir cruciate ligament in basketball (mens and women) (n=180). Henning (13).

New	Old	Definition	Clinical Signs and Symptoms
Paratenonitis	Tenosynovitis Tenovaginitis Peritendinitis	An inflammation of only the paratenon, either lined by synovium or not	Cardinal inflammatory sighs: swelling, pain, crepitation, local tenderness, warmth, dysfunction
Paratenonitis with tendinosis	Tendinitis	Paratendon inflammation associated with intratendinosis degeneration	Same as I, with often palpable tendon nodule, swelling, and inflammatory signs
Tendinosis	Tendinitis	Intratendinous degeneration due to atrophy (aging, microtrauma, vascular compromise, etc.)	Often palpable tendon nodule that can be asymptomatic, but may also be point tender. Swelling of tendon sheath is absent
Tendinitis	Tendon strain or tear A. Acute (less than 2) B. Subacute (4-6 weeks) C. Chronic (over 6 weeks)	Symptomatic degeneration of the tendon with vascular disruption and inflammatory repair response	Symptoms are inflammatory and proportional to vascular disruption, hematoma, or atrophy-related cell necrosis. Symptom duration defines each subgroup:

When treating Achilles tendon pain a correct diagnosis is essential. This can best be achieved by a careful history and a thorough clinical examination. Achilles paratenonitis, i.e. synovial sheath inflammation, is characterized by pain most often on the middle third of the tendon aspects. Pain increases with activity and there is stiffness in the morning after activity, as well as edema and crepitations. The differential diagnosis is tendinosus or a partial rupture, which has a history of sudden onset of pain, pain during athletic activity, very localized swelling and tenderness. The profile of an acute tendon, ligament or muscle injury is seen in Figure 1. When tendon injuries are chronic, they are difficult to manage. The profile characteristic of chronic tendinitis is shown in Figure 2 (17). The implications of these figures should be known by people active in sports.

Fig 1: Hypothetical profile of acute macrotraumatic tissue injury. This profile is typical of an acute partial tendon strain or the pattern of healing in other acutely injured connective tissues such as a lateral-collateral ligament sprain in the ankle. Curved dashed line = pain; curved solid line = tissue healing. **Permission from Leadbetter (17)**

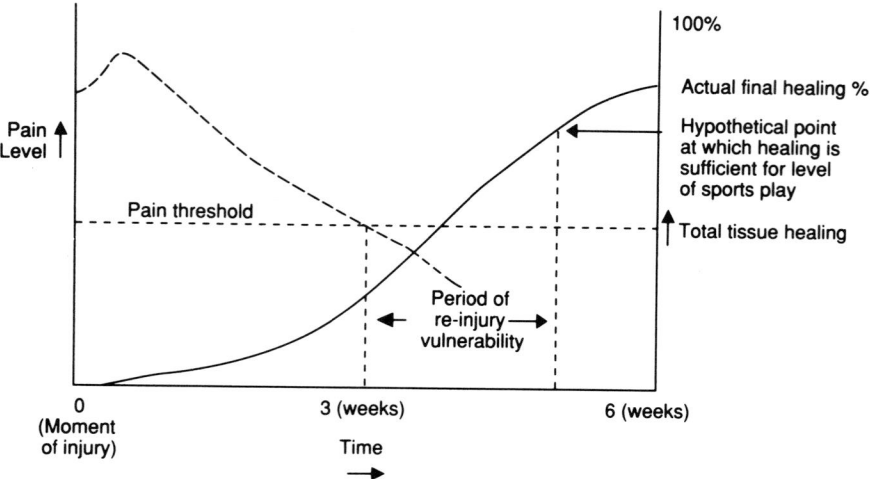

Fig 2: Profile of chronic microtraumatic soft-tissue injury. This profile is typical of overuse tendon injury. Solid line = percentage of tissue damage. **Permission from Leadbetter (17)**

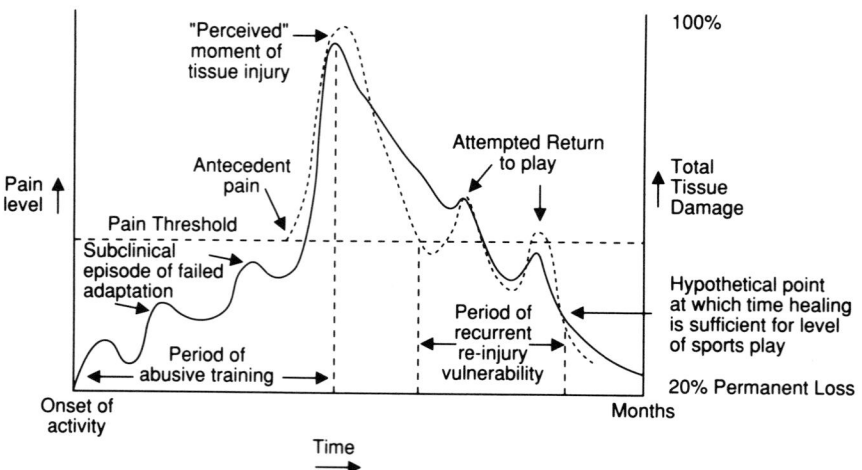

The principle treatment of these injuries is to treat the cause of the injury, and of course, also the symptoms. The degree of pain is supposed to be a dose related response to tissue injury, and can be used as a guide. The relation between pain and rest are show in Table 5.

Table 5: Classification system for the effect of pain on athletic performance. Curwin (11).

Level	Description of Pain	Level of Sports Performance
1	No pain	Normal
2	Pain only with extreme exertion	Normal
3	Pain with extreme exertion and 1 to 2 hours afterward	Normal or slight decreased
4	Pain during and after any Vigorous activities	Somewhat decreased
5	Pain during activity and forcing termination	Markedly decreased
6	Pain during daily activities	Unable to perform

Partial tears do usually not heal for unknown reasons. Allenmark et al. (1,2), has shown that 85% of patients with verified Achilles tendon partial ruptures have remaining symptoms after five years and 74% after ten years. Results with conservative treatment over ten years were acceptable only in 27%, while surgery gave good results in 88%.

> **Message:** A correct diagnosis is the key to a successful management of chronic tendon overuse injuries.

Complete Achilles tendon tear: Concerning complete tears of the Achilles tendon, Kannus and Josza (16) found that 97% of patient with complete spontaneous rupture of the tendons had histological changes. It has also been shown that immobilization has great deleterious effects on tendons and ligaments. In spite of this non-surgery has, with long-term immobilization, become popular.

This treatment gives a good chance of healing with early treatment. This treatment is more successful if it is carried out within the first 48 hours. Non-surgery results in early return to work and involves small costs. There is, however, a risk for re-ruptures and the literature shows in conservatively treated patients that there is a 17,7% risk of re-rupture.

Tendon healing is optimal biomechanically and scar formation is minimized if a strong suture is placed into the tendon. Surgery allows tension in the tendon, which results in a proper orientation of the collagen and, thereby, increased strength. Surgically treated tendons have very small risks for re-ruptures, which in the literature is only 1.5%. Surgery allows early return to sports.

Carter et al. (7) have shown that early mobilization is possible already a week after surgery of the Achilles tendon. Early mobilization with 0 to 20° of plantar flexion is allowed after seven to ten days, and with this aggressive rehabilitation, it is possible to return to full activity in three to five months.

> **Message:** Early motion after a tendon injury results in an earlier return to sports.

2.3 Sports specific activities

Many sports injuries are highly sports specific. There are injuries that are called tennis elbow, jumper's knee, footballer's ankle, rider's strain, etc. This means that these injuries have been associated with a certain sport because of the specific demands in that sport. In order to illustrate how important it is to be well acquainted with the sports as such, and the risks associated with it, we will discuss some aspects of the common injury tennis elbow.161,5

Tennis Elbow: A typical sports specific injury is tennis elbow, which constitutes a diagnostic and therapeutic challenge. Individuals most likely to sustain tendon overuse injuries are those over 35 years of age with a high activity level. They play tennis three times a week or more, at least 30 minutes or more each time.

The etiology of tennis elbow usually involves faulty backhand strokes, but for many players the serve motion can also be a problem. Biomechanical studies have shown that heavy rackets should not be used, at least not when returning back to sports after a tennis elbow. The racket should not be strung more than 52 to 55 pounds and gut strings should be used. The question on vibration is debated, but the vibration diminishes at hand level.

Exercises to promote healing and braces to control the force loads are main elements in the treatment. During the serve, there can be a valgus extension overload syndrome which causes medial tension and lateral compression of the elbow which results in injuries such as medial epicondylitis and ulnar neuritis on the medial side and osteochondritis dissecans on the lateral side. Hyperextension of the elbow at the end of the service motion can cause impingement of the olecranon against the humerus and cause posterior tennis elbow.

> **Message:** Knowledge in and experience of sports are basic requirements for a successful prevention and management of sports specific injury.

2.4 Injury mechanism

To establish etiological factors is usually not enough. The mechanism by which sports injuries occur should also be identified. If the underlying injury causing mechanisms are not analyzed and understood, it is not possible to correctly and successfully treat the injury.

An example of this are injuries to the shoulder that can occur in different ways. For example, injuries experienced by a javelin thrower, tennis player or pitcher are different from those occurring in a swimmer. A pitcher may have a glenoid labrum tear, a javelin thrower a rotator cuff injury and a swimmer an impingement syndrome secondary to instability. The technique used in the specific sports is the base for the injury mechanism. A correct diagnosis is necessary for good treatment. A thorough testing and clinical examination are the key. A definite diagnosis of shoulder injuries, can be secured by MRI (Magnetic Resonance Imaging), or a CT (Cat Scan), arthrogram, which has revolutionized the accuracy of the diagnosis of shoulder lesions. The diagnosis of intra-articular injuries, as well as appropriate treatment can be achieved by arthroscopy.

> **Message:** Different sports have their typical injury mechanism. In order to be able to prevent injuries, it is important to have a profound knowledge of the sport as such and the risks associated with it.

Below we will discuss the injury mechanism in some sports such as skiing, basketball, soccer and American football.

Skiing: In skiing, advances in boot and binding design have lead to dramatic reductions in the production of ankle injuries and tibia fractures, but have been a total failure in protecting knee ligaments (15). Anterior cruciate ligament injuries (ACL) are very common in skiing with 50 per 100,000 skier days. In football there are 60 ACL injuries per 100,000 player days.

The mechanism behind ACL injuries in skiing are very typical for this sport. One is a forward fall which allows the medial edge of the anterior portion of the skis to be engaged in the snow (Figure 2). Another trauma is a backward fall and in some cases only a momentarly loss of control, causing the skier to backwards. Another ACL injury in skiing is when the skier gets back on his or hers skis and suddenly catches the inside edge of the tail of the ski, producing a sudden internal rotation of the hyperflexed knee.

It should be advised that those individuals who are interested in avoiding injury to knee ligaments, especially the anterior cruciate ligament, should consider the use of bindings for the upward release flexibility of the toe.

Basketball is the sport responsible for most injuries to the ACL. Injury producing situations for the ACL in basketball are shown in Table 6. The most common injury mechanisms in basketball are straight knee landing in 29%, plant and cut in 24% and one step stop in 17% (13). A defender in basketball should use proper technique by maintaining a good bent, knee deficit position.

Table 6: Injury-producing situations for the anteroir cruciate ligament in basketball (mens and women) (n=180). Henning (13).

Injury Situation	Total	(%)	Not hit	Hit	PAC	SKL	OSS	TWS	HYP	QTR	Improved Player Technique
Lay-up	22	(12)	20	2	4	8	4	0	1	3	BKL,TSS,BLT
Shifting on defence	22	(12)	20	2	10	1	5	1	1	2	ART,TSS,BLT
Rebound attempt	19	(11)	15	4	0	8	4	3	0	0	BKL,TSS
Dribbling	18	(10)	15	3	5	2	4	3	0	1	ART,TSS
Block shot attempt	15	(8)	15	0	3	10	2	0	0	0	BKL
Jump for a loose ball	15	(8)	14	1	0	10	2	0	1	1	BKL
Loose ball	12	(7)	9	3	1	5	2	0	1	0	BKL
Jump shot	10	(6)	9	1	3	3	3	0	0	0	BKL,TSS
Trying to stop	9	(5)	8	1	4	0	4	0	0	3	TSS,BLT
Other	9	(5)	9	0	2	0	1	2	1	0	
Plant and fake	7	(4)	7	0	7	0	0	0	0	0	ART,BLT,
Landing from a jump	7	(4)	4	3	1	3	0	0	0	0	BKL
Hit	7	(4)	0	7	0	0	0	0	0	0	
Bad pass recovery	4	(2)	4	0	1	2	0	0	1	0	BKL,BLT
Posting up	2	(1)	2	0	2	0	0	0	0	0	ART,TSS
Setting a pick	2	(1)	1	1	1	0	0	0	0	0	ART
Total	180		152	28	44	52	31	9	6	10	
%			84	16	24	29	17	5	3	6	

PAC, Plant and cut; SKL, straight knee landing; OSS, one step stop; TWS, twist; HYP, hyperextended; QTR, other; BKL, bent knee landing; TSS, three step stop; BLT, block turn; ART, accelerated rounded turn.

Soccer: In soccer, the injury producing situations to the ACL are seen in Table 7. ACL injury can occur when a defender is trying to stop in one step. The one step stop is often the player's attempt to stop and reverse direction in one step. Another situation is the plant and cut which involves sudden movement on the straight or near straight leg with intent to change direction in one step.

Table 7: Injury-producing situations for the anteroir cruciate ligament in soccer (n=61). Hit versus not hit: not hit 51 (84%); and hit 10 (16%). Henning (13).

Injury Situation	Total	Improved player Technique
Shifting on defence	12	ART,TSS,BLT
Running, plat to get open or get ball	11	ART,TSS,BLT
Hit	10	
Plant to kick	7	TSS,BKL
One step stop to reverse or change direction	4	TSS,BLT
Foot stuck on artificial turf	3	
Jumping over a downed player	3	BKL
Tackled low	3	BKL,TSS
Landing from a header	2	BKL
Running for ball, bumped off balance	1	BKL
Dribbling ball, got tangled up with opponent	1	BKL,TSS,BLT
Kicked ball the same time as opponent	1	
Knocked off balance	1	BKL
Slipped in mud	1	
Injury situation not known	1	

Injury techniques: plant and cut 22 (36%); one step stop 8 (13%); straight knee landing 7 (11%); twist 2 (3%); hyperextended 6 (10%); and other 6 (10%). ART, accelerated rounded turn; TSS, three step stop; BLT, block turn; BKL, bent knee landing.

<u>American football:</u> The rule changes have reduced the number of ACL injuries (26). Clipping and blocking below the waist on punts and down field and crack back blocking have all been made illegal because they have been identified as instrumental in the production of knee ligament and other lower extremity injuries.

The number and severity of knee ligament injuries decreased in a group of high school football players who had undergone a preseason condition program, when compared to similar groups which had not. Although no certain information proves beyond any doubt that conditioning programs directly strengthen human ACL's or that added strength significance reduces the incidence of injury, it is probable that some benefits accrue.

<u>In physical education</u> classes, the most reported causes of sports injuries are falling/stumbling in 24%, mis-step twist in 22% and kick-push in 18%, induced by the injured party and by other acute problems (40). Most injuries in physical education classes were light contusions and sprains.

> **Message:** It is important in injury prevention programs to direct emphasis of the program to the situation responsible for most of the injuries.

2.5 Research activities

All progress in orthopaedic sports medicine is based on research and clinical experience. In order to secure a correct diagnosis and management, basic clinical research is necessary. In order to evaluate the results of our techniques, outcome evaluations will be more and more necessary.

<u>Ankle ligament injury research:</u> The incidence of ankle ligament injuries is very high: 17 to 21% are soccer injuries, 25% of running and jumping injuries and 56% are basketball injuries. 27,000 ankle sprains occur in the United States each day. 85 % of ankle sprains involve the anterior talofibular ligament (A-TFL). These injuries are often mistreated due to the lack of scientific support in the diagnosis and treatment.

As an example of a comprehensive research program, we would like to present the ankle ligament research program which is carried out at the Department of Orthopaedics and Rehabilitation at the University of Vermont, U.S.A. 1. Ankle biomechanics have been studied showing that strain in the ATFL increases with increasing plantar flexion explaining the injury mechanism (29). 2. Ankle stability tests are needed to evaluate the ankle joint integrity and biomechanics studies have been carried out. The anterior drawer test has been shown to be a selective test for the ATFL. The maximum drawer is at 10° of plantar flexion (31). 3. Studies have been carried out on braces and taping. 4. Proprioception (muscle latency time). 5. Ankle injury risk factors have been studied in a prospective study (5). Risk factors in the study are joint laxity, ligamentous stability, range of motion and strength. It has been found that there is an increased risk for injury with increased eversion/inversion strength and increased plantar flexion strength. The implications of this are difficult to say. The study continues and now also proprioceptive functions are included. 6. Outcome studies are essential for the future. A prospective randomized outcome study taking into account patient satisfaction and cost benefit is being conducted.

Rehabilitation research is an important part in the management of injuries. This is especially true as the rehabilitation can be carried out and influenced by both paramedical and non-medical personnel. There is, however, very little research carried out in this field. At the University of Vermont, research trying to evaluate common rehabilitation activities has been carried out. Strain gauges have been implanted on the anterior cruciate ligament in-vivo after arthroscopic surgery and rehabilitation activities have been carried out. With this technique, it has been impossible to make a comparison of rehabilitation activities based on peak strain values. This is the first objective study where this comparison has been made possible in-vivo (Table 8.) (6).

> **Message:** Research is essential for any development in orthopaedic sports medicine. It may be said that nothing is more vital to the life of a medical and/or sports specialty, than its research program.

Table 8: Results of strain gauge measurements in-vivo of some common rehabilitation activities. With these strain gauge measurements, it has been posible to rank order the rehabilitation activities. Beynnon (6).

RANK COMPARISON OF ACTIVITIES BASED ON PEAK STRAIN VALUES

ACTIVITY	STRAIN
Isoquads @ 15°	5.7%
Squat w/ Sport Cord	5.4%
Squat w/o Sport Cord	4.2%
AROM 44 N Weight Boot	4.0%
Lachman Test (@ 150 N)	3.7%
AROM	3.5%
Simul Hams & Quads @ 15°	3.1%
Isoquads @ 30°	2.5%
Simul Hams & Quads @ 30°	0.7%
Isohams @ 15°	0.7%
All others	0.0%

3. Sequence of Prevention: Measures that Reduce Future Risks and Severity of Sports Injuries.

The sequence of prevention introduces measures that are likely to reduce the future risks and/or severity of sports injuries.

General preventative activities include pre-season screenings, warm-up and cooling down, muscle training and flexibility training, coordination and proprioceptive training.

Specific preventive activities include protective equipment, helmet, braces, orthosis and taping. Examples of prevention are eye guards in squash which decrease the number of eye injuries, high-top basketball shoes have been developed and decrease ankle sprains, the use of mouth guards in field hockey has decreased the incidence of dental injuries and the use of face masks in college ice hockey has reduced the number of facial injuries.

> **Message:** Specific intervention preventive measures can reduce the incidence of injuries.

Health education in schools: One of the strategies in the battle against injuries is aimed at prevention modification of the participants in sports. Health education as a tool in realizing behavioral change can be implemented in school curricula and consequently given by well educated people in physical education and biology (4). The physical education teacher can be a message mediator by educating school age children in practical and theoretical aspects of injury prevention. Although the effects of health education in injury prevention still needs to be proven, there are strong indications that in the short-term, it can be beneficial in reducing the number of sports injuries. A controlled instrumental study has been performed in Holland with special lessons in physical education and biology given concerning injury prevention. Practical topics instructed in these classes were warming-up, stretching exercises, cooling down exercises for ankle stabilization and general coordination and techniques for correct falling. Further education took place concerning adequate sporting shoes, protective materials and first aid in sports (4).

> **Message:** It would seem to be worth while to start with the implementation of health education in school curricula on a more regular basis.

How much activity is too much, is a question that is difficult to answer. It can only be answered by trial and error. Perhaps this factor may also be made accessible by health education invention. Health education will only be effective if it is put forward as a planned strategy.

3.1 Strategies

Strategies for prevention according to the Council of Europe's project includes behavioral approach, the technical approach and organizational approach (36). The behavioral approach is concerned with instruction of education of all those persons participating in sports. The technical approach includes standardization of instrumental and protective materials and safe surfaces, etc. The occupational approach includes strict enforcement of rules by coaches and referees.

> **Message:** Prevention needs a strategy to be effective.

3.2 Final Comments

The burden for society of medical problems including injuries will vary between countries. Diagnostic and treatment methods will continue to improve. There is, however, very little done towards prevention, which should be changed. The best treatment should be prevention. Somebody has said "An ounce of prevention is worth a pound of cure." In other words the future lies in prevention together with well educated and correct management of any injury. Education in orthopaedic sports medicine should, for medical personnel, as well as physical education teachers, therefore, include prevention as there is so much that both medically educated persons, as well as non-medical and allied health personnel can do within this area.

References

1. **Allenmark C, Renström P, Peterson P, Irstam L:** Ten Year Follow-up of Conservatively Treated Partial Ruptures of the Achilles Tendon. Proceedings of the American Orthopaedic Society of Sports Medicine, New Orleans, February 1990.

2. **Allenmark C:** Partial Achilles tendon tears. Clinics in Sports Med 11 (4):759-769, 1992.

3. **Austin GJ, Rogers KD, Reese G:** Injuries in high school physical education classes. Am J Dis Child 134:456-8, 1980

4. Backx FJG, Beijer HJM, Bol E, Erich WBM: Injuries in high-risk persons and high-risk sports. A longitudinal study of 1,818 school children. Am J Sports Med 19:124-130, 1991.

5. Baumhauer JF, Alosa D, Renström P, Trevino S, Beynnon B: A prospective study of ankle injury risk factors. Submitted for Publication to the American Journal of Sports Medicine, 1994.

6. Beynnon BD, Fleming BC, Pope MH, Nichols CE, Johnson RJ, Renström PA, Stankewich CJ: The Measurement of anterior cruciate ligament strain during rehabilitation activities in-vivo. In Proceedings for the 39th Annual Meeting, ORS, Page 308, February 15-18, 1993, San Francisco, CA.

7. Carter T, Fowler P, Blokker C: Functional postoperative treatment of Achilles tendon repair. Am J Sports Med 20(4):459-462, 1992.

8. Clancy WG: Tendon trauma and overuse injuries. In Leadbetter WB, Buckwalter JA, Gordon SL, (eds): Sports-Induced Inflammation. Park Ridge, IL, American Academy of Orthopaedic Surgeons, 1990.

9. Clement DB, Taunton JE, Smart GW, McNicol KL: A survey of overuse running injuries. Phys Sportsmed 9:47-58, 1981.

10. Cook SD, Brinker MR, Mahlon P: Running shoes. Their relation to running injuries. Sports Med 10(1):1-8, 1990.

11. Curwin S, Stanish WD: Tendinitis: Its Etiology and Treatment. Lexington, MA, DC Health and Co, p.64, 1984.

12. Galen Van W, Diederiks, J: Sportblessures Breed Uitgementen. Uitg. De Vrieseborch, Haarlem, 1990.

13. Henning CE, Griffis ND, Vequist SW, Yearout KM, Decker KA: Sport-Specific Knee Injuries. In Clinical Aspects of Sports Injury, Prevention and Care, Volume 5, Renström P, (ed). IOC and FIMS, Blackwell Scientific Publications, Oxford, England, 1994.

14. Ijzerman JC, Van Galen WCC: Injuries in long distance runners. Royal Dutch Athletic Association (KNAU), The Netherlands, 1987.

15. **Johnson R, Renström P:** Alpine Ski Injuries. In Clinical Aspects of Sports Injury, Prevention and Care, Volume 5, Renström P, (ed). IOC and FIMS, Blackwell Scientific Publications, Oxford, England, 1994.

16. **Kannus P, Josza L:** Histopathological changes preceding spontaneous rupture of a tendon. J Bone Joint Surg 73A:1507-1525, 1991.

17. **Leadbetter W:** Cell matrix response in tendon injury. Clin Sports Med 11(3):533-578, 1992.

18. **Lysholm J, Wiklander J:** Injuries in runners. Am J Sports Med 15(2):168-171, 1987.

19. **Macera CA, Pate RR, Powell KE, Jackson KL, Kendrick JS, Craven TE:** Predicting lower-extremity injuries among habitual runners. Arch Intern Med 149:2565-2568, 1984.

20. **Marti B, Vader JP, Minder CE, Abelin T:** On the epidemiology of running injuries. Am J Sports Med 16(3):285-294, 1988.

21. **Mechelen Van W, Hlobil H, Kemper H:** Incidence severity, etiology and prevention of sports injuries. Sports Med 14(2):82-99, 1992.

22. **Mechelen Van W:** Etiology and prevention of running injuries. Thesis, Vrije Universiteit, Amsterdam, The Netherlands, 1992.

23. **Mechelen Van W:** Injuries in Running. In Clinical Aspects of Sports Injury, Prevention and Care, Volume 5, Renström P, (ed). IOC and FIMS, Blackwell Scientific Publications, Oxford, England, 1994.

24. **Nigg B, Segesser B:** The influence of playing surface on the load on the locomotor system and for football and tennis injuries. Sports Medicine 5:378-385, 1988.

25. **Ooijendijk WTM, Van Agt L:** Preventie van hardloopbelssures (The prevention of running injuries). Gen Sport 23(4):146-151, 1990.

26. **Peterson TR:** Blocking at the knee, dangerous and unnecessary. Phys Sportsmed 1(2)46-50, 1973.

27. **Pospeich R:** Analyze von 1000 Unfällen beim Schulsport. Med Sport 21:78-82, 1981.

28. Puddu G. Ippolito E, Postacchini P: A classification of Achilles tendon disease. Am J Sports Med 4:145-150, 1976.

29. Renström P, Wertz M, Incavo S, Pope MH, Ostgaard HC, Arms S, Haugh L: Strain in the lateral ligaments of the ankle. Foot and Ankle 9(2):59-63, 1988.

30. Renström P, Axelsson R, Svensson H-O: Akuta idrottskador på ett centralasarett (Acute injuries in a major hospital). Läkartidningen 77(41):3615-3617, 1980. (R)

31. Renström P, Theis M, Haugh L: Ankle ligament biomechanics: A study of the anterior drawer test. Orthopaedic Research Society, 39th Annual Meeting, February 15-18, 1993, San Francisco, California.

32. Rudd E, Renström P, Beynnon B, Tohyama H: Altered Achilles tendon biomechanics in hyperpronation. American Orthopaedic Association, 26th Annual Residency Conference, Seattle, Orthopaedic Transactions 17(2):455-456, 1993.

33. Sandelin J, Santavite S, Kiviluoto O, Honhanca R: Sports injuries treated in a casualty world. Scand J Sports Sci 2(1):17-20, 1980.

34. Steinbruch K, Lolta A: Epidemiologie von Sportverletzungen. Deutsche Zeitschr. Sports Med 6:175-184, 1983.

35. Toom den PJ, Schurman M: Eon Kostenmodel voor berekening van kosten van ongevalles in de Privesteer. Consumer Safety Institute, Amsterdam, 1988.

36. Vulpen Van AV: Sports for all sports injuries and their prevention. Scientific report, Council, National Institute for Sports Health Care, Oosterbeek, Holland, 1989.

37. Walter SD, Hart LE, McIntosh JM, Sutton JR: The Ontario cohort study of running related injuries. Arch Intern Med 149:2561-2564, 1989.

Educational Aspects in Health Promotion and Adapted Physical Activity: Physicians and Other Health Professionals

Rodríguez, F.A.
Institut Nacional d'Educació Física de Catalunya (INEFC), Universitat de Barcelona
Spain

1. Physical Activity and Public Health

The World Health Organization (WHO) defines health as "complete physical, mental, and social well-being". As this may be considered as a maximalist definition, the Public Health Authority of Catalonia (Generalitat de Catalunya) proposed a slightly modified definition, regarding health as "the highest level of physical, mental, and social well-being, as well as functional capacity, allowed by the social factors in which the individuals and the community are immersed" [9].

In 1977, that international Organization defined a global strategy with the slogan 'Health for all in the year 2000'. Its general objective was that by the end of the century "all the inhabitants in all countries of the world shall have a sufficient level of health as to be able to work and to participate actively in the social life of the community in which they live".

In 1984, WHO-Europe approved the objectives of the strategy 'Health for all in the year 2000 in the European region'. To the classical principle simplified in terms of "adding years to life", the two new trends in this health policy may also be summarized as "adding life to years", and "adding health to life". That simply means that the new challenge in our countries shall be to improve, not only the "quantity", but also the "quality" of life. So, "adding life to years" can be interpreted as trying to improve the quality of life, that is to live in good health, free of diseases, disabilities, and handicaps. Living more years in bad health is not rewarding to people nor convenient for society. "Adding health to life" means to live with positive health, enjoying the highest possible degree of every person's physical, mental, and social capabilities.

Fig.1: Actions in a health system
(Generalitat de Catalunya) [9].

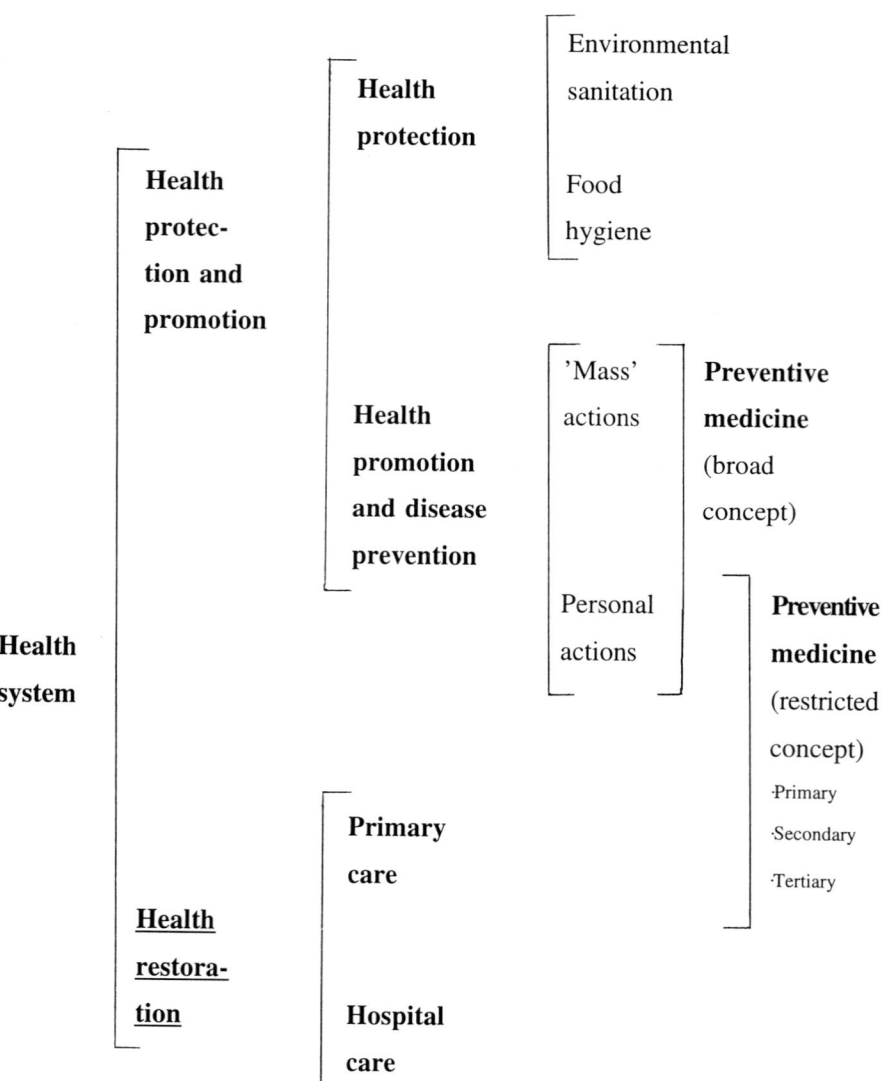

Health and disease are now considered a continuum (Fig. 1).

Health protection is efficient in the so called pre-pathogenic stage of disease, that is when environment and risk factors interact with the host. Health protection measures are generally designed and applied by non-medical health professionals such as engineers, biologists, veterinarians, bromatologists, etc.

Health promotion and disease prevention are efficient in the pre-pathogenic stage, but also in the pathogenic stage, when the morbid stimulus has started to act but the individual is still asymptomatic. It includes three important actions: preventive immunizations and chemoprophylaxis, health education and screenings. Only personal actions are generally undertaken by health professionals.

On the other hand, we may differentiate three stages in prevention. Primary prevention will be effective before the disease has initiated its natural course. It includes health protection and some health promotion and disease prevention measures such as preventive immunizations and chemoprophylaxis and health education, but not screenings. This is already secondary prevention, since the disease has already started, even though the individual may be free of symptoms. The objectives of tertiary prevention are to slow down the course of the disease and to attenuate the disabilities and the sequelae resulting from the pathologic state, and to improve the residual functions.

It has been demonstrated that preventive medicine is always more efficient than curative medicine in a public health system. The increase of life expectancy in good health depends to a large extent on preventive measures -especially primary prevention.

The general principles for public health policies approved by the WHO-Europe in 1984 included: 1) to guarantee equity among individuals, 2) to give priority to health promotion, disease prevention and primary health care, 3) to ensure community participation, and 4) to promote intersectorial and international cooperation.

It is not in the scope of this paper to discuss the impact of physical activity in public health. For a comprehensive review of this matter the reader may refer to an International Consensus Conference on Exercise, Fitness and Health, held in 1988 in Toronto, Canada. The proceedings and the final Consensus Statement were published in a book entitled 'Exercise, Fitness, and Health. A Consensus of Current Knowledge' [3]. A second Consensus Conference took place last year in Toronto.

Nevertheless, it is important to remember that physical activity is a positive influence that tends to further positive health, and that counters an adverse lifestyle. A concomitant of sound health maintenance is likely to be an optimization of longevity, together with an enhancement of the quality of life [3].

Sedentary lifestyles are prevalent in industrialized countries. Persuasive evidence now exists to show that regular physical activity protects against the development and progression of several chronic diseases. These two points suggest that considerable public health benefit would result if sedentary persons became more physically active [1].

This is true for the general population. However it is probably even more relevant for individuals with limiting conditions, as recognized by the International Federation of Adapted Physical Activity (IFAPA) [6].

2. Health professionals, preventive medicine and physical activity

Health professionals, traditionally involved in the treatment and rehabilitation of diseases, are called to have a very outstanding role also in the prevention of diseases and health promotion [2,13]. As mentioned before, health education, preventive immunizations, and screenings are the three fundamental techniques in current clinical preventive medicine. Health professionals (physicians, nurses, pharmacists, social workers, dietitians, physical therapists, respiratory therapists, psychologists, and health educators) are responsible for their application in the clinical and health-care setting [20]. In health education, these professionals have an active educational role as health counselors, but also an important passive or 'exemplary' educational role, acting as 'models' in relation to some habits, both negative (alcohol or smoking) or positive (physical activity) [13].

In the case of the promotion of physical activity, health professionals should be involved at least in the following tasks, directed at apparently healthy, at-risk, and special populations (Table 1): 1) physical activity counseling -and 'exemplary'-passive education-, 2) changing of sedentary behaviour, 3) counseling on physical activity adaptation to special conditions and needs, 4) health appraisal and risk assessment; and 5) exercise testing and prescription.

Table 1: Objectives, roles and tasks of health professionals in the promotion of physical activity.

Objectives:	**HEALTH PROMOTION**
	DISEASE PREVENTION
Adressed to:	**Apparently healthy individuals**
	Individuals at higher risk
	Special populations * chronic disease (tertiary prevent.) * disabled * special conditions (pregnancy, children, elderly)
Health education:	**Physical activity counseling**
	'Exemplary'-passive educational role
	Changing of sedentary behavior
	Counseling on adapted physical activity
Screening and medical practice:	**Exercise information in the medical history**
	Health appraisal and risk assessment
	Exercise testing
	Exercise prescription
	Adapted physical activity prescription

3. The health professionals in rehabilitation and APA

The four highest mortality rates in our countries correspond to four health problems: cardiovascular diseases, cancer, respiratory tract diseases, and accidents. Their morbidity is also very high, and they cause an important proportion of overall disabilities, together with rheumatic and neurological diseases. As progress in scientific medicine has led to considerable improvement in the outcome of formerly fatal diseases and injuries, rehabilitation has gained an important position in the overall system of health care [11]. The need for such services, however, varies greatly for various age groups. Over 30% have become disabled in the middle years of their life, and more than 50% have acquired the disability beyond the age of 65 [11]. With a mean life expectancy of more than 70 years in most of our countries, and with a strong trend towards a progressively older population, the social demands for these services will probably increase greatly. That means larger demands for rehabilitation and APA, since exercise therapy, sports, and other adapted physical activities have become increasingly important in recent years.

Table 2 presents an overall view of the specialized personnel who take part in different settings: clinic, school, and community [11]. This table gives an idea on the variety of training levels, concepts and curricula developed, and also on the modern interdisciplinary approach to APA.

Table 2: Rehabilitation/APA teams in different settings.
(Derived from Tysarowski 1972, cited in [11])

Clinic	Medical doctors
	    General practitioners
	    Specalists (rehabilitation, sports medicine, cardiology, orthopedics, neurology, ORL, geriatrics, psychiatry, rheumatology, oncology, pediatrics, etc.)
	Psychologists
	Special education teachers
	Sport teachers
	Nurses
	Physiotherapists
	Occupational therapists
	Speech therapists, social workers
	Massage and balneotherapy personnel
	Nursing auxiliaries
	International trained aides

School	Teachers Special education teachers Sports teachers Physiotherapists Teaching assistants Full-time and volunteer assistants
Vocational education and training (community)	Administrators Graduate engineers Medical doctors, psychologists Teachers, sports teachers Subject teachers, social workers Master craftsmen Physiotherapists Massage and balneotherapy personnel

The health professionals will have a very specific and relevant role in the service system in the future. It is very clear that they already have it in the area of therapy and rehabilitation in the clinical field on an interdisciplinary professional team basis. But many claim also for community-based organizational and communication structures for implementing the effective team approach. The objectives, roles, and tasks in an overall health system are summarized in Table 3.

Table 3: Objectives, roles and tasks of health professionals in therapy, rehabilitation and APA.

Agents:	Health promotion (according to training level and experience)
Objectives:	**EXERCISE-SPORT THERAPY & REHABILITATION ADAPTED PHYSICAL ACTIVITY SPORT FOR THE DISABLED**

Addressed to:	**Patients**
	   * acute disease
	   * chronic disease
	Special populations
	   * disabled persons (physical, sensory, learning, mental, emotional, multiple)
	   * special conditions (elderly, sedentary)
	   * athletes with disabilities

Roles and tasks:	**Exercise and sport therapy Exercise and sport rehabilitation APA counseling and prescription Counseling and prescription of sport for the disabled Medical assistance for athletes with disabilities**

At this point, a question arises. Does the set-up or the type of institution in which professionals work define their training profile? Or does the educational and training profile define their appropriateness for a certain type of work? Certainly, the organization of rehabilitation and APA is different in the various European countries, and different degrees of integration into the general systems of health care, education, and vocational training exist at the present time. On the other hand, job mobility and diversification seems the general trend in many professional careers, including the health professions [14,15,19].

4. The education of health professionals in health promotion and disease prevention by means of physical activity

As mentioned before, health professionals are called to have a very outstanding role in the prevention of diseases and health promotion. Some sound evidence is available to show that general practitioners can influence exercise habits through counseling and other health education measures [4]. In this respect, education has been regarded as a fundamental issue in order to improve the role of general practitioners. A recent report of the Council of Scientific Affairs of the American Medical Association [2] recommends the inclusion of health education in the undergraduate curriculum. It also stands for continued graduate education of practicing physicians in this important area of preventive clinical medicine. The same also seems to be valid for nurses [18], and for other health professionals [9].

Even though most of the public health authorities stand for the central role in health education of the general practitioners, as well as for the integration of preventive medicine measures into the primary care clinical services, it is also quite evident that this shall also be an important role for other health specialists at almost any other level. This is even more true in the case of those involved more intensively in preventive medicine and other related fields: sports medicine, local public health services, work-site medical services, health screening services, etc. Since the preventive value and application of exercise and sport does not seem to be homogeneously included in the education of these professionals, it seems advisable to provide them with information and training in an appropriate manner i.e., at least true and complete practical information presented in a synthetic way.

In Catalonia, just to mention a close personal experience, an Advising Council on Physical Activity and Health Promotion, serving the Public Health Authority, has been appointed. The Council has initiated its tasks with a survey of the physical activity patterns of the Catalan population, followed by an edited report with the results and a critical overview of the scientific evidence in relation to physical activity and health [7]. A public campaign to enhance the physical activity habits of the general population was then undertaken in a number of high impact mass-media (press, TV, radio, etc.). This campaign, with the slogan "Mou-te, no et rovellis" ("Move, don't rust out") was mainly addressed at increasing their daily activity patterns. The central part of the campaign was developed in 1992, "our" Olympic year, trying to benefit from the positive public image of the Games. This last year we have also been producing a consensus book on physical activity and exercise counseling and prescription ("A guide for the promotion of physical activity", mainly addressed at primary care health professionals [10].

The importance of the initiative at our regional level is reflected by the inclusion on the Health Plan of Catalonia -in the 'Health for all in the year 2000' frame- of two clear objectives: 1) in the year 2000 all health professionals shall be aware of the importance of regular physical exercise for the health of the population, and 2) in the same period, at least 50% of the physicians shall actually undertake physical exercise counseling and prescription to their patients [8,9].

We also consider that specialized education and training of health professionals at a graduate level is an important issue. Interdisciplinary education of public health specialists, sports medicine specialists (graduate education is available and/or recognized only in some European countries) and health education and epidemiology experts is relevant to the progress of scientific knowledge and its application. Our Institute and University actually offer a Master's Course on Physical Activity and Health open to graduate students from the field of medicine, physical education, and others.

With respect to the intersectorial and international cooperation principle, approved by WHO-Europe in 1984, we welcome the initiative of a European Master's Course on Physical Activity and Health, promoted by a group of European Universities under the aegis of the European Network of Sport Sciences in Higher Education. The European dimension of the problem certainly needs the European dimension of higher education and hopefully also research in the near future. It is not very encouraging, for instance, that an international cooperative research project on health and fitness centered on cardiovascular risk factors in European school children has not been supported by any of the European Community instances to which a large group of scientists from the twelve EC countries -and others- have so far applied.

5. The education of health professionals in exercise and sport therapy and rehabilitation

Exercise and sport therapy and rehabilitation is part of the basic training of specialized health professionals in our countries. It exceeds the scope of this presentation to discuss the contents and means of this formation, which is a responsibility of the Schools of Medicine and specialized Institutions; some of these in the various European countries are among the best in the world and have contributed with excellent innovations in many areas. Institutions like Stokes-Mandeville in the field of neurological injuries, or the Deutsche Sporthochschule Köln in heart disease rehabilitation, are two good examples among others. War, an old phenomenon in our continent even present in our days, and more recently the birth of our "motor-driven society", increased accidents and sedentarism, have probably been two decisive factors of different accent.

The systems of education vary among the various countries, but tradition in some cases, and social demands in others, have helped to create generally good training programs in Europe. The rapid and effective change in the rehabilitation of coronary heart disease patients in recent years is a clear example. Research, support to specialized education and training and also economic support to clinical institutions within the health care system will probably improve the current situation.

Two remarks could be made at this point. The first one refers to the need for education and awareness of the importance of physical movement, exercise, and sport on the therapy and rehabilitation processes in many diseases. Some health care systems may lack the necessary coordination as to allow long term physical therapy and exercise. The specialists dealing with a certain condition may not succeed in guaranteeing the continuity of the treatment after the patient has left the clinic or institution. The second one deals with the need for cooperation of personnel with various levels of training in the rehabilitation process. Jochheim [11] underlines the basic requirements for effective teamwork: delegation of responsibility and a well-balanced relationship between equality and acceptance of leadership. Again, the education system has the duty to guarantee that this is well understood and applied by all health professionals.

6. The education of health professionals in APA

Many of the arguments and statements proposed for preventive and therapeutic medicine are also applicable to APA. If one difference shall be pointed out then it is the even more interdisciplinary character of teamwork in APA. The guidelines for efficient cooperative work could be very similar to those just mentioned for therapy and rehabilitation. As a matter of fact, APA experts from different fields have advocated persistently in favor of an interdisciplinary approach [6,16].

Let us look at Sherrill's statement on the role of APA professionals [16]: "Adapted physical activity programs shall be planned and conducted jointly by personnel from hospitals, schools, and communities. The emphasis shall be on developing physical activity attitudes, skills, and habits that will facilitate social integration with family members and significant others in community facilities." He also considers that the training of APA professionals should include theory and practice with all age groups representing the total life span. The same author also states that "Education, broadly defined, includes information about personal exercise needs, counseling to develop positive attitudes about both self and physical activity, supervised practice, and help in changing habits and lifestyles" [17]. If we shall start thinking about people as TABS, an acronym meaning "temporarily able-bodied" -for several reasons but especially looking at the progressive aging of the population-, then we may conclude that APA education, counseling, and prescription shall be included in the formation of all health professionals. Again, we stand for the inclusion of this matter in the curricula of physicians, nurses, psychologists, physical therapists, and the rest of health professionals, active or not in the field of APA. At least a certain level of awareness and basic information and training are absolutely necessary.

The same principle is valid in relation to sport, for the training of health professionals working with patients who may become disabled. If the message for able-bodied people is to develop physically active habits and lifestyles, a positive discrimination shall probably be done with disabled persons for a number of reasons that will not be discussed here. In order to accomplish this goal, basic education and training about sport counseling shall be included in their curricula, and practical information about facilities, community services, clubs, etc. should be provided by the health and community authorities.

As to the medical assistance and scientific support of disabled athletes, this could probably be a part of the training of sports medicine professionals. Ideally, those who are not trained specifically in this medical specialty, but who are vocationally involved, should receive supplementary training in sports medicine. Unfortunately, as far as we know, with some exceptions neither is the case in most of our countries.

A consequence of the interdisciplinary character of APA is the multidisciplinary education of APA professionals. Programs on APA open to graduate students from different fields -medicine, physical education, nursing, physical therapy, etc.- are possibly a good approach to this specialized education. Again, we recognize the excellent initiative of the European Master's Degree on APA. In this case, the lead came from the field of physical education and sports science. This is another example to show that health is too important to leave only in the hands of health professionals.

References

1. American College of Sports Medicine: Guidelines for exercise testing and prescription. Fourth edition. Philadelphia, Lea & Febiger, 1991.

2. American Medical Association: Education for health. A role for physician and the efficacy of health education efforts. JAMA 263:1816-1819, 1990.

3. Bouchard C., Shepard R.J., Stephens T., Sutton J.R., McPherson B.D. (eds.): Exercise, fitness, and health. Champaign, Illinois, Human Kinetics Books, 1990.

4. **Campbell M.J., Browne D., Waters W.E.:** Can general practitioners influence exercise habits? Controlled trial. Br Med J 290:1044-1046, 1985.

5. **Dirix A., Knuttgen H.G., Tittel K. (eds.):** The Olympic book of sports medicine. The Encyclopaedia of Sports Medicine, Vol. I. International Olympic Committee, FIMS. Oxford, Blackwell Scientific Publications, 1988.

6. **Doll-Tepper G., Dahms C., Doll B., von Selzam H. (eds.):** Adapted physical activity. An interdisciplinary approach. Berlin, Heidelberg-New York, Springer-Verlag, 1990.

7. **Generalitat de Catalunya:** Activitat física i promoció de la salut. Llibre blanc. Barcelona, Departament de Sanitat i Seguretat Social, 1991.

8. **Generalitat de Catalunya:** Pla de salut de Catalunya. Departament de Sanitat i Seguretat Social, 1991.

9. **Generalitat de Catalunya:** Llibre blanc. Bases per a la integració de la prevenció a la pràctica assistencial. Barcelona, Departament de Sanitat i Seguretat Social, Doyma, 1993.

10. **Generalitat de Catalunya:** Guia per a la promoció de la salut per mitjà de l'activitat física. Barcelona, Departament de Sanitat i Seguretat Social (in press).

11. **Jochheim K.A.:** Adapted physical activity. An interdisciplinary approach. Premises, methods, and procedures. In: Doll-Tepper G, Dahms C, Doll B, von Selzam H (eds.), Adapted physical activity. An interdisciplinary approach. Berlin, Heidelberg-New York, Springer-Verlag, 1990.

12. **Larson L. (ed.):** The Encyclopedia of Sports Sciences and Medicine. New York, Macmillan, 1971.

13. **Levine D.M.:** The physican's role in health promotion and disease prevention. Bull NY Acad Med 252:2846-2848, 1987.

14. **Magee D.J.:** Physical activity and therapy. In: Bouchard C., McPherson B.D., Taylor A.W. (eds.), Physical activity sciences, pp.205-209. Champaign: Human Kinetics Books, 1992.

15. **Shephard R.J.:** Medicine and physical activity. In: Bouchard C., McPherson B.D., Taylor A.W. (eds.), Physical activity sciences, pp.57-64. Champaign, Human Kinetics Books, 1992.

16. Sherrill C.: Interdisciplinary perspectives in adapted physical activity. In: Doll-Tepper G., Dahms C., Doll B., von Selzam H. (eds.), Adapted physical activity. An inter-disciplinary approach. Berlin, Heidelberg, New York: Springer-Verlag, 1990.

17. Sherrill C. (ed.): Leadership training in adapted physical education. Champaign, Human Kinetics, 1988.

18. Smith J.P.: The challenge of health education for nurses in 1980's. J Adv Nurs 4:531-543, 1979.

19. Steadward R.D., Clifford L.D.: Physical activity for people with physical and developmental disabilities. In: Bouchard C., McPherson B.D., Taylor A.W. (eds.), Physical activity sciences, pp.199-204. Champaign, Human Kinetics Books, 1992.

20. US Preventive Services Task Force: Guide to clinical preventive services. Baltimore, Williams and Wilkins, 1989.

The Impact of Physical Activity in Prevention and Rehabilitation of Cardiovascular and Metabolic Diseases

Rost, R.
Institute of Cardiology and Sports Medicine, German Sport University Cologne, Germany

The significance of the discussion of the health benefits of physical activity becomes apparent in the current crisis of the health care system in Germany which has already exceeded the financial capacity of society. Due to the fact that life expectancy is increasing as a result of the continuous improvement of medical care - among other reasons - more and more older people require better but also more expensive medical care. The same development is taking place in all European countries although the social consequences may differ somewhat as a result of the variety of social systems.

To reduce costs by denying patients necessary and sensible treatment procedures as a possibility for escaping this spiral contradicts all ethical and medical values. The only solution of this problem consists in the prevention of diseases that represent major cost factors. According to mortality statistics these are primarily cardiovascular disorders, which account for about 50% of deaths in our industrialized societies and cancer which is responsible for about another 25 %. The question of the significance of physical activity for health in this preventive context will be discussed in relation to one of the most important disorders from the group of cardiovascular diseases, namely coronary artery disease (CAD) and its metabolic and hemodynamic risk factors. CAD, particularly heart attack, are responsible for every sixth death in the mortality statistics. In the further discussion CAD can be considered to be representative for the entire group of arteriosclerotic diseases.

This discussion is not only important from the medical point of view but it is even more important from the viewpoint of sport and physical education. The change in the age structure of our society also completely changes the clientele which is addressed by sports offers. In the past this has been predominantly the young and powerful man to whom the motivation for physical activity is very different from the reasons to do sports which can be found in elderly subjects who are today the dominant participants in sports. Whereas young people generally are healthy and therefore not interested in the health benefits of physical activity, elderly subjects are largely motivated to participate in physical activity for preventive and rehabilitative reasons. These changes require modifications in the contents of physical education systems. Health aspects today are the dominant arguments in the substantiation of physical education.

However, the simple consideration to prevent health disorders and save health costs by changing life style including physical activity is difficult to prove by scientific methods as a result of the problems of double blind cross over trials in this area. The general belief in the possibility of "running away from heart attack" is therefore frequently challenged by critical opinions. Is this pure belief and wishful thinking or is it a scientifically proven fact? The fact that physical activity can produce injuries and financial costs as well as benefits makes this discussion even more important. A critical cost-benefit analysis is required. Uncritical descriptions necessarily lead to disappointments and discredit the health values of physical activity. Even in the so-called scientific literature such statements can be found. For example the pathologist Bassler (1977) claimed that marathoning establishes "immunity against arteriosclerosis", a statement that leads to the recommendation of competitive marathon running for postcoronary patients. Incidents such as the infamous death of the protagonist of jogging in the United States, Jim Fixx, are in a sense predestinated and lead to sweeping slogans such as "be physically active or stay healthy". A discussion of the health values of sport therefore requires a serious examination of the following counterarguments:

- There is no proof as yet that prevention is possible at all. In their critical overview, McCormick and Skrabanek (1989) come to the conclusion that intervention programs have not led to demonstrable success.

- Prevention only delays disease until a later age and therefore leads to further cost increases.

- The multitude of so-called risk factors discussed in the literature makes health-conscious behavior an attempt to fulfill an almost "mosaic system" of medical rules. McCormick and Skrabanek (1989) compiled 246 risk factors from the literature prior to 1980. The attempt to fulfill the resulting requirements must frustrate even the most conscientious health fanatic. If physical activity is recommended for health reasons, it can only be based on proven facts, if a negative effect due to the distraction from more important health aspects is to be avoided.

- The benefits of sport contrast with its potential to cause not only injuries as mentioned above but also cardiovascular incidents. The greater the number of elderly subjects that are physically active (frequently for health reasons) the more people with preexistent cardiovascular disorders are at risk of suffering heart attack or even sudden cardiac death during sports.

Ulmer, 1989, as well as Moser, 1989, presume that in the end the recommendation of sport for health reasons produces greater costs than benefits.

1. General situation of prevention

All these discussions are frequently carried out on a more ideologic than scientific level and frequently neglect the fascinating amount of experimental as well as epidemiological data which nearly undoubtably prove the health benefits of a positive life style and in particular physical activity. Such doubts are opposed by the realization that effective prevention with respect to CAD has been proven through a surprising development in the United States. The mortality rate of CAD has decreased in North America by 30-40 %. The statement by McCormick et al. that this represents a "secular" development in a certain sense, meaning a spontaneous deviation, does not hold true due to the fact that controversial developments are to be observed in other industrialized, particularly east European countries and that active health consciousness has increased notably in the United States. Estimations show that more than half of the "saved coronary deaths" can be attributed to an improved life-style, which is a greater proportion that can be explained by improved medical therapy including pharmacological treatment, intensive coronary care and invasive measures. An expression of this increased health consciousness observed in the United States, is found in a high general appreciation of physical activity. This is symbolized by the gain of popularity of jogging which is more or less an obligatory act for American politicians in order to demonstrate health and fitness, e.g. electibility. It would certainly be wrong to claim that this is the only or major aspect responsible for the preventive success achieved in North America. The success of nonsmoking campaigns may have much larger impact. On the other hand, strong interrelations exist between physical activity and nonsmoking as well as other aspects of a health-conscious life-style.

In Germany indications for preventive success can also be seen. However, in contrast to the United States a general decrease in cardiovascular mortality cannot be observed although two facts must be taken into consideration in this discussion: The initial level has been much lower than in the United States. In terms of the increased life expectancy and the fact that heart attack is a typical condition in elderly men, a constant level of cardiovascular mortality must already be considered a preventive success.

A detailed analysis of the mortality statistics demonstrates positive trends, e.g. a delay of cardiac death into a higher age (see fig.1.). The rate of unnecessary and from a financial point of view highly expensive death by heart attack in medium age below 65 or even 75, decreases, whereas the number of older people who are dying from CAD increases. This development can also be interpolated as positive. One sceptical aphorism on the value of physical activity indicates that athletes may not grow older but die healthier. Although this should probably not be stated by the unknown authors of this sentence, it can be used to demonstrate the aim of prevention as it should be understood today. In terms of a high life expectancy, not the lengthening of human life span should be considered to be the major aim of prevention but rather the prevention of immature or unnecessary diseases.

Fig. 1 Development of cardiovascular mortality in Germany. The incidence of coronary mortality decreases in medium age groups and increases in old age. This means a shift of coronary death to the end of biological life span and can be seen as success of cardiac prevention. The suspicion that this development is only the direct effect of the longer life expectancy itself (if more people grow older, more elderly people will die by heart attack) can be contradicted by the observation that cerebrovascular death rate decreases even in old age (lower pannel), probably the consequence of a more effective treatment of hypertension e.g. a preventive success as well.

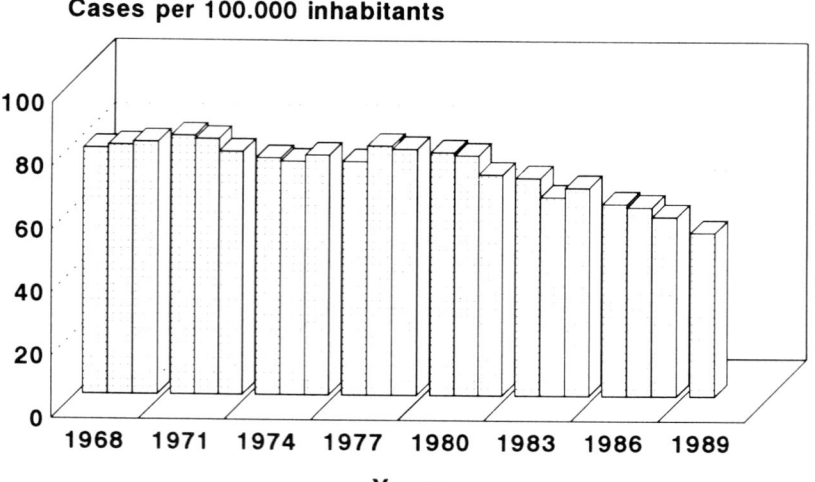

Fatal heart-attacks
males and females aged over 80 years

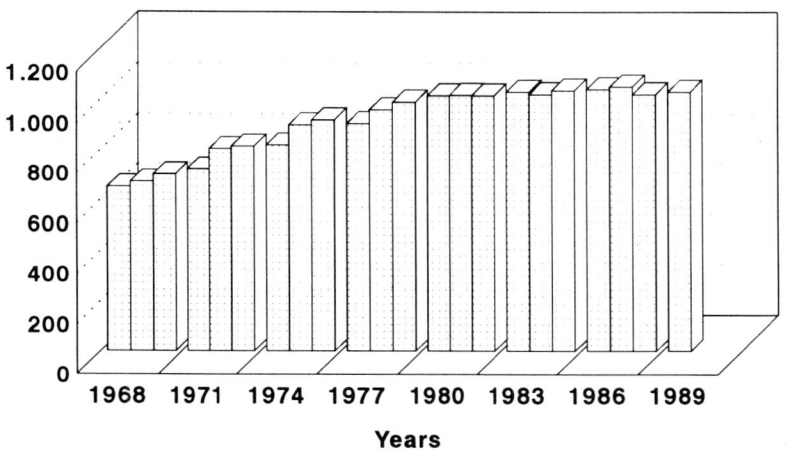

Fatal cases of cerebrovascular diseases
males and females aged over 80 years

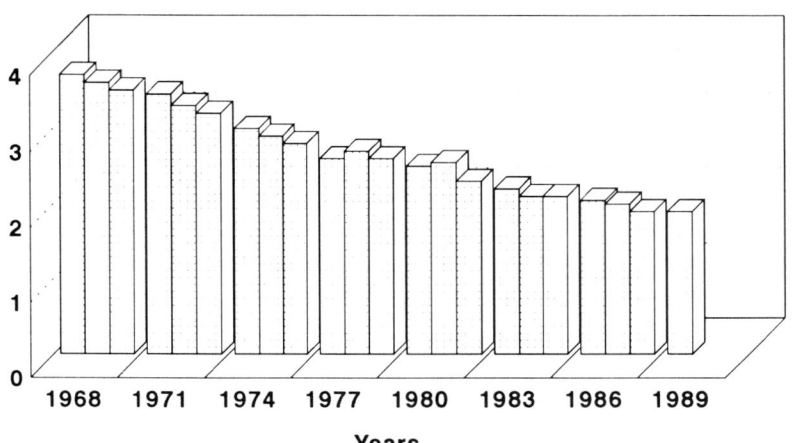

It should be our aim to grow old as healthy as possible, or to use a slight modification of the famous sentence of Sam Fox about sports: The aim of prevention is not necessarily to add more years to our life but more life to our years. A high life expectancy is only sensible if it can be lived in good health. Similarly health must be considered as personal interest as well as social obligation if one regards the high cost of disease today. Keeping in mind that even the best prevention will never prevent death as the natural end and an integral part of life, death by sudden heart attack may be closer to the idea of "dying healthy" than death by cancer. Therefore, as mentioned above, delay of myocardial infarction into older age can be considered a preventive success.

Conversely it can be argued that the shift of death by heart attack into older age may only be the consequence of the larger life span since if there are more elder people more of those should die by myocardial infarction. However, a opposite development can be observed in the second large portion of cardiovascular diseases, ie. cerebrovascular disorders. As can be seen in fig.1 the rate of death by brain stroke decreases particularly in the group of older subjects. This can probably be considered a result of better treatment of hypertension as the main risk factor for apoplexia. If one takes into account the high costs of the treatment of a nonfatal brain stroke, this success of a pharmacological preventive measure contradicts the sceptical opinion that prevention necessarily creates even higher costs. Of course the doubling of life expectancy which has been achieved in the last century can not be obtained free of charge. On the other hand it can be stated that this large life span would already be impossible to finance today if there were no preventive results by changes in general life style which have been observed in industrialized countries over the last two decades.

2. Epidemiological data on physical activity

In the preceding section the general aspects of prevention have been discussed in detail as far as possible since physical exercise has to be discussed from a preventive point of view as an integral part of a health-conscious life style. Arteriosclerosis is probably a multifactorial condition which requests a complex change of life style. On the other hand this situation explains the difficulty of demonstrating the benefits of a single factor such as a physical exercise within this complicated network. In terms of the critical opinions quoted earlier the subsequent questions must be answered:

- Does sport reduce coronary risk? If so, does this occur through a direct or indirect effect, or in other words, does it represent selection or protection? One such selection could be that athletes represent a natural positive sample with respect to health. Are athletes healthier because they engage in sport, or are healthy individuals more likely to engage in sport? Furthermore, a selection could result indirectly from an improved life style because athletes smoke less and follow a more sensible diet, or they are at least supposed to do so. This goal could possibly also be reached without physical exercise.

- If physical exercise represents protection, does it protect in all its variety of forms? For example, can occupational physical activities and sport exercises be equated? Does sport in the form of cross country skiing, for instance, have special significance or is it ultimately unimportant which type of exercise is performed? To answer this question it is unavoidable to know the basic mechanisms by which the health benefits of physical exercise are mediated.

- If sport has a preventive effect against CAD, what is the optimal dose that yields maximum protection, or should exercise be performed according to the motto "the more, the better"?

- Does inactivity really represent a risk factor, or does exercise "only" have the importance of a protective factor if high risk is already present? Does everybody therefore absolutely "need" to engage in sport, or only the individual at higher risk?

- How should risks and benefits of physical activity be balanced from the viewpoint of CAD?

As already mentioned above the correct answer to these questions is difficult to obtain from a scientific point of view, since the classical natural scientific approach of double blind tests can hardly be used in the assessment of life style. Experimental data from animal trials can only be transferred to the human being in a very limited manner and are therefore not discussed here. Statements relating to the benefits of sport therefore refer predominantly to epidemiologic studies. These always leave some doubts as to whether the uncovered relationships can be explained as conditional or causal. However, presently available data are so convincing that it is difficult or even impossible to ignore the health value of physical exercise. However, it must be admitted that sports medicine still owes us detailed answers to many questions.

The following approaches to clinical-epidemiologic investigations are principally available:

1.) The retrospective study of the incidence of CAD depending on the extent of physical activity.
2.) Prevalence studies, e.g., cross-sectional studies of the incidence of CAD in different subject groups with varying extent of physical activity.

3.) Prospective epidemiologic studies which are highly important from a scientific point of view.
4.) Pathological studies, e.g., investigations of the frequency of CAD on the basis of autoptical material.
5.) Rehabilitative studies on the effects on mortality and reinfarction frequency related to CAD, e.g., studies on the health value in the context of secondary prevention of CAD.

As a result of the high interest in the questions presented here, a variety of investigative approaches have emerged in the past. Within the framework of this survey it is not possible to describe these approaches in detail. The reader is referred to relevant overviews, early ones as well as more recent surveys such as Froehlicher, 1977, Hollmann, 1983, Powell, 1987. The majority of previous studies relate to **occupational studies**. One of the most famous trials of this kind and probably the first important study on this topic at all was the investigation of employees of the London Public Transit System conducted by Morris in 1953. This study demonstrated that the coronary mortality rate was lower by a factor of 1.5 for physically active conductors on the double-decker buses compared with the bus drivers. The significance of possible selection factors can be shown very well using this example. While the results were originally interpreted as an expression of a protective effect of physical activity on the job, subsequent analyses were able to show that the bus drivers initially revealed a higher coronary risk initial and therefore chose the less physically demanding job.

In contrast to this study many other similar investigations on the effects of occupational physical activity produced negative results. The ratio of trials with positive or negative results regarding the impact on coronary health is approximately 1:1. For example the Evans County study demonstrated a substantially lower rate of coronary mortality for blue-collar-workers than for white-collar-workers. Similarly, the study by Punsar and Karvonen (1976) is disappointing because surprisingly they were able to show that Finnish lumberjacks, involved in daily hard physical labor, had a significantly higher incidence of CAD than population groups with lower physical demands.

In contrast to sport exercises, occupational, physical exercise is not necessarily a stimulus for a sensible general life style. The high rate of heart attacks in lumberjacks as demonstrated by Punsar and Karvonen could, for instance, be explained by unreasonable diets with high fat contents and by a higher use of nicotine in this group. This conclusion is suggested by Hickey (1975) in his epidemiological study on the connection between physical activity and risk factors (Table 1).

Table 1. Relationship between physical activity and risk factors (Hickey et al., 1975; n = 15171)

Recreational Physical Activity	Cholesterol	Blood Pressure	Relative Overweight (%)	Cigarettes/ Day
Light physical load at work				
Low	238	139/85	7,2	9,4
Moderate	232	137/80	7,0	7,2
Intensive	212	125/80	4.2	5,7
Moderate physical load at work				
Low	234	138/85	7,0	9,8
Moderate	231	136/83	6,4	8,1
Intensive	221	127/80	5,1	7,3
Heavy physical load at work				
Low	228	135/85	6,1	9,9
Moderate	226	134/84	5,5	9,0
Intensive	223	129/84	5,5	6,7

Hickey's cross-sectional investigations revealed a positive influence of physical activity during leisure time on risk factors such as hypercholesteolemia, hypertension, obesity and cigarette consumption, but no effect of occupational physical exercise could be shown with respect to the same factors. However, a fairly recent prospective study by Salonen (1988) indicates a reduction of the relative risk of a cardiac infarct by 30 % for occupational as well as for leisure time activities. The significance of occupational physical activity therefore remains open for discussion.

In contrast to investigations on occupational exercise, studies concerned with **leisure time activities** nearly unanimously demonstrate positive health effects of physical exercise. The most recent and thorough review was provided by Powell et al. (1987). These authors summarized 54 investigations of exercise and CAD incidence published up to 1985 which were considered to be of satisfactory methodological standard. Folsom et al.(1992) added 7 more recent studies and came to the conclusion that these data show fairly convincingly that lack of endurance exercise is a contributing cause of CAD.

The salient epidemiological features of the association between lack of exercise and CAD are, according to Folsom, as follows:

1.) Strength: the risk of CAD is on the average twofold higher in subjects who have low levels of exercise compared to those with high levels.
2.) Consistency: the association between exercise and CAD is generally consistent. Powell et al. concluded that studies with the best methodologies generally showed the strongest relations.
3.) Dose-response: two thirds of the studies that measured exercise at two or more levels demonstrated that the lower the level of exercise, the greater the risk of CAD.
4.) Temporality: the majority of the studies have been prospective, thereby demonstrating that activity level appropriately predates the onset of CAD.
5.) Independence: most studies that simultaneously measured other risk factors have reported that lack of exercise was an independent risk factor for CAD.
6.) Generalizability: Most studies have focussed on middle-aged, white men. Evidence is suggestive that exercise also protects older men, women and non-whites.

After summarizing these general conclusions they shall be elucidated using the most important and wellknown examples:

Morris et al. (1980) following their classical busdrivererror which was mentioned above to the conclusion that a correct answer could only be given on the basis of prospective studies which were carried out by this group with the tremendous number of 17944 medium aged men over a period of 10 years. The results are summarized in table 2.

Table 2. Probability of CHD for the first time within ten years (prospective study by Morris, 1980)

	Athletes	Nonathletes
Nonsmokers	1.50%	3.80%
Cigarette smokers		
11 - 20 daily	4.60%	9.60%
21 or more daily	4.60%	11.60%

Heavy smokers (more than 20 cigarettes daily) who are not engaged in sport can expect an 11.4 % risk of suffering a cardiac event within the next ten years. For physically active nonsmokers, this risk is only 1.5 % and therefore lower by the factor 8. The data of Morris et al. also substantiate the independence of the protective effect of physical activity from other risk factors. Even those who maintain their smoking habits while being involved in sport activities have a clearly decreased risk at 4.9 %, although this is still higher than for nonsmoking, physically active persons by a factor of 3. The conclusion of this study was that a man in the middle age group, which was characteristic for the majority of the selected sample, the frequency of the "biologically premature" cardiac infarct can be reduced by a factor of 8 if the subject succeeds in making recreational physical activity and nonsmoking an integral and natural element of his/her life-style.

The second basic study was performed by Paffenbarger and his colleagues who examined a total of 16936 former Harvard graduates aged 25 to 74 years whose health data were known from university files. They filled out questionnaires every six to ten years concerning their state of health and involvement in physically activity. The data of Paffenbarger et al. show clear dependence of the frequency of heart attacks or the mortality rate related to cardiac infarcts upon the degree of physical activity. Activities were recorded in their various forms, such as walking, running and ball games, and transformed to caloric expenditure in form of "Mets" according to common tables. A mortality minimum of a caloric expenditure of 2000 to 3000 Kcal per week through physical activity was estimated. Subjects with a caloric expenditure of less than 2000 Kcal weekly through physical activity revealed a mortality rate related to coronary events that was elevated by 64 % when compared to subjects with an expenditure exceeding this threshold (Fig.2).

Fig. 2 Physical training and myocardial infarction (Paffenbarger et al. 1978)

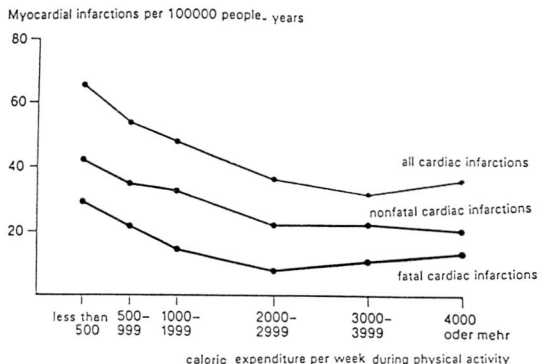

The results given by Paffenbarger et al. (Tab.3) also allow an assessment of the question of whether a decreased cardiac mortality in physically active subjects merely represented a "selection". Those graduates who participated in university sport or other athletic activities in their youth, but who then discontinued their involvement in any kind of physical activity, revealed at least equal or even higher coronary risk to those graduates who never exercised throughout their life-time. Conversely, those individuals who did not engage in sport during their youth, but were physically active later in their life, showed the same protective effect as those who were involved in sport all their life. Therefore, athletes by no means represent a very positive genetic group, as assessed from this viewpoint.

Table 3. Influence of past sport activity on the frequency of cardiac infarct (from Pfaffenbarger, 1978); numbers represent the number of infarct cases per 100.000 life years

	Energy consumption per week		
University sport	< 500	500 - 2000	> 2000
No	70.7	53.3	35.3
Yes	92.7	45.2	35.2
Other sport activities			
< 5 h / week	85.6	54.9	33.3
> 5 h / week	61.2	49.4	28.4

Similarly to the data of Morris, the results of Paffenbarger et al. confirm the independence of physical activity as a protective factor. Classification into selected risk factors shows that those individuals who smoke, suffer from high blood pressure or are overweight are also characterized by an increased protective effect if they are physically active.

A possible criticism of these two classical investigations could be that the description of physical activity is based on subjective declarations. Two more recent trials are therefore related to physical fitness which is considered to be a measure of the degree of physical activity. The validity of this assumption was confirmed by Ekelund et al. (1988) who found a close relationship between physical activity and physical fitness which was assessed in this study by the heart rate during submaximum workload. In their prospective investigation during a period of 8.5 years with 4276 subjects the authors came to the conclusion that a lower level of physical fitness was associated with a higher risk of death by CAD, independent of conventional coronary risk factors.

Similar results were found by Blair et al. (1989). According to their results the probability to die was 3.15 higher for the most unfit than for the fit subjects. If related to cardiovascular death this difference increased to a factor of 7.93. One fascinating result in this study was the fact that the probability to die of cancer was decreased in the physically fit subsample by a factor of 4.3. It remains questionable and out of the scope of this review to investigate if this difference may be the consequence of selection, better health-consciousness or perhaps of positive effects on the immunological system.

3. Secondary prevention

Physical activity has also become an important component of therapy in postinfarct care, i.e., in the area of secondary prevention. In Germany as in all industrialized countries a total shift of attitude occurred after the Second World War in the mid 1960s. Whereas the standard treatment was then generally rest from physical activity during the beginning of the wave of heart attacks after the war, the idea of sensibly dosed and controlled exercise has now generally been accepted. The exercise therapy of cardiac patients in Germany is generally performed in "ambulant coronary groups" (ACG). The explosive development of such groups in Germany is demonstrated in fig.3.

Fig. 3 Number of coronary groups in the Federal Republic of Germany

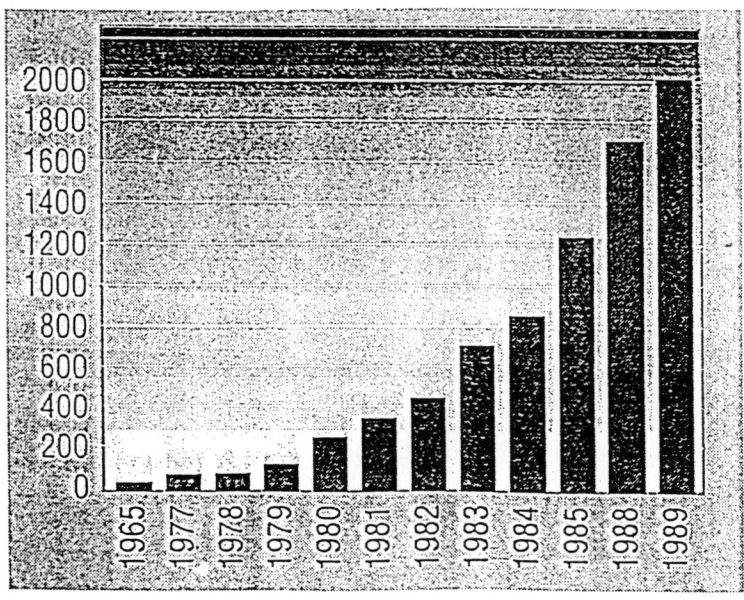

Several randomized controlled trials of exercise in postcoronary patients have been conducted. Although only one investigation showed a significant benefit by itself, pooled data from postinfarction studies indicate that the survival is improved among patients who exercise. O'Connor et al.(1989) performed a meta-analysis of 22 randomized exercise trials involving a total of 4554 postinfarction patients followed for an average of 3 years after randomization. The relative risks in the pooled exercise group vs comparison group there significantly reduced for
total mortality : relative risk 0,80
cardiovascular mortality : relative risk 0,78
fatal reinfarction: relative risk 0,75
sudden death within the first year : relative risk 0,63
(no change in 2. and 3. year)
No effect on nonfatal reinfarction.

4. Mechanism of physical exercise

In the preceding text the relationship between physical exercise and CAD has been discussed. There is a clear and undeniable negative correlation between the degree of physical activity and the frequency of cardiovascular conditions. However, this correlation must not be a causal one. In order to substantiate the significance of exercise for health, and to exclude indirect effects, the mode of operation of exercise must be elucidated. This is also important in order for correct advice to be provided concerning the optimal form of exercise which must be based on an exact knowledge of the mechanisms of sport and exercise on cardiovascular health.

These mechanisms in the past have been seen predominantly in the area of cardiovascular training effects. Since an improvement of the cardiovascular performance capacity can only be obtained through endurance exercise, only these forms of sports or exercises are frequently considered to be "healthy". The preconditions which are necessary to gain such training effects are definite characteristics of duration and intensity of exercise which are fulfilled by typical endurance sports such as running, jogging, swimming, cycling or cross-country skiing. Exercises of lower intensity such as walking or golfing, or of short duration for example in the form of short-interval exercise therefore generally are not considered to be combined with health benefits.

The consequence of this common attitude is frequently counterproductive since it encourages only sporting people to do sport and it discourages those who should exercise for health reasons but who feel incapable of jogging because they are unathletic, overweight and/or suffering by hypertension, arthritis, CAD or other conditions. Conversely this widespread jogging ideology discriminates against the health benefits of non-endurance but widespread types of sports and exercise such as calisthenics, gymnastics and athletic games e.g. soccer, tennis, golf, basketball and many others.

However, this absolutization of endurance sports contradicts the results of most epidemiological results about the benefits of physical exercise. As mentioned above many studies about occupational activities which do not fulfill the characteristics of endurance exercise demonstrate positive effects. If one examines the relationship between the type of leisure time activity and the incidence of CAD in the investigations of Morris or Paffenbarger the results by no means confirm the opinion of the restriction on health benefits of endurance exercise. According to the data of Paffenbarber (Tab. 4), the amount of exercise in terms of its caloric expenditure rather than the form of exercise is important with respect to primary prevention.

Table 4. Decreasing the risk of coronary death through various physical activities (from Pfaffenbarger 1978)

Activity	Relative risk
Climbing steps (appr. 50 steps/day)	1.25
Walking (appr. 5 blocks/day)	1.26
Moderate sport activity	1.08
Intensive sport activity	1.38
Energy expenditure (appr. 2000 kcal/day)	1.64

Such a statement appears logical when the goals of prevention are considered. The major goal of prevention is not the increase of cardiovascular performance but to influence the risk factors which are responsible for the development of arteriosclerotic diseases. These risk factors are predominantly dependent on metabolism, such as obesity, dyslipoproteinemia, diabetes mellitus and hypertension, which correlates with obesity and which, in terms of the metabolic syndrome, is already considered by some authors to practically be a "metabolic disorder".

Therefore with respect to primary prevention, every activity which increases metabolism, e.g. caloric expenditure, brings about health benefits. Endurance loads have the additional advantage of increasing the performance of the cardiovascular system, therefore after an initial stage the same caloric expenditure can be achieved more effectively in shorter time. Conversely these types of exercise are of major advantage in secondary prevention through the improvement of the economy of the cardiovascular system. Heart rate decreases for the same load which means a decrease of myocardial oxygen demand.

The importance of a metabolic consideration of the effects of physical exercise can be clearly demonstrated by the conception of the "metabolic syndrome" which is also called the "Reaven syndrome" after the author who first described this typical accumulation of risk factors. This concept describes the old medical observation that the major cardiovascular risk factors, obesity (particularly the androgenic type) diabetes, dyslipoproteinemia, diabetes mellitus and hypertension are frequently linked together. The common denominator is a reduced sensibility to insuline which results in hyperinsulinemia.

This concept is demonstrated in fig. 4 which takes into account the particular aspects of the necessary balance between energy uptake and energy expenditure, e.g. the sportsmedical aspects. This balance is upset in the industrialized countries by overnutrition and a sedentary lifestyle. In order to reduce the undesired offer of calorie, the cell, particularly the muscle fibre, reduces its capacity of energy uptake by diminishing its sensibility to the hormone which is responsible for energy uptake, ie. insulin. This results in hyperinsulinemia which contributes in a high degree to the manifestation of the above mentioned main risk factors if there is a genetic predisposition.

Fig. 4 The metabolic syndrome as a result of dysbalance between energy uptake and energy expenditure

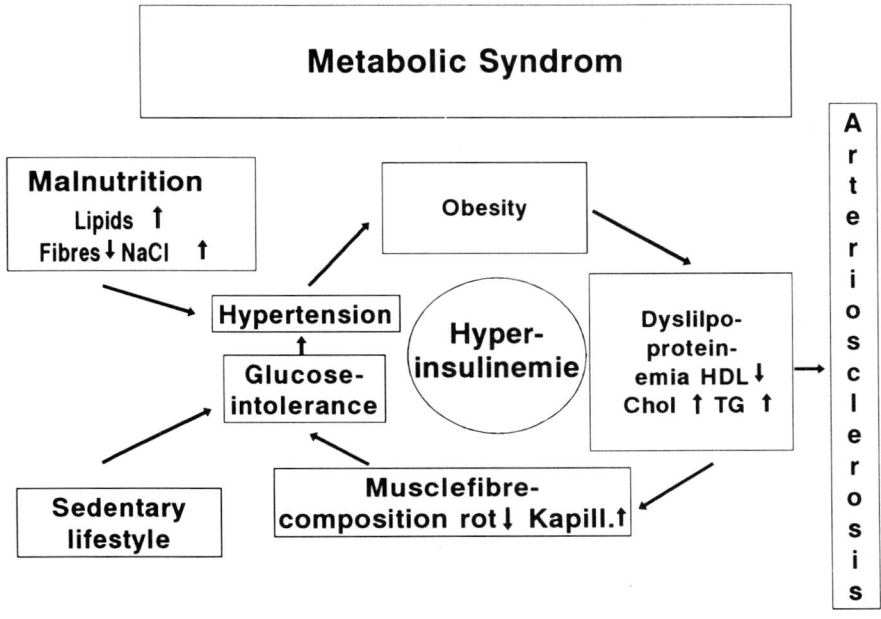

If this unhappy merry-go-round is to be reserved, it is absolutely necessary to turn both setscrews - energy uptake and energy expenditure - not only one of those which is frequently the case. The failure of weight loss only by starvation diet or sensationally offered forms of commercial diets has been experienced by millions of overweight subjects.

A model to explain the mechanism of physical activity is demonstrated in fig. 5. Habitual exercise brings about an increase of carbohydrate uptake in the muscle fibre which results in a decrease of insulin resistance, ie. a reduction in hyper-insulinemia and its negative impact on metabolic and cardiovsacular risk factors. Björntorp demonstrated as early as 1970 the influence of physical activity on insulin resistance and obesity. Conversely physical exercise triggers an increase of fat consumption. This means a degradation of the large VLDL molecules to triglyzerides and free fatty acids which are introduced into the Krebs cycle by the narrow sidepath of betaoxidation. From the remnants which are generated during this destruction of VLDL the HDL molecules are synthesized. Enzymes which are used for this synthesis are increased in athletes, lecithin-cholesterol-acyl-transferas (LCAT) being the most important among them. This metabolic pattern elucidates the increase of HDL-cholesterol in athletes, a most important proof for the health benefits of physical activity.

Fig. 5 Effects of physical activity on carbohydrate and fat metabolism

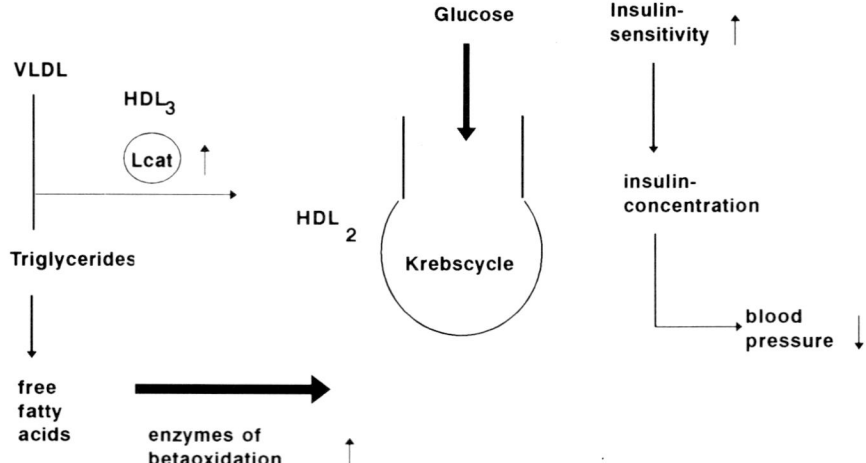

5. Conclusions

Experimental as well as epidemiological data unquestionably demonstrate the preventive effects of physical activity on coronary artery disease (CAP) and its major hemodynamic and metabolic risk factors. The model of the metabolic syndrome points out metabolic factors as the decisive mechanism of these health benefits. Therefore every physical activity which increases metabolic activity is combined with a preventive effect. The optimal amount of physical activity corresponds to 300 - 400 excesscalories used during exercise per day. Tab. 5 illustrates these figures in terms of various athletic activities. On the other hand these positive effects must be balanced against possible hazards such as accidents and injuries which differ widely in different types of sports. Regarding the high incidence of CAD and its metabolic preconditions in the European countries and the high financial burden of our health systems, physical exercise as part of a preventive lifestyle is not only of individual interest in order to pass the large lifespan which is today guaranteed by our high social and medical standard in a healthy way, but it is also social obligation in order to maintain this standard. The facts and considerations summarized in this paper should greatly influence the physical education systems of the European countries.

Table 5. Caloric expenditure for 10 min of sport (average values)

Activity		cal
Bowling		35
Water-skiing		70
Tennis		80
Badminton		80
Table tennis		53
Mountain climbing		80
Fencing		100
Team handball		140
Basketball		140
Trampoline		140
Wrestling, Judo		140
Rowing (50m/min)		20-30
Canoeing (125m/min)		83
Cayaking (125m/min)		68
Dancing	Foxtrot	60
	Rumba, Waltz	70
Running	9 km/h	100
	12 km/h	114
	15 km/h	131
Walking	4 km/h	31
	6 km/h	53
Golf		40-55
Bicycling	10 km/h	28
	20 km/h	78
Swimming	Breaststroke (50 m/min)	113
	Backstroke (25m/min)	70
	Freestyle (50m/min)	140
	Butterfly (50 m/min)	143
Icehockey		200-270
Soccer		230-280
Volleyball		73
Cross-country skiing	6 km/h	112
	10 km/h	151
	14 km/h	231
Alpine skiing	Downhill (tuck)	87
	Slalom	229
Ice-skating	12 km/h	47
	15 km/h	62
	21 km/h	104
Figureskating		50-250

References

1. **Bassler T.:** (1977) Marathon running and immunity to arteriosclerosis. Ann. NY Acad, Sci.3ol,579.

2. **Berg A., Keul J.:** (1985) Influence of maximum aerobic capacity and relative body weight on the lipoprotein profile in athletes Atherosclerosis 55,225.

3. **Björntorp P., de Jounge K., Sjöström L., Sullivan L.:** (1970) The effect of physical training on insulin production in obesity Metabolism 19,631.

4. **Blair S., Kohl H., Paffenbarger R., Clark D., Cooper K, Dupond L.:** (1989) Physical fitness and all cause mortality, prospective study of healthy men and women. JAMA 262, 2395.

5. **Ekelund L., Haskell W., Johnson J., Whaley F., Criqui M., Sheps D.:** (1988) Physical fitness as a predictor for cardiovascular mortality for asymptomatic North American men. New Engl.J.Med. 319,1379.

6. **Folsom A., Ensrud K.:** (1992) Cardiovascular benefits of endurance exercise. In Shephard R., P.O. Astrand (eds): Endurance in sports Oxford Blackwell Scientific publications London Edinburgh Boston Melbourne Paris Berlin Vienna 42o.

7. **Froehlicher V.:** (1977) Does exercise conditioning delay progression of myocardial ischemia in coronary arteriosclerotic disease? Cardiovasc.Clin.8,11.

8. **Hickey N.:** (1975) Study of coronary risk factors related to physical activity in 15171 men. Brit.Med.J. 3,5o7.

9. **Hollmann W., Rost R., Dufaux B., Liesen H.:** (1983) Prävention und Rehabilitation von Herz-Kreislauf-Krankheiten durch körperliches Training. Stuttgart, Hippocrates.

10. **McCormick I., Skrabanek P.:** (1989) Koronare Herzkrankheit kann durch Interventionsmaßnahmen in der Bevölkerung nicht verhindert werden. Lancet (German edition) 1,39.

11. **Morris J., Everitt M., Pollard R., Clave S.:** (1930) Vigorous exercise in leisure-time protection against coronary artery disease Lancet 11,1207.

12. Morris J., Heady J.: (1953) Mortality in relation to the physical activity of work. A preliminary note on experience in middle age. Brit.J.Int.Med.10,245.

13. Moser B.: (1989) Über das Editorial von R. Rost 3/1989 "Können Abstriche am Sterbegeld den Tod unseres Gesundheitsystems verhindern ?" Dtsch.-Z.Sportmed. 40,221.

14. 0'Connor G., Burin J., Yusuf S.: (1939) An overview of randomized trials of rehabilitation with exercise after myocardial infarction Circulation 80,234.

15. Paffenbarger R., Wing A., Hyde R.: (1978) Physical activity as an index of heart attack risk in college alumni. Am.J.Epidemiol. 108,161.

16. Powell K., Thompson P., Caspersen C., Kendrick J.: (1987) Physical activity and the incidence of coronary heart disease 8,253.

17. Punsar S., Karvonen M.: (1976) Physical activity and coronary heart disease in populations from East and West Finland Adv.Cardiol. 18,l96.

18. Reaven G.: (l988) Banting lecture: role of insulin resistance in human disease 37,1595.

19. Rost R.: (l988) Athletics and the heart. London, Year Book Medical publishers Chicago.

20. Salonen J., Slater J., Tuomiletho J., Rauromaa R.: (1988) Leisure time and occupational physical activity: risk of death from ischemic heart disease Am.J.Epidemiol.127,87.

21. Ulmer H.: (1989) Über das Thema Kosteneinsparungen im Gesundheitswesen durch Sport Dtsch.Z.Sportmed. 40,79 und 221.

EUROPEAN MASTER'S DEGREE IN APA:
A WAY OF COMBINING COMPETENCIES

Van Coppenolle, H.; Neerinckx, E.; Vanlandewijck, Y.; Simons, J.; Verwilt, M.
Catholic University Leuven, Faculty of Physical Education and Physiotherapy
Leuven, Belgium

A meeting of the European Association for Research on Adapted Physical Activity in 1988 was the cradle of the idea for a European postgraduate training programme. Five years later, the project has grown out of its infancy: 22 universities from 12 European countries are involved, 67 students enrolled and the structure of the cooperation has been a source of inspiration for other ICP's. The story of a successful ICP...

1. From an Idea ...

The training of sport science students in the field of physical activity for people with a disability wasn't and still isn't an easy task: the field of action is wide, and, in the curricula of most universities, only limited attention is paid to this specific application of human movement. At the end of the eighties, 9 university lecturers discussed the establishing of a cooperation which could solve this problem. This wish and the possibilities offered by ERASMUS gave the initial impetus to the development of a specific training programme.

2. ...towards an ICP!

Several meetings and one application form later, the EMDAPA programme started in the academic year 1991-1992. The programme offers university training in the social, pedagogic and technical aspects of movement activities, adapted to specific populations. Through these adapted movement activities - further called A(dapted) P(hysical) A(ctivity) - therapeutic objectives in the treatment and the training of persons with both psychic or chronically somatic disorders are aimed at, and, through recreational activities and (elite) sport, optimal self-fulfilment is sought.

The objective of the programme is to combine the competencies of a number of European universities in order to offer the students a comprehensive training in the many aspects of APA.

Next to the Faculty of Physical Education and Physiotherapy of the Katholieke

Universiteit Leuven, which hosts the degree, the following 21 institutions are presently involved in the scheme:

- Vrije Universiteit Amsterdam
- Athens University
- Universitat de Barcelona
- Freie Universität Berlin
- Vrije Universiteit Brussel
- Université Libre de Bruxelles
- Université Joseph Fourier Grenoble
- Ruprecht-Karls-Universität Heidelberg
- University of Jyväskylä
- Danmarks Hojskole for Legemsovelser Kobenhavn
- Sporthochschule Köln
- Université de Lille
- Universidade Technica de Lisboa
- Loughborough University
- Université Catholique de Louvain
- Universidad Politecnica de Madrid
- Université de Montpellier I
- University of Northumbria Newcastle
- Nottingham University
- Norwegian University of Sport and Physical Education Oslo
- Eidgenössische Technische Hochschule Zürich

3. Curriculum

The training consists of two stages.

During the <u>first stage</u>, from September till December a multidisciplinary package of theoretical lectures is offered. These lectures, which are held at the host university, consist of the specific courses given by the different experts in APA from the participating universities, completed with a few courses taught by lecturers from the host university.

The courses cluster the main topics of the APA field:

1. Contextual aspects of APA (90h)\par
2. Impairments, disabilities and handicaps (40h)\par
3. Adapted Physical Activity Intervention (130h)\par
4. Research methodology (50h).

The basics of this content have been published in a textbook.

During the <u>second phase</u> an opportunity to specialize is offered. This specialization also takes one semester and is studied at one of the participating universities. During this second stage, the student will gain practical experience and also start a research project that should result in a master's thesis at the end of the training.

4. Scientific Awards

The success of this initiative cannot be denied and therefore new developments will be necessary.

The success is illustrated by the yearly increasing number of students (1991:17; 1992:23; 1993:27) and universities applying for participation. However, quantity cannot be the only standard; fortunately quality has also been proved: the winning of the 'Young Researcher Award' by one of the students at the World Congress of the International Federation of Adapted Physical Activity, Yokohama 1993, can be considered a first indication!

A videofilm "Fitness training as psychomotor therapy in depressive patients", made about the research project of another student has been awarded 'Magna cum Laude' at the International Scientific Film Contest "Medikinale International Hannover 1992".

5. What about the Future?

Moreover, another conclusion must be made. The growing demands of people with disabilities to have qualified trainers and coaches in order to reach higher performance levels (elite sport) and a better quality of sport practice (recreation) emphasize the social relevance of this particular effort. Taking these reassuring conclusions into account, the future seems to be promising. Obviously a cooperation project like this remains 'on the way to'...

First, different partners mean different education systems. Consequently, efforts must be repeated to adapt the programme to the needs of the students. Besides the obvious immediate academic purposes, the publishing of a textbook (fall 1993) must be considered as a first step towards renewed consultation.

A second, and more problematic task will be the pursuit of financial independency. No one can doubt that this programme would not be realized without the Erasmus funding. It was an extraordinary opportunity, which unfortunately won't last. Now it is up to all partners to confirm their involvement through financial support too. Notwithstanding the basic consensus on this topic, it looks as if practice needs some more time. Nevertheless, at this stage of the project, one must hope (and cooperate) to find the necessary willingness. And then money must be available.

Adapted Physical Activity (APA) and Physical Education & Sport Sciences

Vermeer, A.
Free University, Faculty of Human Movement Sciences
Amsterdam, The Netherlands

1. Introduction

This contribution discusses Adapted Physical Activity (APA) research in Europe. This evaluation is a result of personal experiences gained in the 'scientific world' of Physical Education and Sport Sciences. My opinions are also based on a number of observations made when visiting other institutes of Physical Education and Sport Sciences, especially in Europe.
For a better understanding of the content of this contribution, the reader should know that I was appointed to the Faculty of Human Movement Sciences of the Free University in Amsterdam, after a period of eight years of teaching Physical Education in primary, secondary and special schools. The faculty in Amsterdam is the only Faculty of Human Movement Sciences in The Netherlands. Apart from this faculty, there are departments of Human Movement Sciences in:

- the Faculty of Social Sciences of the University of Groningen,
- the Faculty of Social Sciences of the Utrecht University,
- the Faculty of Health Sciences of the University of Limburg, and
- the Faculty of Medicine of the University of Nijmegen.

The Faculty of Human Movement Sciences of the Free University in Amsterdam has six departments: Functional Anatomy, Exercise Physiology, Health Science, Psychology with respect to Human Movement, Educational Sciences and History and Philosophy of Human Movement [2]. My position is in the department of Educational Sciences. It is a clinically- oriented department, one of its focuses being APA. The faculty was founded in 1971 and named 'Faculty of Physical Education'. This name was changed in 1988 into 'Faculty of Human Movement Sciences'. The change from 'Physical Education' into 'Human Movement Sciences' also reflects the development of my personal opinions with respect to the sciences of Physical Education and Sport.

This contribution is based on six statements concerning APA sciences. They are, however, also applicable to Physical Education and Sport Sciences.

1. APA research is an application of fundamental research developed by disciplines such as Functional Anatomy, Exercise Physiology, Psychology and Sociology with respect to human movement in general and to that of persons belonging to special populations in particular. The scientific progress of APA is based on that of these fundamental disciplines.

2. The previous statement implies that APA research consists of fundamental research and the application of the outcomes of this research in intervention.

3. It is difficult for Institutes of Physical Education and Sport Sciences to contribute to the development of Physical Education and Sport Science, including APA, if they do not have the capacities to carry out both fundamental and intervention research.

4. Teachers of Physical Education and sport trainers and coaches, who have completed a programme of Higher Education, should be competent to carry out applied or intervention research. Moreover, some institutes should have opportunities to train students in both fundamental and intervention research. It is not desirable for these students to be competent in teaching PE or sport instruction.

5. Quite a number of European Institutes of Higher Education in Physical Education and Sport are focused almost exclusively on PE and sport, including APA, practice. This is a threat to the development of a European network of Physical Education and Sport Sciences in Higher Education, including APA.

6. The number of international (= English language) academic APA publications from the European continent is too small.

2. APA research is applied research

The first statement to be discussed concerns the nature of APA research. We agree - I suppose - that APA is not a discipline, but a field of study. The question is whether there is a discrete discipline whose aims effect the development of APA theories by means of APA research. The position is taken that Physical Education and Sport Science in general, and APA Science in particular, are applied fields of study. The application concerns the theories and methodology of fundamental disciplines such as Functional Anatomy, Exercise Physiology, Sport Psychology, Sport Sociology, etc. Although it is not a very important remark, this view nevertheless implies that - in fact - a PE/Sport, including APA, Science (singular) does not exist. Applied to APA, APA Science does not have its own body of knowledge. APA research is plural. It consists of an integration of bodies of knowledge of a number of founding disciplines [4]. Therefore, strictly speaking, we should speak about PE and Sport Sciences.

The kind of information that is necessary for the execution of APA research and the method of integration of scientific information depend on the research question and the philosophical viewpoint. Consequently, the scientific progress of PE and Sport Science(s) as applied fields of study is based on that of the fundamental disciplines. I would like to give two examples to illustrate my hypothesis.In APA, teachers and therapists have to cope with questions of the origin and the changeability of the behaviour of children with developmental disabilities. Research that focuses on the interaction between biological and psychological variables is very promising with respect to these questions. A part of the research programme in which I am involved is studying the effects of special nutrition on brain maturation of babies who are born too early or too small, viz. premature and dysmature babies. This part of the research programme is executed by the department of Paediatrics of the Faculty of Medicine. This research is very relevant for us because a direct effect of a better functioning CNS is the enhancement of the visual system, in particular visual acuity. Our part of the research concerns the question as to whether this affects the development of movement coordination, in particular eye-hand coordination and upright locomotion.

Another good example concerns the contribution during this conference of Pederson [3] about the influence of physical activity on the immune system. This kind of very promising research with respect to infectious diseases such as Pfeiffer, and possibly Aids and Cancer, could only be done by biologists, specialized in immunology.

3. APA sciences consist of fundamental and applied or intervention research

The relevancy of fundamental research concerns the application of the outcomes of this type of research in teaching, therapy and instruction and, in general, in intervention. This does not mean that intervention is the application of the outcomes of fundamental research. The outcomes have to be translated into programmes for certain groups of clients of a certain age. In particular, educational and clinical (= therapeutic) sciences, such as Clinical Psychology, provide us with information as to how to do this. These are sciences which integrate fundamental knowledge to be used for educational and therapeutic purposes. This process of integration is subject to standards about what is desirable and to the aim of education or therapy.

This statement can be more provocatively reformulated: Educational and Clinical Sciences are nothing without the relevant fundamental sciences. One of the main aims of Educational and Clinical Sciences concerns the development and the evaluation of educational and therapeutic programmes, in other words, intervention research. The theories and hypotheses for this type of research are rooted in the fundamental disciplines. Intervention research is not developing, but applying theories. The differences between fundamental and intervention research concern methodology. Students who have qualified to become a teacher, therapist or instructor have to be trained in the principles of intervention research within the constraints of a curriculum of 4 to 5 years. Then, they are able to contribute to the further development of available theories, not to the development of new theories. The last aim requires training in the execution of fundamental disciplines.

4. Contribution to theory development

The statement that Institutes of Higher Education will have difficulties in contributing to theory development if they do not have the facilities to carry out fundamental research applies, in general, to those Institutes involved in the training of teachers and instructors, namely, (in the Netherlands), the teacher training colleges of Physical Education and the schools of Physical Therapy. The Institutes of Higher Education which offer a more academic programme do have - in principle - the facilities to carry out fundamental research. In the Netherlands these institutes are called Universities. Thus, in my opinion, it is the primary task of the universities to carry out fundamental research. They have to have the facilities for this type of research. Besides, universities are, quite often, challenged to apply the findings of their efforts. This means that, quite often, they also carry out applied and intervention research.

Of course, I know that not all university faculties and departments are adequately funded to do fundamental research. Many institutes are, with respect to research, almost completely dependant on external grants. Mostly, external grant awarding bodies make demands in terms of the social relevance of the outcomes of the research. In that case, the only solution for such faculties and departments is to develop close relationships with faculties which can offer the fundamental knowledge which is needed. Otherwise, scientifically, one will run dry.

The same applies to the teacher training colleges of Physical Education, the colleges of Physical Therapy and the schools for sport instructors. Students of these institutes of higher education, who are trained to develop and carry out educational and therapeutic programmes, also need to acquire competence in evaluation. They must have the competence not only to execute, but also to evaluate, their interventions. For intervention research they need hypotheses, in other words, theories on which their interventions are based. Fundamental research provides these theories, intervention research can contribute to the indication of the relevance and the refinement of these theories. Intervention research can also contribute to the development of new ideas and hypotheses for fundamental research. It is clear that institutes of higher education which train their students in applied and intervention research, should have a close cooperation with universities carrying out fundamental research. Unfortunately, this is hardly ever the case in my own country. The Netherlands have fine teacher training colleges of Physical Education and schools of Physical Therapy. Only one (Groningen), has a close relationship with a department of Human Movement Sciences of a university (Groningen). In general, in the Netherlands the teacher training colleges of Physical Education are institutes of higher education, like the universities, but they do not train their students in intervention research and they do not cooperate with the faculties and university departments of Human Movement Sciences.

I know very well that not all university colleagues want to promote this kind of cooperation or integration of the tasks of the two types of institutes of higher education. They are afraid of a reduction in academic standards if the universities also have the task of training teachers and therapists. Admission of the Colleges of Physical Education and Sport into the university would lead to an enormous increase in the teaching load of the university professors. This would be at the cost of the time available for research. On the other hand, there are examples of the integration of the undergraduate and graduate level in one institute where we can observe that these institutes can both contribute to applied research as well as to fundamental research. We can find examples of such cooperation in Europe as well as outside Europe, e.g. in the USA.

5. Training of students

It will be clear from the preceding statement that I would like to advocate the inclusion of applied research training in the training of PE and sport students in institutes of higher education. If this is not the case, the status of the PE and sport instruction discipline will suffer. I can again use the situation of my own country as an example.

Until the seventies philosophical approaches were directly translated into educational aims and methods. After this period a purely pragmatic approach was evident in school physical education: (1) PE should teach children that a physically active life style is important for physical health, and, (2) PE should introduce children to the realms of sport, in order to give them the possibility of choosing suitable sport participation at a later age. The theoretical foundation of physical education, i.e. the significance of movement, for children's development in general and for specific aspects of development in particular, such as the development of motor skills, the development of perceived competence and self-efficacy and social development, was neglected. This was also the case in APA. For instance, because of the prosperity of the sixties, in particular based on the enormous amount of gas found in Dutch soil, the development of APA in the Dutch institutes for mentally retarded persons was impressive. All kinds of philosophies could be translated into well-equipped facilities. Measuring of the effects never took place.

In the eighties, both school physical education and institutionalized APA were victims of the first cuts in government expenditure. Although organisations for PE teachers, sport organisations and organisations for APA teachers and movement therapists tried to convince the authorities of the importance of PE, sport and APA, they could not support their argument with results of actual research. This is one reason why the field of PE, sport and APA lost influence. Therefore, it is very important that professionals should be able to substantiate their hypotheses. It is the task of the universities to provide professionals with the right hypotheses and methodologies. Therefore, the universities should carry out both fundamental and applied research. To guarantee relevancy, faculties and departments of Human Movement Sciences should cooperate with professionally-oriented institutes and bodies. A full-time programme of at least four years is needed to train students in both fundamental and applied research. It is impossible to train them at the same time to become a PE teacher, physical or movement therapist or a sports expert.

6. Conditions for the development of a European network

With respect to this statement, I would like to focus in particular on APA. With respect to APA, only a few institutes of higher education in Europe have the facilities described above. As far I can see, only a small number of institutes of higher education in not more than about three or four European countries really have the opportunities to carry out both fundamental and applied APA research. This is a threat to the development of a European network of APA research in Europe. The actual situation is that the scientific APA scene is almost completely dominated by the North American continent. The scientific contribution of Europe to this domain is quite small. Scientific networks of PE and sport sciences, including APA sciences, in higher education have to cope with this problem. At the moment it seems that the number of institutes which are more focussed on PE and sport practice than on research, are in the majority. Let us take the European Masters Degree in Adapted Physical Activity Programme as an example. Three years ago 9 European PE and Sport institutes of higher education developed a one year academic APA programme at a Master's Degree level, subsidised by the ERASMUS programme and excellently organized and hosted by the Faculty of Physical Education and Kinesiotherapy of the Catholic University of Leuven [1]. Students at the universities of Utrecht and the Free University are very enthusiastic about this programme. Nevertheless, the board of studies has to cope with the problem that quite a number of institutes with no tradition of research participate in this programme. Only a few institutes can offer the students who follow this programme participation in ongoing research. We have to discuss what to do. A stricter form of selection? Two degrees: one practically-oriented and one research-oriented? Progress of the field of APA is to a large extent dependant on research and theory development. As we will see in the next statement, the scientific output of Europe in comparison with that of North America is not so great. This implies that priority has to be given to APA research. The networks created by the European Community can make a very valuable contribution in this respect. This does not mean that APA practice should be neglected. However, that is not the first task of a university. My wish is that the group of universities which generated the European Master's Degree in APA, in cooperation with the European Network of Sport Sciences, could promote European cooperation in APA at a Bachelor's Degree level. Such a Bachelor's Degree should include courses in statistics and methodology. After graduation, students could enrol for the Master's Degree programme. The inclusion of institutes with no tradition of research is a threat to the further development of this Master's Degree programme.

7. The academic APA output in Europe

The last statement concerns an evaluation of the international standard of European APA research. There is only one international academic APA journal, the Adapted Physical Activity Quarterly (APAQ). (N.B.: Unfortunately, APAQ is recorded neither in the "Current Contents of Life and Social Sciences" nor in the "Scientific Citation Index". This could be a reason for some researchers not to publish in APAQ but in other scholarly journals.) The board of editors consists of 21 persons. 19 of them are from North America (USA and Canada) and two from Europe (England and The Netherlands). There is no international scientific APA journal in Europe. This does not mean that the number of international academic APA publications in Europe is small. However, many researchers choose to publish in the academic journals of their discipline (Biomechanics, Rehabilitation Sciences, Special Education, etc.). Nevertheless, the number of European academic APA publications is too small for a European APA journal. I can illustrate this by the number of European academic publications in APAQ during the last 5 years.

Table 1: The number of non-North American publications in Adapted Physical Activity Quarterly (APAQ)

	N	%
USA + Canada	126	89
Europe	13	9
-Netherlands (4)		
-England (3)		
-Finland (2)		
-Germany (2)		
-Belgium (1)		
-Norway (1)		
Australia	2	1
China	1	1
Total	142	100

This table also shows which countries contribute, however slightly, to international APA research. This can also be derived from the number of national academic APA journals on the European continent. There are three national academic APA journals in Europe, one in Germany (Motorik), one in France (Motricité) and one in the Netherlands (Bewegen & Hulpverlening). These journals are not purely academic, they also include practical issues with theoretical reflections.

8. Final remarks

For the further development of APA in Europe the standard of research is inadequate. At institutes of PE and Sport Sciences in higher education professionals also have to acquire research competence, in particular competence in applied or intervention research. The primary task of universities is to train students in fundamental and applied research.

References

1. Van Coppenolle H., Simons J., Neerinckx E., Vanlandewijck Y., Verwilt M. (eds.): Textbook European Master's Degree Adapted Physical Activity. Leuven, Acco, 1993.

2. Free University: Human Movement Sciences: Information on Teaching and Research. Amsterdam, Free University, 1992.

3. Pedersen B.D.: Physical Exercise: The Immune System, Cancer and Infectious Diseases. In: Abstract Volume: 2. European Forum Sport Sciences in Europe 1993, pp. 155. Köln, Deutsche Sporthochschule, 1993.

4. Sherrill C.: Interdisciplinary Perspectives in Adapted Physical Activity. In: Doll-Tepper G., Dahms C., Doll B., Selzam H. von (eds.): Adapted Physical Activity: An Interdisciplinary Approach, pp. 23-30. Berlin, Springer Verlag, 1990.

SOCIOLOGICAL ASPECTS OF SPORT AND DISABILITY: CURRENT AND FUTURE PERSPECTIVES

Williams, T.
Loughborough University
UK

1. Introduction

Sociology is an emerging field in the study of sport and disability. While disability sport has been subjected to a considerable amount of attention from biomedical scientists, we know very little about its sociological aspects except in the most crude and one-dimensional sense of individual and common sense interpretations. What we do know has come from the relatively few number of empirical studies which have been conducted within the last ten years in the context of North American adapted physical activity. Much of this research has been driven by the practical concerns and issues that affect the sporting lives of many thousands of individuals but, as a corpus, it is sociologically atheoretical, unprogrammatic and lacking in coherence and direction.

The purpose of this paper is to develop a research agenda for a sociological treatment of sport and disability. This entails a two-part discussion. First, I will examine what is currently on offer as sociological research and make three points: a) the sociology of sport and disability is at the fact-gathering stage of development; b) previous attempts to outline a research agenda have not concentrated on fundamental sociological questions; and c) there is an opportunity to set a European sociological research agenda. Second, I will delineate and clarify a field of study which has two major research activities: a) fundamental research which can build up a field of knowledge; and b) developing praxis based on that knowledge. I am not aware that this has been attempted before and so the task is a preliminary one. I hope that the research agenda, outlined here, can be developed further and implemented through pan-European collaboration.

2. Current Perspectives

Let me start the examination of current research by considering how sociology can contribute to the study of sport and disability. This will benefit the discussion in three important ways. On the one hand, we need to clarify our expectations about sociological research and some of the standards we can use to evaluate current studies. On the other hand, we need to locate those studies within a particular research context; we need to see them as the products of a scholarly community, centred mainly in North America, which has a particular research tradition and a set of operating assumptions that must be highlighted if we are going to lay out a research agenda that has any chance of implementation. In addition, it addresses the question of whether a sociology of sport and disability is important enough to warrant research attention and this, too, should be considered in future discussions about a research agenda.

Sociology can make three important contributions to the study of sport and disability. First, professional sociologists have developed a set of methods that have been tested in countless social contexts. The purpose of these methods, of course, is to make known that which is sociologically unknown and to do so in such a way that the results are credible. Sociological research as the systematic inquiry of the social aspects of sport and disability carried out by a community of inquirers is better than the common-sense notions and received opinions which people develop from their individual position. Second, sociological research offers a view of sport and disability that is very different to the biomedical one which is currently used in adapted physical activity. It rests on a social model of disability which raises different questions, uses different concepts and which forces one to think in different ways, than one would normally do when either practising disability sport or conducting biomedical research in the area. Third, and obviously related to the other two contributions, sociology has the power to challenge the existing beliefs and practices in disability sport. Sociological research very often raises doubts about the things we take for granted and this involves two related processes. These are de-mystification or making known what it is that we take for granted and de-bunking or challenging myths and stereotypes. Sociological research, then, can transcend the one-dimensional, absolutist and dominant view of aspects of our lives that we, or others, regard as social problems, that remain hidden or that we take for granted. Above all, though, its task is to make known something which was previously unknown - in this case, to advance our understanding of how the behaviour of individuals with disabilities in groups is influenced by the social relationships they form, their past experiences and the social settings in which disability sport occurs.

The sociological literature which focuses on sport and disability has been produced in the context of North American adapted physical activity and the characteristics of that social and cultural milieu have influenced its development. The most important of these characteristics is the use of a medical model of disability. Research and practice in adapted physical activity has long been dominated by a functional model of disability which has its origins in medicine, rehabilitation and illness. The assumptions of the model are based on the view of disability as a 'personal tragedy' and they place an overwhelming emphasis on the individual as an organism 'adapting' to the environment. Understanding the activity 'problems' which the individual has by virtue of some kind of physical, sensory or intellectual deficit has been, naturally, the domain of researchers in sciences which focus on, for example, exercise physiology, biomechanics, psychology and motor control and they rely heavily on quantitative research methods and statistical analyses. This tradition has had a great deal of influence on the development of the sociological literature because not only has research been undertaken by researchers who have been socialized, professionally, in contexts and by agents which utilise the personal tragedy model of disability and which value particular research methods (eg. graduate training, academic journals) but much of the sociological material is located within psychological studies under the rubric 'social and psychological aspects of adapted physical activity'.

2.1 Research Overview

Prior to 1980 there were very few studies in the sport and disability literature which professed to be sociological although quite a number of them offered 'social' material. There were a number of studies, for example, which focused on students in physical education and recreation and their attitudes toward people with disabilities and there were other studies which focused on integration, on barriers to participation and on sexuality. Attention was directed to therapeutic recreation and adapted physical education and, in the main, the articles tended to offer reports of programmes and discussions of some of the issues which confronted practitioners. Their emphasis was on effective intervention strategies and especially the use of sport and physical activity as vehicles for the socialization of individuals with disabilities. They championed sport and physical activity as contexts in which individuals could establish sexual relationships and learn the basic social skills which others, the able-bodied, take for granted. The activities were functional, in the sociological sense, but while there can be no doubt that they provided many practical guidelines, there was very little empirical research informing these discussions and what research there was tended to be atheoretical (for an excellent review of the therapeutic recreation research at this time, see 11). For the most part the studies provided a pragmatic, descriptive, view of the social aspects of adapted physical activity that remains popular in those journals which have practical concerns (eg. Palaestra).

In the period since 1980 the research literature has increased considerably in both quantity and quality. It exhibits a number of interesting characteristics. The first, and arguably the most important, is that the majority of studies have focused only on those topics which have relevance to disability. The sociological interest of the literature is centred on the importance placed on the differences which result from the presence or absence of the material conditions of impairments and the effects those differences have on the lives of sports men and women and the ways in which disability sport is structured. In particular, there are four categories of topics which have been the most popular (see Table 1). These are studies on culture (mainly attitudes towards the integration of individuals with disabilities), referent groups (mainly emphasising different impairments), social context (mainly opportunities and barriers to participation) and social processes (mainly socialization via and into sport, participation and integration). By far the most common are studies on social processes.

Table 1: Frequency of Major Themes in the Sociological Literature on Sport and Disability

Themes	Frequency
Foundations	18
Aktivities	24
Culture	64
Health & Lifestyle	11
Referent Groups	46
Social context	40
Social Procecces	103
Total	306

The second, and perhaps the most evident characteristic, is that research has become much more empirical than was the case before 1980. There has been an increase in the use of different research methods, together with quite sophisticated research designs and statistical analyses, which have changed the corpus from a small assortment of interesting articles on 'social' aspects to a fairly large and growing collection of studies on 'sociological' aspects. As a result a lot of pioneering work has been done in the examination of a number of disability relevant themes. Large amounts of factual information have been collected and used to make known a number of trends or patterns among large numbers of athletes on a range of topics. It is noticeable, too, that the topics which were found to be practically important in the early years have continued to claim research attention but additional topics have been included as the disability experience and sport in modern western societies undergoes social transformation. Studies on attitudes, integration, the barriers to participation, and socialization via sport are still important and they continue to be examined but they have been complemented by studies which consider, for example, socialization into sport and participation.

The third characteristic has been the continuing domination of the medical model of disability but to a lesser degree of late. This is evident, for example, in the overwhelming emphasis on impairments as analytic categories and a focus, especially, on groups of individuals with cerebral palsy, learning difficulties, spinal cord injuries and sensory and visual impairments. However, in the last few years there has been a noticeable shift away from rehabilitation and 'personal tragedy' toward examinations of disability sport per se. As more empirical studies are undertaken so the results draw more and more attention to the ways in which structured inequalities within particular societies are affecting the daily sporting lives of men and women with disabilities. As a corpus, then, the literature is leaning toward a more sociological model of disability which locates the origins of disability not with the individual but with society.

The fourth characteristic, and perhaps the most consequential for future developments, is the lack of sociological paradigms used in the literature. There are some studies which incorporate functionalist assumptions when they make use of theories (eg. a social learning approach to socialization) in a heuristic and very limited way but there are very few studies which make explicit use of the recognised sociological perspectives. Most studies are atheoretical and this is problematic because in the absence of sociological paradigms and the theories which they support then all facts appear as relevant as any others to the researcher and to the practitioner. It becomes very difficult, then, for research to develop in a manner which is both systematic and cumulative and this is illustrated with some of the limitations which are evident in the literature at the present time. For example, there has not been much new information generated that was not or is not known to many practitioners; there are few studies which de-mystify disability sport or which challenge the myths and stereotypes surrounding sports men and women with disabilities; nearly all of the studies have been done in the United States and one could argue that much of the information they have produced is useful only in the United States; and research is descriptive and random. All these are symptoms of a field which is going through the fact-gathering or preparadigm stage of its development (cf. 9) and this is surprising because there have been several attempts in the past decade to introduce sociological theory and to outline a research agenda.

2.2 Previous Research Agendas

One of the reasons that descriptive research is problematic, in this case, is that an excess of random facts inevitably lead to chaos. Not only is this a problem of quantity (ie. too many facts), but it is also a problem of quality in that all facts appear to be equally relevant. Description, of course, has a very important theoretical task to perform in the research process because it is a necessary pre-cursor of explanation. The development of a sociology of sport and disability, then, must begin with a description of the phenomena which claims the attention of the group interested in studying it. This is a vital step in the process because without it we would not know on what we should focus our attention but there comes a time in the development of a field when there are so many facts that, in the absence of some organizing process, further research only adds to the chaos and the mass of facts which continue to be collected actually get in the way of understanding. Fact-gathering needs to be ordered in some way and this has been recognised by at least two researchers in the past - Howard Nixon and Karen DePauw - who, between them, have made several contributions to the generation of a research agenda that could structure research in the field.

Nixon's contributions have varied in form and content. His first contribution was to edit a special issue of Arena Review in which he brought together a set of theoretically informed treatments of a number of relevant sociological themes. These included: sport involvement and stigma (17); sports and the political movement of persons with a disability (7); mainstreaming and sport (8); sport, leisure and recreation skills (3); the Special Olympics (16); adjustment of athletes to career-ending injuries (10); physical impairment and psycho-social disability in professional baseball (2); and sport and elderly individuals with disabilities (4). This compilation is significant because it appears to have been the first explicitly sociological treatment of sport and disability. The ways in which the authors approached the subject matter illustrated clearly that when research is theory-driven a set of topics and research questions are produced which are different to those which guide research when it is practice-driven. Because they are theoretically informed the sociological analyses are supported by explanatory structures that derive their power from generalizations in a way that practice-driven research cannot match. As a result they were insightful and should have prompted an incorporation of theory in the work of other researchers. Unfortunately, what they offered was not programmatic. They were a collection of articles which showed how a sociological analysis can be undertaken and they were missing a rationale together with an explication of basic sociological questions which might have helped to bring some order to the field.

Nixon's other contributions have centred on the topic of integration. There were two main attempts and in both cases his aim was to encourage more attention for disability sport from sociologists of sport. In the first (13) he outlined some of the potentially salient personal attributes and background parameters (i.e., type and severity of disability and amount of sports background) and sports structure parameters (i.e., type of sport, amount of disability adaptation, and degree of competition) that could affect the extent to which integration efforts in sport result in genuine integration and a reduction in the stigmatization and 'handicapped' minority status of people with disabilities. In the second (14) he set out a concise explanation of the sociological approach to disability in general that highlights very clearly the ways in which the minority status of people with disabilities is manifested in society through, for example, inferior treatment, segregation, stereotyping and the erection of personal barriers. He goes on to discuss labelling and stigmatisation and makes reference to the ways in which people with disabilities are relegated 'to a socially disadvantaged status' (14, p.165). He places great importance on the identification of contextual variables which lead to labelling and stigmatisation (eg. power, resources, social distance, community tolerance and the stimulus properties of the disability such as severity, visibility and type). He sees research problems in terms of practical problems and discusses, for example, exclusion, discrimination, the myth of inferiority, restricted opportunities, integration, etc. Indeed, there is a very practical orientation in the issues and questions for research which he outlines at the end of the paper. These revolve around three concerns:

> (a) how to proceed with integration through sport of disabled people into the mainstream of society; (b) what types of sport and sports programs to develop for the appropriate integration of disabled people into sport and society; and (c) how to incorporate competition and opportunities for success and failure into sports programs involving disabled people. (14, p.171)

In both of these works Nixon's contributions to a theoretical foundation are invaluable but they are applied only to one particular research problem. They are useful to an understanding of the practice of integration and many of the concepts are highly relevant in a general sense but they are limited, in their explication, to the one research problem.

DePauw's (5) attempts to bring order to the field are based on a reversion to a practice-driven agenda which would echo research from a decade before were it not for the way in which it was generated. Her first contribution is a much more sophisticated and informed agenda than that which was used prior to 1980 because it came about as a result of deliberations by the Subcommittee on Research, U.S. Committee on Sports for the Disabled in 1985. The Subcommittee, through a survey, sought the views of athletes with disabilities, professionals and coaches on appropriate topics for a number of research areas. Sociological aspects were included although they were joined with psychology and some were subsumed under other research areas such as 'legal, philosophical and historical bases of sport' and 'demographics of sport for the disabled' (5, pp. 296-297) and a list of specific topics resulted - the impact of sport upon athlete, family and society; sport role models for young people with disabilities; influences of age, gender, ethnicity and disability upon sport participation; society's perceptions and awareness of sport for individuals with disabilities; influence of onset of disability upon sport participation; international comparisons of sport programmes; gender differences; incidences of discrimination; and comparisons with able-bodied patterns of recruitment, scholarships, professional sport (5, pp. 295-297). This is still an attempt to resolve practical problems and to sensitize researchers through issues but it is much more programmatic in the range of topics considered and their relevance to disability sport in the 1980s. The topics are quite specific and at least make extensive use of sociological concepts.

Her second contribution (6) addressed research opportunities and it differed from the previous one because it was based on a review of the related literature. She noted that research activity in the 1980s had become sport specific, disability specific, performance enhancing and discipline oriented. Sociology, for perhaps the first time in the general literature on adapted physical activity, was differentiated from psychology and three future sociological research directions were highlighted. They were

> (c) sport initiation - research on the reasons for and extent of participation in sport, effect upon participation in youth sport programs, recreation, and leisure activities; (d) effects of sport - research on the values of and specific sociological, psychological, and physical benefits of participation and competition upon functional capacity for sport and activities of daily living; and (e) influences upon sport - research on the historical, philosophical, legal, and societal factors influencing sport and athletes with disabilities. (6, p.83)

In addition, she offered several practical suggestions for future research action. These were: multi-disciplinary team research; interagency cooperation; computer modelling; and information links and database sharing (6, p.83).

These attempts by both Nixon (13,14) and DePauw (5,6) to structure the field have introduced sociological concepts and research topics but they are limited. They have not asked the broader and perhaps more fundamental sociological questions which address the notion of difference and which focus on the social origins of disability. They have not considered the ways in which sport might reinforce, legitimate, or challenge those differences, nor have they shown how the sociology of sport and disability can progress to a paradigmatic stage of development. There is an evident need, then, for the introduction of sociological perspectives and an indication of how they might be applied to the study of sport and disability. In particular, the point needs to be made and illustrated that different sociological perspectives generate different research questions.

2.3 European Research

Europeans can contribute to the development of a sociology of sport and disability. In North America the research agenda used to conduct even cursory sociological examinations of sport and disability has been heavily influenced by the quantophrenia of adapted physical activity (cf. 18), by medicine and by the functionalism of mainstream sociology in the United States. A European sociology of sport and disability, such as it is at the present time, has a different set of forebears that relies far more on the distant traditions such as Marxism and phenomenology as well as the more immediate influences of cultural studies. Indeed, there is much to be gained from the recent works of writers such as Oliver (15) and Morris (12) which offer powerful analyses and critiques of disability on which a sociological account of sport and disability can be modelled. The direction of this sociological work can be influenced, of course, especially if it is funded by European institutions, by problems which are peculiar to sport and disability in the European context (eg. migration, political differences). There is an opportunity, therefore, for Europeans to set their own research agenda far removed from some of the influences, but not all (eg. medicine), which helped to shape the early years of sociological study in the North American context of adapted physical activity.

There are a number of factors, however, which may affect the manner in which Europeans can contribute to the development of a sociology of sport and disability. Perhaps the most important is the small critical mass of European researchers and their geographical dispersion. There is only a small number of researchers in Europe (approximately eighteen, see Table 2) and they are currently working on eighteen projects which are directly or indirectly related to the social aspects of adapted physical activity; in some countries, as far as I am aware, there is no research being done on the social aspects of sport and disability.

Table 2: European Researchers Currently Working on the Social Aspects of Adapted Physical Activity (19)

Researchers	Institution	Country	Topics
Zbynek Janecka Hana Válková	Palacky	Czech Republic	Social aspects of children with disabilities (7-11 yrs)
Josef Kábele	Prague	Czech Republic	Lifestyle of wheelchair basketball players
Vlasta Karásková Hana Kostihová	Palacky	Czech	Leisure and family environment of children with dyslexia
Martin Kovár Maria Kyralová	Písek Prague	Czech Republic	Lifestyle of individuals with paraplegia
Josef Kvapilík	Prague	Czech Republic	Lifestyle of individuals with learning difficulties
Jiri Simice	Prague	Czech Republic	Leisure and young people with visual impairments
Tarja Kolkka	Jyväskylä	Finland	Gender, women and wheelchair basketball
Jean-Paul Genolini	Lille	France	Disabled representation in sport
Gudrun Doll-Tepper	FU Berlin	Germany	Attitudes toward integration of people with disabilities Biographies of athletes with disabilities
Heike Tiemann	FU Berlin	Germany	Women and disability sport socialization
Klaus Schüle	DSHS Köln	Germany	Wheelchair basketball participation
Jürgen Schwier	Oldenburg	Germany	Sport socialization of visually impaired young people
Roni Bolotin	Dis. Vets Org. Tel Aviv	Israel	Social situation of veterans with spinal cord injuries
Pedro Ruiz	INEF, Barcelona	Spain	Integration and lifestyle of athletes with disabilities Impact of Paralympic Games on attitudes of able-bodied
Trevor Williams	Loughborough	England	Sport and spinal injury units Wheelchair sport subcultures Disability sport socialization

The active researchers are located, mostly in universities, in seven different countries and, except for the individuals in the Czech Republic, probably do not have contact with each other in their work. On the one hand, then, collaboration should be easily accomplished, given the relatively small number of researchers, but on the other hand their geographical dispersion makes it extremely difficult to work closely together on common projects. Some of the researchers are working on similar topics or at least topics which overlap to some extent (see Table 2) and, in particular, two themes seem to dominate the European work.

These are

> **lifestyle** (being studied by Kábele, Karásková, Kostihová, Kovár, Kyralová, Kvapilík and Ruiz)

and

> **socialization into sport** (being studied by Kolkka, Tiemann, Schüle, Schwier, Williams).

In addition, quite a few researchers are focussing their research on wheelchair sports (eg. Kábele, Kovár, Kyralová, Kolkka, Tiemann, Bolotin and Williams). There would appear to be some common ground, therefore, on which to base collaboration - at the very least, researchers should be sharing their results; at the most, they should be cooperating on joint projects. Both would be desirable, of course, because while the cultural relativity and cultural pluralism of Europe are such that they make it difficult to develop generalisations, the diversity of the Community provides an opportunity, through collaboration, to study disability sport in many different social contexts.

3. Future Perspectives

Let us move on, now, to a consideration of the future. It is a future, I believe, in which the sociology of sport and disability can only be developed effectively in two collaborative arrangements. The first is a collaboration between sociologists (or at least researchers interested in the social aspects of sport and disability) that would foster the exchange of information and encourage the initiation of joint research projects on a pan-European basis. The second is a collaboration between practitioners and sociologists. We have seen above how the sociology of sport and disability has been practice-driven and that many topics important and relevant to disability sport have been identified by practitioners (5) but I would argue that the time has come, now, for sociologists to take a much more active role in setting the research agenda while being cognisant of the concerns of practitioners and working closely with them. In the case of both of these collaborative arrangements there are two major research activities: fundamental sociological research which will develop a field of knowledge we can term 'a sociology of sport and disability' and developing praxis to show practitioners how sociological research can make a difference in the sporting lives of men and women with disabilities. These two research activities are mutually supportive; in fact they provide two necessary conditions for knowledge in a neo-pragmatist epistemology (cf. 1) - laying down a conceptual framework (sociological paradigms, concepts, questions) and using it (application).

3.1 Fundamental Sociological Research

There are, in this case, two parts to developing fundamental sociological research. The first is to list a set of basic sociological topics or themes on which research can be focused. These would include:

1. the social organisation, referent group behaviour and social interaction patterns that occur in disability sport settings (for example how they are created, maintained and changed);
2. the relationship between disability sport and other spheres of social life (for example the family, education, politics, the economy, the media, religion, medicine, and community services);
3. the cultural, structural, and situational factors affecting disability sport and the sport experiences of individuals with disabilities (for example lifestyle, access to transport, income, attitudes of the able-bodied, values, beliefs, ideology); and
4. the social processes that occur in conjunction with disability sport (processes, for example, such as socialization, stigmatization, participation, integration, social stratification, sexuality, and social change).

The second part is to make explicit use of sociological perspectives. There are several which would be extremely useful and their job in the research process is to provide specific research questions and relevant concepts, to guide the collection of data and to provide interpretations of information. They are aids in our attempts to understand disability sport and with them we can develop strategies which may bring about social change. Each perspective offers a different set of assumptions about how societies operate, the important social features which must be considered and how those features are related to others. A researcher might choose one or another perspective because its assumptions tend to coincide with their own or because it can produce different and perhaps more penetrating insights. Consider the following.

1. A functionalist perspective assumes that societies are systems that operate on the basis of consensus and common values. Disability sport is functional when it contributes to the working of the system. It is viewed as a source

of inspiration for members of the system. On both a personal and a social level it provides a context in which children and adults with disabilities learn the values and skills necessary to live in a society; in which the relationships with other people with disabilities and with the able-bodied can be established and strengthened; and in which the individual can be rehabilitated or at least improve their health and fitness. Disability sport, then, has a positive function.

2. A conflict perspective assumes that societies operate on the basis of coercion and the manipulation of individuals. Disability sport is related to alienation, exploitation, sexism, racism and handicapism. It provides a context, usually a segregated context, in which one group exercises social control over another; in which the interests of a power elite are maintained at the expense of the interests of the powerless majority; and in which sport is a distorted form of physical activity that hinders the production of a humane and creative society. Disability sport, then, is an opiate; it masks the true interests of people with disabilities and diverts attention away from other, important, aspects of social life which are much more problematic.

Clearly, both of these perspectives are used implicitly in a few studies in the current literature. Functionalism, for example, fits very well with the use of disability sport as a rehabilitative tool and elements of a conflict perspective are inherent in those critiques of the inclusion of able-bodied athletes and athletes with minimal disabilities in disability sport. Their use, however, needs to be much more explicit and systematic if the field is going to develop.

3.2 Developing Praxis

A sociology of sport and disability is not some academic discipline which occurs only in the confines of institutions like universities. It is the study of how real people with disabilities produce, reproduce and transform their sporting lives and so it must be affected by and, in turn, affect those people. The position I am adopting here is captured best by Marx's 11th thesis on Feuerbach which stated "The philosophers have only interpreted the world in different ways; the point is to change it". The purpose of a sociology of sport and disability, therefore, is to make a difference in the sporting lives of disabled men and women and this can be done if the basic knowledge can be generated. This is to say we must interpret the world of disability sport so that it can be changed and this means that the sociological information has to be used.

There are at least three ways in which the sociological information on disability sport can be used. The first is to use the information in the education of students and the training of administrators. In particular we can use the detail of the disability sport context to put over several principles which guide a sociologist when he or she examines a problem.

1. *It is important to consider other points of view.* Different factors affect the sport participation of people with hearing impairments, visual impairments, paraplegia, quadraplegia, cerebral palsy, and so we need information on how people with these different impairments manage their lives, what is important to them, etc.
2. *It is important to weigh the available sociological evidence.* Social life is definitely not simple and so as well as considering one other view we need to consider all other views. We should gather as much information on the particular problem as we can and then evaluate the sources of that information to make informed decisions.
3. *It is important to be cognisant of the sociological research methods relevant to solving particular problems.* In weighing up the evidence we need to know how credible is the information we already have and we need to know what methods can be used to collect information that is needed but which we do not yet have. All research methods, of course, have their strengths and weaknesses but it is not a question of methods being right or wrong - rather of them being more or less useful in addressing specific research problems in particular contexts.
4. *It is important to ask embarrassing questions.* Sociologists have a practical role to play in de-bunking established social practices. They act like the sand in one's underwear after a visit to the beach because they are trained to recognise contradictions which, when they are made public, can cause some personal or social discomfort. One could ask, for example, why it is that athletes with disabilities need able-bodied organizers when groups of wheelchair racers can travel without them all to races all round the world (eg. Florida, Sydney, Berlin, Heidelberg, Boston, etc.). They make their own travel arrangements, hire vans, book rooms, and do everything independently and yet when they travel to the Paralympics or to other official events they are usually accompanied by 'carers'.

The second way of using the sociological information is to de-mystify disability sport. De-mystification can lead to the emancipation of people with disabilities by involving them in sociological research and by informing them of the sociological results which would be relevant at both the personal and social levels. This is effective in raising awareness and changing some behaviours. We know from our sociological research programme at Loughborough, for example, that when we involve sports men and women with disabilities, so that research is practised as a dialogic act, then it raises consciousness about oppression and oppressive agents (eg. the role of the media and its manipulative properties) and the promotion of self-help. Moreover, providing sociological information can increase awareness leading, for example, to an increased politicization of the collective (eg. organizing support for an Association's programmes within the voluntary membership and among external organizations) or to an understanding of how power operates within social groups. At the very least, the outcome of using the information in this way is that it would allow a disability group to control its own destiny within a framework of disability sport that, in most countries, is controlled by the able-bodied.

The third way of using the information is in the development and implementation of policies which affect disability sport development programmes. Anyone with experience of Government departments, or even with large sports organizations, will know that administrators often mistake their own experiences for the experiences of others. These experiences and interpretations are used to formulate social programmes which affect the sporting lives of people with disabilities. But there is often a gap between the formulator's interpretation and the lived experiences and interpretations of the programme recipients. Sociological research can bridge this gap but, having said that, it is in this area that the shortcomings of the current North American studies are most evident because each country must undertake its own study of participation to generate basic knowledge. It is a fundamental sociological principle that a phenomenon can only be understood by situating it in its social context. This means that not only will particular issues and problems be relevant in specific social contexts but on a European level there is much to be gained from comparative studies of sport and disability. There is much to learn, both practically and theoretically, from studying the the ways in which disability sport is structured in the different European countries, which issues are more important and which intervention strategies are effective in particular social conditions. The most important thing, though, is that any sociological study worthy of the name would add the views of people with disabilities to the consideration of policy and programming. It is information on their experiences and interpretations which is, too often, missing and which sociological research can add.

4. Conclusion

Let me end by stating that I see the future in a positive way. The most important thing, I believe, is to recognise the problem. The study of the social aspects of sport and disability is gaining momentum, in North America and in Europe, but it will be more or less effective to the extent that we, as a collective, can develop a relevant research agenda and advance the field to a paradigmatic stage. In Europe this means, on a practical level, that we must increase the number of sociologists who can and who wish to study disability sport and we must foster collaboration between them. Developing the research agenda, sharing information and initiating pan-European sociological projects are all necessary to the sociology of sport and disability in this context but it is not something which I must do or that you must do. It is, rather, something which we must do together.

References

1. Bosley, R.: On Truth: A neo-pragmatist treatise in logic, metaphysics and epistemology. Washington, University Press of America, 1982.

2. Brandmeyer, G.A.,Alexander, L.K.: Physical impairment and psychosocial disability in professional baseball. Arena Review 8: 46-53, 1984

3. Carmichael, D.L.: Sport, leisure and recreation skills for the handicapped: a broader perspective. Arena Review 8: 35-40, 1984.

4. Danigelis, N.L.: Sport and the disabled elderly. Arena Review. 8: 68-79, 1984.

5. DePauw, K.P.: Research on sport for athletes with disabilities. Adapted Physical Activity Quarterly 3: 292-299, 1986.

6. DePauw, K.P.: Sport for individuals with disabilities: Research opportunities. Adapted Physical Activity Quarterly 5: 80-89, 1988.

7. Hahn, H.: Sports and the political movement of disabled persons: examining nondisabled social values. Arena Review 8: 1-15, 1984.

8. Jansma, P., Gayle, G.W.: Mainstreaming the handicapped into sports: prerequisites and benefits. Arena Review 8: 27-34, 1984.

9. Kuhn, T.S.: The structure of scientific revolutions. Chicago, University of Chicago Press, 1984.

10. Lerch, S.H.: The adjustment of athletes to career ending injuries. Arena Review 8: 54-67, 1984.

11. Lewko, J.H.: Specialized knowledge and the delivery of leisure services to the disabled. Leisure Science 1: 131-146, 1978.

12. Morris, J.: Able lives. London, The Women's Press, 1989.

13. **Nixon, H. L.:** The creation of appropriate integration opportunities in sport for disabled and nondisabled people: A guide for research and action. Sociology of Sport Journal, 1: 184-192, 1984a.

14. **Nixon, H. L.:** Handicapism and sport: New directions for sport sociology research. In N. Theberge, & P. Donnelly (eds), Sport and the Sociological Imagination: refereed proceedings of the 3rd Annual Conference of the North American Society for the Sociology of Sport, Toronto, Canada, 1982, November (pp. 162-176). Fort Worth, Tex., Texas Christian University Press, 1984b.

15. **Oliver, M.:** The politics of disablement. London, Macmillan, 1990.

16. **Orlove, F.P., Moon, M.S.:** The Special Olympics program: Effects on retarded persons and society. Arena Review, 8: 41-45, 1984.

17. **Snyder, E.E.:** Sport involvement for the handicapped: Some analytic and sensitizing concepts. Arena Review, 8: 16-26, 1984.

18. **Sorokin, P.A.:** Fads and foibles in modern sociology and related sciences. Westport, Con., Greenwood Press, 1956.

19. **Williams, T.:** European Research Register 1993. European Association for Research into Adapted Physical Activity, 1993.

Action Field 4

Physical Education

The Art and Science of Teaching Physical Education

Almond, L.
Loughborough University
UK

1. Introduction

The title of this paper presents me with several problems. The key words are art and science, but are they opposite, complementary, a synergy or two different sides of a coin? I propose to examine both of these terms in order to demonstrate a clear relationship but also to reveal important pedagogical elements which are missing.

Finally, I shall use this analysis to present a model of sport pedagogy and describe a number of key components which reveal their richness and their potential for disciplined inquiry by researchers and practitioners.

2. The Art of Teaching

We often hear people referring to teaching as an art form, but what do they really mean? Can teaching be considered as an art in the sense that a painting, a sculpture or a dance performance is recognised as art? Are there different conceptions of 'art'? If we examine the dictionary, we find that art refers to a number of conceptions. I present just two of them. It can be:

(1) "practical skill, or its application, guided by principles" or
(2) "human skill and agency": application of skill to production of beauty and works of creative imagination.

It is clearly the first conception that people refer to when they speak of the art of teaching, because the primary purpose of teaching is not the production of beauty or a work of creative imagination. However, there are times when teaching can clearly demonstrate acts which are creative, full of imagination and artistic but these are extrinsic and not fundamental to the primary purpose of teaching. Best (1) puts it another way when he writes that;

"It is distinctive of any art form that its conventions allow for the possibility of the expression of a conception of life situations." (p.115)

He goes on to point out that the arts are concerned with contemporary moral, social, political and emotional issues. It is intrinsic to the notion of an art form that it can at least allow for the possibility of considering issues of social concern. The teacher or coach does not have the possibility of expressing through their medium their view of life situations. Though you may counter this by saying that teaching and coaching can display numerous examples of real life tragedy and drama and exemplify moral, social and political issues in abundance. To counter this argument, it needs to be pointed out that the central convention of art, in contrast to teaching, is that the object of one's attention is an imagined object.

Before I complete this account of 'the art of teaching' I would like to spend a little time on the notion of the teacher as artist. One of my early mentors was a scholar called Lawrence Stenhouse (9) who was one of the first people to formulate the notion of the teacher as a researcher or more significantly he articulated an approach to research based teaching. He proposed that:

> "the expression of educational ideas in curricular form provides a medium for the development - and if necessary the autonomous medium for the development - of the teacher as artist." (p.158)

He goes on to make the point that teachers 'learn through the critical practice of their art'. This analogy with art is expanded further when he illustrates how the sketch book of good artists shows their exploration and interpretation of ideas which leads to revision and an adjustment to their art; he also proposes that artists become stereotypical or derelict when they cease to develop in this way. Stenhouse relates this analogy with teaching, but perhaps this happens also to researchers as well as to teachers and coaches. He concludes his analogy with this point when he writes:

> "But note that a good repertory company is also concerned with the development of its actors as artists and of the skills and arts of its technicians too. And the medium of this development is the very same medium as that which entertains - motivates - and educates its audience." (p. 160)

Thus, it could be said (a.k.a Stenhouse) that teachers not only learn their art, but also learn through their art, where the gymnasium, playing field or pool is the theatre and also the laboratory which places the teacher (or coach) in the key position.

I make this point because Stenhouse's analogy refers to the (progressive) development of the teacher through what they teach. He is not proposing that teaching is underpinned by principles applied from an external source. Teaching and its development comes from the careful scrutiny of one's practice where teachers submit their practice to critical reflection, analysis and interpretation.

Thus, it would seem from my brief account and explanation of art that the 'art of teaching' refers to the way in which a practical skill, or its application, is guided by principles. If you can accept this account, what kinds of principles are being referred to? and are they scientific or moral principles (or both)?

3. Science and Research

Let me turn now to science and take a closer look at what it represents. When I speak of science I am referring to research and a 'family of methods' which share the characteristics of disciplined inquiry. In an attempt to define disciplined inquiry Cronbach and Suppes (2) suggest that:

> Disciplined inquiry has a quality that distinguishes it from other sources of opinion and belief. The disciplined inquiry is conducted and reported in such a way that the arguments can be painstakingly examined. The report does not depend for its appeal on the eloquence of the writer or on any surface plausibility. (p.15)

They go on to point out that what is important about disciplined inquiry is that its data, arguments and reasoning are capable of withstanding careful scrutiny by members of the scientific community. In other words it is not enough to be systematic and scrupulously careful in the way that you pose questions and articulate appropriate ways of answering these questions, what you do in your research must be open to further testing by one's peers, available for scrutiny and criticism, subject to high levels of routine scepticism and open (and responsive) to alternative interpretations of one's findings. This process plays a crucial role in checking the validity of the findings of particular studies and making judgements of adequacy. It lies at the heart of the justification for research as a source of knowledge.

This brief outline raises a further question because disciplined inquiry can refer to basic (sometimes referred to as pure) research and applied research. This dichotomy between basic and applied research reflects a distinction between two types of work. In basic research the scientist generates fundamental generalised knowledge directed towards the research community which is translated into practice by the applied scientist who demonstrates its relevance beyond the research community. In one sense it serves to reinforce the separation of theory and practice. In another sense, it raises questions about what is crucial in research and its relationship to practice and who should do research.

It raises questions also about the justification of publicly funded research that does not make some contribution to the needs of non-researchers or as Hammersley (3) points out

"Research must be judged not just in terms of its validity but also on the basis of its relevance to practical concerns (p.248)".

Hammersley (3) makes the point that one reason for the division of labour among researchers is that it is often not possible to answer questions that are directly relevant to practical problems adequately through any one single piece of research. Research directed at practitioners is best served by drawing on a wide range of studies not simply on one. This point is reinforced by Martens (5; p.96) when he writes that scientists are often not interested in the task of making knowledge accessible and useful to practitioners, nor are they rewarded in academia. They also appear to have little understanding of how their research can be applied to real-life problems. His answer is the proposal that a new breed of scholar is emerging, he calls them a 'knowledge integrator' who is capable of synthesising both the world of scientific research and real-world demands of practitioners, or, I would suggest, someone who is capable of disciplining research with the problems of practice. This point is interesting because recently there have emerged a number of journals, particularly from Human Kinetics which are about applied research. One product of these initiatives is the emergence of a debate about what constitutes basic and applied research and their roles within sport sciences and physical education (see Yiannakis and Greendoffer, (10)). This debate is most interesting and deserves not only careful scrutiny but the proposal of alternative conceptions. I am only sorry that my presentation today cannot attempt to do this, such a radical alternative would take too long to present.

Let me turn now to:

4. Art and Science: an unfulfilled relationship

So how does my discussion of art link with that of science? In one sense Stenhouse's notion of 'teacher as artist', who learns through their art, has a strong association with a view of research as disciplined inquiry. However, there is another sense in which art and science are related. Let me return to my earlier discussion on art and what it means. From the dictionary art can be a practical skill, or its application, guided by principles. I believe this is the main issue, what is meant by guiding principles? Clearly research on the 'teaching -learning process and context' can provide plausible and credible claims supported by the criterion of validity and also relevance which can contribute to the generation of theoretical insights disciplined by the problems of practice. These insights can serve as tentative guidelines (open to further judgement and criticism) to inform practice and stimulate intelligent practices. In the same way the sport and exercise sciences can generate further insights to inform practice. The production of these guiding principles to underpin and inform practice will require the 'knowledge integrator' with their special skills and insights. In one sense they need to be 'generalists' but also specialists in understanding practice, the problems of practice and the needs of teachers. However, the empirical sciences cannot help us to generate procedural principles which are implicit within value claims, we need much more than research and science in our search for procedural principles.

Within our institutes of higher education the profession has tended to concern itself with the generation and production of scholarship and research in the educational sciences and sports sciences whilst the practitioners have dealt with technical matters. This has often been at the expense of generating a coherent vision of Physical Education. **What is the point of being concerned with the effectiveness and efficiency of teaching if what is being taught is of little consequence or not worthy of being a significant end to pursue?** These are judgements that technical concerns and science are unable to answer, yet they represent an aspect of our work that we cannot ignore.

We need to help teachers of physical education acquire a vision of worthy ends to pursue together with an understanding of their practical and ethical relevance in the form of guiding principles. This is vision of Physical Education must illustrate its richness, vitality and potential for making a worthwhile life possible, highlight its significance and relevance and provide a real guide to professional practice which informs our understanding of what can be done and why. Such a commitment would be sterile unless it also generated ethical routes for realising this potential and provide practical guidelines for action. This is a very tall order and may explain why it has not been attempted.

Thus, I would want to argue that a teacher's practical skill underpinned by guiding principles (the 'art of teaching'), and its association with science, has three essential components (there may well be others). These represent components of a pedagogy which guides practical action:

i. a vision of worthy ends to pursue
ii. he educational sciences and sport sciences which provide sources for developing informed practice
iii. caring and ethical principles of procedure

and grounded in the realities of practice.

This account of the art and science of teaching Physical Education provides the basis for locating my own thinking about Physical Education in schools and practical action in curriculum development within a particular English and also personal view of Sport Pedagogy. It is this perspective that informs the final part of my presentation which represents a model of Sport Pedagogy which draws on my examination of the art and the science of teaching.

5. Sport Pedagogy

In the following diagram I am proposing that Sport Pedagogy is concerned with several distinctive components that are interdependent. The first component is the generation of practical ideas. In this aspect of research, which I call creative research, I am proposing that those colleagues who are involved in a systematic and critical appraisal of practical activity areas such as games, swimming, athletics, dance or adventure pursuits, which provide new or alternative teaching frameworks and perspectives that can be used in schools, are engaged in an activity worthy for consideration as a form of research. The same case can and should be made for coaches. This creative enterprise involves a process of critical appraisal of existing curricula, the generation of alternative theoretical perspectives which are tested in practical situations, the communication and presentation of these proposals to practitioners as critical peers and the submission of these ideas to challenging questions amongst a range of critical audiences.

The second component, 'generating informed and intelligent practices', is associated with creative research because it needs to be part and parcel of the whole process of generating new ideas, but it can go beyond it. In order to develop their work, achieve coherence and attain the status of informed and intelligent practice, teachers need to be able to draw upon the work of colleagues engaged in research on problems in educational settings and other colleagues who work in a sport sciences' context. Too often developments and new insights within these disciplines have not been easily translated into the teaching situation, often resulting in teachers seeing them as irrelevant and sometimes harmful. Thus, it takes a person with very special skills and insights to translate empirical research into realistic practical possibilities in actual situations. It requires someone with detailed knowledge and understanding of practical contexts, the concerns and problems of teachers and/or coaches, as well as an interest in improving pedagogy. This kind of person could be Marten's (5) 'knowledge integrator' or someone concerned with the transfer of knowledge.

My third component is central to all major research interests within Sport Pedagogy and forms a substantial element of international conferences and journal articles relating to the teaching of physical education. These educational sciences (also the sport sciences) with their focus on the teaching-learning process and context, have three distinct paradigms which Sparkes (8) in his informative and illuminating account of the paradigms debate calls the positive (empirical-analytical), the interpretative and the critical. Popkewitz (6) in an earlier text made the same essential points. It needs to be pointed out that each of these paradigms contains further specific forms of inquiry which makes the task of a 'knowledge integrator' a rather daunting prospect highlighting the magnitude of translating research into forms that not only inform practice but generate intelligent practices.

This presents a real problem because we often make a distinction between researchers and practitioners, because it may well be a relationship that the profession engenders and reinforces. The relationship between researchers and those in educational settings (the practitioners) who are usually the objects of research, is neatly encapsulated by Kemmis (4) when he writes:

> "These politics are revealed nowhere more clearly than in reports of research, which are frequently written about people involved in education rather than for them, and addressed to people outside the situations studied rather than within them." (p.7)

Kemmis goes on to speak about the positivist perspective which uses the third person 'them' (or he or she) when they write about the objects of their research in which they attempt to explain people's actions. Reports of their research are written for people outside the setting usually the researchers or policy-makers and not generally for the people the research is all about. The interpretivist uses the second person 'you' and speaks to these people and aims to understand people's actions. He contrasts this with the critical theorist who attempts to speak 'for' or 'with' people in which they are both products and producers; their aim is to develop or improve people's actions. Whether the critical theorist achieves this aim is quite another matter, from my own experiences and reading of the literature I am not yet convinced. The central point of Kemmis's paper is that the separation between the researcher and the practitioner needs to be bridged.

Let me turn now to my fourth component, one in which research in pedagogy and physical education has little to offer us at present. When I speak of the teaching-learning process and the context in which teachers have to make ideas accessible to their pupils, I am referring also to the process whereby new developments in the form new ideas and alternative practices need to be made accessible to teachers through inservice courses and further training opportunities. Here we have to deal with scepticism, different levels of understandings, ideological positions which inform a person's priorities and practical resistance to any form of change. All these factors need to be addressed in helping people to transform their practice and make informed changes. In one sense, this form of further education and training, is a kind of social marketing besides the educational and psychological process of making ideas accessible and helping people understand the implications for their practice in order to implement informed changes. I would argue that this educational process affords considerable scope for the pedagogue and also for research (see the Prochaska and DiClementi model, (7)).

Finally, my last component is concerned with the process whereby ideas need to be implemented into practice. There is very little research in physical education and few guidelines available to inform practice, yet innovation and change have been a significant aspect of many teachers' lives recently. This is a neglected area of research in physical education and I would argue that it represents one of the most significant aspects of any model of Sport Pedagogy. Is this a legitimate target for researchers who do research on teaching learning situations, teachers and their content or is it the province of the practitioner?

6. Concluding comments

In this presentation I concluded my analysis of the art and science of teaching physical education by proposing that there are three essential components:

i. a vision of worthy ends to pursue which guides our practice of what to teach and informs how we teach,
ii. educational sciences and sport sciences which provide a range of sources for developing informed practices,
iii. caring and ethical principles of procedure need to be formulated which will inform a teacher's practice.

However, these three components must be grounded and disciplined in the realities and problems of practice. In this way the art of teaching and the science that underpins and informs practice represent a close relationship that enhances teaching.

In addition, I have used my account of the art and science of teaching to generate a model or framework of Sport Pedagogy. It represents a personal perspective which highlights aspects of Sport Pedagogy that need further debate In one sense it is an agenda for clarification of what constitutes Sport Pedagogy; in another sense it is just a personal view that invites critical comment.

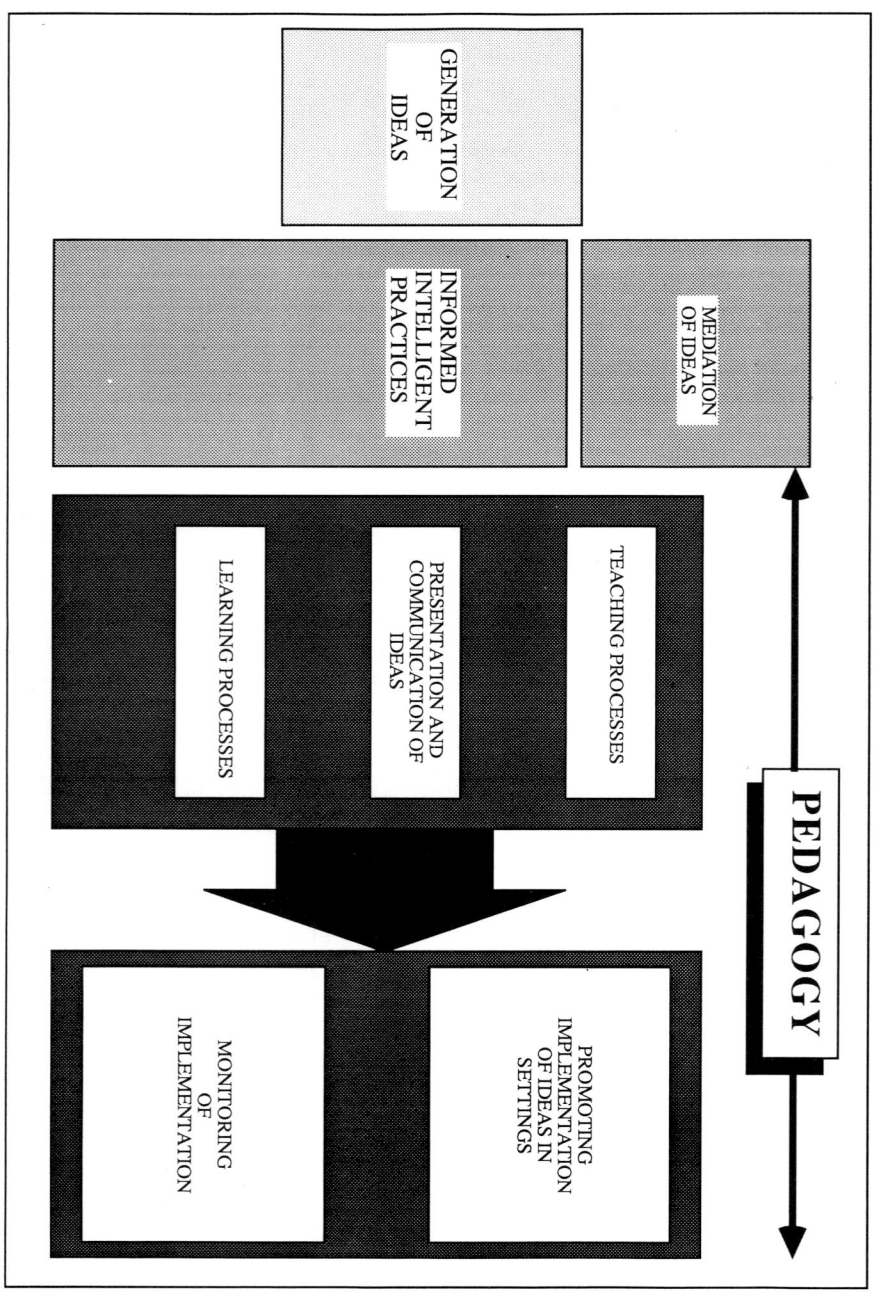

References

1. **Best, D.:** Philosophy and Human Movement. London, George Allen and Unwin, 1978.

2. **Cronbach, L.J., Suppes, P. (eds):** Research for tomorrows' schools: Disciplined inquiry for education. New York, MacMillan, 1969.

3. **Hammersley, M.:** On practitioner ethnography. In: Hammersley, M.: What's wrong with Ethnography?, pp.135-155. London, Routledge, 1992.

4. **Kemmis, S.:** Developing Critical Communities of Teachers through Teacher Education. Seminari sobre Formacio del Professorat i Renovaceo Pedagogica Valencia 1992.

5. **Martens, R.:** Knowledge Problems in Physical Education. Quest 42: 93-99, 1990.

6. **Popkewitz, T.S.:** Paradigm & Ideology in Educational Research. London, The Falmer Press, 1984.

7. **Prochaska, J.O., DiClemente, C.C.:** Towards a Comprehensive Model of Change. In: Miller, W.R., Heather, N. (eds.) Treating Addictive Behaviours, pp.3-27. New York, Plenum press, 1986.

8. **Sparkes, A.C. (ed.):** Research in Physical Education and Sport: Exploring Alternative Visions. London, The Falmer Press, 1992.

9. **Stenhouse, L.** (1983) Curriculum Research and the Art of the Teacher. In: Stenhouse, L. (1983) Authority, Education and Emancipation. (pp.155-62). London: Heinemann Educational Books.

10. **Yiannakis, A., Greendorfer, S.L. (eds.):** Applied Sociology of Sport. Illinois, Human Kinetics Books, 1992.

Youth and Sport in Europe: Implications for Physical Education

Brettschneider, W.-D.
Institut für Sportwissenschaft, Freie Universität Berlin
Germany

1. Youth, sport and Europe - problems and chances

The[1] political, social, and cultural landscape in Europe has changed enormously over the last few years: the disappearance of the East-West conflict, the growing concerns regarding ethnic identity and regional autonomy, the ambivalence between rejecting and supporting a common European policy, which can be found in various countries. These events of the last few months clearly show that the Europeans have continued oscillating between integration and disintegration, as they have done for the past 2500 years (10).

Now, what is the role of sport and Physical Education in this process of Europeanization? i.e. in this tension between the quest for togetherness and a closer union among the peoples of Europe and the strong sense of cultural identity which corresponds to natural and historical communities (such as ethnic groups or countries). I will try to deal with these questions by looking at the sports culture of young people in Europe and its implication for Physical Education in schools.

Focussing on youth, sports and Europe means speaking about problems and chances. Let me start with the problems:

Youth: In many, if not all European countries, the integration of young people into society as well as the conveying of traditional values and norms from one generation to the next has become more and more difficult. In various West European countries adolescents have to face the fact that they can no longer rely on secure traditional ties such as family, community, religion or nation. Adolescents of today are, unlike their parents' generation, called upon to be the producers and writers of their own biographies. As this is hardly possible at school, the motor of individualization runs on high revs in leisure time. It is here that young people build up an identity and find a specific and individual style of life (1). In the East European countries this development is not completely the same. Yet, the trend towards individualization and the search for a growing spectrum of biographical options can be identified here as well. The striving for individualistic lifestyles, materialistic gains and life goals might occasionally be interpreted as reaction and provocation against conventional educational aims of the older generation.

Sport: To speak about adolescent sport means to an increasing degree, to speak about a system which is at present in the process of change. The distance between top-level sport and its moral, recreational sport as an element of every day life, the commercial allure of fitness training and Physical Education in schools which searches for a balance between tradition and innovation is ever-widening. Sport is disintegrating. The change is evident at the level of participants, the kinds of sport activities, the underlying configuration of motives and the integration of sporting activities into the individual lifestyle. These changes have paved the way for a broader understanding of sport. We must take leave of the myth of a unified sport culture and we must recognize that sport has become a highly diversified social phenomenon (4, 12).

Europe: What do we mean when we say Europe? The European Community of Twelve, which is mainly an economic and monetary entity whose domestic borders have recently opened? Do we mean former Western Europe or the Council of Europe, the Europe of twenty-six member states, whose aim is to cooperate in the areas of culture, environment, education and sport, law and human rights, or do we mean the geographical area labelled Europe? Whatever is meant by Europe, it always includes problems, problems involving ethnic minorities and difficulties in cultural, religious, economical and social areas which hinder the growing togetherness of the European Community.

But, to discuss youth and sport culture in Europe also means to talk about chances and hopes.

Youth: Youth today might have its problems but is also a carrier of hope. Although young people are neither the opinion leaders in a society, nor the instigators for social and cultural change, they do determine the direction of development in decisive ways. Whoever deals with the future and wants to develop visions, must recognize the role of today's youth in Europe's process of integration.

Sport: While we accept sport as no longer something uniform, we are in a position to use the opportunities that result from its diversity and its cultural relativity. In my opinion sport can be portrayed as a seismograph. By observing the readings produced the present situation of sports in individual European countries becomes clear. Simultaneously we receive impressions from many other social areas of life. Sport guarantees - as literature does - an exceptional inside look into the feelings and thoughts of people, their hopes, dreams and fears. Especially as sport symbolizes society's situation, it makes present difficulties in our cultures recognizable and allows the problems to reach the surface. At the same time it becomes evident, where the opportunities for sport lie and how they may be realized.

Europe: Europe portrays itself not only as a giant economic area or as a piece of the map, where ethnic and political contrasts flare. Europe also means shared cultural heritage and ideas. But the sought-after the so-called "European house" requires more than an idea as foundation. Whoever wants to move in and live there together needs information about Europe. Commitment to Europe presupposes knowledge about Europe. What is required, in addition, is the willingness to get to know your neighbours, to accept and tolerate their different ways and to learn from them. Europe can be understood and discovered only through the meeting of Europeans - especially young Europeans.

With these annotations in mind, the question is raised as to the role sport and Physical Education can play in the process of Europeanization, i.e. with respect to cross-cultural learning and international understanding. In the following I will focus on three different concepts of sport and analyse them in relation to the question of their role in the process of cultural and social integration between the youth of Europe:
- top-level sport as the traditional domain of young people
- recreational sport as an attractive element in the lives of adolescent youth and
- school physical education as a forum for cultural tradition and cultural innovation.

As the majority of papers given at this conference focus on countries of the European community I would like to shift the emphasis and have a closer look at our East European neighbours.

2. The international sport - contradictory and overestimated

There are only a few speeches by sport officials and pedagogues on the international scene that pass up the chance to stress the significance of sports as a bridge between peoples, its importance as a forum to promote international understanding, peace and goodwill or as a possibility for further education. However, whoever opens the newspaper after international sporting events, will not always find comments so much in favour of international sport meetings as it was the case on the occasion of the track and field world championship in Stuttgart a couple of weeks ago. He will also find hints that sports do not always bridge the gap, but sometimes widen it. Modern sport is primarily characterized by two principles: by cooperation and by competition. Always, when we seek to reduce the character of sport to one feature, we fail to notice the other equally important feature belonging to sport. Love - so we say - makes a person blind; the love of sport should not lead us into blindness but make us aware of the various and often contradictory facets of sport.

We should be aware that the second aspect - that of competition - cannot be separated from the deep structure of the European culture. It can be shown that international competition has its main roots in what might be called Eurocentric or Western culture. Here, we find the origins of the over-emphasis of the principles of competition, which often leads to the assumption that only success, only victory counts. The interweaving between European culture and top-level sports can be convincingly proven by referring to the work of GALTUNG (7, 8).

My first example concerns the conception of space.
European culture conceives of space in terms of centre-periphery. The Western world in the centre, seen as the source of what matters. Most of the sports that exist across the world originate in Europe, mainly in Greece and England. The multiplicity of other forms of sport, from African dances to non-competitive Eastern movement forms, in contrast, plays only a subordinate role.

Let's look at the conception of time.
In Europe, time is conceived of as something dramatic: a beginning, progression, crisis, catharsis, downfall. Above all, concepts such as "to save time" and "time is money" can be seen as guiding principles of the industrial society. This concept can be recognized also in institutionalized sport. Everything is focussed on the competitive event - make or break, heaven or hell, win or fail.

My third example refers to the conception of interpersonal relationships.
These relationships in European culture can be characterized above all by two distinctive features, which can also be combined: namely the <u>vertical</u> and the <u>individual</u>. These are the properties that determine the nature of competition. The more complex the society the richer the hierarchy in its social system. Society makes the defeat of others legitimate, and this is reflected in sport.

This necessarily simplified presentation is meant neither as an argument for cultural pessimism nor as an attack on competitive sport - my respect for individual and collective cultural achievement is too great for that. My basic point is that the dimensions stated above, including their reflection in sport, constitute a specific configuration. This configuration expresses a central feature of European culture, namely a stronger orientation towards competition than towards cooperation.

All European countries - in the West as in the East, in the South and in the North - have contributed to this common European legacy in varying degrees. Knowledge as to the interrelations between competitive sport and the European civilization can help to muffle unreasonably high expectations and prevent misunderstandings. A certain homogeneity, that is determined by rules, is a feature of this internationalized and institutionalized sport. But also the seemingly identical sport experiences generate different interpretations, which throw light on the traditional thought and the cultural development in their respective counties. There are many studies in the field of cultural anthropology to afford empirical proof for this assumption (9). International sport undoubtedly makes communication easier. Based on a universal language it disregards linguistic borders, having no need for translations. But it surely cannot be the instrument that automatically solves the problems. It surely cannot be the panacea for European integration.

3. Recreational sport as a seismograph of social and cultural development

The variety of sport and its multitude of interpretations are best revealed by examining recreational sport, rather than in international top-level sport, which is characterized by a certain homogeneity.

Throughout Europe there are numerous examples of games and sports that are unique to one culture: Hurling in Ireland, pesapallo in Finland, pelota in the Pyrenées or palkovana from the Czech and the Slovak republics are less well-known and rarely played outside their culture of origin. We do not find these forms of games and sports in the schedules of international sport events.

Yet, apart from these culture-specific forms, a constantly increasing number of sports are shared by many cultural groups. Migration, ethnic pluralism and internationalization - so typical for Europe today - have contributed to the perception, that sport is one of the universally shared pursuits of the world. The same rules are accepted in the last corner of our global village and guarantee the same structure of sports. Yet, internationally imposed rules do not lead to identical interpretations in different cultural context. Moreover, sport as a whole is to be seen as a microcosm of our societies, enabling us to study their structures, processes and problems. It is a form of cultural expression which helps us to gain an insight into the history of thoughts and traditions of specific cultural and social contexts (14).

In order to demonstrate the interconnection of social and cultural developments on the one hand, and the concepts of sport on the other, I choose to make an example of the current situation in Germany. Here we are able to view clearly the various consequences political, social and cultural postwar developments have had (and continue to have) on sport. In addition, I am sure, that some central results from West and East Germany can be generalized and applied to Western and Eastern Europe. My third reason for choosing Germany as an example is simply the availability of information. Two representative surveys comparing East and West German youth - one of them carried out in the period of transition (1990), the other one after the unification in 1991 - can be solidly used to form the basis of my interpretation (2, 6, 3).

For a better understanding of the following results, it is necessary to consider the fact that long before the peaceful revolution, a revolution had already taken place in the minds of the younger generation. Unnoticed by the public partly due to the influence of West TV, the lifestyle and attitude towards life of the GDR youth had been continuously changing in the last decade. The extent of "Westernization" is clearly to be seen: youths in both East and West treasured the individuality of their lifestyles, the importance of leisure time, fashion and personal wellness. These were precious assets for young people in East Germany, just as they were for the majority in the West.

Now to sport involvement: Fitness studios or exotic leisure pools did not exist in the East. Even the many varieties of modern dance or body styling, very attractive to girls were not offered. Since in the former GDR almost everything was organized, informal sports activities, the most natural thing in the world for those in the West, were poorly represented in the East. The participation rates clearly show the difference: 22 % of the youth in the West jogged regularly, in the East only 15 %. For aerobics and various forms of dance the ratio was 14 % West to 6 % East. In swimming 31 % to 17 %; table tennis 14 % to 9 % (6).

These findings referring to informal activities, mark a total contrast to the findings referring to institutionalized sports. Here, the level of participation of the East German youth in sports such as athletics, handball and volleyball was 2 to 3 times as high as compared to the West.

The attention paid to sports among West German youth is far less than that in the East. An analysis of the significance of sports shows how big the differences are. While two thirds of the East German youths attach great importance to sports, only 1/2 of the West German youth feel the same. This result reflects the importance of sport in the former GDR.

It is interesting to note, and it may surprise many, that when it comes to the question of active sports involvement in their leisure time, only two thirds of the East participate against the 80 % in the West.

These findings are only surprising at first glance. The apparent discrepancy is quickly resolved: Sport was ubiquitous in the consciousness of the East German teenagers: on the one side was top-level sport, whose success could be identified with; on the other side, sport was part of a controlled and organized leisure time. Contrary to this, participation in sport was not without boundaries: sport activities were limited mainly to the traditional institutionalized sport such as track and field, handball or gymnastics. More modern sports such as tennis, squash or badminton, which are especially appealing to both sexes in the West, were either not supported for ideological reasons or not offered in the East because of the missing infrastructure. In the West the diversity of sports offered as recreational activities also makes exercising more attractive. When comparing sports concepts and sports involvement you see a clear distinction between East and West.

Similar differences arise when asking the question what youth is actually seeking in sport. The gratifications and the motives related to performance, effort and competition find much more approval with the East German youth than with their peers in the West. On the other hand, West German youth put more emphasis on well-being, relaxing and having fun. They are not interested so much in training and commitment.

We may say that in the West of Germany there is a kind of cultural reformulation of sport in process. As to the youth in the East of Germany, their sport concept shows that the idea behind it is like that which was characteristic of the FRG in the sixties and seventies. Presumably there will be a swift adjustment in sport as in leisure and recreation activities in general between East and West.

We suspect that the apparent East-West differences, with regard to sport concepts and involvement, are not only valid in Germany but also in varying ways to the differences between Western and Eastern European countries. Through the first reports on the transformation process from the Czech and Slovak Republics, Poland or Hungary, we see that, especially in sport, a speedy alignment between East and West is happening. Here too we can see, certain social developments, - changes in lifestyle - having a strong impact on sport and sport concept and vice versa. Yet, we should not forget that - for at least 4 decades - different norms and values have been internalized. And these norms are still in our heads.

We may keep in mind that at present specific differences between the East and the West are still dominant. But at the same time, a new sport concept with new meanings and values - reflecting tendencies towards individualism and hedonism instead of group solidarity - seems to be emerging levelling the former distinctiveness. Whether such developments are really desirable, is a totally different question.

4. Physical Education as a forum for valuing tradition and encouraging innovation

Now I turn to Physical Education in schools as the last part of my lecture. Here I will concentrate especially on the situation of P.E. in those East European countries which have taken leave from the socialist way of education and who have turned to a democratic outlook on life. I am doing this for two reasons: Firstly, I wish to sensitize my Western European colleagues to the problems, P.E. teachers and their students are confronted with, problems resulting from the process of political, social and cultural transformation, which is at present taking place. Secondly, I would like to encourage sport pedagogues as well as P.E. teachers in Eastern European countries not to adapt too quickly what is offered by the West. Not all that glitters is gold. This proverb is valid for P.E. concepts as well.

Let me begin with a look into the past. Independent from the noteworthy and exceptional individual features of various Eastern European school systems, there was a high level of agreement on the pedagogical concepts of P.E.. This can be explained by their adherence to the shared ideas of Marxism and Leninism. I will attempt to point out the characteristics of these concepts. In doing so I plead for your understanding concerning necessary generalizations (11).

1) Physical education, in which the relation between social, educational and sport concepts was reflected, was committed to following and promoting a normative view of man - the so-called socialistic personality with all-round education of mind and body.

2) The relationship between individual and society was characterized by the dominance of the so-called objective demands of the society. As a result Physical Education in the schools was seen from a utilitarian perspective. Above all, it had to prepare for work, defence and physical fitness, whereas anthropological considerations were left to fade into the background.

3) P.E. was characterized by concentration on a very limited number of institutionalized sports outlining historically developed sport.

4) Efficiency and intensity of the P.E. programme as well as the tendency of measuring and evaluating the process of learning in the genuine pedagogical field were other characteristics.

5) As my last point I would like to mention the organizational interweaving of school P.E. and sport involvement outside school.

It would be easy to demonstrate the interrelation between these characteristics of P.E. and the Marxist analysis of work and labour.

This was the situation in school P.E. in most Eastern European countries. This is what most teachers taught and students experienced. But this ideology, whose characteristics were clearly reflected in P.E., has lost its significance. It does not exist anymore.

Reference point of pedagogical thought and action is no longer the question: What are the objective needs of our society? The central theme shifts now to the individual, who wishes to experience the world by movement, games and sport. This change in the system of reference surely leads to uncertainty for teacher and student. New lines of orientation are necessary and inevitable.

In order to develop a new concept for P.E. a few questions have to be answered. The first question is simple: What do young people look for in sport? The answer is not as simple: They take part in sport for the sake of exercise and physical well-being. They hope that sport will have a positive effect on their fitness, their health and their figure. People wish to express something by moving; they would like their movements to be masterly, impressive and aesthetic. They see sport as a field of action in which they can set a goal for themselves, compare themselves with others and reach the limits of their own possibilities. In sport, adolescents look for situations which are exciting. They are looking for the feel of risk and adventure, the enjoyment of uncertainty, and afterwards, the feeling of relief. In sport, adolescents also see an opportunity to enjoy the company of other people in an atmosphere which makes it easy to communicate (13).

My second point refers to sport activities. P.E. is not a sacrosanct place apart from every day-life. Physical education is always - and can never be anything other than - an encounter with every day reality, a presentation of what children and adolescents experience in the field of movement, sport and games as part of their world. And this world is experienced not as a homogeneous whole, but in all its various features and aspects. We find institutionalized sports; we find forms of movement culture, that are unique to one culture; we find informal sport activities which vary in different social settings and situations.

The more complex the social world of movement and sport and the more differentiated the subjective appeals of sport are, then the more important the pedagogical filter becomes. Namely to make accessible to the young people those elements of our movement and sport culture, which might be important for the development and the well-being of the individuals.

This can be achieved neither by a biologically oriented concept of physical exercise related to fitness and adaptation of body systems, nor by a concept of sport socialization and its emphasis on institutionalized competitive sport. Neither can the task be fulfilled by concepts that instrumentalize movement and sport activities for educational purposes, nor can the goal be attained by a concept, that offers a so-called "movement grammar", based on certain movement topics such as body, weight, time, space etc. (5).

Those who wish to bring together individual and society, and see movement and body on the one side and the social reality of sport on the other side as central reference points for pedagogical decisions, will have to take into account the consequences of their position in educational practice. They will have to arrange P.E. lessons in such a way that sport with all its many facets and with all its different meanings, becomes understandable and available for as many students as possible. They will have to strive for a balance between cultural tradition and cultural innovation. All this means that we need to emphasize diversity and openness rather than unity and uniformity.

The pedagogical norm for the arrangement of P.E. lessons in such an understanding aims at the ability to act in the various fields of movement and sport.

This means that participants need to have at their disposal a broad and flexible repertoire of abilities, patterns of movements and skills, which should guarantee access to the whole realm of movement, play, games and sport. They should also enable them to have experiences with their own body which go beyond athletic activities.

The participants should be able to understand and also to practise sport in varying situations and social contexts, and with different meaningful orientations. In short: to recognize movement culture and sport as a part of our socially constructed reality.

My last point: Participants should be able to keep a distance from sport, and to teach participants to be critical of the reality of sport, for example of the sometimes egocentric ideas of the sport federations, the growing influence of economic interests, the excessive demands of the media. This way we should be able to protect the principle of openness in sport.

5. Conclusion

In my paper I have concentrated on the interrelationship between games and sport on the one hand and social and cultural contexts on the other hand. We have seen institutionalized competitive sport reflecting the deep structure of shared European culture. As internationalized competitive sport is not a world that remains separate and apart from others, so recreational sport is not a privileged sanctuary from real life. Referring to Eastern and Western Germany as exemplars I have tried to point out to what extent sport involvement and sport concept are permeated and influenced by the dominant political and cultural mainstreams.

Adolescent sport as a configurational whole is characterized by diversity, as well as the sport cultures in the individual European countries and ethnicities. With this in mind and with a view of man - which is democratic and humanistic - we should strive for protecting the principle of openness in sport and in P.E. Sport is probably one of the most powerful transfer mechanisms for culture and structure ever known to mankind (8).

The best way to tackle the many problems inherent in the process of Europeanization would be to find a balance, a balance between globalization and localization, and a balance between tradition and innovation.

We all live under one sky, but we look at different horizons. With this in mind a helpful guideline for overcoming the obstacles in the process of European integration would be: unity through diversity.

References

1. **Beck, U.** (1986): Risikogesellschaft. München: Suhrkamp.

2. **Behnken, J. et al.** (1991): Schülerstudie '90. Jugendliche im Prozeß der Vereinigung. München: Juventa.

3. **Brettschneider, W.-D.** (1992): Unity of the nation - unity in sports? Paper presented to ISCPES-conference on Sport in the Global Village. Houston, USA.

4. **Brettschneider, W.-D. and Bräutigam, M.** (1991): Sport in der Alltagswelt von Jugendlichen. Frechen: Rittersbach.

5. **Crum, B.** (1992): Competing orientations for PE curriculum development: The trend towards a consensus in the Netherlands and an international comparison. In: T. Williams, L. Almond, A. Sparkes (eds.) (1992): Sport and Physical activity. Moving towards excellence. London: Spon.

6. **EMNID** (1991): Sport- und Freizeitverhalten - ein Ost-West-Vergleich. Bielefeld: EMNID.

7. **Galtung, J.** (1982): Sport as carrier of deep culture and structure. Current Research on Peace and Violence, 5 (2-3), 133-143.

8. **Galtung, J.** (1992): Sports and culture. Paper presented at the conference on Kulturen der Welt. Bonn, Germany.

9. **Harris, J.C. and Park, R.J.** (1983): Play, Games and Sports in Cultural Contexts. Champaign, Ill. Human Kinetics Publishers.

10. **Hartmann-Tews, I.** (1992): Europe - cultures and structures. Paper presented to ICHPER-Conference. Prague, Czechoslovakia.

11. **Hummel, A.** (1992): Zum Sportunterricht in den Ländern der ehemaligen sozialistischen Staatengemeinschaft. Berlin (in press).

12. **Kamphorst, T.J. and Roberts, K. (eds.)** (1989): Trends in sport. Amersfoort: Giordano Bruno.

13. **Kurz, D.**(1990): Sport mehrperspektivisch unterrichten. Wann und wie? Paper presented to conference on Sport zwischen Tradition und Zukunft. Bayreuth, Germany.

14. **Standeven, J.** (1992): Games, Culture and Europeanisation. Paper presented to ICHPER-Conference. Prague, Czechoslovakia.

Footnotes

[1] Modified version of the unpublished keynote address presented at ICHPER Conference on Physical Activity for a Better Lifestyle in a New Europe, Prague 1992.

TEACHING TEACHERS: AIMS, METHODS AND CONTENTS

Carreiro da Costa, F.
Technical University of Lisbon
Portugal

Learning how to teach does not begin with pre-service courses nor doesn't it end with an undergraduate degree. Learning how to teach is a lifelong process. So, I would like to examine "teaching teachers" as part of a larger teacher education continuum starting with a pre-training phase, moving through pre-service and induction phases, continuing within in-service phase until teacher retirement.

Pre-training, pre-service, and induction are considered periods that have the potential to significantly influence how teachers develop their professional skills and orientations (52). Consequently, viewing learning how to teach as a process of a large continuum, it becomes clear that teacher preparation in all phases need to function both as logical extensions of the previous phase, and by its turn influencing the following phases.

We need to be conscious that prospective teachers begin to learn about physical education, teaching and schooling in primary and secondary schools, through early experiences that they have faced as students during 12 years and more than 10,000 hours, exposed to patterns and ideas of teaching and schooling. For students teachers, long apprenticeship of observation (36, 41) undertaken as a pupil at school as well as play and sport experiences outside the school context (16, 32), join with stereotypical cultural practices in physical education and sport, to equip them with a knowledge of teachers' work. These formative impressions of teaching and physical education and sport practices shape their professional learning and teaching views. Moreover, it enables them to develop specific socialization strategies to lead the intended impact of teacher education programs, strongly influencing what they extract from teacher education and their teaching experiences. This period of beginning to learn some of the more visible professional values that will influence futures phases is the pre-training phase (68).

Pre-service phase, or initial teacher preparation, includes course work and all the operations used to prepare prospective teachers for entry into a teaching career (39). If this teacher education phase does not modify pre-existing images of schooling and teaching that student teachers hold, these early conceptions will provide a continuing influence over the pedagogical perspectives, beliefs, and behaviours of physical education teachers.

Induction phase includes the entire process by which the beginning teachers are brought into the profession, and some systematic assistance is sustained for at least one school year (28). The transition from student to teaching is a critical question. In the teaching, beginners are expected to do essentially the same job on their first day of employment as veterans. Research suggest that when beginning teachers are not supported, much of them begin to question their own effectiveness and their decisions to become teachers.

In-service phase includes education and training activities engaged by certificated teachers who intend to improve more effectively their professional knowledge, skills, and attitudes in order that they can educate and promote children's development and learning.

"Teaching teachers: aims, methods and contents" is not an easy theme. Unfortunately, physical education does not represent a professional culture, the body of knowledge used to make professional decisions and to carry out professional tasks (51). Instead of a "culture of professionalism" (36), physical education is marked by a lack of consensus, not only about the mission and goals of the field but also about the nature of its subject matter, as well as aims, contents and processes of physical education teachers preparation (1).

Furthermore, such "culture of variability" points out multiple and contradictory answers regarding *"What is a successful teaching in physical education?", "What is a good physical education teacher?",* and *"How can we produce good physical education teachers?".*

In this paper I would like: (a) to analyse the plurality of conceptual orientations and approaches for teacher education as well as in general education, and in physical education; (b) to describe my point of view concerning the expected aims and contents of teaching teachers programs in physical education; (c) To call for attention that teachers learn to teach not only through formal teacher preparation but also through what has been called the socialization process; (d) finally, to refer some modus operandi which contribute to educate and train the professional physical education teacher as the one who has both technical and reflective competence and performs in a critical, ethical and moral manner.

Yet, before beginning to develop these topics, I would like to point out the following. The professional performance of the physical education teacher requires many functions. In this lecture, however, we will focus our discussion on the teacher education and training for teaching function.

Thus, when we speak of **teaching** teachers, we are referring to the orchestration of knowledge, skills, tasks, methods in the special ways that lead regularity to the changes we call learning how to teach. **Content** designates collectively the knowledge, skills, and dispositions that the teacher educator intents the teacher (prospective, novice or veteran) to acquire. **Methods** refer the processes of the program such as procedures and arrangements that teachers educators employ to accomplish the aims of the teacher education program.

1. Conceptual Orientations in Teacher Preparation

When we ask "What must be the aims, contents and methods in teacher preparation?", the meaning of the question and the basis of the answer emanates from our paradigmatic assumptions.

In fact: "All teacher education is a form of ideology. Each program is related to the educational ideology held by a particular teacher educator or teacher education institution, even though the relationships may not be made explicit" (Spodek, 1974, cited by Zeichner, 66: pp. 3).

This ideology concerns different views of teaching, learning to teach, teachers and schooling, it represents a personal conception about theory and practice relationships, as well as the relationship between research and action. These different views constitute what Zeichner (66) names alternative paradigms of teacher education.

Feiman-Nemser (22) prefers to name these conceptual alternatives that frame teacher education as "conceptual orientations", that is, "a set of ideas about the goals of teacher preparation and the means for achieving them" (pp. 220). She categorizes the plurality of orientations and approaches in teacher preparation in five conceptual orientations: (a) academic, (b) practical, (c) technological, (d) personal, and (e) critical/social.

Each orientation has a focus or thesis that highlights a particular conception of good teacher and teaching, underlines specific aims to teacher education, and valorizes specific educational and training processes.

1.1 The Academic Orientation

The *academic* orientation underline the fact that teaching is primarily concerned with the transmission of knowledge and development of understanding. Consequently, this orientation emphasizes the teacher's role as an intellectual leader, a scholar and a subject matter specialist. A good teacher is the one that has a profound knowledge of subject matter. On the other hand, learning to teach is viewed as a process including knowledge of facts, concepts, procedures that define a given field and understanding of how these pieces fit together.

Lee Shulman's (56) ideas represent a new and contemporary view of academic orientation and express a challenge to historically dominant notions in this orientation. He argues that teachers need more than merely exposure to subject matter. They need what he names *pedagogical knowledge*, that is, useful ways to conceptualize and understand what makes learning some topics difficult or easy for students of different ages and backgrounds.

1.2 The Practical Orientation

The *practical* orientation focuses attention on the elements of craft, technique, and artistry that skillful practitioners reveal in their work (22: pp. 222). Consequently, a good teacher is the one that reveal professional artistry, this is, "the kind of competence practitioners sometimes display in unique, uncertain and conflicted situations of practice" (55: pp. 22). Teaching is conceptualized as a process of research and experimentation. We learn to teach by reflection-in-action, and reflection-on-action.

Donald Schön is the author whose contribution is the most important. His works "The Reflective Practitioner" (54) and "Educating the Reflective Practitioner" (55) have contributed to expand in the field of teacher education the theories about epistemology of practice.

1.3 The Technological Orientation

The *technological* orientation focuses attention on systematic procedures that provide teachers with specific teaching skills. The primordial goal is to prepare teachers who can carry out the tasks of teaching with proficiency. There are two approaches within this conceptual orientation: (a) one originating in behaviourist tradition; (b) another clearly shaped by cognitivist position.

The first approach assumes that learning to teach involves the acquisition of principles and practices derived from the scientific study of teaching, fundamentally from the research on what constitutes effective teaching. Teaching competence is defined in terms of performance and by reference to what happens to the students being taught (57). Consequently, a good teacher and the teacher effectiveness are similar concepts.

The second technological approach that has been gaining evidence is the metaphor of the teacher as a decision maker. This is a deliberative orientation (22, 33) so-named because good teaching and programs are viewed as resulting from the good deliberations and subsequent actions undertook by teachers. In this approach, research findings on teacher effectiveness and on teacher planning are used as "principles of procedure" in order to help prospective and in-service teachers to make informed and thoughtful decisions, in the hope that, through introspection and analysis, teaching can be enhanced (15).

1.4 The Personal Orientation

The *personal* orientation points out that learning to teach is constructed as a process of learning to understand, develop, and use oneself effectively. The teacher's own personal development is a central part of the teacher preparation (22: pp. 225).

This orientation, like the others, is very diverse. However, all personal variations seek development of the self as the key to competent teaching; they seek to develop *psychological maturity* of prospective teachers. Teacher education is considered a process of becoming rather than the mastery of a set of competencies. They emphasize the reorganization of perceptions and beliefs over the mastery of specific behaviors, skills and content knowledge (66). Thus, prospective teachers are stimulated to point out their learning needs and are viewed as active agents in determining the objectives and contents of their professional education. However, the growth towards psychological maturity is not viewed as an inevitable process; it is seen instead as a development that must be stimulated by a safe and supportive learning environment.

1.5 The Critical/Social Orientation

The *critical/social* orientation emphasizes the political and ethical dimensions of teaching and considers teacher education as a part of a larger strategy to create a more just and democratic society. Thus, the teacher is viewed both as an educator and a political activist.

This orientation is assumed through different designations, such as "progressive education", "critical pedagogy", "emancipatory teaching" and "student empowerment". Critical inquiry involves questioning those presented truths as granted for. It involves: (a) looking for unarticulated assumptions and seeking for new perspectives; (b) learning to make decisions about teaching and learning based upon perceived ethical and political consequences and awareness of alternatives. Teaching skills are considered also important. However, they are not valued as ends in themselves, but rather as means to bring about desired ends.

In short, from this point of view the fundamental task of the teacher education is to develop prospective teachers' capacities for reflective action: *Why do it? Where are we going to?*

2. Conceptual Orientations in Physical Education Teacher Education (Pete)

All the conceptual orientations and approaches in teacher education that we early referred to do not tell us how teacher education is practiced. They only inform us the way in which it is conceived, thought about, and theorized. On the other hand, some of those orientations have yet little or no practical reference within physical education.

Bain (1,2) refers three theoretical positions in physical education teacher education. Two dominant perspectives: behavioral paradigm and occupational socialization theory. In addition, she refers that a critical perspective is emerging.

2.1 Behavioral Paradigm

Behavioral paradigm is like the technological orientation I referred before. It aims to develop and improve effective teaching skills from research on teaching effectiveness. Prospective and practicing teachers must learn and improve teaching skills and strategies related to pupil achievement. Books like "Developing Teaching Skills in Physical Education" by Daryl Siedentop (57), "Enseignement des Activités Physiques et Sportives. Observation et Recherche" (46); "Pédagogies des Activités Physiques et Sportives" (47) and "Analyser l'Enseignement pour mieux Enseigner" (48) by Maurice Piéron are excellent examples of a technological orientation in physical education.

2.2 Occupational Socialization Perspective

Occupational socialization perspective "includes all of the kinds of socialization that initially influence persons to enter the field of physical education and that later are responsible for their perceptions and actions as teacher educators and teachers" (35: pp. 107).

This perspective points out that learning to teach in physical education is a lifelong process that involves different kinds of influences, such as early physical education and sports experiences, significant others, societal common-sense on physical activities, teacher formal preparation, schools' organizational socialization, and culture. In conclusion, occupational socialization helps us to understand how teachers are socialized throughout their lives, which are the most significant agents, and how socializing influences occur. Therefore, we can deliberately use appropriate training strategies in order to increase programmatic goals.

"Socialization Into Physical Education: Learning to Teach" a book edited by Thomas Templin and Paul Schempp (61) is an excellent example of the socialization theoretical perspective in physical education teacher preparation.

2.3 Critical Theory Perspective

Critical theory perspective in physical education teacher education is like the critical/social orientation I described before. Prospective and in-service teachers are prepared to consider not only pedagogical, but also political, economic, and ethical/moral dimensions of daily practice. They are involved in action research in which they attempt to improve educational practice through analysis, dialogue, and strategic action (29).

There are two excellents books that express this orientation. One of them is "Improving Teaching in Physical Education" by Richard Tinning (62). The other one is "A Reflective Approach to Teaching Physical Education" by Donald Hellison and Thomas Templin (26).

2.4 Traditional Perspective

Although in most cases the curricular structure of physical education teacher education courses is organized on a technical rationality model of science (37, 42, 53), and despite a growing body of research is based on the behaviorist paradigm, as well as the amount of information that it was possible to gather about teaching effectiveness (5, 8, 46, 57), the technological or behavioral training approach to physical education teacher education has not been widely adopted and implemented by pre-services and in-services programs (1, 39, 40, 58).

As Siedentop (58) points out "While the "technician" metaphor has increasingly dominated much of the literature and rhetoric of teacher education, it seems not to have been reflected in actual program change" (pp. 9). In fact, teacher education literature in physical education points out that teacher education programs have not made use of existing knowledge (1, 39, 40). Contents and processes of programs are selected based on tradition, logic, personal commitment and inspiration (39: pp. 5).

Consequently, it seems that learning how to teach in physical education is mainly based on "traditionalistics" thesis (29). According to this view, teacher education is primarily a process of professional socialization and induction in school observing and modeling the cooperative teacher. There is a notion that with time and experience a natural process of improvement will occur. To teach physical education it's enough to have a little common sense, a good knowledge of the subject mater, and some intuition.

This is a non theoretical conception of teacher education, where knowledge about teaching is accumulated largely by trial and error and the dominant pedagogical knowledge might be called "craft pedagogy" (64). Beginning with these initial experiences, student teachers learn to think that the way to learn more about teaching is through trial and errors, not through careful thought and scholarship.

This non theoretical tradition of teaching and teacher education in physical education is responsible for the little influence on the way of thinking and on teaching capacity of prospective and in-service teachers. Moreover, this traditional view contributes to what Bart Crum (16, 18) calls the "Self Reproducing Failure of Physical Education".

3. The True Problem In Pete

Nowadays there is a growing controversy between those who stand for the "critical pedagogy" (18, 20, 29, 42, 63) against the pedagogy that has dominated the physical education discourse - the "performance pedagogy" (63): A pedagogy anchored on principles of behaviorist paradigm.

In my opinion, to oppose "performance pedagogy" versus "critical pedagogy" is not the right question because, unfortunately, teaching skills is not being deliberately or systematically developed and improved in most courses of physical education teacher education. On the other hand, inquiry, although not being a new idea, has often been forgotten, as if the teaching process could be developed regardless of ideas and values.

In my point of view, the true problem, the first and most central problem in physical education teacher education is how to convince all of us, university administrators, professors, teacher educators, and prospective, novice, and veteran physical education teachers that:

(a) Teaching competence is an ethical and moral question.
(b) Teaching competence is a question of professional dignity and credibility.
(c) Teaching competence is a question of professional survival.
(d) Teaching competence is mainly a consequence of the teacher education quality, and of the support given during teacher professional career. On the other hand, it is a consequence of the conditions under which teachers carry out their work (19).

Once more we are faced with a philosophical question. Each one has his own conception of teaching competence.

However, if we go back to the five conceptual orientations in teacher preparation, we see they offer a rich variety in points of view whenever we want to define and to focus aims and practices of our own physical education teacher education programs.

Although each orientation emphasizes different issues and priorities, I think these orientations are not mutually exclusive. None of them offer a fully developed framework to guide teacher preparation. However, all orientations constitute a source of ideas that can help us to reflect on expected aims for our teacher education programs, as well as to examine more systematically teacher education practices in physical education as they relate to the type of teachers we hope to prepare.

4. Teaching Teachers: Aims And Contents

Now I would like to summarize my point of view concerning the expected aims of teaching teachers programs in physical education. To define aims for teacher preparation is implicitly to answer the following question: **What kind of teachers must we educate and train?**

In my opinion, we need to conceptualize physical education teachers as persons who have the following characteristics:

4.1 Teachers with a profound scientific and pedagogical knowledge, knowing about and knowing how to do, that is, experts in teaching physical education

It must be emphasized that a highly mastery of a subject matter is not a sufficient condition for achieving teaching effectiveness or teaching expertise. Teaching expertise demands both to be a master of the subject area and to be a highly skilled teacher (59).

Shulman (56) proposes that the knowledge base for teachers include seven categories of knowledge. Four of these categories include appropriate information for all teachers, regardless of subject-matter speciality:

(a) *general pedagogical knowledge;*
(b) *knowledge of learners and their characteristics;*
(c) *knowledge of educational contexts;*
(d) *knowledge of educational ends, purposes and values.*

Three categories of teacher knowledge that are specific to the subject area:

(e) *Content knowledge* - mastery of subject matter. Within physical education, knowledge of content field is usually interpreted as knowledge about movement (1: pp. 765).
(f) *Curriculum knowledge* - the particular grasp of the materials and programs that serve as "tool for trade" for teachers.
(g) *Pedagogical-Content knowledge* - that special amalgam of content and pedagogy that is specific of teachers, their own special form of professional understanding.

In classroom teaching "There has been recent concern that the disciplinary knowledge that beginning and many experienced teachers possess poorly equips them for this transformation process" (14: pp. 305).

I verified in a process-product study (6, 7, 12) that less effective teachers were characterized by weak instruction, teaching errors, and providing pupils with high rate of inappropriate feedback.

Bain (1) points out that "Despite the apparent programmatic emphasis on the science of movement and on pedagogy, research testing physical educators' knowledge in these areas indicates that neither experienced teachers nor graduating seniors meet standards established by experts" (pp. 765).

Furthermore, the new academic orientation hold by Shulman (56) calls the attention of teacher educators back to the "professional treatment of subject matter". It challenges the familiar division of labor between arts and science faculty and teachers educators and suggests a new conception of subject-matter treatment. It calls for an integration of scientific and pedagogical learning and call for new conceptualizations and new institutional arrangements between scientific and educational departments.

In fact, we can question the relationship between theory and practice as it is generally conceptualized in pre-service training. Russell (50) argues that typical "theory into practice" perspective might generate considerable confusion and dissatisfaction among student teachers. As students struggle to find the relevance of taught theory they may resort to dismiss it in favour of unreflective practice and the imitation of observed classroom routines.

4.2 Teachers with both a large repertoire of teaching skills and technical virtuosity

Teaching implies instrumental know-how. Teachers need to dominate a large repertoire of teaching skills that enables them to achieve physical education goals, and to face the demands of every day life in the gymnasium.

Research on teacher effectiveness has underlined that most effective teachers present a much more large repertoire of teaching kills as well as a great flexibility in the educational relationship (5, 6, 46). A successful teaching requires the teacher's ability to articulate a very large number of diagnostic, instructional, managerial and therapeutic skills, tailoring behavior in specific contexts and situations to the specific needs of the moment, in order to create the pupils the best conditions of learning (4,8).

On the other hand, descriptive research on teaching has shown some problems in teaching physical education in schools (46). Studies centered on pupil behaviour have shown that pupils in many physical education classes spend an alarmingly small amount of time engaged in motor activity. Furthermore studies on teachers' self efficacy (44, 45), as well as studies about the evaluation of teachers' pedagogical needs (43) refer that they present, even after a long time of experience, concerns about their teaching, namely discipline, pupil motivation, and class control.

This teaching repertoire does not come naturally to prospective and in service teachers. It can only be acquired in structured learning to teach processes. Furthermore, Borg, Kelly, Laryer & Gall make a deep logical case remark training:

"How much confidence...would you have in a surgeon if you knew that he had never perfected his techniques...and never practiced under the guidance of an expert the specific skills needed in a given operation - if, in fact, he had learned surgery by listening to lectures gives by someone who had not performed an operation...and had been graduated from medical school largely on the basis of ability to pass multiple-choice tests?" (pp. 24; cited by Cruickshank & Metcarf, 15: pp. 471).

Research shows that training is a powerful process for enhancing knowledge and skills. Prospective and in-service teachers can be wonderful learners. Teacher educators may use many procedures in order to develop and improve teaching skills, such as: microteaching; analysis of teaching; behavior modification; simulation; peer coaching; supervision; selfanalysis; etc. Bruce Joyce and Berverly Showers (30, 31) outline the components of effective teacher training.

4.3 Teachers who believe both that good teaching is important and that their fundamental role is to teach pupils how to learn

The purpose of pre-service teacher education is to prepare qualified teacher who are eager to improve professional practice and who have been socialized into believing that good teaching is important. In fact, pedagogical optimism is a characteristic of more effective teachers, that is, to believe that all pupils can learn and that we can teach them (4).

To promote student learning is the prime goal of teaching school physical education. Unfortunately, research suggests that teacher preparation has shown some lack of capacity in training physical education teachers motivate to organize, in an intentional way, the teaching-learning activities aiming the "accomplishment of students competencies for lasting and satisfying participation in movement culture" (18).

There is evidence to support that prospective, new, and experienced teachers hold a non-teaching perspective (3, 9, 39). Many teachers are not convinced that students' learning constitute the most important purpose of school physical education. Consequently, there is also evidence to think that socialization process in the school context serves to reinforce to a large degree the idea that successful teaching is defined in terms of keeping students participating (busy), with minimal misbehavior (good), while providing an enjoyable experience (happy) (49).

The majority of the schools and programs of teacher preparation fail to promote a teaching conception at the end of their programs (5,10, 13, 17). As teacher socialization theory points out, "Unless formal training can modify preexistent images of teachers and teaching, future teachers will practice what their teachers did" (21: pp. 154).

Thus, teacher educators must encourage prospective teachers to question their assumptions about teaching and reinterpret their past experiences in physical education, through a reflective approach centered in:

(a) the promotion of a critical appraisal of school physical experience;
(b) the promotion of an inquiry oriented experience of all school conditions and practices as they exist in future workplaces (classroom level, relationship between the PE teaching staff, and school level);
(c) the promotion of a reflection about the present, that is, about course orientation regarding institutional constrains pushing students to enter in teacher occupation.

Yet, teachers educators in developing and improving habits of thought may use procedures such as: case study; simulation; inquiry; life stories; teaching analysis; clinical supervision; role playing; etc.

4.4 Teachers prepared to continuously and accurately examine themselves and the results of their work, and to make adjustments accordingly

Teaching in physical education is characterized by variability, complexity, and uncertainty, as well as by foreseeable situations that may be previously controlled. Such reality requires both problem-setting and problem-solving capacities (34). "In face of variability, uncertainty, and complexity of practice, future practitioners must learn the importance of continuous problem-setting activities and ways in which these activities will result in different alternatives in different work organizations" (37: pp.174).

Teachers must be able to drive their teaching through a technical, practical and critical rationality. Van Manen (65) has described these three different domains of reflection as follows:

Firstly, in technical reflection, the concern goes to the efficiency and effectiveness of the means used to attain ends that remain unquestioned.

Secondly, in practical reflection, the main task is to explain and to clarify the assumptions and to underline teaching activity and to assess the adequacy of the educational goals towards which the activity leads.

Finally, critical reflection incorporates moral and ethical criteria into discourse about practical action.

We should be aiming to create a learning environment in our teacher education programs that emphasizes and promotes in prospective and in service teachers a reflection on these three domains. We reject the view that the "critical" is somehow separate from the "technical" and "practical" gymnasiumbased reality of student and teachers reality.

We need teachers capable to distinguish good from unacceptable educational practice. We need hard-headed teachers with guts to face professional activity with curiosity, energy, and a non-routinary teaching practice. In short, we need a reflective teacher that views his own learning as part of the job of teaching, and believing that to improve his teaching as a collective undertaking.

Once more we must be conscious that becoming a learning teacher is not only a matter of individual disposition. Reflective teaching, teaching analysis, action research, selfanalysis, self-improvement, peer coaching, etc., are procedures that teachers educators can use as knowledge as well as strategies aiming to equip student and in-service teachers with the knowledge, skills and confidence to continue their professional development.

4.5 Teachers that perform accordingly to ethical and moral principles

Teaching skills is good but can not replace ideas and values. In fact, "Teaching is not defined by the technical skills of its practitioners, but instead by the educative intentions and moral purposes with which they undertake their work" (23:pp.139).

Teaching quality is also a kind of social justice. I verified that less skilled pupils in school physical education can accede to high learning levels whenever they are provided with adequate opportunities to learn (6, 11). That is why, physical education in school must be thought as an education project aiming the cultural integration of all youngsters in order to give them opportunities to acquire the required social-culture competencies (18).

Unfortunately much of what stands for physical education in our schools is uneducative. Exclusion instead of integration is often the rule. Education requires a moral code for teaching. To call for a moral code to teaching and teacher education demands that school can provide equal access and equal receipt quality for all students (60:pp.310).

Teachers must be educated not only to develop an intelligent performance, aiming to produce fairer learning conditions, felt as more human and satisfying by all students, but also to acquire a critical awareness that "Any structures or practice that interfere with the simultaneous goals of equity and excellence, that perpetuate preexisting social and economic inequalities, are subject to critique and elimination" (60:pp. 310).

Inquiry, action research, case study, group discussion, teaching analysis, etc., are procedures that alone and in combination can contribute to accomplish that aim. It is important to remark that some of the procedures we have been referring are obviously more appropriate to achieve some aims than others. However, the procedures do not determinate by themselves what kind of aims can be achieved, but instead the purposes to which they are applied. That is what justifies the adequacy or the link with the competence we want to develop and improve.

If we go back to our initial question "What kind of teachers must we educate and train?", I would conclude that we need to conceptualize **physical education teacher as a subject mater expertise, a professional that has both technical and reflective education, performs on a critical, ethical and moral manner, and presents disposition to continue developing and improving his work efficacy allowing profession dignity.**

Many of you will agree with me, certainly many won't. Many others will say that we aren't proposing anything new. I think that the latter may be right. However, there are signs that most of the PE training courses have failed to accord a speech of intentions with a coherent and real one, consequent in contents and in proceedings.

Locke (39, 40) points out that teacher education programs in physical education mostly had low impact. "The effects, if any, just get washed away when graduates enter full-time teaching" (40: pp.9). This leader of the physical education teacher education wrote that we must recognize that "we have done such a poor job on helping teach learn in preparation programs" (pp. 10).

Yet, we must notice that to refer that teacher education has low impact is not to assume that all PETE programs have low impact in all students. On the other hand, it is important to remark that the lack of impact of teachers education programs is not a determinism, but a consequence of the characteristics of some programs.

It seems that this lack of impact can be explained mainly as a consequence of absence of systematic training procedures to provide prospective teachers with specific teaching skills, considering programs fragmentation and teacher education staff' conceptual and ideological cohesiveness, and also because teacher educators tend to underestimate values and beliefs of teaching and schooling carried in by prospective students to the formal preparation.

Fortunately, teacher education research has identified not only the deep causes of teacher preparation programs, but also described the characteristics of high impact programs. There is a large consensus that the characteristics of effective teacher education programs are as following (1, 24, 38, 39, 61):

(a) a conceptual cohesiveness within PETE faculty;
(b) an explicit educational design;
(c) emphasis on procedural knowledge;
(d) adequate selection of skills concerning to the demands of the workplace;
(e) teacher education commitment;
(f) close attention to preconceptions of prospective teachers; and
(g) a strong support within induction phase.

5. Final Remarks

From the lot of the presented considerations, I should like to underline the following aspects:

1. The initial teacher preparation programs have a low impact upon students and upon future teaching practices in school.
2. The inefficacy of the teacher preparation programs does not constitute the sole factor in the reproduction of the teaching habits, but it does constitute a determining factor.
3. Nevertheless, the research on teacher education has shown that:
    a) There are consequent programs and that all of them can be improved.
    b) Many teacher educators, in own individual way, are doing an excellent work.
4. In order to improve initial teacher preparation programs, I think there are some conditions that we must bear in mind:
    a) The need of an holistic conception that might gather aims, means and all agents of education.
    b) Consequently, only a whole program operated by a group of like-minded teacher educators (in which people, process and policy all together push towards the same goals) can achieve strong effects.
    c) The need that all who truly believe in the importance of the teacher training engage themselves in a critical analysis comparing their own beliefs, values and educational practices in PETE and find out if they are using consistent knowledge and correct alternatives.

Shirl Hoffman (27) wrote that physical education was "a disconnected society of professionals and academics in search of ways to 'reconnect'" (pp. 17).

I believe that the challenge for excellence the net work is facing may be a true effort that might contribute to a unifying conceptualization about the missions and goals of our field, so that:
   - fragmentation gives way to collaboration and integration;
   - deprofessionalization gives way to professionalization;
   - extermination and death give way to the growth of Physical Education in the European schools.

References

1. Bain L.: Physical education teacher education. In: Houston W.R. (ed.): Handbook of Research on Teacher Education, pp. 758-781. New York, Macmillan Publishing Company, 1990.

2. Bain L.: Research in sport pedagogy: past, present and future. In: Williams T., Almond L., Sparkes A. (eds.): Sport and Physical Activity. Moving Towards Excellence, pp. 3-22. London, E & FN Spon, 1992.

3. Borys A., Fishburne G.: A comparison of pre-service and in-service teachers' conceptions of successful teaching. In: Lirette M., Paré C., Dussureault J., Piéron M. (eds): Intervention en Éducation Physique et Entraînement. Bilan et Perspectives, pp. 41-46. Québec, Presses de l'Université du Québec, 1990.

4. Brophy J., Evertson C.: Learning from teaching: A developmental perspective. Boston, Allyn and Bacon, 1976.

5. Brophy J., Good T.: Teacher behavior and student achievement. In: Wittrock M. (ed.): Handbook of Research on Teaching, pp. 328-375. New York, Macmillan Publishing Company, 1986.

6. Carreiro da Costa F.: O Sucesso Pedagógico em Educação Física. Estudo das Condições e Factores de Ensino-Aprendizagem Associados ao Êxito numa Unidade de Ensino. Dissertação de doutoramento não publicada. Lisboa, F.M.H.- Universidade Técnica de Lisboa, 1988.

7. Carreiro da Costa F.: Caracterização da intervenção pedagógica de dois grupos de professores com níveis de sucesso distintos no ensino de uma técnica desportiva. In: Bento J., Marques M. (eds.): As Ciências do Desporto e a Prática Desportiva, pp. 329-348. Porto, Faculdade de Ciências do Desporto Educação Física-Universidade do Porto, 1991.

8. Carreiro da Costa F.: A investigação sobre a eficácia pedagógica. Inovação 1: 9-27, 1991.

9. Carreiro da Costa F., Carvalho L., Onofre, M, Dinis J.: As representações de sucesso e de insucesso profissional em professores de educação física. Boletim da Sociedade Portuguesa de Educação Física 4: 11-30, 1992.

10. Carreiro da Costa F., Pestana C., Dinis J., Carvalho L.: Physical education and sports students' expectations of future professional activities. Paper presented at the *«1992 Olympic Scientific Congress»*, Malaga, Spain, 1992.

11. Carreiro da Costa F., Piéron M.: Teaching learning variables related to student success in an experimental teaching unit. In: Telama R., Laakso L., Piéron M., Ruoppila I., Vihko V. (eds.): Physical Education and Life-Long Physical Activity, pp. 304-316. Jyväskylä, The Foundation for Promotion of Physical Culture and Health, 1990.

12. Carreiro da Costa F., Piéron M.: Teaching effectiveness: Comparison of more and less effective teachers in an experimental teaching unit. In: Williams T., Almond L., Sparkes, A. (eds.): Sport and Physical Activity. Moving Towards Excellence, pp. 169-176. London, E & FN Spon, 1992.

13. Carreiro da Costa F., Carvalho L., Pestana C., Dinis J., Piéron M. (1993). Physical education and sport first and fifth years students' expectations of future work activities. Paper presented at the «AIESEP' 93 International Seminar on 'The training of reflective teachers in reflective practice of physical education'», July 15-19. Trois Rivières, Quèbec, Canada, 1993.

14. Carter K.: Teachers' knowledge and learning to teach. In: Houston W. H. (ed.): Handbook of Research on Teacher Education, pp. 291-310. New York, Macmillan Publishing Company, 1990.

15. Cruickshank D., Metcalf K.: Training within teacher preparation. In: Houston W. R. (ed.): Handbook of Research on Teacher Education, pp. 469-497. New York, Macmillan Publishing Company, 1990.

16. Crum B.: The self reproducing failing of physical education. In: Telama R, Laakso L., Piéron M., Ruoppila I., Vihko V. (eds.): Physical Education and Life-Long Physical Activity, pp. 294-301. Jyväskylä, The Foundation for Promotion of Physical Culture and Health, 1990.

17. Crum B.: Shifts in professional conceptions of prospective physical education teachers under the influence of preservice professional training. In: Telama R., Laakso L., Piéron M., Ruoppila I., Vihko V. (eds.): Physical Education and Life-Long Physical Activity, pp. 286-294. Jyväskylä, The Foundation for Promotion of Physical Culture and Health, 1990.

18. Crum B.: Convential thought and practice in physical education teacher education: Problems of teaching physical education and selected implications for change. Quest (accept for publishing), 1993.

19. Doolittle S., Schwager S.: Socialization and inservice teacher education. In: Templin T., Schempp P.(eds.): Socialization Into Physical Education: Learning to Teach, pp. 105-121. Indianapolis, In: Benchmark Press, 1989.

20. Evans J.: Research pedagogy and reflective teaching. In: Williams T., Almond L., Sparkes A. (eds.): Sport and Physical Activity. Moving Toward Excellence, pp. 41-51, London, E & NF Spon, 1992.

21. Feiman-Nemser S.: Learning to teach.In: Shulman L., Sykes G. (eds.): Handbook of Teaching and Policy, pp. 150-170. New York, Longman, 1983.

22. Feiman-Nemser S.: Teacher preparation: Structural and conceptual alternatives. In: Houston W. R. (ed.): Handbook of Research on Teacher Education, pp. 212-232. New York, Macmillan Publishing Company, 1990.

23. Fenstermacher G.: Some moral considerations on teaching as a profession. In: Goodlad J., Soder R., Sirotnik R. (eds.): The Moral Dimensions of Teaching, pp. 3-25. San Francisco, Jossey-Bass, 1990.

24. Fuller F., Rown H.: In: Ryan K. (ed.): Teacher Education, pp. 25-52. Chicago, University of Chicago Press, 1975.

25. Graham G.: The developing physical education teachers and coach: Empirical and research insights. In: Lirette M., Paré C.,Dussureault J., Piéron M. (eds.): Intervention en Éducation Physique et Entraînement. Bilan et Perspectives, pp. 87-99. Québec, Presses de l'Université du Québec, 1990.

26. Hellinson D., Templin T.: A Reflective Approach to Teaching Physical Education. Champaign, Human Kinetics Publishers, 1991.

27. Hoffman S.: Therapy for an ailing profession. Journal of Physical Education, Recreation & Dance 9: 17, 1985.

28. Huling-Austin L.: Teacher induction programs and internships. In: Houston W. R. (ed.): Handbook of Teacher Education, pp. 535-548, New York, Macmillan, 1990.

29. Kirk D.: A critical pedagogy for teacher education: Toward an inquiry oriented approach. Journal of Teaching in Physical Education 5: 230-246, 1986.

30. Joyce B., Showers B.: Improving inservice training: The messages of research. Educational Leadership 37: 379-385, 1980.

31. Joyce B., Showers B.: Student Achievement Through Staff Development. New York, Longman, 1988.

32. Lawson H.: Toward a model of teacher socialization in physical education: The subjective warrant, recruitment, and teacher education. Journal of Teaching in Physical Education 3: 3-16, 1983.

33. Lawson H: New directions for research on teacher education and school practice in physical education. International Journal of Physical Education 20: 8-14, 1983.

34. Lawson H.: Problem-setting for physical education and sport. Quest 36: 48-60, 1984.

35. Lawson H.: Occupational socialization and the design of teacher education programs. Journal of Teaching in Physical Education, 5: 107-116, 1986.

36. Lawson H.: From rookie to veteran: Workplace conditions in physical education and induction into the profession. In: Templin T., Schempp P. (eds.): Socialization Into Physical Education: Learning to Teach, pp. 145-164. Indianapolis, In: Benchmark Press, 1989.

37. Lawson H.: Beyond positivism: research, practice, and undergraduate professional education. Quest 42: 161-183, 1990.

38. Locke L.: Research on teacher education for physical education in the U.S.A., Part II: Questions and conclusions. In: Telama R., Vastala V., Tiainem T., Laakso L., Haajanen T. (eds.): Research in School Physical Education, pp. 285-320. Jyväskylä, The Foundation for Promotion of Physical Culture and Health, 1983.

39. Locke L.: Research on teaching teachers: where are we now? Monograph. Journal of Teaching in Physical Education, 1984.

40. Locke L.: Research and the improvement of teaching: the professor as the problem. In: Barrette G., Feingold R., Rees C., Piéron M. (eds.): Myths, models & methods in sport pedagogy, pp. 1-26. Champaign, Human Kinetics Publishers, 1987.

41. Lortie D.: School teacher. Chicago, Chicago University Press, 1975.

42. Mackay J., Gore J., Kirk D.: Beyond the limits of technocratic physical education. Quest, 42: 52-76, 1990.

43. Oliver B.: Teacher and school characteristics: their relationship to the inservice needs of teachers. Journal of Teaching in Physical Education, 7: 38-45, 1987.

44. Onofre M., Carreiro da Costa F.: The self-efficacy concept of physical education teachers in interactive teaching. An exploratory study. Paper presented at the «1992 Olympic Scientific Congress», Malaga, 1992.

45. Onofre M., Carreiro da Costa F.: (1992b). O Sentimento de capacidade na intervenção pedagógica de professores de educação física. Comunicação apresentada no «IV Congresso da Sociedade Portuguesa de Educação Física», Oeiras, 11-12 de Dezembro, 1992.

46. Piéron M.: Enseignement des Activités Physiques et Sportives. Observation et Recherche. Liège, Presses Universitaires de Liège, 1988.

47. Piéron M.: Pédagogie des Activités Physiques et du Sport. Paris, Ed. Revue EPS, 1992.

48. Piéron M.: Analyser L' Enseignement Pour Mieux Enseigner. Paris, Ed. Revue EPS, 1993.

49. Placek J.: Conceptions of success in teaching: Busy, happy, and good. In: Templin T., Olson J. (eds.): Teaching in Physical Education, pp. 46-56. Champaign, Human Kinetics, 1983.

50. Russell T.: From pre-service teacher education to first year of teaching: A study of theory and practice. In: Calderhead J. (ed.): Teachers' Professional Learning, pp. 1334. London, The Falmer Press, 1988.

51. Schempp P., Martinek: Collaborative research in physical education. Journal of Teaching in Physical Education 7:208213, 1988.

52. Schempp P., Graber K.: Teacher socialization from a dialectical perspective: Pretraining through induction. Journal of Teaching in Physical Education 11:329-348,1992.

53. Schein E.: Professional Education. New York, McGraw-Hill, 1973.

54. Schön D.: The Reflective Practitioner. New York, Basic Books, 1983.

55. Schön D.: Educating the Reflective Practitioner. San Francisco, Jossey-Bass Publishers, 1987.

56. Shulman L.: Knowledge and teaching: Foundations of the New Reform. Harvard Educational Review 57: 1- 22, 1987.

57. Siedentop D.: Developing Teaching Skills in Physical Education (2nd ed). Palo Alto, Mayfield Publishing Cy, 1983.

58. Siedentop D.: The modification of teacher behavior. In: Piéron M., Graham G. (eds.): Sport Pedagogy, pp. 3-18. Champaign, Human Kinetics Publishers, 1986.

59. Siedentop D., Eldar E.: Expertise, experience, and effectiveness. Journal of Teaching Physical Education 8: 254-260, 1989.

60. Sirotinick K.: Society, schooling, teaching and preparing to teach. In: Goodlad J., Soder R., Sirotnick K. (eds.): The Moral Dimension of Teaching, pp. 296-323. San Francisco, Jossey Bass, 1990.

61. Templin T., Schempp P. (eds.): Socialization into Physical Education: Learning to Teach. Indianapolis, In: Benchmark Press, 1989.

62. Tinning R.: Improving Teaching in Physical Education. Geelong, Deakin University Press, 1987.

63. Tinning R. (1992). Teacher education pedagogy: Dominant discourses and the process of problem-setting. In: Williams T., Almond L., Sparkes A. (eds.): Sport and Physical Activity. Moving Towards Excellence, pp. 23-40. London, E & NF Spon, 1992.

64. Tom A.: Teaching as a Moral Craft. New York, Longman, 1984.

65. Van Manen M.: Linking ways of knowing with ways of being practical. Curriculum Inquiry 6: 205-228, 1977.

66. Zeichner K.: Alternative paradigms of teacher education. Journal of Teacher Education, 34: 3-9, 1983.

67. Zeichner K., Tabachnick B.: Are the effects of university teacher education 'washed out' by school experience? Journal of Teacher Education, 32: 7-11, 1981.

68. Zeichner K., Gore J.: Teacher socialization. In: Houston W. R. (ed.): Handbook of Research on Teacher Education, pp. 329-348. New York, Macmillan Publishing Company, 1990.

Continuous Formation in Europe

Cilia, G.
Istituto Superiore Statale di Educazione Fisica
Rome, Italy

1. Introduction

Many pedagogues agree on the opinion that continuous formation comprises Education during adulthood, learning to read and write, and Schooling.

If we consider adult education as an active faculty within Continuous Formation, we must highlight its peculiar character implying individual choice and free participation. When considering the basic process of learning to write and read, we'll immediately focus its character of urgency together with its political and cultural motivations. If we consider Schooling, we'll notice that it is featured by both urgency and free choice. Learning is a necessary process for the individual formation, as necessary as the free development of one's own personality.

As a direct consequence we can infer that Continuous Formation is made up of choice and freedom, as well as of individual participation and general motivation. However, all the above stated components within continuous formation are overtaken by an extremely peculiar and rich inner force. Within the dynamics of such inner force characterizing the process of continuous formation, we notice that the process of learning to write and read has gone through a chance: once a primary need, a participation process, and a managing phase, it now comes to be a force modifying society.

Adult education must tend to change from free choice drive into need for general - not just personal - improvement of a fairer society.

Schooling should aim at finding a space (within the need for learning) for all inner growing urges and creative stimuli, requiring understanding of the future - our children's future.

Needlees to say that Adult Education is increasingly widespread all over the world, while at the same time adjusting into the role of a public "service".

In this role of public service, Adult Education has inevitably lost its go. Past struggles and sacrifices endured have lost their charismatic sense, while new communication techniques based on discussion made the old conception of Adult Education appear obsolete.

Whenever defending that Adult Education must tend to include (besides free participation and social change) a feature of primary need and the commitment needed by general involvement, we hint to the role of moral support Adult Education has always been featured by and must continue to be based on. That is, the cultural need for a rational force, the objective of which is to take full possession of one's own historical and political role.

Adult Education meant as personal "service" to individual desires and interests mainly helps to inject innovative systems into the traditional ones: it has nothing to do with Continuous Education.

We think that learning to write and read should aim at improving cultural and interpersonal relationships; and also at opening the debate within society, so as to become the main reason for social changes.

The process of merely learning to read and write, apart from real life, i.e. separated from adult interests, work and condition is only a means and has nothing to do with Continuous Formation.

When we consider "leisure time" as a sort of balance area between everyday working fatigue and free time rest (in other words the span of time dedicated to man's creativity), we defend the need for a space reserved for living in full freedom. Leisure time, meant as pastime or easy fruition of the advantages offered by the society of consumerism, is by no means part of the Continuous Formation process.

Finally, as regards School, Continuous Formation is separated from obsolete curricula and "notionalism". Continuous Formation nowadays demands for democratic teaching methods and inter-disciplinary as well as multi-disciplinary approaches. Pupils should be trained to observation and reasoning, which means be trained to shift from the conception of "storage", to that of "change" into a new reality.

Continuous Formation does not consist in one specific type of Education such as Adult Education, Learning to read and write, Schooling. But it consists in a sum of elements from the above described types of Education.

Continuous Formation is to be found in the relationship between the various educational systems: between studying and working, education and society. It stimulates a different conception of life, seen as a continuous vertically - oriented in-depth investigation, aiming at perfection. Therefore it can no longer be considered as a sort of Education confined to childhood or adolescence, but as a permanent process. Continuous Education also promotes an upwards directed educational policy; in fact it is not just a privilege for a restricted elite, but part of the rights of every citizen.

"Vertical" dimension is a "quality" dimension expressed in the process of free conquest of individual freedom. "Quantity" is the "horizontal" dimension expressed within the ethical order (i.e. global desire of justice).

The re-proposition of the cultural component within Education is the big event in Continuous Formation. As Husserl (5) used to say, Education promotes a "new project of knowledge".

The cultural component within Continuous Formation implies a rediscovery of the cultural implications in everyday working activity and in the effort required by studying hard. The cultural component, as a specific target in man's evolution is part of Adult Education as rational intentionality; it is part of the process of learning to read and write as pure intentionality, and part of leisure time as pure intention, or creative intention.

Continuous Education therefore shows the path to follow: a dynamic revision not only of man, but also of society.

Continuous Formation, together with its operational implications (the process of Learning to read and write, Adult Education, and Schooling), are not free from the need of self-determining, when confronted with the antinomy Reality-Education. The process goes through various stages highlighting the following recurring basic principles shared by each faculty, including Continuous Formation: consciousness of the environment, participation, and research.

2. The process of learning to read and write as consciousness of one's own environment

A new birth implies the creation of a new environment. A progressive knowledge of his/her own environment by the newly born human being gradually guides him/her towards knowledge and consciousness. Being conscious of the environment is a gradual conquest of one's own "self". After establishing the initial relationships out of the vague picture of a surrounding environment, the baby learns to distinguish objects, human faces, sounds, colors, movements, and language.

Throughout the years the child will learn a second language: written language, and will be able to transmit thought.

The kernel of education consists in the child's patient effort to record life, to reproduce events, thoughts, images, feelings of his/her human experience through symbols and gestures.

The relationship between conscience and environment consists of three basic processes.

First comes the consciousness of environment induced through education, as already stated above. The subject through a confused static acceptance, eventually gets to a dynamic acquisition of the environment.

Follows the recognition of the other human beings within the environment: in other words the subject gradually acquires cognition of the external reality, and he/she will go from recognition to critical verification and evaluation of the outer world.

Finally, a process is created through personal involvement of the subject as well as of many other subjects operating in the environment and of the environment itself. This process aims at breaking with the traditional illiterate environment through creation of a new environment, where the subject can freely act and have time to think.

3. Adult education as relationship

Relationship is made possible by the existence of many thinking subjects operating in a common environment. Education is therefore a "relationship" among all existing cultural and social implications.

Relationship is based on language, dialogue, participation. Dialogue is first of all inner, then inter-individual: the final "dialogue with reality" implies the capacity to share a common substratum with all other individuals. The environment may be thought of as a substratum. We all live within the environment, each of us with his own personality. Since it is our own environment, it will later be assumed into our consciousness. Day after day, our personal experience realizes itself within this consciousness of the environment.

In the educational process carried out apart from schooling as well as in traditional School Education the teacher's availability to dialogue with pupils crucial. While reasoning, the difference between teachers and pupils is often removed. As regards Adult Education, everybody can take the role of teachers, provided that he/she assumes full responsibilities for his/her choice.

As regards Adult Education, the type of participation is crucial. We agree with Meister's classification (8), and report it as follows:

a) actual participation (family, religion, neighbourhood)

b) spontaneous participation (freeing of the fancy-creative element)

c) voluntary participation (cultural, political associations, and Unions)

d) promoted participation (by public administration).

4. Schooling as research

In Continuous Formation, research is a particular method to face cultural problems from the point of view of the above stated environment conscience, and of the relationship between participation and management.

Research consisting in the everyday effort of learning, the patient desire to learn, to observe and to start anew from the beginning -whenever necessary- appears to be the method featuring Continuous Formation.

The objective of Continuous Formation through research is getting to success. However, a possible failure must be taken into account. Doubting is a basic characteristic of the difficult art of teaching.

Different questions come to our mind: What shall we teach? How have we got to teach it? Which is the objective of research in Continuous Formation? Free thinking, critical skills, development of personal opinions. But the major trends within Continuous Formation are: the Right to Study, the recognition of experience as knowledge, the equivalence between manual labour and intellectual activities.

5. Objectives of Continuous Formations

Traditionally, education could not be acquired unless during a limited period of time comprising childhood and adolescence. Nowadays, it tends to be a continuous process throughout each individual's life - or it wouldn't answer the urgent needs of both people and society.

Education cannot ignore social changes such as the increased length of human life, social and demographic modifications, scientific progress. Continuous changes in private and in public life oblige the individuals to adjust to them. Man faces increasingly numerous different responsibilities needing a Continuous Formation process, which is a special kind of education allowing the individuals to participate actively in social life.

Continuous formation is based on different methods. Traditional Education, Schooling, Experimentation, Practical Formation, Team Groups, Mass Media, Physical Education, Sport.
At the same time, the content of Continuous Education is rapidly expanding not just within a specific school area, but rather as an activity affecting different sectors of life.

The increase of leisure time in adulthood, for example, helps carry on the process of education and renders it specially necessary - if we correctly perceive the meaning of leisure time. Schooling and life are to be considered a whole and complementary contribution to Education.

Schooling and the Educational Process which is carried out outside Schooling (children, adolescents, adults) cannot be independently conceived as separated.

Education during childhood, for example, is not concluded with the achievement of a "diploma", but it should be carried on throughout one's life.

6. Proposals for Continuous Formation

The true global dimension of Continuous Formation comprises formal and informal education.

They both contribute to a new conception of Education, made up of different components such as politics, economics, society, which were not considered relevant by Traditional Education.

B. Schwartz (11) (Strasbourg 1970) maintains that first of all the youth should be taught to exploit the educational means outside the School. They should be educated to continue their formation by themselves, when they reach adulthood.

As a first thing, teaching should be varied: it should be made up of lectures, followed by a period of training to discussion, a period of time devoted to critic, and eventually a period in which the students learn to work on their own or in groups.

Then, the teacher must motivate the students as much as possible, explaining them that Education is useful to face everyday situations. But, still more important is the possibility to establish a tight correlation between what is taught and what is needed in real life, in absence of which the student feels frustrated.

As regards the methods to follow, Schwartz maintains that Audiovisual Aids and Conferences are the most useful means to "inform" and to promote discussion.

H. Jeanne (3) in her work "L'Education permanente facteur de mutation" is conscious that the structure of Adult Education, its methods need and imply an important change in current school strategies. We will observe on inversion of trend. School strategies will -from now on- influence Adult Education.

Jeanne (3) proposes a new educational strategy based on various independent levels, irrespective of the pupils' age. This strategy is based on the end of traditional Education and of the empiric diffusion of knowledge. Jeanne (3) maintains the need for a democratic approach.

Bonacina (1) in his "Project '80" summarizes his opinion in the three following points:

1. extension of education to the whole population through a pluralistic educational system.
2. creation of a system of communication, information, and of creative and critical participation within any single social situation.
3. promotion of an autonomous cultural development.

The philosophy of "Project '80" in Bonacina's opinion, should stick to the following principles:

a) Extension of the educational activity to the whole population through an everlasting Continuous Formation process.
b) Educational Activity promoting the capacity of communicating, of learning, of critically participating to social reality, apart from any form of authoritarianism.
c) Autonomous cultural development in the field of research on sport and recreational activities.

7. Teacher Formation

Two introductory notes should be forwarded before dealing with Teacher Formation.

The first is a socio-political note. Nowadays, we are going through a period of deep changes. From a model of "advanced industrial society", the society shifted into a "post-industrial" society. The passage was so swift that no adequate cultural or scientific remark on the event was possible until present.

The characteristics of the advanced industrial model were based on objectives and goals until present officially considered valid, though actually inadequate. The objectives of formation have deeply changed from an educational viewpoint.

The basic educational system, in charge of providing pupils with the necessary capacities, skills and qualifications to find a job was once Schooling.

Each individual's total amount of time in the mid-sixties was divided into work, study, and leisure.

During the sixties, society can be depicted as a Church with three naves: work, study, and leisure. Then, the Technological and Economic Progress built up the "Post-Industrial" Society.

The criteria and values of the new society have deeply changed. But also the use of leisure time is different. The role of Education was deeply modified. Such is the big crisis we are facing now not only in Italy, but also all over Europe.

Nowadays, in Europe and particularly in Italy, School is no longer what it was in the mid-sixties.

The Teacher Formation system can be easily summarized into two major trends:

1. The public trend providing a scholastic formation and only a limited amount of correlated activities apart from schooling.
2. The private trend consisting of a minimum amount of scholastic formation and a lot of complementary activities.

Needless to say that in the last ten years, teachers educated within the private system had a higher chance to find a job.

In the post-modern society the Government crisis is evident. Such crisis is a threat against political, economical, cultural and social cohesion in our Country. The role of Government is doubtless weaker, to the advantage of different private as well as public institutions controlling and managing what should be administered by a Central Power. All this affects the problem of teacher formation and of refresher courses.

Right now, a teacher is a person looking for his/her own cultural, professional, and ethic and social identity.

He/she is a cultural operator trained to perceive dangers, above all that coming from television and video-culture; suffering the influence of family crisis and of father-mother as well as son-daughter relationship.

Family crisis on one side, remake of the formative principles on the other; massive pervasiveness of TV and video culture are causing not just a big problem at an updating level, but deep confusion as far as the change of the educator's professional and cultural identity is concerned. The new educator is a cultural operator very much alike a freelance engineer. He is no longer teaching how to speak and write. He is someone capable of planning curricula, evaluating tests and - above all - producing results ready for further social appreciation.

The educator is no longer just a lecturer. He is also capable of spotting the right objectives, finding out the right tools, and judging results.

8. Role of the Physical Education Teacher

We'll now say something about the P.Ed. Teacher, taking for granted all philosophical, cultural and didactical debates splitting opinions over the last 50 years.

We are therefore not going to speak about the philosophy of sport, but rather about the P. Ed. teacher's role, as related to the other teachers'.

I think that a P.Ed. teacher's specific role is to be identified in his/her "bodiness", that is self-respect and self-estimation, evaluation of his/her own integrity, as related to post-industrial society.

Post-modern society is based on show. There's no longer culture as such; there exist cultural shows: there's no longer sport as a competitive or non--competitive activity, but sponsored sport shows are telecast on world-diffusion programs. There are no longer sportsmen, but a cult exists which could be defined as "neo-pagan body cult" based on aesthetic surgery, on one's appearance, on one's commercial look.

By means of virtual images (our future reality), man is able to materialize his own thoughts onto a screen through an expert system and to build his own historical reality.

He is no longer the one who acts, but according to present models, he need only have a pleasant appearance (possibly obtained by means of aesthetic surgery or cosmetics). The goal is to improve his/her appearance on the occasion of a TV telecast.

"Bodiness" is now at risk of becoming a virtual information. It took 250 years of fights to solve the antinomy between body and soul. Now that we conquered the right, the role, the dignity of bodiness, we are at risk of losing that right again. In fact, it is no longer a person made of flesh and bones what we are watching, but a telecast image manipulated by telematics and video culture.

Such is the defy, throughout the nineties, by the P.Ed. Teachers who wish to renew their role, their content, their professional task in order to regain bodiness and therefore to rescue their existence.

Educators must strive to reach three objectives:

1) defending the dignity and the importance of their job;
2) get used to team-work to pass individualism;
3) operate a cultural revolution to assess man's crucial importance as related to structures and processes.

References

1. **Bonacina, F.**, Educazione Permanente, Strasburg, Conseil de l'Europe, 1970.

2. **Claparede, A.**, L'education fonctionelle, II ed, Neuchatel, 1946.

3. **Jeanne, H.**, L'éducation permanente, facteur de mutation in Education permanente, Strasbourg, Conseil de l'Europe, 1970.

4. **Hely, A.S.M.**, Tendenze nell'educazione degli adulti, Roma, Armando, 1966.

5. **Husserl, E.**, Idee per una fenomenologia pura, trad. di Alliney, Torino, 1960.

6. **Lefebvre, H.**, Au delà du structuralisme, Paris, Editions Anthropos, 1971.

7. **Mchale, J.**, The Future of the Future, New York, 1965.

8. **Meister, A.**, Alphabétisation et development, Paris, Editions Anthropos, 1973.

9. **Myrdal, G.**, An Intenational Economy, London, Routledge & Kean Paul Ltd., 1956.

10. **Schiller, F.**, Lettere sull'educazione estetica dell'uomo, Firenze, La Nuova Italia, 1970.

11. **Schwartz, B.**, Réflexions prospectives sur l'education permanente, Strasbourg, Conseil de l'Europe, 1970.

A Critical Review of Competing PE Concepts

Crum, B.
Institute for Social Research, Tilburg University
The Netherlands

1. Introduction

Since the eighties the education systems in most European countries have to cope with serious problems. The combination of economical scarcity and a decline of respect for schooling in general and the teaching profession in particular, resulted in a lower priority for education and consequently in serious cuts in the educational budgets. The retrenchments on the one hand and the emergence of new school subjects (e.g. computer science) on the other, led to renewed discussions about the desirable content of the core curriculum. "Back to basics" became a widely heard slogan. Subjects, which had traditionally an accepted position in the core curriculum, are now questioned as to their continuing relevance.

One of the traditional school subjects now under pressure is physical education. Some educational experts don't consider physical education any longer as one of the basics of general education. They believe, that what is done by school physical education could better be left to other agencies (e.g. sport clubs). Moreover, politicians, public opinion and educational authorities increasingly display scepsis about the outcomes of physical education (PE).

The PE profession should not remain passive in the face of this criticism and scepticism. First, it is necessary to fight against misconceptions that mislead the authorities in their judgments on the importance of PE and then convincing arguments should be put on the table to underline the extraordinary relevance of good movement and sport education in 21rst century schools. However, it is at least equally important to look at home for the cause of the attacks on the position of PE; that means: to be self-critical. In doing so it might become evident that the profession has also to blame itself for the public scepticism and criticism. To blame itself, because of the conceptual confusion that still ravages PE teacher education as well as PE curricula and PE practices. To blame itself, also because of the striking discrepancies between the rhetoric about PE objectives on the one hand and the disappointing practical output on the other.

I do emphasize that there is a conceptual confusion in the PE profession, because I believe that this confusion -- and in particular the ongoing influence of two well-known, traditional PE ideologies -- plays an important role in the 'self reproducing failing of PE' (see Crum, 1990, 1993b). It seems to me that there is no other subject with more conceptional disagreement and confusion than PE. The history of PE is characterized by a continuing external struggle for recognition as well as by a continuing internal competition between different PE concepts. Therefore, a critical review of competing PE concepts could be an important step in a process of self-criticism.

In a first section, I will deal with two preliminary questions, namely (a) What is meant by 'PE concept'?, and (b) What are the functions of a PE concept?. Then, I will develop my classification of competing PE concepts. Finally, I will critically review the distinguished concepts.

2. What is meant by 'PE concept' and what are its functions?

From professional PE teachers it should be expected, that they deal rationally and methodically with the alternatives for the arrangement of their classes. The questions they are confronted with, can be reduced to four main categories, namely:

- The justification-question: why should PE be a part of the core curriculum of a school?
- The objectives-question: which aims should be realized in PE?
- The methods-question: how should PE classes be arranged to realize the chosen objectives?
- The evaluation-question: how can the quality of the given PE classes be assessed?

These four questions and the given answers should be seen as interrelated. The answer to the justification-question should have direct implications for the answer to the objectives-question. Then, the choice for a particular set of objectives should have clear consequences for the answers to the methods-question. Finally, the answers to the evaluation-question should be affected by the views referring to the justification issue and the decisions on objectives and methods.

The intended connection is not automatically accomplished. Therefore it is needed that the reflection on PE as a school subject, on planning decisions, the interaction with students and the evaluation work are guided by a clear frame of reference. Such a frame can be called 'a PE concept'. Thus, the term 'PE concept' refers to the more or less coherent set of views concerning the identity and function of PE as a school subject. As such a PE concept is an abstract construct. It is a reconstruction of the thinking which can be deduced from the practical professional speaking and acting of a physical educator or a construct that is designed in the strict theoretical reasoning of a scholar. A PE concept, that is expressed in the professional speaking and acting of a practitioner, is a 'spoken or lived concept'. In contrast, the PE concept of a theoretician, that is designed as a prescription of the desired identity and function of PE, is a 'discursive concept'. It might be evident, that a discursive PE concept has an idealtypical character and can be expected to be a coherent and consistent set of thoughts. On the contrary, a spoken or lived PE concept often tends to express a mixture of prejudices, experiential rules and theoretical elements. I emphasize that this paper deals only with idealtypical, discursive PE concepts.

A coherent and consistent PE concept can fulfil at least four functions: (1) a justification function, (2) a heuristic function, (3) an innovative function, and (4) an instrumental function. I will present a brief explanation per function.

A society in continuous change leads to changes in the task of the school. Therefore, a particular school subject cannot claim eternal life. Again and again a subject can be asked to justify its position in the curriculum. In the past 10 years PE is put into that position in a number of European countries. A plausible and convincing justification of PE in the schools of today and tomorrow is only possible on the basis of a well-founded PE concept.

A PE concept is a heuristic device. As such it can function as a 'map' that leads, for example, a process of curriculum development into the right direction. It has steering power, because it puts basic criteria at the disposal of the deciders.

Because society and culture are in continuous change and because students of tomorrow are different from those of the present, innovation of PE is again and again required. A clear PE concept shows the way on the slippery innovation path, it helps to separate the wheat from the chaff in the trendy innovation proposals.

Finally, a PE concept can function as a support instrument for the daily planning of the PE classes. If things go alright at school level, the daily work is guided by a workplan, and this plan is based on an explicit PE concept.

The foregoing refers mainly to the function of a PE concept for curriculum development and daily practice. However, PE concepts also play a role in PE teacher education and in research on teaching PE. A few words concerning the relation between a PE concept and research on teaching PE are in place, because this relation is rather tricky. At first sight one might think, that there is a simple, direct, one-way line from didactical research, through theory formation, toward the formation and evaluation of a PE concept. However, it is not that simple. The relation is more complex, because empirical research on PE teaching itself already starts from assumptions about the identity and the function of PE. Researchers are prejudice-ridden, although they are not always conscious of their tacit PE concepts. Their concepts, tacit or explicit, affect the research questions as well as the design of the research. So, the relation between a PE concept and PE research is reciprocal. At the one hand research can be directed to testing the empirical tenability of a PE concept, while at the other hand such research always starts from a tacit or explicit PE concept.

Figure 1 shows the central function of a PE concept for curriculum and practice, teacher education and research, as well as the connections between research, teacher education and school practice (Crum, 1993a).

Fig. 1: The central role of PE concept and the connections between research, teacher education and curriculum and school practice.

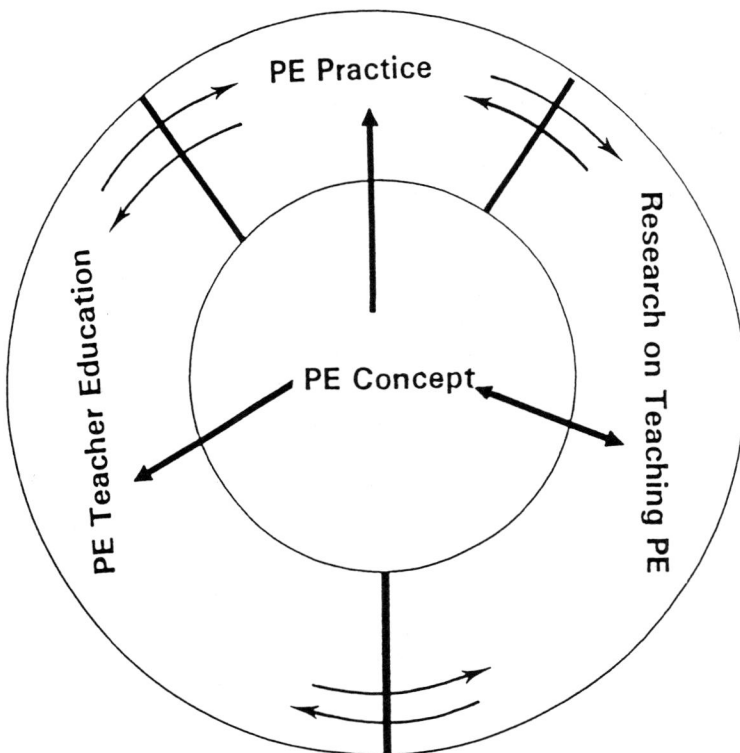

3. A classification of competing P.E. concepts

Now, I come to my classification of existing PE concepts, in particular PE curriculum concepts (cp. Crum, 1991, 1992). I start from the assumption, that decisions concerning the school curriculum in general are largely based on value-bound views concerning:

(a) children and their potential and desirable development,

(b) the social-cultural state of affairs and the expected, respectively desired changes in the social-cultural context;

(c) the task of the school; and finally

(d) considerations concerning the connections between (a), (b), and (c).

This assumption can be specified for each particular school subject. A specification of this assumption for PE leads to the thesis, that PE ideologies can be characterized by their implicit and/or explicit assumptions and beliefs concerning (1) corporality and human movement; (2) movement culture; and (3) physical education as a school subject. Education is a normative problem and so are decisions concerning the content of a curriculum. Since value judgments differ and since views on mankind, society and the school as an institution differ, curricula will differ. My starting point is schematically represented in figure 2.

Fig. 2: the relationship between fundamental views and curriculum decisions

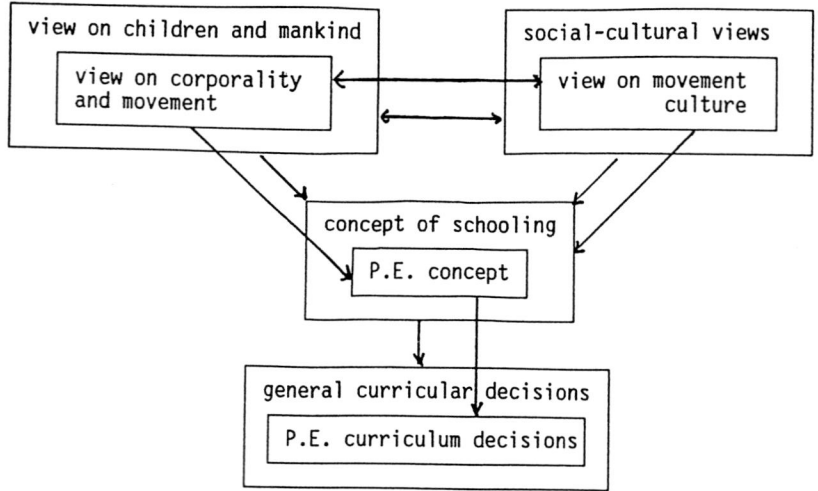

In the upper right box of the scheme, you read the term "movement culture". This is a literal translation of the Dutch term "bewegingscultuur" (in German: "Bewegungskultur"). In the Netherlands as well as in Germany this term is generally accepted as useful. However, the term is rather uncommon for English speaking people. Since the term will regularly be used in my explanations, I better try to explain what is meant with "movement culture" before I continue.

The term "movement culture" refers to the way particular groups of people deal with their corporality and the desire or need to move, apart from the moving behaviour that is necessary in the frame of labor and life maintenance. So "movement culture" contains the collection of movement behaviour phenomena in the context of leisure. The term tries to express the same idea as terms such as "eating culture" or "housing culture". These terms refer to the way particular groups deal with a well defined problem and their potential for acting. "Movement cultures" are man-made and changeable. They vary dependent on time and place. For example, in the movement culture of the fifties windsurfing and jogging were unknown elements. While skiing and mountaineering are important elements in the Swiss and Austrian movement culture, they are less important in the Dutch.

Contemporary movement cultures are rather complex and different. However, due to the mediatization of our societies (think e.g. of the influence of Eurosport) they grow towards one another. Since the beginning of the 20th century competitive sport has formed an important and powerful element of the movement culture of the Western world, but under influence of the 'sport for all' idea other elements have emerged. Think e.g. of: disco-dancing, jogging, playing ballgames in the street, exercising in a fitness centre, adventure sports such as hang-gliding and rafting, recreational play and sport, Tae-kwon-do etc..

Now back to the scheme. Against the background of the scheme, I put the following two questions when examining physical education ideologies and the related curriculum documents:

1. What are the tacit or explicit views on (a) corporality and movement, (b) movement culture, and (c) PE as a school subject, which form the conceptual basis?
2. Is the perspective of the upper left box or the perspective of the upper right box dominating? In other words: are the considerations concerning "personal development" more important than the considerations concerning "social-cultural goals" or is it the other way around?

On the base of the second question, I initially distinguish three PE curriculum orientations which are mainly based on assumptions concerning the upper left box, largely neglecting the perspective of the upper right box and one orientation, which is mainly based on assumptions concerning the upper right box. Finally I identify a fifth orientation in which a balance is strived for between the upper left and the upper right approach.

These five PE curriculum orientations can be labeled as follows (Crum, 1991, 1992):

1. the biologically oriented training-of-the-physical concept;
2. the pedagologistic ('bildungs'theoretical) education-through-movement concept;
3. the personalist movement education concept;
4. the conformist sport socialization concept;
5. the critical-constructive movement socialization concept.

4. The biologically oriented training-of-the-physical concept

The biologistic PE concept has its origin in the system of the Swedish gymnastics. Per Henrik Ling viewed the development of the body-instrument by means of well-chosen movements as the objective of his system of "Swedish gymnastics". In the beginning of the century, this system took roots in Europe as well as in North America. Of course under influence of changing scientific insights and also due to developments in the panorama of diseases, the original ideas were adapted now and then. However, the basic idea remained the same.

This basic idea has its roots in the view that the human body is a machine, an instrument, and that movements can improve the quality of that instrument. PE is especially seen as important, because the social context contains all kinds of threats to the development of a well-functioning body-machine. Think of tuberculosis in former days and of obesitas and coronary diseases in modern times. The theoretical frame of reference of this concept is found in the medical-biological disciplines, which are more or less characterized by mechanical and physical reductionism. Considerations concerning movement (sports) as a social-cultural domain hardly play a role in this conceptual model. The main principle of the concept is implied in the insight, that the human body develops the more it is charged by physical exertion; if human beings don't exercise or exercise too less, disturbances of organic development and decline of organic capacity are the result. Due to the increase of coronary diseases and the new healthism, there is in many countries an obvious revival of this way of thinking.

Curricula, which are constructed in the line of this concept, have the following characteristics:

* The objectives are formulated in terms of effects of training of anatomical and physiological variables: improvement of flexibility, cardiovascular endurance, muscular power and muscular endurance.
* Content description is in terms of exercises for the improvement of flexibility, cardiovascular endurance and muscle power and endurance (The exercises are classified according to body-parts.
* Main methodological principles are: keep them busy with a high level of exertion and frequent repetitions of simple exercises.
* Pupil-tasks are formulated rather as training tasks (that are tasks directed to biological adaptation of the body-machine) than as learning tasks (that are tasks directed to enlargement of personal competence).
* Product evaluation by means of standardized fitness tests is emphasized.

In order to avoid misunderstandings, I point to the following. In some countries there is now a trend to construct curriculum elements directed to teaching and learning concerning the relationship between movement/exercise/sport and fitness/health. The idea is that by doing so, youngsters can acquire competencies in order to be self responsible for health-oriented exercise and sport. This trend is not rooted in the biologistic PE concept. It rather fits with the "critical-constructive movement socialization" concept.

To indicate the orientation toward PE teacher education of the concepts, I refer to a recent classification of conceptual orientations to generic teacher education of Feiman-Nemser (1990). This way the orientation of the "training-of-the-physical" concept should be labeled as 'academic' and 'technological'. That is to say that the emphasis in the program is on the biological disciplines and on the development of training effectiveness skills.

This concept induces a research orientation characterized by a technical knowledge-constitutive interest (see Habermas, 1968) and by questions and designs aimed at the development of a training technology.

5. The pedagologistic education-through-movement concept

The origins of this concept lie in the Philantropinism and GutsMuths' ideas on "Leibesübungen" and also in the so called "Austrian School of PE". In the German speaking regions this concept is labeled the "bildungstheoretische" concept.

The basic assumption is, that movement is an outstanding medium for exploration, communication and general personal development. While in the biologically oriented concept the "biological adaptation" function of movement is put in the centre, here the emphasis is on the "explorative" and "communicative" functions of movement. The "explorative" function refers to the datum, that especially young children make contact with and explore and enhance their world by moving and manipulating. The "communicative" function refers to the datum, that human beings can exchange messages and learn social roles by movement and play.

The advocates of this concept deeply believe that movement, play and sport have very special potentials for the cognitive, personal and social development of children. Therefore, they legitimate PE on the basis of its supposed potential for personal and social development. The main motto is not "learning to move" but "moving to learn".

This conceptual model also ignores explicit considerations concerning the movement culture. Personal and social development are viewed as timeless and contextless categories. This concept finds its main theoretical frames of reference in phenomenology, hermeneutic pedagogy and humanistic psychology.

The curricular consequences of this line of thinking are the following:

* Objectives are formulated in abstract terms of general personal development. Apart from the formation of movement and posture, the aims are: character building (will-power, perseverance, discipline), and social and aesthetic formation.
* Content description is in terms of the traditional catalogue of gymnastic, play, sport and dance. It is assumed that these activities as such - contain a rich educational potential.
* The main methodological principle is: organize these activities orderly and in good atmosphere. The idea of the so-called "functional formation" (funktionale Bildung) is rather influential. This idea says, that the desired pedagogical outcomes will be automatically produced by just arranging the movement activities of the traditional catalogue in a good and orderly atmosphere.
* Process evaluation, based on criteria such as order, atmosphere and child-orientation, is emphasized; there are no substantial directions for product evaluation.

The orientation to teacher education of this concept is 'practical'. This means that the emphasis is on traditional craft and that there is a strong reliance on a practice in which the teacher educators and the cooperating teachers are important role models.

The related knowledge-constitutive interest is also 'practical'. This concept induces hermeneutic and interpretive scholarly work, in particular on questions concerning basic assumptions, justification, objectives and content of PE.

6. The personalist movement education concept

Due to its pedagogical orientation this concept is related to the foregoing concept. However, there is an important difference. Here the justification of the subject is not derived from developmental aspects which have nothing directly to do with movement. The justification of PE is based on the idea, that the development of movement competence as such is an important datum in the development and the life of an individual. Hence, the essence of the subject is seen in the teaching and learning of movement as a personal way of being. Here the motto is not "moving to learn", but "learning to move".

Within the "personalist movement education" concept two variations should be distinguished. They differ in their view on human movement. One stream (the Anglo-Saxon "movement education" tradition according to the ideas of Laban) starts from a so-called substantial body concept (emphasizing the body as a substantial object) and a related biomechanical view on human movement. The other stream (the movement education concept that is influential in the Netherlands) starts from the assumption of a "relational" body concept (the body as a subject) and the idea that human movement should be interpreted as meaningful behaviour (cp. Gordijn, 1968; Tamboer, 1985, 1993).

This concept also emphasizes the personal development aspect. Here too, explicit considerations concerning the social-cultural aspects of movement and sport are lacking. The theoretical frames of reference are: phenomenology, hermeneutic pedagogy, humanistic psychology and general teaching theory.

This concept leads to the following curricular consequences:

* The objectives are formulated in terms of the realization of a personal movement competence and identity.
* The content description depends on the chosen movement concept. In the Anglo-Saxon "movement education" tradition the content is organized on the basis of the idea that movement can be viewed as transposition in time and space of the body or bodyparts. This results in a content catalogue that looks like a grammar of body-movements. In the continental movement education tradition by contrast, the content is organized in movement themes based on the meanings that can be realized in movement acts.
* Important methodological principles are: orientation to the individuality of the student and guided discovery.
* Process evaluation is dominant.

With reference to Feiman-Nemser's classification, here the orientation to teacher education can be labeled as 'personal'. The emphasis is on an individualized, personal-meaning based orientation to growth as a teacher.

The research orientation of this concept is more or less the same as that of the 'pedagologistic' concept: a 'practical' knowledge-constitutive interest, hermeneutic and interpretive studies directed to clarification of assumptions, objectives and content.

7. The conformist sport socialization concept

This concept can largely be seen as a reaction to the vagueness and the "stratospheric thinking" of the "education-through-movement" concept. The excessive and abstract effect claims of the latter were for many in the profession implausible and impracticable and evoked the need of a more realistic concept. Two factors played a stimulating role in the development of a new concept. First, the emergence of a society-oriented general curriculum theory and second, the growing power of organized, competitive sports as a social system. They led to a concept that in German speaking regions has been labeled as the "Didaktik der reduzierten Ansprüche" (the didactics of reduced pretentions) (Kurz, 1977).

Advocates of this concept start from the following basic ideas:

(a) the school is pre-eminently an agency for the transference of cultural techniques; and
(b) organized sport is a relevant and important social-cultural domain and youngsters should be introduced in the values, rules and techniques of that domain.

This concept shows an obvious dominance of the social perspective. However, the view of the social reality is uncritical. The dominance of competitive sport and its elite and selective character are taken for granted. There is a clear orientation towards the status quo. The conformist concept is characterized by a no-nonsense style. The emphasis is rather on 'socialisation into sport' than on 'socialisation through sport'.

There are no explicit considerations concerning individuality and everybody's right to develop a personal identity. The learning individual is merely seen as a role-taker and the role-making aspect is denied. The theoretical frames of reference for this concept are functional sociology, kinesiology, behavioral analysis and general teaching theory.

The curricular reflection of this concept has the following characteristics:

* The objectives are formulated in terms of physical fitness and technical and tactical capabilities needed for participation in the well-known sport disciplines.

*   The content description is organized according to the techniques and tactics of the most popular forms of sport.
*   The main methodological principles are teacher orientation, efficiency and control.
*   Product evaluation is emphasized and done by means of testing of well-defined sportskills, tactical control and knowledge of official rules.

The orientation to teacher education of this concept is 'academic' (emphasis on subject matter knowledge such as kinesiology, motor learning theory and sportpsychology), 'technological' (emphasis on teacher effectiveness skills) and also 'practical' (emphasis of own sport skills of the teacher students).

This concept induces a 'technical' knowledge-constitutive interest and empirical-analytical process-product research.

8. The critical-constructive movement socialization concept

This concept has in common with the conformist sport socialization concept, that it also stems from scepticism concerning the plausibility of traditional PE legitimations and the connected objectives. The question about PE's utility value is here also a starting point. The basic ideas, however, are different. They are:

(a) the school is not only an agency for cultural adaptation, but also for cultural innovation;
(b) participation in movement culture according to personal possibilities and needs is an important factor for the quality of daily life;
(c) competitive sport is only one mode of movement culture and the dominance of this mode should be criticized because of its selective and excluding traits;
(d) the uniqueness of an individual should be acknowledged; the learning individual is not only viewed as a role-taker but also as a role-maker.

This way of thinking displays a search for balance between the individual and the social-cultural perspective. Theoretical frames of reference are symbolic interactionism, critical theory, humanistic psychology, cognitive psychology and general teaching theory.

This concept results in curricula with the following traits:

*   The objectives are formulated in terms of the techno-motor, socio-motor, and reflective competences, that are needed for a personal and social satisfying, life-long participation in movement culture (also with regard of the individual responsibility for physical fitness and health).

* The content is thematically organized. A movement activity (e.g. a particular sport) is developed from different viewpoints as a theme of teaching and learning.
* The main methodological principles are: thematic and methodological openness, pupil orientation and problem orientation.
* Process as well as product evaluation is seen as important; the latter is done according to individual standards.

The orientation to teacher education can be labeled as critical/social. The emphasis is on PE as a moral obligation to pupils and society, on the context of PE and on issues such as inclusion and equity. "Learning to reflect" (see Crum, 1993c) is seen as a basic principle of the PETE program. Learning to reflect on ethical, social and political issues related to PE, on values and objectives, on assumptions and consequences of the teaching act and on analysis and evaluation of the teaching.

This concept leads to a 'critical' knowledge-constitutive interest. The research induced by this concept leans on critical theory and on cognitive theory. The research can be empirical-analytical as well as naturalistic, process-product research as well as research on teacher socialization and teacher thinking.

9. A critical review of the first four concepts

I start with a longer critical comment on the two concepts, that have been and partly still are the most influential in the tradition of our profession, namely (a) the biologistic "training-of-the-physical" concept, and (b) the pedagogistic "education-through-movement" concept.

That the training-of-the-physical concept is still very influential, appears from the formulations of many contemporary national PE curriculum documents. Often "taking care of the physical development and fitness" is stated to be the main goal of PE. If this is documented in offical curricula, it is not surprising that the "training-of-the-physical" concept gets shape in daily practice at schools. Physical educators, who conceive their job according to this ideology, strive for classes with a high activity level. Therefore -as I mentioned before- they look for exercises which are well-known to the students and can easily be repeated. In conducting their classes, they build on rules of thumb as: "to keep them busy", "to make them sweat", "to tire them out". If they attach importance to systematic evaluation and can find time for it, they use standardized fitness tests in order to assess the outcomes of their work. In doing so they profile themselves rather as fitness trainers than as teachers. They act as fitness engineers, handling their students like car mechanics handle the bodies and engines of cars.

This view has put our profession off the scent and has led physical educators into a cul-de-sac. I have two arguments for this contention. The first argument is based on motives of principle. The first starting point is, that the school is an institutionalized agency designed to produce important, lasting changes in competence repertoires of youngsters in order to prepare them for participation in culture. The second assumption is, that teachers are hired to teach children the knowledge and skills, which enable them to participate in society as productive, responsible and healthy members. Given these basic assumptions, it is difficult to see how a process, that only aims at direct improvement of physical fitness, can be regarded as an educational process. A PE program that is designed in order to train the body-machine is a corpus alienum amidst the teaching and learning oriented school subjects. As a consequence it runs the serious risk of being rejected. Not everybody will be convinced by this fundamental consideration concerning the essentials of educational work. If one starts from another assumption concerning the essentials thereof, the argument can be put aside.

The second argument is a very pragmatic one and cannot easily be ignored. It focuses on the question, whether the objectives that are stated according to the "training-of-the-physical" concept are realistic. Thanks to research done in the domain of exercise physiology we know now, that the traditional claims about the fitness outcomes of physical education programs cannot be substantiated. Moreover we are able to explain, why this is so. In this respect two points are of decisive importance. First of all, exercise physiology informed us about the requirements to which a program has to come up with in order to develop respiratory and cardio-vascular efficiency, muscular strength and endurance and flexibility. An experienced and well organizing physical educator needs at least 3 times a week 30 minutes for the execution of such a training program. Moreover, in order to estimate the real value of such a program, the effects of the holiday-breaks and the fact that a class consists of kids with rather different initial fitness levels should be taken into consideration.

These problems lead to the following conclusion. Given the requirements for a program effectively aiming at improvement of physical fitness on the one hand, and the total set of PE objectives, the number and the heterogeneity of the students in a class, the number of classes a week and the holiday-breaks on the other hand, it is evidently unrealistic to assume that PE programs can substantially contribute to direct improvement of the fitness of school children (see e.g. Klausen/Rasmussen, 1983; Verschuur, 1987, 191).

I summarize the considerations referring to the question, whether the claims of the "training-of-the-physical" concept are realistic, by means of a metaphor:

a physical educator who believes that PE can produce substantial fitness effects, can be compared with a person who expects to see more in broad daylight with the help of a pocket-torch.

After this indictment against the biologistic concept, I can be shorter concerning the "pedagologistic education-through-movement" concept. The pocket-torch metaphor also fits with regard to this concept. For it cannot be seen how the timely restricted experiences in PE classes could have a substantial impact on cognitive, emotional, social, aesthetic or character development compared to the amount and intensity of experiences that are collected in interactions with peers and family members. I think that these pretentious claims can only be understood as classical attempts to gain a respected position as a school subject. As a starting point for the design and execution of PE programs they are as deceptive as the fitness claim of the "training-of-the-physical" concept.

First and foremost, the two ideologies are essentially different in their fundamental assumptions concerning the body, movement, children and education. However, they display also noticeable similarities. The following points are noteworthy:

* Both concepts are based on a mind-body dualism.
* In both concepts movement is seen rather as the mean than as the object of the intervention act. In the first case, movement is seen as a mean for body building and body shaping; in the second case, movement is seen as a mean for character building and personality shaping.
* In both concepts the idea of compensation is predominant. In the first case, compensation of the lack of physical activity in everyday school life; in the second case, compensation of the lack of "real education" in the other school subjects.
* Both concepts are constructed during PE's struggle for public recognition. As such both are characterized by strong rhetoric and pretentious claims for outcomes. Even though evidence now shows that these claims cannot be substantiated under school conditions, the PE profession returns to fitness and character building whenever called on the carpet by public opinion (paraphrasing Siedentop, 1983, p. 39).
* And last, but not least, both concepts induce non-teaching PE practices. The biologistic ideology leads to PE as fitness training. The pedagologistic ideology, with its abstract objectives and vague practical indications and its idea of "functional formation", easily seduces physical educators into thinking, that it is merely their task to arrange classes that have the character of supervised recess or entertainment.

It is high time for the physical education profession to distance itself from the "training-of-the-physical" and the "education-through-the-physical" myths.

While the first two concepts easily lead to non-teaching practices, the remaining three concepts have in common that their practical consequence is "teaching" and hopefully also "learning". However, the three considerably differ concerning the question what should be learned and how the learning processes should be arranged.

The "personalist movement education" concept has the shortcoming that the definition of objectives is done without explicit reference to the social-cultural context and that consequently the choice of the learning content is done without explicitly taking into account what is going on in the actual movement culture. The development of a personal movement identity is so strongly emphasized, that cultural developments are largely neglected as points of reference. By doing so physical education runs the risk to become an isolated movement sanctuary which has little to do with the real world of movement/-exercise/sport outside the school.

The "conformist sport socialization" concept suffers from the opposite problem. Here the shortcoming is, that the existing sport reality is accepted as the only point of reference, that the teaching is only directed at transference of culture and not at culture innovation. Moreover, teaching practices according to this concept generally are teacher-oriented. Themes and methods are viewed as closed, and pupils are very much under teacher control and scarcely get opportunity to act in an independent and creative way.

The official PE curriculum documents almost never reflect just one of the reviewed concepts. Commonly they display a cocktail of some of the concepts; rather frequently a cocktail of elements of the "biologistic", the "pedagologistic" and the "conformist" concept (see Crum, 1991).

You will have noticed, that I'm not an adherent of one of the four reviewed concepts. I am a convinced advocate of the fifth concept, the one that is called "the critical-constructive movement socialization concept". I think that only this concept can offer a plausible justification of the relevance of PE in present and future schools, serve as a heuristic instrument for the development of useful curricula and as a basis for PE teacher education and research on teaching PE.

References:

1. **Crum B.J.:** The Self Reproducing Failing of Physical Education. In: Telama R. et al. (eds.), Physical Education and Life-Long Physical Activity, pp. 294-303. Jyväskylä, The Foundation for Promotion of Physical Culture and Health, 1990.

2. **Crum B.J.:** Physical Education as part of the core curriculum in secondary education; a limited, comparative international survey. Enschede, National Institute for Curriculum Development The Netherlands, 1991.

3. **Crum B.J.:** Idealtypische Konzepte von Sportunterricht - eine Klassifikation. Sportpädagogik 16: 2, 29-32, 1992.

4. **Crum B.J.:** Over vakconcepten - functies, wortels en classificaties. In: Rijsdorp K., Bonnier B. (eds.), Handboek Lichamelijke Opvoeding en Sportbegeleiding III. Deventer/Antwerpen, Van Loghum/Slaterus, 1993a.

5. **Crum B.J.:** Conventional Thought and Practice in Physical Education: Problems of Teaching and Implications for Change. Quest, 45, 3, 339-356, 1993b.

6. **Crum B.J.:** The urgent need for reflective teaching in PE. Keynote address to the AIESEP-seminar on 'The Training of Teachers in Reflective Practice of PE', Trois-Rivières, Québec, Canada, July 1993 (1993c).

7. **Feiman-Nemser S.:** Conceptual orientations in teacher education. East Lansing, MI, Michigan State University, National Center for Research on Teacher Education, 1990.

8. **Gordijn C.C.F.:** Inleiding tot het Bewegingsonderwijs. Baarn, Bosch & Keuning, 1968.

9. **Habermas J.:** Erkenntnis und Interesse. Frankfurt, Suhrkamp, 1968.

10. **Klausen K., Rasmussen B.:** Effect of Five Physical Eduation Lessons a Week on some Anthropometric and Physiological Variables in School Children. In: Telema R. (ed.) Research in School Physical Education. Jyväskylä, 1983.

11. **Kurz D.:** Elemente des Schulsports. Schorndorf, Hofmann, 1977.

12. Siedentop D.: Physical Education: introductory analysis. Dubuque, Brown, 1983.

13. Tamboer J.W.I.: Mensbeelden achter Bewegingsbeelden. Haarlem, De Vrieseborch, 1985.

14. Tamboer J.W.I.: Sport and Motor Actions. Journal of the Philosophy of Sport (in print), 1993.

15. Verschuur R.: Daily physical activity and health; Longitudinal changes during the teenage period. Haarlem, De Vrieseborch, 1987.

Unemployment and Occupational Opportunities

Dietrich, K.
Fachbereich Sportwissenschaft, Universität Hamburg
Germany

1. Introduction

Beginning in the 1970s throughout Western Europe there were big social problems. Physical education teachers could not get positions in schools after their university studies. The rising number of teachers training students on one side and the diminishing number of school pupils on the other side produced more and more unemployed teachers.

This development took place in all subjects of our public schools and also in physical education.

In the first part of my report I will speak about an investigation, that analysed the problems of examined P.E. teachers. The empirical study about unemployment and occupational opportunities will give us an impression about the situation in 1985.

In the second part of my report I will try to characterise the job market in the field of sport and describe the changing situation of the qualification system.

2. What jobs are found by unemployed P.E. teachers ?

In the investigation in 1985 (Dietrich/Heinemann/Schubert 1990) we made the attempt, to answer the following questions:

- What jobs are found by unemployed P.E. teachers?
- Of what value are their university qualifications?
- What sportrelated jobs are offered on the job market?
- What grade of professionalisation can be identified?

In a questionnaire we asked 1350 just examined P.E.-teachers about their occupations. What we didn't expect was, that less than 10% declared to be unemployed. But it is not true to say that all the others would have a full-time job. Between the situation of employment and unemployment we can find a wide range of occupations and of possibilities to earn money.

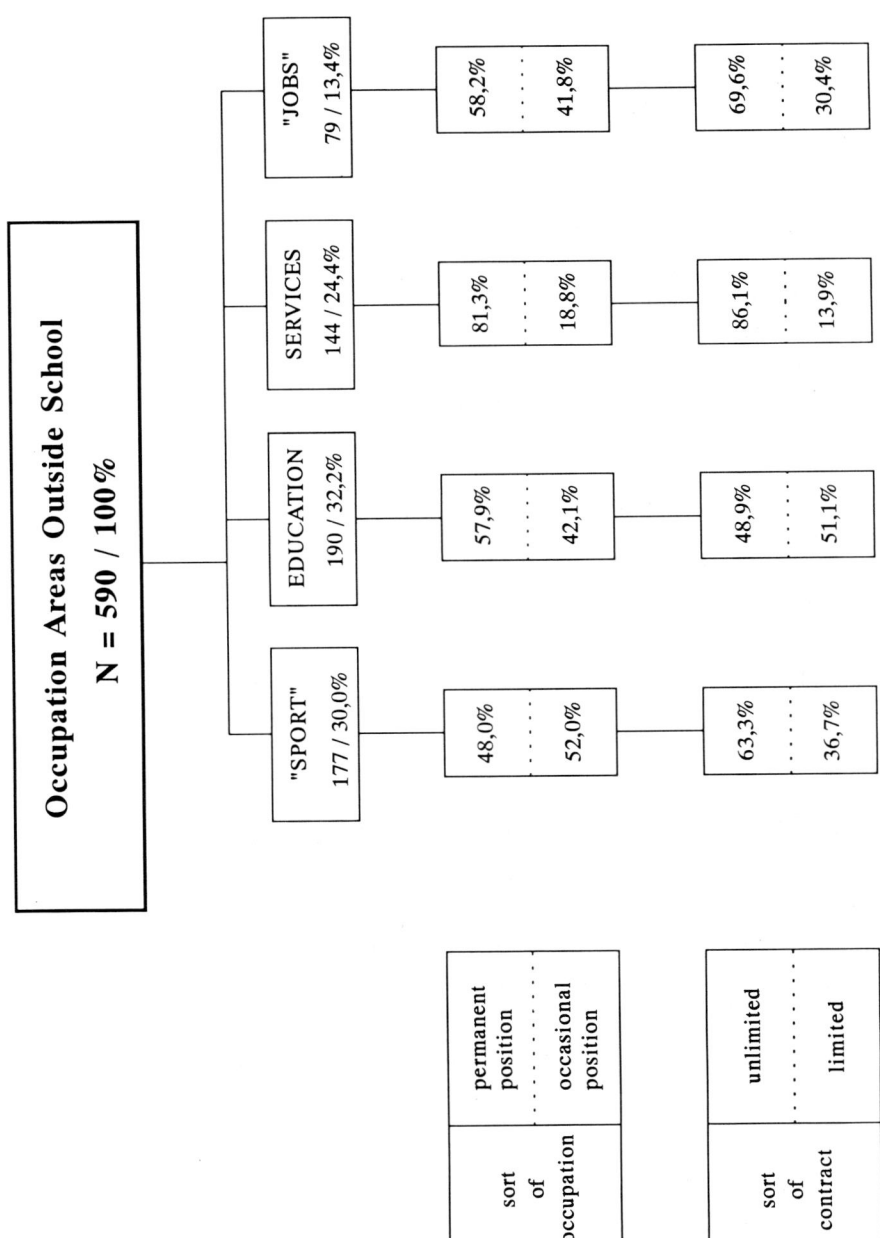

40,2% of all examined teachers had got a job in school; only little more (43.8%) have found a position outside of school.

Let's have a look on this group of 590 persons, who found employment in fields they didn't prepare in their studies in university. We can distinguish four different fields of occupations as the following picture shows:

- Most of the university-leavers (32,2%) are working in educational fields (all form of teaching activities in several institutions - but not in sports), where they can employ educational and didactical qualifications;
- Only 30% are working in the field of sport (as trainer or coach in clubs, commercial fitness-centers - in sport shops or as sportjournalists);
- (24,4%) are working in special services (interpreter, journalist, shop assistant, insurance seller, computer technician);
- and at least the rest (of 13.4%) is working in small jobs (like taxidriver etc.).

It is not only important to have any job; for the unemployed persons it is important, to find a job of high quality. There are occasional occupations as well as full-time jobs; jobs in a fixed position as well as changing short-time jobs. Looking at our picture we can see the differences between the occupation fields:

The chance to get a full-time job is much better in special services than in the field of sports; even in the field of small jobs the situation is better. Similarities we can find in the limitation of an occupation. In the field of sports the jobs are limited more frequently than in the field of education and in special services.

3. Of what value are their university qualifications?

In the german concept of teachers training there are three qualification fields: studies in sport and sport science, studies in an other subject of school, and studies in educational sciences. All these qualifications are especially orientated on the demands of schoolwork. This makes the P.E. teachers unflexible to work in other fields. Lets take some examples to verify this statement.

- the pedagogical orientation of teachers behavior form a barrier to work in commercial sportcenters with its economic pattern; only 16,9% of those persons working in the field of sport decided to work in commercial sport institutions and mostly they stay there for only a short time;
- P.E. Teachers have deficits in the field of management, marketing and economical practise;
- the special demands of - for example - fitnesstraining in a sport center cannot be solved without additional qualifications;

- to work in sport clubs P.E. teachers for example as trainer or exercise leader are on one side overqualified and underpaid on the other side;

The personal reaction to these facts is a high grade of unsecuredness about the value of qualifications gained in university studies; it is a so called Qualificatio-nabivalenz that defines the situation of unemployed P.E. teachers.

This explains the fact that those persons who have gained additional qualifications have much better chances to find a position in sport outside schools. Important are the licences of sport organisations as exercise leader, trainer or coach but also the experience persons can get in a long time socialisation process practising competition sports. Nearly 50% of those people who work in the field of sport have two or more licences from several sportorganisations.

But there are also language-knowledge or the ability to handle computers to increase chances to get positions. Our investigation shows, that persons with additional qualifications have also better chances to get an unlimited position.

4. What sport related jobs are offered on the job market?

In an other part of our investigation we analysed the job market looking especially on the commercial sport market. Expecting a wide range of occupational opportunities, we found various possibilities of occupations. In Hamburg there are more than 450 special offers in this area.

This table may give you an overview:

Commercial Sport offers

(Hamburg 1985)

N = 450 / 100%

Big sport centers	7,1%
Fitness and body building studios	13,3%
Asian competition sports	4,7%
Dance and balletschools	9,8%
Modern dance and gymnastics	13,3%
Sportschools for one sportdisciplin like sailing, boxing, horse riding	9,8%

Sport and tourism	4,9%
permanent offers of single persons with a special competence	8,0%
non permanent offers of single persons with a special competence	9,6%
institutions with additional sport offers	8,9%
others	10,7%

You can see various occupational opportunities but it is the question, if these are jobs for P.E. teachers after four years' university studies. To characterise job market in sport it is not only important to know the number of occupations; it is also important to find out what qualities the jobs have. Asking the persons concerned we found out:

- they are working mostly in dependant jobs,
- without a job contract,
- in a limited position,
- with small amount of wages,
- looking for a better job (especially in school).

What may be important: in the field of sport there are less chances to get a good job than in the other fields of occupation I showed you in the picture before.

Since the 1980s the job market has changed in a process of professionalisation and deprofessionalisation. To explain this statement we must look at those marks that indicate the level of professionalisation. The following list of indicators shows the grade of institutionation of an occupation and the grade of professionalisation:

Indicators for Professionalisation

Formation/Qualification

- special knowledge (autodidactical or from institutions)
- Course of formation (private, established, academical)
- Examination (different levels)
- Science related to the occupational field

Regulation for entrance

- Licences
- Selection following achievement criteria
- Steps of promotion
- Regulated career

Organisation

- labor union
- Job ethics
- network of participants (national, international)

Legal status
- state protected job name
- position with a guaranteed salary
- regulated working time
- high estimation in public scene

If everybody is able to manage daily-life demands we wouldn't say, he is doing a job. Characteristic for an established job is a set of special knowledge, and regulated courses of formation. This may be very different:

P.E. teachers must run a definite course of about 4 years; the knowledge is produced by established sciences like geography, sport science and educational sciences.

A sportjournalist has different possibilities; he can go an autodidactical way or step by step as a volunteer; he can take private schoolcourses, may be in the institution of a publisher or in a university course (like Hamburg or Cologne).

The entrance into job is very simple for a sportjournalist. The most important criterion is his experience. A P.E. teacher has to run a university course, with a state controlled examination; he must absolve a second examination as the last step to run a regulated career.

The organisation of the members of a job field is another indicator for the grade of professionalisation. The journalists have a member union, but not an own labor union. Job ethics can be found as well in the group of journalists as in the group of P.E. teachers.

The job in the area of medicine is a most obvious example for a professionalisation on a high level and is still developing in a process of specialisation and differentiation. In sport journalism for example we can notice an opposite development:

In the big media town of Hamburg there are many offers to get occupations on the job market of the mass media; the reaction is deprofessionalisation: there are many entrances into the job field on different levels; there are opportunities for personal engagement and the chance for a step by step promotion.

Nevertheless we established a curriculum for sportjournalism in Hamburg like we can find it too here in Cologne. It is like a professionalisation from above. And I think it is useful especially for higher level positions.

5. What is the structure of the job market in the field of sports?

The job-market in the field of sports is diffuse and sometimes contradictionary: on one side we can find various occupations with good chances to earn money, but on the other side there are bad chances to get a permanent job with possibilities for a promotion and a regulated career.

One reason of this situation is not only the level of profession, but also the type of occupation: occupations in the field of sport are mostly characterised as personorientated services. The disadvantage of these occupations are highly evident:

- This service depends on a direct interaction between the person who offers the service and the person who takes it;
- the result is the achievement of both; not only of the person who offers the service;
- the result often cannot be evaluated exactly and in an objective way;
- it is difficult to calculate the demand in this services because it is the free choice of people in their leisure time;
- it is difficult to create a permanent relation between an offer of these services and a constant demand.

It will take some years till the job market in the field of sports will clarify and the various occupations will get professionalised to different job images.

6. What factors determine the further development of job market?

Heinemann has fixed some factors that determine the further development of the job market.

He characterises the job market as an open and mostly unregulated field. Its development depends on the following factors:

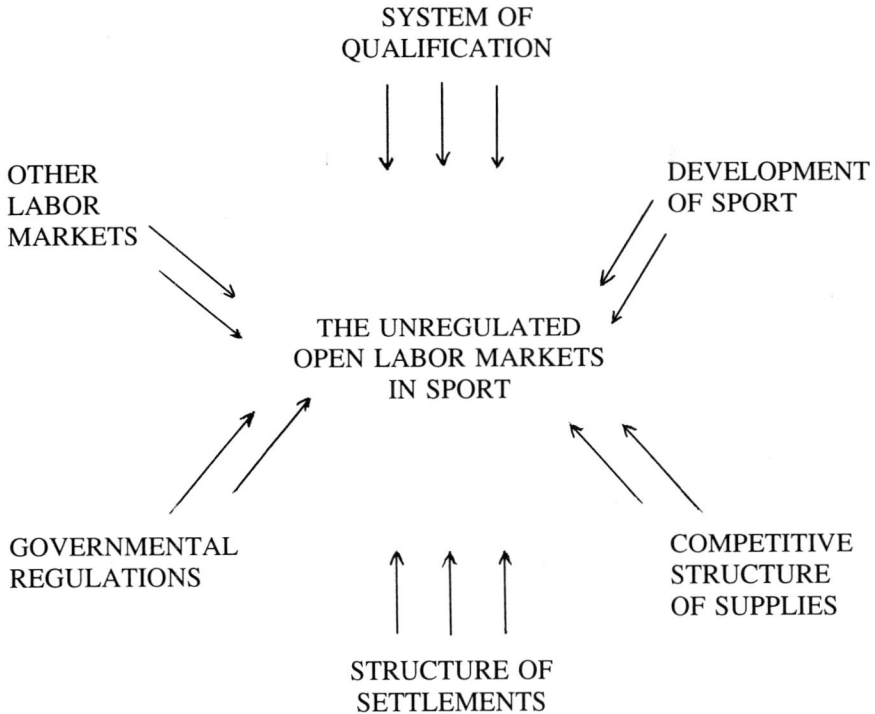

- the systems of qualification
  the structure of formation
  the grade of professionalisation

- the development of sport
  functions of sport in society
  public acknowledgement

- the competitive structure of supplies
  different demands
  number of offers

- structure of settlement
  types of occupations
  hierarchy of occupations

- Governmental Regulations
  Institutionalisation of qualification
  legal status of the job

- other labor markets
  technology
  Commercial markets

7. The actual development and open questions.

Looking at the actual development we can say:

During the intervening years after our investigation in 1985 the situation has changed. The qualification system and the job market system are still unbalanced and there are great variations in both these systems between different european countries. But in the meantime we can see many activities and tendences of change. Lets give some remarks to this statement:

- there are many trials in the universities to develop new curricula with special orientation into a new job market. I take the example of Hamburg with studies in three professional directions: Leisure, factory and permanent formation (I), social work, handicapped and third world (II) and media and journalism (III); other important fields of study in other universities are: sport management (Bayreuth); ...

- beside these university activities we can find many Courses and international Seminars (f. example in the subject area: Sport and management) with the tendency to establish permanent studies in this area. IST-Institute in Münster);

- special Erasmus programs are running between several European countries: for example "Sport, economy, society" between the universities of Rome, Leicester, Lyon, Hamburg and Barcelona.

- in the frame of European network there works the Commission III with the special task to clarify the European jobmarket, to look for necessities of compensations of differences and to open the way to an European job market.

European unification and free choice on the jobmarket create new challenges for all organisations involved in the formation and distribution of people studying sport sciences.

References:

1. Heinemann, K./Schubert, M.: Honoriert der Arbeitsmarkt sportwissenschaftliche Qualifikationen? In: Sportwissenschaft. H. 1, Tübingen 1989.

2. Heinemann, K./Dietrich, K./Schubert, M.: Akademikerarbeitslosigkeit und neue Formen des Erwerbsverhaltens. Weinheim 1990.

Physical Education within the School Curriculum: A Beautiful Dream?

Hardman, K.
University of Manchester
UK

1. Introduction

Throughout history, physical (activity) education has been considered an important component of education and the educational process. This has been manifested in statements in support of physical education within educational practice from Antiquity to Modernity. The continuing presence of physical education in curricula, grounded, since Antiquity, in the Aristotelian concept of 'harmonious balance' and variously linked with preparation for the rigours of life, healthy well-being, enhancement of quality of life, socialisation, politics, militarism, nationalism, conformity, social control through promotion of obedience to authority etc., character building and other instrumental outcomes, implies that it has passed the 'test' of time. But, has it? In the present century, physical educators have repeatedly been called upon to defend and justify the inclusion of physical education as part of the school curriculum. The arguments proffered have met with only limited success, since in many countries physical education is not accepted on par with seemingly superior academic subjects concerned with developing a child's intellect. Whatever pupils views of physical education, many School Directors place it "near the bottom", being seen less "..as a substantial part of general education" and "..more like an annex" (Naul, 1992, p.13.). 'Academic' subjects are highly rated in schools, whereas 'practical' subjects like physical education are placed conventionally towards the bottom of a hierarchical order of knowledge. Fasting (1992) has indicated that as competition increases between school subjects "..physical education seems to be one of those subjects that is falling behind" and "..If administrators need to reduce the number of classes in a subject, physical education is often chosen" (p.46).

2. Global Concerns in Physical Education

2.1 'Reality' and 'Truth of Fact' and 'Dream'

Ideals expressed by educational philosophers, educational institutions and educators, and in ideological statements of governments, together with principles expounded in 'official' documentation, often belie the actual realities of situations and implementation of policy and practice. This is evidenced in the increasing global concerns about the state and status of physical education (some commentators would argue that physical education is in crisis) and the issues to which they give rise as the end of the second millennium A.D. draws nigh. What now appears to be the plight of an hitherto 'essentially' regarded school curriculum subject, begs the question whether physical education in schools is but a wishful dream of interest-vested practitioners. **What is the reality?** Comparativists are well aware of the pitfalls of taking things at face value - things are not always what they seem to be. Certainly, far from accepting idealistic documentary and sometimes politically inspired statements, the 'truth of fact' should be questioned.

A number of examples suffice to illustrate the 'truth of fact' thesis. In the domain of physical education, we read (Smulders, 1987), on the one hand, that Belgian schools have three physical education lessons per week, but on the other hand the practice is up to three lessons. According to 'Annex D' of the England and Wales National Curriculum Proposals' (1991a, p.82), physical education, in the three cycles of the primary phase of French schools, is allocated five 'hours' per week; elsewhere, a French source reports there is a credibility gap in the operation of the weekly programme: schools are required to teach the subject, but resources do not always allow this to happen: the 'tiers-temps pedagogique' is 'a beautiful dream'. 'Annex D' also indicates compulsory physical education lessons in the secondary phase colleges and lycees with optional additions of sporting activity in sports centres. To some extent, this is at odds with some research findings (Hardman and Mallalieu, 1986), that in some schools distanced from Paris, up to 90% of pupils in some schools had no compulsory physical education, though some 30% did engage in voluntary sporting activity. Also in 'Annex D', there is a brief overview of physical education in Germany (pp.83-84): it suffers from ambiguities, generalisations and interpretations based on 'official' documentation and minimal school-based observational experience in Bavaria, which, at the time, was itself in the process of revising its curriculum guidelines. Bavaria (as any non-Bavarian will eagerly testify) is not typical of all Länder: each Land has its own "Guidelines" for physical education, and on curriculum time alone, we would find variations between individual Länder, a situation that has prevailed in the post 1949 Federal Republic. The variations in the Federal Republic have reflected the cultural autonomy enjoyed by each Land, political demographics, and earlier, the legacies of American, British and French influences. The 'Annex' statement that "Sport..is called physical education in Germany" is a misrepresentation of the truth: 'Sport' as a term on the timetable, has significant pedagogical connotations, an important feature totally overlooked.

From 'truth of fact', I move to the 'dream' theme. Clearly, there is no one unique physical education delivery system common to all countries; there are similarities, differences and variations in process and product orientation based in politico-ideological, socio-cultural, economic values and norms and ecological settings, (hence, caution is necessary in identifying problems and offering solutions). Thus, policy and practice are more often than not 'localised' and not 'globalised'. Nevertheless, there are world-wide problems and controversies within the field, which suggest that there are global concerns, especially in regard to subject status, erosion of curriculum time, insufficient/-inadequate financial, material and personnel resources, and either a predisposition against sporting competitive activity or the promotion of the few (sporting elite) with the concomitant neglect of the participation of the many. The following illustrative exemplars drawn from selected European countries and other continental regions of the world demonstrate the magnitude of the problems.

3. The Parlous State of Physical Education

3.1 An historical dimension

Historically, the field is replete with references to, and examples of, the parlous state of physical education: H.M.I. Jolly (1876) voiced "..the neglect of Physical Education" (p.3) in the U.K.; its discredit under the National Socialists and sublime status in 1945 Germany and post 1949 Federal Republic, in the period when the Deutsche Olympische Gesellschaft and Deutscher Sportbund both drew public attention to the deplorable situation of the subject in schools; its marginal position in the primary school curriculum in Scotland (Scottish Education Department 1980; Committee on Primary Education 1983); and the Swedish Education Minister's suggestion (1990) that physical education disappears from the curriculum as a compulsory subject in secondary schools (and this in a country with a distinguished record of school physical education); it did not happen, but the mere fact of its consideration was a cause for alarm.

3.2 Scandinavian perspective

The Swedish situation was sufficiently alarming for one Norwegian scholar, (Karhus, 1992) to observe that amongst some Norwegian physical educationists, there is a fear of the 'Swedish Ghost' i.e. effective reduction of time for physical education in optional programmes, because of increasing competition from other subject areas, which has resulted in some Swedish Secondary schools no longer offering physical education as an 'option' and others offering fewer classes. In the Scandinavian context, Fasting (1992) comments that many teachers "..have had (problems) in the legitimization of the subject" (p.46). The status of physical education as a core subject in Norway still leaves teachers feeling that it "..is left somewhere behind the subjects that really count" (Karhus, 1992, p.1), especially given that teachers can teach physical education without formal institutional physical education training and "..Headmasters very seldom involve themselves pedagogically in P.E. They hardly know what is happening - 'it is gym, the pupils like it, you fix it" (Karhus, 1992, p.2).

3.3 A European perspective

Shifting to the mainstream European scene, there are many examples of the strains and tensions that physical education and physical educators are experiencing. Indeed, at the European Network Forum in Portugal, LaPorte (1991) commented that physical education had been pushed into a defensive position, was suffering from budgetary controls and lack of time, was undervalued by authorities and had become unstable because of influences and pressures from groups with vested interests in sport and fitness.

(i) In Belgium, according to Smulders (1992), there is a trend, especially in Catholic denominational schools, of diminution of time-tabled physical education lessons; curriculum reorganisation has seen physical education placed within the area of Fine Arts, where expression, cooperation and creativity rule, and sport and competition have been phased out.

(ii) Almost mirroring this development is the situation in Scotland : the Scottish Education Department has placed Physical Education alongside Art, Drama, and Music within an 'Expressive Arts' area, despite opposition from the professionals. Primary school phase teachers perceive physical education concerned essentially with functional activities such as games, gymnastics and swimming, and only marginally with expressiveness, rating aesthetic appreciation lowly in a list of objectives (Jess, 1992). Thus, there is conflict between teachers and the Education Department, epitomised in gaps between official 'Guidelines' and teachers' perceptions. Furthermore, Jess (1992) reports that many primary schools do not have adequate facilities for physical education classes - 70% rely on a multi-purpose hall, which is also used for school lunches, assemblies, concerts, drama etc. - (a scenario also typical of England and Wales), that radio broadcasts account for a large proportion of P.E. time in Infant programmes, and that there is a problem of curriculum continuity because of the number of class teachers involved (normally seven), the majority of whom do not share information, indeed, physical education is rarely discussed at staff meetings.

(iii) In France, the earlier reference to the 'tiers-temps pedagogique' as a 'beautiful dream' was recently reinforced by Bonhomme (1992), when he reported that in Primary (Elementary) Schools, 72% have less than two hours physical education per week and that 50% of children are taught by a sports coach. Other problems in France have related to quality of facility provision in schools and the intellectually demanding curriculum, one outcome of which is that physical education is merely seen as a diversion or even as "a necessary evil in order to pass examinations" (Rigby, 1978, p.4). The obligation, after 1974, on schools to form 'Association Sportives' to offer voluntary sport was viewed by the Physical education teachers' union as undermining the broadly based curriculum. Indeed, it was even suggested (Brackpool, 1977) that the French government allowed a sub-standard situation to develop, favouring the development of a sports elite at the expense of a genuine physical education programme for all children in schools.

(iv) The plight of physical education appears even worse in Greece, where many schools have minimal, if any, facilities for the subject. Until very recently, the curricula are reported as written in a language that many teachers could not understand, with statements so vague that presumptions as to meaning had to be made. The curricula also provided contradictory guidance, e.g., freedom in movement was recommended and then static tasks prescribed; swimming was to be carried out where possible but no further guidance was proffered - perhaps, it was realised that possibilities were severely limited: at the time, in Salonika, for instance, there was but one pool for one million people; there is also doubt expressed as to whether public school teachers were actually qualified to teach swimming. The curriculum also recommended that during inclement weather, physical education should take place in the classroom, where non-complex ball games could be practised; obviously this type of space is inadequate for such activity and many lessons were simply cancelled.

(v) Martin's (1972) assertion that "..The flood of recommendations, action programmes, promotion plans etc. is a sure indication of the need for reform of the system", perhaps still has relevance in present-day Germany, for according to Naul (1992), some west German models need evaluation at a time when each new Land in the eastern part of the country is respectively basing its school system on such suspect models through 'partnerships' with Länder in the west. The open strategies and fun-oriented teaching methods (the dominant ideals) introduced by some west Germans as "missionaries of democracy", have caused some east German physical educators and sport pedagogues to have understandable doubts in accepting all the new teaching approaches when discipline and performance orientation are neglected (Porschutz, 1991), and when they observe the physical education teaching of some

'Besserwessis'. (Re)unification of Germany presented an opportunity for reflection in physical education. The former GDR had already undertaken curricula reform (1989-90), which has been overlooked by many west German sport pedagogues at a time when "...rethinking physical education is overdue in West German States" (Naul, 1992, p.17). In the East, physical education has been largely seen as a socialist relic of the former GDR competitive sport system; physical education is now regarded as "less important and having only minor significance in school education like it is more or less in West Germany" (Naul, 1992, p.18); the trend is to replace specialist teachers by non-specialists; discipline, order and performance have largely disappeared from the teaching situation; physical education has changed from "an important main subject to an unimportant minor subject", with the result that many teachers have let pupils do what they want rather than intervening, for risk of "accusation of being an authoritarian ex-socialist" (Naul, 1992, p.18); the 'open instructional methods' introduced, have produced conflicts and chaos with teacher confusion on methods and pupils faced with unfamiliar lesson formats. By no means did all aspects of physical education in the former GDR only relate to socialist ideology, just as in the Federal Republic there was (and is) not an unquestionable standard of physical education, which should be adopted in its entirety for a new beginning in the East. Renewal in the new Länder was an opportue occasion for overhaul and improvement of physical education within the general framework of education in the whole of Germany, if only to meet societal changes and in the name of contributing positively to shaping a better future.

(vi) In England and Wales, where the greatest stimulus to change in the last decade has arisen from Party policy embedded in political philosophy, calling for greater efficiency from contracting services, a national curriculum has recently been imposed on the education delivery system, in which, the entitlement of the child is secured to physical education as a compulsory 'Foundation Level' subject.

Notably, physical educationists had no control over the national curriculum nor the selection of the Working Party set up by central government to construct a curriculum and express its form and content. The Working Party's parameters of action were set down by the Secretary of State for Education, highlighted by, for example, the timetable time to be allocated to physical education within the national curriculum. All requests to the Secretary of State to stipulate this were rejected - it was non-negotiable. Additionally, Working Group members were frequently reminded of 'resource implications' of recommendations: e.g. in the response to the Interim Report (Department of Education and Science, 1991a), the group was asked to reconsider the economic 'feasibility' of the proposals and implored to ensure that the final report recommendations were realistically related to the general level of school funding which could reasonably be expected to be available (Department of Education and Science, 1991b); effectively, the Working Group was being 'asked' to construct a curriculum based in economic viability and not educational desirability and is reminiscent of the Newcastle Commission remit of 1861, when it was requested to make recommendations for a sound, but economically cheap system of 'popular' education. Some members of the Working Group opposed the request, but "..their actions were strongly framed by the policy statements of more powerful others" (Evans, Penney & Bryant, 1993, p.8); there was tension between a broadly based curriculum 'available to all children' and harsh economic realities.

In essence, the finally approved version of the National Curriculum in Physical Education (a compromise by the Working Group and National Curriculum Council) provides access to a broad and balanced range of experiences with opportunities to achieve and pupils to be told what they have achieved. It is much too early to assess the physical education curriculum impacts - it was only introduced into schools in September, 1992 - but the struggles and conflicts during the national curriculum planning process are also apparent in its implementation in schools, for, apart from the competing demands to meet the requirements of Core and Foundation subjects, there is the context of scarce resources and many teachers in the Primary phase of education (age 5 to 11) inadequately prepared for the P.E. Curriculum requirements: together, these factors may mean that 'entitlement' and 'flexibility' are incompatible with one possibility being that delivery is compromised.

The inclusion of Physical Education in the National Curriculum for schools in England and Wales did represent a victory (albeit with a deal of compromise) for a strong physical education lobby in the battle to retain its statutory obligatory status, when government sense and common sense came to prevail. Any euphoria may, however, be short-lived, for the 'war' is not yet over - the Secretary of State for Education, reacting to professional pressures on a range of curriculum, attainment target tests and examination issues, is currently reviewing the overloaded curriculum, and there may well be some positive discrimination in favour of the 'Core' curriculum areas (English, Mathematics and Science) at the expense of the lesser important 'Foundation' subjects.

(vii) In the wider European arena, some aspects of the problems in Germany are also manifested in the Czech and Slovak Republics, where the re-orientation of the concept of school physical education (ideas on humanism, democracy and freedom) has brought elements of liberalisation, an orientation in physical education which builds only on pupils' interests and neglects knowledge of young people's needs, as well as former scientific research studies.

Currently, this is witnessed in several schools, where pupils only want to engage in activities they are specifically interested in, and many pupils see the physical education teacher solely as an activity organiser. Recent changes in theoretical conceptions designed to create more positive attitudes towards physical activity engagement have not been realised in practice, and are epitomised by low participation rates in leisure activities in and out of school. The danger of replacement of a centralised bureaucratic system of compulsory physical education based on orders, guidelines and norms, stifling development of independence, initiative, innovation and creativity, with no scope for voluntary-based physical activity (it had no theoretical or practical infrastructure) by decentralisation with risks of 'ad hoc' disparate outcomes exists.

School physical education is undervalued as a subject: school senior management shows little interest in it and its contribution to the general development of pupils is not adequately appreciated; physical education teachers are considered inferior, less capable and less skilful and "regrettably...criticisms are well founded because of the poor quality and superficial nature of their work, lack of motivation and anomie towards other teachers" (Antala, Sedlacek & Sykora 1992, p.21).

3.4 A Middle East perspective

Inferior subject status and curriculum time reduction is also endemic in the State of Kuwait, where Behbehani (1992) reports that physical education "has become less important than other curriculum subjects" (p.34), allocation of time has been reduced from three to two lessons in Year 4 and is down to one lesson in Year 9 (third year of High School), it no longer features on the Final School Certificate, lessons are cancelled as examinations draw near, there is a reaction to females teaching boys in Elementary Schools and recently built schools have no indoor provision for physical education, resulting in lessons being cancelled during bad weather conditions (Behbehani, 1992, pp.34-35).

3.5 An African perspective

Some of these problems pale into relative significance in some African countries, especially where Islam is the dominant religion practised. Muslim scholars associate physical education and sport with the evils of gambling and alcohol and have stated conditions for participation: development of strength, health and fitness for Islamic Jihad (Holy War) if necessary; skill and technique for self-defence; non-interference with prayer; and women's exercise to be performed with all parts of the body covered and unobserved by men. Several countries adhere to these conditions with the consequences that physical education does not feature in some curricula, (e.g. Chad, Libya, Mali and Niger); where teachers are female Muslims, physical education is not taught even when it is on the curriculum (e.g. Kenya, Nigeria, Uganda) and there are no co-educational classes; where there is extra-curricular sport, females are non-participants (parental opposition and hindrance of clothing); there is no physical education during 'Ramadan'; and physical educators are regarded as satanic agents indulging in play rather than in prayer and worship (Kamiyole, 1993 pp.29-31).

The situation is less dire in Kenya. Nonetheless, familiar symptoms of physical education's malaise are much in evidence. Apart form a 1933 British Syllabus, the immediate post-Independence Kenya lacked a modern official syllabus as well as trained personnel, and suffered gross inadequacies of facilities and equipment. In 1973, the national Inspector of Physical Education (actually a music specialist!) approved guidelines for secondary schools, but many schools continued to offer physical education on the basis of the attitudes and interests of Head Teachers, most of whom argued that there were no career opportunities in physical education; thus, students were urged to follow courses which facilitated access to 'white collar' jobs or into higher education: "..Physical education was regarded as a subject without academic significance" (Wamykoya and Hardman, 1992, p.30). Even after the intervention of President Kenyatta with a directive making physical education a compulsory subject and an associated campaign to raise its level and profile, some Head Teachers had physical education lessons timetabled only for inspection purposes (with only two Inspectors to oversee physical education in the whole of the country, such lessons are a rarity), preferring instead other subjects during scheduled physical education time. The formal education process continues to be associated with an academic curriculum tied to examinations. The general populace believes that education is a means of selecting and socialising members of an intellectual elite to maintain standards of cultural excellence. Hence, physical education is conceived of as non-intellectual, subsidiary to 'academic' subjects serving as a means of social training or as a means of compensating for the rigours of academic work (Wamykoya and Hardman, 1992, p.32.)

3.6 An Australian perspective

Many of the problems referred to in the European, Middle East and African contexts also occur in other regions of the world. In October, 1991 a Conference was held at Deakin University, Geelong, Australia with the theme "Crisis in Australian Physical Education". According to the conference delegates "a crisis in physical education...is occurring in the areas of early childhood, primary, secondary and tertiary education" (Alexander and Sands, 1991). In the State of New South Wales, a newly elected Liberal (Conservative) State Government initiated curriculum reform in 1988, which placed physical education within 'Personal Development, Health and Physical Education' (comprising Health, Physical Education, Life and Career Studies and Home Science), one of eight Key Learning Areas in an integrated curriculum, proposed to replace the traditional subject approach. A study reported by Williams, (1993) indicates problems of Key Area 'ownership' and 'control', whether the Area is integrated or specialist oriented; devalued status of Personal Development (it has no defined syllabus, is a 'filler' on the timetable, and no professional qualifications are required to teach it), inability of Home Economics and Personal Development teachers to cope with the syllabus, loss of physical education status and perhaps loss of time, no support system, no in-service teaching, and no teacher training courses to prepare intending teachers for this Area. Riley (1992), focusing on the State of Victoria, argues that physical education has declined since 1981, when the newly elected Labour Government implemented a change in philosophy linked with a 'tightening of the economic belt'. The Physical Education Branch of the Ministry of Education was closed; reorganised teaching and curriculum strategies were introduced in schools with devolved powers and suddenly specialist physical education teachers found career pathways ended. Morale deteriorated, higher expectations of teachers were coupled with less support; and marginal developments sponsored by outside agencies producing exciting packages emerged to fill a void in schools with Sports Development Officers giving 'one-off' motivational lessons, which were "more like talent identification sessions" (Riley, 1992, p.12). The State Government attitude is seemingly aptly summed up in a Ministry Support Centre Day Seminar on "How to become an Instant P.E. Teacher" (Teacher Gazette 1989). The Victoria State situation may well strike a chord with colleagues familiar with a range of initiatives introduced and developed after 1981 in the United Kingdom, since when there has been increasing government (Conservative) intervention in educational and sporting circles. European colleagues may empathise with the position in Victoria in relation to the all-powerful 'God', "Sport", particularly its highly competitive form. How often do we see the neglect of physical education in the pursuit of greater glory through sport? In too many countries, elite athletes in school settings are a main focus of interest and energies - this is a neglect of the many. Without doubt, development of children's excellence is a proper objective and striving for it is as worthy of support as any other human endeavour, but physical education should not be a 'slave to sport'; physical educators should be concerned first and foremost with all-round development and are not merely performance-orientated sports coaches!

3.7 An American perspective

In the United States, the 'erosion' of physical education is seen in a crisis of identity in Higher Education as demonstrated by a) the proliferation of different titles and b) the separation of academic disciplines from practice (teaching in schools) to gain academic credibility - perhaps this is a way for scholars to avoid the stigma of being thought of as 'gym. teachers'! In schools, 75% of all States possess K-6 grade level requirements in physical education, but 50% do not specify time or activity guidelines (Bucher and Krotee 1992); in grades 7-9, more than 80% require physical education, with 60% recommending time/unit specification, but activity selection guidelines are locally set; in grades 10-11, only 25% require physical education (Mitchell and Earls, 1987). Research (Krotee 1992), conducted in the State of Minnesota, showed that 45% of sample respondents listed lack of motivation and negative attitude of students towards physical education, and lack of respect towards the teacher. This introduces another dimension - that of quality of the physical education service being delivered - and one that is apparently not peculiar to Minnesota, if the President of FIEP is accurate in his intimation that daily teaching in some European schools, where physical education is supposedly well established, does not inspire confidence that children will enter adulthood with knowledge, skills, attitudes and habits for the hoped-for active life styles adopted (Andrews, 1993).

4. Future Directions

4.1 The role of Physical Education

The various 'snap-shot' country scenarios presented inevitably provide a somewhat distorted image of physical education in schools. The "truth of fact" probably lies in a less negative direction. Nevertheless, if Physical Education is to have a real future and not remain just a "beautiful dream", one optimistic view must be that only by confronting the issues and planning for the future we can change the present situation. The rigidity and resistance to change of educational systems, especially by the critically important agents involved, the teachers, must be overcome. It should be remembered that education facilitates a preparation for the future, whilst preserving the significant legacies of the past. As social etc. values become more egalitarian and educational opportunities increase, the nature of educational provision will inevitably change. The speed and direction of change will depend on the relevance of the educational 'product' to further technological advances and to the increasingly emphatic social demand for educational opportunities to provide for life-time changes as well as resource redistribution. Consequently, education should respond to the needs of optimally developing individuals' capabilities and provide opportunities for personal fulfilment and social interactions, essential in peaceful human coexistence. Physical Education should be more involved with the process of personal fulfilment in the future. A key feature here is development through 'instrumental' body and self-concepts which, in turn, affects behavioural perceptions of self-competence, self-adequacy, self-fulfilment and self-actualization.

4.2 Curriculum Reappraisal

There is an abundance of literature on the philosophy of Physical Education in the broad process of Education, but it is not the intention here to restate it, but rather to suggest that this area of the curriculum is ripe for reappraisal both in regard to its fundamental purposes in view of social and peer culture changes, and to the pedagogic processes that might best bring about these purposes. Some commentators emphasize the need for educators at large and physical educators in particular to recognise the importance of understanding and reflecting on the post-modern youth culture in structuring a relevant curriculum. Recent research around the world in the domain of physical activity indicates changing activity patterns of adolescents with gender differences levelling out, sport culture and sport settings becoming more differentiated, traditional activities in decline, and greater awareness of what is being sought (Brettschneider and Brutigam, 1990). Clearly, these trends have implications for the future of physical education curriculum planners, not only in Germany, but also in a host of other countries (many of these are in Europe and the industrially developed world), where similar changes can be detected.

Any reshaping of physical education, however, should recognise local and cultural diversities, traditions as well as different social and economic conditions and incorporate a range of aspects related to the all-round and harmonious development of the individual within society; at the very least this should include Health and Fitness, Moral Issues and Quality of Life. Physical Education programmes have taken on responsibility for equipping school children with knowledge about, and methods for, developing health and fitness. Teachers need to rationalize the provision of health-related fitness in the school curriculum, to relate this provision to subsequent adoption and practice, and above all not to regard this provision as a substitute for an integrated programme of physical education which has, or ought to have, wider and more intrinsic purposes. It may well be that physical educators should develop an appropriate rationale and capacity for establishing the foundation for self-care of the functioning body, since body image and concepts are increasingly likely to play a greater role in the psychology of personal stability, which underpins personality and social effectiveness. In March 1993, Mr. Jacques Delors, Chairman of the UNESCO International Commission on Education for the Twenty-First Century, pointed to "a weakening of the great value systems which have guided societies for so long"; he called on education to contribute to "...the emergence of common values which the recent progress of democracy entitles us to hope for, also to a better understanding of others..". Physical education has long laid claim in <u>moral</u> education widely interpreted. Such virtues as co-operativeness, fair play and honesty are fundamental in the concept of 'homo ludens'. It would seem that physical education is uniquely placed to inculcate best practice in many of the related and desirable moral virtues, but efforts and resources will need to be increased significantly to have a greater impact. Furthermore, research will be required here to identify the best pedagogic methods by which to achieve greater success.

The term <u>'Quality of Life'</u> has different meanings for those living in developed and privileged societies from those in underdeveloped and underprivileged societies. Common to both, however, is that education represents a way of achieving a better quality of life. Even in impoverished areas, where many live at the margins of life, there are incessant pleas for improved basic educational delivery systems for all; this will only be secured through massive resource allocation and appropriate management. Within this basic education system, physical education should be utilised to attract people to the joy and pleasure of engagement in physical activity, from which self identity via competence may be forged and self assurance, and fulfilment be gained. Thus, as in the so-called developed world, where education <u>is</u> Quality of Life, individual human potential resulting in higher order satisfactions and achievement of self actualization - issues central in current debate and focus of curriculum planning in physical education - could be facilitated.

If the status of physical education is to be improved as a school subject, physical educators will have to be thoroughly prepared for it. Status will not be freely granted by those who jealously safeguard their superior position. If significant others are to be persuaded of the real importance of physical education, then it is necessary to realise that this entails more than a commitment to an essential enterprise and delivery of a quality curriculum, it requires the application of political skills and arguing the case at local, through national, to international levels: policy makers, decision takers, committee members, administrators, other subject colleagues and 'clients' need to be lobbied and convinced that physical education is "an authentic educational activity" (Kirk, 1987, p.147).

4.3 'Roads to Rome'

To this end, whilst all roads do not lead to Rome, many do. The Forum of European Physical Education Associations has already made a declaration (1991) of intent:

a) no education without physical education (physical education is to be promoted and defended as a core curriculum subject);
b) promotion of the academic study and practice of physical education as an important discipline in its own right;
c) information exchange on physical education in Europe as a basis for lobbying national governments and European agencies;
d) exploration of a minimum European curriculum and securance of resources to implement it;
e) promotion of in-service training courses for teachers, supported by Governments and Institutions;
f) development of links with influential European bodies with vested interests in physical education.

The Madrid Declaration is a positive step forward, but it is only one of the 'roads to Rome'. Perhaps, there is a role here also for the European Network. However, physical education has to be rethought not only in a European, regional, but also in a broad global context. A truly international lobby for the cause of physical education would not go amiss. The announcement (February, 1993) of a UNESCO International Commission on Education for the 21st Century addressing one central all encompassing question: what kind of education is needed for what kind of society of tomorrow; and aiming "..to study and reflect on the challenges facing education.. and to formulate suggestions and recommendations..which can serve as an agenda for renewal and action for policy-makers and officials at the highest levels" (p.4), provides a potential international vehicle to promote the essential contribution of physical education within 'tomorrow's education on another road to Rome.

An indispensable component in any future developments in physical education in schools is research and evaluation, for which "international cooperation is a prerequisite for (its).. universal and well balanced promotion" (UNESCO, 1979) - yet another road to Rome, and one that amongst others should at a very minimum consider the conceptual aspects of physical education.

The journey to Rome is a task for all physical educators and research pedagogues. It represents a challenge to improve the status, state and quality of physical education in schools, a challenge which should not ignore the Past, but should learn from it, for together with the Present, it will help shape a more positive future.

References

1. **Alexander K., Sands R.A.:** Report of the Recent Conference at Deakin University on the Crisis in Physical Education in Australia. Victoria College, November 1991.

2. **Andrews J.A.:** The Work of the Fédération Internationale d'Education Physique (FIEP) and its Contributions to World-wide Developments in Physical Education and Sport. Hardman K., (Ed.), (1993), Proceedings, International Sports Science Summit: 'Towards a Richer and Healthier World through Sports Science'. Nafferton, Educational Studies Ltd.

3. **Antala B., Sedlacek J., Sykora F.:** (1992), Topical Problems of Physical Education in Schools in Czechoslovakia. British Journal of Physical Education, Vol.23, No.4, Winter, 1992. pp.20-22.

4. **Behbehani K.:** (1992), Physical Education in the State of Kuwait. British Journal of Physical Education, Vol.23, No.4, Winter. pp.33-35.

5. **Bonhomme G.:** (1992), The Training of P.E. Teachers in France. Paper, SCOPE Conference, 'The Training of Physical Education Teachers - The European Dimension'. University of Warwick, 27-29 November.

6. **Brackpool G.:** (1977), The Development of Physical Education and Sport in France. M.A. thesis, University of Liverpool.

7. **Brettschneider W.D., Brutigam M.:** (1990), Sport in der Alltagswelt von Jugendlichen. Rotterbach.

8. **Bucher C.A., Krotee M.L.:** (1992), Management of Physical Education and Sport. St. Louis, Mosby Year Book Inc.

9. **Committee on Primary Education**: (1983), Primary Education in the Eighties. H.M.S.O.

10. **Department of Education and Science/Welsh Office:** (1991a), National Curriculum Physical Education Working Group Interim Report. London, H.M.S.O.

11. **Department of Education and Science/Welsh Office:** (1991b), Physical Education for Ages 5-16. Proposals of the Secretary of State for Education and Science. London, H.M.S.O.

12. **European Physical Education Associations:** (1991), Declaration of Madrid. 27 October.

13. **Evans J., Penney D., Bryant A.:** (1993), Theorising Implementation: a Preliminary Comment on Power and Process in Policy Research. Physical Education Review, Vol.16, No.1, Spring. pp.5-12.

14. **Fasting K.:** (1992), The Prince Phillip Fellows Lecture - 'The European Tradition and Current Practice in Physical Education'. British Journal of Physical Education, Vol.23, No.4, December. pp.44-48.

15. **Jess M.C.:** (1992), The Provision and Perception of Physical Education by Primary Class Teachers: Report of a Survey carried out in Fife Region, February 1991. Manchester Metropolitan University, October.

16. **Jolly W.:** (1876), Physical Education and Hygiene in Schools. Paper presented at the British Association, Glasgow, September.

17. **Kane J.E.:** (1993), UNESCO International Commission on Education for the Twenty-first Century. A Preliminary Reaction from ICSSPE. West London Institute. March.

18. **Karhus S.:** (1992), The Norwegian School System - its Role in Norwegian Society - and Physical Education in the National Curriculum Guidelines in the Secondary School. Paper, SCOPE Conference, 'The Training of Physical Education Teachers - The European Dimension'. University of Warwick, 27-29 November.

19. **Kamiyole T.O.:** (1993), Physical Educators' Albatross in African Societies. International Journal of Physical Education, Vol.XXX, No.2. pp.2931.

20. **Kirk D.:** (1987), The Orthodoxy of Rational-Technocracy and the Research Practice Gap: a Critique of an alternative view. Unpublished Paper, Department of Human Movement Studies, University of Queensland.

21. **Krotee M.L.:** (1992), Physical Education in the United States: Overview, Issues and Problems. British Journal of Physical Education, Vol.23, No.4, Winter, 1992. pp.7-10.

22. **Martin D.:** (1972), Schulsport in Deutschland. Schorndorf, Hofmann Verlag.

23. **Mitchell M.F., Earls R.F.:** (1987), A profile of State requirements for Physical Education K-12. The Physical Educator, Fall. pp.337-343.

24. **Naul R.:** (1992), The Training of Physical Education Teachers in Germany. Paper, SCOPE Conference, 'The Training of Physical Education Teachers - The European Dimension. University of Warwick, 27-29 November.

25. **Naul R.:** (1992), German Unification: Curriculum Development and Physical Education at School in East Germany. British Journal of Physical Education, Vol.23, No.4, Winter. pp.14-19.

26. **Porschütz W.:** (1991), Selbstandigkeit, Leistungsstreben, Ordnung. Diskussion der notwendigen Komponenten im motorischen Lern- und Übungsprozess. Sportunterricht, 40. pp.377-381.

27. **Rigby F.:** (1978). The Place of Physical Education and Sport in a Centralised System - France; Physical Education Review, Vol.1, No.1, Spring, pp.53-58.

28. **Riley C.:** The Rise and Fall of Physical Education in Victoria, Australia. British Journal of Physical Education, Vol.23, No.4, Winter. pp.11-13.

29. **Scottish Education Department:** (1980), Learning and Teaching in Primary 4 and Primary 7: a Report by H.M. Inspectors of Schools. H.M.S.O.

30. **Smulders H.:** (1992) Physical Education and Sport in Belgium. Unpublished manuscript.

31. **Teachers Gazette:** (1989). December UNESCO, (1993), International Commission on Education for the Twenty-first Century. 15 February.

32. **Wamykoya E.K., Hardman K.,** (1992), Physical Education in Kenyan Secondary Schools. British Journal of Physical Education, Vol.23, No.4, Winter. pp.30-33.

33. **Williams P., Williams M., Bertram A., McCormack A., Guray C., Brenton R.:** (1993), Implementing a New Integrated Curriculum in Australia: the Views of Head Teachers, Physical Education. Physical Education Review, Vol.16, No.1, Spring. pp.31-40.

PROFESSIONAL QUALIFICATIONS IN PHYSICAL EDUCATION

Laporte, W.P.R.
Hoger Instituut voor Lichamelijke Opvoeding, Universiteit Gent
Belgium

1. Introduction

This talk on professional qualifications will concern only what is still commonly referred to in most countries as "physical education". It is about physical education teaching at school, as part of the educational system for children from 6 to 18 years old.

I do not intend to elaborate on differences in concept and terminology, which are a major point of discussion, especially here in Germany, involving such terms as sports pedagogy, Sportunterricht, Schulsport, Schulsportpädagogik etc. (for a discussion of these, see Karlheinz Scherler 1992 and Dietrich Kurz 1992 in the journal "Sportwissenschaft").

Never before has there been so much talk and discussion about qualifications and professionalism among teachers in general and among P.E. teachers in particular. It cannot be denied that this is partly a reflex of the ever growing demands of our society. However, it is also related to a kind of educational crisis which, in many countries, has turned the educational system itself into a subject of hotly contested debate.

Therefore, to talk about quality and professionalism today is also a sign of instinctive self-preservation. It is probably also related to the uncontrolled growth of P.E. and sports schooling which has occurred in a number of countries. This has led to overproduction and consequently a degree of competition on the job market. In the USA, this has even caused the introduction of selection systems, as fully described in the "Journal of Teaching in P.E." monograph under the title "Teacher Testing and Teacher Competence" (Griffey and Oliver, 1990).

It is clear to all of us that the term professional qualifications refers to the qualifications required in order to practise a profession or to hold an office in an expert way.

Each person who performs his/her task with a high degree of knowledge, capability and efficiency, can therefore be called a professional. This applies to manual labour as much as it does to "higher functions".

However, there is a hierarchy of professions and as a result, the practitioners of some professions are almost automatically referred to as professionals. Medical doctors, lawyers, notaries and engineers are automatically considered to be professionals, and they are esteemed and paid as professionals; all this because they belong to an exclusive, expert and highly-trained group.

The question could arise as to whether the teaching profession in general has that status, and whether the P.E. teacher has a professional status within the group of teachers. This is certainly not always the case and as proof we can point to a series of initiatives which aim at polishing the image of the teaching profession in general and the profession of P.E. teacher in particular : for example, the professionalization movement of the "Carnegie task force on teaching as a profession", the "Holmes group" in the U.S.A. and the OECD's continuous concern for more quality teaching. We should also bear in mind the repeated call for quality in our own subject, which was heard during the last AAHPERD(1)-congress in Washington, its theme being "QP^2 : Quality programs, quality professionals". Finally, we can point to the permanent concern of ICHPER, which has created a special committee for "International curriculum standards for professional preparation of Physical Education Teachers".
And last but not least, we can note that the European Physical Education Association (EUPEA) wants to be involved in the discussion on the quality of teaching and teacher training.

I would like to discuss the following points :
- what does "professional" mean ?
- the extent of the teacher's professionalism in general.
- the extent of the P.E. teacher's professionalism.
- what does society expect from the P.E. teacher ?
- how can P.E. teacher training and more specifically the
  European Network, cope with this ?

2. What does "professional" mean ?

We can, according to Darling-Hammond et al. (1983) distinguish:

- <u>teaching as labour</u> : carrying out a program planned and programmatically organised by administrators.
- <u>teaching as craft</u> : requiring a repertoire of specialized techniques.
- <u>teaching as profession</u> : the teacher needs not only specialized techniques but should judge when these techniques should be applied and hence a body of theoretical knowledge.
- <u>teaching as art</u> : based not only on professional knowledge and skills but on a set of personal resources which are unique, novel, unconventional and unpredictable.

According to Perkin (1983) a profession could be described as a "desirable and dignified occupation of intellectual training and a largely mental exercise".

The OECD-report "The Teacher and Educational Change : a New Role" (1974) sums up the characteristics of a profession :

1. a whole of systematically ordered and transferable theoretical knowledge (<u>expertise</u>).

2. authority to perform independently all tasks in the field of the profession and authority to make eventual decisions (<u>autonomy</u>).

3. prestige recognized by society (<u>status</u>).

4. fundamental orientation towards service to society, which is usually formalized through an <u>ethical professional code</u> and a professional organization, which controls the application of this code.

5. professional culture, supported by <u>formal organizations</u> and informal, fraternal contacts as well as by institutional relationships.

Furthermore we should bear in mind the following variables (Harries-Jenkins (1970)) :

- <u>the structure</u> of the profession: the degree of specialization and exclusiveness.

- <u>the context</u>: for instance, the size of the professional group : the smaller, the more exclusive.

- <u>the conditions for membership</u>: the higher the required schooling, knowledge and conditions of entry, the more we deal with a profession.

There is no doubt at all that the status of professional is more obvious with doctors, magistrates, notaries, lawyers, engineers, architects, chemists, veterinary surgeons and, of course, also with university professors than with teachers. But how professional is the teacher and what are the obstacles which get in the way of this professionalism?

3. The teacher's professionalism

When we apply all the above mentioned conditions to the teaching profession, we immediately find that there is not the same degree of professionalism as there is with a medical doctor or a notary :
- teachers do not have a professional code;
- in many countries, training is not sufficient to achieve cultural development;
- professional organizations aim at syndicalism rather than at concern for quality for the profession;
- the professional group is far too large to be exclusive;
- social status is rather low, which is often reflected in low salaries.

However, in some aspects teachers do have the characteristics of professionals. First of all, we can point to educational expertise and to the serving nature of the profession, although it must be admitted that the level of the former is not everywhere equally high. As for the teacher's autonomy, this is restricted to the classroom. Outside the classroom, the teacher is usually only a semi-professional, in that she/he has to share this autonomy with colleagues, school boards and parents.

During the last few years, the problem of professionalization has come to the forfront of discussion.

The OECD (1990) takes a very great interest in quality teaching and consequently in professional teachers. Quality teaching can, following OECD, be obtained by :
- a smooth influx of new, motivated, well-trained teachers;
- responsibility to society (amongst others, to parents); This implies a change from a closed school to an open school;
- teachers who are able to work in a creative and independent way and who possess a broad range of professional skills;
- offering an attractive career, opportunities for promotion and better salaries;
- attracting teachers who are able and who are willing to perform, inside or outside school, tasks apart from their teaching task.

In the USA the following factors are cited as obstacles to the professionalization of the teaching profession :
- expens,
- feminization of the profession,
- difficulties in describing professional requirements,
- opposition on behalf of the political world and parents, who refuse to hand over control over schools to professionals,
- dominance of bureaucrats and administrators over underqualified teachers,
- low status and great diversity of training-institutes,
- small contribution of high-status universities to teacher training.

Additionally, the professionalization tendency is also criticized from within, by the teachers themselves. There are two main strands of criticism from this quarter. One strand, although it is theoretically in favour of professionalization, claims that the tendency is actually one of professionalization of professors, lecturers and instructors rather than of teachers, and that it leads to the promotion of research at training institutes rather than the improvement of practice in schools. The other strand rejects professionalization altogether. This view claims that, since it inevitably involves research-based rationalization and research-based educational practice, it would cause education to become too technical and not focussed clearly enough on the child's personal and social background and needs.

4. How professional is the P.E. teacher ?

4.1 Expertise

A P.E. teacher has to be an expert in educating and forming children and young people in the field of human movement and physical activities. This implies:

- that he should possess a thorough knowledge of pupils' general development and in particular, of their motor development.
- that he should possess knowledge and skills concerning movement culture.
- that he should have didactic competence in order to activate learning processes in the field of human kinetics and physical fitness, based upon development. In this way, he should contribute to modelling people who are able to function independently as democratic citizens.

In our profession we know a lot of examples defining or describing expertise or competence in our field (Oliver, 1990).

For too long, P.E. training-institutes have been obsessed with the so-called expertise of sports-club trainers, which has resulted in the transferring of a decoction of sports expertise to schools.

4.2 Autonomy

With increasing frequency, responsibilities for education are being handed down from higher management or decision making levels to school level. At school, the P.E. teacher has to possess a large amount of autonomy in order to organize his teaching. His high training-level, which provides him with expertise, allows him to plan and realize his teaching within a school curriculum in an autonomous way, although this should happen in co-ordination with other autonomous teachers.

4.3 Prestige-status

Prestige and status depend on related factors.

The P.E. teacher's prestige and social status depend on his personality and on the motivation, dedication and expertise he shows.
Prestige and status also depend on the group the teacher belongs to. That is, they depend on how active the P.E. teachers' association is, on the journal which is edited by them, on the journal's quality, on the association's representation in educational systems, on national and international contacts, on congresses, refresher courses, and so on. They are also determined by the level of education or schooling, by research related to the training, and by all national and international contacts of the training-institutes.

As a matter of course, prestige and status also depend on the degree of social relevance which citizens and people in charge attribute to P.E. as a school subject.

4.4 Ethical orientation and service to society

Besides transferring knowledge and teaching skills, the educational system is an outstanding environment for learning socially relevant attitudes. In this way, the school environment has a serving character.

Without doubt, the subject P.E. is sui generis particularly suitable for learning social skills and acquiring ethical attitudes. Moreover, physical education is being used in projects for health education, multicultural education, and so on.

4.5 Professional culture and formal organizations

It is quite clear that in this respect physical education overshadows many other teaching disciplines. In most countries, P.E. teachers' organizations have existed since the turn of the century, and international organizations such as FIEP (2) and ICHPER-SD (3) have come into being (in 1923 and 1958 respectively).

Scientific organizations such as ISCPES (4) and institutional organizations such as AIESEP (5) have also been created. In addition, national and international professional journals of academic stature are regularly published. "The Journal of Teaching in P.E.", the "Journal of Comparative Physical Education", "Quest" an the "International Journal of Physical Education" are good examples, although it should be noted that these journals have yet to improve their status and ranking in citations indexes.

Each year, congresses are being organized at which scientists and field-workers exchange information and communicate research results and practical experiences.

In this way, our field has developed a professional culture which not only contributes to the quality of physical education, but which also contributes to the status of P.E. (of course, the existence at these rather positive elements do not mean that we should not continue to improve quality of our organisations, congresses and journals).

4.6 Structure - specialization - exclusiveness

Expertise has already been noted as a requisite characteristic of a P.E. teacher. The distinctive nature of this expertise should now be made clear. P.E. teachers are not trainers, and trainers are not P.E. teachers. On this point, public opinion is often confused and this misunderstanding needs to be clarified urgently. Because of the huge impact of sports on physical education, the difference is not always clear. To the public, sport is practised both at school and in sport clubs, and one distinguishes no formal differences. And we have stimulated this confusion, for example here in Germany, where the word "Leibeserziehung" has been replaced by "Sportunterricht". As already mentioned, German terminology is still a matter of debate.

P.E. has tried to benefit from the status of sport. However, in doing so, it has lost part of its identity. As a result, even the people in charge of it sometimes argue that P.E. lessons should no longer be a part of the school curriculum and that it is enough if children have opportunities to go to sports clubs after school.

This narrow view, in which the role of P.E. is merely to initiate pupils in the practice of sport, constitutes a refutation of distinctiveness. Furthermore, it means that the P.E. teacher is not a professional, because any trainer could do the same, perhaps even better. It follows from this that any P.E. teacher who wants to be a professional must be, first and foremost, a good educator.

4.7 The size of the group

The group of teachers in general is considerable and this causes difficulties in achieving a high degree of professionalism.
However within the group of teachers, the proportion of P.E. teachers is rather small. Moreover, the position of the P.E. teacher within any one school, when he/she is the only one who teaches P.E., is exclusive.
There is some discussion about the relative merits of exclusive P.E. teacher-training as opposed a combination of this and training in other disciplines.
In this context, and in the context in which it is accepted that high qualifications are important to the quality of teachers, a rather obvious fact should be noted. The actual level of a specific professional qualification will be higher when a single subject is studied full time over four years than when two or three fields of study are followed over the same period.

4.8 Conditions of entry

I have already pointed out that the degree of professionalism corresponds to the level of teacher-education. Although P.E. teacher-education has existed in Europe since the beginning of this century (1908 Ghent), we are still confronted with several lower levels of education in this field.
In some countries, it takes place solely at university (France, Germany). In others, it also takes place at a lower level separate from university education (Austria, Belgium, Denmark, Portugal). In a few, there is no university-level education at all (Italy, The Netherlands, Switzerland).

The OECD has pleaded for university-level education because the teacher's tasks have become so much larger and because, as a result of this, a far greater amount of many-sidedness and flexibility is required. These attributes, it is felt, are best guaranteed by university-level education. Such a system also implies that the entry level for university will be a first threshold, which is in itself a kind of quality selection.

4.9 Summary

In summary, an application of the criteria for professionalism shows that the P.E. teacher meets most of them. What is needed in the future is some necessary adaptations in order to upgrade the professional image of P.E.. These will be achieved in the context of new challenges which will certainly be imposed upon education.

5. New social challenges at school

5.1 From an economic, social and cultural point of view, ever growing demands are made on schools and teachers. Schools, and therefore also teachers, should adjust to these rapid societal changes.
On the one hand, modern industry requires more and more highly qualified people; on the other hand, our community asks for more attention to be given to social phenomena such as multiculturalism, social disadvantage and drugrelated problems, and to social goals such as the integration of disabled people and equality of the sexes.

5.2 The sporting world puts pressure on school and P.E. to prepare young people for competition.

5.3 Social and economic status are linked to educational level. As a result, parents want their children to be educated to a high level, even if they do not possess the necessary aptitude. If these young people fail, this is attributed to a failing in the school system.

5.4 When both parents work, education within the family often fails. Moreover, because single parenthood has become quite common, the responsibility for general, moral and social education is passed on to the school.

5.5 The authorities expect from schools, and more specifically from P.E., that they should help in solving the problem of our youth's decreasing fitness.

6. Adapted professionalism

The teacher's responsibilities are becoming broader and his-/her tasks are getting more and more complex.

Besides transferring knowledge and skills in a particular field, the teacher is expected to perform several other duties.

According to a recent Dutch report (Heinstra 1993), a teacher will have to possess the following skills in the near future:

6.1 General professional qualifications

The ability to :
- plan, organize, perform and evaluate this teaching.
- support learning processes and development processes on a pedagogical and educational level.
- develop curricula and teaching material.
- be innovative.
- be a spokesperson for educational values.
- do research on education.

6.2 Substantial professional demands

- social expertise: knowledge of, involvement and participation in cultural and social events.
- instrumental expertise: knowledge of the subject, pedagogical, didactic, social and ethical skills, and organizing qualities.
- task expertise in relation to broad utility within the school organization. A larger differentiation in tasks and functions could offer more perspectives to the teacher.

6.3 Social and ethical qualifications

Because there is no teaching without values and because a lot of educational tasks are no longer family matters, the teacher should adhere to a professional code. This involves responsibilities:

- towards himself, as a human being and as a teacher;
- towards his pupils;
- towards his colleagues;
- towards society.

The above series of qualifications is deduced from the professional roles and tasks which a teacher will have to perform in the future. What is notable about them is that one particular qualification runs through them like a continuous thread. This is the ability to reflect on one's own everyday professional practice. This ability is important because it is a precondition for the development of professionalism.

Although this skill in <u>introspection</u> has been heavily stressed over the last few years, the concept of a critical attitude is not new to our field. The work in the seventies of the wellknow Frankfurter Arbeitsgruppe and of Knut Dietrich in the journal "Sportpädagogik" are examples of earlier attention to this aspect.
It is striking that in July of this year, an AIESEP-seminar was held in Trois Rivières in Canada with as its main theme "The training of Teachers in Reflective Practice of Physical Education". At this seminar, Bart Crum (1993) gave a lecture on "the urgent need for reflective teaching in physical education".

7. A professional code as a keeper of professionalism ?

These days more and more voices are heard among teachers demanding that a professional code should be drawn up, following the example of other professions such as the medical. This professional code, it is claimed, could watch over professionalism in the following ways (Heinstra, 1993).

- It could be an instrument to improve quality of teaching.
- It could demonstrate to the outside world what serious work teaching actually is, and it could also be a means to monitoring professionalism.
- It could standardize all phases of professional qualification, from initial training to the highest degree of professionalism.
- It could provide arguments in support of professional demands regarding conditions of employment reflecting the profession's status.

These ideas raise a number of questions. For example:
- who is to draw up such a code ?
- should it be a general teacher's code or should there be several codes specific to disciplines? I can easily imagine that certain items would apply to a P.E. teacher but not, for example, to a mathematics teacher.
- is the code to have national, European or worldwide coverage ?

Our professional organizations, both national and international, will have to think over matters such as these.

8. Consequences for teacher training

8.1 If we want to achieve a high degree of professionalism, then the first requirement is that the teacher's training for this professionalism should correspond to this aim.

8.1.1 <u>Intellectual, cultural and personality development</u> turn the teacher into a highly educated individual, who is able to fulfil his task in an independent and creative way.
Mere specific subject related knowledge and mere technical or sports skills cannot result in professionalism.

8.1.2 <u>Thorough professional knowledge</u> entails providing an insight into the backgrounds of the sciences which support the discipline.

8.1.3 This professional knowledge is partly acquired by a fair amount of <u>practical expertise in the motor activities</u> which are relevant for P.E. teaching.

8.1.4 It is only through <u>extensive pedagogical and didactic preparation</u> that the student can master the skills which are necessary to enable him to perform his/her pedagogical task and his/her cultural transfer in the most efficient way.

8.2 The kind of professionalism we have in mind can only be achieved in <u>highly qualified institutions</u> of academic stature, where training and research stimulate each other. It should be clear that this research has to be relevant for P.E. and that it has to support teaching. Far too often, research at our universities stands apart from P.E. and only serves high-performance sports.

8.3 <u>Selection of the students</u>

8.3.1 The intake of P.E. students who want to become P.E. teachers should meet certain criteria. Besides their sufficiently high level of intelligence and general education and their sporting capabilities, their motivation to become a teacher should also be taken into account. In fact, it seems that a student's strongest motivation is often his/her interest in sports rather than that in a teacher's pedagogical task. Crum (1990) has pointed this out as a possible reason for the lack of interest in P.E. within the educational system.

8.3.2 During the years of study, a selection has to be made based upon academic outlook, sporting, pedagogical and didactic skills. However, a discussion of training models, curricula and their contents, the relative merits of training or several subjects etc. would lead us too far afield. Once again, I refer here to the international curriculum standards for professional preparation of Physical Education teachers proposed by the curriculum committee of ICHPER.

9. A professionalisation model

Determinants in Professionalisation of P.E. Teachers

DETERMINANTS IN PROFESSIONALISATION OF P.E. TEACHERS

TEACHER TRAINING INSTITUTE

- EXPERTISE
- AUTONOMY
- PROFESSIONAL AND GENERAL CULTURE
- DEVOTION AND SERVICE TO SCHOOL AND SOCIETY

P.E. TEACHER

P.E. PROFESSIONAL ORGANISATION

SCHOOL

SOCIETY

Professionalism is influenced by five main determinants.

1. **The personality of the teacher**, including his/her compentences motivation and dedication.

2. **The teacher training Institute.** This provides knowledge and skills so that the starting competencies of the beginning teacher can evolve into real professionalism. The higher the level of training, the higher the potential level of professionalism.
   Teacher training should have close contacts with both school and also the P.E. teacher organizations in order to receive feedback and adjust programs accordingly. Teacher training institutes should organize in-service training in close collaboration with the schools and the professional organization.

3. **The school** has to give opportunities to the teacher to become a professional by granting autonomy and by providing facilities to participate in in-service training sessions.

4. **The P.E. teacher association** has a responsibility to the teacher and to the profession to disseminate information by editing a journal and also by representing the profession in society at large. P.E. associations should monitor the quality of P.E. and should guarantee, in collaboration with teacher training institutions, the scientific level of, and the ethical guidelines for, P.E. teaching.

5. **Society**: the P.E. teacher should be fully aware of what is happening in society in order to adapt his teaching to its needs. Professional teachers will be highly valued by society if P.E. is fulfilling the needs of society. More over he/she should be involved in services to society in and outside his school job.

10. Conclusions

The call for more professionalism and better care for quality in the teaching profession is getting louder and louder. This is a sign of the growing awakening of consciousness among teachers, educational policy makers and several social structures. To physical education, professionalism will appear to be a question of to be or not to be. Either P.E. will be handled in a professional way, and as a result its status and recognition will both grow, or P.E. will play only a minor role in education. In this paper, I have deliberately not written about objectives and contents, about curricula at schools and during the teacher training period. These are matters which should be discussed elsewhere. But we have to remember that professionalism is a process which needs to be supported by several authorities or bodies.

1. Training programmes for teachers, preferably at universities, bear a great deal of responsibility in this, because they have to provide a good output of young people who have all capacities necessary to become good professionals.

2. Teachers have continuously to improve their professionalism through reflection, reading and research.

3. The school system has to look after and to control the teaching quality of its teachers.

4. Teachers have to be backed up and have to get additional in service training through external support.

5. Authorities have to provide solid legislation, which improves the relationship between teachers, schools and inspectors. They also have to guarantee fair salary arrangements; it is clear that quality teaching by professionals should be valued.

6. It is the main task of a professional organization to act as an informant and a stimulus to the teacher. Moreover, a professional organization has to represent its subject and uphold its image.

7. The responsible professional bodies such as EUPEA, ICHPER, AIESEP and the European Network should find solutions for the implementation of high professionalism in P.E..

References

1. AAHPERD, QP^2-Quality Programs, Quality Professionals. AAHPERD National Convention, Washington DC., 1993.

2. Crum B.: The Self Reproducing Failing of Physical Education. In: R. Telama, L. Laakso, M. Piéron, I. Ruppola and V. Vihko (Eds.), Physical Education and Life-long Physical Activity. Jyväskylä, 1990.

3. Crum B.: The Urgent Need for Reflective Teaching in Physical Education, AIESEP-Seminar, Trois-Rivières, 1993.

4. **Darling-Hammond L., Wise A., Pease S.:** Teacher Evaluation in the Organisational Context : A Review of the Literature, Rev. of Educ. Re search, Vol. 53:3, 285-328, 1983.

5. **Griffey D., Oliver B. (ed.):** Teacher Testing and Teacher Competence. Monograph of the Journal of Teaching in Physical Education, Vol. 9:3, Champaign, Human Kinetics, 1990.

6. **Harries-Jenkins:** Professionals in Organizations. In: J. Jackson (ed.): Professions and Professionalization. Cambridge, 1970.

7. **Heinstra R.J.:** Beroepscode voor Leraren ... een Opmaat voor Kwaliteit. Velon-Tijdschrft, 14:3, 48-54, 1993.

8. **Hellison D.R., Templin T.J.:** A Reflective Approach to Teaching Physical Education, Champain, Human Kinetics, 1991.

9. **Holmes Group, Tomorrow's Teachers :** A report of the Holmes Group. East Lansing. MI., 1986.

10. **ICHPER,** International Curriculum Standards for professional preparation of P.E.-teachers. Working Draft F. Grebner, 1993.

11. **Kurz D.:** Sportpädagogik als Teildisziplin oder integrativer Kern der Sportwissenschaft. Sportwissenschaft 2:145-154, 1992.

12. **OECD,** The Teacher and Educational Change : a New Role. Paris, OECD, 1974.

13. **OECD,** The Teacher Today. Tasks, Conditions. Policies, Paris, OECD, 1990.

14. **Oliver B.:** Defining Competence : the case of Teaching, J. of Teaching in Physical Education 9:184-188, 1990.

15. **Perkin H.:** The Teaching Profession and the Game of Life. In: P. Gordon (ed.) Is Teaching a Profession ? London, Institute of Education, University of London, 1983.

16. **Scherler K.:** Sportpädagogik - eine Disziplin der Sportwissenschaft. Sportwissenschaft 2:155-166, 1992.

17. Solmon M.A., Worthy T., Lee A.M., Carter J.A.: Teacher Role Identity of Student Teachers in Physical Education : An Interactive analysis. J. of Teaching in Phys. Educ. 10: 188-209, 1990.

Footnotes

[1] **AAHPERD :** American Aliance for Health, Physical Education, Recreation and Dance.

[2] **FIEP :** Fédération International d'Education Physique.

[3] **ICHPER-SD :** International Council on Health, Physical Education, Recreation, Sport and Dance.

[4] **ISCPES :** International Society of Comparative Physical Education and Sport.

[5] **AIESEP :** Association International des Ecoles Supérieures d'Education Physique.

Sportpedagogy as a Science

Meinberg, E.
Pädagogisches Seminar, Deutsche Sporthochschule Köln
Germany

1. Sportpedagogy as a science

All the themes and the problem areas which are concealing themselves behind this title can only be presented in a very reduced and superficial way. Who wants to claim seriously, provided with a small amount of time, that he is able to present a final polished picture of the European theory of sportpedagogy? That would be nothing but presumptuous. Therefore, you cannot expect from my explanations a stock-taking of theories of European sportpedagogy which are, in part, completely different or hardly developed. The term "sportpedagogy" already contains its very own difficulties: Is the term, for example, identical with the term "physical education" and how is the term "sportpedagogy" related to the term "Körperkultur"(culture of body), an expression preferred in East-Europe. It is difficult to speak at all about the European sportpedagogical science itself and in general.

It is, nevertheless, the duty of the international community of scholars to come to an understanding of what sportpedagogy as a science could mean. And it is that which I want to address in my lecture. I intend to up a programmatic frame for the sportpedagogy as a special science by searching for cultural phenomena in common. My intention is to qualify such problems which, independent of the prevailing culture, have to be considered, if the claim is made for sportpedagogical science and research.

2. The idendity of discipline of the sportpedagogy: aspects

I am interested in an identity of discipline of a common European sportpedagogy. Based on this interest, I am going to list the important areas which emerged structually from the sportpedagogy as a science.

2.1 The character of the science

At the beginning there is undoubtedly the question about the character of the science of sportpedagogy. What kind of science is this sportpedagogy? Can you put sportpedagogy in the common schemes and classifications of the other fields of science - or is the sportpedagogy probably of such an incomparability that the sportpedagogy holds an extraordinary character of its own? You can answer this question in a simple and, at the same time, concise way: Sportpedagogy refers to human behaviour or, more precisely, to the sportive/playing actions and behaviour in connection with the educational behaviour that the sportpedagogy tries to penetrate and to understand (the scientific behaviour is also a field of the sportpedagogy as I will demonstrate in my considerations). The different forms of behaviour and actions are the center of the sportpedagogy. Therefore, the sportpedagogy can be called a science of behaviour. Naturally, the use of this term is connected with a lot of complicated questions which cannot be answered easily. For example: How does a science of action/behaviour compare to the Arts and to the social sciences which are not mentioned here?

According to the wide-spread division of sciences into natural sciences and the Arts and then recently into social sciences, sportpedagogy tends toward the social sciences and the Arts which interpret human behaviour from different points of view. Both - the social sciences and the Arts see their justification in this task.

Not without reason J.S. MILL named, what is mainly entitled "Geisteswissenschaften" in the German language area, "moral sciences"; it is hardly possible to express the relation to human behaviour any clearer.

But of course, research of sportpedagogy is not restricted to human behaviour in general but to carefully selected types of behaviour and to the sportive and playing actions which can be characterized mainly by the phenomenon of movement. Although this uniqueness stands always in a close relationship to human behaviour in general.

You can see this fact from another point of view: The fertile humus soil of the sportpedagogical science is undoubtedly the practice. If you look a little bit closer into this practice you will find out that this practice consists of more than one practice and of a variety of incalculable situations. Therefore, sportpedagogy can be considered as a practical science. You can say that sportpedagogy owes its right to exist to an extraordinary practice. As the present demonstrates, the theory receives its impulses from a very dynamic sports and playing practice. But at the same time the theory, despite all organizational established complications, is interested in influencing the practice in a positive way, so that - I hope you will accept at this place the introduction of the always questionable term "dialectics" - it could come to an interaction between theory and practice. But because of many reasons this is not necessarily so.

The naive view is commonly held in Europe that it is an obligation of the practical sciences to develop theories which could easily be transferred to the practice (what kind of practice ?); or even more simple is the view that the sportpedagogical theory could offer a reference book full of solutions and that the sportpedagogical theory has nothing more to do than to pick out the right solution. This view is a misunderstanding of the sportpedagogical theory.

No sportpedagogical theory will ever be able to record and embrace the sportpedagogical practice completely. The theory has got a special character, even if it tries hard to strive for the whole, the theory still remains, with regard to the practice, a fragment. The theory, based on carefully selected criteria, always perceives only certain aspects and levels of the practice and is far away from embracing the whole sportpedagogical practice. Therefore the sportpedagogical theory is not able to fulfill all the wishes and the hopes of its listeners. But what can be and should be expected in general from a "sportpedagogical" theory as a science rooted in practice?

The next sentences have to be regarded carefully: The sportpedagogical theory observes with scientifically blurred eyes the sportpedagogical practice, it describes and explains to achieve that the different kinds of practice become more acquainted with each other and to become more understandable to each other. The sportpedagogical theory is determined to improve the understanding and tries at the same time to make innovations possible with the help of its knowledge. But an absolutely necessary condition to achieve this is the work of developing a theoretical framework. Unfortunately sciences are condemned or obliged to create theories. With the help of these theories it might be possible to learn to interpret sportive/playing behaviour as an expression of human beings. The creation of theories, both, small and big, detailed and complex as well as abstract and concrete, those that concern the past and those of an utopian future, regional and nation-wide, empirical and non empirical is the first civic duty of the sportpedagogy as a science. Precisely it is this obligation that should be taken seriously by the so called sportpedagogical theorists. These sportpedagogical theorists are a circle of scientists in which - as we can notice to our deepest regret - a peculiar shyness against theories is clearly visible. Moreover, it seems as if, in this circle, the committed and passionate creation of theories, which is not to be mixed up with the esoteric, is a superfluous stigma ridden business. But probably it is also due to the fact that sportpedagogy is comparable with a declining star in the hierarchy of reputation. Reluctance towards theories can be very harmful.

You can say that sportpedagogy is a "Handlungswissenschaft" which derives its questions from the different kinds of "active" practice, which the sportpedagogy mainly wants to purify and to change, if it is wanted. According to scientific standards this attempt of purification and changing is based on various results in observation, description, explanation and comprehension. In this intention the sportpedagogy interrelates with the other "Handlungswissenschaften" and therefore does not deserve at all any right to exclusiveness. The "sportpedagogy" fits in the frame of all the other practical sciences, but at the same time, the sportpedagogy does research of special kinds of the sportive and playing "Bewegungshandeln". Because of this extraordinary research sportpedagogy differs from the other sciences. The speciality of the sportpedagogy results from the description of its subjects and themes.

2.2 The subject matter of sportpedagogy

In a first approach the subject matter of sportpedagogy is sportive and playing actions. What is considered as sportpedagogy is the combination with and the relation to the pedagogical acting. As a result of long lasting conventions the pedagogical acting is equated with education, lessons, development and learning. Pedagogical situations are in some ways always connected with requirements which have the general aim to support the personal development of the adolescents - or as SCHLEIERMACHER has formulated it in a timeless and unsurpassable way: "education is the influence of an older generation on a younger one."

However, for what is said here, there exists another version which is worded in general terms and is suitable to reach agreement in the whole of Europe about this delicate question: sportpedagogy's working field is undoubtedly the educational process embracing sportive and playing actions. These educational processes require theoretical uncovering and practical support. Educational process encompasses - this is an important additional remark - educational processes as well as learning- and developing processes. To summarize this in a formula you can say: the subject matter of the sportpedagogy as a theory is the chances of education, embedded in various sportive and playing situations, as genuine practices of individual life styles.

Although further explanations are not necessary in this auditorium, it might be important to mention two things:

The supremacy of the educational category which did not have the best reputation in the last few years and was deformed more than once, at least in the German language area, automatically shows a big European heritage - namely the tradition of the educational theory - which, to avoid all misunderstandings right from the beginning, should not be continued uncritically or even be glorified. Nevertheless, you can not conceal the fact that the cradle of the modern sportpedagogy is in Europe and that the modern sportpedagogy was disseminated in this intellectual climate. Representatives of this intellectual climate are ROUSSEAU or PESTALOZZI.

Both - among other important persons (for example: W. von HUMBOLDT) - increased in their emphatic demands for "genuine production of human beings", for genuine individualization, the value of the sensory and the value of the body. They considered the body as an object which is educable and as an object which is necessary to educate.

With this opinion view, PESTALOZZI and ROUSSEAU showed the actual sportpedagogy the frame for its subject matter, which is so important for the character of sportpedagogy.

Reminiscence also shows that even young sciences like in our case sportpedagogy (offspring and branch of the pedagogy anyway) stick to traditions as to regarding to the field of research and they are interested in restoring old results of the research. But you have to point out that sportpedagogy does not come to terms with the role of the Keeper of the Holy Grail. It is absolutely clear that things (results of research) are not restored for eternity. Especially the development of the young sportpedagogy is a good example for the expansion, nuanciation and the modification of the field of research. So you can say that a new and progressive aspect is always added to an old and static aspect. Anything else would be very surprising because it is the special or extraordinary character of a "Handlungswissenschaft" to stand in a close contact with the practice. This practice can be characterized, especially in the European countries, as a very dynamic one and as a practice full of changes.

2.3 The methodology

One fact is absolutely clear: Sportpedagogy has got, like all the other sciences, an invariant-variant object of research. It is even clear that the sportpedagogy has to elaborate its object of research in a suitable way and not at discretion if it wants that its results will be accepted or taken seriously. Sportpedagogy achieves this appropriateness by basing its researching results on the generally accepted researching methods. To put it in other words: Sportpedagogy is obliged to researching methods which are necessary instruments for the sportpedagogy's scientific work. The fact that "clean" research within the sportpedagogy depends on a reflecting awareness (consciousness) of methods and influences the quality in a positive or negative way is a well known fact. Since I have not got the time to make an excursion in researching methods, I would like to point out three important aspects:

The scientific theoretical theorem that there exists some kind of correspondence between the chosen object of research and the prevailing method, that you can not find out everything with one or with the same method, should be of an absolute validity for the sportpedagogy, too.

The fact I have just mentioned above stands in very close relationship to the following aspect, namely that sportpedagogy as a science has to deplete the whole repertoire of existing theories to do justice to its subject matter. (The claim that sportpedagogy has to develop its own researching methods because of its extraordinary character came up in the sixties from time to time. This demand should be put to the relicts of the pioneer time and should be buried straight away).

A major task of the sportpedagogy is to explain and understand the different pedagogical important and sportive kinds of practice. Therefore the hermeneutical group of methods is playing an important role which does not mean that the position of the other methods is devaluated. The hermeneutical methods, often denounced, even today, as the "softies" in the repertoire of methods, are the prevailing ones; at the latest since the objectivity, which seems to remain inviolable for the hermeneutic for ever, is exposed as being close to the myth, and even intelligent natural scientists have used the "postulate of unsharpness" already since the 1/3 of the century.

2.4 Researching types

Sportpedagogical research gains its knowledge, in contrast to the pure acting of the sportpedagogical practising teacher, from sticking to the methodological rules and from trying to put them into practice. The purpose of research could be, and that is not a secret, of different nature. Not only the fact that they are obeying more or less strictly a certain method but also the fact that they are trying to connect their targets with certain types of research is characteristic for the sciences. The distinction between pure research and applied research, a really classical disjunction, which points at the same time at an allocation of the science is well known in this context. Just let me mention three aspects in this context.

For a few years you can observe that (comp.: report of the ministry of research and development) the pure research - this kind of research which is not aiming at a concrete and direct area of application but is not doing researches only for the sake of research as it is perceived from time to time - is forced onto the defensive. Further you can observe that the financial resources will be cut more and more. (This is in accordance with the opinion recently uttered in the budget debate of the "Bundestag" [German Parliament] in 1993: " we need a gentle correction: more applied research - less pure research; more prose - less lyrics"). In fact you can hardly express this more lyrically. Of course the scientists worry about the fact that a further weakening (undermining) of the pure research would be unresponsible and that the heart of the science would be destroyed - because it is proved that a lot of results, based on the work of pure research, are of or probably could be later of an important relevance. You can say casually that science without pure research would be like Cologne without the cathedral (Cologne Dome).

Therefore it follows that applied research is favoured today. The consequence of this is that now the science is mainly judged from its usefullness; at the end the science will be, as everything else, submitted to the laws of the market and will be or should be product orientated. The economical discourse is covering - like a huge shadow - the science more and more. Categories (economical terms) like marketorientation, profitability, profit orientation, and maximation of profit have become important for the science.

(This unmistakable tendency becomes visible in the ministerial supported emergence of sponsoring the science which can often be compared with an external order for science. Foundation chairs which are often established for a special purpose - namely to make one's own practical research - are a good example for the increasing influence of the sponsoring on the sciences).

All these are indisputable indicators for the dominance of a market orientated and applied science; it is not an accident that pure research is mainly located in institutions which do not belong to the university. Utilitarianism and pragmatism are the main characteristics of current research.

At the end this fact contains a development which can lead to or has already led to an expansion of the traditional distinction between pure and applied research for what we can call "service science". This kind of science is influenced by external interests and is regarded as a satisfaction of a specific practical need. Therefore, this is science temporally limited and is chosen for the direct practical usability. If my trendanalyse will be accepted, we are confronted with a science triad at the moment: to say it in a more precise way, we are confronted with pure research, which should become more and more applied, with applied research, which becomes productorientated and we are confronted with the so called "service research", which is permanently forced up and has clients who do not belong to a university. What kind of role does the sportpedagogical science play in this context?

Does the sportpedagogy fit in this panorama of research? Does sportpedagogy cultivate pure research or is this something completely strange for the sportpedagogy? You can nearly suppose that, if you consider the restraint behaviour of those in questions of theory, who are working with this science. What can pure research mean within the sportpedagogy? Is this alignment for a practical science not necessary? Does sportpedagogy know the phenomenon of the service research? Or is it not correct that this type is left out of consideration in case of a science which is busy with extremely complex pedagogical and educational processes? I wonder if it is possible to develop European large-scale projects which could point out the conditions of a possible cooperation between the pure and applied research in the case of the sportpedagogy and even rehearse this at very concrete examples. This would be, because of reasons of progressiveness, very helpful for the "sportpedagogy" as a science.

2.5 Kinds of knowledge

My last considerations were also used to encourage the sportpedagogy, more than usual, to concentrate on its deepest inner life and to occupy itself with the own scientific identity because this is a necessary precondition to pursue the practical ambitions in a single-minded and profitable way. To achieve this there is undoubtedly an additional step necessary. It is important for the sportpedagogy to find out what kind of knowledge it tries to create or helps to create. Because: Symptomatic for science is knowledge, that teaches us the linguistic feeling already. And symptomatic for knowledge is the occurrence of plurality of them. The distinction between sciences is that they insist on different kinds of knowledge; not each science knows the same - by the way this would be a very desperately boring monotony.

Analogous to the different researching types it is also possible to come up with knowledge typologies. Especially sciences should differentiate between different kinds of knowledge. Of course this happened from time to time already. (comp.: SCHELERs division in: " Bildungs- , Herrschafts- and Heilswissen" and also behind HABERMAS' teachings of "recognition guiding interests" conceals a specification of knowledge). But this is not on the agenda of the sportpedagogy and, therefore, it is necessary to reflect about the most important types of knowledge. I think that we can differentiate between at least four types.

1. Knowledge of orientation:
Crucial is: Knowledge of orientation is a kind of knowledge which remains in a more general-abstract sphere (this includes reflection about the sense of competitive sport, of physical education and about the sense of certain models etc.).

2. Handlungswissen (Knowledge of acting):
The "knowledge of acting" is on a more concrete level compared to the knowledge of orientation. This kind of knowledge is both, more detailed and more understandable than the knowledge of orientation, but above all the "knowledge of acting" is situative minded. "Knowledge of acting" is a kind of knowledge of the situation, even though it appears with the claim of being generalizationable. (The knowledge used for teaching preparations belongs to the knowledge of acting - this can be distinguished from the technological knowledge).

3. The technological knowledge:
The technological knowledge, as a special version, is not to be mixed up with the term "high tech". It has its roots in the Greek word "techne", it is technical knowledge, that means something like skilfulness or - referring to the ancient Greeks again - it is close to the word "poiesis" which means the manufacturing of knowledge. In the end technical and technological knowledge means the

"know how" in the sportpedagogy. A perfect example for this kind of knowledge is the method, which has in the subject physical education one of its most popular field of work.

4. The self reflexive knowledge:
A total different form of knowledge is the self reflexive knowledge. That special kind of knowledge does not refer directly - as opposed to the other kinds of knowledge - to sportpedagogy, but it refers to a level above that and introduces the scientific knowledge created by the sportpedagogy itself. This sportpedagogical knowledge - therefore, you can call also meta knowledge. Anyway, why is this knowledge which you can not find in the common terminologies necessary?

To put it in a nutshell: to envisage the possible consequences of an expulsion of knowledge which orientates towards scientific parameters. (I would like to demonstrate this with the help of an simple example: Let's suppose that the sportpedagogy advices grown ups the torture of competitive sports. The behaviour could be called self reflexive at that moment, when the sportpedagogy involves possible consequences of its advice and begins to produce knowledge then. The success of the current claim for an estimation of the consequences of scientific results depends in a strong way on the fact if the sciences are capable of producing self reflexive knowledge).

Finally we can say: the different kinds of knowledge, between which I have differentiated, are related with one another - probably with a little bit more phantasy you can develop more schemes with additional classifications and subgroups. You can not exclude an assignment of different kinds of knowledge from the existing different kinds of science. But probably this could be a field of work, where pure research is responsible for the basic knowledge and applied research could help to create the knowledge of acting.

2.6 Sportpedagogy in the context of other sciences: neighbouring disciplines

Sportpedagogy is on the one hand influenced by the pedagogy and on the other hand influenced by the science of sports:
Sportpedagogy is both - part of the pedagogy and part of the science of sports. The science of sports itself is divided in a conglomerate of subdisciplines, but the pedagogy's grade of differentiation is, because of its age, much more distinctive than the one of the science of sports. The result is that the sportpedagogy has some "blood relatives" and that the number of the siblings is enormous and rich of variations (for example: the "Freizeitpedagogy", is as well a sister of the sportpedagogy as the sportsmedicine, the "Kriminalpädagogik" and the sportssociology). It is not surprising that the contact or the communication

to the just enumerated disciplines is closer, more fertile and more intensive than to other disciplines to which the sportpedagogy has either no relationship or a very sporadic one. Sportpedagogy has to approach or has to go towards the different sciences (a "word" of JEAN PAUL is handed down: to talk about education means, at the same time, to talk about everything). Sportpedagogy has to borrow knowledge from here and there; so sportpedagogy has to come into contact with the philosophy or the psychology - but not to the extent that the sportpedagogy loses its own character. What sportpedagogy needs are complementary sciences and not mega sciences by which the sportpedagogy loses its own character.

If you try to enclose and to label the surrounding of the neighbouring disciplines which are closely related to sportpedagogy, you can describe the sportpedagogy as a special kind of a somatic pedagogy, which stands out from the others because of its emphasis on the corporeality.

2.7 The social function of the sportpedagogical science

I would like to finish the "Tour-Parforce-Ride" through the area of science by giving a short comment on the specific characters of sciences: sciences do not move or exist in a vacuum, they are not hostile to society but socially accepted, and what is very important they are very useful for the development of society. The system of sciences is a function of society and takes on, at the same time, an important function of this society, namely the production of knowledge. In times of financial or economic crisis science becomes aware of her integration in the system of society at the latest. Science is a very public affair and often receives help from the public - without this help the enterprise of science would not be possible. Scientific research is always financially supported in every European country. Science accepts this help but it also gives it back. But what does this science give back? Science gives back that kind of science which is absolutely necessary for the continuation of society. Society needs the science to survive - this is one of the main functions of science. Without doubts science is accountable to the public. Therefore, the social function of science includes the moral acting of the person who does scientific research.

How much the scientific activity includes a special moral quality shows the existence of the law of freedom of the science in Germany and in other places. Freedom, for many the greatest good of human beings, is tied together with science (but also with art). This is, compared with other occupations, a privilege which can not be appreciated enough. And who possesses this privilege should be willing to show special moral engagement and not only raise the voice when shortenings of the privileges are to be feared. Freedom is tied together with responsibility so that scientists have to be responsible in a certain way. But this necessary responsibility often leads to abuse.

Science can expect from society and from politics protection of the freedom, but on the other hand society must rely on that science does not abuse that freedom. Let us believe RHEINARD MEY, a famous German Song writer, that only above the clouds freedom is unlimited.

Finally, please allow me to point out two eminent important principles that are tied together with the freedom of science. To avoid that the use of this freedom is not converted into arbitrariness every scientist of the sportpedagogy is obliged to prove the relevance of his respective object of research. The scientist has to question him- or herself if society can make use of his or her researching results, because sciences have a serving function towards the human community in the sense of the world community. Sciences have to perceive a serving function. This function is the measure of the ideas, the approaches and the results of the sportpedagogy. The sportpedagogy - and this is the second aspect - has to make a genuine contribution to the humanization and not to the destruction of society. This is very demanding and everybody knows that it is very difficult to fulfill this, and therefore everything necessary has to be done to make a preceding possible, without loading the burden of humanization of the human conditions onto the sciences alone. The social function and duty of the "sportpedagogy" as a science in this only world consists also of the continual admonition that a misregard of the body means at the same time a misregard of the human being. I can't and I don't want to find another closing word.

References

1. **Meinberg, E.:** Hauptprobleme der Sportpädagogik. Darmstadt 1991.

2. **Ders.:** Zum Ansatz einer verstehend-beschreibenden Sportpädagogik. In: Brehm, W./Kurz, D. (Red.): Forschungskonzepte in der Sportpädagogik. DVS-Protokolle Nr. 28, 37-56. Clausthal-Zellerfeld 1987.

3. **Ders.:** Sportpädagogik als Wissenschaft - Entwicklung und Ansatzpunkte. In: DENK, H./HECKER, G. (Hrsg.): Texte zur Sportpädagogik. Teil II, 10-34. Schorndorf 1985.

Physical Education Teacher Training
- Historical Perspectives -

Naul, R.
University of Essen
Germany

1. Introduction

Famous universities employed fencing and riding instructors in many European countries even before the year 1800; on the premises of the university these gentlemen taught their students the art of fencing and horseback-riding, and these students passed their skills on to others (cf. Krüger 1989). Physical education had a tradition in all European countries, particularly due to the aristocratic education and knightly religious exercises, which the sons of the haute bourgeoisie experienced after 1750. However, the writings mainly of French doctors and pedagogues such as Tissot and Rousseau had the first long-lasting impact on the European intellectual history and the new beginning of a bourgeois physical education before and after the French Revolution (1789) (cf. Bernett 1960).

Indeed, many stimuli and ideas, which can be found in the first textbooks on a new, bourgeois physical education, originated in France; they were recognized and acknowledged rapidly across Europe and had a large influence on the beginnings of physical education teacher training in many countries during the early 19th century.

Two keystones for this development were the literary works and instructional activities of Johann Heinrich Pestalozzi (1808) from Switzerland and Friedrich Christoph Gutsmuths (1793) from Germany. Their systems of pedagogical (GutsMuths) and elementary gymnastics (Pestalozzi) determined the beginnings of physical education teacher training across Europe. They gave many European fellows, in Denmark and Sweden as well as in Spain, and even the grandfather of reformed public schools in England, Thomas Arnold, ideas for their own activities (cf. McIntosh 1968 ,pp. 28, 79; ,Smith 1974, pp.80).

However, the foundation for the beginnings of state-supported physical education teacher training did not emerge from intellectual historical consideration; rather, it was a result of the political and social situation that many European countries were in after 1800. Napoleon Bonaparte ruled over many European countries through occupation and skilled policy of alliances. In almost all countries drastic state reforms in administration, military, and education were initiated, either as a consequence of Napoleon's occupation, or as a national unification and renewal against this occupation, or as a new beginning after the regained liberty and independence and as protection against future military conflicts and territorial losses.

During the entire 19th century, including the period between 1850 and 1870, and in the 20th century before and after World War I the reorganisation of the military before and after the periods of military conflicts was a real impetus and stimulus for the support of physical education and physical education teacher training in many European countries. This mechanism transferred the good words and pedagogic ideas of Gutsmuths and Pestalozzi as well as of their numerable successors to the social reality of physical education teacher training in most European countries. In the following I will focus on the intellectual and structural historical development of physical education teacher training, and I would like that you take in mind the special connection to their real historical differentiations.

2. The First Systems of Physical Education Teacher Training

The systems of Gutsmuths and Pestalozzi became the first basic systems of European physical education teacher training. When Frans Nachtegall opened his private gymnastic institute in Copenhagen in 1799, he had studied Gutsmuths "Gymnastics for the Youth" either in German or as a Danish translation. He adopted his system and it became the basis of instruction for the first state physical education training school in Europe, which was established in Copenhagen in 1804. This Military Gymnastics Institute was expanded with a civil department for training elementary school teachers in 1808. Only 6 years later, in 1814, when Napoleon's era came to an end, gymnastics became a compul-sory subject in Danish elementary schools, which was a novelty in Europe. Meanwhile, Gutsmuths' successor, Per Henrik Ling from Sweden, had already stepped into Nachtegall's shoes. Per Henrik Ling went to Nachtegall's private institute in Copenhagen in 1799 and stayed there for about 5 years. Ling took Gutsmuths' ideas to the University of Lund after 1804, continued to study anatomy and physiology and elaborated his own system later (cf. Georgii & Liedbeck 1840). In 1813, the Swedish King agreed to open the Royal Central Gymnastic Institute (CGI) in Stockholm, and Ling was elected director of the new institute, which opened its doors for a first training course for officers one year later. This Central Gymnastic Institute of Stockholm became the most important and leading of this kind in Europe for about one century (cf. Leonard 1947; pp. 148; de Genst 1949, pp. 158).

After 1800 Pestalozzi's system of gymnastics and method of instruction was studied and accepted by many visitors, military personnel, and educators from many European countries in order to renew their national military and educational systems. In 1806, two years after the foundation of the first Military Gymnastic Institute in Copenhagen, the "Real Instituto Militar Pestalozziano" was founded in Madrid and Voitel, a Swiss national, was elected the first director. A year later Senor Amoros y Ondeano took over the institute, started his courses, and developed a system based on Pestalozzi. In 1810, Amoros brought his ideas to Lisbon in Portugal, and when he left Spain after Napoleon's brother Joseph was forced to resign as the King of Spain in 1814, Amoros emigrated to Paris. He became the founder of physical education training in France, and worked as the head of the newly established "Gymnase Normal Militaire" from 1817 to 1837, to which a civil department was added in 1820. But la methode amorosienne survived in France after the school has been closed. It more or less remained as a basis for another 60 years of teacher training at the Military Gymnastic School of Joinville, established in 1852 (cf. de Genst 1949, pp.304).

The Bostonian Phoklion Heinrich Clias became a supporter of the Gutsmuths and Pestalozzi system for the early physical education training schools in Europe. He went to Paris in 1817 and challenged Amoros, failed, received no official support, and went to the city of London in 1820. In England he was made an officer and taught the Pestalozzian system and method to military students at the Royal Military School and to students of Charterhouse Public School (cf. Wildt 1964, pp.39; Groll 1970, pp.59).

Neither the Gutsmuths system nor the original Pestalozzi system of physical education had a strong influence in Germany. When Friederich Ludwig Jahn and his companion Ernst Eiselen developed their German gymnastics after 1811, the Prussian Ministry of Education gave it some attention at first. However, due to the political "Ban of Turnen" which started in 1820 and lasted for more than two decades, there was no particular gymnastic teacher training with state sponsorship in Prussia. In 1847, the first institution opened its doors for one year headed by Major Rothstein: the "Central Institute for Gymnastic Teaching in the Prussian Army". However, this first institute, did not adopt any kind of a German system, instead it became probably one of the first European institutes which assimilated the new Ling system (cf. Großbröhmer 1993, pp.70).

Nevertheless, German gymnastics in the tradition of Jahn and Eiselen became popular around Europe. In Greece, for example, it became the first basis for physical education training just after the state's "rebirth" in 1830. The Munich Panhellenic professor Thiersch, German translator of Pindar, and a strong supporter of the Jahn student Maßmann, went to Greece with two gymnastic teachers from Munich in 1833. They instructed officers and students in Naupila. In Italy and the Netherlands there were early German gymnastic influences on physical education teacher training as well. In the same year, 1833, Rudolf Obermann, from Switzerland, began teaching German gymnastics at the Military Academy of Turino. He became a strong supporter of the Spieß system and the director of the first Normal School of Physical Education in Italy, established in Turino in 1860 (cf. Wildt 1972, pp.233 and pp.312; de Genst 1949, pp.254 and 261). In the Netherlands Gutsmuths' writings were well taken, but physical education teacher training was not affected until the appearance of the immigrant Karl Euler in 1848 (cf. Lommen/Kramer 1987, pp.38;).

3. Early Structure of Physical Education Teacher Training

The Gutsmuths and Pestalozzi systems were implemented cross-nationally at the first military physical training schools. However, both systems had been adapted and modified very early by Per Henrik Ling and Amoros. In comparison to their systems the Jahn/Eiselen system of gymnastics gained less international influence on physical education teacher training programmes. In many European countries those systems of early physical training were also introduced in some general teacher seminars and normal schools.

The second step in the historical development of physical education teacher training was the introduction of gymnastics and physical training as a compulsory subject at general teacher seminars and normal schools for elementary and secondary school teachers.

In some European countries participants of the teacher seminars received more than a programme related to physical training; the programme was expanded with a course including instruction of anatomy and physiology as well as internships in teaching physical exercises. From personal physical training via a course of instruction related to organizing physical exercises, the development led to a degree as a physical education teacher, which could be taken at general teacher seminars and normal schools for teachers.

In order to receive an overview of the early historical development of physical education teacher training in the different European countries I have began to collect and evaluate data of a variety of international sources (e.g. Bollansee 1921; Euler 1896; Wildt 1972; de Genst 1949; Krüger 1985; Ueberhorst 1976; Kramer & Lommen 1987; Leonard 1947; van Dalen & Bennet 1971; Lindroth 1993; McIntosh 1968; MTW 1882-1920; MTSS 1921-1924; LÜ 1925-1932 ; Smith 1974; Thiemer 1914).

However, the table with the data is still incomplete for some European countries. For that reason I only include data for those countries which I could verify between different sources. The table documents the years of establishment when physical education training was established at military and naval schools as a first step, and the emergence of physical education teacher training courses at general teacher seminars or normal schools as a second step.

Table 1: Physical Education Training in Military Schools and Normal Schools of Teacher Training

	Military Schools	Normal Schools
B	1886	1854
D	1847 (1851)	1827
DK	1804	1818
F	1817 (1852)	1887
GB	1822 (1862)	1840
GR	1892	1834
I	1833	1861
N	1870	1869
NL	1814	1851 (1881)

In Luxemburg, Finland and Ireland national military schools did not exist during that time period. Finland was controlled by Russia and Ireland under British rule up to World War I, and Luxemburg was politically liaised with Belgium after 1868. In Begum, Greece, and Norway physical education as a subject of general teacher training emerged earlier than in national military schools. Most European countries included physical education training within their military or naval schools before 1850. However, first attempts in France (1817), England (1822), and Germany (1847) failed and were not officially reestablished until the 1850s/1860s.

Again, Denmark and Sweden were the first countries to establish physical education courses in general teacher seminars. But in Germany and Greece gymnastics were also added to the study course of teacher seminars before 1850. In many European countries P.E. was incorporated in general teacher education between 1850 and 1870. However, in the Netherlands this was initially a private initiative by the organization "De maatschappij tot nut van het algemeen" and it was not until 1881 that the Dutch state government took responsibility for the inclusion of physical education in general teacher education like the French ministry did in 1887.

In England the situation was very different in comparison with the state supported development on the European continent. Some institutions included physical training like Battersea Normal College in 1840 on a private basis, and Archibald MacLaren started to drill military personnel in the Military

School at Aldershot in 1862. Many of them became the first drill masters at elementary and secondary schools. In general, P.E. teacher training started before P.E. became a compulsory subject in the European schools.

Table 2: Year that P.E. Became a Compulsory Subject in European Schools

	Elementary Schools	Middle Schools	Secondary Schools
B	1879	1850	1842
D	1847		1860
DK	1814	1828	1828
F	1880	1868	1868
GB	1944		1902
I	1878	1862	1859
L	1861	1872	1888
N	1879	1869	1869
NL	1889	1863	1879

Denmark (1814) and Sweden (1824) were the first countries where P.E. became a compulsory subject by law and where P.E. was taught; naturally, it did not cover the entire country at this early stage. In Greece, German gymnastics were introduced into some schools very early; however, P.E. was state-regulated only some decades later as it was the case in some other Southern European countries. England is probably the only European country where P.E. officially did not become a compulsory teaching subject until just recently, when the "National Curriculum" was introduced in the late 1980s (cf. Amstrong 1992!). However, after 1900 many English and Scottish schools, also elementary schools, included P.E. lessons for their students; particularly the London School Board became a strong supporter of school physical education after 1880. Therefore, I assessed the 1902 "Model Course of Physical Training" for the secondary schools and the McNair report (1944) for the elementary school level as landmarks for compulsory P.E. in Great Britain. (cf. McIntosh 1968, pp. 148 and 252 ; Smith 1974, pp. 106 and 148).

Most European countries introduced P.E. as a compulsory teaching subject by law in their schools between 1850 and 1880, just parallel to the efforts made to implement training courses and degrees for P.E. teachers into the regular teacher seminars and normal schools. However, until now it remains difficult for some countries to assess when P.E. has become a compulsory subject in school. Some countries implemented P.E. officially for secondary schools comparably early (e.g. Greece, Spain), but with no or little support for the dissemination into schools; on the other hand, there were countries where local or regional school boards supported the introduction of P.E. earlier than official support was given.

4. Systems of Physical Education Teacher Training

The Swedish system of Hjalmar Ling, son of Per Henrik, and of his successor Törngren, the French Amoros/Laisne-system, the German Spieß/Maul-system and so-called "Arnoldism" (c.f. Mangan 1981), which means the British education of character values of sports and games, became the four most influential systems and methods for physical education teacher training throughout Europe after 1850 up to World War I.

Indeed, the Ling system became the most common and influential system throughout Europe. Acceptance and adoption of the system began in the 1840s. In 1843 the German major Rothstein, and again with lieutenant Techow in 1845, attended a course in the CGI in Stockholm and brought the Swedish system to Germany as basis for the Prussian gymnastic teacher instruction of the 1850s. In 1845, a French commission went to Stockholm as well to provide a report for the Ministry of Education. A year later the famous coworker of Per Herink Ling, Carl August Georgii, went to Paris and lectured Swedish gymnastics for half a year. In 1849, he resigned at Stockholm Gymnastic Institute as a teacher and emigrated to Great Britain, where he stayed for 28 years. Georgii became the strongest supporter of the Ling system in England since the 1850s. He opened a private institute in London and -following his example- more than half a dozen another Swedish gymnastic teachers opened private institutes in the city of London until 1870 (cf. Wildt 1972, pp.189).

Most of the European countries adopted the Ling system for physical education teacher training after 1880, and it had a long standing tradition in many of the later physical education university departments until the 1950s and 1960s, particularly in Belgium, France, and southern European countries.

To give a brief overview of the most dominating system in European P.E. teacher training, I will try to identify time periods when the Ling was implemented for national P.E. teacher training in the different European countries.

Table 3: Adoption of the Ling System for P.E. Teacher Training

B	1870
D	1850
	1900
DK	1880
E	1920
F	1880
GB	1850
	1880
GR	1900
I	1890
IRL	1900
N	1820
NL	1910
P	1910
SF	1840

Like Rothstein in Germany of the 1850s many outstanding P.E. teachers and scholars became promoters of the Ling system in their countries: Docx and Vleminckx in Belgium in the 1870s and 1880s joined by Sluys; Björnstadt in Norway after 1870, Demeny and Lagrange in France in the 1880s and particularly in the 1890s after their visits in Stockholm; the Swedish lady Bergmann-Österberg in England of the 1890s and later, Mosso in Italy in the 1890s who all became supporters of the Ling-system. After 1900 it was Joas Gomes d' Oliveira in Portugal and Ioanidis Chryssaphis in Greece, August Ferdinand Schmidt in Germany who also became supporters of the Ling and modified Ling/Törngren-system. The same applies to Hubert van Blijenburgh in the Nederlands after 1910 and to Leal d'Oliveira again in Portugal of the 1930s. These gentlemen and scholars became well known internationally as promoters of physical education teacher training oriented towards the Swedish Ling and Törngren systems in their countries.

Between 1870 and 1900 a strong British influence on the national physical education systems became evident in many European countries. Athletics and games in the British Public Schools were studied by many foreign teachers and scholars and were evaluated as an excellent educational and physical supplement to the different gymnastic exercises (cf. Andrieu 1990,pp.21; Hamer 1989, pp. 449; Lindroth 1993, pp. 116).

In comparison to the strong Swedish and British influences on European physical education training programmes the influence of German school gymnastics of Spieß and Jaeger remained relatively small. Aspects of German gymnastics were adopted and incorporated in P.E. teacher training programmes mainly in Belgium, the Netherlands, and Italy (cf. de Genst 1949, pp. 375 , 360 and 261; Kramer & Lommen 1987, pp.22; Wildt 1972, pp. 174, 169, and 223) whereas la methode de Joinville influenced more or less teacher training programmes between 1850 and 1880 in Spain, Portugal and Greece (cf. de Genst 1949, pp. 255, 278.)

In order to give a brief overview of the different European influences that each country in Europe received from abroad during particular time periods, I prepared some profiles for selected countries.

Table 4: Great Britain

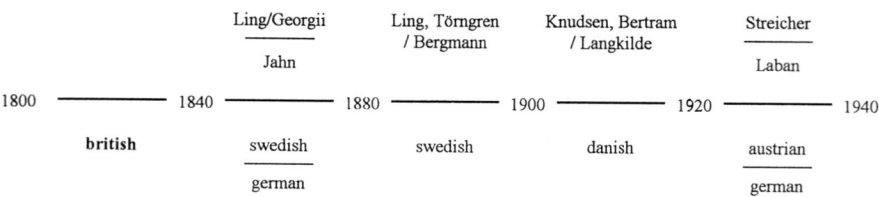

The profile for Great Britain (GB) documents Swedish and German influences in P.E. after 1840, particularly supported by the Swedish Ling student Georgii and others. After 1880 a stronger Swedish impact become visible through Mrs. Bermann-Österberg, the founder of the first P.E teacher normal school. The adoption of the Swedish system for school gymnastics continued after 1900; however, Langkilde was responsible for a strong influence of the Danish school of gymnastic on teacher training and physical training in the Royal Army. After World War I the natural method renewed instruction in P.E., and the Austrian School of Margarete Streicher and Karl Gaulhofer as well as the German Laban style of dance gained support.

Table 5: France

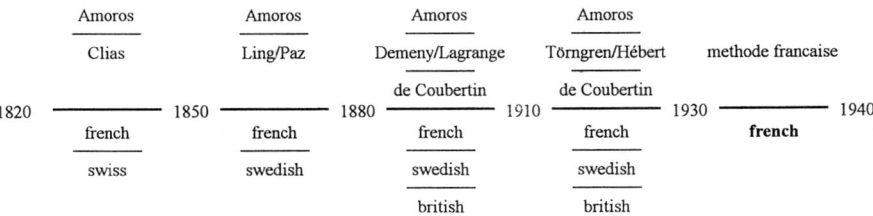

Although there has been a long standing tradition of the Amoros system in France, influenced by the Swiss Pestalozzi system which was also promoted by Clias, there has also been a long-term influence on the different European streams of physical education. Particularly the Swedish gymnastic system gained much support by French scholars such as Paz, Demeny and Lagrange between 1850 and 1910. After 1880, the British model of public school education experienced strong support as well, at first by Baron de Coubertin. Including la methode naturelle developed and promoted by Hebert, the different approaches were combined to the so-called French method, which documents a national identity after many years of physical education development in teacher training.

Table 6: Netherlands

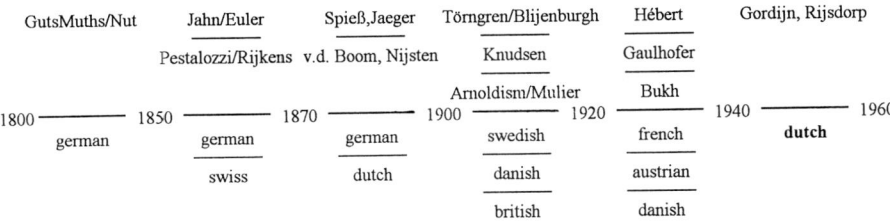

In the Netherlands international influences on physical education teacher training began after 1800, when the philanthropic ideas of Gutsmuths were taken and promoted especially by the van Geuns and who became the Dutch translator of Gutsmuths and the social organisation "de maatschappij tot nut van het algemeen". The German gymnastic system of Jahn/Eiselen and the Swiss system of Pestalozzi were promoted by the German immigrant Karl Euler and by Rijkens, a Dutch national. After 1870, German school gymnastics of Spieß and Jaeger were modified by van den Boom and Nijsten, who created something like a Dutch version of German gymnastics. Between the turn of the century and 1920 Swedish, Danish and British influences dominated. Hubert van Blijenburgh became the "Ling of the Netherlands" and Mulier followed the British model of sports. After World War I the movement associated with the natural method of P.E. instruction was adopted following the ideas of Hébert, Knudsen and Bukh; in particular, the Austrian School had a strong impact in the 1930s, when Karl Gaulhofer was appointed as a professor in P.E. at the University of Amsterdam. After World War II an independent Dutch system of physical education teaching developed; it was derived from the various pre-war influences of the different foreign natural methods. These physical education approaches of Gordijn and Rijsdorp are less known internationally. Nevertheless, the Dutch approach was adopted by some German colleagues in the field of school physical education in the early 1980s.

Table 7:   Greece

	Jahn/Pagon		Amoros/Phokianos		Ling/Chryssaphis	
1830	———	1860	———	1900	———	1930
	german		french		swedish	

In Greece we find different time periods with foreign influences. Between 1830 and 1860 the Jahn/Eiselen gymnastic system was promoted by Pagon who graduated as a gymnastic teacher in Munich. After 1860, Phokianos became a strong supporter of the French Amoros-system, which also dominated school physical education up to 1900. After the turn of the century Chryssaphis introduced and expanded the Swedish system in teacher training.

Table 8: Germany

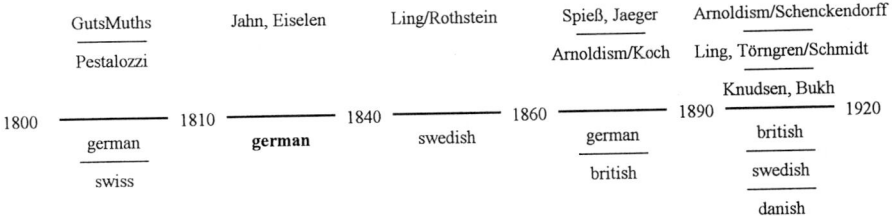

The first international influence in Germany, which is represented here by the state of Prussia, began with the Pestalozzi system. It was incorporated for the first time into teacher training by Zeller. After 1810 the Jahn/Eiselen gymnastic system dominated for about 30 years. This period of time is the only one without foreign influences. The Ling system had its first impact in the 1840s and dominated physical education teacher training for about a decade in the 1850s, when Rothstein became director of the Central Gymnastic Institute in Berlin. Between 1860 and the 1890s the Spieß/ Maul and Jaeger system of gymnastics strongly dominated in teacher training. In school physical education, however, the British idea of athletics and games was strongly supported predominantly by Koch even before the 1890s. After 1890 von Schenckendorff became the most influential political supporter of the English sport and games movement. In physical education teacher training a second phase of Swedish influence began after 1900, when the famous physician Schmidt promoted postural exercises. There also was a slight influence of Danish gymnastics before World War I, which became stronger after 1920.

Table 9: Denmark

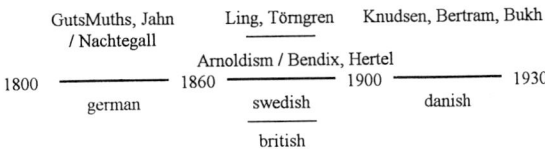

In Denmark the German GutsMuths system was implemented by Nachtegall after 1800. There was a long standing tradition of that system for teacher training until the 1880s. It was somewhat expanded by German gymnastics.

After 1880 the Ling system was adopted and removed influential due to the efforts of Törngren and Thulin until the 1930s. However, a remarkable development began after 1900, when Knudsen, Bertram and later Bukh in the 1920s created a new system, the Danish school, which became popular in many European countries and received its strongest support in England.

The Danish as well as the French and Dutch examples illustrate an important result of the different cross-national assimilations of the various systems that existed in Europe. Almost every European country developed its own national P.E. system, either in the 19th or 20th century, and either before or after having received international influences. There are some P.E. and sport historians like de Genst (1949, pp.380) in Belgium, Kramer & Lommen (1987, pp.7) in the Netherlands, or Gilbert Andrieu (1990, pp. 50) in France, who assessed their national systems of physical education and teacher training as "eclecticism" because they represent a mixture of the former original models of the systems. Taking another perspective regarding such diverse systems, an outcome is that they all document real national identity: la methode francaise did include the Amoros system, the Ling system, the natural method of Hebert and the instruction of English sports. La methode belge is another example, which includes beside the Amoros and Ling system the German gymnastics of Spieß and Jaeger, which in turn was a national mixture of the Jahn/Eiselen system and the Spieß system promoted by Happel and Cuperus. The same happened in Scandinavia where Norwegian and Finish gymnastics were developed to combine the strong Ling impact with the benefits of German gymnastics. In Italy Emillio Baumann's system of P.E. teacher training is another example for the establishment of a national system that includes different European influences. Therefore, I believe that from a European perspective we need "eclecticism" in order to combine the best aspects of our diverse national systems.

5. Advanced Structure of Physical Education Teacher Training

With the development of basic systems of P.E. teacher training after 1850 until World War I the structure of the physical education training schools advanced and extended to a more professional and academic level.

As mentioned earlier a first step was the establishment of military or naval schools with departments for civil students, as a second step P.E. training programmes and courses were included in schools for general teacher training. The third step of development was the founding of independent P.E. teacher training schools. Normal Schools for P.E. teacher training in Europe either emerged from the civil departments of military schools or general teacher training schools, or were simply founded independently as separate institutions, predominantly after 1870. However, the independent schools for P.E.

teacher training were not established on a academic university level.
Eventhough some universities in Europe for example in Finland, Greece, Spain, and Germany offered P.E. teacher training courses before 1900, the nature of the teaching degrees was non-academic, and P.E. was not accepted as an academic subject. In some countries universities courses offered before 1900 provided an equivalent opportunity for acquiring a P.E. teacher degree because of the decline or lack of Normal Schools for P.E. teacher training (e.g. Spain). In Germany short courses for a degree as a gymnastic teacher were brought to the universities after 1890 in order to attract local university students to become a gymnastic teacher as well (cf. Großbröhmer 1993, pp. 200).
To my knowledge physical education training was associated with the academic world before World War I in close relation with medical institutes or faculties only in Denmark (Copenhagen 1909) and Belgium (Brussels 1904 and Gent 1908) (cf. Laporte 1984). A more academic restructuring of the Royal Central Gymnastic Institute in Stockholm was discussed after 1912 (cf. Thiemer 1914, pp.24), however, it took more than 20 years until the new status was accepted in 1934 (cf. de Genst 1949, pp. 176).
The incorporation of physical education into regular academic university teacher studies began in the 1920s and 1930s in most European countries, when the university P.E. departments and faculties developed as a fourth step. The next table gives an overview of the aforementioned third and fourth step of institutional development in P.E. teacher training.

Table 10: First European P.E.T. Normal Schools and University Institutes

	P.E. Normal Schools	P.E. Institutes
B	1874	1904
D	1877	1924
DK	1828	1909
F	1928	1933
GB	1884	1933
I	1884	1923
N	1859	1927
NL	1852 (1912)	1925
S	1864	1934

The first Normal School for P.E. teacher training in Europe was established in Denmark in 1828; 100 years later the Institutes Regionaux d'Education Physique (IREP) were founded in France. Again, the development in Scandinavia (Sweden, Norway) began earlier than in other parts of Europe. Most of the countries established their first independent P.E. Normal School between 1870 and 1890. There was an early private initiative in the Netherlands in the 1850s which was similar to the one in England by Madame Bergman-Österberg in 1884. On a official state level the development started later in both countries.

The temporal differences between the establishments of P.E. institutions on a university level is smaller. Between 1920 and 1940 many European countries, which did not establish P.E. as an academic subject in their universities before, brought physical education teacher training into the framework of academics. The situation was different in England where Carnegie College became the first P.E. College for men in 1933. In some countries like France, Italy, Spain, and Portugal this process did not end until the 1970s. Meanwhile, other European countries developed a fifth step in the 1950s and 1960s. Some university departments and faculties of P.E. were transformed and expanded into independent Universities for Physical Education and Sport Sciences, which offered all academic degrees. One of these very first P.E. universities offering doctoral degrees in sport science was the German University of Physical Culture at Leipzig established in 1950. Today such universities with full academic courses and degrees exist in Norway, Denmark, Hungary, and in Germany in Cologne.

6. The Dissemination of Cross-National Influences in P.E. Teacher Training

Just as we can identify the different systems of physical education teacher training before and after 1850 with the different institutions that trained students, we can also distinguish main dissemination strategies for cross-national developments.

Before 1850 most cross-national influences in Europe came from adventurers, political or economic refugees, and immigrants. I like to give you two examples: the Bostonian adventurer Phoklion Heinrich Clias and the German immigrant Karl Euler.

Table 11: Curriculum vitae of Phoklion Heinrich Clias

Boston 1782 - Coppet 1854

1791	education	Groningen	(NL)
1803	prisoner of war		(GB)
1806	teaching	Groningen	(NL)
1807		Heerenveen	(NL)
1808		Amsterdam	(NL)
1809		Oldenburg	(D)
1810		Mecklenburg	(D)
1811		Gottstadt	(CH)
1815		Bern	(CH)
1817-1819	P.E. courses	Paris	(F)
1821-1826	P.E. courses	London	(GB)
1827		Bern	(CH)
1841	P.E. teacher training	Besancon	(F)
1843-1848	supervisor of gymnastics	Paris	(F)
1848-1854		Coppet	(CH)

At the age of 9 Clias, born in Boston as the son of a Swiss immigrant to the U.S.A., was brought to Groningen for advanced education, where he escaped later from the school to become a sailor. It is reported that he was an English prisoner of war before he came back to Groningen in 1806; it was then that his teaching career of gymnastics began with the strongest influence by Gutsmuths. He taught in the Netherlands at different places (e.g. in Amsterdam) and then he went to Germany for two years. When he came to his father's country, Switzerland, in 1811, he probably became well acquainted with the Pestalozzi system for some years before he left for Paris in 1817 for the first time. In Paris he challenged Amoros ,as it was mentioned before, and went to London for a couple of years. He was quite successful in England, was made an officer of gymnastic instruction, and taught his style of German-Swiss gymnastics to students of Charterhouse Public School. After 1827 he lived again in Switzerland for more than 14 years, then he became a successful instructor in teacher training and school gymnastics in the French city of Besancon. Later he was the city supervisor for school physical education in Paris for some years. In 1848 he returned to Switzerland where he died in a small village close to Lake Geneva in 1854. I am sorry that his remarks are incomplete for many reasons. One of his biographers, Rühl from

Germany, called him a plagiator in 1896, because he copied Gutsmuths and Pestalozzi in their writings. Nevertheless, Clias has been assessed as a good qualified and successful gymnastic teacher in any place where he worked in Europe, and he is known as an early promoter of physical exercises for girls.

Table 12: Curriculum vitae of Karl Euler

Trier 1809 - Brüssel 1885

about 1830	teaching	Berlin	(D)
1835		Breslau	(D)
after 1835		Königsberg	(D)
1840		Danzig	(D)
1843	P.E. courses	Köln	(D)
1845		Mannheim	(D)
1846		Karlsruhe	(D)
1847	teacher course	Luxemburg	(L)
1848		Diekirch	(L)
1848		Amsterdam	(NL)
1849		Utrecht	(NL)
1851	P.E. teacher courses	Leuwaarden	(NL)
1851-1859		Haarlem	(NL)
1860		Bruxelles	(B)
1863	P.E. teacher courses	Bruxelles	(B)

Euler was educated in gymnastics by Jahn's companion Ernst Eiselen in Berlin. After short stays in Breslau, Königsberg and Danzig he came to our host city of the 2nd European Forum, Cologne. Euler was the founder of the first Cologne gymnastic club in 1843 and he became the pioneer of school gymnastics in Cologne grammar schools. Financial and social problems forced him to move to the South. Due to some political problems of the "revolutionary" Turner movement in the state of Baden, he left for Luxemburg where he became one of the first gymnastic instructors. Because Luxemburg was under German rule during that time period, Euler left for the Netherlands during the revolution in 1848. He taught gymnastics in Utrecht and Leuwaarden before the Dutch Minister Thorbecke elected him to teach gymnastics in the Haarlem Rijksnormaalschool for teachers in 1851. In some respect Euler became a founder of physical education teacher training in the Netherlands and also in Belgium after 1860. Cuperus and Sluys became his Belgian students, who both highly influenced school gymnastics and physical education teacher training in Belgium in later years.

There have been many early promoters of European physical education teacher training like Clias or Euler. Johann Seegers from Belgian for example, became the first fencing master at the University of Bonn in 1819. Seegers was also accepted by the regional Prussian school authority of the lower Rhine district to teach gymnastics in grammar schools. Due to his efforts, school physical education was introduced here in Cologne in 1839, and in other cities of the lower Rhine valley around here like Krefeld, Bonn, and Duisburg, even before the "Ban of Turnen" was abolished officially. When remembering men like Euler, Seegers or Georgii, Baumann, Nycander and others it seems to me that working and living abroad as a physical education teacher was less restricted in many European countries about 100 years ago than it is in the closer European Community of today.
However, other forms of dissemination of physical education systems for teacher training throughout Europe, which took place particularly after 1850, should also be mentioned.

When physical education gained more attention by state authorities, officers and teachers were sent to leading European institutes to study their systems of teacher training. Also students from abroad went to those institutes and graduated there. Leading teachers and scholars from abroad received invitations by state ministries and physical education organizations to lecture and bring along a student group to demonstrate their system of training. The leading institute visited by foreign students, teachers, study commissions, and other people was the Central Gymnastic Institute of Stockholm until World War I. Nearly all famous European physical educators were there during the 19th century, French, Belgians, Germans, English, Spanish, Portuguese, Greek etc. On the other hand, many Swedish gymnasts went abroad and worked quite successfully in other European countries. Victor Balck, for example, one of the famous teachers of GCI and later IOC member, took groups of gymnasts to Belgium, England, France, and the Netherlands in order to demonstrate their system of physical education teacher training in 1870s, 1880s and later. After 1900 Knudsen, Bukh and Agneta Bertram form Denmark continued with gymnastic clincs abroad, like Karl Gaulhofer and Margarete Streicher from Austria did the same in the 1920s and 1930s in Denmark, England, the Netherlands, and Germany.

The most influential physical educators in Europe visited and studied each other in order to learn from the different systems of teacher training. Hjalmar Ling for example, went to Paris in 1854 to continue his study of anatomy with the famous French physician Claude Bernard at Hotel Dieu, and then continued on to Berlin to learn more about the German gymnastic system. Edward Thring, the Headmaster of Uppingham Grammar School, who studied German gymnastics employed a German gymnastic teacher in Uppingham in

1859 to supplement the teaching of athletics and games.
The leading physical education scholars of the past already had their European network including seminars, clincs, combined projects etc. without any official links or bureaucratic organization. They simply wanted to learn from each other to expend and to improve their expertise, and they were successful because most of them were able to read and understand three to four European languages.

7. Conclusions

The following "Map of Development" gives an overview of the historical and institutional structure of the system of P.E. teacher training in Europe.

Table 13: Historical Map of Development

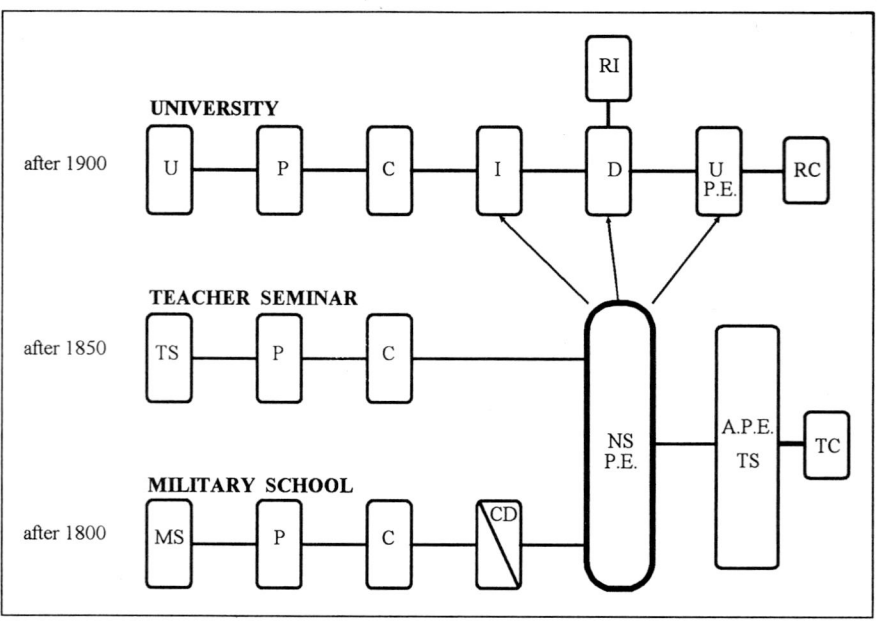

Summarizing the development of more than 150 years of professional and state supported P. E. teacher training in Europe we can identify an institutionalization process from Military Training Schools to P.E. and Sport Science Universities with all academic degrees.

There are three levels of systems: those which developed after 1800, the military schools (MS)-, mainly after 1850 -the teacher seminars (TS) or normal schools , and finally those emerging after 1900 -the university departments (U). However, there are similarities between the three systems with respect to the process of development: from physical training programmes for the students (P), via courses (C) of P.E. teaching to full degrees for P.E. teachers. In many military schools civil departments (CD) were established before independent Normal Schools for P.E. teacher training (NS P.E.) were founded either as a next step of both military schools and general teacher seminars or as newly founded institution. After World War I universities institutes (I) and departments of P.E. (D) were established which led to independent P.E. universities (U P.E.) in the 1950s including research institutes (RI) and research centers (RC) at universities and sport science universities within the last decades.

In some countries Normal Schools of P.E. and Colleges, particularly in the UK were also converted into university units with institutes and departments; some other P.E. Normal Schools developed to Training Schools or Academies of P.E. where trainer and coaches were trained (A.P.E. TS) , sometimes in conjunction with a special training center (TC).

The final question is: "What can we learn from the historical perspectives of P.E. teacher training for our European Network of the Higher Institutes of Physical Education?"
I believe we can learn three important things:

1. European physical education teacher training needs the eclecticism of our national systems in order to prevent and to develop diversity, which must, however, consist of more similar features between the study programmes.

2. European physical education teacher training needs more international input in our national study courses. Foreign language skills for students and teachers must be improved. Courses in theory and practise must include more features of the European dimension we historically have in nearly all teaching subjects.

3. European physical education teacher training must improve expertise, which means that training should not be dominated by a single system or national approach. Instead, it means that the European dimension of any topic we teach must be incorporated in order to give our students the best what European physical culture and sport science can offer today.

And what about us, the teachers and scholars? I believe, that we should reduce any bureaucratic obstacle to come closer together, to become more flexible and mobile, to share our knowledge at conferences, research clincs, and summer schools. We should make more experiences abroad and publish our results of research on a more international level. If we can make this a reality, then we all can benefit from each other and improve the European exchange process crossnationally.

References

1. **Andrieu A.:** L education physique au XXe siecle: Une histoire des practiques. Joinville-le-Pont, Libraire du Sport, 1990.

2. **Armstrong N. (ed.):** New Directions in Physical Education, vol.2 Towards a National Curriculum. Leeds, Human Kinetics Europe, 1992.

3. **Bernett H.:** Die pädagogische Neugestaltung der bürgerlichen Leibesübungen durch die Philanthropen. Schorndorf,Hofmann,1960.

4. **Bollansee A.:** Contribution a l'Histoire de l'Education physique en Belgique. Lierre, Joseph Van In & Cie, 1921.

5. **de Genst H.:** Histoire de L'Education Physique, Tome II. Bruxelles, A. de Boeck, 1949.

6. **Euler C.:** Enzyklopädisches Handbuch des gesamten Turnwesens und der verwandten Gebiete, 3 Bde. Wien & Leipzig, 1894-1896 (Key words: Belgien, Dänemark, England, Frankreich, Griechenland, Italien, Niederlande, Norwegen, Preußen, Schweden, Spanien,).

7. **Georgii C.A., Liedbeck P.J.:** Gymnastikens allmänna Grunder af Ling, dels af Författaren, dels enligt, dels yttersta vilja. efter dess död, redigerade och pa trycket utgifna. Upsala, Leffler & Sebell.

8. **Groll H.:** Systematiker der Leibesübungen, Wien, Österreichischer Bundesverlag, 1970.

9. **Großbröhmer R.:** Die Geschichte der preußischen Turnlehrer. Aachen, Meyer & Meyer, 1993.

10. **Gutsmuths J.C.F.**: Die Gymnastik für die Jugend. Schnepfenthal: Buchhandlung der Erziehungsanstalt 1793.

11. **Hamer E.**: Die Anfänge der "Spielbewegung" in Deutschland. London, Arena, 1989.

12. **Kramer J.P., Lommen N.**: Geschiedenis van de Lichamelijke Opvoeding in Nederland. Zeist, Jan Luiting Fonds, 1987.

13. **Krüger A.**: Die Universitätsprofessoren für Reitlehre: Die Anfänge der organisierten Wissenschaft vom Sport an der Georg-August-Universität Göttingen. In: Lämmer,M. Renson,R., Riordan,J. (eds.) Proceedings of the XIIth HISPA Congress, pp. 241-252. Sankt Augustin, Richarz, 1989.

14. **Krüger A. (Hg.)**: Leibesübungen in Europa. London, Arena, 1985.

15. **Laporte W.**: 75 Jaar Lichamelijke Opvoeding aan de RUG. Gent, Archief RUG, 1984.

16. **Leonard F.L.**: A Guide to the History of Physical Education (3rd ed.). Philadelphia, Lea & Febiger, 1947.

17. **Lindroth J.**: Gymnastik med Lek och Idrott. Stockholm, HLS Förlag, 1993.

18. **LÜ** (Monatschrift für Leibesübungen) 44 (1925) - 51 (1932).

19. **Mangan J.A.**: Atheticism in the Victorian and Edwardian Public School. Cambridge, University Press, 1981.

20. **McIntosh P.**: Physical Education in England since 1800. London: Bell & Sons 1968.

21. **MTSS** (Monatsschrift für Turnen, Spiel und Sport) 40 (1921) - 43 (1924).

22. **MTW** (Monatschrift für das Turnwesen), 1 (1882) - 39 (1920).

23. **Pestalozzi J.H.**: Ueber Körperbildung als Einleitung auf den Versuch einer Elementargymnastik, in einer Reihenfolge körperlicher Uebungen. Aarau: Sauerländer 1807.

24. **Smith W.D.:** Stretching their Bodies, The History of Physical Education. London, David & Charles 1974.

25. **Thiemer:** Die Turnlehrerausbildung im Ausland und Inland. In: MTW 33 (1914), 19-27, 50-58, 97-105.

26. **Ueberhorst H.:** Geschichte der Leibesübungen, Bd.5, Leibesübungen und Sport in Europa. Berlin, Bartels & Wernitz, 1976.

27. **Van Dalen D.D, Benett B.L.:** World History of Physical Education (2nd ed.). Englewood Cliffs, NJ, Prentice Hall, 1971.

28. **Wildt K.C.:** Daten zur Sportgeschichte, Teil 2 Europa von 1750 bis 1894. Schorndorf, Hofmann, 1972.

29. **Wildt K.C.:** Auswanderer und Emigranten in der Geschichte der Leibesübungen, Schorndorf, Hofmann, 1964.

Educational Research in Physical Education

Piéron, M.
University of Liège
Belgium

It is usual to consider teaching as an art, which requires a bit of a wise Judgment, a good knowledge of the subject matter and intuition. When dealing with the teaching of physical education, it is advisable to consider the need for safety measures. Analysing the question under a research approach, this view is undoubtedly too restrictive. There is little doubt that a part of pedagogy is artistic and that pedagogical talent can be viewed as stemming from inner powers. However, real artists try to master their art. They base their talent on knowledge and improve their techniques through information and research. Although it may be true that Pedagogy is not entirely a science in the restricted sense of the word, Pedagogy is considerably enriched and refined by a multitude of scientific contributions. It is a domain particularly favourable to investigation and verification of hypotheses drawn from experiments inside and outside its own field.

Like medicine or other highly qualified professions, education is a practical art and an applied science, a sequence of changing actions designed to reach specific objectives through thoughtful strategies. Pedagogy is a body of theories and rules aimed at guiding teachers and educators in their daily actions. It is multidisciplinary. It deals with aims and objectives, with relationships on a one to one basis or with groups, with various means to reach the objectives. There are multiple viewpoints when trying to define Sport Pedagogy. In their vocabulary, Piéron, Cheffers & Barrette (1982) listed at least eight different definitions. There are probably almost as many conceptions of sport pedagogy than researchers or theoreticians involved in the area. National or regional cultural aspects exert a strong influence on the way pedagogy and teaching physical education in particular are considered. However some general trends emerge. Some researchers are engaged in the behaviourist paradigm, others are oriented toward socialisation research, and use the critical theory as perspective, some use the quantitative paradigms, other prefer a qualitative approach.

Since the beginning of the seventies, a research endeavour focusing on the events occurring in the physical education class has attempted to develop a new dimension in the scientific approach to teaching physical education and sport. This research is characterized by a strong belief in the prominent role played by teachers in the educational enterprise. In attempting to identify abilities and strategies effectively used by teachers, investigators have maintained a constant interest in improving practice in physical education classes and in improving teacher preparation.

The systematic analysis of physical education teaching has been largely inspired by research trends in general education. Big names from experimental pedagogy like Flanders, Bellack, Joyce, Dunkin & Biddle, Rosenshine, Berliner, and Doyle in the English speaking countries and De Landsheere or Dussault in the French speaking countries have largely inspired those researchers applying educational research paradigms appropriate to the study of teaching physical education.

Authors, like Locke & Dodds (1984) and Silverman (1991), consider that the educational research in physical education can be subdivided into two broad categories:

1. Research on teaching: <<... focuses on the teaching and learning process as directed by teachers. RT-PE includes inquiry into the pre-active (planning), active (execution), and post-active (reflection) phases of instruction.>> (Silverman, 1991)
2. Research on teacher education: <<...examines the preparation and development of pre-service and in-service teachers. That research includes study of the effectiveness of teacher training programs, teacher socialisation, method for providing feedback to teachers, and the process of in-service teacher development.>> (Silverman, 1991).

I shall deal with these two aspects in this paper.

Research in pedagogy and more especially in the area of teaching physical education seems to be characterized by sudden bursts of enthusiasm toward some topics, then dropping out after a more or less extended period of time. Frequently, this occurs after asking excellent questions, but only answering a few without exhausting the bulk of pertinent problems. Fortunately, several university departments have sustained a coherent research programme approach over many years.

As it was observed in other human and social sciences, like psychology and sociology, research in pedagogy of physical education has borrowed most of its paradigms and models in the field of classroom pedagogy. Within this context it frequently happened that the specific about physical education was forgotten. Research on teaching physical education has used several paradigms which I shall briefly describe. They have been adopted and sometimes specifically adapted to physical education teaching. These paradigms gave a theoretical base for investigation and provided a framework to interpret the findings. They determined the type of data to collect.

1. Paradigms

For many years, research studies have been organized around two models or paradigms: the <<Descriptive - correlational - experimental loop>> (Rosenshine & Furst, 1973) and the Presage-Process-Product paradigm. The latter presented and adapted by so many authors ultimately made it quite difficult to identify the initiator. Mitzel (1960) was one of the first authors to present the paradigm.

The <<Descriptive - correlational - experimental loop>> entails at least three main elements:

1. The development of means and procedures which allow description of teaching under its quantitative and qualitative aspects;
2. Correlational studies wherein the descriptive variables are related to pupils learning gains or to changes in attitude or motivation;
3. Experimental studies wherein significant variables identified in correlational studies are tested in situations rigorously controlled. They search for causality.

Describing was a first step in understanding what is occurring in a physical education class, before relating behaviour and events to outcomes or before setting up an experiment.

1.1 Presage-Process-Product (Figure 1)

Presage variables concern the characteristics of the teacher. Process variables concern the activities occurring in the gym or on the sports field during teaching periods. The aim is to identify what the teacher and the pupils are doing during the teaching-learning process. We stand at the point where three series of variables converge. They are those pertaining to persons delivering the teaching, those who are receiving the teaching, and the conditions in which the teaching occurs. Product variables concern the outcomes of teaching. Two other types of variables linked to the process also merit consideration. Context variables concern the teaching environment and the conditions to which the teacher should adjust. Programme variables are within the decision making power of the teacher: types of objectives, nature of content, and pedagogical directions for evaluation.

Fig. 1: *A model for the study of physical education teaching*

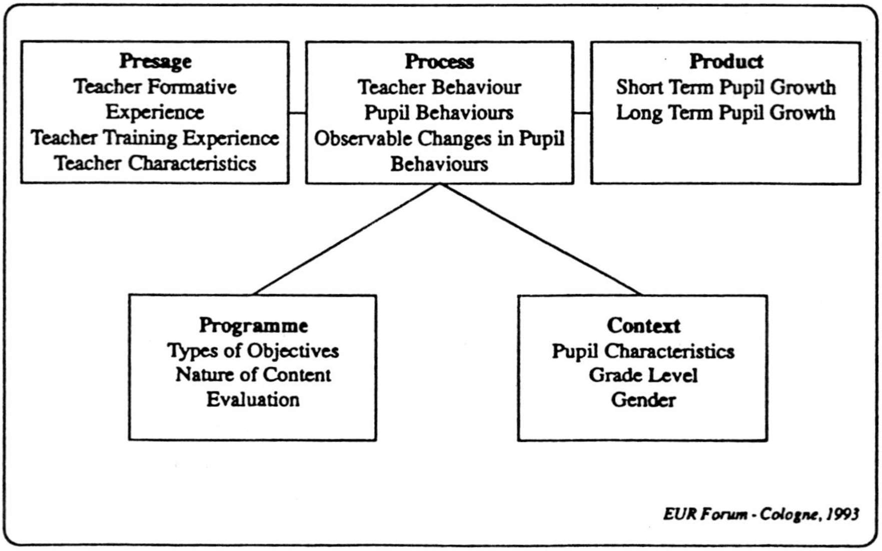

Presage	Process	Product
Teacher Formative Experience	Teacher Behaviour	Short Term Pupil Growth
Teacher Training Experience	Pupil Behaviours	Long Term Pupil Growth
Teacher Characteristics	Observable Changes in Pupil Behaviours	

Programme	Context
Types of Objectives	Pupil Characteristics
Nature of Content	Grade Level
Evaluation	Gender

EUR Forum - Cologne, 1993

1.2 Quantitative and qualitative research

The process was seen as a black box, or something like <<terra incognita>> and the focus was placed on describing the process. Quantitative and qualitative methods were used to fulfil this objective.

Quantitative methods are usually associated with systematic measurement, experimental, quasi-experimental and correlational methods, statistical analysis and mathematical modes. Qualitative methods are associated with naturalistic observation, ethnography, life history, and narrative reports.

The teaching situation is of such a complexity that no single research approach is totally satisfactory. Observing what is happening in a class with category systems do not allow description of the whole teaching process or to allow full interpretation and understanding of the phenomenon under observation.

1.3 Ecological paradigm and ethnographic observation

Qualitative research provides an alternative to the quantitative mode of describing and understanding what is occurring in a physical education class. In the naturalist paradigm, realities are multiple, holistic, and constructed by participants. Under the qualitative label one finds approaches slightly different but pertaining to the same family: ethnographic, participant observation, case study, interpretative, symbolic interactionist, etc. The primary significance of qualitative research on teaching concerns issues of content rather than issues of procedure. One central concern is the nature of classrooms as socially and culturally organized environments.

Qualitative research involves: (1) intensive long-term participation in a field setting; (2) careful recording of what happens in the situation (field notes and other kinds of documents); (3) subsequent analytic reflection on data gathered. Qualitative field work research involves being thorough and reflective in noticing and describing events in the field setting, and in attempting to identify the meaning of actions in the events from the various points of view of the participants. Fieldwork methods are thought to be inductive. Specific categories for observation are not determined in advance of entering the field setting as a participant observer. The researcher identifies conceptual issues of research interest before entering the field setting. However, induction and deduction are in constant interaction.

Interpretive methods using participant observational fieldwork are appropriate when one needs to know more about:

1. The specific structure of occurrences rather than their general character and overall distribution;
2. The meaning-perspectives of the particular actors in the particular events;
3. The location of naturally occurring points of contrast that can be observed as natural experiments when we are unable logistically or ethically to meet experimental conditions of consistency of intervention and of control over other influences on the setting;
4. The possibility to search for hypothetical and specific causal linkages not identified by experimental methods, and the development of new theories about causes and other influences on the patterns identified in survey data or experiments.

Fieldwork is best at answering questions, like:

1. What is happening, specifically, in social action that takes place in this particular setting?
2. What do these actions mean to the actors involved when the actions take place?
3. How are the events organized in patterns of social organization and learned cultural principles for the conduct of everyday life.

4. How are the events being observed, related in this setting as a whole (i.e., the classroom) particular in relation to happenings at other system levels outside and inside the setting (e.g., the school building, a child's family, the school system);
5. How do the ways of everyday life in this setting compare with other ways of organizing social life in a wide range of settings in other places and at other times? (Erickson, 1986).

Like the quantitative approach, ethnographical observation does not escape criticism. Siedentop (1987) lists such criticisms as: (1) the absence of any mechanism for public verifiability of primary data; (2) the temptation to make implicit attribution of causality; (3) the central role attributed to intentions; (4) the philosophical or educational bias of the investigator.

1.4 Mediating processes paradigm

The mediating process paradigm research focuses on implicit processes that pupils use to mediate instructional stimuli and to produce learning outcomes. A third factor was introduced between the process and the product of teaching, allowing for the inclusion of mediating elements.

Two aspects of mediation are considered:

1. The pupil's motor activity, his/her motor engagement necessary to master the tasks set forth by the teacher; a large part of research based on pupil observation is based on these premises.
2. The motivational, affective, and cognitive aspects of pupil thinking during learning. Pupil information-processing responses to the instructional stimuli intercede in the direct link between teacher behaviour and pupil outcome assumed in the process-product paradigm.

Affective aspects of pupil thought may influence the quality of the engaged time during the lessons. Ultimately, pupils' outcomes may be affected by their thoughts. The mediating process implies that teachers do not influence achievement but, cause pupils to behave and think in certain ways.

1.5 Expert vs beginner paradigm

Berliner (1986) developed attention towards the expert vs beginner paradigm in education. Through systematic analysis of the expert physical education teacher, information is sought to explore the journey that beginners may follow in order to be successful in their teaching.

2. Collecting the research data

Earlier comment indicated that an accurate description is necessary to understand any phenomenon. Every science has passed through this process. The development of procedures and instruments to describe, register, and analyse, go parallel with understanding. Teaching physical education is no exception. Two types of information contribute to the description of teaching and what is closely related: (1) information from observable behaviours or teaching strategies and (2) information which is not directly observable, in some way hidden, like values, attitudes, concerns, and decision making mechanisms or thinking processes of teacher and pupils during teaching.

The first type of information is gathered through observation (live or through the use of video-tape recording), the second type of information necessitates the questioning of the subjects.

In the beginning, the research endeavour in the study of the teaching of physical education focused upon accessible data. Techniques of systematic observation were extensively used.

2.1 Observation

In classroom research, Evertson & Green (1986) described four phases of using observation as an approach to study educational processes. The evolution was mirrored in physical education, but with a few years delay:

1. There was an exploratory phase in which the focus was a consideration of whether teacher-pupil interaction and other related instructional behaviours could be reliably and validly identified. In physical education, this phase started around the end of the sixties;
2. A period of instrument development, and of descriptive, experimental, and training studies;
3. A period in which studies of teacher effects explored teacher behaviours that relate to pupil outcome. This research trend is frequently referred to as the process-product approach.
4. A period of expansion occurred where alternate approaches, theoretical and methodological advances, and convergence across research directions in the use of observational techniques to study teaching emerged.

Observation is a method of collecting data which intends to represent the reality as reliably as possible. The care taken in defining events to observe and the carefully designed training of observers, made observation a rigorous data collecting method. In teaching activities, it has the advantage of bearing a larger ecological validity than questionnaires or interviews. However, it is necessary to keep in mind its limits.

There are different purposes in observation leading to differences in strategies for observation, levels of systematization, and levels of formality. These factors lead to differences in design and implementation.

Cheffers (1978) distributed current systems under two broad headings:

1. Inductive, where the systems materialize and attain a form only after a series of observations have been made. Examples are anecdotal recording, critical incidents, ethnographical data, etc.;
2. Deductive, where a formula pre-exists and interpretations are made through that formula. Most deductive systems develop as a result of an inductive process.

In the deductive applications, observers use two types of observation schedule allowing either a sequential analysis or a multidimensional analysis. In the first analysis, every observation is considered through an unique viewpoint and linked to the preceding and to the following events. Data is dealt like a chain of events. Interaction analysis systems are the typical example of this sequential approach. In the multidimensional analysis, specific events are studied under several points of view. Feedback is a teachers' intervention frequently analysed through this procedure.

2.2 Questioning

Hidden data which are qualified as <<invisible data>> are gathered by means of various questioning techniques. This datum concerns teachers and pupils. With teachers, questions attempt to consider: (a) what they think to be effective teaching; what is a good session, what are their concerns about teaching; (b) questions are raised in relation to their decision making process; on their reflective thinking during every phase of teaching whether it pre-active and / or interactive.

Two aspects are analysed in pupil thinking: the affective facet of a physical education session (like or dislike, perception of effort) and the cognitive aspect (what kind of thinking occurs during the action or when a specific skill is being performed).

Questionnaire and interview techniques are well known. The first was systematically used in curriculum research. The second under its various forms has been used more frequently since the success of qualitative approaches.

Three other techniques are also used for research purposes:

1. The critical incident technique;
2. The thinking aloud technique. Subjects are asked to verbalize their thoughts as they complete a task;

3. The stimulated recall technique: it is used to investigation cognition. Subjects view a video tape of a lesson and respond to interview questions about their thoughts during class.

Data collected through self-reports need to be checked carefully. What a subject thinks and what is reported as thoughts may differ.

3. Research themes and findings

3.1 Describing what is happening in a physical education class

Two areas concern what is occurring in a physical education class: (1) the behaviour of the participants, teacher and pupils; (2) the affective and reflective thinking of both.

In the domain of behaviour, three questions were directly asked:

> (1) Is it possible to observe classroom events with acceptable levels of reliability and validity?
> (2) Does the intra-individual variability of teaching events allow us to state that the teacher and pupil behaviour corresponds to usual teaching behaviours?
> (3) Does the daily reality observed in the class correspond to research findings on teacher effectiveness or the principles of good teaching or to curriculum theory?

3.2 The teacher

3.2.1. Behaviour

In the behaviour area, research studies aimed at analysing: (1) a general profile related to teacher behaviours; (2) specific teacher behaviour under viewpoints like task presentation or feedback; (3) high inference behaviours like enthusiasm; (4) teacher-pupil interaction; (5) management and control of the class.

The profile of teacher's interventions has been described. It deals with teaching instructional functions like task presentation and feedback, class organization and management, silent observation and affective functions. Significant differences were observed between experts and novices (Howe & Jackson, 1985; Piéron, 1982) or according to program and context variables. Some specific functions were investigated through multidimensional observation schedules.

Several teacher's interventions or skills have been thoroughly investigated. Feedback is a typical example. Task presentation, class management and control have started to be of concern to researchers. However, in this paper, only one thoroughly investigated area of research will be dealt with. Studies on feedback and their implications to practitioners will be analysed.

Feedback is component of learning models for skill acquisition (Gentile, 1972; Magill, 1989; Schmidt, 1992; Singer & Dick, 1974) as well as in models for teaching effectiveness (Bloom, 1979; Carroll, 1963). Feedback is located at the crossroads of the learning and teaching processes. In teaching, informative feedback exceeds a mere knowledge of results or information gained about the correctness or incorrectness of ones' behaviours. Informative or augmented feedback is information given to a learner to help him/her repeat correct behaviours, eliminate incorrect behaviours, and achieve the desired outcomes. The need for informative feedback to improve and sustain performance is an essential learning experience. Instructional theorists traditionally have viewed teacher feedback following a learner's response as a critical pedagogical operation.

In observational studies linking teacher behaviour, pupils behaviour and pupils learning gains, it was observed that more effective teachers provided their pupils with more frequent specific feedback (Carreiro da Costa & Piéron, 1990b; Phillips & Carlisle, 1983; Piéron & Piron, 1981). However, the relationship between observed feedback and the improvement of performance is not a straight one. To benefit from feedback, it is necessary that the individual pupil be able to understand the message, to process it and be able to put it into practice.

Feedback follows after a series of teacher decisions. Within this decision making process, two aspects are of special relevancy: identifying performance errors and delivering the message. Analysts started by studying the message. Observation systems usually take into account the intent, the content, the direction, the general and specific referent of the message. The follow-up of the message could be part of the study. I am convinced that its apparent effect on pupil performance, its appropriateness to the learner, its perception and memorization, are worthy avenues and areas of research and will be a focus for future research.

Feedback exerts two main functions:

1. As reinforcement to strengthen correct performance. Feedback reinforcing a response increases the probability that it will happen in similar condition in the future. In this case, reinforcement and motivation are associated;
2. As information to correct errors. It bears a message related to performance errors and to the most appropriate ways to correct them: identifying correct parts in the movement, explicating the origins of errors, describing

the necessary means to implement the corrections or developing reasons to change.

Delivering feedback comprises several elements forming a chain: observing pupil in such a context that performance error can be identified and the nature and the cause of the error can be determined. Several factors influence this whole process, more especially the pupil observation. There seems to be general agreement in models and paradigms of the teaching process that observation of pupil learning behaviours should be an important skill for teachers. The content of the feedback message depends largely on the teacher's ability to analyse the skill, to determine those factors critical to proficiency at a particular stage of learning, to identify the aspects of the response which are preventing the learner from attaining the skill objectives and to provide feedback related to these factors (Barrett, 1979a,b, 1983; Craft, 1977; Hoffman, 1983).

Observation is a special skill; it involves more than just watching what is going on. Alertness, sensitivity, and ability to identify and to assess a range of behaviour and relationships, are crucial components. A key to useful observation is knowing what should be seen. Diagnosis skill or skill analysis is defined as the act identifying errors in learner's performance. This is considered an essential competency for the physical education professional. One interesting question concerns the relationship between kinesthetic experience and diagnosis ability.

Research in this area is based on hypotheses which advance that teacher's diagnosis skill depends on: (1) his/her own skill in the specific motor ability taught; (2) his/her knowledge of this skill.

The ability of subjects to analyse skill is examined following their exposure to varied level of experience in the sport speciality. It was evidenced that the diagnosis skill necessitates both a thorough knowledge of the subject matter and a personal practical experience (Girardin & Hanson, 1967; Imwold & Hoffman, 1983; Harari, 1986; Harari & Siedentop 1990). The general assumption underlying studies in this area is that the teacher must have a thorough knowledge of the skill technique, the standards of performance, and sport specific context, to make an accurate diagnosis. It was also shown that it was possible to acquire this skill through a specific preparation (Kniffen, 1985). This skill is hardly generalizable, that means that a transfer to other subject matter is not automatic (Biscan & Hoffman, 1976).

As stated by Hoffman (1977): <<teachers who cannot identify critical errors, or who can identify the errors but cannot correctly interpret their significance in relation to goal attainment in the ski?1, are destined to commit serious mistakes as they move into the prescriptive phase of teaching>>.

3.2.1 Teacher thinking

Research on teacher's thinking is a relatively newborn topic in the field of physical education, although authors presented papers on the topic ten years ago (Hanke & Treutlein, 1983). For most part, this research is devoted to describe teachers' planning and decision making during instruction (changing strategies and organization of the class, giving feedback, and disciplining). Research showed for example that planning did not emphasize objectives or pupils' needs but was more concerned with the selection of tasks.

It is assumed that attitudes, values, and concerns influence what teachers do in their classes. It is necessary to understand their decisions in the planning and the interactive phases of teaching. Recently, several questions were investigated by means of questionnaires, or by the critical incident technique and interviews.

What is the conception of teaching effectiveness? What is a good physical education lesson? What are the concerns of teachers in teaching? What are the stressing events in teaching? Some of these questions are specific to in-service teachers, other are addressed to pre-service and to in-service teachers. Answers are compared between different kinds of teachers.

The comparison of experts and novices has been shown to be an effective technique for uncovering the cognitive processes used in planning decisions (Housner & Griffey, 1985) and interactive decisions.

3.3 The pupil

3.3.1 Pupil behaviour

Analysis of teaching physical education gathered different types of data leading to implications for reflective teaching and implementation:

1. Quantitative data informing on the level of pupil participation or the proportion of pupils engaged in physical activities;
2. Quantitative data on the level of pupil engagement in various educational or sport specific settings;
3. Quantitative data completed by information on the quality of engagement (failure success ratio);
4. Qualitative descriptions of the type of participation in the tasks.

The first three kinds of information can be used in planning a session. They bring attention to organizational problems. Some sport specialities induce a very low pupil engagement.

Knowing the types of participation facilitates the identification of individual pupils creating discipline problems to teachers or of other pupils ready to contribute to a favourable climate.

The concept of time concerns the teacher as well as the pupil. Management of time allocated to physical education in the curriculum is one of the teaching functions. Time is mainly considered at the class level for teachers. In pupils, it is considered as from an individual viewpoint. Time is related with teaching effectiveness. Time spent on task is linked in the quantitative studies completed in the area of pupils' behaviour.

Research emphasizing pupil behaviour intends to match the quantitative aspects of the engagement with its quality to predict success in learning objectives or with its level intensity when fitness is the main objective. The specification of the task to learning objectives is of prominent importance. Data gathered through pupil/athlete observation is rich in information useful to teachers or coaches.

3.3.2 Pupil thoughts

One of the mediating factors of pupil outcomes, the role of time was fairly well investigated. The mediating role of the cognitive processes is just about to be investigated. It is related to the information processing in learning physical education tasks.

Actually, researchers attempt to gather two types of information of pupil thoughts:

1. Thought related to their perception of the lesson. Pupils are asked to what extent they have enjoyed the session, how they feel about the level of intensity of activities, what is the meaning of teachers' intervention, how much of the task presentation do they have retained. Data is sought either in quasi experimental settings or in natural settings. These thoughts are related to the affective and perceptive aspects of the lesson;
2. Thoughts related to the performance of motor skill.

Questions addressed by researchers are <<What thoughts do pupils report having while performing the assigned tasks; what types of strategies do they report during practice; to what extent are pupils aware of physical education lesson content?>>

Analysing pupils thoughts, their perceived competence, their perceptions of achievement goals, their attention, their perceptions of teacher behaviours could bring more light on their achievements and achievement potential.

4. Identifying variables related to teaching effectiveness

It is particularly difficult to identify criteria of teaching effectiveness. There are many sources of variation and there is a large part related to specification, due to the influence of objectives, of educational settings, of subject matter taught, and many other factors, known or unknown.

However, it is tempting to ask direct questions and to offer some answers in looking at what is occurring during a teaching session: <<Amongst the behaviours and strategies observed during teaching, is there any difference between the most and the least effective teachers?>> and <<Are there significant relationships between behaviours observed during teaching and pupil outcomes?>>.

The Experimental Teaching Unit is a research design used to study teaching effectiveness. It is a series of lessons on a topic of general interest given to the grade level of the pupils to be taught by the teachers in an experimental context. The Experimental Teaching Unit model mandates a semi-controlled setting (sometimes a micro-setting) in which the content to be taught is standardized. In Experimental Teaching Unit studies, the learning environment can be reduced in terms of time, space, number of pupils. They are characterized by:
1. A learning objective set forth by teachers;
2. A measure of pupil learning developed specifically to appraise the instructional content taught which is administered before and after Experimental Teaching Unit lessons are taught (pre- and post-test);
3. A teaching period;
4. Systematic observation of selected teacher and pupil behaviours conducted during the Experimental Teaching Unit lesson.

It is necessary to point out that considering learning objectives is only a fragmentary view of what teaching objectives could be. Educating children is more than teaching sports skills. Other objectives deserve to be pursued. Moreover, learning gains are not necessarily considered as priority objectives by teachers or by pupils. However, there are at least two reasons to retain learning as a criterion. These are advanced:

Fig. 2: *Model of classroom process (adapted from Yerg, 1981)*

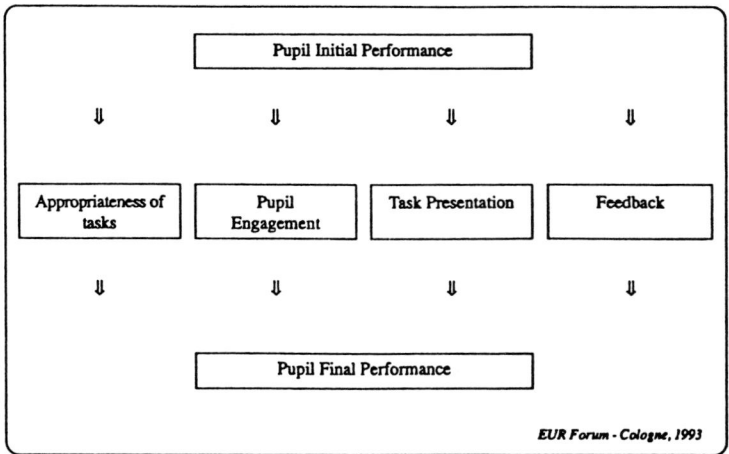

1. Learning is one of the school missions and an objective to all subject matters, including physical education. The role of the school is not limited to allow recreation by the pupils. Physical education is not just another form of recess;
2. The attitude of pupils towards the school is largely dependent on their success in subject matters taught. In his study of teaching effectiveness. Bloom (1979) found that attitude was responsible for approximately 20% of the final variance of pupil outcomes.

Helping pupils to improve their sports skills within a climate of success is undoubtedly part of teaching effectiveness. Variables responsible for learning will be sought within the process of teaching, in events occurring in the classroom. Let us stop for a while at the research methodology used in teaching effectiveness. Although there are variations in design, it is possible to review the Experimental Teaching Unit studies according to their main components: tasks to be learned by pupils (the content of the Experimental Teaching Unit), length of the teaching period, pupil and teacher characteristics and the size of the class taught. Two approaches were typically used to process data and to identify variables related to teaching effectiveness:

1. A correlational approach. Process-product studies intend to identify relationships between, on the one side, teaching behaviours and strategies observed during the action in the gym and, on the other side, pupil outcomes (Figure 2). For years, the correlational approach made substantial progress shifting from a micro-setting to a natural educational environment.

2. A comparative approach. Comparisons are made for:

Fig. 3: *Comparative model in the study of teaching effectiveness*

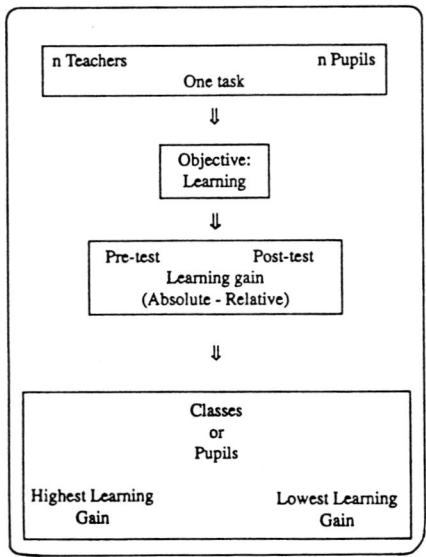

a. Teachers whose classes are making the highest progress with teachers whose classes are making the lowest progress (Carreiro da Costa & Piéron, 1990a,b; De Knop, 1983; Graham, Soares & Harrington, 1989; Phillips & Carlisle, 1983; Piéron & Piron, 1981);

b. Pupils learning gains. In that approach, behaviours of pupils with the highest learning gain are compared to behaviours of pupils with the lowest learning gain (Figure 3).

The model for analysis is relatively simple. It seeks an answer to the question <<What makes a difference between more and less effective teachers?>>.

Research based on Experimental Teaching Units (ETU) has gathered data and produced results worthy of consideration. Although some differences exist in the design of the studies, they can be summarized and discussed according to several topics including:

1. The improvement of learner performance. The teaching conditions of all the studies have resulted in some pupil learning gains except when tasks to be performed were too complex and inappropriate to the pupil ability levels;
2. The influence of entry levels. The relationship between the entry and final levels is generally high. However, it decreases when the teaching duration period is increased;

3. The motor engagement time. Many studies have showed that time on task is important in pupil learning. However, it was found that this unique variable was not satisfactorily predictive. The quality of the pupil engagement is so important that the formula<<Busy, Happy and Good>> cannot guarantee conditions for significant progress in pupil achievement. The adequacy of any treatment must be considered under several aspects namely:
    a. The specificity of activities to facilitate a significant transfer from the activities performed in the ETU toward the final learning objective;
    b. Taking into account the pupil's individual differences: the <<interaction aptitude-treatment>> explains that every pupil cannot benefit from the same kind of activities or from the same teacher interventions. The adequacy of the tasks to the pupil skill level is a key to its success;
4. The feedback provided by the teacher to the pupil: several studies found a significant relationship between feedback and pupil learning gains when the quality of performance was considered rather than its quantitative aspect.

The possibility to generalize results in teaching effectiveness research depends on the teaching conditions in terms of:

1. Tasks practised by the pupils during the teaching period: a large variety of tasks being used: from simple to complex, in open and in closed skills, in individual and in team sports;
2. Length of the ETUs: they ranged from a few minutes to a full unit of teaching lasting for several weeks and in one case for three years (Graham, Metzler & Webster, 1991);
3. The pupils and teachers involved in the ETU: pupils from kindergarten to university level and pupil teachers to master teachers.

In general, studies have been characterized by a clear trend to become closer and closer to the real teaching conditions. The problems facing the researchers and the implications of these studies for pre-service and in-service teachers led me to believe that this chapter of investigations is yet far from being completed. This research question will be improved through a higher adequacy of research instruments, an enrichment of the learning situations, and by considering more carefully, methods used by the teacher.

5. Teacher preparation

As with the other domains considered so far, data concerning teacher preparation are gathered by means of observation and questioning.

Fig. 4: *Research themes in teacher preparation in physical education*

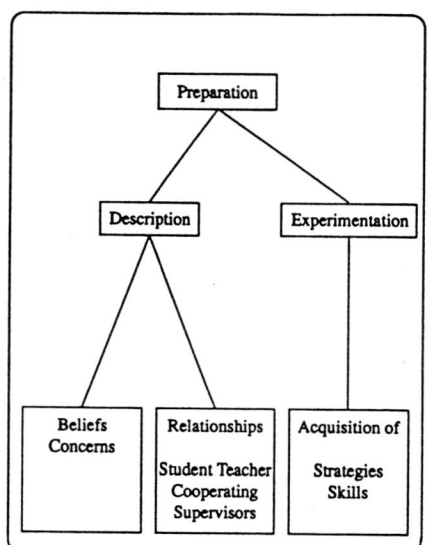

In the domain of teacher preparation, two research avenues have been explored (Figure 4). One is experimental and is concerned with questions like: <<Is it possible to learn teaching skills, teaching strategies and teaching styles?>> or <<How efficient are the preparation techniques which are usually used?>> The second area of research is descriptive. The purpose is to investigate how the student passes through the program, the impact of the program, the impediments to the program which effect the students. Socialisation and Induction are two words representing research themes in the field of teacher preparation. They deal with factors influencing teachers during the preparation and their first experience in teaching.

5.1 Acquiring teaching skills and strategies

After identifying teaching skills, it was natural to seek application in the preservice preparation or the in-service training. Two research methodologies have been largely used in studying the learning of pedagogical skills:

1. Comparing experimental and control groups: the control group follows a specific preparation based on the learning of some observation system, on clear definition and demonstration of typical teaching behaviours. In addition, subjects receive an objective feedback from the observer. A common hypothesis is: the preparation to teaching analysis or the training to

use an observational system will make teachers more conscious of their invention and help them to improve the teacher-pupil interaction.

Fig. 5: *Research model used in the study of the acquisition of teaching skills: Experimental versus controlgroups*

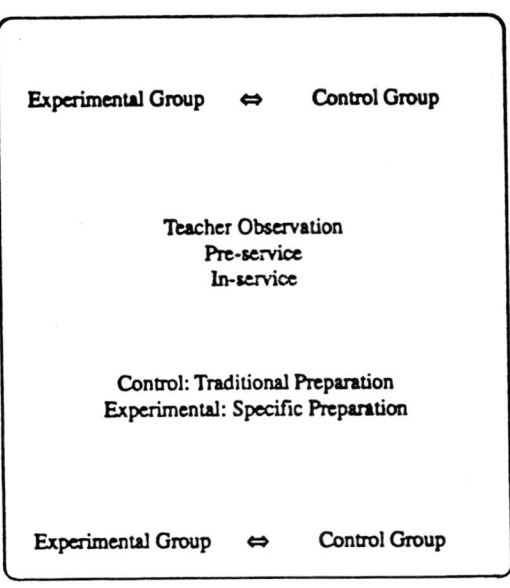

2. Behaviour modification using the multiple baseline design and specific intervention to modify target behaviours. This research methodology has been systematically used (Siedentop, 1981). It is based on specific interventions aimed at the acquisition of well defined behaviours. Without entering into a detailed view of teaching skills, it emphasizes variables related to teaching effectiveness namely feedback, climate of the class or pupil time-on-task. Moreover, it allows us to individualize the preparation in matching trainee characteristics and intervention. This methodology induces a search for causality. The behaviour modification is related dynamically to the intervention and modification.

Studies actually completed can be distributed in four main categories whose aims are:

1. Changing the whole picture of the teaching relationship as it occurred in interaction

Fig. 6: *Research model used in the study of the acquisition of teaching skills: Multiple baseline design*

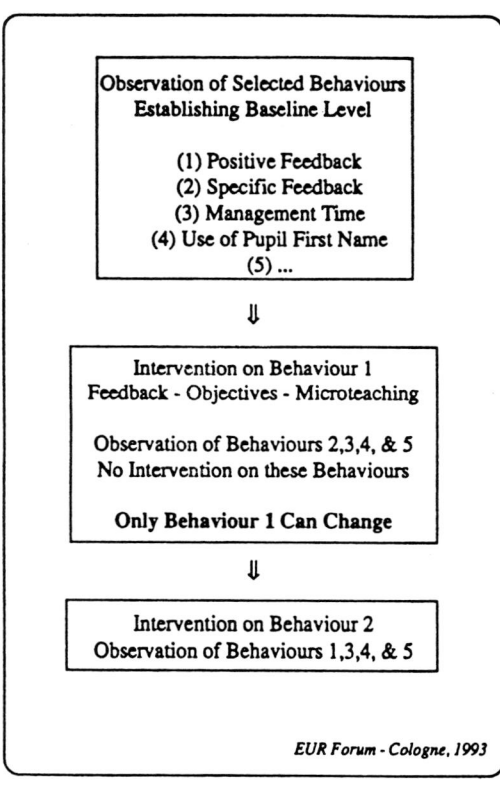

2. Modifying some specific teacher behaviours. Increasing the feedback rate, increasing the frequency of positive and approving statements, decreasing the negative reactions to performance and behaviours, using more frequently the pupil's first name, decreasing the length of silent observation and organization periods... These are just a few examples of the target behaviours;
3. Increasing the pupil motor engagement time in physical education classes;
4. Acquiring high inference teacher behaviour, e.g. enthusiasm.

From all the studies, it must be retained that teaching behaviour or teacher pupil interaction can be changed by specific programmes or by behaviour modification techniques using the multiple baseline design. However as with all types of learning, there is a trend to forget more or less rapidly the strategie or the skills learned by these programs.

In the descriptive aspect of research on teacher education, two themes are addressed with an increasing frequency. The first research interest deals with beliefs and concerns of future teachers. They are compared between individuals at different stages of their teacher preparation or of their professional experience. Prospective physical education students, student teachers, experienced teachers, and expert teachers are questioned on the intended outcomes of teaching physical education, the elements of the instructional and managerial context, what good teachers do when they are teaching, what an effective lesson is, etc.

1. Are teachers' perceptions about what constitutes effective teaching consistent with those characteristics identified in the teaching effectiveness research literature?
2. Do teachers describe their feelings of success in terms that reflect effectiveness as defined by research?
3. Do in-service and pre-service teachers differ in their perceptions of effectiveness and success?

Unsuccessful teaching incidents are related almost exclusively to pupil misbehaviour, and pre-service teachers perceived they had no control over these circumstances. Arrighi and Young (1987) found pre-service teachers' perceptions of effective teaching related more to administrative or discipline-oriented issues rather than subject matter content, instructional method, or pupil achievement. Success in teaching was related to positive pupil feedback and attitudes, and less attention was paid to improved skill performance.

From questionnaires and the answers to open questions, four main areas were defined:

1. The instructional activities related to planning, observational skills, feedback, pupils motor engagement, evaluation, and motivation;
2. Control and management of the class with safety procedures, material and equipment, and administrative routine;
3. Content dealing with the activity specific knowledge;
4. Personal characteristics like aptitude to teaching, patience, enthusiasm, flexibility of behaviours,...

Schempp (1985) suggested that physical education student teachers defined competence in teaching as the ability to control pupil behaviour and incompetent teaching as the lack of such control. Views from the different types of teachers diverge frequently. However, there are some discrepancies between findings of the research completed to date. These findings should bring our attention to the importance of matching a meaningful perspective of teaching shared by teacher educators and the limited view of the trainees.

Other questions are also addressed in recent investigations. Let us give a few examples: What are the features of educational situations that beginning physical education teachers experience as successful and problematic and why? What is the nature of relationships between the first year teachers and their administrators, students, peers, and pupils' parents? How similar are the beginning teachers' behaviours and concerns to those held by expert physical educators? What type of support do pre-service teachers expect from teacher mentors?

The student teaching experience has been considered as the most meaningful experience in the teacher preparation. However, some doubts have been cast on its real effectiveness. Authors like Zeichner (1980) stressed that: <<Most criticisms of the present practice center around the argument that field-based experiences are conservative institutions which serve merely to socialize prospective teachers into established patterns of school practice>>.

The most commonly used approach for analysing the impact of the student teaching experience is to measure student teacher attitudes, by questionnaire, before and after the experience. Conclusions are drawn from the comparison of pre- and post-scores.

Some pessimistic views have been exposed from these investigations. Concerns of student teachers are mainly self oriented. Notification of unsatisfactory performance, threat of personal injury, disagreement with supervisor are frequently at the top of the rankings. The other view shows that concern toward pupils is low in the ranking of student teachers.

Analyses of the relationships between each element of the student teacher - cooperating teacher - university supervisors triad were completed by various research techniques like systematic observation of the supervision conference, critical incidents, questionnaires, and interviews. Here are some examples of the questions addressed by researchers: What do these teachers see as the role of the co-operating teacher and university supervisor during the student teaching experience? What events during the student teaching experience are viewed as successful and problematic by the co-operating teachers? What impact do the co-operating teachers perceive they will have on the student teachers and vice versa?

The student teaching experience exerts only a slight influence on these concerns.

Quantitative and qualitative descriptive analyses of teaching have confirmed the large gap between pedagogical theories and the daily reality of physical education classes. However systematic observations have contributed to gather data that provide a sound basis to teaching methodology. Teaching physical education can be based on reality rather than on unrealistic expectations. To date, some of the research findings have been disseminated and applied in teacher preparation and in in-service training.

In the near future we can expect that multiple data collection processes and improved strategies will add insight to the process of teaching and teacher preparation. A lot of problems are still ahead. They must be dealt with by in--depth analyses and longitudinal or long-term studies. Let us cite some of these problems: high inference teaching qualities (enthusiasm, clarity, class management), discipline and burn-out problems, teachers' induction into the career, teacher decision-making in pre-active and inter-active phases of teaching, the appropriateness and quality of teacher intervention and of student participation...

6. **What is happening in Europe? Where are we going in relation to the research on teaching physical education and the research on teacher education?**

Differences in culture, language and economic development make the construction of an European model a difficult task. At a different level, sport pedagogy research is also facing difficulties arising from language barriers, educational concepts, and the diversity of school environments in Europe.

They are many cues showing that in the study of teaching physical education, many pedagogues are reluctant to collect any kind of data. This statement is reflected around Europe. Reviewing the literature, I found more papers presenting models, developing and criticizing ideas, than papers presenting quantitative and/or qualitative data (Piéron, 1986; Piéron, Cloes & Delfosse, 1992).

In preparing this paper, I found some evidence that European researchers were involved in many aspects of the research on teaching physical education or on teacher education.

The teaching process in physical education has been described through a number of different approaches:

(1) Teacher-pupil interaction. It was a subject of research for several years, beginning the systematic observation of physical education classes (Heinila, 1979, 1980, 1983; Underwood, 1978, 1979, 1980, 1988).

(2) Teacher and pupil behaviour. Detailed descriptions of physical education classes have been provided at the elementary and secondary levels (Carlier, Ghos, Renard, 1992; Carlier, Radelet & Renard, 1991; Carlier, Renard, Ruwet & Swalus, 1987; Demarteau & Piéron, 1978; Florence, Dawance & Renard, 1991; Hardy, 1993; Piéron, 1982; Spackman, 1986a, 1986b; Scheiff & Ren-

ard, 1991, 1992; Scheiff, Renard, Roelandt & Swalus, 1987; Swalus, Carlier, Florence, Renard & Scheiff, 1987; Telama, Paukku, Varstala & Paananen, 1982; Whitehall & Underwood, 1991). For example, Telama and his collaborators used a multidimensional approach combining behavioural observation, interviews to collect pupils and teachers' perceptions of physical education lessons along with physiological data. The number of schools, classes, teachers, and pupils was remarkably high. The <<Expert vs Beginner>> paradigm was used several years before that Berliner (1986) draws attention to the paradigm (Piéron, 1982). Feedback, a teacher intervention of prominent importance, was observed through multifaceted systems in intact classes, and in more controlled settings. The structure, the observable response of the pupils, and their perception of the feedback message was amongst the categories of the analysis. Class control and management, constantly a concern of beginning and experienced teachers in a new subject of descriptive studies (Hardy, 1992, 1993; Piéron & Brito, 1990; Piéron & Emonts, 1988). Descriptors of quantitative and qualitative designs were combined to investigate the teaching of swimming (Hardy, 1990).

(3) Teacher thinking was advocated and theorized before becoming a <must> in international research on teaching (Hanke, 1983). The relationship between student satisfaction and selected process variables was investigated by Delens, Renard & Swalus (1987). Students were asked about various aspects of their perception of the lessons (Crum, 1986, 1987; Telama et al., 1982).

Process-product studies were completed in experimental teaching units in micro settings and intact classes (DeKnop, 1983, 1986; Behets, 1991, 1993; Piéron & Piron, 1981). For example, Carreiro da Costa & Piéron (1992) used a multifaceted approach (behaviour, attitude, and motivation) to collect the data and to relate such aspects to pupils' outcomes.

Only a limited number of studies were devoted to the preparation of teachers in the two main aspects usually considered:

(1) The acquisition of teaching skills (Cloes, 1987; Delgado Nogeira, 1989 / 1990; Piéron & Wauqier, 1984).
(2) The effects of the student teaching experience on values, attitudes, and concerns of future physical education teachers (Behets, 1990; Piéron, Brunelle & Tousignant, 1989), and the concerns or anxieties of beginning physical education teachers. Problem situations in teaching physical education were identified by the critical incident technique (Telama, Lahde & Kurki, 1980).

Although a pretty large number of research subjects tackled by European researchers in the area we have considered, the level and the extent of this research remain too limited for several reasons.

★ Numerous studies could be categorized as <<one-shot>> studies. They cannot contribute substantially to the building of a coherent body of knowledge. Only a few university departments were involved in a systematic research endeavour.

★ The number of qualified researchers is too limited. We still are far away from attaining a <<critical mass>> allowing substantial developments.

★ There are relatively few opportunities to publish research findings in journals specific to sport pedagogy. It seems appropriate to remind oneself that in the USA, a tremendous development of research on teaching physical education and on teacher education was observed after the creation of the journal of Teaching Physical Education and in relation to the publication of several proceedings from AIESEP international congresses.

References

1. **Arrighi, M., & Young, J.** (1987). Teachers perceptions about effective and successful teaching. Journal of Teaching in Physical Education, 6, 122-135.

2. **Barrett, K.** (1979a). Observation for teaching and coaching. Journal of Health Physical Education and Recreation, 50, 1, 23-25.

3. **Barrett, K.** (1979b). Observation of movement for teachers - A synthesis and implications. Motor Skills: Theory into practice, 3, 2, 67-76.

4. **Barrett, K.** (1983). A hypothetical model of observing as a teaching skill. Journal of Teaching in Physical Education, 3, 1, 22-31.

5. **Behets, D.** (1990). Concerns of preservice physical education teachers. Journal of Teaching in Physical Education, 10, 66-75.

6. **Behets, D.** (1991). Teacher enthusiasm and effective teaching in physical education. Physical Education Review, 14, 1.

7. **Behets, D.** (1993). Teaching behaviour of student, teachers and pupils' skill level in an ETU setting. Physical Education Review, 16, 1, 12-18.

8. **Behets, D.** (1993). Systematic observation training for preservice physical education teachers. The physical educator, 50, 87-94.

9. Berliner, D. (1986). In pursuit of the expert pedagogue. Educational Research, 15, 5-13.

10. Biscan, D., & Hoffman, S. (1976). Movement analysis as a generic ability of physical education teachers and students. Research Quarterly, 47, 161-163.

11. Bloom, B. (1979). Caractéristiques individuelles et apprentissages scolaires. Bruxelles: Ed. Labor.

12. Capel, S. (1992). Anxieties of beginning physical education teachers. Paper presented at the 6th ICHPER Europe Congress, Prague, Czechoslovakia, July 15-19.

13. Carlier, G., Ghos, P., & Renard, J.P. (1992). Le contenu enseigné. In, Analyse de l'enseignement de l'éducation physique au secondaire. Université Catholigue de Louvain, 1-14.

14. Carlier, G., Radelet, K., & Renard, J.P. (1991). Sources de variations des feedback et leur perception par les élèves. Revue de l'Education Physique, 31, 137-176.

15. Carlier, G., Renard, J.P, Ruwet, A.M., Swalus, P. (1987). Etude du répertoire d'exercices observés en salle. Sport, 30,1, 117, 29-36.

16. Carlisle, C., & Phillips, A. (1984). The effects of enthusiasm training on selected teacher and student behaviors in preservice physical education teachers. Journal of Teaching in Physical Education, 4, 64-75.

17. Carreiro da Costa, F., & Piéron, M. (1990a). Teaching learning variables related to student success in an experimental teaching unit. In, R. Telama, L. Laakso, M. Piéron, I. Ruoppila, & V. Vihko (Eds.), Physical education and life-long physical activity. Jyväskylä: The Foundation for Promotion of Physical Culture and Health, 304-316.

18. Carreiro da Costa, F., & Piéron, M. (1990b). Comparaison de deux enseignants classés selon les progrès de leurs élèves. Revue de l'Education Physique, 30, 57-63.

19. Carreiro da Costa, F., & Piéron, M. (1992). Teaching effectiveness: Comparison of more and less effective teachers in an experimental teaching unit. In, T. Williams, L. Almond, & A. Sparkes, Sport and physical activity. Moving towards excellence. The Proceedings of the AIESEP world convention. London: E & FN Spon. 169-176.

20. Cheffers, J. (1978). Systematic observation in teaching. In, M. Piéron (Ed), Towards a science of teaching: Teaching analysis. Liège: AIESEP, 7-30.

21. Cloes, M. (1987). Identification et modification de comportements enthousiastes d'enseignants en éducation physique. Thèse de doctorat en éducation physique, Université de Liège.

22. Cloes, M., & Piéron, M. (1989). Identification des comportements enthousiastes de l'enseignant perçus par des élèves lors de séances d'éducation physique. Revue de l'Education Physique, 29, 7-16.

23. Crum, B. (1986). The use of learner reports for exploring teaching effectiveness in physical education. In, M. Piéron, & G. Graham (Eds.), Sport pedagogy, the 1984 Olympic Scientific Congress proceedings, vol. 6. Champaign: Human Kinetics, 97-112.

24. Crum, B. (1987). Professional profiles of physical education teachers and students' learning. In, G. Banette, R. Feingold, R. Rees, & M. Piéron (Eds.), Myths, models & methods in sport pedagogy. Champaign: Human Kinetics, 143-149.

25. Craft, A. (1977). The teaching of skills for the observation of movement: Inquiry into a model. Unpublished doctoral dissertation, University of North Carolina at Greensboro.

26. De Knop, P. (1983). Effectiveness of tennis teaching. In, R. Telama, V. Varstala, J. Tiainen, L. Laakso, & T. Haajanen (Eds.), Research in school physical education. Jyväskylä: The foundation for promotion of physical culture and health, 228-234.

27. De Knop, P. (1986). Relationship of specified instructional teacher behaviors to student gain on tennis. Journal of Teaching in Physical Education, 5, 2, 71-78.

28. Delens, C., Renard, J.P., & Swalus, P. (1987). Etude des liens entre la satisfaction des élèves et différents paramètres observés. Sport, 117, 37-43.

29. Delgado Nogeira, M.A. (1989/90) Influencia de un entrenamiento docente durante las practicas docentes sobre algunas de las competencias del profesor de educación física. Doc. diss., Univ. Granada.

30. Demarteau, M., & Piéron M. (1978). Analyse des communications verbales entre un professeur d'éducation physique et ses élèves. In M. Piéron (Ed.), Towards a science of teaching: Teaching analysis. Liège: AIESEP, 98-124.

31. Erickson, F. (1986). Qualitative methods in research on teaching. in, M. Wittrock (Ed.), Handbook of research on teaching (3rd Ed.). New York McMillan, 119-161.

32. Evertson, C., & Green, J. (1986). Observation as inquiry and method. In, M. Wittrock (Ed.), Handbook of research on teaching (3rd Ed.). New York: McMillan, 162-213.

33. Florence, J., Dawance, V., & Renard, J.P. (1991). La présentation des exercices dans l'animation de la séance d'éducation physique au secondaire. Revue de l'Education Physique, 31, 51-56.

34. Gentile, A. (1972). A working model of skill acquisition with application to teaching. Quest, 17, 3-23.

35. Graham, G, Metzler, M., & Webster, G. (1991). Spezialist and classroom teacher effectiveness in children's physical education. A 3-year study. Journal of Teaching in Physical Education, 10, 321-426.

36. Graham, G., Soares, P., & Harrington, W. (1983). Experienced teachers' effectiveness with intact classes: An ETU study. Journal of Teaching in Physical Education, 2, 2, 3-14.

37. Hanke, U., & Treutlein, G. (1983). What P.E. teachers think: Methods for the investigation of P.E. teacher cognitions in teaching process. In, R. Telama, V. Varstala, J. Tiainen, L. Laakso, & T. Haajanen. Research in school physical education. Jyväskylä: The foundation for promotion of physical culture and health, 31-37.

38. Harari, I. (1986). Relationships among knowledge, experience, and skill analysis ability in gymastics. Doct. diss., Ohio State University.

39. Harari, I. & Siedentop, D. (1990). Relationships among knowledge, experience and skill analysis ability. In, D. Eldar & U. Simri (Eds). Integration or diversification of physical education and sport studies. Wingate Institute: The Emmanuel Gill Publishing House, 197-204.

40. Hardy, C. (1990). Investigations into the teaching of swimming in secondary schools. Doc. Diss., Loughborough University of Technology.

41. Hardy, C. (1992). Pupil misbehaviour in physical education lessons. Bulletin of Physical Education, 28(2), 59-67.

42. Hardy, C. (1993a). Teaching behaviours of physical education specialists. Physical Education Review, 16,1, 19-26.

43. Hardy, C. (l993b). A content analysis study of types of student misbehaviour and teacher reaction in physical education classes. Paper presented at the International Conference, teacher Education: From practice to theory, Tel Aviv, Israel, June 27 - July 1.

44. Heinila, L. (1979). Analyzing systems in the evaluation of the teacher - pupil interaction process in physical education classes. In, T. Tammivuori (Ed.), Evaluation. International congress of physical education, July 1976. Helsinki: Finnish society for research in sport and physical education, Publication 64, 37-58.

45. Heinila, L. (1980). Developing a system (PEIAC/LH-75) for describing teacher-pupil interaction in physical education classes: Objectivity and content validity of coding. In, G. Schillings, & W. Baur (Eds.), Audiovisuelle Medien im Sport. Moyens audiovisuels dans le sport. Audiovisual means in sports. Basel: Birkhauser Verlag, 361-370.

46. Heinila, L. (1983). Developing a system (PEIAC/LH-75) for describing teacher - pupil interaction in physical education classes: Construct validity and sensitivity. In, R. Telama, V. Varstala, J. Tiainen, L. Laakso, & T. Haajanen (Eds.), Research in school physical education. Jyväskylä: The foundation for promotion of physical culture and health, 124-132.

47. Hoffman, S. (1983). Clinical diagnosis as a pedagogical skill. In, T. Templin, & J. Olson (Eds.), Teaching in physical education. Champaign, IL: Human Kinetics, 35-45.

48. Housner, L., & Griffey, D. (1985). Teacher cognition: Differences in planning and interactive decision making between experienced and inexperienced teachers. Research Quarterly for Exercise and Sport, 56, 45-53.

49. Howe, B., & Jackson, J. (1985). Teaching effectiveness research. Victoria, British Columbia: University of Victoria.

50. Imwold, C., & Hoffman, S. (1983). Visual recognition of a gymnastics skill by experienced and inexperienced instructors. Research Quarterly for Exercise and Sport, 54, 149-155.

51. Kniffen, M. (1985). The effects of individualized videotape instruction on physical education majors ability to analyze select sport skills. Doct. diss., Ohio State University.

52. Locke, L., & Dodds, P. (1984). Research on teaching teachers: Where are we now? Journal of Teaching in Physical Education. Monograph 2, 1-85.

53. Magill, R. (1989). Motor learning. Concepts and applications. Dubuque: Wm. C. Brown.

54. Phillips, D., & Carlisle, C. (1983). A comparison of physical education teachers categorized as most and least effective. Journal of Teaching in Physical Education, vol. 2, 3, 55-67.

55. Piéron, M. (1982). Analyse de l'enseignement des activités physiques. Bruxelles: Ministère de l'Education Nationale et de la Culture Française.

56. Piéron, M. (1986). Analysis of the research based on observation of the teaching of physical education. In, M. Piéron, & G. Graham (Eds.), The 1984 Olympic Scientific Congress Proceedings. Vol. 6, Sport Pedagogy. Champaign, IL: Human Kinetics, 193-202.

57. Piéron, M. (1992). Pédagogie des achvités physiques et du sport. Paris: Ed. Revue EPS.

58. Piéron, M. & Brito, M. (1990). Analyse d'incidents d'indiscipline survenant dans des classes de l'enseignement préparatoire (10-12 ans). In, J. Duran, J.L. Hernandez, & L. Ruiz (Eds.), Humanismo y nuevas tecnologias en la educación física y el deporte. Madrid: INEF, 113-117.

59. Piéron, M., Cheffers, J., & Barrette, G. (1990). An Introduction to the terminology of sport pedagogy (Vocabulary used in research in teaching and Coaching). Liège: ICSP.

60. Piéron, M. & Emonts, M. (1988). Analyse des problèmes de discipline dans des classes d'éducation physique. Revue de l'Education Physique, 28, 1, 33-40.

61. Piéron, M., & Piron, J. (1981). Recherche de critères d'efficacité de l'enseignement d'habiletés motrices. Sport, 24, 144-161.

62. Rosenshine, B., & Furst, N. (1973). The use of direct observation to study teaching. In, R. Travers (Ed.), Second handbook of research on teaching. Chicago: Rand Mc Nally, 122-183.

63. Scheiff, A., & Renard, J.P. (1991). Analyse de l'enseignement de l'éducation physique dans le secondaire. Paramètres de temps de la séance. Sport, 135, 167-177.

64. Scheiff, A., & Renard, J.P. (1992). Analyse de l'enseignement de l'éducation physique dans le secondaire. Les comportements des élèves. Sport, 139, 153-159.

65. Scheiff, A., Renard, J.P., Roelandt, E., Swalus, P. (1987). Etude des paramètres de temps de la leçon. Sport, 117, 19-28.

66. Schempp, P. (1985). Becoming a better teacher: An analysis of the student teaching experience. Journal of Teaching in Physical Education, 4, 158-166.

67. Schmidt, R. (1988). Motor control and learning. A behavioral emphasis. Champaign: Human Kinetics.

68. Siedentop, D. (1981). The Ohio State University supervision research program summary report. Journal of Teaching in Physical Education, Introductory Issue, 30-38.

69. Siedentop, D. (1987a). Sport pedagogy research: Methods and assumptions. In, H. Rieder, & U. Hanke (Eds.), The physical education teacher and coach today, Köln, Bundesinstitut für Sport, vol. 1, 295-310.

70. Silverman, S. (1988). Relationships of selected presage and context variables to achievement. Research Quarterly for Exercise and Sport, 59, 35-41.

71. Singer, R., & Dick, W. (1974). Teaching physical education. A systems approach. Boston, MA: Houghton Mifflin Cy.

72. Spackman, L. (1986a). The systematic observation of teacher behaviour in physical education: The design of an instrument. Doct. Diss., Loughborough University.

73. Spackman, L. (1986b). The systematic observation of teacher behaviour in physical education. Physical Education Review, 9, 2, 118-134.

74. Swalus, P., Carlier, G., Florence, J., Renard, J.P., & A. Scheiff(1987). Analyse de l'enseignement de l'éducation physique à l'école primaire. Sport, 117, 12-43.

75. Telama, R. Lahde, S. & Kurki, H. (1980). Critical incidents and problem situations in teaching physical education. In Schilling, G. & Bauer, W. (Eds) Audiovisuelle Medien im Sport. Moyens audiovisuels dans le sport. Audiovisual Means in Sports. Basel: Birhauser Verlag, 237-254.

76. Telama, R., Paukku, P., Varstala, V., & Paananen, M. (1982). Pupil's physical activity and learning behaviour in physical education classes. In, M. Piéron, & J. Cheffers (Eds.), Studying the teaching in physical education. Liège: AIESEP, 23-35.

77. Telama, R., Varstala, V., Tiainen, J., Laakso, L. & Haajanen, T. (1983). Research in school physical education. Jyväskylä: The foundation for promotion of physical culture and health.

78. Underwood, G. (1988). Teaching and learning in physical education: A social psychological perspective. London: Falmer Press.

79. Whitehall, C., & Underwood, G. (1991). A case study of the behaviour of pupils of high and low motor ability in primary school games lessons. Bulletin of Physical Education, 27(3), 24-33.

80. Zeichner, K. (1980). Myths and realities: Field based experiences in preservice teacher education. Journal of Teacher Education 31, 6, 45-55.

Physical Activities out of the School System Educational Aspects

Telama, R.
University of Jyväskylä
Finland

1. Introduction

In most European countries Physical Education is a compulsory subject at least at some age. Physical education in school is significant because it reaches almost all young people. Even though the time reserved for Physical Education may be limited, it still makes it possible to try to encourage children and young people to become more social and have a physically active way of life. Physical Education also aims at educating children and young people and promotes the development of self concept and social development.

Physical education outside school may be quantitatively more frequent for many school-aged children, but it does not reach everyone. In discussing children's and young people's sports, one of the essential dimensions is the organization of activity. In physical education outside school a distinction should be made on the one hand between young people's spontaneous physical activity organized by young people themselves, and on the other hand, organized sports organized by adults.

In many countries, such as the Nordic countries and Germany, organized sports are often provided by sport clubs. In addition to sport clubs, some countries, such as the United Kingdom and Portugal, also have well organized extra-curricular sport activities which, because of their competitive and selective nature, correspond to sport club activity. In addition, sport in many countries is organized by other organizations than sport organizations.

2. Participation in physical activity and sports outside school

Before going into the educative aspects of physical activity outside school, I would like to briefly discuss the number of school-aged children participating in physical activity outside school. It is usually very difficult to obtain a clear picture of the situation in various European countries just by studying the percentages of participation in unorganized sports or sports in general. It seems to be the case that in most countries, a major part of young people participates at least once a week in physical education outside school. In Finland and

Sweden the figures are 75 to 80 percent among fifteen-year-olds (16, 34). In most European countries about 50 percent of young people participate in physical activity outside school at least twice a week. This correlates with the frequency of school physical education in most countries (32).

It is also relatively common to participate in physical activity organized by sport clubs. In the Flemish part of Belgium and in Sweden more than half of the boys participate in activity organized by a sport club and the percentage of participation among boys in many other countries is also close to 50 percent (Scotland, Germany and Finland). (9, 12, 16, 28, 34). In all European countries there is a difference between boys and girls in the participation in organized sports, but in the Nordic countries the difference is smaller than in other countries. In the Nordic countries there is not much difference anymore between the sexes in the participation in organized sports. Organized sports has become more and more popular in recent years and for instance in Sweden the participation of girls has increased more in relation to boys (34).

In Finland the number of young people participating in unorganized sports is slightly bigger than the number of young people taking part in activities organized by sport clubs. In many countries the situation is reversed. (34).

3. Organized and unorganized sports outside school as an educative environment

As the previously presented facts indicate, a large proportion of school-aged children take part in physical activity outside school, and in most countries more than 50 percent of young people participate in it at least as often or even more often than in school physical education. The number of those participating in organized sports is also relatively high. The most actively coached young people in sport may spend about ten times more time in training than in school physical education. Physical activity outside school has proven to be a significant factor from the point of view of young people's physical, mental and social development. How these possibilities can be used depends on many factors which will be analysed next.

When I talk about sports as an educative environment, my starting point is the teleological view on the growth and development of man where developing individuals are seen as subjects of growth rather than objects of various educative measures.

Although the possibilities of coaches and instructors to function as educators in organized sports outside school are principally the same as for teachers at school, I see education in sports as aiming at creating a safe and enjoyable environment of growth and organizing stimuli which promote development.

What then are the important characteristics pertaining to the development of an individual which can be expected to be developed in physical activity or sports? In this context, I shall discuss self concept and self esteem, sociability and morals which, according to research are linked to physical activity and sports. It should be pointed out that physical activity outside school might be of great importance in the development of a child's independence and healthy life style. I shall analyse enjoyability and mental security as important factors of the environment of growth, the relationship between ability on the one hand and challenges and expectations on the other, the emotional and motivational atmosphere, cooperation and competition, the significance of dialogue and communication and the need for independent action. As factors influencing the environment of growth I shall discuss the roles of adults in children's sports, the effects of the competitive system and the significance of sub-cultures in sports. All of these are affected by the existing social values of society, the ideals and problems of top level sports and above all, the mass media in sports. In the present paper I shall not go into these social factors.

The division of organized and unorganized sports is essential from the point of view of the above mentioned factors. For this reason I shall discuss these factors in view of the organization of activity.

4. Enjoyment, perceived competence and self-esteem

One of the most important features of a good environment of growth is its enjoyability and mental security. The fact that sports is an enjoyable environment is supported by its popularity. Physical activity is by far the most popular active leisure-time activity and organized sport is also very popular and its popularity has increased during the last decade. On the other hand high rates of drop-out and factors causing drop-out indicate that there might also be problems concerning the enjoyment of sport. Enjoyability is based on the fact that it is possible to have so many kinds of positive experiences in sports, such as excitement, the pleasure of learning new things and the joy of success, and the experience related to social relationships.

Sport psychology has traditionally been attempting to point out the long-term effects of physical activity and been less interested in immediate experiences. Chalip & al. (10) noted, however, that "from the point of view of significance to a person's development, it might be argued that the sum of immediate experiences is as important, or more so, than the long term "effects" sport psychology has been attempting to identify."

An important factor from the point of view of enjoyability and mental safety has to do with self-concept and expectations towards one's own competence. One enjoys most the kind of activity where the demands of the activity are in

the right relation to what one believes one is able to do, that is to say perceived competence. If the demands are too easy, this leads to boredom. Too high demands can cause anxiety. The most common factors causing anxiety in children's sports are external expectations aimed at the child by adults, and the pressure to participate.
On the other hand the positive attitude of parents increases enjoyment in sports and is in relation to the positive experience of competence (40, 41, 51, 54).

In children's informal sports, perceived competence and challenges are usually in harmony. This might also be the case in most organized sports, but in the activity organized by adults it is possible that they aim at too high expectations when the level of competition is high. A study by Chalip & al (10) in which they compared situations in school physical education, in organized sports and in children's informal sports shows clearly that competence and challenges are balanced best in children's own sports and thus the possibilities for flow experience are greater. In formal sports and in school physical education the challenges are too big in relation to competence.

The results of studies concerning drop-out in sports also indicate that the emphasis on success decreases enjoyment and increases drop-out (17, 40, 45, 57, 60).

In sport psychology there is plentiful research on the effect of physical activity and sports to self concept and self esteem. As Gruber's (24) review showed, participation in physical activity and sports as such does not affect self concept very much, but instead some separately designed programs and teaching methods can affect it positively. For instance programs emphasizing fitness have been noted to have a positive effect. In discussing the significance of this kind of observation from the point of view of the development of an individual's personality and mental health it is important to analyse the connections with self esteem because self esteem is very important from the point of view of mental health. The observation of cognitive psychology that the perceiving of reality is more important to personality than reality itself, is also interesting from the point of view of the connections between sports and self concept. It has been shown that measured physical fitness does not necessarily correlate with self esteem, and the intermediary factor is perceived fitness or perceived competence. Therefore, what is of importance for self esteem is how one experiences one's own features and not the real features (36, 55, 56). Even though perceived competence has been found to be a relatively stable feature, pedagogically it is possible to direct children's and young people's assessment of competence towards a more realistic direction. We have found that for primary school children daily physical education programs caused perceived competence to become more realistic (49, 50).

Susan Harter (27) has made a pedagogically interesting observation in establishing that the connection between perceived competence and self esteem depends on how important the individual considers the field of competence to be. High competence assessment supports self esteem only when the feature which is the object of competence assessment, such as fitness, is considered to be important. A person who considers social relationships and appreciation of friends important and who regards himself as socially skilled, has high self esteem even though his perceived competence would be lower in some other fields. If success in competitions and good results are emphasized in children's sports, young people may also consider success important even if they do not regard themselves as good sportsmen. This can lead to a conflict between perceived competence and the importance of fields of competence, which is a threat to self esteem.

This is closely linked to the studies of cognitive psychology on the criteria of the assessment of competence and the relationship between competence assessment and motivation. According to the criteria of competence assessment, there are two different kinds of target orientation: mastery and competitive orientation. In mastery orientation the individual regards good performance, learning and advancement as important; regardless of what his own performance is in relation to others. In competitive orientation one's own performance is compared with the performance of others. (15, 46). Pedagogically important is the concept of motivational climate in which the concepts of mastery climate and competitive climate can also be distinguished. A mastery oriented individual can maintain his motivation more easily in both climates in spite of his own perceived competence. A competitive oriented individual is motivated only if his perceived competence is high (46).

The adults who organize sports can regulate motivational climate by drawing attention to the definition of success, what is appreciated, how the child is evaluated and how mistakes are being treated etc. (1). Pedagogically more recommendable is the mastery climate because the motivation is higher, even though the individual's skill or perceived skills are limited. Mastery climate guarantees experiences of success and competence and experiences which strengthen self esteem for most children. Mastery orientation has been found to correlate positively with enjoyment and negatively with boredom experienced in sport (14). Research data indicates that in children's and young people's sports competitive climate prevails and it seems that the role of adults in maintaining it is significant. There are not many data on the motivational climate of children's informal sports but it seems to vary greatly according to each situation. A mastery climate appears more frequently in informal sports than in formal sports.

5. Social development in sports

According to the old education principles in upper class Britain, sports has an inherent educational value. Consistent with this principle, participation in competitions and sports develops such virtues as courage, honesty, unselfishness, and determination, and in general it promotes the particpant's social and moral education (37). This conception has prevailed until recently in spite of the fact that sports has changed and so have social circumstances and values. Although in many countries the objective of school is to make children more social with the help of physical education, there is very little data on the socially educative effect of physical activity and sports.

The objective of social education is to develop social skills such as the skill to communicate and cooperate and the skill to make social observations and social attitudes such as empathy, and the wish to take other people into consideration. The skill to take roles and the skill to position oneself in another person's situation and the understanding of the consequences of one's own actions are a prerequisite for ethical development.

The basis of social education lies in the theory of action. Social skills and attitudes are learnt in social action, interaction with other individuals. Play, games, and sports offer wide possibilities for this. In interaction with others young people learn to understand, internalize and make use of positive social behaviour in practicing the skills which are needed in working with various kinds of people (13). Cooperative activities not only create prosocial interactional behaviour but also give the feeling of enjoyment (23).

The socially educative real effect of physical activity and sport has been diminished by the old belief that sports as such is socially educative. Beliefs such as "team games have a socially educative effect" are still being repeated. Being a member of a team seems to teach the first steps of such social skills as adaptation to common rules and cooperative action, but there is hardly any data on the effects of team games on real prosocial behaviour. A prerequisite for prosocial behaviour is cooperation, taking other people into consideration, helping others and compliance with common rules (22, 29).

Prosocial behaviour depends on the specific type of human interaction. Good evidence of this are the results of some Finnish research. (30, 31). The object of the study was the development of helping behaviour and social relationships in school physical education. There were three test groups and a control group in the study which lasted a complete school year. One test group individually followed the instructions of the teacher and another worked in pairs helping each other and giving advice to each other according to the Mosston's reciprocal style (39). In this group, the students were able to choose their own pairs. The third test group worked in pairs like the second group but the pairs changed after a period of time. In other words they had to work with many different students. All three study groups had the same content of syllabi. The control group received normal teaching, the content of which was not predetermined but was taken note of. Helping behaviour was measured by using a questionnaire which was validated by video observation. Social relationships were measured with a sociometric questionnaire.

Helping behaviour and social relationships clearly developed much better in a group where the students worked in pairs and changed their pairs than in other groups. The results show that prosocial behaviour is learnt especially by working together with different individuals. Another condition is interactional cooperation, that is to say giving advice, guiding and helping the other. In physical activity and sports the interaction between individuals is often superficial parallel activity and not real cooperation.

Games, playing and sports no doubt offer good possibilities for social interaction which helps to develop prosocial attitudes and behaviour. Sports is, however, above all a means, and its efficiency depends on what kind of interactional situations can be created in it. The Finnish research concerned school physical education but reciprocal teaching styles have also been successfully tested in sport training (11). Usually the traditional sport training has been and probably still is rather coach-centered while the interaction between sportsmen is practically nonexistent.

The basic element of sports is competition. It might cause problems from the point of view of social education because competition is the opposite of cooperation. In Sherif's socialpsychological study (52), the significance of competition and cooperation to social behaviour is well described. In a summer camp the boys were divided into two similar groups. During many weeks the groups competed daily on a winning/defeat principle and winning was well rewarded. The competitions began in a gentlemanly way but quite soon hostility between the groups begun to surface. Hostility appeared as aggressiveness even outside competitive situations. The competitions were finished but the hostility between the groups remained. Only after the groups had to work for a common goal in fixing a burst pipe and organizing food supplies, did peace return between the groups.

Sherif's study reveals not only the significance of cooperation but also the elements of competition which might be problematic from the point of social education. Competition as such need not be a problem, but the overemphasizing of the significance of competition for example with good prizes and prolonged competitive situations between the same individuals or groups, definitely constitutes a problem.

Competition has been defended in connection with education, for instance by the fact that one learns self control and a correct attitude towards success and failure. In competitive sports one can also learn target-oriented behaviour and to strive to achieve the target one has set for oneself. More important than competition as such is the attitude towards competition. Problems usually arise when the importance of competition is overemphasized.

A problem in organized sports may arise from the different conceptions of adults and children towards competition. Adults who organize sports, look at competition in the long term and often emphasize the significance of competition and success while children look at it as momentary action. Action is important for children. Although children enjoy winning, they still usually prefer to play in the losing team than to sit on the reserve bench of the winning team. When researching the moral thinking of children in morally problematic situations in soccer, it was found that goals and winning were important but nobody wanted a conceded win. In other words children do not prefer winning over playing as such. (58).

There must be at least some cooperation in children's own games and sports because they organize the activity themselves. It seems that the significance of competition remains within the bounds of what is reasonable.
On the other hand children's own activity can be socially selective and some individuals may be kept out which can to a certain extent be avoided in organized sports.

6. Moral development and sports

Arnold (2) has presented three hypotheses on the connection between sports and moral development. The first hypothesis is based on the traditional British conception of sports as morally developing as such. According to the second hypothesis, sport is a world of its own and it has no connection with the real world. The third hypothesis indicates that competitive sport is immoral. It has not been shown that sport as such would help to develop moral thinking. On the contrary the morals of sportsmen have been shown to be lower than the morals of non-sportsmen (4, 7, 8, 20). This does not necessarily indicate that sport is unethical in itself. In the light of research Arnold's second hypothesis according to which sport is a world of its own is more likely. This shows in the way that sports situations are judged from a morally less exacting viewpoint than other life situations (3, 61). This is also connected with the so-called Dr Jekyll and Mr Hyde phenomenon in which the calm familyman turns into an aggressive fighter on the field (5). The same change comes over the parents of competing children outside the field (42).

It has been established that children playing tough contact games are more aggressive than other children (48). This may be explained with the selection of the players. On the other hand, it has been shown that in icehockey for instance violence has nothing to do with street violence (53).
Sport may form a world of its own where morals exist guided by game reasoning.

This means that sport in itself is very probably not morally educative or harmful. In this context it should be pointed out that I am talking about children's and young people's sports and I shall not discuss the problems arising from the double morality of top level sports. It is more important to study sports as a means of moral education than to study the moral significance of sports as such.

In modern society the teaching of morals based on only one ideological or moral viewpoint does not work anymore. Habermas (26) has pointed out that contracts based on voluntary communication become increasingly important in the solving of conflicts between individuals as the traditional authority crumbles. Several other theoreticians on morals and justice have underlined the significance of communication and dialogue (19, 43). In order to develop moral thinking, guidelines applicable to physical education and sports have been developed on the basis of theories based on dialogue (18, 25, 33). These methods have also been found to be useful in developing children's moral thinking (6, 47).

The significance of sports as a means of moral education lies in the fact that in sports there are genuine conflict situations familiar to young people which can be solved through discussion. The problem with organized sports, however, is that when adults organize activity, superwise the following of the rules, and solve conflicts, the dialogue between children is almost nonexistent. An example is the attitude towards rules.
When playing with each other, children must control that the rules are complied with themselves and they must also solve conflict situations by themselves. Rules are broken but less so than in sports organized by adults. In children's sports, rules are the cohesive force. If they are not complied with the activity dissolves. This also emphasizes the responsibility of the individual as a member of the game community. When adults control that the rules are followed this easily leads to a situation where the moral responsibility is delegated to the umpire, coaches and rules. The rules may become a factor which restricts winning.

In the project Ethical Values in Sport and Young People under the Sports Committee of the Council of Europe young soccer players were presented with the following situation: during a game a player is roughly tackled. He is probably injured and is stretched out on the field. The referee does not see the situation and the game continues. The opposing side has the ball and they are about to make a goal. What would you do if you were the player who has the ball? (35). Almost all of the players which we interviewed said that as a first alternative they would take advantage of the situation, they would not stop the game and they would not notify the referee. In most cases the reason given was that it is the referee's role to see what is happening and to stop the game (58). Sportsmen as well as coaches have been found to delegate responsibility to the referee (5, 21, 38). It has been said that playing is like taking a moral holiday (44).

7. Conclusions

The role of adults in organizing children's sport is very significant. Children learn new skills from adults which they can make use of in their own leisure-time activities. When the adults take care of the organization, the children can concentrate on developing their sport skills. With the help of training methods and their own behaviour, adults can also guide the social and ethical development of the child as well as the development of the child's personality. The adults are, however, a part of the organization in children's sport and they are being pressured by the management of the sports, the competitive system and various sub-cultures in the field concerned. Therefore, it is understandable that the adults might get carried away and start overemphasizing the significance of competition, organize activity very strictly and forget that children's sport is mainly for children and not the other way around. Because children's spontaneous games and sports have their own educative function, they should be the object of research and enough facilities should also be reserved for it.

I would like to conclude by making some recommendations on developing physical activity and sports outside school:

Activity organized by children themselves should also be increased in organized sports.

Children's spontaneous physical activity and sports must be provided for in public places of physical activity.

The competitive system should be the object of attention. The significance of competition must not be overemphasized in training and coaching. Children do not need high level competitions.

A mastery oriented motivational climate should be created in children's sports.

Instruction methods which are based on interaction between children should be used more frequently in children's coaching.

To prevent the harmful effects of professional sub-cultures in top level sports, a new sub-culture should be created in children's sports. This subculture would contain its own norms, rules and behavioural patterns.

References

1. Ames C.: Achievement goals, motivational climate, and motivational processes. In: Motivation in sport and exercise. (Ed: Roberts, GC) Human Kinetics, Champaign, Illinois, 161-176,1992.

2. Arnold P.J.: Moral aspects of an education in movement. American academy if physical education papers 19, 14-21, 1986.

3. Bredemeier B., Shields D.: Divergence of moral reasoning about sport and everyday life. Sociology of Sport Journal 1, 384-387, 1984.

4. Bredemeier B.J., Shields D.L.: Moral growth among athletes and nonathletes: a comparative analysis. The Journal of Genetic Psychology 147(1), 7-18, 1985.

5. Bredemeier B.J., Shields D.L.: Values and violence in sports today. The moral reasoning athletes use in their games and in their lives. Psychology Today 19(10), 22-25, 28-29, 32,1985.

6. Bredemeier B.J., Weiss M.R., Shields D.L., Shewchuk R.M.: Promoting moral growth in a summer sport camp: The implementation of theoretically grounded instructional strategies. Journal of Moral Education 15(3), 212-220, 1986.

7. Bredemeier B.J., Weiss M.R., Shields D.L., Cooper B.A.B.: The relationship of sport involvement with children's moral reasoning and aggression tendencies. Journal of Sport Psychology 8, 304-318, 1985.

8. Bredemeier B.J., Weiss M.R., Shields D.L., Cooper B.A.B.: The relationship between children's legitimacy judgments and their moral reasoning, aggression tendencies and sport involvement. Sociology of Sport Journal 4(1), 48-60, 1986.

9. Brettschneider W.D.: Youth and sport in Germany. Paper presented at ICSSPE Sport and Leisure Seminar "Youth and Sport", Bosö, Sweden May 7 to 8 1993.

10. Chalip L., Csikszentmihalyi M., Kleiber D., Larson R.: Variations of Experience in Formal and Informal Sport. Research Quarterly for Exercise and Sport 55, 109-116, 1984.

11. Cox R.L.: A systematic approach to teaching sport. In: Sport Pedagogy. The 1984 Olympic Scientific Congress Proceedings 6 ed. (Eds: M. Pieron; G. Graham) Human Kinetics Publishers, Inc., Champaign: Illinois, 109-115, 1986.

12. De Knop P., Vanreusel B., Theeboom M., Wittock H.: Children and youth sport in Belgium. Paper presented at ICSSPE Sport and Leisure Seminar " Youth and Sport", Bosö, Sweden May 7 to 8 1993.

13. Deline J.: Why can't they get along? Developing cooperative skills through physical education. Journal of Physical Education, Recreation and Dance 62(1), 21-26, 1991.

14. Duda J.: Motivation in sport settings: A goal perspective approach. In: Motivation in sport and exercise. (Ed: GC. Roberts) Human Kinetics Publishers, Champaign: Illinois, 57-91, 1992.

15. Dweck C.S.: Motivational processes affecting learning. American Psychologist 41, 1040-1048, 1986.

16. Engström L-M.: Children, youth and sport in Sweden. Paper presented at ICSSPE Sport and Leisure Seminar "Youth and Sport", Bosö, Sweden May 7 to 8 1993.

17. Feltz.D.L., Petlichkoff L.: Perceived competence among interscholastic sport participants and drop-outs. Canadian Journal of Applied Sport Sciences 8, 231-235, 1983.

18. Figley G.E.: Moral education through physical education. Quest 36, 89-101, 1984.

19. Gauthier D. (Ed.): Morals by agreement. Oxford University Press, Oxford, 1975.

20. Goncalves C.: Fair play and youth sport participants. In: Physical education and life-long physical activity. Reports of Physical Culture and Health ed.Vol. 73. (Eds: R. Telama; L. Laakso; M. Piéron; I. Ruoppila; V. Vihko), Jyväskylä, 137-143, 1990.

21. Goodger M.J., Jackson J.J.: Fair play: coaches' attitudes towards the laws of soccer. Journal of Sport Behaviour 8(1), 34-41, 1985.

22. Gottman J., Gonso J., Rasmussen B.: Social interaction. Social competence and friendship in children. Child Development 46, 709-718, 1975.

23. Grineski S.: Children, games and prosocial behavior. Insight and connections. Journal of Physical Education, Recreation and Dance, 20-25, 1989.

24. Gruber J.J.: Physical activity and self-esteem development in children: A meta-analysis. American academy of physical education papers 19, 30-48, 1986.

25. Haan N.: Two moralities in action contexts: relationship to thought, ego regulation and development. Journal of Personality and Social Psychology 36(3), 286-305, 1978.

26. Habermas J.: Moral consciousness and communicative action. The MIT Press, Cambridge, Massachusetts, 1991.

27. Harter S.: The construction and conservation of the self: James and Cooley revisited. In: Self, ego and identity: Intergrative approaches. (Eds: Lapsley,DK; Power,FC) Springer, New York, 43-70, 1988.

28. Hendry L.B., Love J.G.: Youth and sport in Scotland. Paper presented at ICSSPE Sport and Leisure Seminar "Youth and Sport", Bosö, Sweden May 7 to 8 1993.

29. Johnson D.: Student-student interaction on School outcomes. In: The Social Psychology of Learning. (Ed: McMillan,J) Academic Press, New York,123-157, 1980.

30. Kahila S.: Opetusmenetelmän merkitys prososiaalisessa oppimisessa. Studies in Sport, Physical Education and Health ed. Vol. 29. Jyväskylän Yliopisto, Jyväskylä. 132 pages 1993.

31. Kahila S., Telama R.: Effects of cooperative method on helping behavior in physical education lessons. In: The physical education teacher and coach today. Vol. 2. (Eds: H. Rieder; U. Hanke) Bundesinstitut für Sportwissenschaft, Köln, 220-230, 1988.

32. King A.J.C., Coles B.: The Health of Canada's Youth. Views and Behaviours of 11-, 13- and 15- year-olds from 11 countries. Health and Welfare Canada, 1992.

33. Kohlberg L.: A Cognitive-Developmental Approach to Moral Education. The Humanist 32, 13-16, 1972.

34. Laakso L., Telama R., Yang X.: Youth sport in Finland. Paper presented at ICSSPE Sport and Leisure Seminar "Youth and Sport", Bosö, Sweden May 7 to 8 1993.

35. Lee M.: Experts group on Ethics in Sport and young people. Summary of agreed interview procedures, StraŸbourg, Council of Europe, DS-SR (90) 22, 1990.

36. Lintunen T., Leskinen E., Oinonen M., Rahkila P.: Relationships between physical fitness, perceived fitness and self-esteem: a follow-up study of 11-15- year-old adolescents. Poster presented at the Eleventh Biennal Meetings of International Society for the Study of Behavioral Development (ISSBD) 3-7 July 1991 in Minneapolis, Minnesota, USA, 1991.

37. McIntosh P.C.: Physical education in England since 1800 (rew.ed.). G.Bell & Sons Ltd. Englanti, London, 1968.

38. McIntosh P.C.: 41st European Teacher's Seminar on "Education against Violence" the Potential of Fair Play in Sport. Donaueschingen, 10-15 October 1988. Report (reported by McIntosh). Council for Cultural Co-operation. Strasbourg, 1988.

39. Mosston M., Aahworth S.: 3rd ed. Merrill Publishing Co, Ohio, 1986.

40. Ommundsen Y.: Self Evaluation, Affect and Dropout in the Soccer Domain. A Prospective Study of Young male Norwegian Players. The Norwegian University of Sport and Physical Education. Department of Behavioral Sciences in Medicine. University of Oslo, 1992.

41. Ommundsen Y., Vaglum P.: Soccer competition anxiety and enjoyment in young boy players. The influence of perceived competence and significant others' emotional involvement. International Journal of Sport Psychology 22, 35-49, 1991.

42. Partington J.T.: Psychology of sport and motor behavior:research and practice. Proceedings of the Canadian society for psychomotor learning and sport psychology. In: Sport values. The Jekyll and Hyde syndrome. (Eds: Wankel, LM; Wilberg,RB) Fourteenth annual meeting, University of Alberta, Edmonton, Alberta, 129-136, 1982.

43. Rawls J.: Oikeudenmukaisuusteoria. Juva,WSOY, 1988.

44. Reddiford G.: Morality and the games player. Physical Education Review 4(1), 8-16, 1981.

45. Roberts G.C., Kleiber D.A., Duda J.L.: An analysis of motivation in children's sport: The role of perceived competence in participation. Journal of Sport Psychology 3, 206-216, 1981.

46. Roberts G.C.: Motivation in sport and exercise: Conceptual constraints and convergence. In: Motivation in sport and exercise. (Ed: Roberts,GC) Human Kinetics, Champaign, Illinois, 3-29, 1992.

47. Romance T.J., Weiss M.R., Bockoven J.: A program to promote moral development through elementary school physical education. Journal of Teaching in Physical Education 5(2), 126-136, 1986.

48. Roos R.: Do rough games hinder kid's moral growth? Physician and Sportsmedicine 14(12), 31-34, 1986.

49. Sarlin E-L.: Päivittäisen liikuntaohjelman yhteydet peruskoulun 1.-3. luokkalaisten koettuun fyysiseen ja yleiseen pätevyyteen sekä motoriseen kuntoon, pallonkäsittelytaitoihin ja voimistelutaitoihin. Liikuntapedagogiikan lisensiaatintutkimus, Jyväskylän Yliopisto, 1992.

50. Sarlin E-L., Telama R., Bovellan A-K., Romppainen A-M.: Effects of Daily Physical Education on Motor Fitness, Ball Handling, Gymnastic Skills and Perceived Physical Competence among Elementary School Children. In: Physical Education and Life-Long Physical Activity. (Eds: Telama,R; Laakso,L; Piéron,M; Ruoppila,I; Vihko,V) Reports of Physical Culture and Health, Jyväskylä, 501-507, 1990.

51. Scanlan T.K. Lewthwaite R.: Social psychological aspects of competition for male youth participants:IV. Predictors of enjoyment. Journal of Sport Psychology 8, 25-35, 1986.

52. **Sherif C.M.:** The social context of competition. In: Joy and sadness on children's sports. (Ed: Martens,R) Human Kinetics Publishers, Champaign, Illinois, 81-97, 1978.

53. **Smith M.D.:** Violence and sport. Butterworths, Toronto, 1983.

54. **Smith R.E.:** Toward a cognitive-affective model of athletic burnout. Journal of Sport Psychology 8, 36-50, 1986.

55. **Sonstroem R.J.:** Planning for self-esteem change through exercise. In: Sport for All. (Eds: Oja,P; Telama,R) Elsevier Science Publishers B.V, New York, 355-363, 1991.

56. **Sonstroem R.J., Morgan W.P.:** Exercise and self-esteem:rationale and model. Medicine and Science in Sports and Exercise 21(3), 329-337, 1989.

57. **Sternberg, Horn T.:** Coaches' feedback and changes in children's perceptions of their physical competence. Journal of Educational Psychology 77(2), 174-186, 1985.

58. **Telama R.:** Ethics in sport and young people, The Finnish pilot study. (unpublished), 1991.

59. **Telama R., Laakso L., Yang X.:** Physical Activity and Sport Participation of young Finns. Scandinavian Journal of Medicine and Science in Sports 3, 4, (in press), 1993.

60. **Weiss M.R., Bredemeier B.J., Shewchuk R.M.:** The dynamics of perceived competence, perceived control, and motivational orientation in youth sport. In: Sport for children and youths. (Eds: Weiss,MR; Gould,D) Human Kinetics Publishers, Inc., Champaign, Illinois, 1986.

61. **Weiss M.R., Bredemeier B.J.:** Moral development in sport. Exercise and Sport Science Reviews 18, 331-378, 1991.

Summary of the Interview of Conference-Participants by Students of the Specialism "European Sport Studies"

Tokarski, W.; Petry, K.
German Sport University
Cologne, Germany

During the Cologne Conference students of the specialism "European Sport Studies" performed the task of checking the conference participants' knowledge concerning the European institutions and programmes and of rendering their attitude towards European developments in the field of sport and politics more transparent.

By the help of a semi-standardized questionnaire, which was presented in German, French, English and Spanish, a total of 87 participants from nine European countries had been interviewed.

Most of the persons interviewed were working in academic fields, either in the function of professors or as lecturers. There were only a few representatives of governmental and non-governmental sport organizations.

The main interest of the congress participants interviewed was focussed on (high) performance sport. The state of knowledge of these congress participants concerning the European sport institutions and organizations proved relatively homogeneous: Most of the interviewed candidates were able to name up to three institutions or organizations. However this only applied to institutions to which they had some sort of direct connection themselves.

Most of those interviewed could identify the European Network and ERASMUS and one institution of higher learning in their own country.

Institutions which are responsible for the (European) Programmes such as the European Union, the Council of Europe, the CDDS, the Sport Forum, the European Sport Conference, etc. were only known to a very small number. Activities of the European Union in the field of sport could only be identified by every second participant interviewed. Here, too, ERASMUS and the European Network were the most frequent entries.

Only one of three candidates was able to identify contacts for questions related to sport and Europe in his own country. Here governmental bodies (ministries, offices,...) were named in prominent position.

Projects with a relevance to Europe at institutions where the candidates interviewed were working themselves, were identified by more than 50 % of them. And here, apart from individual activities, ERASMUS cooperations were dominant, too. Five institutions cooperated in courses for the (European) Master's Degree.

The future of Europe was seen as fairly positive by 60 % of those interviewed, the rest preferred to have a rather different opinion.

The result of the interview - even if it cannot claim to be of a representative nature - clearly shows that the ERASMUS-Programme of the European Union is the most widely known item within the different institutions of Higher Learning in Europe. This fact may be attributed to a large extend to the foundation of the European Network of Sport Science in Higher Education.

In order to shape the European development in sport itself to a far greater extend by the institutes of the sport science institutions, the mediation and transmission of the results of their scientific investigations to a larger public - e.g. by the Network - would be a further positive step in the right direction.

SCIENTIFIC COMMITTEE

Head   Camy, J.
                    Mester, J.

Members   Alfermann, D.
                    Appell, H.-J.
                    Barreiros, H.
                    Claude, R.
                    Doll-Tepper, G.
                    Elvin, I.T.
                    van Gerven, D.
                    Hackforth, J.
                    Klissouras, V.
                    König, W.
                 † de Marées, H.
                    Meinberg, E.
                    Persyn, U.
                    Piéron, M.
                    Rodriguez, F.A.
                    Rost, R.
                    Scherler, K.
                    Tokarski, W.
                    Wilke, K.

LOCAL ORGANIZING COMMITTEE

Head   Mester, J.
General Secretary   Ritzdorf, W.

Bureau   Seibert, B.
                          Velhagen, Ch.

Members
Gerling, I.
Knicker, A.
Krause, W.
Richter, H.
Scharfenberg, A.
Stein, N.

Layout Conference Proceedings
Herbeck, K.
Seibert, B.
Velhagen, Ch.

Address
Deutsche Sporthochschule Köln
2nd European Forum
Büro des Rektors
Carl-Diem-Weg 6
D-50933 Köln
Phone: +49.221 - 4982 385/200

Fax: +49.221 - 4995 505

Authors: (only first authors listed) Page

Almond, Len	462
Åstrand, Per-Olof	162
Bambuck, Roger	10
Bilard, Jean	288
Bouchout, Jean-Pierre	174
Brettschneider, Wolf-Dietrich	472
Carreiro da Costa, Francisco	484
Cilia, Giuseppe	506
Claude, Raymond	180
Crum, Bart	516
De Knop, Paul	32
Dietrich, Knut	534
Doll-Tepper, Gudrun	298
Elvin, Ian T.	309
Engel, Lis	193
Govaerts, France	55
Hackforth, Josef	69
Hardman, Ken	544
Hollmann, Wildor	317
Kirchgässner, Helmut	205
König, Walfried	18
Kozel, Jürgen	215
Laporte, Willy	561
Loret, Alain	86

Madella, Alberto 232
Martínez Ferrer, Josep Oriol 336
Meinberg, Eckhard 577
Mester, Joachim 245
Naul, Roland 588
Pedersen, Bente Klarlund 347
Peitersen, Birger 360
Piéron, Maurice 611
Pociello, Christian 95
Reilly, Thomas 260
Reischle, Klaus 271
Renström, Per A.F.H. 370
Roberts, Kenneth 113
Rodriguez, Ferran A. 395
Rost, Richard 409
Rubingh, Berend 126
Sobotka, Werner 133
Standeven, Joy 137
Telama, Risto 643
Tokarski, Walter 659
Van Coppenolle, Herman 431
Vermeer, Adri 434
Wagner, Philip 153
Williams, Trevor 443